ENGINEER TO WIN

Carroll Smith

Motorbooks International
Publishers & Wholesalers Inc
Osceola, Wisconsin 54020, USA   ®

STATEMENT OF NON-LIABILITY

Our society has reached the point where I am advised that, in order to protect myself from possible lawsuits, I should include a statement of nonliability in this book. Since I believe that the human being is wholly responsible for his or her own actions, I strongly object to this necessity and to the morality that has spawned it. However, I would object even more strongly to being sued—so here it is:

The price of man in motion is the occasional collision. Motor racing is dangerous. In order to be competitive in this business it is necessary for both man and machine to operate at the outer edges of their respective performance envelopes. The closer we come to the edge, the greater the risk of falling off. This book is about improving the performance of the racing car and its driver. It deals with the deliberate exploration of the outer limits of traction—and of materials. The closer the racing car approaches its theoretical potential, the greater the chances become of paying a sudden-stop type penalty when anyone involved in the exercise makes an error in judgment.

If, while attempting to apply any of the ideas, procedures or advice contained in this book, you should come unstuck—or your racer should break—it will be as a result of your own conscious decision. I disclaim responsibility for your actions—and for your accident.

Carroll Smith

First published in 1984 by Motorbooks International Publishers & Wholesalers Inc, P.O. Box 2, 729 Prospect Avenue, Osceola, WI 54020 USA
© Carroll Smith

Printed and bound in the United States of America.
Book and cover design by William F. Kosfeld.
Cover photograph by Marc Sproule.

Motorbooks International is a certified trademark, registered with the United States Patent Office.

2 3 4 5 6 7 8 9 10

Motorbooks International books are also available at discounts in bulk quantity for industrial or sales-promotional use. For details write to Special Sales Manager, Motorbooks International, P.O. Box 2, Osceola, Wisconsin 54020.

Library of Congress Cataloging in Publication Data
Smith, Carroll.
    Engineer to win.
    Bibliography: p.
    1. Automobiles, Racing—Design and construction.
I. Title.
TL236.S518   1984   629.2'28   84-16526
ISBN 0-87938-186-8 (pbk.)

DEDICATION

I have been privileged to know and to work with many of the movers and shakers of the past quarter century of motor racing. Two of them stand out in my memory: Carroll Shelby and Phil Remington. Shel because he just plain refuses to be beaten, because I have never known anyone who enjoys life quite so much as he does, because he proved to the world that we Americans can DO IT if we only try hard enough, and most of all because he gave those of us who worked with him more rope than I had ever believed possible (and more than I have seen since).

Rem stands out for different reasons. The way the world is supposed to work is that craftsmen, scientists and philosophers pass their accumulated knowledge on to the next generation. Of course it doesn't work that way—especially in racing where egos are very liable to get in the way.

As a craftsman, Rem is a legend. But he is much more than a super craftsman. He has the God-given gift of inspiring those who work with him to do more and better work than they had ever believed was in them (all successful leaders have this gift; it is known as leadership). He has passed on his vast knowledge to a couple of generations of racers who all seem to feel that, for a time at least, they have been apprenticed to a legend. We have, and we are the better for it—both as racers and as human beings.

FOREWORD

After reading ENGINEER TO WIN, I am given new reason to take an even closer look at my race cars than I have in the past. I would like to think that my finishing record was due to good maintenance and good preparation. I now realize that I have been very lucky. We (racers) have ALL been very lucky.

When the rear wing breaks and falls off (where the single pylon mount is fish-mouthed and welded to the tubular wing spar) and you crash; or when the stub axle breaks (at the base of the first thread), the corresponding wheel and tire exit, and you dig up the countryside; or when the front antiroll bar link breaks (where the rod end gets clinched into the sloppy clevis) and you snap into oversteer and oblivion—you would tend to think that the parts just broke, and you would be correct. Carroll will explain to us that, while you may be correct, someone along the line is at fault—either through negligence or through ignorance—and the failure or breakage was both predictable and preventable. End of discussion!

Parts DO break, and that's that. Parts will ALWAYS break, and that's that. Parts do not have to break or to fall off, and Carroll shows us the "hows," the "whys" and the "whens" (well, ALMOST the "whens") in ENGINEER TO WIN.

The object of our (the racers') exercise is to win races. If that fails, the secondary objective is to finish the races that we start. The third objective is to bring the car (and driver) back in one usable piece. If we have done our homework—and if we have done everything just right—we can succeed at all three. We can't always win, but if we ingest

what Carroll is trying to impart to us through his books, we WILL be able to consistently manage the second and third objectives—and that is a BIG plus.

I have had the enlightening and educational pleasure of working with Carroll on numerous occasions, and I feel that I am a better owner, mechanic and person for it (although by Carroll's standards and decrees I am still and always will be a "rookie"). Together we haven't always won. But we've usually come pretty close, had fast, safe and well prepared race cars—and we have had a hell of a lot of fun.

Carroll Smith is a unique and talented individual. We should all be grateful that he has taken both the time and the effort to further educate us with ENGINEER TO WIN. Carroll is a good teacher, but WE have to be willing to learn. Learn from him, and the next time you see him in the pits, thank him.

With ENGINEER TO WIN Carroll has not redesigned the wheel (it rolls and does pretty much what it is supposed to do, and he normally leaves those sorts of things alone). He has, however, vividly shown us why (and just about when) the wheel will fall off the car if we let it—then he tells us how to prevent it.

Thank you, Carroll Smith!

Tim Fortner

INTRODUCTION

Admirable though they may be in other respects, RACERS DO NOT READ—at least about the technical aspects of racing (or about the technical aspects of anything else; PLAYBOY and ON TRACK are the racer's reading norm). The exchange of technical information among racers is thus largely limited to verbal contact and, usually, to discussion on a one-to-one basis. This sweeping generalization may go a long way toward explaining why racers are forever reinventing the wheel.

While little of the specialized body of knowledge concerning the dynamics of wheeled racing vehicle performance exists in print (with the notable exception, of course, of TUNE TO WIN), there are NO secrets when it comes to mechanical design; the selection, use and treatment of structural materials and/or components; or in the techniques of fabrication, machining, welding and joining. It is all in print and it is all in English.

Nonetheless, all too often I see the wrong materials and/or the wrong components used. Or I see the right stuff used with the wrong techniques. And I see racers—intelligent, dedicated and competent racers—making mechanical mistakes in areas that have been common knowledge for years. As a parallel I see the vast majority of off-road racers struggling to learn the very basics of chassis and suspension design and using, for God's sake, SWING AXLES! (At the front that is; at the rear they have progressed all the way to VW-based trailing arm independent setups.) Lest you deduce from the foregoing that this regrettable tendency is restricted to the "do it in the dirt" group (who work harder AND have more fun than the rest of us), I invite you to consider how many of the "leading edge of automotive technology" designers of the Formula One circus forgot all about the torsional rigidity of the chassis when they all fell in love with ground effects a very few years ago—and how long it took the majority of these individuals to remember that a torsionally rigid chassis is the very basis of vehicle cornering performance and control.

I think that a large part of the problem, at least in the United States and in Australia, lies in the fact that most racers have a built-in "anti-engineer" prejudice. The general feeling seems to be that engineers—and, by association, engineering knowledge and techniques—are too theoretical for the hairy chested REAL WORLD of motor racing. I know that every time I arrive to do a consulting job with an operation that I have not worked with before, I have to overcome this prejudice one more time—usually by a combination of getting my hands dirty and figuring out a quick solution to at least one of the problems that led to my being called in to start with.

I am among the first to state that MANY engineers—especially those of the electronic, semiconductor and hypersonic fluid flow persuasions—ARE too theoretical for our particular (or peculiar) world. This fact does not, however, condemn engineering—or even engineers. It most certainly does not condemn engineering knowledge and/or engineering practice and procedure. Think about it the next time you walk aboard a commercial jet aircraft!

Anyway, some eight years ago I wrote and published PREPARE TO WIN in an effort to place as much as possible of the knowledge available concerning the science of race car preparation into one understandable and reasonably concise volume. A few years later, in TUNE TO WIN, I attempted to do the same thing with the art of vehicle dynamics. These efforts seem to have been successful. The reviews have been favorable, the mail plentiful and flattering. We have sold more books than anyone believed possible; we have made some reasonable money—and the books continue to sell.

All of the information contained in PREPARE TO WIN and TUNE TO WIN is still valid and none of it is outdated. The world, however, continues to turn—and in the God-knows-how-many race cars, test days, bull sessions and races since I delivered the typescripts to the printer I have learned a fair bit. Some suppliers have gone away and others have taken their places. There are new products, new materials and new techniques that the racer should know about—and we have learned more about some of the old ones. Ground effects came into being, partially matured and are, thank God, in the process of dying. It is, in short, time to update the information.

I considered rewriting the books; that is, bringing out "new editions." But there is not enough new information to warrant a real rewrite and a quick and dirty update would be a cheap shot. So I decided to do an "addendum." I started to compile the new stuff that I have learned over the past few years plus a few items that I left out on the first go-around. It didn't work. It didn't work because I was spending too much time trying to explain what has come to be known as "materials science" in a helter-skelter, piece-work sort of way. I finally decided that the only sensible thing for me to do was to (one more time) jump in where angels fear to tread and to write a basic metallurgy and strength of materials book for the racer, and THEN discuss the specifics of our usage of the materials. Of course, some of the material that follows is just what I started out to do—a listing of some of what I have learned about both preparation and vehicle dynamics in the years since I wrote the first two books.

Somehow each book that I write seems to end up being more technical than the last. This is probably due to the fact that I started with the simple subjects, and have run out of them. My advisers in the publishing world maintain that the current subject is too technical for the "average racer" (whoever he or she may be) and that I am going to lose my shirt. I don't think so. One sin that I have never been guilty of is that of underestimating my audience. While the racer may not be particularly willing to dig through textbooks and technical publications in search of general information, his or her thirst for knowledge that specifically relates to success in racing is unlimited. I sincerely hope that my estimation of the situation is correct, as I am working on both DESIGN TO WIN and DRIVE TO WIN, as well as on THE GREAT STREET CAR BOOK. No, I don't know when ANY of them will appear—I am still a full-time racer and a part-time writer.

All the best,

Carroll Smith

CONTENTS

CHAPTER ONE

INTRODUCTION TO METALLURGY

ME (AND YOU) AND MR. MURPHY

Thanks in part to the poster industry, I am certain that all of my readers are familiar with Mr. Murphy and his law(s). I am a long-time admirer of the good Mr. Murphy; so much so that I married one of his daughters and have sired a couple of his grandchildren. I do not, however, feel that the ever-growing anthology of his probably apocryphal dictums, however germain they may be, should be known as Murphy's LAWS. LAWS they were never meant to be, and most emphatically are not! Murphy meant to remind us—the engineers, mechanics, fabricators, welders, machinists, drivers and pilots of the world (in short, those who deal intimately with the potentially deadly combination of man and machine in motion) that the price of human error and/or oversight in any branch of engineering can be (and often is) very high indeed. His words—his original words, that is, not the cutesy imitations that have proliferated in the past few years—are priceless and should be engraved on the inner surface of every racer's and airman's eyeballs.

As I recall, his original pronouncement was, "If anything can go wrong, it will." This was very quickly expanded to, "If a part can fail, it will—and it will do so at the most inopportune time and place possible." What Murphy actually meant was that, due to the innate perversity of inanimate objects, we must design each and every part of our aircraft so well that it WILL NOT FAIL. Then we must manufacture it, install it, inspect it and maintain it in the same way. We must do all of this because IF WE DO NOT, THE AIRPLANE IS GOING TO FALL OUT OF THE SKY.

Murphy was actually an early aviator. He could easily have been a racer—the two species are very similar in nature and outlook. The rest of Murphy's real laws are variations on the same theme, which leads us to Smith's second law of motor racing: THERE IS NO SUCH THING AS MATERIAL FAILURE—ALL FAILURES ARE HUMAN IN ORIGIN.

By definition, any component that is properly designed, properly manufactured from the correct grade of the correct material, properly installed, inspected and maintained and is not overly abused in service WILL NOT FAIL DURING ITS DESIGNED SERVICE LIFE. If it DOES fail (without being involved in a crash), then it was either underdesigned, badly manufactured, improperly installed and/or maintained, or it was grossly abused. In any case, the primary cause of failure was HUMAN ERROR. Metal cannot think. Therefore metal can neither be blamed nor held responsible.

With the exception of those which are immediately preceded by violent meetings between metal and metal or between metal and stone, OUR component failures can be divided into five basic and overlapping classifications:

Design Faults
Manufacturing Errors
Installation Errors
In-Service Inspection and Maintenance Errors (or Omissions)
Operator Abuse

Design faults and oversights have only three possible causes: ignorance, carelessness and/or laziness. Each of us has been and will again be guilty of all three. Ignorance includes, but is not limited to, incomplete appreciation of:

(a) The operating conditions and loads to be encountered.

(b) Normal, to-be-expected shortcomings of materials, manufacturers, operators and maintainers.

(c) Incomplete gathering of information regarding the physical characteristics of the chosen materials under the conditions to be encountered, such as reaction to temperature, vibration, fatigue, heat treating, plating, corrosion, normal surface defects and a host of other factors (including believing the salesman).

Laziness and carelessness are so closely related (at least in my case) that I will treat them as one. One of Murphy's "laws" states that, "The probability of a dimension being omitted from a drawing is directly proportional to its importance." Design laziness includes such things as not calling out bend or machining radii, not doing at least a rough stress analysis if there is ANY doubt, not calling out specific heat treating details, not calling out specific materials, or fastener grades, or welding rods, or whatever—the list of possibilities is endless. My personal favorite sin lies in not checking my drawings in detail. Usually the guy who makes the part or the man who installs it will catch mistakes in this area (except with respect to wall thicknesses and heat treats) and the omission will cost money and embarrassment but will not cause physical risk. There is, however, no excuse.

Inspection and maintenance failures are failures of omission. An adequate part can fail only if it is not properly inspected and maintained. THERE IS NO PART OF THE RACING CAR WHICH CAN BE SAFELY INSTALLED AND FORGOTTEN ABOUT, including rivets and welds. Every part should be on a specific inspection schedule and a specific replacement schedule. I do not want to hear that the (select one or more of the following) piston, valve, gear, valve spring, bearing, rod, crank, or whatever failed because it had been in there too long. I pay the engine builder to make damned sure that no part of the engine is in there too long! By the same token, I am not going to tell either the car owner or the driver that the gear, axle, hub, bearing, wishbone, CV joint or whatever failed because it was too old (i.e. had exceeded its fatigue life). I get paid to make sure that this DOESN'T happen. If it does, the buck stops with me, the fault is mine and I take the flak. The same is true of the mechanics' FU's. I take the flak from the payer and the person at risk, and then I have a private chat with the creator of the FU. If he is worth keeping around he already feels so stupid, guilty and generally inadequate that the chat will consist mainly of disuading him from suicide. On the other hand, if he doesn't feel that way, he is GONE.

Abuse is normally applied by the occupant of the cockpit, as in hitting something, missing a shift(s), locking brakes, overrevving and so on. But not always! It is hard to blame the driver when a bolt falls out, or he runs out of brake fluid (or pads), or the Schraeder valve in the tire isn't tight. . . .

As John Donne said centuries ago, "No man is an island, entire unto himself." Failures usually have more than one cause and they are usually interrelated. Almost all non-accident race car component failures are fatigue failures, which means (as we shall see) that there was at least SOME warning which went either unseen or unheeded. Further, most of the parts which fail because they were underdesigned or badly manufactured were pretty obviously not up to the job to start with. IF SOMEONE HAD TAKEN THE TIME AND TROUBLE TO THINK ABOUT IT MUCH THEY WOULD NOT HAVE BEEN ON THE CAR!

Everyone involved with motor racing must be a jack-of-all-trades. The mechanics must recognize insufficient or misplaced radii—and have an eagle eye for cracks. The machinists and fabricators must recognize bad or insufficient design—and be willing to point it out when they see it. The engineers and designers must be willing to listen to criticism from the shop floor—and to respond to it. In this most egocentric of all occupations there is no room for the insecurity caused by the oversensitive ego. For my own part, my first (and last) feeling when one of my goofs is detected before it gets on the car is one of immense gratitude to the detector. On the other hand, the surest way to get fired from any race team that I am running is to state, "I knew that that part would fail"—after it has.

So, when the control arm fails on the north bank at Daytona, whose fault is it? It is the designer's fault, IF he knew that the part was going to be used on the high banks. It is also the chief mechanic's fault because he should have seen that the design was not sufficient to withstand the loads imposed by the banking. AND it is the fault of whoever is in charge of the operation because he should either have seen the inadequacy himself or hired someone who could. It could even be the driver's fault if he didn't tell anybody about the curb that he clouted hard in practice. Whosoever's fault it may be, two things are perfectly certain:

(1) It was NOT the wishbone's fault.

(2) It doesn't really matter whose fault it was; it happened. What DOES matter is that all of those involved learn from the failure so that it cannot happen again. The most incredible thing in motor racing is to watch an experienced and supposedly competent person replacing a part which has just broken with another one just like it (known in some circles as "the Pommy syndrome"). I once heard a man say, "What the hell, parts break." I don't work with him anymore. Parts DO NOT BREAK—we break them.

In some cases it is difficult to convince the car owner and/or his beancounter that an expensive part that looks (and tests) just fine should be trashed simply because it has accumulated some seemingly arbitrary number of hours of service time. Of course these people have never been in either an aircraft or a racing car that was in the process of crashing because a critical part had just failed from fatigue. . . .

Murphy's last words were, "Never underestimate the power of group effort to botch up even a good design." What can happen here is that the designer may be simply too lazy to bother calling out a specific radius on a machined part. His rationale goes like this, "Joe is a good machinist. He knows better than to make a part with a sharp corner. Not only is there no need for me to call out a radius here, but, if I do, Joe is liable to feel insulted."

So the radius call out is left off the drawing.

When Joe is making the part he thinks, "It sure looks like this part needs a radius here. But Peter is a damned good Engineer—if he wanted a radius here, he would have called one out. So I'll just make the part to the print."

So the radius is left off the part.

Bill, the mechanic installing the part, thinks, " Boy, this looks wrong! But Peter designed it and Joe made it—they are both competent and experienced, so it must be right. I'll just put it on like I was told to."

So the part gets on the car.

You may think that this is an improbable scenario, if not an impossible one. An example is in order. The one race that Shelby's Ford GT Mk II's lost over the years was the 24 hours of Daytona in 1967. All of the transaxles failed. They all failed in the same place after very close to the same number of MINUTES of service (quality control was superb). Hank Gregorich was the Chief Engineer of the transmission and chassis division at the time—and a damned fine engineer (and human being) he is. For years after the incident, one of the input shafts that had failed where the radius was omitted hung on his office wall. These same shafts were then in their third year of manufacture—with no design changes. Just one bad batch slipped through manufacture, inspection and installation. We lost a motor race. We were humiliated. We ALL learned. We never lost another motor race!

The last words on the subject of component failure are usually those of the driver. Inevitably these words are, "Oh, shit!" These have been the last words of far too many of my friends. I sincerely hope that this book may go a little way toward preventing these being the last words of more of my friends (and yours).

Anyway, if we are to prevent parts from failing, we must all have some knowledge of HOW and WHY parts can fail. Since most of our parts are made from metal, it follows that we must all have some familiarity with basic metallurgy. And so here we go. . . .

THE REAL INTRODUCTION TO METALS AND METALLURGY

I think that I did a pretty good job on the metal working side of things the first time around, in PREPARE TO WIN. Those readers who wish to explore the subject further will find a list of recommended books and pamphlets in the appendix. One work deserves special and specific mention: Ron Fournier, one of the best fabricators that I have ever known (and one of the nicest people) has now written his own RACE AND CUSTOM CAR METAL FABRICATOR'S HANDBOOK, which was published by the ubiquitous (and generally excellent) HP Books in December of 1982. The book is outstanding—buy it! It is, in fact, so good that it has completely removed any temptation I may have felt to expand on my previous coverage.

What I did NOT do in either of the previous books was to discuss the various metals that we use—their origins, properties, alloys, designations, heat treatments, recommended uses and the like. Many of you have written or called asking for just that; a short and simple course in basic ferrous and nonferrous metallurgy. Besides, I have seen enough of the wrong metals—or the wrong alloys of the right metals or the wrong heat treatment of the right alloys—used, often with disastrous results, to convince me that I should attempt the subject. It is not going to be short and, despite my best intentions and efforts, it may not be terribly simple. Bear with me if I get a bit pedantic.

There are two separate but necessarily interwoven branches of metallurgy: extraction metallurgy (the separation of metals from their ores) and physical metallurgy (the changing of metals from their pure states, in which they are typically soft and weak, into useful conditions of hardness, toughness and strength).

It can be argued that, from the practical point of view, we racers are not really much concerned with physical metallurgy and not at all with extraction metallurgy (unless we should find ourselves among the survivors of Armageddon). After all, while it has only been in the past few centuries that scientists have had any success at all in figuring out the hows and whys of metallurgy, many of the practical aspects of the art (including, but not limited to, ore reduction, annealing, quenching, tempering and carburizing) have been common knowledge among metalsmiths for millennia. Even today a complete and scientific understanding of physical metallurgy escapes us.

I do not agree with those who feel that theoretical knowledge is unnecessary. I believe that, both in order to do our jobs properly and to derive the maximum satisfaction from our lives, each of us should strive to learn as much as possible about the practical aspects of the materials and the tools with which we work. I also believe that we each should have some appreciation of the origins of the materials which we use and of the human creativity and effort that has gone into their development and production.

I also do not agree with the often-stated dictum that there are no craftsmen today, that the workman has lost respect for his material. There ARE still craftsmen around. And the craftsman has not only respect but also a sort of romantic (almost mystic) feeling for his material, whatever that material may be. It is the noncraftsman—the assembly line worker, the person whose work is noncreative—who has no respect for the material with which he works. How could he have?

THE NATURE OF METALS

We each learned in high school that all matter is composed of atoms. Mother Nature has arranged that there are about 100 different kinds of atoms, most of which will not concern us in this book. We call the different kinds of atoms ELEMENTS. Each element is unique in its ATOMIC STRUCTURE and all of the atoms of any given element are identical. Atoms can exist in three states:

(1) As pure elements, each with its own unique physical and chemical characteristics. Iron, for instance, is a

soft and weak metal. Carbon is a hard and very strong, but brittle, nonmetal.

(2) As a mixture or a solution of different elements. In this case the characteristics of the mixture will generally be a combination of the characteristics of the constituent elements. Steel, for example, is a solution of carbon in iron which combines some of the ductility of iron with some of the hardness and strength of carbon.

(3) As a chemical compound in which the individual atoms of the constituent elements have combined in definite proportions and in a definite structure to form a new substance whose physical and/or chemical characteristics may be completely different from those of its constituent elements. As an example, sodium (a soft white metal) combines with chlorine (a green, poisonous gas) to form sodium chloride which we know as common table (or sea) salt.

Mr. Webster defines a metal as "any of a category of electropositive elements that are usually whitish, lustrous, are able to deform plastically without breaking and which exhibit high tensile strengths combined with moderate levels of elasticity." Translated, this means that metals exhibit the following characteristics:

(1) They are good conductors of both heat and electricity. If, for instance, you pick up a lump of metal in one hand and a lump of stone in the other, the metal will feel colder to your touch than the stone if both are below body temperature, and warmer if both are above body temperature. This ability to conduct heat (and electricity) with unusual efficiency is due to the presence of a large number of "free electrons" within the atomic structure of metals. This is of no great interest to the racer, except when he is wiring the car. In this case he must remember that, as the temperature of a metal increases, its electrical resistance also increases; i.e., its ability to conduct electricity decreases. This is why we need LARGE wires from the battery to the starter. It takes a lot of current to crank the engine over; the transmission of this current through the starter cables heats the wires; the heating of the wires decreases their ability to conduct current so the starter motor turns over more slowly and the engine won't start. This example will serve as our first practical application of metallurgical knowledge.

(2) Metals are lustrous. This means that they reflect light well and/or that they shine well, a characteristic of interest only when we find ourselves polishing the tub or the wheels, in which case we usually wish that it weren't so. (About the only good thing that I can find to say about Dymag wheels is that they are black and so do not require polishing.)

(3) Metals as a family are generally able to undergo a considerable amount of plastic deformation without rupture (or failure). This is one of the keys that makes metals useful to us. It is this characteristic that allows metals to be beaten and/or rolled into sheets, bars and rods, drawn into wire and formed into useful shapes.

(4) Metals are elastic. This simply means that, when a metal has been deformed by an applied load, the metal will return to its original shape and size when the load is released (assuming that the metal was loaded within its elastic limits). This ELASTICITY allows metal structures to resist failure under high levels of load and stress. A properly designed and fabricated metal structure will distribute a severe impact load by yielding slightly in the area of the applied load, thus distributing the load throughout the structure. A ceramic or reinforced plastic structure under the same conditions would probably crack and/or fracture in a brittle manner. As you might expect, we will be looking into this subject at considerably greater depth later on.

(5) Metals are characteristically strong. Without strength, metals would be relatively useless as structural materials. Fortunately the Creator foresaw this and endowed metals with their characteristically high tensile strengths, making them perhaps the most useful and versatile of all groups of elements.

Before we go any further into our investigation of metals, we must pause and define some of the terms we will be using to describe their properties:

HARDNESS is the property of resisting penetration. Normally, the hardness of a material varies directly with its strength—the harder the material, the stronger it will be, and vice versa.

BRITTLENESS is the tendency of a material to fracture without changing shape. Technically, brittleness is the property of resisting any attempt to change the relative positions of the atoms within the structure of a material. Unfortunately hardness and brittleness enjoy a close relationship—the harder (and therefore the stronger) a material is, the more brittle it is liable to be. Brittle materials exhibit poor shock load resistance and are therefore not suited to our use.

MALLEABILITY is the exact opposite of brittleness. A malleable material can be severely bent (the technical term is "permanently distorted") without rupture. As a point of interest, the most malleable of the metals is gold. Unfortunately malleable materials tend to be weak.

DUCTILITY is very similar to malleability. It is the property of some materials that allows them to be drawn out to thin sections without breaking, like taffy (or wire). We normally use the term "ductility" to mean BOTH ductility and malleability. The harder and stronger a metal is, the less ductile it will be; the softer and more ductile the material, the weaker it will be.

TOUGHNESS of a material is defined as the total amount of energy that the material can absorb before failure. It is a measure of the material's ability to resist impact or shock loads. It is the opposite of brittleness.

Having looked at the general nature of metals, investigated some of their characteristics and defined a few of the basic terms, it is time to begin our more detailed investigation into their structure and behavior.

THE CRYSTALLINE STRUCTURE OF METALS

Although they certainly look and feel like solid entities, all metals are actually POLYCRYSTALLINE in structure; that is, they are composed of cohesive groups of CRYS-

TALS. A crystal is defined as an orderly and repetitive arrangement of identical CRYSTAL UNIT CELLS which are in turn each composed of a fixed number of atoms arranged in an unvarying pattern in space. These unit cells join to form a regular and repetitive CRYSTALLINE SPACE LATTICE.

As an indication of the numbers and sizes involved, let's consider the structure of one of the more common metals, copper. Each unit cell of copper is composed of nine atoms arranged in the shape of a cube, with one atom at each corner and one in the geometric center of the cube, as illustrated by FIGURE [1].

One gram of pure copper contains 2,370,000,000,000, 000,000,000 (237 × 10 to the 19th power) unit cells. To put things in some perspective, the smallest object that can be distinguished by the unaided human eye, under ideal conditions, is about 500,000 atoms in diameter.

The basic structure of the crystals—the actual arrangement of the atoms into unit cells—is, logically enough, termed the CRYSTAL STRUCTURE of the metal. Since the individual crystals (which we usually call "grains") are normally far too small for us to see, they are examined through a microscope (at magnifications ranging from 100 to 1,000 times and more). Crystal structures with grains small enough to require this sort of treatment are referred to as MICROSTRUCTURES. Some castings have grain structures made up of crystals large enough to be seen with the naked eye. These are called MACROSTRUCTURES and are of little interest to us. I will not mention the word again.

This is probably as good a time as any for me to state that there is no such thing as a "molecule" of metal. Metals have atoms and they have unit cells and they have crystals, but they do not have molecules. In fact, one of the characteristics that distinguishes the family of metals from other elements is that they are "monotomic"; that is, their crystalline structure is made up of individual atoms, not of molecules.

By their very nature, crystals do us some favors. They are organized little devils; the arrangement of particles (atoms) within any given crystal is orderly and predictable. Each atom vibrates or does its thing around a fixed point, and these points are cleverly arranged in a regular pattern in three-dimensional space. What is more, the pattern repeats itself so that crystal unit cells can join each other in an orderly fashion in a modular, three-dimensional crystalline space lattice. This regularity is due to a phenomenon known as the CONSTANCY OF ANGLE which states that, in any crystalline substance, the angle included between any two adjacent faces of the crystal must be equal, and that this angle will remain constant throughout the substance. This is easy enough to visualize in two dimensions, as illustrated by FIGURE [2].

We can come up with an almost infinite number of regular shapes which will satisfy this requirement: the equilateral triangle, the square, the rectangle, the regular pentagon, the regular hexagon and so on. Each of these two dimensional figures has an AXIS OF ROTATIONAL SYMMETRY passing through its geometric center and perpendicular to its plane.

One of the ways in which we describe and analyze the symmetry of any geometric shape is by specifying its axes of symmetry. This is done by counting the fractions of a rotation required to carry the figure to a position that is completely congruent to its original position (i.e., a position in which it would be completely hidden from view were the original placed directly in front of it).

Figure (2): Some of the plane shapes which satisfy the "constancy of angle" requirements.

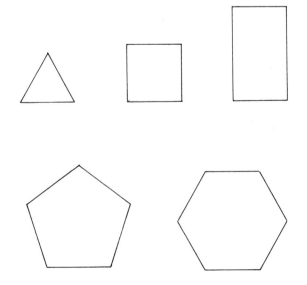

Figure (1): Nine copper atoms forming a cubic crystal cell of metallic copper.

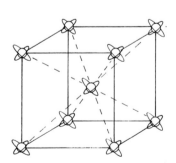

Obviously one complete rotation of any two-dimensional figure will satisfy congruency. As shown in FIGURE [3] one third of a full rotation will return an equilateral triangle to congruency. We therefore state that the equilateral triangle has a THREEFOLD AXIS OF ROTATION. The square requires one fourth of a full rotation and so has a fourfold axis. The rectangle requires one half of a rotation and has a twofold axis while the pentagon and the hexagon require only one fifth and one sixth of a rotation respectively and so are described as having fivefold and sixfold axes of rotation.

THE CRYSTALLINE LATTICE

Still visualizing in two dimensions let's take a look (using FIGURE [4]) at how we can stack or build a lattice using plane shapes which possess constancy of angle. Note that these lattices exhibit the same axes of rotational symmetry that the single figures displayed; that atoms at the corners or along the edges of a single figure are ''shared'' by the other figures having the same corners and/or edges; that it is not possible to construct a lattice using figures with a fivefold axis of rotation or with figures having more than a sixfold axis. Attempts to do so are shown in FIGURE [5]. With two-, three-, four- and sixfold axes of symmetry we have exhausted the possibilities of lattice construction.

Figure (4): Two-dimensional representations of symmetrical crystal lattices.

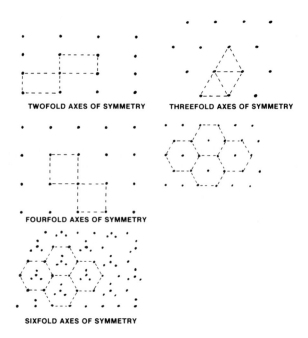

Figure (3): Axes of symmetry for some plane shapes displaying constancy of angle.

Figure (5): Attempts to build symmetrical lattices from figures with five, or with more than six, axes of symmetry are doomed to failure.

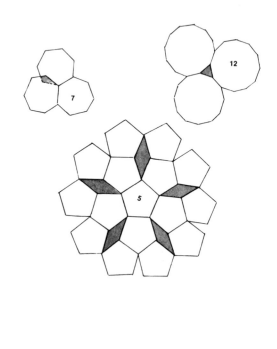

THREE-DIMENSIONAL SYMMETRY

Everything that we have discussed with regard to two-dimensional symmetry carries over into three dimensions. It merely gets harder to visualize (and to draw). Crystals of metal (or of anything else, for that matter) cannot have either a fivefold axis of symmetry or an axis of symmetry greater than sixfold. This simplifies things more than a bit. As a typical example, consider the hypothetical simple cubic crystal shown in FIGURE [6].

In three-dimensional space this cube has LOTS of axes of symmetry: SIX twofold axes (through the centers of each of the six pairs of opposite edges), FOUR threefold axes (through the four pairs of opposite cube corners) and THREE fourfold axes (through the centers of the three pairs of opposite faces). The only way that I have ever been able to understand this concept is to construct a cube from cardboard or foam and pierce the thing with needles or welding rod until I am satisfied. I'll be damned if I can figure out a way to show it clearly in a drawing. I don't even want to consider trying to show the axes of any other crystal configuration (cubes are easy) but you can play with foam and cardboard until you have the concept of three-dimensional axes of symmetry mastered. The important part is to realize that, although each "module" or "unit cell" of the three-dimensional space lattice can be rotated every which way about its various axes of symmetry; when the rotation is stopped, it will still fit perfectly into the crystal lattice, rather like square Legos.

FIGURE [7] is a schematic representation of how a simple cubic unit cell builds into a cubic space lattice. Note that every atom (with the exception of those at the outside corners of the lattice) is shared by at least two unit cells and that the atom in the center of the space lattice is common to ALL of the unit cells shown. Each of the crystal unit cells can be fitted into its proper position within the lattice by a rotation about any of its axes of rotation; and it will fit perfectly, sharing edges and atoms in a unitary structure.

THE STRUCTURE OF THE CRYSTAL UNIT CELL

Just as there are a limited number of possibilities for the shapes that can form a lattice, so there are limited possibilities for the arrangement of the atoms within the cells that comprise the crystals. My trouble in this area lies in my difficulty in visualizing the atoms themselves. After all, no one (at least no one I know) has ever SEEN an atom!

As a long time science-fiction fan I have no trouble at all visualizing our planet whirling in orbit around the sun, and our moon orbiting earth and the other planets orbiting the sun, each with its own satellites, while the whole mess—solar systems, comets, asteroids, Han Solo, Princess Leila, E.T. and all—rushes through space. I have a hell of a lot of trouble looking at my own fingernail (or a part of the race car) and realizing in my heart that this seemingly solid object is mainly empty space simply because it is composed of countless atoms, each of which is in turn comprised of a dense nucleus surrounded by a "cloud" of electrons, each of which is whirling in its own little orbit around that nucleus. AND that the space between the nucleus and the orbit of the electrons, which makes up the vast majority of all space, is EMPTY! My brain knows that this is true, but my heart (or some other unreasoning part of me) is boggled by the concept.

Figure (7): A hypothetical, simple cubic unit cell and a cubic crystal space lattice composed of eight unit cells. Note that, with the exception of those located at the outside corners, each atom of the structure is shared by at least two unit cells while the central atom is shared by all eight unit cells.

Figure (6): Hypothetical, simple cubic crystal.

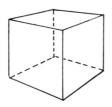

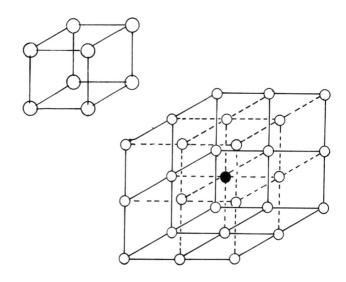

Anyway, the atoms that make up the crystal unit cell can be arranged so that the cell will be body-centered, face-centered or close-packed. These three basic crystal unit cell structures develop from the geometry of layers of efficiently stacked spheres of uniform size. In order to simplify the necessary visualizations of crystalline structures in the pages to come I will often represent the individual atoms as solid spheres while, in other drawings, either unit cells or individual crystals may be shown by cubes.

One more time we will call upon our old friend the easy-to-draw cube to illustrate. Iron (as well as copper) has a BODY-CENTERED cubic unit cell. In this case, as shown by FIGURE [8A], one atom is located at the geometric center of the cell and is surrounded by eight other atoms, one at each corner of the cube. In FIGURE [8A] I have purposely exaggerated the distance between the atoms of the cell in order to make their arrangement clear. In actuality

the atoms are virtually touching each other, as shown by FIGURE [8B] in which the individual atoms are represented by solid spheres. Again, an actual cube may be of benefit in the visualization.

Another possibility is the FACE-CENTERED cubic structure. Aluminum has a face-centered cubic structure in which an individual atom occupies the center of one face of a cube and is surrounded by 12 other atoms—one at each corner of the cube and one at the center of each of the other faces. Obviously the face-centered cubic crystal cell contains more atoms than its cousin, the body-centered cell, so the atoms are more closely packed as shown in FIGURES [9A] and [9B].

The next possibility is the CLOSE-PACKED hexagonal unit cell arrangement. Magnesium has such a structure, as does the orange or apple display at your local supermarket.

Figure (8A): Body-centered cubic unit cell. Distance between atoms is exaggerated for clarity.

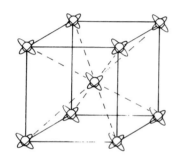

Figure (9A): Face-centered cubic unit cell, with distance between atoms exaggerated for clarity.

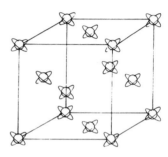

Figure (8B): Body-centered cubic unit cell using spheres to represent atoms.

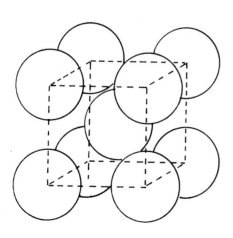

Figure (9B): Face-centered cubic unit cell using spheres to represent atoms.

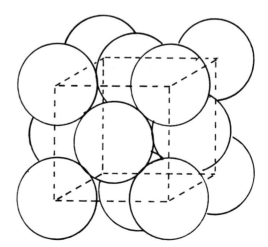

The structure of the close-packed hexagonal unit cell is depicted by FIGURES [10A] and [10B], which also depict, step by step, how the unit cell is made up from stacked planes of atoms. These CRYSTALLOGRAPHIC planes are simply the planes in which the atoms are naturally arranged in the greatest numbers. The arrangement of the planes differs with the type of unit cell structure. The three

Figure (10A): Close-packed hexagonal crystal unit cell, with distance between atoms exaggerated for clarity.

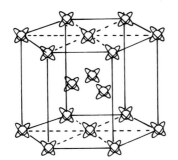

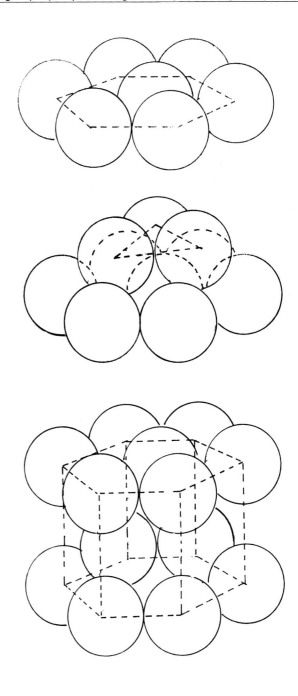

configurations in which we are interested are shown schematically in FIGURES [11], [11A], [12] and [13].

There are other symmetrical crystal forms. I am not going to describe them. Roughly 60% of the common metals crystallize in a cubic pattern and about 30% crystallize on a hexagonal pattern. The three basic structures that I have described cover most of the metals in which we have a direct interest. I feel these three also illustrate the principles involved as well as they can be illustrated. It is important to realize that, regardless of the configuration of the crystal unit cell, as the lattice is built up, the atoms along the edges and faces of the individual cells are SHARED with the adjacent cells, so that the lattice becomes an integrated structure as illustrated by FIGURE [14].

The physical or mechanical properties of specific metals largely depend upon the type of space lattice that they form as they solidify from the liquid state. In general, the more closely packed the atoms in the unit cell, the harder and stronger the metal. Therefore metals with a face-centered lattice tend to be ductile, shock resistant and easily worked. Metals which have a body-centered lattice tend to be stronger but less ductile. And, finally, those with a hexagonal close-packed lattice tend to be very strong and hard but brittle, with limited ductility or toughness.

Regardless of the configuration or atomic structure, the whole mess is held together by very strong electrical forces. The nucleus is composed of positively charged protons and neutrally charged neutrons, while the orbiting electrons are negatively charged. To the best of my knowledge no one knows exactly what electrons really are; they are variously called "waves," "particles," "negative

Figure (11): Crystalline planes of body-centered cubic crystal lattice.

Figure (12): Crystalline planes of a face-centered cubic lattice.

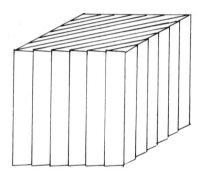

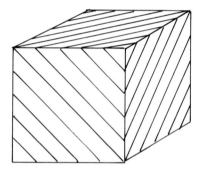

Figure (11A): A face-centered cubic crystalline space lattice with one corner sliced to expose a crystallographic plane of atoms; corresponds to Figure (9B).

Figure (13): Crystalline planes of a close-packed hexagonal lattice.

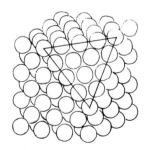

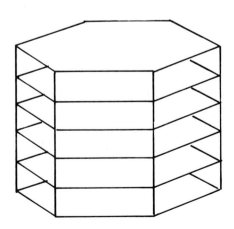

charges of electricity" and, lately, "quarks." (For our purposes, we are going to consider the electron to be an infinitesimally small particle of matter which has a negative electrical charge.) Opposites attract, so the whole little system is kept in equilibrium by electricity—similar to the way in which gravity and velocity interact to keep satellites in earth orbit.

THE STRENGTH (AND THE WEAKNESSES) OF CRYSTALLINE STRUCTURES

The atomic structure of crystals shows an orderliness and perfection that is unique in nature. Theorists tell us that a perfect crystal of virtually any metal is stronger than even the strongest alloy steel that man has yet developed. As an example, it has been proven that a single perfect crystal of

iron has an ultimate tensile strength of 1,900,000 psi while normal metallic iron has an ultimate tensile strength of about 4,000 psi and our strongest practical steels are presently about 320,000 psi. This is why artificially grown filaments or "whiskers" of metallic substances (such as boron) and nonmetals (such as carbon) are so strong when properly oriented and used in "composite" materials.

However, it can be demonstrated that real-life crystals of metal do not even approach the theoretical strength of a perfect crystal of the same metal. The reason for this is that the crystal structure of metals, although regular and orderly, is a long way from being perfect. Virtually all crystalline structures in nature contain imperfections—sometimes minute imperfections—and these imperfections play at least as important a part in the determination of the physical properties of the real-world metal as does the structure itself. If metals were comprised of single crystals this would not be so—but they are not.

GRAINS OF METAL

Under normal circumstances any piece of metal will consist of a large number of small crystals (or grains) rather than one large one. Like Legos, each of these crystals will be made up from identical unit cells but, like Legos constructions, the crystals may NOT be uniform in either size or shape. Therefore each crystal will not be perfectly aligned with its neighbors like bricks in a wall, rather, there will be voids between the grains like the spaces between the stones in a dry stone wall. Even if the grains WERE uniform in size and shape, there would still be imperfections in the structure. For example, suppose you were to dump a whole bunch of identical solid shapes into a box; no matter how much you shake the box the shapes will not align themselves perfectly and there will be voids between them.

In the crystalline structure of metals this lack of uniformity and imperfection of structure is a natural consequence of the way in which metals solidify into crystals from the liquid state (since all metals are refined from their ores by a process involving lots of heat, they first appear in liquid form).

THE GROWTH OF CRYSTALS

In the liquid state the atoms that comprise our metals are confused, wandering around at random and bumping into each other. As the liquid metal begins to solidify (actually the metals "freeze" and change "phase" just as liquid water freezes into crystalline ice), the atoms begin to grow together into orderly crystals in several areas at the same time (just as lumps of slush begin to form in a pail of freezing water). These first CRYSTAL NUCLEI form crystal unit cells which join together into crystalline space lattices. The lattices then continue to grow at the expense of the ever decreasing volume of liquid (it's a bit like watching Pac-Man eat the opposition) until they run into each other. At the point of collision, growth of the crystal lattice stops, although it continues elsewhere until the liquid is completely solidified. At this point the crystals become the

Figure (14): Crystal space lattice built up from face-centered cubic unit cells, showing how adjacent cells share edge and corner atoms to form an integrated lattice.

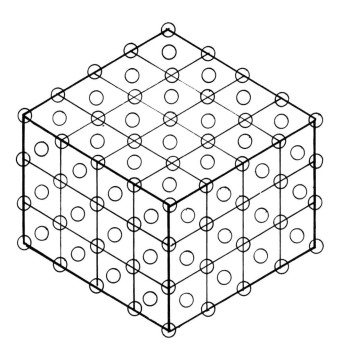

"grains" of the solid material. The process is shown in FIGURE [15] and schematically in FIGURE [15A].

Each crystal of the solid substance is termed a "grain" and its interface with each of its neighboring grains is termed a GRAIN BOUNDARY. Each and every grain of the solid is joined to its neighbors AT ALL POINTS along its boundaries. The actual location of the grain boundaries, as well as the size and the shape of individual grains, is determined simply by where the separately growing crystals happen to meet during solidification. It is for this reason

that individual grains usually have irregular and noncrystallographic shapes. Planar crystal faces (like a diamond) simply cannot be formed when each grain shape is randomly determined by the chance arrangement of its growing neighbors. However, when a section is sliced from a crystalline material, etched, polished and photographed under a microscope, the CROSS-SECTIONS of the grains so depicted are liable to look a lot more uniform than the grains themselves really are. FIGURE [16] shows how this

---

Figure (15): Steps in the solidification of a crystalline solid from the liquid state.

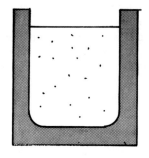

FORMATION OF CRYSTAL NUCLEI IN MELT AT BEGINNING OF SOLIDIFICATION.

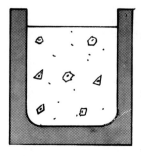

PARTIAL SOLIDIFICATION, CRYSTAL NUCLEI AND GROWING CRYSTALS IN MELT.

GROWING CRYSTALS HAVE MET. SOLIDIFICATION COMPLETE. CRYSTALLINE SOLID FORMED.

Figure (15A): Growth of crystal unit cells into crystalline grains.

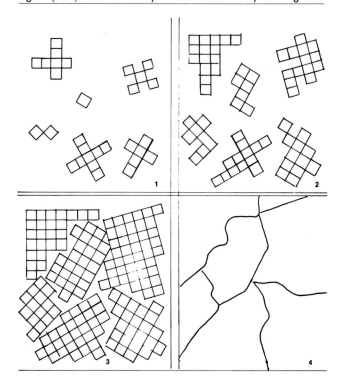

Figure (16): Why the crystals of a sectioned, etched and polished specimen appear more uniform than they actually are. *The Oxy-Acetylene Handbook*, Linde Division of Union Carbide Corporation.

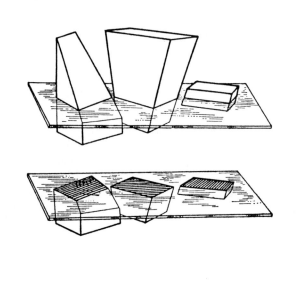

24

can come to pass. To me, these microphotographs of crystals and grain structures resemble nothing so much as the grained vinyl tile found in every motel bathroom in the world, as in FIGURE [16A].

Some years ago—when I was in college, students were a lot less antimilitary than they are now—an instructor in basic metallurgy used an analogy with soldiers to explain the alignment or orientation of crystals within a solid. I have never run across one that is as clear so, with apologies to a long-departed professor at the University of Rochester, I will steal the analogy.

Visualize a drill field on which several hundred trained soldiers, assigned to two different groups, are randomly placed, as shown in FIGURE [17A]. When one group is commanded to fall in it does so. These troops are represented as X's. In this case we arrange for them to form up in separate formations as PLATOONS on their preassigned platoon guides. However, we have also arranged that the platoon guides will not be in alignment with each other. We now have the situation shown in FIGURE [17B]. When the unassigned troops, represented by O's are given the order to fall in, being well trained, they will attach themselves to the nearest platoon as continuations of that platoon's formation and alignment.

Everything goes along nicely and in an orderly fashion until the extended platoons begin to collide because they are not aligned with respect to each other. The leftover soldiers, unable to find a position for themselves that will be aligned with both platoons, become confused. The best that they can do is to find a compromise position—so we end up with the majority of the soldiers in perfect formation but with a significant number trying to fill up the voids caused by misalignment, and only partially succeeding. Further, dislocations exist between platoons where there is insufficient room for a soldier. Further still, the platoons, due to the joining of random numbers of extra soldiers, are no longer of equal size or even of similar shape.

This is a two dimensional representation. Imagine the soldiers as fish of different shapes and sizes in the sea. The fish themselves are three-dimensional and they are able to move freely in three-dimensional space. If they were to be given the same training and the same commands as the soldiers, the result would be a three-dimensional crystalline fish structure complete with boundaries, intersections and voids.

Figure (16A): Aluminum grains enlarged 10,000 times.

Figure (17): Platoon analogy illustrates solidification of crystals.

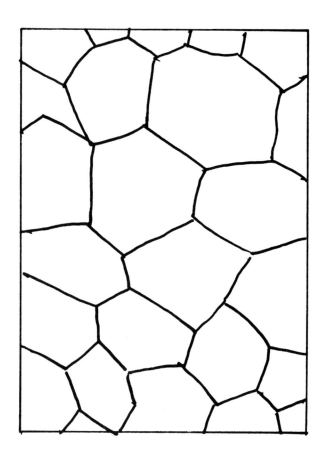

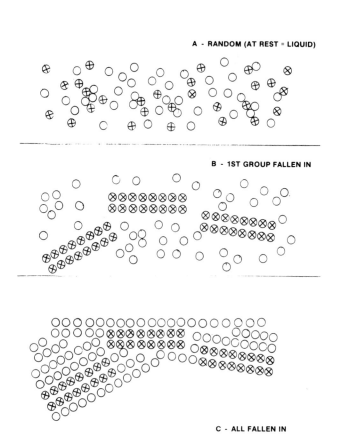

A - RANDOM (AT REST = LIQUID)

B - 1ST GROUP FALLEN IN

C - ALL FALLEN IN

Pretty much the same state of affairs exists in the world of metallic crystal structures. While a given crystal may be most impressively regular, the actual, real-world metal consists of a conglomerate of small crystals, not one big one. Since the crystals or grains grow sort of all willy-nilly with respect to each other, their attempts at alignment are imperfect and there are, inevitably, misfits as well as boundaries between adjacent crystals or grains as shown by FIGURE [17D]. A group of crystals with no grain boundaries between them would simply be a single large crystal. Further, although the internal arrangement of the atoms in all of the crystals of a given metal or metallic alloy must be identical, the external shape of the individual crystals may be very different (as may their sizes), again contributing to imperfect fits between individual grains of the metal. Grain boundaries (as well as the size of individual grains) are a major factor in the determination of the physical properties of metals.

FIGURE [18] is a two-dimensional representation of a grain boundary done with a circle template. Researchers and university students do it with soap bubbles between planes of glass. The reader can do the same thing with marbles. In fact it is probably a pretty good idea for the reader who has come this far to do so. Playing with three-dimensional (or even two-dimensional) toys is the best way that I know of to really grasp a concept.

Anyway, we are not really sure just what goes on at the borders between adjacent crystals or grains. We assume, from experimental results, that there is some sort of interlocked or interlocking border line where the atoms that make up the last unit cells of one crystal change their orientation from the atoms of the adjoining crystal. Or, there may be some unattached "free" atoms floating along the border and serving as a noncrystallized adhesive between adjacent crystals. At any rate, we do know that many crystalline grain boundaries are a great deal stronger than they have any right to be (even though they do not approach the theoretical strength of a single crystal).

VACANCIES IN THE LATTICE

In addition to the boundaries between the individual grains of a crystalline substance, there are also normally a certain number of gaps or vacancies within the crystalline lattice (no soldier found his way here, in or out of formation). FIGURE [19] shows vacancies in a two-dimensional representation of a crystal lattice. These vacancies can be either small (a single or maybe a few atoms missing) or they can be fairly large (multi-vacancies) in which case several atoms would be necessary to fill the void and the whole lattice is liable to be relaxed or disordered in the immediate area of the vacancy. Small vacancies are inevitable, but we really do not need multi-vacancies in our structural materials—unless, of course, we can figure out some very clever way to fill them with something that will enhance the properties of the metal. More about this later—suffice for now to state that the vacancies may, under some circumstances, be helpful.

Figure (17D): Aluminum grains enlarged 5,000 times.

Figure (18): Grain boundary in two-dimensional representation.

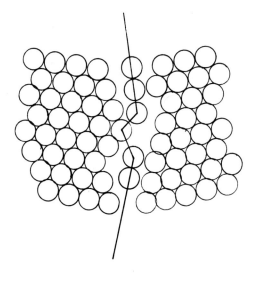

DISLOCATIONS

A dislocation in the lattice is not dissimilar to a grain boundary. In the case of the dislocation two adjacent cells, instead of nesting, have sort of butted against each other creating a "semi-boundary" or an area where the adjacent atoms do not line up perfectly. The result is an extra plane—or partial plane—of atoms extending from the dislocation. This sort of "edge dislocation" also illustrated by FIGURE [19A] can significantly reduce the crystal's ability to withstand stress.

We will return to the crystalline nature of metals, or at least to the behavior of metals due to their crystalline nature. But before we go further it is time to examine the actual atomic structure of our metals and the nature of the interatomic bonds that hold them together.

THE PLASTIC DEFORMATION OF METAL

One of the major characteristics that makes metals more useful to engineers than, say, minerals, is their unique ability to undergo large plastic deformations without rupture. In other words we can form the damned things into shapes that, after they are formed, will be strong, tough and resistant to both shock and fatigue. This seeming magic comes about because the crystal structure of metals (unlike that of minerals) is relatively tolerant of structural imperfections. Metals form strong but FLEXIBLE bonds across grain boundaries. Nonmetallic crystals may form strong bonds across boundaries, but they do not form flexible ones and so are very liable to rupture across grain boundaries whenever a stress is applied. For our investigation into why this is so we should touch, briefly, on the structure of the atom itself and on the nature of the interatomic bonds that hold our universe as well as everthing and everybody in it together.

THE STRUCTURE OF THE ATOM

We are all more or less familiar with the concept that everything is a collection of tiny little atoms flying around in close formation and that each individual atom consists of a NUCLEUS around which orbit a number of ELECTRONS, much as the moon orbits the earth and the planets orbit the sun. The nucleus is comprised of some number of PROTONS, each of which has a positive electrical charge ($+1$) and some number of NEUTRONS, which have no charge. The orbiting electrons each have a negative electrical charge (-1). The MASS of the nucleus is many thousands of times greater than that of the electrons, but the space enclosed within the electron orbits is many thousands

---

Figure (19): Vacancies and edge dislocations within the crystalline lattice.

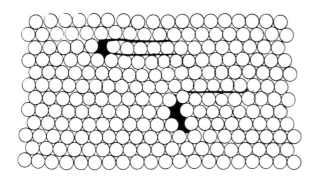

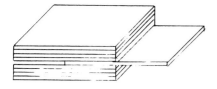

Figure (19A): Edge dislocations formed by joining of irregular crystal surfaces.

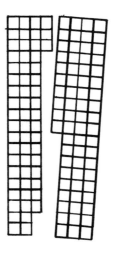
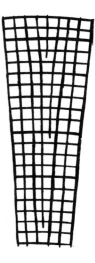

of times the volume of the nucleus. FIGURE [20] shows the relationship between the nucleus and the electrons of a few familiar atoms, such as hydrogen, the simplest atom in nature.

We know that, electrically speaking, opposites attract and that the electrostatic attraction between positively charged protons and negatively charged electrons is what holds the universe and everything in it together. Atoms of different elements have different numbers of neutrons, protons and electrons and, consequently, different weights.

The atomic number of any element is simply the number of protons in its nucleus. For example, hydrogen, has exactly one proton and a corresponding atomic number of 1. The hydrogen nucleus has a positive electrical charge of ($+1$). Orbiting this simple nucleus is a single electron with a negative electrical charge of (-1). Overall the atom is electrically neutral. More complex (or heavier) atoms have more protons, more neutrons and more electrons to match their protons. As examples, sodium has 11 protons and an atomic number of 11, chlorine has 17, iron 26, uranium 92 and so on.

This picture that I have painted of the atom as a dense nucleus surrounded by tiny orbiting electrons is accurate—the nucleus' diameter is typically 1/10,000 to 1/100,000 of the diameter of the outermost electron orbit, and so dense that one cubic centimeter of tightly packed nuclei would weigh 100,000,000 metric tonnes (a metric tonne is 1,000 kilograms, or 2,200 pounds). Accurate my picture may be—but it is incomplete.

There are several possible orbital distances and inclinations—somewhat like the earth satellites with which we are becoming familiar. In fact, like the satellites, the orbital distance from the nucleus depends on the amount of energy with which the electron in question is charged. Unlike the earth satellite, however, there is a finite (fixed) number of orbits available to the electrons; rather than being infinitely variable in diameter they vary only in fixed finite steps. Further, the maximum number of electrons that can fit into any given orbit is limited. As you would expect, the farther the orbit from the nucleus the greater the amount of energy required to maintain the electron in orbit—just as you would expend more energy whirling a rock about your body on the end of a long string than you would whirling the same rock at the same rpm on a short string.

Mother Nature is not only very intelligent, she is also very lazy. One of the irrevocable laws of nature is that the higher the total energy contained in any physical system, the less stable the system will be. Being lazy, Nature always tries to achieve the lowest available energy state, with all components as close to a state of rest as can be arranged. For this reason, the available electron orbits closest to the nucleus are filled first (this is not quite technically correct because in some circumstances a higher orbit MAY require less energy, but we are not going to go into THAT!) and electrons select the higher orbits only after the lower ones have been filled.

The energy level of electrons depends not only upon the placement of their orbit but also upon the atomic number of the element in question. The higher the atomic number of an element, the more protons are present in its nucleus and the greater the total positive electrical charge. This causes the orbiting electrons to be more tightly bound or attracted to the nuclei of the heavier atoms and causes a corresponding DECREASE in the energy levels of all of the particles in these heavier atoms.

At any rate, the electrons in the outermost orbit of any atom are highly charged and relatively unstable little devils. Like highly charged and unstable people, there is not a lot of fidelity in their makeup!

Figure (20): Basic atomic structure of simple atoms.

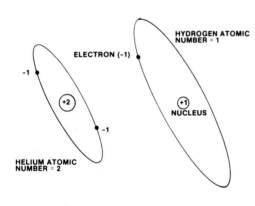

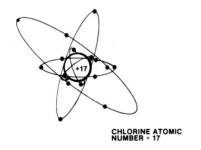

THE ATOMIC BOND (IN GENERAL)

SOMETHING must hold all of the atoms of any given element, alloy or compound, together. We have seen that the electrostatic attraction between the positively charged protons in the nucleus and the negatively charged electrons in orbit about it hold the atom together. But each atom is, by definition, electrically neutral and so, since there is no attraction between neuters, it would seem that electrostatic attraction CANNOT bond individual atoms together into the clumps that make up matter. Wrong! It is indeed the old "attraction between opposites" that binds our world together, but in methods more complex than the simple ± relationship that we have seen in the case of the individual atom.

Strangely enough, the complex and dense nucleus of the atom is pretty much a fixed entity—both in makeup and in charge (except, of course, when it comes to nuclear fission, without which we would ALL be better off). The neutrons and even the protons don't have much to do with the formation of interatomic bonds (except, of course, that the protons do provide the positive charge without which nothing would work—it's a little bit like the father's role in conception and childbirth).

On the other hand, the busy little electrons in the process of whirring about in their chosen orbits, can and do interact with the electrons and orbits of other nearby atoms. They can interweave orbits and, being faithless little devils, they can even desert their own nucleus and either go off with another, share a common nucleus or even share their affections and attentions among a whole group of nuclei. In so doing they form interatomic bonds of varying flexibilities, strengths, and longevities.

THE IONIC BOND

When an atom, for whatever reason, loses (or is deserted by) one of its electrons it winds up with one more proton in its nucleus than it has electrons in orbit and so, instead of being electrically neutral, becomes positively charged. Since it is no longer electrically neutral it is no longer, strictly speaking, an atom. By losing an electron it has become a positively charged ION. The electron that deserted the nucleus is not capable of existing on its own; it must join the electrons in orbit about another nucleus. In so doing, another ion is formed. This one, possessing an extra electron, is negatively charged. These two newly formed ions, one positive and the other negative, are electrostatically attracted to each other; whereas the original atoms, being neutral, were not. A stable compound can be formed from the resultant ions.

As an example, consider our old friend, easy-to-draw table salt (sodium chloride). Table salt is actually a simple compound formed by the reaction of sodium (Na, atomic number 11) with chlorine (Cl, atomic number 17). Each atom of sodium gives up one electron to a corresponding atom of chlorine resulting in the formation of a positively charged ion of sodium (Na+) and a negatively charged ion of chlorine (Cl−). Electrostatic attraction binds the two together to form the familiar cubic sodium chloride crystal (NaCl) of FIGURE [21]. This is termed an IONIC BOND.

Figure (21): The ionic bond of sodium chloride.

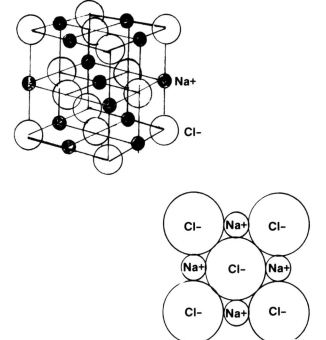

TWO-DIMENSIONAL REPRESENTATION OF THE SODIUM CHLORIDE IONIC BOND.

What has actually happened is shown in FIGURE [22]. A single, high-energy and unstable electron in the outermost orbit (also termed the ''energy shell'') of the sodium atom jumped to the outermost orbital shell of the chlorine atom. In order for this event to take place, several conditions had to exist simultaneously:

(1) The deserting atom had to have a higher energy level than was called for in the orbital shell to which it jumped.

(2) The atom to which the electron jumped had to have a lower overall energy level than the deserted atom (i.e. a higher atomic number).

(3) The orbital shell to which the electron jumped had to have room for it.

So, loosely attached electrons jump from high to low energy levels, and in so doing change electrically neutral atoms into electrically charged ions. Opposites attract and so sodium chloride is an integrated and stable crystal structure. In order for any IONIC BOND to exist in a stable state, the bonded condition must represent a DECREASE in energy over the unbonded state. Sodium chloride is stable simply because the straying electron gave up energy in its jump (the energy was transformed into heat) and the resultant compound of NaCl has less total energy than the individual atoms of Na and Cl had. Lazy, old Mother Nature likes this state of affairs.

The ions in an ionically bonded crystalline substance naturally align themselves into a structural matrix such that the attracting forces between ions with opposite electrical charges are stronger than the repelling charges between ions with like charges. However, ionic bonds are not really very strong to start with and they are inescapably intolerant of structural irregularities. In order for the ± attraction to work, any ionically bonded compound must strictly alternate positively charged ions with negatively charged ions within its structure. The displacement of a single ion within the lattice will result in a +/+ and −/− relationship, which is a repelling rather than an attracting situation.

Ionically bonded compounds are therefore not well suited to structural uses. Besides, in order for an ionic bond to form at all, there must be at least two atoms present—one to give up an electron and one to gain it. In order for this electron transfer to occur we have seen that the two atoms must have different energy states (atomic numbers). This means that the atoms cannot be of the same element. Since we know that metals DO exist as crystalline solids in the pure state we must search elsewhere for the bonding method used to hold the individual atoms of our metals together.

Figure (22): Two-dimensional representation of a sodium chloride reaction.

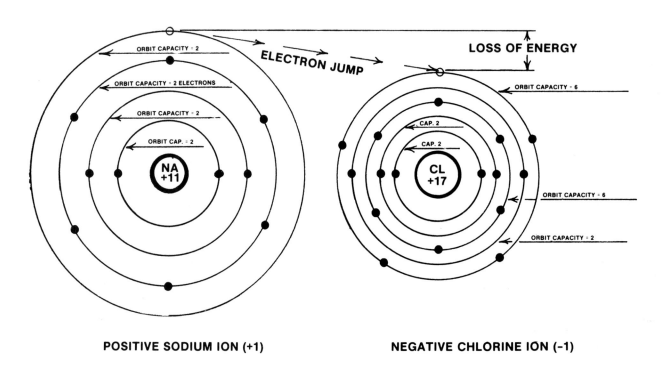

POSITIVE SODIUM ION (+1)   NEGATIVE CHLORINE ION (−1)

THE SHARED ELECTRON OR COVALENT BOND

The next atomic bond that we will consider is the shared-electron bond, also known as the COVALENT BOND. To begin the investigation I will ask you to accept one premise as fact: When two atoms are somehow brought close enough together that their electron orbits (or energy shells) can actually interact, the energy states of the orbiting electrons may be altered and, under some circumstances, this alteration can result in the formation of atomic bonds between atoms of the same element (it can also occur between atoms of different elements).

What actually happens is that electrons, rather than orbiting about a single nucleus, are shared between two nuclei—it is a sort of a "figure eight" interwoven orbit. The most common example is perhaps the diamond, a crystal of pure carbon. The crystalline structure is unusual, not to say weird. Each atom of carbon forms four covalent bonds with four surrounding carbon atoms and in EACH of the bonds it shares two electrons with each neighbor. FIGURE [23] schematically depicts in two dimensions the diamond covalent bond as an interweaving of electron orbits.

In the covalent bond both the distance apart and the angular relationship between the atoms involved are critical. The crystals so formed tend to be very strong indeed but, alas, along with the strength goes excessive hardness (the diamond is the hardest substance known to man). They are remarkably intolerant of crystalline imperfections of any sort. As an example, a polished rod of laboratory glass will support, under perfect conditions (which include a lack of oscillations to the extent that the experiment must be performed in still air), a tensile load in excess of the capacity of our strongest alloy steels. However, should the rod be touched, even lightly, by a sharp object while it is subjected to high levels of stress, it will not only fail, it will explode! We had best forget about the covalent bond and continue our search for a bonding method suitable for use with structural metals.

THE METALLIC BOND

The METALLIC BOND is different! It is, in fact, unique to the family of metals. It is this bond that imparts to metals their unique combination of strength, elasticity and ductility. In any given metallic crystal, the outer orbital shell of EACH atom is missing a few electrons. In other words, the metallic atoms are not strictly atoms at all but are actually positively charged metallic ions. Two questions immediately arise: Where are the missing electrons? and, Since all of the ions are positively charged, and likes repel, why doesn't the crystal fly apart?

The answer to the first question supplies the key to the second. The detached electrons are, in fact, still present (and busy) within the crystal. One of the characteristics of metallic crystals is that the atoms (or, strictly speaking, the ions) are packed very closely together in space. This some-

what alters the rules of the game. The extremely close packing of the nuclei causes a change in the energy relationships. Under these conditions, the lowest energy level for the outermost (highest energy and most unstable in the orbital sense) electrons is no longer a fixed orbit around a single nucleus but becomes a sort of wandering random orbit or series of orbits throughout the entire crystal! At any given time there are enough electrons (those in fixed orbit plus sufficient wanderers) in the vicinity of each nucleus to maintain both individual and collective neutrality of electrical charge. The particles which would seem to be positively charged ions are, in effect, neutrally charged atoms of the metal.

At the same time, the circulating electrons form the flexible "adhesive" that bonds the atoms together with very strong but flexible interatomic bonds into a crystalline lattice which is remarkably tolerant of structural imperfections. These interwoven random orbits, by their very circulating nature, allow any disturbing force to be spread over all of the bonds, and so resist unbonding stress by flexing or distortion of the lattice structure. Moreover, any local disturbances to the circulation of the electrons throughout the crystal structure tend to be almost self healing.

These semifree electrons are simply not present in the structure of minerals and so cannot come galloping to the rescue like cavalry in reserve when they are needed to reinforce the bonds across the grain boundaries. It is important to realize that only a few electrons from each atom are ranging freely throughout the crystal. Most are still contained in their regular orbits about their very own nuclei.

Figure (23): Two-dimensional schematic representation of the covalent bonding of the diamond crystal.

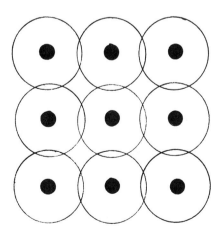

FIGURE [24] shows a couple of different attempts to represent the metallic bond schematically. It may help to think of the roving electrons as sort of an elastic mortar bonding the bricks of a wall together; an elastic mortar that is in constant circulation among the bricks and is temporarily attached to each. FIGURE [25] is a cartoon of the bonding of the metallic crystal with the bonds represented as coil springs; FIGURE [26] schematically illustrates the difference between the atomic bonds of minerals and crystals.

As a point of interest: For the past several pages we have been looking into the dreaded field of QUANTUM MECHANICS. Admittedly our look has been both incomplete and oversimplified. Hopefully it has been understandable. If so, it should serve not only to acquaint the reader with some of the basics of the atomic structure and bonding of metals, but to also partially dispel the clouds of fear that tend to surround most bodies of scientific knowledge.

If all scientific writers and teachers could (or would) write and teach with the clarity and simplicity of Isaac Asimov, we would all be better off and our nation would not be behind in any aspect of the technology race. At most

levels physical science is, if not simple, at least understandable in principle. We are merely afraid of it—just as I was scared to death of computers until Dave Head forced me to spend a couple of hours using his word processor (now I cannot believe that I ever tried to write without one). I truly believe that the normal human being can learn anything that he or she sets his or her mind to. Our problem is a combination of laziness and lack of self confidence. Pity!

SUMMARY

In the real world metals are a collection of atoms which fly around in very close formation and are arranged in a regular and repetitive fashion into crystal unit cells of various shapes which are, in turn, built up, Lego-like, on a regular and repetitive three dimensional lattice structure into crystals of metal which we call grains. The real metals do not exhibit anywhere near as much strength as theory tells us that they should. But they form strong and flexible interatomic bonds which allow us to form them into strong and useful shapes while they are in the solid state, whereas we cannot do the same with stone, glass or ceramics.

Figure (24): Schematic representation of typical hexagonal and cubic metal crystals. Circles represent ions with a slight positive charge arranged on a regular lattice. Wandering negatively charged electrons (or their habitat) are indicated by the shaded portions. The absence of these electrons from their normal orbits is responsible for the positive charge of the metal ions. The electrons range freely throughout the crystal, orbiting all of the nuclei as a group instead of as individuals. There are always enough electrons, either in regular orbit about each nucleus or wandering in its vicinity, to result in a neutral charge.

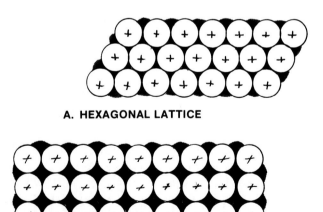

A. HEXAGONAL LATTICE

B. CUBIC LATTICE

Figure (25): Elastic nature of metallic interatomic bonds represented as coil springs.

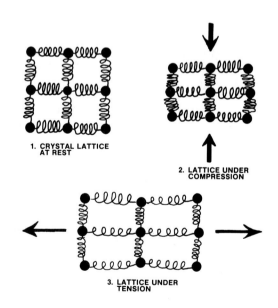

1. CRYSTAL LATTICE AT REST

2. LATTICE UNDER COMPRESSION

3. LATTICE UNDER TENSION

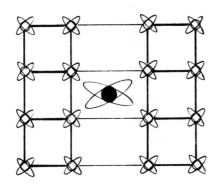

**IRREGULAR MINERAL
CRYSTAL AT REST**

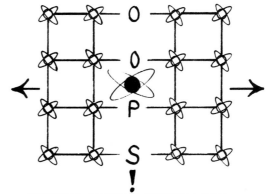

**MINERAL CRYSTAL UNDER LOAD.
BRITTLE LATTICE CANNOT DISTORT.
ATOMIC BONDS FALL ACROSS DISCONTINUITY.**

**IRREGULAR METALLIC
CRYSTAL AT REST**

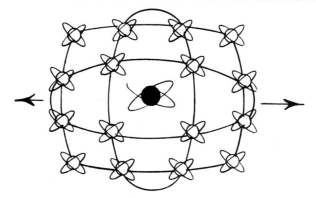

**METALLIC CRYSTAL UNDER LOAD.
STRONG ATOMIC BONDS ACROSS
DISCONTINUITY ALLOWS LATTICE TO
DISTORT, SHARING LOAD AMONG MANY BONDS.**

CHAPTER TWO

PLASTIC AND ELASTIC DEFORMATION OF METALS

THE PLASTIC DEFORMATION OF METALS

In the preceding chapter I pointed out that the ability of metals to undergo plastic deformation (or a permanent change in shape) without rupture is one of the characteristics that makes metals our most versatile and useful structural materials. The next question is, of course, "HOW?" The answers are not simple, nor, at the time of writing, are they entirely understood, at least by practical engineers like me. A basic understanding of what is actually happening when we form metals will, however, go a long way toward preventing mistakes during forming and consequent structural failures. So bear with me.

To start with, the reduction in strength between the theoretical single metal crystal and the actual collection of crystals that comprise real metals is, as we have seen, largely due to imperfections—grain boundaries, vacancies and dislocations—in the structure of the crystal lattices involved. These seeming defects, however, are not ALL bad. It is, in fact, these very imperfections in the actual structure of our engineering metals which impart to them the ductility, malleability, shock and fatigue resistance which make them useful.

What happens is this: When we bend a sheet of metal we are actually rearranging the structure of its crystal lattice, either in tension or in shear. Shear is easier to visualize (and to draw) with our two-dimensional lattice, so we are going to, at least at first, use shear as our example.

Once upon a time, not so very long ago, physical metal-

Figure (27A): Two-dimensional representation of simultaneous slip in a cubic crystal lattice.

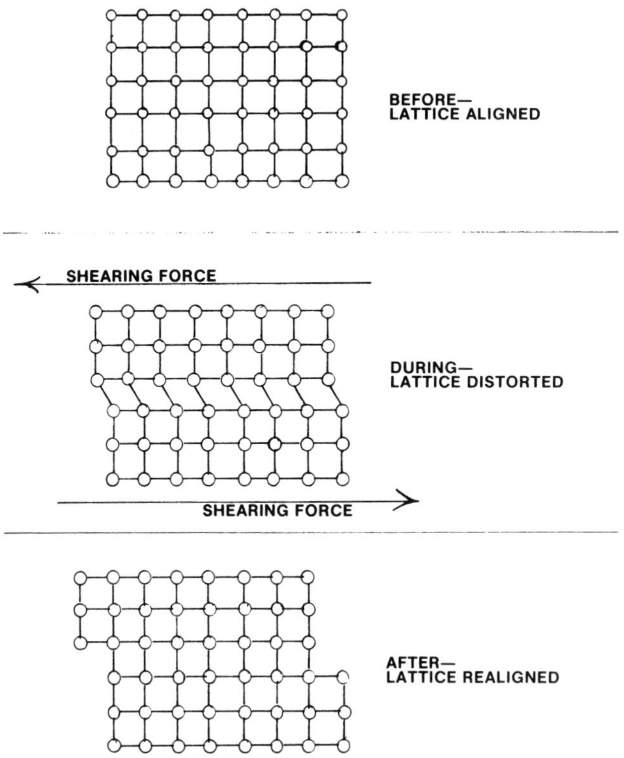

BEFORE—
LATTICE ALIGNED

SHEARING FORCE

DURING—
LATTICE DISTORTED

SHEARING FORCE

AFTER—
LATTICE REALIGNED

35

lurgists believed that, as we bent the sheet, a simultaneous slip occurred between two adjacent crystallographic planes of atoms which ended up realigned. This is schematically represented in FIGURES [27A] and [27B]. It is a convenient and relatively easily understood concept: when we bend the metal the adjacent planes of unit cells sort of slide along on one another until everything is realigned and we are back to square one, except that we have achieved a different (and stable) shape.

Unfortunately this simple theory is not valid. When technology advanced to the point that the theorists could actually measure the strength of the bonds between the atoms of a crystal and accurately predict the forces that would be required to produce this simultaneous slip they found, to their enormous surprise, that the theoretical force required was SEVERAL THOUSAND TIMES the actual force which would produce the deformation in practice. DRAT! One more time practicality had outstripped theory.

As one who is very liable to make the prototype part and THEN make the working drawings, this sort of thing always tickles me; even though, when examined closely and in the long run, it always works out to be a triumph for the theorists. What actually happens is that the structure of the metal takes advantage of the discontinuities within its structure to allow CONSECUTIVE SLIP of (or between) adjacent rows of atoms or cells. FIGURES [28A], [28B], [28C] and [28D] schematically illustrate what happens using our familiar two dimensional lattice.

The very presence of a dislocation of any sort introduces an area of high energy within the lattice. This area can also be viewed as one of low stability. The area surrounding the dislocation is less stable than the rest of the lattice and it can be moved, upset or altered with a lesser amount of applied stress than would be required to change the arrangement of a perfect lattice. Under stress the dislocation will move across the crystal—ONE LATTICE SPACE AT A TIME—until the top rows of atoms in the lattice are aligned with the bottom rows. Note that the effect is exactly the same as if the simultaneous slip described in FIGURE [27] had occurred. However, since the slip actually takes place consecutively, stretching and reorienting only one set of atomic bonds at a time, the force required to produce the change is much less. Since the dislocation has been removed from the lattice, we now have a perfect crystal and, theoretically, the metal should be stronger than it was before we distorted it.

To insert a welcome bit of practical application, this is exactly what happens when metal "work hardens" through being cold worked. The metal DOES become stronger. Unfortunately the increase in strength is accompanied by an increase in hardness which embrittles the metal. Normally, however, as one dislocation is removed through plastic distortion, more are created and the net effect is usually nil; the metal is no stronger after the dislocation has been moved than it was before. It is, however, no weaker, and that is the crucial point. This unique ability to permanently deform under stress (rather than break) and to retain that deformation (or new shape) when the stress that produced the deformation has been removed, is what allows us to shape and form the metals that make up the very structure of our industrial society.

It should be becoming evident about now that there is a definite tradeoff between the ductility, or formability, of a metal and its actual strength. The stronger the crystal lattice, the stronger and less ductile (or more brittle) the metal. This is absolutely true. The whole purpose of physical metallurgy is—through alloying, thermal treatments of various sorts and some types of cold working—to control the type of dislocations, their size, number and mobility in order to influence the tradeoff between breaking strength and ductility in our favor. Sometimes we go so far as to form structural shapes, especially complex shapes, from a metal or an alloy in a ductile but relatively weak condition and then increase the strength of the already formed part by thermal treatment.

Figure (27B): Three-dimensional representation of simultaneous slip in a cubic crystal space lattice.

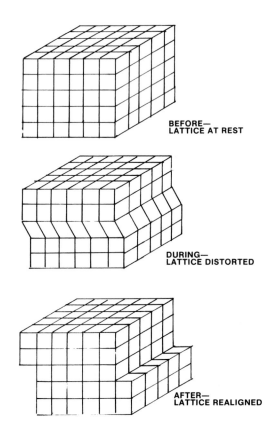

BEFORE—
LATTICE AT REST

DURING—
LATTICE DISTORTED

AFTER—
LATTICE REALIGNED

DISLOCATION MOVEMENTS (AND BARRIERS TO THEM) WITHIN THE CRYSTAL

A dislocation can move unhindered across the crystal lattice because the lattice itself, being crystalline, is a regular structure. If a barrier were to be placed in the path of the dislocation its movement would necessarily stop. Another dislocation in the path of the moving dislocation serves as a perfectly adequate barrier. Metals which contain virtually no dislocations are extremely ductile (in fact, most metals in their pure state, with very few dislocations, are so soft and weak as to be structurally useless). Metals which contain a moderate number of dislocations are reasonably ductile and formable. Unfortunately, increasing the number of dislocations within the structure of a metal will not, by it-

Figure (28C): Same crystal lattice undergoing consecutive slip, due to force F'/F. Slip started at front of lattice and has progressed to plane A-B-C-D.

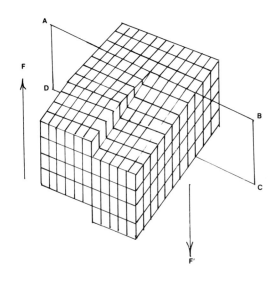

Figure (28A): Two-dimensional representation of simultaneous slip.

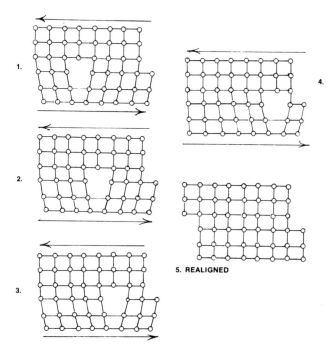

Figure (28D): Same crystal space lattice after completion of slip, showing permanent and stable change of shape.

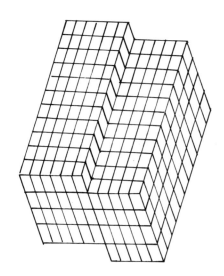

Figure (28B): Hypothetical cubic crystal lattice with no dislocations or vacancies.

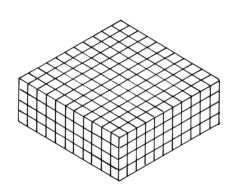

self, increase the strength of the metal—only its brittleness. In fact, we will discover as we go on that great numbers of dislocations within the crystal lattice inevitably lead to the dreaded "metal fatigue."

We have seen that real world metals consist of numerous single crystals or "grains," and that at the intersection of these grains the crystal lattice is disordered. These "grain boundaries" are also very effective barriers to the movement of dislocations. The larger the grain size the farther apart these barriers will be and the more ductile will be the metal. For example, when metals work harden, what ACTUALLY happens is that, as the metal is repeatedly hammered (or bent, as the case may be) the individual crystals or grains are physically broken down into smaller and smaller grains. This moves the grain boundaries closer together and physically limits the movement of the discontinuities, causing the metal to become harder and more brittle. Eventually a point is reached when the metal loses enough ductility that it can no longer be formed. At this point the original grain size and ductility must be renewed by reheating the metal and allowing it to cool slowly (annealing).

If pure metals are so soft and weak as to be structurally next to useless, and if we cannot get much of a strength increase by fooling with the grain size or the number of dis-

locations, then we must come up with some other method in order to arrive at a useful condition. The method used is termed "alloying." When we combine a metal in an intimate mixture with small portions of different metals (or, sometimes, nonmetals) the basic crystal lattice can be modified or distorted, making it difficult for dislocations to move along it. We will return to alloying in some detail later.

THE ELASTICITY OF METALS

We have seen that it is the PLASTICITY of metals that allows us to form metals and their alloys into useful shapes. This is all very convenient, but if metals were completely plastic in nature then our metal parts, no matter how convenient their shape, would lack the STIFFNESS that is necessary in order for us to make structures capable of resisting the loads that we wish to impose upon them. Fear not! All has been arranged by the Master Engineer in the sky.

The study of ELASTICITY is simply the study of the relationship between STRESSES and STRAINS in solid materials. In essence, the study of elasticity is the study of STIFFNESS.

In the learning process we must define the terms which we will use before we begin the study of any body of

Figure (29): Load, stress and strain.

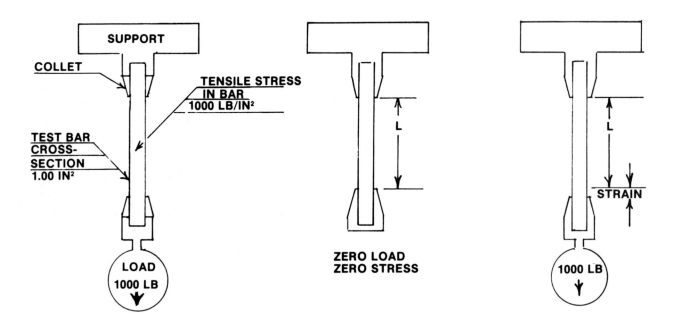

knowledge. Since no one likes definitions (they are just as boring to write as they are to memorize), I try to hide them within the text. Sometimes I fail. It is now time for a couple of undisguised definitions:

To the nonengineer, stress and strain are frightening words—but only because, a century ago, Sigmund Freud and his disciples, realizing that engineering terminology was both precise and convenient, applied the language of structural engineering to the distressed mental states of mankind. Since none of us are comfortable with the notion of mental disorder, the theft of OUR terms by the shrinks has rendered the words scary. In the discussion of loads and strengths, stress in a structure (or in a material) is simply the applied LOAD divided by the cross-sectional area of the loaded part. If a bar with a cross-sectional area of one square inch is supporting a load of 1,000 pounds in tension then the tensile stress within the bar is 1,000 pounds per square inch, as illustrated by FIGURE [29]. Strain, also shown in FIGURE [29], is merely the deformation produced, in this case an elongation in a material (or in a structure), by the application of a stress. There is nothing complex or scary in that.

Intuition, to the engineer, is instinct tempered and matured by experience. Much of what follows we already know by intuition. In order for us to raise the results of our engineering above the level represented by instinct, we must first "formalize" some of the concepts that we think we understand already.

The behavior of ELASTIC materials contrasts with that of PLASTIC materials in that an elastic material which has been distorted by the application of a load will return to its original size and shape when the stress produced by the load is removed. A plastic material will not; it will remain, at least to some extent, distorted when the load and the stress that it produced has been removed. Depending upon the level of stress imposed, many solid materials (especially metals) exhibit BOTH plastic and elastic behavior. It is this duality in the nature of metals that allows us to use them as structural materials. If they weren't elastic they could not withstand the loads that we wish to impose upon the structures which we build from them. Also, if they weren't plastic at some higher level of stress we could not form them into satisfactory shapes from which to fabricate the structures.

MR. HOOKE

One of the first men to approach metallurgy from an analytical point of view was the English mathematician Thomas Hooke who, in 1680, formally stated what engineering man had known intuitively forever: "The strain of any material is proportional to the load applied to it." He, being a scholar, actually stated his law as an anagram in Latin which, since no one had managed to break his code, years later he translated as, "as the force, so the extension" (they talked funny in those days!). Today we have simplified Mr. Hooke's law to "the strain of any material must be proportional to the stress within it." In other words, if an applied tensile stress of "×" psi will stretch or compress a given test specimen 1 unit of length, then a stress of 1.5× will produce an elongation (or a compression) of 1.5 units and a stress of 2× will produce a deformation of 2 units and so on. Clever man, Mr. Hooke. With that one deceptively simple statement he formalized the basis of all structural engineering—bridges, ships, race cars, aircraft, space vehicles or whatever.

HOOKE'S LAW OF PROPORTIONALITY is, however, true only within those limits of both stress and strain which define the ELASTIC LIMITS of any given solid material—that range of stress and strain within which the strained material (or a shape or a structure formed from the material) will return to its original size and shape when the load which produced the strain is released.

If we graph the stress/strain relationships of ALL atomic bonds, we end up with an endless set of similar curves, each in the shape of FIGURE [30]. As structural engineers, the only region of this curve in which we are interested is the FIRST ONE PERCENT of elongation; this is the upper limit of the portion in which Mr. Hooke's law applies. In this region the curve is actually a straight line (if it were a curve strain would not be proportional to stress).

In the "tensile testing" of a material, a specimen bar of the material is mounted in a tensile testing machine and a steadily increasing tension load is applied until the specimen parts. While the level of stress is being increased, continuous and precise measurements of the specimen's length are taken. If we plot the actual relationship between stress

Figure (30): Stress/strain curve of typical interatomic bond.

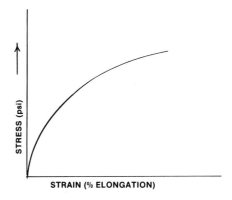

and strain in a typical metal we end up with the graph in FIGURE [31].

Note that while stress, along the vertical axis of the graph, is expressed in psi, strain, measured along the horizontal axis, is expressed in percent elongation—a new term. PERCENT ELONGATION is the difference in length of a test specimen before it has been subjected to a tensile stress, and the length measured while it is subjected to a given level of stress, expressed as a percentage of original specimen length (usually 2''). When we are speaking of the mechanical properties of a given metal or alloy, percent elongation is the difference between the original length and the length measured after the specimen has ruptured; this is used as a relative indication of ductility.

This graph is usually termed a STRESS/STRAIN diagram and is characteristically made up of two distinct stages, labeled O-A and A-C on the graph. During the first stage, Origin to A, the curve is essentially a vertical, straight line (its slope is vastly exaggerated in the drawing simply so that the slope can be seen at all). For most metals the distance O-A along the HORIZONTAL axis of the graph is no more than one part in a THOUSAND (0.001'' per inch of specimen length or a percent elongation of 0.1). The stress level at the corresponding point on the vertical axis is a function of the mechanical characteristics of the metal or alloy in question. At any point within this area the material will always obey Hooke's law: Strain will be directly proportional to stress and if the applied load is released the specimen will return to its original length and dimensions. This is termed the elastic stage of the material, and point A defines its upper limits of both stress and strain. In the stress department this point is termed the ELASTIC LIMIT of the material, and is defined as the maximum stress that a material can withstand without a permanent deformation remaining after the load that caused the stress has been released. The accurate determination of the precise location of the elastic limit of a given material is difficult. It is, however a simple matter to measure the level of stress which will produce a given percent elongation in any given material. For reasons of simplicity and ease of measurement, rather than attempting to measure the precise elastic limit of materials, metallurgists and engineers use the YIELD STRENGTH of a material (defined as the stress at which a material exhibits an arbitrarily chosen specified percent elongation (.002'' per inch of original specimen length is the normally chosen figure) to indicate the upper limit of the elastic region.

The second stage of the stress/strain diagram, A-C, is called the ''plastic stage'' of the material. When the stress level falls within this area the strained material will not return to its original shape and dimensions upon release of the

Figure (31): Idealized stress/strain diagram for a hypothetical metal.

Figure (32): Return curve when load is relaxed after metal has been strained beyond its elastic limit.

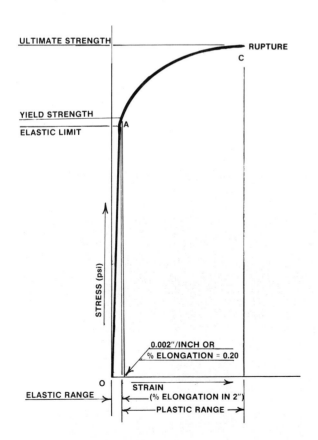

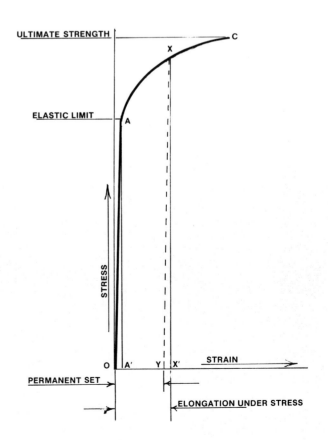

load but will exhibit some amount of permanent elongation, or "set." The curve ends abruptly at point C for the simple reason that, at this level of stress, the interatomic bonds holding the specimen together are stretched as far as they will go. The bonds run out of elasticity, snap, and the specimen ruptures in tension. The stress within the material at this point is termed that material's ULTIMATE TENSILE STRENGTH and is defined as the maximum stress that the material can withstand without failure. It is expressed (in this country) in psi.

If, at any level of stress between points A and C on the curve, the load is released the return graph to stable dimensions will be a straight line whose slope will be parallel to O-A and the material will exhibit a "permanent elongation," or set, even in the absence of stress. This is shown graphically in FIGURE [32].

Note that the material, even after it has been strained beyond its elastic limit, still does its damndest to return to its original dimensions. When stressed, the elongation was the distance O-X' measured along the horizontal axis; when the stress is relaxed the material contracts a distance of X'-Y resulting in a permanent "set" of distance O-Y.

Some metals, most notably iron and its derivative, low-carbon mild steel, possess a sharply defined YIELD POINT, that level of stress at which there takes place an increase in strain WITHOUT any increase in load. In this case, as illustrated by FIGURE [33], the stress/strain diagram exhibits a characteristic horizontal area (labeled A-B on the graph) in which things are somewhat confused in the stress and strain department. This area is essentially a horizontal line along which the metal will continue to elongate, even though the stress is held at a constant level.

This characteristic of iron may have been sent to confuse us! None of the rest of our structural materials possess a distinct yield point; neither do the high-carbon and/or alloy steels. In fact, as shown in FIGURE [34], the higher the carbon content of a given steel the higher the ultimate tensile strength (more about this later) and the less distinct the yield point until, at some level of carbon content, the distinct yield point disappears altogether.

In the design and study of structures we are interested only in the behavior of our materials within the elastic stage represented by the area O-A. The plastic area is for the forming of metals, not the resistance of applied loads. If we should design a structure so that the elastic limit, A, of the material(s) chosen will be exceeded, then the structure will yield or fail under load and we will have either underestimated the loads involved or overestimated the strength of our materials—either way we lose!

EXCEEDING THE LIMITS

All structures are designed so that no component will ever develop a stress or a strain that will exceed the elastic limit of the material under the maximum predicted load(s).

But, since SOME assumptions are always necessary; SOME joints are inevitable; practical considerations will require SOME less-than-optimum section changes; SOME

Figure (33): Idealized stress/strain diagram for a hypothetical mild steel, showing distinct yield point.

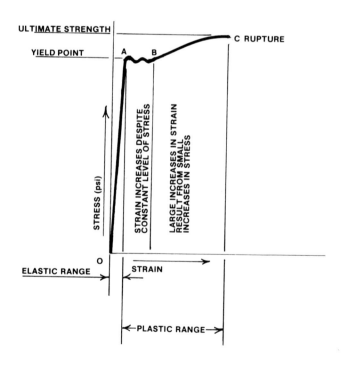

Figure (34): Idealized stress/strain diagrams for various ferrous metals. In each case A = elastic limit, B = yield strength, and C = ultimate tensile strength.

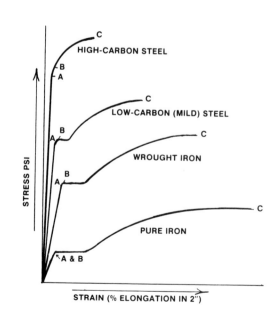

manufacturing tolerances must be allowed; SOME errors will occur in construction/fabrication and post treatment; SOME in-service abuse is inevitable. And, because all intelligent structural engineers are devout cowards, various factors are applied to all stress calculations: We have weld factors, joint factors, heat treat factors, material factors, quality control factors and the ever popular Jesus factor. Me? I design by the book and the book factors and then I multiply by 1.0 to 2.50 AFTER I have applied all of the book factors. We DO hit things and we DO drop things, and engineers, fabricators, machinists and heat treaters DO have bad days. And I REALLY dislike component failure.

For these reasons, all well-designed structures can accept loads in excess of the posted maximum simply because the engineers involved are always conservative. But there is another factor to be considered: We know that if the stress in a polycrystalline metal is increased to a level above the elastic limit of the metal then the metal will deform plastically as the stress continues to rise. Interestingly enough, this rise in stress reflects an increase in the strength of the metal brought about by the creation of crystalline dislocations by the plastic deformation. If the load is relaxed from any point on the stress/strain curve above the elastic limit (say point (b) of FIGURE [33]) and then reapplied, the new load will have to build up a stress in the material equal to level (b) before plastic deformation will begin again.

This is what is happening when a spring, an antiroll bar or an axle shaft "takes a (visible) set"—somebody screwed

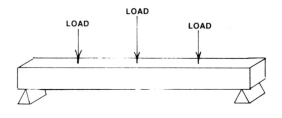

Figure (35): Simple rectangular beam in bending.

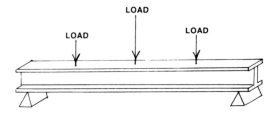

Figure (36): I-beam in bending.

up, either in design, manufacture or quality control and what you have is JUNK. It is junk because it was either designed badly or it was manufactured badly. The fact that the stress in the part may never reach a level that will cause elastic deformation to begin again is beside the point. The best that can be said about the product is that its fatigue life will be limited by the incompetence of its designer/producer. Some manufacturers, especially of springs and torsion bars, will tell you that ALL springs take an initial set in service and that after they have done so they will be good forever. These people are either misinformed or lying. No torsion bar (or axle) should take a discernible initial set after it leaves the factory in which it was born. Proper coil springs are preset by the manufacturer and will not take a set once they are in your hands. If they do, take your business elsewhere.

In addition, depending on factors of shape, load and materials, SOME structures may be able to accept loads considerably in excess of those calculated to be the maximum acceptable simply because the shape chosen was inefficient to start with! Consider the rectangular, solid-wooden beam loaded in simple bending shown in FIGURE [35]. At the point in the loading of the beam at which the upper and lower fibers of the beam (which are, respectively, in tension and compression) have reached their yield stress, the vast majority of the central or core fibers are still relatively lightly stressed and so are in a position to accept more and more load as the beam deflects farther. Thus, we enter an area in which the overall level of STRESS remains constant while STRAIN increases with load simply because the center of the beam is lightly stressed. This is a very inefficient way to design a beam and, with the exception of wooden beams, it is simply not done anymore.

On the other hand, if we substitute the I-beam of FIGURE [36] for the rectangular beam of FIGURE [35], since most of the lightly loaded central fibers are simply not there, almost all of the bending stress will be resisted by the top and bottom flanges—the vertical web existing mainly to separate these flanges.

While the efficiency of the I-beam (its weight/strength/stiffness ratio) is vastly superior to that of the solid rectangular beam, its excess-load-carrying capacity is much reduced, simply because it contains nowhere near so much unstressed material. The same is true of the tubes and thin-walled shell structures from which we construct our racing cars. In addition, as we increase the ultimate tensile strength of the materials we use, the yield point inevitably creeps closer to the ultimate tensile strength (we lose ductility) and the plastic stage of the material becomes, on a percentage basis, narrower—and less forgiving. It doesn't pay to fool around with increased loads for either race cars or aircraft; they are too efficiently designed to begin with (or at least they should be).

This is also why our antiroll bars are tubular rather than solid. When we twist a solid bar, the fibers of the metal are stretched by being rotated about the center of the bar. This is what torsion is all about. FIGURE [37] shows graphically that all of the fibers in the bar go through the same ANGULAR distortion. However, when we are speaking about LINEAR distortion (or STRAIN) the displacement of the fibers increases with the distance that the individual fiber is located from the center of the bar. In the linear sense, the outer fibers are stretched a much greater distance than the inner ones. Since stress and strain don't know about angular displacements, linear is all that counts and in any torsionally loaded shaft, the inner fibers are along for the ride.

This means that we can get rid of a lot of weight while maintaining most of the original torsional resistance by simply deleting the lightly stressed core of the bar, i.e. by substituting a tube for the bar. What is actually happening here is that we are arranging for the stress within our antiroll bar (which is a simple torsion bar) to be more evenly distributed.

If we look at FIGURE [38], the arrows indicating the level of stress at the center of the solid bar are very short indeed. The center of the bar is free loading; it makes a major contribution to weight but only a minor contribution to strength (or torsional resistance; in this case, stiffness). If we increase the outside diameter of the bar and delete the center, we end up with a tubular bar in which all of the material is more-or-less evenly stressed. Fortunately it is in the nature of things that the outside fibers will virtually always be more highly stressed than the inside. This is in our favor simply because almost all cracks will therefore originate on the outside surfaces of our parts where, with a little bit of luck, they can be detected BEFORE failure occurs. For the same torsional resistance, we have significantly reduced the weight of the bar.

The same basic design truths apply to the efficient design of axles, drive shafts, coil springs, beams and any other structure or component loaded in bending, torsion or com-pression. Delete the lightly stressed inside fibers and save weight, sometimes lots of weight. The other side of the coin is the fact that in making the structure more efficient we inevitably reduce the width of its plastic stage (the amount of warning we get before failure). This means simply that the designer must bear in mind the experience level and the capability of both the people who are going to construct his device and the people who are going to use it! There ain't no free lunch (there never was) and there is no sense at all in giving a set of prints for a Formula One car to people whose skills and experience are at the figure-eight/demolition derby level.

We should, however, design ALL of our structures so that they will bend before they break (i.e. so that the material will yield well before it ruptures). This way we keep the cars (and the people) in one piece a lot longer. This is, of course, the reason behind the telltale lines that some of us paint on drive shafts and antiroll bars, and why we are forever inspecting things visually, by magnetic particle and/or dye penetrant or by x-ray. We want to know when they yield or when fatigue cracks begin to develop so that we can replace them before they break.

For SMALL amounts of strain the stretch/recover cycle is almost infinitely repeatable. The load and resultant stress can be applied and released literally millions of times with the same result. This elastic behavior of solids is the basis of all structural design and engineering. What is actually happening here is that the interatomic bonds which hold the atoms of all solid substances together are, to some extent, elastic. If we visualize the crystal space lattice of a typical metal as consisting of rigid atoms connected by coil springs which represent interatomic bonds we will see something

---

Figure (37): Solid shaft in torsion, showing unequal distribution of stress.

Figure (38): Concentric hollow shaft in torsion, showing more uniform distribution of stress.

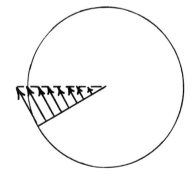

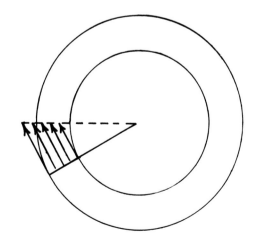

similar to FIGURE [39] which is, of course, simply a reprint of FIGURE [25] and the whole thing will, I hope, become instantly clear—at least in principle. In practice it really IS that simple.

Another way of visualizing the difference between plastic and elastic behavior is to use the familiar cubic crystal lattice in FIGURE [40]. In the first frame we see the lattice at rest, with no stress imposed. The second frame shows a load imposed which strains the lattice, causing deformation—but the stress developed is below the elastic limit of the material and when the load is relaxed the lattice returns to its original dimensions. Frame three shows the load and resultant stress increased to a level in the plastic range of the material; slip has occurred and when the load is relaxed a permanent deformation will be evident due to the slip; as shown in frame four.

MR. YOUNG

So far as I can determine, for 120 years Mr. Hooke's contribution to engineering had no practical impact at all—until Thomas Young, an English physicist, realized in 1800 that the elastic properties of a given MATERIAL could be isolated from the behavior of a STRUCTURE made from that material AND that each elastic material has its very own unique and individual CONSTANT OF ELASTICITY, which is a measure of the material's "springiness" (the ability of the strained material to return to its original shape and dimensions when the load is relaxed). The larger the modulus, the larger the stress that can be imposed without exceeding the elastic limits of the material. Young re-expressed Hooke's law as, "for any material, stress divided by strain is equal to CONSTANT."

So, YOUNG'S MODULUS (which is simply imposed stress divided by percent elongation) is a measure of the relative stiffness of MATERIALS, whereas the stiffness of a STRUCTURE is a function of both the modulus of elasticity of the material(s) used AND the shape of the structure. Young's modulus is often called the MODULUS OF ELASTICITY. The two terms are interchangeable.

In order to arrive at a practical value for this dimensionless constant, Young's Modulus (or the Modulus of Elasticity) is defined as the stress required to DOUBLE the original length of a test specimen of the material in question; i.e., to achieve a strain of 100%. With any structural material this is a pretty damned big number! The Modulus of Elasticity of aluminum and its alloys is about 10,500,000 psi, while the Modulus of Elasticity for all steels is about 30,000,000 psi. Obviously any structural material will part or break long before its length is doubled under a tensile load. In fact, the elastic limit of ALL of our current structural materials is exceeded long before an elongation of 1% is reached; after that the material goes plastic, and the structure goes limp.

Figure (39): Elastic nature of metallic interatomic bonds represented as coil springs.

Figure (40): Progressive deformation of cubic crystal lattice.

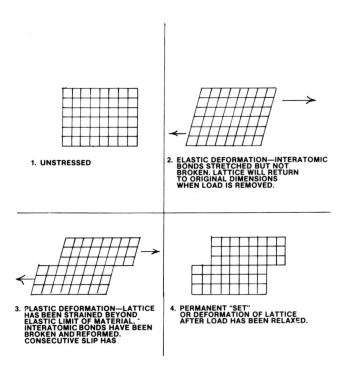

1. CRYSTAL LATTICE AT REST

2. LATTICE UNDER COMPRESSION

3. LATTICE UNDER TENSION

1. UNSTRESSED

2. ELASTIC DEFORMATION—INTERATOMIC BONDS STRETCHED BUT NOT BROKEN. LATTICE WILL RETURN TO ORIGINAL DIMENSIONS WHEN LOAD IS REMOVED.

3. PLASTIC DEFORMATION—LATTICE HAS BEEN STRAINED BEYOND ELASTIC LIMIT OF MATERIAL. INTERATOMIC BONDS HAVE BEEN BROKEN AND REFORMED. CONSECUTIVE SLIP HAS

4. PERMANENT "SET" OR DEFORMATION OF LATTICE AFTER LOAD HAS BEEN RELAXED.

STIFF DOES NOT NECESSARILY IMPLY STRONG

The MODULUS OF ELASTICITY of a material is, then, actually a measure of the stiffness or elasticity of the ATOMIC BONDS within a given material and is therefore a measure of that material's relative stiffness. We do not build structures from materials with low Moduli of Elasticity simply because such structures would sag under any reasonable load.

The STRENGTH of a material, on the other hand is a relative measure of the stress required to rupture the atomic bonds within the material. We do not make structures from weak materials simply because such structures would break under load.

Together, the two properties of stiffness and strength define the physical properties of a solid material. For instance:

> STEEL is strong and stiff
> COPPER is strong and flexible
> FIBERGLASS MADE FROM CHOPPED STRAND MATT AND RESIN is weak and stiff
> LEAD is weak and flexible

SUMMARY

I think that one of my summaries is in order here. A solid is considered to be elastic if, after a change of shape due to an external load, the body returns to its original size and shape when the load is relaxed. Plasticity, in the metallurgical sense of the word, is the ability of a metal to be deformed beyond its range of elasticity without fracture; the result is a permanent change in shape. These two related properties are the most significant of all of the characteristics of the family of metals. Plasticity gives us the ability to form metals into useful shapes and elasticity allows us to use metal fabrications as load-bearing members in our structures.

Depending upon the level of stress imposed, all metals exhibit both elastic and plastic behavior. We are interested only in the properties of materials in their elastic range. This range is defined by the elastic limit of each material—that stress below which the material will obey Hooke's Law of Proportionality which states that the strain (or linear deformation) of any material must be proportional to the stress which causes it. Each metal (and each alloy) has its own characteristic Modulus of Elasticity, defined as the stress which would be necessary to double the length of a test specimen of the material. Although this doubling is clearly impossible with any of the structural metals, the Modulus serves as a very useful indication of the relative stiffness of our structural materials.

While the stiffness of a material is clearly important to its suitability for use as a structural material, it is not the entire picture. We must also consider the strength of the material in question. Because a material is stiff does not necessarily mean that a structure made from it will be strong—at least in all circumstances. Consider, for example, a long thin sheet of glass loaded as a beam. . . .

STIFFNESS VERSUS WEIGHT

When we are designing a structure we are usually interested in other factors in addition to stiffness; weight, for instance. Some interesting aspects of the great scheme of things surface when we begin to compare the stiffness of any of our structural materials with their specific gravities. In order of ascending specific gravity, some of the structural materials used in aerospace are:

Material	Specific Gravity	Modulus of Elasticity (psi)
Aircraft-quality spruce	0.50	1,900,000
Magnesium	1.7	10,000,000
Carbon filament	2.3	110,000,000
Boron filament	2.3	60,000,000
Aluminum	2.7	10,500,000
Steel	7.80	30,000,000

There is nothing particularly surprising about this table. However, when we divide the Modulus of Elasticity for each material by its specific gravity, we DO get some surprises:

Material	Modulus of Elasticity ÷ Specific Gravity	Ratio (Steel = 1.00)
Spruce	3,800,000	0.99
Magnesium	5,900,000	1.54
Carbon filament	47,800,000	12.84
Aluminum	3,880,000	1.01
Steel	3,840,000	1.00

The surprises here are not that carbon filaments are so stiff for their weight (so long as we ignore the resin matrix which is necessary to make structures from the filaments), nor even that magnesium looks so good when compared with steel, but that, weight for weight, we could build just as STIFF a structure from either wood (aircraft-quality spruce, in the direction of the grain only) or aluminum as we can from steel.

Of course the ratio of stiffness to weight is far from being the full story in the selection of a structural material. Many factors must be considered, including cost, joinability, fabricatability, behavior at high and low temperatures, repairability, resistance to corrosion and, above all, strength and resistance to fatigue.

If we tabulate the same materials with specific gravity versus ultimate tensile strength instead of Modulus of Elasticity, we get a different view of things:

Material	Ultimate Tensile Strength (psi)	UTS/sg	Ratio (Mild Steel = 1.00)
Aircraft spruce	20,000	10,000	1.05
Magnesium (AZ 31B)	43,000	25,300	2.41
Carbon filament	280,000	122,000	11.60
Aluminum (6061-T6)	42,000	15,500	1.48
Aluminum (2024-T3)	65,000	24,000	2.29
Aluminum (7075-T6)	83,000	31,000	2.95
Titanium	180,000	39,600	3.77
Steel (SAE 1020CD)	82,000	10,500	1.00
Steel (4130 @ RC30)	136,000	17,500	1.66
Steel (4340 @ RC44)	208,000	26,500	2.52
Steel (300M @ RC52)	270,000	34,600	3.30

This table is also interesting. While we may be able to come up with a wooden structure that is just as stiff and just as strong as a mild steel one, we sure as hell are not going to come up with any wooden structure that will even approach the strength of one made from an alloy steel and heat treated. On the other hand, if we were to use aluminum alloy 7075-T6, we could equal both the strength and the stiffness of mild steel—if we could join it as well. Titanium, going strictly on weight, strength and stiffness, makes the rest of the metals look silly. But this is still only a part of the picture.

Consider a part as simple as a racing brake disc top hat or bell. On the surface of things, it looks like titanium is the only way to go; it will produce a lighter, stronger, stiffer part than either aluminum or steel. This happens to be absolutely true, IF your operation can afford the titanium and knows how to machine it. If I were building either a Formula One car or a champ car, I would seriously consider the use of titanium in a lot of areas. However, it is unlikely that I will ever design or build either of the above and I do not consider titanium to be cost effective in lesser classes of racing. The usual solution is to use aluminum.

The low-tech people use 356 castings heat treated to the T6 condition. This is a giant mistake: The stuff is weak to start with and butter at operating temperature. The inevitable result is disc run out, an inconsistent pedal and an unhappy driver. The higher-tech people machine their top hats from billets of aluminum bar stock, often 7075-T6 be-

cause it is the strongest and the hardest of the "normal" aluminum alloys. On the surface this would seem to be a good and logical choice. It is not! It is, in fact, a poor choice because 7075 loses both strength and hardness at the operating temperature of brake discs. The proper aluminum alloy for disc brake top hats is 2024-T4 simply because its mechanical properties at operating temperature are far superior to those of the other aluminums. So the high-tech people, like Mac Tilton, machine their top hats from 2024-T4. This is not, however, in my opinion THE answer.

For years I went along happily making my top hats from 2024 and replacing them when the drive dogs became too worn for further use. Some years ago I was in Australia and needed to make top hats. While the food, the beer, the wine, the racing, the sailing, the friendships and the birds in Australia are better than those of any other country where I have spent much time, there is a VAST shortage of alloys, either steel or aluminum. I made my top hats from 1020 mild steel. Imagine my surprise when I found that, for equal strength, I had come up with a part that was only a few ounces heavier than the same part in aluminum. Further, when the dogs wore, I simply welded on more material and remachined (with a file, when necessary). Of course we had to hog out a lot of steel, which took time and it would have been considerably easier and less expensive in terms of man hours to make them from 2024.

If I were to make top hats again, in the United States, I would give serious thought to asking Jim Meyer (who appears again and is identified later in the book) if he had forging dies that would come close and, if he said yes, machining them from forged blanks of 4340 and then heat treating or, if the forging dies were available, of making the top hat integral with the hub. Either way I would end up with a part both lighter and stronger than the same part from aluminum. It would be stable at temperature and I wouldn't have to hog out so much material that they would be uneconomical to manufacture. And I could repair them when the dogs wore.

I have gone through this little exercise, not to convince anyone to make 4340 (or even 1020) brake top hats, or even to show how clever I am, but to illustrate my point that the selection of the optimum material to use is seldom simple and that, while a reasonable material choice may very well be easy, a great many factors must be considered before the right choice can be made. Of course, in many cases there is no single RIGHT choice and the final choice becomes a matter of judgement rather than of calculation.

CHAPTER THREE

IRON AND STEEL MAKING

Iron is one of Nature's more abundant chemical elements. In its pure form it is, in miniscule amounts, essential to our biological well being—and of little other practical value. When, however, it is combined with small quantities of other elements, iron—along with its derivative, steel—becomes the most versatile and useful of man's tool-making and structural materials and the literal framework of our industrial society—to say nothing of most of our racing cars.

The iron-making process begins with the mining of iron ore, a brown or rust-colored rock which contains oxides of iron which are, unfortunately, combined in a nonhomogenous mix with other, unwanted, elements. The richest grades of iron ore contain up to about 65% iron but we have mostly used these "high grade" ores up and have to content ourselves with the lower grades, which require considerable pretreatment in order to make them suitable for iron making. After the ore has been dried and crushed to a powder, as much of the unwanted mineral content as possible is removed by physical and/or chemical processes and the remnants are either pelletized or sintered to a uniform size. The ore is then reduced, or SMELTED, to produce an impure grade of metallic iron known as PIG IRON. The smelting takes place in very large (upwards from 100 feet tall) vertical furnaces termed BLAST FURNACES, illustrated by FIGURE [41].

THE IRON SMELTING BLAST FURNACE

The materials used in the blast furnace are: iron ore, coke (coal from which the volatile components have been

Figure (41): The iron-smelting blast furnace. The charge of iron ore, coke and limestone is loaded through the double-valve system at top. Superheated air from a gas heater is "blasted" in at bottom. Gases are collected at the top, filtered and reused to heat air. Molten pig iron and slag are drawn off at the bottom.

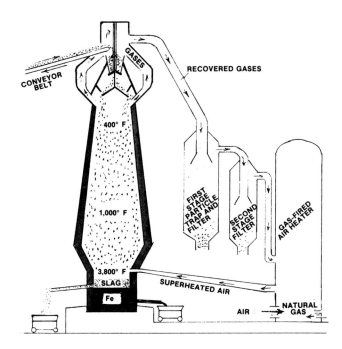

distilled in a "coking oven" in the absence of air—coke is to coal as charcoal is to wood), crushed limestone (which acts as a "flux," combining with most of the unwanted minerals remaining in the ore to form a "slag" which is physically separate from the metal) and vast quantities of air. The ore, coke and limestone are loaded (or "charged") into the top of the furnace in alternating layers, several tons at a time. The air, preheated in a gas furnace to about 1300 degrees F, is then blown (or "blasted") upward through the charge under considerable pressure. The super-heated air reacts with and causes the coke to burn, at a temperature high enough (approximately 3800 degrees F) for the coke to reach incandescence. In the process, carbon monoxide gas is formed ($2C + O_2 = 2CO$) and rises rapidly through the charge, combining as it goes with a portion of the iron oxides in the ore to form metallic iron and carbon dioxide ($FeO + CO = Fe + CO_2$).

This INDIRECT reduction takes place in the upper half of the shaft at temperatures below 1500 degrees F—well below the melting point of iron. The metallic iron so formed is combined with impurities into porous solids called "sponges" made up of metallic iron and slag. These sponges seep downward through the charge and finally melt when they reach the "zone of combustion" just above the hearth where the temperature reaches its maximum of 3800 degrees F. At this temperature, as we have noted, the coke reaches a state of incandescence. This leads to the DIRECT reduction of the remainder of the iron oxides in the ore by physical contact with the incandescent carbon ($FeO + C = Fe + CO$). The by-product of this reaction is carbon monoxide gas which then rises through the charge, contributing to the indirect reduction of the oxides in the upper portion of the shaft. The molten iron collects at the bottom of the hearth where it is drawn off at intervals of several hours. Most of the impurities contained in the original ore are combined during the process with the limestone flux to form a molten slag which floats on top of the iron and is drawn off separately (and used as an aggregate in concrete and brick making). The hot gasses are collected at the top of the furnace, purified and used to partially preheat the incoming charge of air.

The iron-smelting process in the blast furnace is continuous; once a blast furnace is started, it is normally kept in operation for a period of several months. Depending on the size of the unit, an individual furnace's production of pig iron varies from less than 500 tons to more than 2000 tons—per day. To reduce one ton of iron ore in a modern blast furnace typically requires about 1000 pounds of coke, 600 pounds of limestone and 4500 pounds of air. The result is about 1120 pounds of pig iron, 800 pounds of slag and 6000 pounds of recovered gases. As you would expect, recent developments in blast furnace technology have concentrated on improving the energy ratio of the process.

Pig iron, as produced by the blast furnace, is not a particularly useful material. During the process of direct reduction the iron picks up significant amounts of carbon (3.5% to 5.8%) from the incandescent coke, making it brittle. It also contains, at best, lesser but excessive amounts of silicon, manganese, phosphorus and sulfur. When solidified, pig iron is hard, brittle, nonhomogenous and virtually unmachinable. Its microstructure is full of all sorts of nasty things.

Useless as it may be, pig iron is the raw material for all of the subsequent iron- and steel-making processes. At one time it was cast into ingots (called "pigs" because of their fancied resemblance to a litter of piglets suckling from the mother sow) directly from the hearth and transported to the refining furnaces or converters in solid form. In order to conserve the energy required to remelt the pigs, current practice is to convey the pig iron, in the molten state, directly to the refining furnaces.

CAST IRON

The generic term "cast iron" refers to metallic iron in which is dissolved more than 2% of carbon (the most that iron can hold is about 6%). Steels are defined as iron with less than 2% carbon dissolved within their matrix. The various cast irons are almost the only ferrous metals that can be poured (or "cast") while in the molten state, into molds where they solidify into finished or semifinished parts of varying sizes, shapes and complexities (either solid or hollow). This obviates the necessity for machining or forging the shape from the solid form or fabricating it from several pieces and joining them together. Obviously if a satisfactory part can be cast—even if it must be finish machined—it will be more economical to produce than an equivalent fabricated, forged or machined part.

We, the racers, have a strong tendency to downgrade cast iron as a component or structural material. We think of it as heavy, relatively weak and, in some ways, crude. As often happens we are not entirely correct. There are some material functions, even within the restricted framework of motor racing, that cast irons fulfill as well as, or better than, practical alternatives—and at notably less cost.

At the time of this writing, despite the successful use by a few of the really-big-buck Formula One teams of carbon filament disc brake rotors, good old gray cast iron is still the best available material for racing (or any other automotive or industrial, and most aircraft) brake discs.

During the late and much lamented Shelby/Ford Le Mans program we must have tried every metal and alloy known to man—including flame-sprayed copper on cast iron, a couple of wrought stainless alloys and plasma coatings. We ended up with a curved vane rotor designed by Phil Remington and cast from good old gray iron. Admittedly the program ended 15 years ago but, except for the carbon composites (which I and every other racer would use if we could afford them) nothing has changed except that Automotive Products has come up with a "spheri-cone" disc which costs even more than the normal ventilated unit (and works better in extremely high temperature applications) and that Bob Gregg, by the simple expedient of manufacturing state-of-the-art rotors in the U. S., has brought the price down to something resembling a reasonable level.

Anyway, the vast majority of all automotive and industrial engine blocks, cylinder heads, transmission and differential housings, brake discs, calipers and drums—along with a pretty fair percentage of camshafts, followers, pump housings and exhaust manifolds—are still made from various grades of cast iron. Further, given sophisticated metallurgy and advanced casting techniques, it is a damned good material for most of them. As an example, a large engine lathe may contain several hundred separate iron castings ranging in size from cams and control wheel knobs weighing a few ounces to the main frame which may weigh tons. Less well known is the fact that a great many RACING engine blocks (including both of the current Formula Two engines and the BMW and Renault Turbo Formula One engines) feature cast iron blocks. For that matter, the normal material for the exhaust-side turbocharger housing (automotive, racing and aircraft) is a high-alloy cast iron. Industrial uses are endless, from pump housings to back hoe swing arms. Most machine tool frames, ways and beds are manufactured from cast iron. More uses are being developed daily. If you think of cast iron as a "crude" material, I will guarantee that a visit to a modern iron foundry will change your mind!

Be that as it may, OUR uses for cast iron are definitely limited, and rapidly becoming fewer. Since the "energy crisis" (which we—ostrich-like—seem to have forgotten about) can only get worse, I believe that, except for a few very specialized components, the future of cast iron in the transportation industries is grim. It is very unlikely that any of my readers will ever have occasion to make casting patterns or to cast anything from iron—or any other metal. So I am not going to go into the techniques and procedures of the foundry at all. However, a brief investigation of some of the properties of the various cast irons and the metallurgical techniques used in their production will serve as a logical introduction to our study of the production and properties of ferrous metals.

THE REFINEMENT OF PIG IRON

We have already determined that pig iron, as it issues from the blast furnace, is not fit for engineering use. To convert pig iron to "base metal" (the raw material of the iron foundry) I learned in college (admittedly some years ago) that pig iron was remelted, partially decarbonized and refined, either in a specialized type of blast furnace termed a "cupola," or by "puddling" (stirring molten pig iron in the presence of an oxidizing atmosphere). Until I started to write this chapter I never gave the process another thought. It seems that things have changed: Pig iron is now too expensive to be used in the production of cast iron (cost of energy again, plus the fact that we have used up most of the high-grade ores). For some years after this state of affairs came about, the foundries cheerfully melted down old engine blocks and the like. Even those have now become too scarce to be a dependable supply, and now the cast iron industry obtains the majority of its raw materials by melting and refining STEEL scrap in electric furnaces and then adding carbon in the form of graphite. Sometimes I just do not understand the way in which our economy is supposed to work.

THE ROMANCE BETWEEN IRON AND CARBON—PART ONE

For our purposes we will divide the engineering ferrous metals into two broad classes: cast irons and steels—both of which are, of course, ALLOYS OF IRON AND CARBON. The strength, hardness and toughness that make the ferrous based metals useful to us are profoundly influenced by the remarkable sensitivity of the physical and chemical properties of iron crystals to relatively small percentages of carbon dissolved within their matrixes (actually, the sensitivity is to the movement of dislocations within the crystal space lattice). This sensitivity to dissolved carbon is, in fact, the very basis of ferrous metallurgy. In order to understand this rather complex interrelationship—and its various effects—we must look somewhat deeper into the intimate relationship between carbon and iron.

There are several distinct types of cast iron. Within each type there are several possible grades. The different types of cast iron are distinguished by the form in which the majority of the dissolved carbon appears within the iron matrix. It can appear either as some form of GRAPHITE or as IRON CARBIDES. The grades within each type of cast iron are distinguished by the structure and the relative hardness of the iron (and, usually, silicon) matrix within which the carbon is dissolved.

To begin with, grains of essentially carbon-free metallic iron are called FERRITE. Ferrite readily forms a solid solution with other metals in which the other metals (typically silicon and some manganese) are completely dissolved in the iron. Ferrite itself, being essentially pure iron, is soft, ductile and tough. The addition of silicon makes it harder, stronger and less ductile (or more brittle). In fact, since cast irons contain higher percentages of silicon than most steels (it helps to precipitate the carbon out of solution) cast irons typically machine better than steels. The ferritic matrix of ductile and malleable cast irons provides their characteristic high ductility, toughness and shock resistance.

Some irons, when etched, polished and examined under magnification, have a deep and lustrous whitish appearance almost like that of a pearl. This appearance is due to the alternating layers of soft ferrite and hard IRON CARBIDES that make up the matrix—known, logically enough, as PEARLITE. This laminate structure of alternate hard and soft layers (shown in FIGURE [42]) is both very strong and very tough—rather like a laminated wooden beam.

If certain irons are cooled very rapidly the metal will solidify with all of the carbon combined with iron as particles of iron carbide, also called CEMENTITE. These particles are exceptionally hard and, while they are extremely wear resistant and thermally stable, they are also very brittle. Naturally enough, they impart these qualities to the irons whose matrixes are dominated by cementite.

There are six separate and distinct types of cast iron: gray iron, white iron, malleable iron, ductile or nodular iron, compacted graphite iron, and the family of high-alloy irons.

GRAY IRON

Gray iron is the most common form of cast iron used in the foundry. A scanning electron microscope photo of its microstructure (magic!) is reproduced in FIGURE [43]; the insert shows an etched sample of gray iron enlarged 100 times.

Gray iron is basically a matrix (lattice) of iron and silicon in solid solution interspersed with particles of carbon in the form of very thin interconnected FLAKES of graphite. Because more carbon can be dissolved in molten iron than can be dissolved in iron in its solid state, the graphite is precipitated out of solution with the iron during the cooling process. The mechanical properties of gray iron are affected by the amount of carbon present (i.e., how much space the flakes actually take up in the matrix), the size and distribution of the flakes and by the hardness of the metallic matrix. All of these factors can be varied and controlled by adjusting either the silicon and/or carbon content of the iron and/or the cooling rate of the casting. Simply put, the higher the carbon and/or the silicon content and the slower the cooling process, the more and larger will be the graphite flakes and the softer and weaker will be the matrix.

Like most materials in flake form (corn flakes, for instance) the graphite flakes themselves are both weak and brittle and the volume that they occupy within the matrix has little mechanical strength. The presence of the graphite in flake form does, however, give grey iron its excellent castability and machinability so that complex parts, both solid and cored, with varying cross-sections can be readily cast and economically finish machined. The material has modest tensile strength values (up to about 55,000 psi, ultimate), good wear resistance, excellent internal vibration damping ability and thermal stability and good resistance to galling. It is economical to produce, cast and finish. It is used for most machine tool bases, ways and housings, automotive and truck disc brake rotors (both solid and ventilated), internal combustion engine cylinder blocks and heads and for the vast majority of everyday household and industrial cast iron products that do not require high tensile strength (all cast irons exhibit good compressive strength).

WHITE IRON

If the composition of a molten grey iron is just right (very low silicon content) and the cooling rate is rapid enough, the metal will solidify with the carbon content of the iron in the form of granules of iron carbide, rather than as graphite flakes. This microstructure, magnified 100

Figure (43): The graphite flake structure of gray iron (scanning electron microscope photo). *Iron Castings Handbook*, the Iron Castings Society, 1981.

Figure (42): An etched sample of gray cast iron magnified 2,500 times to show the characteristic laminate structure of pearlite. Pearlite is composed of alternate layers of ductile ferrite and hard but brittle cementite. The dark shapes are sulfur contained as manganese sulfide. Linde Division of Union Carbide and *Metallurgy*, by Johnson and Weeks, American Technical Society, 1977.

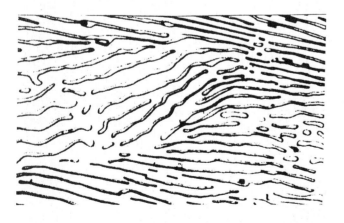

times, is shown in FIGURE [44]. Iron carbide or cementite is, as we have seen, an exceptionally hard and brittle compound. The resultant iron, known as WHITE IRON, is virtually free of graphite and is also hard and brittle—as well as virtually unmachinable. It does, however, exhibit great compressive strength and outstanding resistance to wear and abrasion and so does find limited use in the manufacture of farm, earth-moving and mining equipment. Its utility is increased by the technique of "chill casting" in which the formation of iron carbides—or a controlled combination

of iron carbides and graphite flakes known as "mottled iron"—can be formed at selected areas on and near the surface of gray iron castings by localized rapid cooling of the mold—as shown in FIGURE [44A].

A great many automotive camshafts and cam followers (tappets) are manufactured this way—the result is a tough part with a hard and wear-resistant surface. The other side of the coin is that the mottled iron sections must be ground to their finished dimensions since the carbides are not machinable by other methods. With cams and tappets this is no great disadvantage as we have not come up with any other way to finish the wearing surfaces anyway. The major use for white iron castings is, however, as a starting point for the production of malleable iron castings.

MALLEABLE IRON

Malleable irons are the toughest of the cast irons, exhibiting tensile strengths and ductilities comparable to those of the low-carbon steels. As shown by FIGURE [45] the

Figure (44): A polished and etched sample of white iron at 100 diameters magnification. The white constituent is iron carbide. The gray areas are pearlite. The Iron Castings Society.

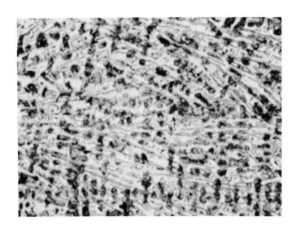

Figure (45): Graphite formations in malleable iron (scanning electron microscope photograph). The Iron Castings Society.

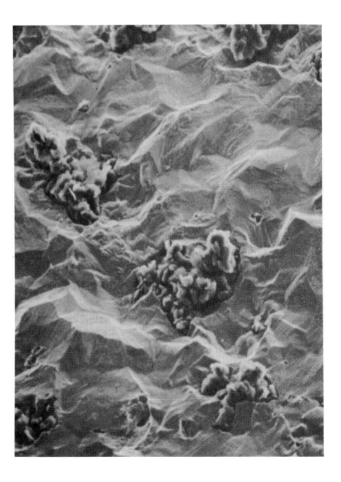

Figure (44A): The etched section of an iron casting at a corner where predetermined rapid cooling caused the formation of hard, white iron. The Iron Castings Society.

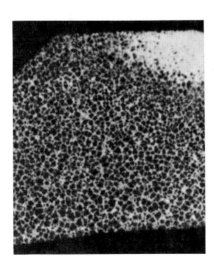

microstructure of malleable iron is distinguished by the presence of almost all of the carbon in the form of irregularly shaped lumps (nodules) of graphite which are interspersed throughout the matrix of the iron but are not interconnected.

This unusual structure is achieved by heat treatment of white iron castings in the solid state. After the castings have been removed from their molds they undergo a lengthy annealing process—beginning at a very high temperature (above 1650 degrees F). During the process the iron carbide contained in the white iron dislocates as free carbon which is then precipitated in the iron matrix as irregular nodules of graphite. The basic matrix structure can be controlled during heat treatment in order to vary the mechanical properties of the resultant malleable iron.

Although there are definite limitations to both the thickness and the complexity of the castings that can be produced in malleable iron, its strength and toughness make it popular for the production of hand tools (including the C-clamps of which you are certain to own several), industrial and automotive heavy-duty brackets, hangers, axle housings, drive yokes, a great many connecting rods, most brake calipers and so on.

It is interesting to note that, by fooling around with heat treatment, we have progressed from reasonably strong but fairly brittle gray iron, through very brittle white iron, and tricked-up ductile gray iron with hard mottled iron wearing surfaces to strong and really tough malleable iron. These physical metallurgists are clever folks!

DUCTILE OR NODULAR IRON

Ductile or nodular iron—called spheroidal graphite (SG) iron in England—was discovered (and appreciated) during the 1940's. However, economical and reliable metallurgical and foundry techniques for its production and use were not developed until the 1950's. Accordingly, nodular iron castings did not really begin their still increasing rise in engineering popularity until the early 1960's. One of the best-publicized early uses was the hollow cast iron crankshaft of the English Ford 105E engine—first of the production super-short-stroke engines and the dominant engine in the European Formula junior circuit where I cut my professional eyeteeth. This engine could also lay some claim to being the foundation stone on which Keith Duckworth and Mike Costin have built the Cosworth family of truly outstanding racing engines. The simple fact that we had to replace the stock hollow cast crank with one carved from a steel billet (NO ONE in those days could afford forging dies) as soon as we started to use more than about 7700 rpm with regularity does not detract from the metallurgical achievement of Ford of England.

As illustrated by FIGURE [46] the microstructure of nodular iron differs from that of the other irons in that ALL of its carbon is contained in the form of tiny SPHERICAL NODULES of graphite which are evenly dispersed throughout the matrix but are not connected with each other at all. These graphite microspheres can make up as much as 10% of the total volume of the iron but, because of their

shape and their isolation from each other (the resultant spherical voids have no sharp edges and are effectively localized), they have only a minimal effect on the mechanical properties of the iron while imparting to it both excellent castability and very good machinability.

Now second only to gray iron in tonnage produced, nodular iron is far-and-away the most ductile of the cast irons. It also combines exceptional tensile strength for a castable material with a very high modulus of elasticity, so that very stiff but shock-resistant structures can be cast from it. Further, it is eminently castable so that these structures can be complex. It even has good corrosion resistance and elevated temperature properties. Its matrix can be closely controlled by varying the chemical composition and/or the cooling rate to produce different grades and it can be alloyed with such elements as nickel, molybdenum and vanadium to further enhance its already outstanding mechanical properties. Ultimate tensile values range from about 60,000 to over 160,000 psi with yield strengths in the 40,000 to 145,000 range and percentage elongations from 18% down to less than 1% at the top of the tensile-strength range.

Figure (46): Nodular graphite particles in ductile or nodular iron (courtesy of the scanning electron microscope). The Iron Castings Society.

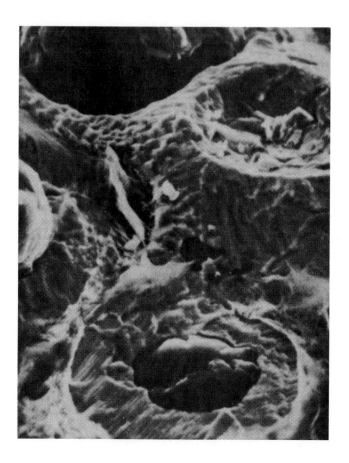

Even though the production of nodular iron castings is complex and expensive, its unique (among castable metals) mechanical properties have led to the rapid and continuing expansion of its uses in industry. The trucking and transportation industries have been quick to appreciate nodular castings as lighter and stronger replacements for complex steel weldments and for their ability to produce complex structural shapes—both cored and solid—that are strong, light and cheap. Examples include such critical components as crankshafts, gears (including ring and pinion sets) and front suspension steering knuckles.

COMPACTED GRAPHITE IRON

Like nodular iron, the structure of compacted graphite iron was discovered during the 1940's. Development in this case was a bit slower and only recently has it become feasible to produce it commercially. Its structure (see FIGURE [47]) is distinguished by the presence of graphite in the form of interconnected blunt flakes (somewhere between the wispy flakes of gray iron and the lumps of malleable iron). It looks rather as if someone had hammered the hell out of gray iron's graphite flakes. Not surprisingly its physical characteristics are in between those of gray iron

Figure (47): Compacted graphite iron. The Iron Castings Society.

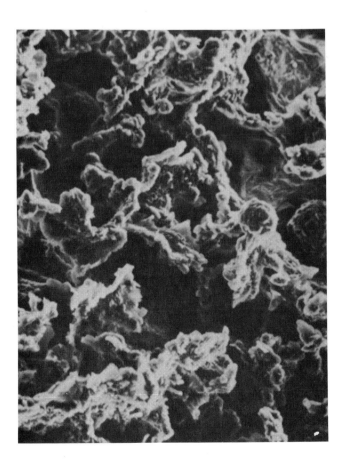

and ductile iron. Compacted graphite irons possess tensile strengths close to those of malleable and ductile irons (although with considerably less ductility) combined with castability rivaling that of grey iron. This allows complex castings with intricately cored molds to be made from a stronger grade of iron than was previously possible. Typical uses include gears, automotive and industrial brake drums, high pressure hydraulic valve cylinders and bodies, and heavy-duty housings of various types.

HIGH-ALLOY IRONS

Most types and grades of cast iron are commonly alloyed to some extent with other elements in order to modify the physical and/or chemical properties of the base iron to suit specific requirements. In the very specialized family of "high-alloy irons" the alloy content is so great (up to 36%) that these characteristics are not merely modified but are fundamentally changed in order to meet severe and specific operating conditions and requirements. These requirements include high resistance to corrosion, maintenance of physical properties at either very high or very low temperatures, high ratios of thermal stability and anticorrosion properties at extreme temperatures and extreme resistance to wear and abrasion.

While the production of high-alloy cast irons is specialized and expensive, their ability to deliver the required characteristics as a castable metal makes their use economical in many industrial applications—including the handling of both abrasive and corrosive materials. Typically these irons are produced by alloying grey, white or ductile iron with:

Nickel and/or silicon for corrosion resistance.

Nickel, silicon, aluminum and/or chromium for high heat resistance.

Nickel-chromium, chromium or molybdenum-chromium for resistance to wear and abrasion.

The most widely used high-alloy irons are the Ni-Resist family of gray and ductile irons alloyed with nickel, silicon, chromium and molybdenum. Ni-Resist irons are used throughout the petroleum, chemical and steam energy industries as pumps, housings, turbines, valves and valve stems; as well as in the transportation, racing and aircraft industries as exhaust-side turbocharger housings and exhaust manifolds.

WROUGHT IRON

All of this cast iron technology is quite recent. The sophisticated cast irons were not available to our ancestors, for the simple reason that they had no way to make a fire hot enough to melt iron. All that even our immediate ancestors had was pig iron and, later, very impure gray iron; these, having strength only in compression and being inherently brittle, were not particularly suited for structural use. The structural ferrous metal from the beginning of the Iron Age more than 3000 years ago until the middle of the 19th century was wrought iron.

Wrought iron is simply pig iron that has been purified by one of two incredibly laborious processes: forging or puddling. Forging came first (in fact the origins of iron forging are lost in the mists of prehistory). To begin with, a "blank" is cast from pig iron, heated to white heat and hammered or forged to literally squeeze the slag and impurities from the iron. In the process, a great deal of the carbon content is reduced by oxidation. In the very beginning, instead of casting an iron-forging blank, a number of small sponges, or "blooms" from primitive blast furnaces were forge welded together at white heat to form the blank. No matter how the forging blank was formed, as it cooled it was reheated, folded over to expose fresh surfaces to the hammer and reforged—and reheated—and refolded—and reforged—until the master smith finally judged that it had reached the ideal proportions for its intended use. For the first few millenia the forging was done by hand, presumably by apprentices or slaves. In the Middle Ages mechanical forging hammers, powered by water wheels, were developed which allowed the use of larger blanks, less muscle power and more brainpower. The process was, however, still slow, and only a few hundred pounds of wrought iron per day could be produced by even the best of forges.

In the late 18th century an Englishman named Henry Cort developed the coke-fired puddling furnace in which a molten pool of pig iron could be mechanically stirred with long iron paddles called "rabbles" which were inserted through ports in the furnace walls. The puddler stirred iron oxides into the molten pig iron and kept on stirring while the oxides (reacting with the carbon in the pig iron) removed most of the carbon from the iron in the form of carbon monoxide gas. The release of the gas agitated or stirred the molten iron into a "boil" which drove most of the slag out. As the carbon content was reduced, the melting point of the evermore-pure iron continuously increased from its original 2100 degrees F to about 2800 degrees F. Since the temperature of the furnace was below the increased melting point, the metal began to solidify into a pasty mass. At this point it was rolled up into a rough ball and removed from the furnace. Believe it or not a skilled (and very strong) puddler could convert about a TON of pig iron in a day. There were MEN on the earth in those days (and desperate, hungry men they must have been)! Puddling, mind-bogglingly crude and laborious as it seems to us, was a quantum leap forward in terms of quantity of production.

After the pasty ball of semisolid iron was removed from the furnace it was hammered to remove some of the remaining slag. (The steam hammer came along in the early 19th century, its development spurred by the success of puddling in producing larger quantities of wrought iron than could be handled by water-mill-powered trip hammers.) The iron was then reheated and passed, still hot, through a series of rollers which squeezed it into bars which could then be either forged or further rolled into shapes and/or plates as desired. The plates and bars were then further shaped and joined (either by riveting or forge welding) into structural girders, tubes, boilers, ship's hull plates and the like. Wrought iron was also rolled into I-beams and used as railroad track. The rolling process elongated the remaining slag content into stringy longitudinal threads which actually added to the strength and toughness of the finished product.

In the process iron oxides in the form of scale fell off the steel and these were added to the pig iron being puddled to promote oxidation.

The wrought iron so produced was a tough and ductile material with moderate strength (20,000 to 40,000 psi, ultimate). This doesn't sound like much strength by our standards, but it was a hell of a lot better than anything else that was available until Henry Bessemer came along in the 1850's. It was also remarkably resistant to corrosion (as witness the anchors that are regularly recovered from centuries of immersion in salt water).

Wrought iron bars reinforced the marble temples of Greece and Rome. Wrought iron was the major structural metal used by our civilization from about the 14th century until the development of the Bessemer process in 1856. It was wrought iron that made the Industrial Revolution possible at all and it was the development of the puddling process that made it practical. Carbon steel does just about everything better and more cheaply than wrought iron, so we don't use much wrought iron today. Because of its softness, ductility and inherent resistance to atmospheric corrosion it does find some limited uses in pipe and ornamental iron. It is interesting to note that what little wrought iron is produced today is made in puddling furnaces—mechanized, of course—but still recognizable as direct descendants of Mr. Cort's original devices.

STEEL AND STEEL MAKING

"Carbon steel" is, technically, metallic iron to which a small amount of carbon (up to about 1.7%) has been added in order to increase the strength, hardness and malleability of the iron. In practical terms, carbon steel is merely pig iron from which most of the impurities have been removed and whose carbon content has been REDUCED in order to improve ductility and fatigue resistance. "Alloy steels" are carbon steels to which minute amounts of specific alloying elements have been added in order to improve certain physical characteristics of the resultant steel.

"Steel refining" is the generic term used to describe the process of purifying pig iron, reducing its carbon content and alloying the result in order to produce a homogenous steel of predetermined chemical composition and resultant physical or mechanical characteristics. The raw materials are pig iron (in both solid and molten form), iron ore, selected steel scrap, limestone and, of course, the various alloying elements. The refining can be accomplished in an open-hearth furnace, a Bessemer converter, a basic oxygen furnace or in one of several types of electric furnaces.

THE BESSEMER PROCESS

In the working lifetime of my great-grandfather, a metalsmith, carbon steel was limited by the laws of supply and demand to the production of specialized items—edged tools and weapons, rifle barrels and the like. The man who changed all that was Henry Bessemer. In the mid-19th century the good Mr. Bessemer, an English metallurgist, searching for a way to produce a better and more dependable grade (and larger quantities) of carbon steel in order to meet the ever-growing demand for railroad track, boiler plate and rifle barrels, developed the ''air-refining'' process for converting pig iron to steel that bears his name to this day.

Actually, Bessemer was trying to improve (or at least to speed up) the puddling process of wrought iron production. He applied a blast of hot air to the bottom of the pool of molten pig iron in a puddling furnace and found that not only did the blast of air very quickly remove the silicon and carbon from the pig iron (which was what he was trying to accomplish) but that the heat produced by the oxidation of the impurities was sufficient to keep the metal molten. Further, the temperature of the molten iron was actually raised into the steel-producing range BY THE HEAT OF OXIDATION. He at once realized what he had accomplished and the age of steel was upon us.

Sir Henry was not only a very good engineer and metallurgist, he was also a very astute combination of businessman and politician. His great inspiration (or rather the intelligent application and exploitation of it) earned him both knighthood in an age when they were hard to come by and an enormous personal fortune.

The Bessemer converter (see FIGURE [48]) is a large, pear-shaped vessel which is mounted on trunnions so that it can be tilted. Capacities vary from about 5 tons of pig iron to more than 50 tons. The converter itself is lined with refractory brick. (A refractory material is one which does not undergo significant physical change at elevated temperatures; in other words, one that does not burn, melt or break down. The famous tiles on the space shuttle are a high tech refractory material.) In use, the converter is tilted and loaded (or charged) through its mouth with molten pig iron to which lime has been added as a flux. It is then rotated back to vertical, and pressurized air is injected into and blown through the molten iron through a series of ceramic tubes or ''truyeres'' in the bottom of the vessel. The

Figure (48): The Bessemer converter.

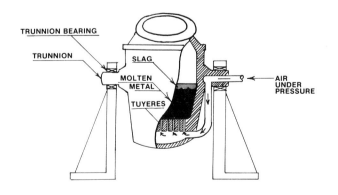

oxygen content of the air burns some of the carbon (and most of the other impurities) present in the iron and thus refines the pig iron into carbon steel. The lime causes the oxides formed during the burning process to separate and collect on the surface of the molten steel as slag.

When the oxidation has progressed to the stage where the carbon content has been reduced to the level desired in the finished steel (this point is judged, believe it or not, by the color of the flame blasting forth from the open mouth of the converter—the Bessemer conversion is a pretty spectacular process!), the air blast is stopped, the converter is partially tilted and the slag is poured off. The vessel is then tilted the rest of the way and the molten steel is discharged into a ladle from which it can either be poured into molds where it solidifies into ingots (which are sized and shaped for ease of subsequent processing into finished mill products) or it can be conveyed, still molten, directly to the mills for processing. To obtain the desired chemical composition of the finished steel, alloying elements are added either during the blow or during the pouring process.

The Bessemer conversion of iron into steel takes place in a matter of minutes—without fuel—and the resultant steel has a uniform chemical composition. Further, unlikely though it may seem, the carbon content can be controlled very closely. The Bessemer process virtually revolutionized the industrial world, reducing the price of steel to a small fraction of what it had been, bringing about a quantum leap in volume of steel production and opening up whole new worlds to structural engineers.

The air-reduction process of steel refining was very popular during the latter half of the 19th century and well into the 20th. However, the process is not very good at removing some of the impurities commonly found in pig iron which has been smelted from low grade ores—the resultant steels tend to be highly oxidized and dirty. As we have mostly used up the known supply of high-grade ores, the Bessemer process has fallen into disuse. Besides, the Bessemer process cannot use very much unmelted scrap in the charge simply because the heat generated is not sufficient to melt it.

So poor old Henry's name is about to pass from current technology into the history books. Still, his process (and his wealth) outlasted his long life, and that is about all a man can reasonably ask. In contrast consider the case of William Kelly of Kentucky who, working completely independently of Bessemer, developed the exact same process within weeks of Bessemer's breakthrough (and patents). His rewards, tangible and otherwise, totaled right next to zilch. He, like a great many supremely talented racing drivers I have known, simply didn't make it happen!

OPEN-HEARTH STEEL

While Bessemer in 1856 was definitely the first to develop a practical method of refining steel, he was not the only man working on the problem. A very few years later William Siemens developed the open-hearth method of refining steel, in which the necessary oxidation is induced by the oxygen present in the iron oxides (ore) which make up a part of the charge. The open hearth furnace (see FIGURE [49]) is first loaded with ferrous scrap, limestone and iron ore. This "basic" charge lies on an open hearth where it is melted by direct exposure to a gas flame which continuously sweeps its surface. The molten pig iron, which comprises the majority of the charge, is added after the basic charge has melted.

During the subsequent refining (which goes on for hours), nearly all of the carbon, silicon, phosphorus and manganese contained in the iron—along with most of the sulfur—are reduced and combined with the limestone of the basic charge to form a slag which floats on top of the molten metal and protects it from reoxidation. The charge is allowed to continue its reaction until oxidation has reduced the carbon content to the percentage desired in the finished steel. The furnace is then tapped from the bottom. The steel flows into a ladle from which it is either poured into ingot molds or taken directly to the mills for further processing. Alloying elements are added either just before the furnace is tapped or while the steel is flowing into the ladle.

Open-hearth-furnace capacities vary from 100 net tons to more than 500 tons. Each "heat" requires from four to ten hours, depending both on the size of the furnace and the amount of carbon desired in the finished steel. This time can be decreased by the addition of oxygen to the furnace during the refining period. A wide range of high-quality carbon and low-alloy steels can be produced by the open-hearth process, and it allows the use of scrap and/or iron ore in quantities of up to 80%. This feature has been of considerable interest for almost a century, simply because our highly industrialized society somehow manages to produce ferrous scrap more cheaply than we can smelt iron ore! The steel produced by the open-hearth furnace is slightly more consistent than that produced by the Bessemer process.

For all of these reasons the open-hearth furnace was the dominant steel-making method until the rising cost of both labor and energy doomed it to obsolescence in the immediate post-World War II period. Japan and Germany, with their steel industries in ruins, pretty much avoided the open-hearth furnace when they rebuilt. Financed by our Marshall Plan dollars they concentrated on the basic oxygen and electric furnaces. Our steel industry, on the other hand, did not modernize—partially through ostrichlike ignorance, partially through greed and partially because of a lack of incentive (from the tax point of view) to do so. Our steel industry—and our entire nation—is now paying the price for this historic shortsightedness.

THE BASIC OXYGEN PROCESS

Similar to the Bessemer process, the basic oxygen process of steel making takes place in a vessel (shown by FIGURE [50]) which is similar in both size and shape to the Bessemer converter. After the vessel has been charged with molten pig iron and (sometimes) from 12% to 30% ferrous scrap, high-speed jets of pure oxygen are introduced to the top surface of the charge through water cooled lances. At the same time burnt lime and fluorspar (calcium fluoride) are introduced to form the slag. The oxygen reacts with the charge to cause very rapid oxidation of the carbon, manganese and silicon contained in the pig iron and the generation

Figure (50): The basic oxygen furnace.

Figure (49): The open-hearth steel-making furnace. Gaseous fuel is blown through hot brickwork at A. Air is blown through hot brick at B. Preheated gas/air mixture burns at C, melting with charge on hearth. Exhaust gases heat brickwork regenerators D and E. When regenerators A and B cool, the flow of gas and air is reversed, and D and E preheat the fuel.

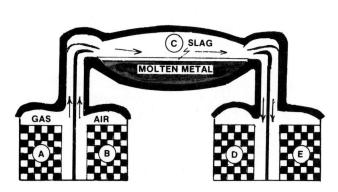

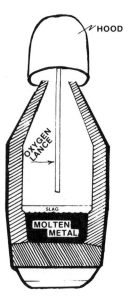

of very high temperatures which melt the scrap, form the slag and refine out the carbon. Again, alloying elements are added either just before the furnace is tapped or while the steel is being poured.

The steel produced by the basic oxygen furnace is comparable in every way to that from the open-hearth process. The basic oxygen furnace is not fussy about raw material and, since no fuel or heat source is required and the charge presents a very low surface-to-volume ratio, the charge is converted with a high degree of chemical and thermal efficiency.

The relatively recent escalation of the cost of both fuel and scrap has reversed the historic advantages of the open-hearth steel-refining furnace. The dramatic rise in the cost of energy has also served to increase the cost of operation of the electric furnaces and so the basic oxygen process is becoming more and more popular for the production of carbon and low-alloy steels, actually achieving a worldwide majority about 1975. FIGURE [51] shows current steel production by method of refinement.

ELECTRIC STEEL REFINING

The major alloying elements which are added to carbon steels in order to create the so called ''high-grade'' or ''exotic'' steel alloys are: chromium, manganese, molybdenum, titanium and vanadium. They are normally added in the form of ferro-alloys, most of which are more readily oxidizable than is iron itself, making it impossible to produce these high-grade alloys by the open-earth, Bessemer or basic oxygen process. (The result of an attempt to do so would be the creation of a MIXTURE of metallic iron and the alloying element, rather than a steel ALLOY.) In order to produce these high-alloy steels it is necessary to reduce the oxygen activity in the furnace and to increase the temperature so that the alloying elements become more reducible in relation to carbon.

The ever-increasing demand for uniform batches of high-alloy steels led to the development of the various types of electric steel-making furnaces which satisfy both of these requirements. Since there is little, if any, flame involved in the electric melting process, the furnace temperatures can be increased without fear of furnace damage and, since oxygen is not required for the maintenance of combustion, the atmosphere in which the refining takes place can be closely controlled and its oxygen content reduced to a practical minimum. It is also possible to control the temperature within the furnace to closer limits with the electric furnace than with other types. The letter ''E'' as a prefix to a steel designation indicates that the steel has been refined in an electric furnace, as in E4130.

THE ELECTRIC ARC FURNACE

The first of the electric steel-making processes was the electric arc furnace developed to meet the demand for high-alloy tool steels in the very late 19th century. Fortunately the development of modern tool steels coincided with the production of vast amounts of cheap electric power through hydroelectric plants. The electric arc furnace, illustrated by FIGURE [52], is simply a closed furnace lined with refractory brick and containing large graphite electrodes which extend through its roof.

In operation the electrodes are lowered into close proximity with the initial charge of ferrous scrap and/or solidified pig iron. The current is then switched on, striking an arc from the electrodes to the charge. The intense heat of the arc, aided by the heat radiated back from the walls and the roof of the furnace, melts the charge and brings about the deoxidation process. When the charge is mainly melted, burnt lime is added as a flux to form the slag. At this time,

Figure (52): The electric arc steel-making furnace.

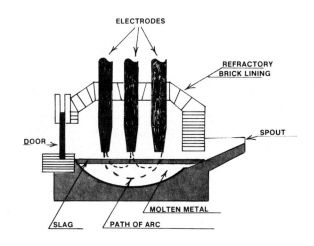

Figure (51): U.S. steel production by various methods in tons × 1,000 and as a percentage of total production.

YEAR	BASIC OXYGEN FURNACE	OPEN HEARTH FURNACE	ELECTRIC FURNACE
1965	22,879 Or 17.5%	94,193 or 72%	13,804 or 10.5%
1970	63,330 or 48.2%	48,022 or 36.5%	20,162 or 15.3%
1975	71,801 or 61.6%	22,161 or 19%	22,680 or 19.4%
1978	83,484 or 60.9%	21,310 or 15.6%	32,237 or 23.5%

U.S. steel production by types of steel in tons × 1,000 and as a percentage of total production.

YEAR	CARBON STEEL	ALLOY STEEL	STAINLESS STEEL
1965	117,000 or 89%	13,318 or 9.9%	1,493 or 1.1%
1970	117,000 or 89%	12,824 or 10%	1.279 or 1%
1975	100,360 or 86%	1,517 or 13%	1,111 or 1%
1978	116,916 or 85%	18,161 or 13.6%	1,954 or 1.4%

if desired, an additional charge of raw iron ore can be added. Alloying elements are added near the end of the refining process. Temperature is controlled automatically by varying the height of the electrodes above the charge. The molten charge is stirred, either mechanically or by magnetic induction, to speed the deoxidation process.

Furnace capacity is considerably less than that of the open hearth but the refining process is fast. The electric arc furnace can be scaled down to allow the economic production of as little as a few hundred pounds of steel, and the furnace itself can be manufactured cheaply enough to allow individual furnaces to be reserved solely for the production of specific alloys—a feature of some interest in the manufacture of experimental and low-demand alloys. More importantly, the furnace can operate efficiently with a cold charge consisting largely of unrefined iron ore, thus reducing the need for blast furnaces, the energy to operate them and the handling equipment necessary to convey pig iron (solid or molten) from the blast furnace to the refining furnace. This is the major reason, until the cost of energy production soared a few years ago, it looked as if the electric arc furnace would replace all of the other types for the production of carbon and low-alloy steels, as well as being the major source for the high-alloy steels for which it was designed.

THE ELECTRIC INDUCTION FURNACE

Developed in the 1920's, the electric induction furnace has just about taken over the production of high-alloy tool steels. No actual refining takes place during this process; it is a "dead melt" situation in which the charge never comes into contact with the heat source. As shown in FIGURE [53], the melt takes place within a closed crucible

Figure (53): The electric induction furnace.

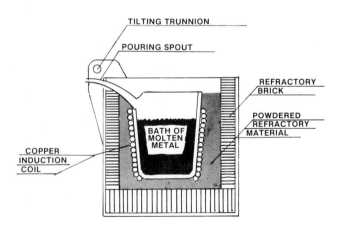

which is in turn contained within an insulated furnace. The charge actually makes up the secondary side of an electric transformer. The primary side is a water-cooled copper tube wound around the crucible and connected to a monster power source. Low-frequency induction coils are used in production, while high-frequency furnaces are used in laboratory work, small-batch production and induction heat treating.

The charge may consist of an ingot of steel, pieces of selected steel scrap (or a combination of both) and the required alloying elements. Regardless of the composition of the charge, what goes in is what comes out; the process is limited to melting and mixing, no refining takes place.

VACUUM MELTING

No matter what refining process is used in the production of a steel, it is usually poured from the furnace into molds where it solidifies into ingots of specific sizes and shapes which are designed for ease of subsequent processing into the final form of the steel, be it sheet, wire, plate, bar, tube or forged shape. In addition to the desired alloying elements and the inevitable impurities, all molten steels contain a certain amount of entrapped gas, chiefly oxygen. As the steel solidifies in the ingot molds some of this gas escapes from its surface as bubbles but some does not make it out and is trapped within the solid steel in the form of hollow spots called "voids." The result is an ingot which, while its surface may appear perfectly normal and homogenous, is to some extent porous. The resultant steel, termed "rimmed steel," is perfectly suitable for a number of processes (those that entail considerable rolling during which the internal voids are squeezed and welded shut). Sheet rolling and wire drawing are two examples that come to mind.

Rimmed steel is not, however, suitable for processing into forms which do not require severe rolling-bar stock or forging billets, for instance. Liquid steel that has been deoxidized (usually by the addition of manganese, silicon or aluminum to the melt) so that little or no oxygen remains in solution is termed "killed steel." Depending upon the amount of remaining oxygen it can be either partially or completely killed, and it is used in the production of bar stock, forged billets and tubing (and for very ductile sheet stock which will be subjected to deep drawing or other severe forming operations). However, there lives not a machinist (or an inspector) who has not found a void while machining an expensive part—usually on the final cut. Further, the byproducts of the deoxidation remain in the killed steel as oxide inclusions, which are as bad as voids from the structural point of view (except that there are many fewer of them) AND knock the hell out of cutting tools.

What to do? X-ray inspection of steels during manufacture avoided a lot of disappointments. But, the aerospace industry's requirements for high-quality, homogenous and pore-free alloy steels of great uniformity, purity and refinement of grain size grew to unprecedented levels during World War II and the period immediately afterward. It became obvious that something new had to be done. The demand was met by the development of the vacuum melting process, in which an alloy steel from an electric furnace is remelted, degassed and poured in a vacuum. The lack of an atmosphere during the process prevents reoxidation of the steel but the biggest single advantage of the vacuum melt process is that it permits the use of carbon dioxide as a deoxidizing agent.

Carbon dioxide has the singular property of leaving the molten steel completely, but it is not an effective deoxidizer at atmospheric pressure. Under vacuum it becomes enormously effective and vacuum-melted steels have now become the accepted norm for aerospace use—particularly when forging is contemplated. The same is true for racing use. Most competent racers now use vacuum-melted 300M or vacuum-melted 4340 for critical forgings such as hubs and drive shafts. FIGURE [54] illustrates vacuum melting and shows that it is also possible to combine the electric induction furnace and the vacuum-melting process in one operation.

THE ELECTRIC ARC VACUUM FURNACE

Two types of electric-arc vacuum furnaces are used for the production of alloys of those elements which are easily contaminated by exposure to air: the consumable arc furnace, in which the negative electrode is composed of the metal to be melted, and the nonconsumable arc furnace with a tungsten electrode. It would be senseless to attempt to carry out these purifying melts in a furnace lined with refractory brick from which the steel would pick up impurities of various sorts so, in both cases, the charge is placed on a relatively thin, water-cooled hearth and the entire furnace is lined with water-cooled copper. In operation the furnace is evacuated prior to beginning the melt and maintained under vacuum until the melting and alloying process is completed. Most of the high-alloy steels are now melted, alloyed and poured under vacuum simply because of the exceptional purity and homogeneity of the resultant steel. Some, like 300M, are double- and triple-vacuum-melted to previously unknown levels of purity.

Figure (54): The vacuum induction furnace. Charge is induction melted and cast into ingots under vacuum.

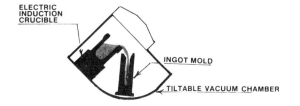

ELECTRIC INDUCTION CRUCIBLE

INGOT MOLD

TILTABLE VACUUM CHAMBER

THE WORKING OF STEEL INTO USEABLE FORMS AND SHAPES

With the exception of powdered and sintered metals (which are of no interest to us), all of the shapes available in ferrous metals begin as molten metal, in which form it is of no use to the engineer, let alone to the racer. Before we can use the stuff, molten steel must be processed into useful shapes from which we can machine, forge or fabricate the parts that we need. The processing is done in the steel mills of song and story.

From the refining furnaces, molten steel can either be cast into ingots for later processing into useable forms or it can be conveyed, still molten, directly to the processing mills. In either case, the shaping processes are very similar: Ingots and billets are shaped into bars, sheets, plates or wire by various mechanical processes such as rolling, forging and extruding. The metal undergoes plastic deformation by being stressed beyond its elastic limit. In the process, the physical characteristics of the metal are improved by breaking up the "as cast" crystal structure and "refinement" of the grain size.

This mechanical working can take place either at temperatures which are close to the ambient air or at elevated temperatures. Basically a metal which has been plastically deformed at a temperature which is low in relation to its melting point is considered to be cold worked while those that have been deformed at temperatures approaching their melting points are hot worked. The mechanical properties of the finished product will depend to some extent on the temperature at which it was formed. The yield strengths of almost all metals decrease notably with increasing temperature, so that a given amount of deformation can be achieved at much lower stress levels if the material is hot worked rather than cold worked. We know from practical experience that a steel bar which we cannot do anything at all with at room temperature will bend like taffy at red heat. For this reason, all operations involving large changes in shape—whether by forging, stamping, pressing, rolling or extruding—are normally carried out at elevated temperatures.

Almost all of the energy expended in the hot working of metals is dissipated as heat, leaving the metal's crystal structure largely unaffected and the metal ductile. On the other hand, while most of the energy expended in the cold working of a metal is also dissipated in the form of heat, some part of this energy remains within the crystal structure of the metal itself as "strain energy" in the form of various distortions of and dislocations in the crystal space lattice. Therefore, cold working, by decreasing the grain size and increasing the number of dislocations in the crystal lattice of the metal being worked, can increase the strength and hardness of the finished product—sometimes to a notable extent—at some cost in ductility.

THE SHAPING OF STEEL INGOTS INTO MILL PRODUCTS

I am fully aware that the whole subject of steel making and steel processing is both vast enough and complex enough to make the various steps difficult to visualize. I think that my text and illustrations are good, but I feel that some sort of reasonably comprehensive "overview" is needed. For once, I got lucky. While doing the basic research for this portion of the book I ran across some truly outstanding graphics published by The American Iron and Steel Institute (1000 16th Street, Washington, D.C. 20036). I have received permission to reprint excerpts from its STEELMAKING FLOWLINES. FIGURE [55] follows the subject from ore, coal and limestone to sheet, tube and bar.

The shaping or working process all starts either with molten steel or with cast ingots which have been heated to a uniformly high temperature in a "soaking pit." Next the ingots are rolled (or the molten metal is cast and then rolled) into partially finished shapes: SLABS (which will be made into plates, sheets or tubes), BLOOMS (which will become structural shapes) and tube rounds, or BILLETS (for the production of bar stock and wire).

STEEL SHEET

Steel sheet and strip are produced by progressively reducing a slab to the desired final thickness through hot-rolling mills. The better grades of steel sheet are hot rolled only to an approximation of final thickness and then cold rolled to final dimensions. Annealing and/or other thermal treatments before, during and after rolling are carefully controlled to produce a specified quality of finished sheet. Plate (sheet more than 1/4'' thick) is produced in the same way.

BAR AND ROD STOCK—WIRE

Bar stock, rod, angles, I-beams and other shapes are also rolled to specified dimensions through progressive hot shaped rollers. Again, the higher grades are hot rolled only to approximate size and are cold drawn through hardened dies to their final dimensions. Hot-rolled round bar stock is also extruded, under unthinkable pressure, into wire. Special "tube rounds" are hot rolled and then used in the production of seamless pipe and tube.

Figure (55): A flowline of steel making. American Iron and Steel Institute.

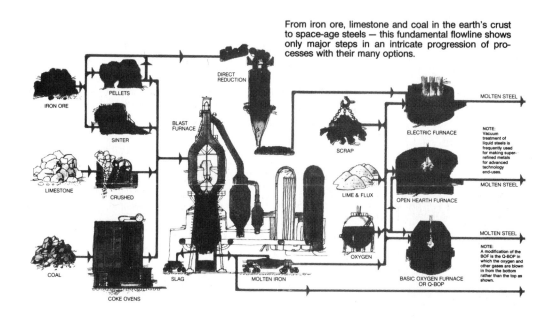

From iron ore, limestone and coal in the earth's crust to space-age steels — this fundamental flowline shows only major steps in an intricate progression of processes with their many options.

TUBE AND PIPE

Seamed tubing and pipe are roll formed from strips of sheet or plate and then welded. Seamless tubing (and pipe, which is merely tubing with thick walls intended primarily for the conveyance of liquids), on the other hand is pierced by a pointed mandrel while being fed by angled rollers and then either hot or cold finished. In any case the processes have always seemed so unlikely to me that I feel that some pictures of the processes are needed. Accordingly, FIGURE [56] illustrates the various processes by which tube and pipe are formed from flat or bar stock.

STRUCTURAL SHAPES

Structural shapes—angles, zees, I-beams and the like—are hot rolled through progressive grooved rollers. Roll forming can also be used as a cold-working process for the production of very precise shapes from steel strip—but that is a fabrication technique, not a mill process.

HOT VERSUS COLD

As you would expect, the different mill forming processes result in steel mill products of varying qualities and properties:

CARBON STEEL SHEET can be purchased either hot rolled or cold rolled. FIGURE [58] (shown later) shows significant differences in mechanical properties between the two. I do not want to know about hot rolled steel sheet. Admittedly it IS more malleable and therefore easier to form, but it comes complete with scale, is not as uniform as cold rolled, is considerably less strong and is liable to contain some slag inclusions.

ALLOY STEEL SHEET can be purchased, hot rolled or cold rolled, in either the annealed-only or the annealed-and-normalized condition. The annealed is easier to form while the annealed-and-normalized is stronger. In either case I use cold rolled.

BAR STOCK in diameters up to about 4'' is usually available either hot rolled or hot rolled and cold finished in

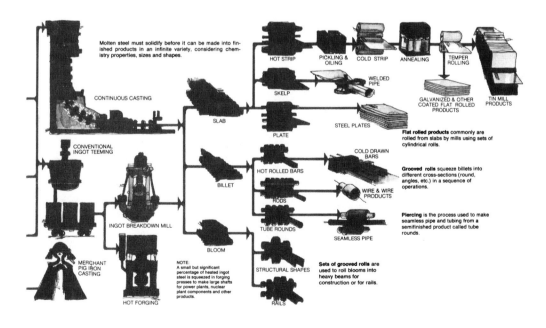

either carbon or alloy steels. Alloy steel bar is sometimes available in one of several heat-treated conditions. The cold-finished bars have ultimate tensile strengths significantly higher than hot-rolled bars, yield strengths up to 100% greater, are straighter and have a much better surface finish. The larger bars are available hot rolled and machine straightened only (it takes a lot more force to cold work metal than it does to hot work it and there are limits to the forces available to process steel in commercial quantities). My basic feeling here is that, except for flywheels (which I no longer make because Mac Tilton makes them better and cheaper than I can), I have no use for large-diameter bar stock. I order cold-finished bar stock which is both

stronger and better finished. It also usually machines a bit better.

CARBON STEEL TUBING can be ordered as COLD DRAWN SEAMLESS, in which case it will be drawn from SAE 1018 steel; as DRAWN OVER MANDREL (DOM), in which case it will be drawn from 1020 steel, be just as strong and just as well finished and a good bit cheaper. It also comes as ELECTRIC RESISTANCE WELDED (ERW) tube, which is produced from SAE 1020 steel unless the wall thickness is 16 gauge or lighter, in which case it is made from SAE 1010. HOT FINISHED SEAMLESS tubing is made from SAE 1026 and is considerably less expensive than cold drawn tube. It is also not as strong, scaly and less dependable. COLD DRAWN AND BUTT WELDED TUBE is found occasionally in some sizes and is considerably stronger and better finished than ERW. One thing that has to be watched out for is that the industry bends a lot of carbon steel tubing to make lots of things and so most carbon steel tubing is available in the annealed condition—woe to him who does not detect it before he builds the part. I have a very good friend who once got an entire roll cage cut, bent, fitted and tacked before he realized that his merry men were working with annealed boiler tube. The other thing that we don't want is "free machining tubing." I currently use round carbon steel DOM mechanical tubing for most things other than suspension links (there I use E4130N and stress relieve and heat treat after welding). For roll cages I use either 4130 or DOM 1020. I do not want to know about hot-finished tubing because I do not want to clean it. I am old enough to remember the days when English ERW tubing was liable to split along the weld seam. As a matter of principle (or, possibly, stubbornness) I do not use ERW or butt welded tube on the race car; although, since it is a lot cheaper, I use it all over the trailer and the shop.

ALLOY STEEL TUBING is generally available in either the normalized or the annealed condition.

I do not generally keep any stock of material of lesser quality than I am willing to use on the race car (with the exception of ERW square tube which everyone who works for me knows does not get used on the car). The reason is very simple: I cannot possibly look at every piece of material that someone is going to make a part from. Mr. Murphy's well-known laws assure me that, if I keep junk around, someone, someday, is GOING to make a critical car part from it. Smith's less-well-known corollary states, "If it isn't available, it isn't going to find its way on to the race car." The same applies to worn parts, bent parts, fasteners and everything else that is not judged good enough to go on the car. If you wouldn't put it on the car to start a race with, SCRAP IT! The only exceptions that I allow to this rule are worn out rod ends and spherical bearings which I keep at home for tooling and the inevitable "junk box" of nuts, bolts, washers and gubbins that I keep around, also for tooling.

STEEL DESIGNATIONS

A standardized four-digit identification and designation system is used for all steels produced and used in the United

Figure (56): Different methods of manufacturing tube and pipe from flat or bar stock. *Manufacturing Processes*, seventh edition, by B. H. Amstead, P. E. Ostwald and M. L. Begeman, John Wiley and Sons, 1977.

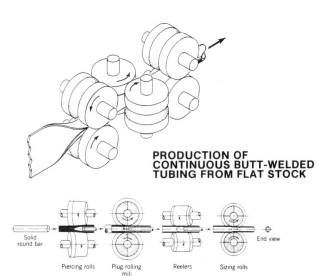

PRODUCTION OF CONTINUOUS BUTT-WELDED TUBING FROM FLAT STOCK

Solid round bar

Piercing rolls   Plug rolling mill   Reelers   Sizing rolls   End view

Principal steps in the manufacture of seamless tubing.

Rotary seamless process for large tubing.

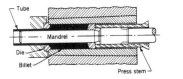

Extruding a large tube from a heated billet.

Tube
Mandrel
Die
Billet
Press stem

States. I only wish that it were in use worldwide. We divide steels into two broad categories: carbon steels and alloy steels.

CARBON STEELS

There are four classifications of carbon steels. They are identified by the first two digits of the designator:

10xx—nonresulfurized carbon steel. This series is the basic structural "low-carbon" or "mild" steel.

11xx—resulfurized carbon steel. These are the free machining steels. They are inherently brittle and are of no interest to us. We should make a mental note of the designator so that we can avoid the group.

12xx—resulfurized and rephosphorized carbon steel—likewise to be avoided.

15xx—nonresulfurized, high-manganese carbon steel. This is the basic carbon steel used for low-cost forgings. It is of interest to us only because the auto industry tends to use it for such things as suspension knuckles, which WE overstress and bend.

In each case the last two digits of the designator indicate the approximate midpoint of the carbon content. Thus, SAE 1010 contains 0.08% to 0.13% carbon, while SAE 1020 contains 0.17% to 0.23%. As always, the higher the carbon content the higher the ultimate tensile strength—and the lower the ductility.

ALLOY STEELS

Alloy steels are also identified by a four digit number. In this case the first two digits indicate the MAJOR alloying element or elements:

13xx—Manganese-1.75%

40xx—Molybdenum-0.20% or 0.25%

41XX—Chromium-0.50%, 0.80% OR 0.95% PLUS Molybdenum 0.25%

43xx—Nickel-1.83% PLUS Chromium 0.50% or 0.80% PLUS Molybdenum 0.25%

44xx—Molybdenum-0.53%

46xx—Nickel-0.85% or 1.83% PLUS Molybdenum 0.20% or 0.25%

61xx—Chromium-0.60% or 0.95% PLUS Vanadium 0.13% or 0.15%

86xx—Nickel-0.55% PLUS Chromium 0.50% PLUS Molybdenum 0.20%

87xx—Nickel-0.55% PLUS Chromium 0.50% PLUS Molybdenum 0.25%

88xx—Nickel-0.55% PLUS Chromium 0.50% PLUS Molybdenum 0.35%

92xx—Silicon-2.00%

SPECIFIC STEELS

It would take an entire (and sizeable) book to list ALL of the carbon and alloy steels in use today. Fortunately only a few are of direct interest to the racer.

CARBON STEELS

SAE 1010-1015 This is the most common of the low carbon or mild steels. It is generally available as hot-rolled or cold-rolled sheet and it is used to form ERW tube in wall thicknesses below 0.065''. Both formability and weldability are excellent. Like all of the low-carbon steels, 1010-1015 does not respond to heat treatment. Its strength levels are moderate and it was never intended to be used as a primary structure—lawn furniture, trailer frames and tooling only!

SAE 1018-1020 This is a very popular grade of low-carbon structural steel. It is available as hot-rolled or cold-finished bar, as ERW tube in wall thicknesses of 0.063'' and up, as cold-drawn-seamless and DOM tube. It welds and forms very well and, while it does not respond to heat treatment, it can be case hardened by carburizing. I use it for just about everything other than suspension links—usually as DOM round tube or as cold-rolled sheet.

SAE 1025 This is the best of the low carbon steels. To the best of my knowledge it is now available only as seamless round tube—and that rarely. Before 4130 was developed, 1025 was the standard aircraft structural tubing. We don't use it simply because it is difficult to find and, if a tube fabrication deserves something better than 1020, it deserves to be made from 4130 and heat treated.

SAE 4130 Best known of the family of CHROME-MOLY steels, 4130 is often considered, in racing circles, to be the ideal steel for all high-strength/high-stress applications. IT IS NOT! In thin sections (that is, in tube or sheet form) its unique combination of excellent tensile strength, toughness and response to mild heat treatment combined with its good formability in the annealed condition and its outstanding welding characteristics make it virtually unbeatable for fabrications subject to high stress levels. It is critical that all welds be stress relieved. I prefer the use of OXWELD 32 CMS welding rod with 4130 for the simple reason that it both normalizes and heat treats well in conjunction with 4130. Many welders prefer to use a stainless rod, but the high nickel content of stainless welding rods means that the weldment will not respond well to heat treatment. Since I believe that not heat treating 4130 fabrications is DUMB (if you don't heat treat you end up with an expensive part with the same strength as 1020—and brittle weld areas), Smith's law says to use the heat-treatable rod for EVERYTHING. I heat treat 4130 fabrications to Rockwell C Scale 26 to 30 and no higher. This results in an ultimate tensile strength of about 130,000 psi with sufficient ductility that I do not have to worry about brittle parts.

The other side of the 4130 coin, often unknown to (or at least unappreciated by) the racer, is that it possesses poor deep-heat-treating characteristics and has an inborn dislike of varying cross-sections. These characteristics make 4130 a poor choice for machined or forged parts—it doesn't forge very well anyway. It also doesn't machine very well, at least in the normalized condition—too gummy. Those people who make hubs, steering knuckles and the like from 4130 are kidding themselves—and their customers. It doesn't make very good shafts, either, as in drive shaft, or axle, or torsion bar.

SAE 4140 This is a deep hardening chrome-moly steel with excellent impact resistance, fatigue strength and general all-around toughness. It is commonly used for small-aircraft forgings. I use it in bar form for all of the little gubbins and small parts that we are always machining. It doesn't weld as well as 4130 but it does weld satisfactorily. Welded to 4130 tube or sheet, with Oxweld 32 rod, a 4140 machined component can be heat treated to the same spec as 4130.

SAE 4340 This is the nickel-chrome-moly deep-hardening steel that we SHOULD use, in its vacuum-melted configuration, for our hub forgings, drive shafts, axles and the like. Its tensile strength, toughness, fatigue resistance, excellent deep-heat-treating characteristics and very high tolerance of stress reversals (which is just another way of saying that it has excellent fatigue resistance) make it just about unbeatable. It is also weldable (with care and a lot of pre- and post-heat) and eminently forgeable. In use it should be heat treated to the 180,000—200,000 psi range, maximum—although it can be taken to 220,000 psi without significant loss of toughness. The hardness range between Rockwell C Scale 46 and 48 should be avoided with this steel as it becomes brittle in this range.

SAE 4340 MODIFIED This is, as you would expect, very similar to 4340. In fact, this is as good a time as any to demonstrate the significant effects of seemingly insignificant changes in the chemical composition of steel alloys by throwing in a chemical composition table, FIGURE [57].

The addition of a trace of vanadium and an increase in the silicon level (while they have no notable effect on the hardness, strengths, or ductility of the resultant alloy) work miracles in the toughness and resistance to fatigue, producing a steel which, in the 270,000 to 300,000 psi range, is the toughest, most impact resistant and most fatigue resistant of the usually available steels. Unfortunately, even in the normalized condition, it is a bear to machine. Reducing the

hardness by reducing the level of heat treatment or by tempering has the curious effect of reducing the tensile strength WITHOUT increasing the ductility or toughness.

The most common use of this outstanding steel, also known as 300M, is for military and commercial aircraft landing gear. We use it for hubs, for drive shafts, axles and torsion bars—when we can afford it (or when we cannot afford NOT to use it). At its normal, heat-treated hardness level of Rockwell C 52/56 it is hard enough that we can and do run roller bearings directly on its surface. While the material is great, the heat treating is tricky. There is a very real danger of surface decarburization which can only be avoided by copper plating prior to heat treat. The ONLY heat treat specification for 300M is MIL H 6875, but there are tricks to every trade. MIL H 6875 calls out a two-hour quench at 575 degrees F. Doubling the quench time to four hours will notably increase the ductility and fatigue resistance of the finished product. Another trick is to absolutely forbid the heat treat shop to perform Rockwell or Brinell hardness tests on the actual part, supply a ''test coupon'' of the same material and cross-section WIRED to each part and insist that the coupon be heat treated along with the part and that all hardness tests be done on the test coupon. This is a good idea with ALL parts heat treated much above Rockwell C 40.

SAE 6150 This is the chrome vanadium steel that most of our suspension springs used to be made from. Its machinability is poor and it is not weldable, but its tensile strength is excellent and its fatigue resistance is superb. It is also widely used in the aerospace industry for high-strength forgings with widely varying sections where uniform heat treating is not possible.

SAE 9254 This is the chrome silicon steel from which racing car suspension springs are cold wound NOW. Its tensile strength and fatigue resistance are superior to those of 6150 and its heat-treating properties are much better. Anyone who makes race car springs from anything else is kidding you. For that matter anyone who claims to make race car springs and whose name is not Rockwell International is kidding you!

THE HIGH SILICON, NICKEL CHROME STEELS These are usually known by trade names such as Hi-Tuff and Stress Proof. They contain up to about 3% silicon and are, as the names suggest, tough as hell. They are popular for stock car and off-road racing axles—and the alloys are very suitable for these applications. They are not as good as 4340 M or even 4340, but they are also a damned sight cheaper and, especially where the minimum weights imposed are high, the fact that a part with the same strength and fatigue resistance can be made lighter by using a better steel may be a lot less significant than the cost difference. However, these steels are tough only because of the high silicon content, which is mainly in the form of longitudinal fibers or strings of silicon. This limits the efficient (and safe) use of the alloys to parts with minimal section changes and virtually no transverse machining (we don't want to cut the longitudinal strings that make the stuff tough to start

Figure (57): Comparison of the chemical compositions and the physical characteristics of SAE 4340 and SAE 4340 modified alloy steels.

CHEMICAL COMPOSITION

	Carbon	Manganese	Phosphorus	Sulfur	Silicon	Chromium	Nickel	Molybdenum	Vanadium	Copper
Vacuum Melt SAE 4340	.43	.74	.006	.002	.30	.77	1.81	.24	0	.19
Vacuum Melt 4340 Modified	.43	.86	.01	.001	1.68	.78	1.78	.37	.06	.13

with, do we?). They also don't like being bent very much because that may rupture the silicon strings. Mind you, I have made a lot of street car antiroll bars from Stress Proof with excellent results and pretty severe bends—but in this case the bends are almost, by definition, in lightly stressed areas.

THE MARAGING STEELS For some years now there has been a lot of ballyhoo and general BS about the exotic alloys known as the precipitation-hardening maraging steels. These very high nickel (up to about 18%) steels alloyed with cobalt and molybdenum are reputed to be THE answer to a racer's prayers: Tensile strengths up to 350,000 psi with high-yield strengths, good formability, machinability and excellent impact resistance are the major claims. And the claims are all TRUE. What they don't tell you in the book (or in the rumor mill) is that the maraging steels don't like stress reversals. Their fatigue resistance under conditions of reversed stress is not good. Since stress reversals are what a lot of racing car components are all about, the scrap bins outside of the high-buck team workshops (and the verges of a lot of racetracks) are littered with exploded half-shafts, torsion bars and gears made from miraculous maraging! Actually, the torsion bars would probably be superb IF they were always put back in the same position so that the stress could not be reversed. I won't let the stuff in the door!

Unfortunately one has to be very careful when calling out a metal specification. For instance, one of the most popular of the maraging steels is called VASCOMAX 300, and a great many people who should know better think that VASCOMAX 300 is the same stuff as 300M. A lot of racers have gotten themselves into real trouble in the hub, drive shaft and torsion bar department through this little area of confusion. We are going to go a bit deeper into the maraging steels when we discuss alloying in general—not because I consider them to be useful now, but because I feel that they definitely represent the wave of the future, after some further development takes place.

THE STAINLESS STEELS These are ferrous alloys which contain 10.5% or more chromium, as well as other alloying elements. They are exceptionally resistant to corrosion and, in general, tend to retain their mechanical characteristics at high temperatures. Most of them are nonmagnetic. The chromium imparts corrosion resistance to the stainless steels by combining with oxygen in the atmosphere to form a thin and transparent protective film of chromium oxide on the surface of the metal. This film is both stable and self renewing so that the corrosion resistance is permanent. A number of alloying elements are added to the basic iron/carbon/chromium alloy to enhance specific mechanical characteristics. The stainless steels are divided into four basic families:

(1) The austenitic stainless steels of the 300 series are basically chromium/nickel alloys which are nonmagnetic, do not respond to heat treatment but can be hardened by cold working. They display excellent corrosion resistance and are unusually formable. They are generally available in sheet and tube form.

(2) The ferritic stainless steels of the 400 series are straight chromium alloys. They are magnetic, do not respond to heat treatment and can only be moderately hardened by cold working. They exhibit good ductility and corrosion resistance.

(3) The martensitic stainless steels are chromium-based alloys that are magnetic, have reasonable ductility and good corrosion resistance AND are hardenable by heat treatment. Some of them can be heat treated to tensile strengths exceeding 200,000 psi.

(4) The precipitation hardening stainless steels are chromium/nickel alloys which can be hardened to very high strength levels by solution heat treatment and ageing. (We will go into solution heat treating and ageing in our discussion of aluminum alloys.)

STAINLESS AND THE RACER

While the corrosion resistance and elevated temperature properties of the various stainless steels make them popular in the aerospace, food handling and chemical industries, we racers really don't have much use for them. For almost all of our applications, either steel or nonferrous alloys do the job as well if not better—and at lower cost. The only stainless that I ever use is austenitic type 321, an alloy originally developed to stop the cracking of piston-engined aircraft exhaust systems. It makes truly outstanding race car exhaust systems, if the money is available. In my present case—ever since I made my decision not to work full time for the big teams—the money is usually not available and I use 1020 DOM. The stainless is lighter and more fatigue resistant, but except for turbocharged engines and long-distance racing (neither of which I do any more, at least for now), the stainless is simply not cost effective. It is not sand bendable, so the exhaust system must be fabricated and welded from a selection of mandrel bends and straight lengths. The bends are expensive because the material itself is expensive; there are no bends in stock anywhere; none of the tube benders want to know about it; and when you do find someone willing to bend it, you pay a giant setup charge. If you decide to make a stainless system (or to have one made) remember that, regardless of what the man who agrees to do the job may say, 321 is the ONLY stainless alloy suitable for the job.

FIGURE [58] tabulates the approximate mechanical values as well as the relative machinability of the steels that we commonly use—in a variety of possible conditions. The values are approximate simply because that is the way that testing of metals goes—it never repeats very exactly and no two authorities ever seem to agree on ANYTHING within a few percentage points.

By now it should be pretty evident that there is more to the selection of the RIGHT steel for a specific purpose than is immediately obvious. A certain amount of both knowledge and judgement is required in order to make an intelligent decision. Often this knowledge and judgement is lacking when the decision is made. The results are seldom good. Recently, I was shown a failed suspension arm pivot pin. The failed item was a homemade replacement for the stock item which had gone away in a crash. When I expressed considerable surprise that the part had failed without the car having hit something and asked what the material was, the man in charge replied, "It's the best stuff you can get—ROLLED STEEL!" I didn't know whether to kill him or to just sit there and cry. As a matter of fact, that particular incident planted in my mind the idea for this section of the book.

Another man, vastly experienced, who should have known better, finally got tired enough of bending the front suspension stub axles on his production-based racers to go to the expense of having replacement items machined from billet. When he showed me the unfortunate results of the first attempt to run the new parts, I naturally asked what the material and heat treatment were. He allowed as how it was "good stuff—steel." It turned out that he had delivered a brand-new stock part to a machine shop with instructions to copy it in "steel." In the face of ignorance, Murphy's laws always prevail. The machine shop used a convenient chunk of resulfured and leaded free-machining bar stock. The resultant part, while expensive, was nowhere near as strong, as stiff or as fatigue resistant as the stock item. . . .

On the other side of the coin (to illustrate what applied intelligence, knowledge and experience can accomplish),

Jim Meyer (of Jim Meyer and Associates, Metallurgical Consultants) who, among other things, supplies most of the hub and other forgings to the leading champ car, GT and Formula One teams (see Appendix) was once called upon to solve a problem having to do with the frequent bending of the steering knuckle on a factory off-road team racer. There was no time available for a new part and previous attempts to weld stiffness onto the stock part had failed (as such attempts usually do). Jim took an educated guess as to what the material was (no one knew, and there wasn't time to find out), called out a really radical heat treatment followed by a severe shot-peening procedure—and it worked! Murphy did, however, prevail. Delighted with the quick and easy fix, the team, against Jim's advice, did not redesign the part, or even upgrade the material. The heat-treated and shot-peened stock part (replaced after each event) worked just fine until THE BIG RACE (which just happened to be a lot longer). Metal fatigue caught up with ignorance and optimism and all of the parts bent. It just goes to show that HIRING a knowledgeable consultant is only half the battle; you also have to LISTEN to him.

Figure (58): Approximate mechanical properties of common steels.

	Steel	Condition	Tensile Strength (PSI) Ultimate	Tensile Strength (PSI) Yield	Percent Elongation	Machinability—On A Scale of 100	Rockwell Hardness	Reduction of Area %
Bar Stock	1018	Hot Rolled	69,000	40,000	38%	50	B72	52%
	1018	Cold Drawn	82,000	70,000	20%	65	B85	65%
	1020	Hot Rolled	69,000	40,000	38%	50	B72	52%
	1020	Cold Drawn	82,000	70,000	20%	65	B85	65%
	4130	Hot Rolled & Annealed	86,000	56,000	29%	65	B90	57%
	4130	Cold Drawn & Normalized	98,000	87,000	21%	65	C19	52%
	4130	Water Quenched @ 1550° F Tempered @ 1000° F	146,000	133,000	17%	Not	C31	50%
	4140	Hot Rolled & Annealed	89,000	62,000	26%	57	B91	58%
	4140	Cold Drawn & Normalized	102,000	90,000	18%	66	C19	50%
	4140	Oil Quenched @ 1550° F Tempered @ 1000° F	153,000	131,000	16%	Not	C32	45%
	4340	Hot Rolled & Annealed	101,000	69,000	21%	45	C15	45%
	4340	Cold Drawn & Normalized	111,000	74,000	18%	55	C19	42%
	4340	Oil Quenched @ 1550° F Tempered @ 1000° F	182,000	162,000	15%	Not	C32	40%
Sheet & Tube	1010	Hot Rolled/Drawn	47,000	30,000	39%			
	1010	Cold Rolled/Drawn	60,000	45,000	38%			
	1018	Hot Rolled/Drawn	68,000	40,000	39%			
	1018	Cold Rolled/Drawn	82,000	70,000	20%			
	4130	Hot Worked & Annealed	85,000	65,000	20%			
	4130	Cold Worked & Normalized	95,000	75,000	15%			

CHAPTER FOUR

ALLOYING AND HEAT TREATMENT OF STEELS

THE MECHANICAL PROPERTIES OF STEELS (AND OTHER METALS)

We have reached the point where we are ready to investigate how our steels are formulated, alloyed and processed to achieve certain specific properties and strength levels. Before we can discuss the subject with any degree of understanding we need to define the terms used to describe the properties we are trying to achieve. Bear with me once more—this time I am even going to REPEAT some definitions.

LOAD is the overall force to which a material or a structure is submitted in supporting the weight of a mass, or in resisting an externally applied force or system of forces. In this country load is usually expressed in pounds.

STRESS is an applied force or system of forces that tends to deform a body or a structure. It is usually expressed as UNIT STRESS—the applied load divided by the area over which it is applied (i.e., the cross-sectional area of the material or the portion of the structure which is resisting the load). We will express unit stress in pounds per square inch (psi).

INTERNAL STRESSES are the stresses present WITHIN the crystal structure of a material that has been strained by cold working. They are independent of and cumulative with working stress, so they can provide some nasty surprises. Internal stresses can usually be relieved by annealing or normalizing.

STRAIN is the elastic deformation of a body caused by stress.

ELASTICITY is the property that a material exhibits by returning to its original size and shape after it has been deformed (strained) by an applied stress. Each material has a definite point termed its ELASTIC LIMIT, beyond which the material cannot be stressed without undergoing permanent distortion. The object in designing any structure is to keep the stress level at all times below the elastic limit of the material used. The elastic limit of a material is described as the maximum unit stress that the material can withstand without undergoing a deformation which will remain after the load has been released. In this country it is normally expressed in psi.

ELASTIC DEFORMATION is a TEMPORARY change in dimension caused by stress. A material or a component that has undergone elastic deformation will return to its original dimensions when the stress is removed, IF it has not exceeded its elastic limit. Good examples include the bow (as in bow and arrow), the wing structure of a 747 in a gust and the coil spring of an automobile.

THE MODULUS OF ELASTICITY is the stress required to make a tensile test specimen of a given material double its original length. This is an artificial visualization or constant, simply because, with almost all metals, the test piece will have broken long before its length will have been doubled. The modulus of elasticity is, however, a vital factor in the calculation of the strength of materials. Purely as a matter of interest, within the physical limits of elasticity of almost all metals, elongation is very small in proportion to original length and we usually assume it to be zero.

THE ULTIMATE TENSILE STRENGTH of a material is the maximum tensile (stretching) load per unit of cross-sectional area that the material can withstand before rupture. We will express it in psi.

THE YIELD STRENGTH of a material is the tensile load per unit of cross-sectional area at which the material exhibits a specific limiting permanent set or elongation. It is thus different from (and greater than) the ELASTIC LIMIT. It is commonly used rather than the elastic limit simply because it is easier to measure.

THE YIELD POINT is the load per unit of cross-sectional area at which there occurs a NOTABLE increase in deformation without any increase in load. It is of interest to metallurgists and theoreticians, not to racers.

HARDNESS is the property of resisting penetration. The hardness of metals can usually be increased either by cold working or by heat treatment (or by both). Normally an increase in the hardness of a metal is accompanied by a fortuitous increase in ultimate tensile strength and an unfortuitous corresponding increase in brittleness. Hardness is measured by sinking a hardened steel ball (of standard diameter and hardness) into the surface of the metal being tested, under a precisely measured standard load. The re-

sulting indentation is then measured and assigned a number from the standard Brinell or Rockwell hardness scale that corresponds to its dimensions. For every material, there is a definite correlation between hardness and ultimate tensile strength. Therefore, by measuring the hardness of a part, its approximate tensile strength can be obtained from a table without the necessity of cutting a tensile specimen or destroying the part. It is, however, standard practice to physically test a small percentage of critical parts after heat treatment. Hardness tables are made from paper—and paper will not cushion a meeting between an aircraft and a mountain—or a race car and a wall. FIGURE [59] is a standard hardness-versus-tensile-strength table for steels.

DUCTILITY is very similar to malleability. It is the property of some metals which allows them to be drawn out without breaking. We normally use the term "ductility" to mean both ductility and malleability. Naturally, the harder and stronger a metal is, the less ductile it will be and, the softer and more ductile the metal, the weaker it will be. This seeming dead end is resolved in the engineering of structures by the thermal treatment of metals and their alloys. For example, many aircraft (and some race car) parts are formed from aluminum alloy 2024 in the "O" or dead-soft condition. Readily formable in this annealed state, 2024 has an ultimate tensile strength of only 26,000 psi—

Figure (59): Hardness versus approximate tensile strength of steels.

Rockwell Hardness		Brinell Hardness		Ultimate Tensile	Notes
"C" Scale	"B" Scale	Tungsten Ball	Steel Ball	Strength (psi)	
-	79	140	136	70,000	1018/1020 Steel, Hot Rolled
2	86	165	160	81,000	1018/1020 Steel, Cold Rolled
6	89	177	171	85,000	E4130N Steel—Annealed
8	90.3	184	177	88,000	
12	93.4	199	190	93,000	
14	94.9	206	197	97,000	E4130 Steel—Normalized
16	96.2	214	206	100,000	
18	97.5	222	215	103,000	
22	100.2	241	235	112,000	E4340 Steel—Normalized
26	-	264	259	123,000	E4130 Fabricated Suspension
30	-	293	286	136,000	Components are Heat Treated to this Level
34	-	329	318	150,000	Machined 4140 Components are Heat Treated to this Level
38	-	365	357	170,000	4130 Tubular Anti-Roll Bars are Heat Treated to This Level
40	-	385	377		
42	-	417	405	181,000	E 4340 Hubs, Axles, Torsion Bars
44	-	427	419	194,000	
46	-	452	442	208,000	"Temper Brittle" Range of 4340 Steel—Avoid
48	-	479	464	221,000	
50	-	508	488	237,000	300 M Hubs,
54	-	544	-	256,000	Torsion Bars
58	-	601	-	285,000	Axles
60	-	627	-	298,000	
				311,000	

balsa wood. However, when the formed parts are heat treated to the T-3 condition the tensile strength more than doubles (to 65,000 psi). In the T-3 condition, while the strength level of 2024 is eminently suitable for aircraft structures, it is virtually unformable. The same characteristics hold true for all of the heat-treatable alloys, both ferrous and nonferrous. The usual measure of ductility is percent elongation in a standard 2.00'' tensile test specimen. Any metal or alloy with a percent elongation of more than 18% is readily formable.

PERCENT ELONGATION is the difference in length of a test specimen of a given material after it has been ruptured by a tension load and its original length (usually 2''), expressed as a percentage of the original specimen length. It is used as an indication of the relative ductility of two materials.

REDUCTION OF AREA is the difference between the original cross-sectional area of a test specimen and the least cross-sectional area of the same specimen after it has ruptured in tension. It is also a convenient indication of relative ductility.

TOUGHNESS is a measure of the total amount of energy that a material can absorb before failure. It is a measure of the material's ability to resist impact or shock loads. The unit measure of this vital quality is called the MODULUS OF TOUGHNESS and is defined as the amount of energy absorbed per unit VOLUME, up to the breaking point. Unfortunately these figures are obtained from impact tests whose accuracy and practical interpretation are subject to both doubt and debate. The boffins occasionally slip one through on us, like the maraging steels that we will discuss later.

ENDURANCE LIMIT of a material is defined as the limiting stress below which the material will withstand an indefinitely large number of cycles of stress without failure.

PROOF STRESS is the maximum stress that a material can withstand without resulting in a permanent elongation of more than 0.0001'' per inch of original specimen length. Again this is of no practical use to the racer and I mention it only because we occasionally see it in tables of mechanical properties.

ALLOYING

We know that metals in their pure form are so soft and weak as to be structurally useless to the racer. They are made strong, hard and tough by "alloying" pure metals with small amounts of other metals, or even of nonmetals. The elements which make up alloys are usually soluble when in the liquid state and will completely dissolve in each other—as, for instance, alcohol, sugar and some delightful and doubtless unhealthy trace elements dissolve in water to make wine. Come to think of it, wine making is not unlike metallurgy. Unlike wine, however, metallic alloys are not very useful to us in the liquid state—and the rules change in the solid state.

ALLOYING ELEMENTS

Some of the more common alloying elements and the basic properties that their presence imparts to steel are:

CARBON increases hardness, hardenability and tensile strength but decreases ductility and toughness.

CHROMIUM increases tensile strength, toughness, hardness, hardenability and resistance to both wear and corrosion.

COBALT increases tensile strength and hardness and, like a catalyst, it increases the effect of some of the other alloying elements.

MANGANESE increases tensile strength, hardness, hardenability and wear resistance. Improves forgeability and increases the rate of carbon penetration during the carburizing process.

MOLYBDENUM increases tensile strength, hardness, toughness, hardenability, machinability, corrosion resistance and strength at elevated temperatures.

NICKEL increases strength and hardness without impairing toughness and ductility. Increases corrosion resistance.

SILICON increases toughness and improves weldability.

SULFUR increases machinability but decreases weldability, ductility and toughness.

TUNGSTEN increases strength, hardness and toughness, particularly at elevated temperatures.

VANADIUM increases strength, hardness and resistance to impact and shock. Because it retards grain growth of the resultant alloy. It allows much higher requenching temperatures to be used and so improves the hardening properties of tool steels.

THE NATURE OF ALLOYS

Most metallic alloys are SOLID SOLUTIONS. In order for any solid solution alloy to exist, several basic requirements must be met—the first of which is, logically enough, that the alloying element(s) must dissolve completely in the base metal—IN THE SOLID STATE. In the solid solution both the dimensions and the shape of the crystalline space lattice of the base metal (i.e., the solvent) are altered by the presence of atoms of the alloying element(s) [the solute(s)]. Both the concentration and the position of the atoms or ions of the alloying elements present within the crystal space lattice of the resulting alloy, as well as the changes that they cause in the type and shape of that lattice, are crucial to the properties of the alloy. There are two basic possibilities:

THE SUBSTITUTIONAL SOLID SOLUTION

When the atoms of the solvent and the solute metals are of approximately the same size, and the metals have the same crystal unit cell structure, the solute atoms can take the place of some of the solvent atoms within the crystal lattice of the base metal, resulting in the creation of a SUBSTITUTIONAL SOLID SOLUTION. Substitutional solid solutions behave very much like pure metals, except that the differences in atom size alter the characteristics of the lattice, making dislocation movement more difficult than it was in either of the unalloyed metals. The difference is, however, not liable to be very great. The crystal lattice of the substitutional solid solution is schematically illustrated by FIGURE [60].

THE INTERSTITIAL SOLID SOLUTION

If, on the other hand, the atoms of the solute are much smaller than the atoms of the solvent, they can and do fit into the spaces or INTERSTICES between the atoms of the solvent and form INTERSTITIAL SOLID SOLUTIONS. That these interstitial spaces do exist—even in planes of close packed atoms—is schematically shown by FIGURE [61]. But the spaces are necessarily very small and there are not a lot of metals whose atoms are small enough to fit into the interstices of the typical metallic space lattice. There

are, however, some nonmetallic elements, including carbon, hydrogen, nitrogen and oxygen which DO form interstitial solid solutions with some of the metals. In fact the interstitial solid solution of carbon in iron is the basis of all ferrous metallurgy. No matter how small the atoms (or ions, as the case may be) of the solute may be, there is simply not very much room in the interstices of the crystal lattice of the base metal. The percentage of the alloying element that can physically be present in the alloy is generally limited to less than one percent. FIGURE [62] is a diagrammatic representation of the interstitial solid solution. It shows the distortion of the crystal lattice caused by the presence of the interstitial atoms which are, of course, occupying space that would normally be empty.

THE MECHANICAL MIXTURE

There is a third possibility. When the components of an alloy are not soluble in each other and so cannot combine with each other, a MECHANICAL MIXTURE may be formed, in which each element of the alloy solidifies independently of the other, not allowing the other to enter into its crystal space lattice at all. The alloy that results will consist of individual regions of the individual components—and these regions will be mechanically separable. These EUTECTIC mixtures are common among the structural ferrous alloys.

ALLOTROPIC METALS

Some metals are able to change their crystal structures WHILE IN THE SOLID STATE. These metals are said to be ALLOTROPIC in nature. The change in structure is always caused by a change in temperature—and the temperature at which the change takes place is unique to and characteristic of the individual metal and to the individual change in microstructure.

Figure (60): The substitutional solution: Minority (solute) atoms replace majority (solvent) atoms at random locations in crystal space lattice.

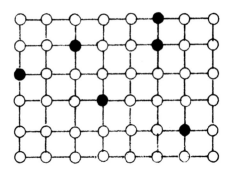

Figure (61): Available interstitial sites between planes of close-packed atoms in crystal space lattice.

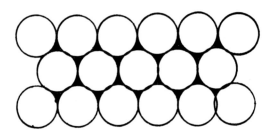

Figure (62): Interstitial solution with minority atoms occupying spaces between majority atoms, thus producing a distorted lattice.

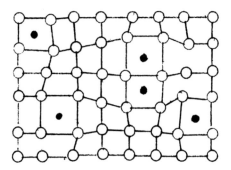

THE SOLIDIFICATION OF PURE METALS

During the time that metals (and alloys of metals) are changing from the liquid state to the solid state, changes take place in their structures that have a profound effect on the mechanical properties of the resultant solid metals. We have seen that when pure metals solidify, crystallization begins simultaneously at various places within the liquid. The exact way in which crystallization actually begins is still a bit uncertain, even to the metallurgists. It is generally felt that because the atoms of the liquid metal are in very close proximity to each other and are in continuous random motion, some small number of them will inevitably arrange themselves in the proper formation at the right point on the cooling temperature curve to form a crystal unit cell of the metal. This theory always reminds me of the old, "If you sit enough monkeys down at enough typewriters and keep them there long enough, sooner or later one of them will write the Bible" theorem. However, the sheer number of atoms involved makes this random process of arrangement seem at least somewhat plausible.

Anyway, once a single unit cell has somehow come into existence within the cooling liquid, other nearby atoms will attach themselves to the first group—in the proper orientation—and a crystal space lattice is formed. As the freezing process continues, more and more atoms attach themselves to more and more lattices (in the form of crystal unit cells) until solidification is complete. In the case of a pure metal this process will take place at a constant temperature as shown in the graph of FIGURE [63].

Solidification will begin when the liquid metal is cooled to its freezing point and the temperature of the metal will remain constant until crystallization is complete. During the freezing process, a "heat of solidification" is given off from the liquid at the exact rate and in the exact quantity required to maintain the "slush" at a constant temperature. Therefore, in the time between the beginning of solidification and its completion, the liquid and solid phases of the metal will coexist at a constant temperature, just as ice and water do. You will never convince ANY woman of this, but a glass of ice water will have a temperature of exactly 32 degrees F whether it is composed of 99% water and 1% ice or 99% ice and 1% water.

The forming crystals do not grow uniformly in all directions throughout the liquid. Instead, crystal growth progresses in a sort of treelike fashion. This continuous formation of crystal branches is termed "DENDRITIC GROWTH" from the Greek word for tree, "dendron." The resultant crystals are known as DENDRITIC CRYSTALS. The trees themselves are known as DENDRITES and are shown in FIGURE [64].

The dendrites grow in a three-dimensional pattern. As solidification progresses, each branch continually increases in diameter AND forks into new and smaller branches until an interlocking system of crystal "trees" is formed in which each of the ever-growing dendritic "branches" is surrounded by liquid metal which progressively freezes—to both form new and smaller branches and to increase the size

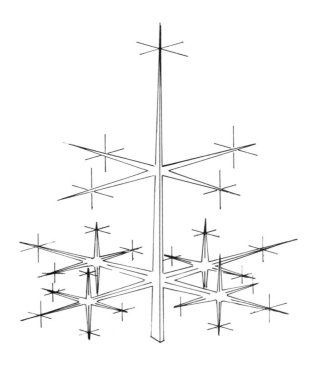

Figure (64): The crystal dendrite.

Figure (63): Cooling curve for pure metal. Freezing (or crystallization) takes place at a constant temperature. Thermal arrest, or change of phase line, is horizontal.

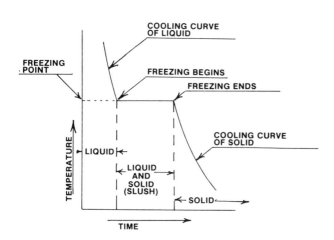

of the existing ones until all of the liquid metal has solidified and a solid, interlocking crystalline structure has resulted. FIGURE [65A] shows the process. FIGURE [65B] shows the final result: a homogenous polycrystalline solid metal.

THE SOLIDIFICATION OF THE SOLID SOLUTION ALLOYS

In the case of the solid solution alloys, which are composed of different elements, each of which has its own melting point; freezing, instead of taking place at a constant temperature, will occur over a RANGE of temperatures, as illustrated by FIGURE [66].

The early stages of the solidification process are similar to the freezing of pure metals. The major difference is that the first solid metal alloy that is formed as the alloy freezes is richer in the constituent which has the higher melting point. In other words, the CENTERS of all of the dendritic branches will be of a different composition than the outer layers. Further, the composition of the later branches to form will be different from that of the earlier (and thicker) branches. The result is a nonhomogenous physical composition which results in unfortunate variations in the mechanical characteristics of the solidified alloy. The term given to this phenomenon in the freezing of the solid solution alloys is CORING and it is almost unavoidable in the microstructure of the cast billets of metallic alloys which are often the end product of the older steel refineries. The continuous casting process used in the newer mills reduces the problem considerably.

Coring in cast billets can be reduced by extending the time required for solidification but this is expensive. Typically this nonhomogenous microstructure is corrected just prior to mill processing of cast alloy billets by heating the billets to a temperature just below the melting point of the constituent with the lowest melting point and holding the billet at that temperature in a "soaking pit" long enough for the constituent elements to diffuse evenly throughout the billet. The name given to this process is, logically enough, DIFFUSION. It is defined as "the slow elimination of differences in concentration in miscible gasses, liquids or solids brought into intimate contact with each other by gradual and spontaneous mixing." A common example is the diffusion of tobacco smoke in air. Homogeneity of composition and structure is further improved by the mechanical working (rolling and/or forging) that takes place during the mill processes, followed by appropriate thermal treatments to relieve some of the internal stresses set up within the microstructure of the alloy by the working.

TYPES OF ALLOYS

There are three basic types of metallic alloys that are of interest to us. They are usually classified on the basis of the mutual solubility of the elements involved:

TYPE ONE—All of the constituent elements which comprise the alloy are completely soluble in each other in both the liquid and the solid states. Crystals freezing from the liquid state of these alloys will be comprised of all elements in solid solution with each other, either substitutional or interstitial.

TYPE TWO—The constituent elements are soluble in the liquid state but not in the solid state. When the molten alloy solidifies it does so as virtually pure crystals of the individual elements in a mechanical mixture.

Figure (65): Formation of crystal dendrites (A) is the first step in the growth of a polycrystalline structure (B).

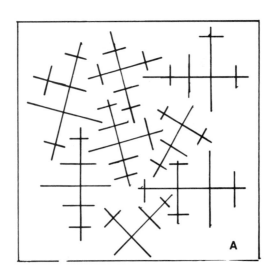
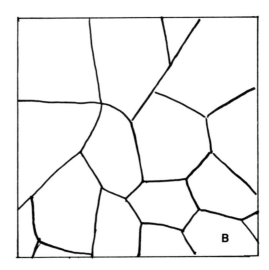

TYPE THREE—The constituent elements are completely soluble in the liquid state but only partially soluble in the solid state. In this case, depending on the composition of the alloy in the liquid state, the result may be a solid solution, a eutectic mixture or a combination of the two.

These three basic types do not exhaust the possibilities. Even in the liquid state, not ALL metals are soluble in each other. Lead and copper as used in many shell bearing applications are a common example of insoluble metals. Standard bearing bronze is manufactured by mechanically mixing a quantity of lead as thoroughly as possible in molten copper and then freezing the mixture before the lead has a chance to separate out. The lead ends up as slippery little globules evenly dispersed throughout the copper.

SUMMARY (SO FAR)

I have opened this alloying can of worms about as far as I want to open it. I do not feel that this book is the place to go into the details of how alloys are actually formed. Talented and dedicated men spend their working lifetimes studying the subject and we racers have no real need to understand the details of the processes. It is, however a fascinating subject and if I ever need to fill some space in a book (this one is fast getting TOO full), I may someday devote a whole chapter to it. I do feel, though, that we need to understand the basic principles and the objects of the exercise.

The idea is to enhance some of the mechanical characteristics of the metal in question by the addition of relatively

small percentages of alloying elements (usually called ''hardening phases'') to the crystal matrix of the base metal. These hardening phases can form substitutional solutions, interstitial solutions or mechanical mixtures with the base metal. Most of our structural metals are able to hold a higher percentage of alloying elements dissolved in the liquid state than they are able to retain in the solid state. When we dissolve more of an alloying element in the molten base metal than can be retained in solid solution, particles of the excess alloying element precipitate out of solution as the alloy cools. The result is a combination of a solid solution alloy and a eutectic mixture (grains of the alloying element interspersed in the solid solution alloy). Most of our structural alloys are of this type.

A RETURN TO THE FAMILIAR GROUND OF GRAIN BOUNDARIES

It is now time to revisit the grain boundaries which we learned about in Chapter One. But this time we are going to look at things from a slightly different point of view. You will recall that when we were first discussing the existence and nature of the boundaries between grains or crystals of metal I stated that, under certain circumstances, we could make use of these boundaries to enhance some of the mechanical characteristics of our metals. These grain boundaries are really pretty damned complex. Although they are actually the random intersections of three-dimensional crystals (because grain growth during crystallization continues until the adjacent grains actually collide), the boundaries are infinitely small in width with only minimal mismatching. In microphotographs—such as FIGURE [67], which is an enlargement of the polycrystalline structure of etched high-carbon steel—we see them as dark lines between the crystals and it is therefore easy to think of them

---

Figure (66): Cooling curve for solid-solution alloy. Freezing occurs over a range of temperatures, and thermal arrest is a curve.

Figure (67): Microstructure of sectioned and etched high-carbon steel.

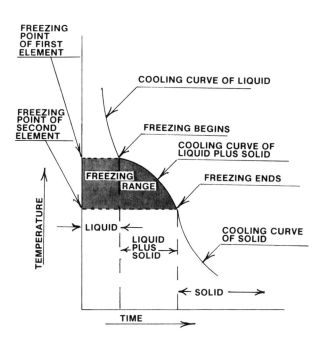

as having finite width. In actuality the average diameter of a single crystal in FIGURE [67] is unimaginably (at least to me) small and the width of the grain boundary is beyond human comprehension. Nonetheless they do exist and their nature is critical to the final mechanical properties of both pure metals and alloys.

In the case of pure metals the relationship is the simple one which we discussed in Chapter One: By their very existence, they act as barriers to dislocation movement and so increase the strength of our metals. The smaller the grain size, the more barriers there will be to movement of dislocations through the crystal lattice and the stronger, but less ductile, the metal will be. Of course it works in reverse and, in general, the larger the grain size, the more ductile, but softer and weaker the metal will be.

However, when we are talking about multiphase alloys, the picture changes. When any excess alloying element precipitates out of solution with the cooling base metal, it has to go somewhere. If it cannot remain in solution it must either crystallize as separate relatively large grains in a eutectic mixture or find its way into the boundaries between the grains of the solid solution alloy, either as tiny grains or as planes of atoms. If it crystallizes as separate large grains we have a mechanical mixture, or "inclusions" in the alloy. Such an inclusion is shown in FIGURE [68]. As we learned in our investigation of cast iron this can be either good or bad.

If, on the other hand, the "second phase precipitate" forms tiny separate crystals in the grain boundaries and between the slip planes of the first phase (as illustrated by FIGURE [69]), the tiny hardening-phase crystals can act as pins or keys to discourage relative movement between ad-

jacent grains and so add markedly to the ultimate strength of the alloy. In this case, as you would expect, they also decrease the ductility of the metal. If, instead, they should form a plane or partial plane of atoms in the grain boundaries of the base metal, as in FIGURES [70A] and [70B], they will isolate the grains of the solid solution alloy from each other and will PROMOTE relative movement between adjacent grains—and, structurally speaking, we are in big trouble. Love lube between the grains, we don't need!

WINDING UP

In the investigation of alloys we are concerned with the structure and the mechanical properties of pure metals when ions of another metal (or nonmetal) are added to them. The composition, microstructure and behavior of alloys is more complex—and less understood—than that of the pure metals. In fact, most alloys have been arrived at by the time-honored, "Let's try this and see what happens" method. Metalsmiths knew HOW to make alloys to satisfy many given mechanical requirements for millennia before the physical metallurgists began to learn WHY the alloys behaved as they did. Although the birth and development of the microprocessor has taken a lot of the guesswork out of the investigation process, I am delighted to say that a lot of this "suck it and see" experimentation still goes on, only now we call it "basic research."

HEAT TREATING

Heat treating is one of the most misunderstood and misused terms in all of metallurgy. For example, I have been informed by a supposedly well qualified and competent fab-

Figure (68): Carbon inclusion along a grain boundary of ferrite.

Figure (69): Excess second phase element precipitates from solution (in small quantities) in boundary layers of first phase as particles tend to "pin" or "key" grains together.

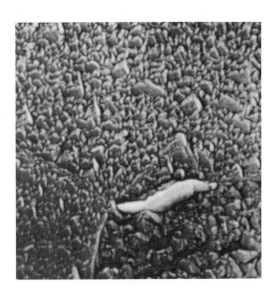

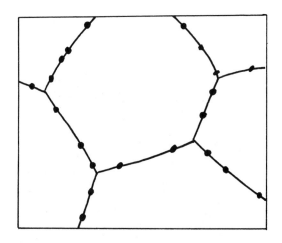

ricator that the heat treatment call outs on some of my drawings of suspension linkage parts to be made from E4130 steel tube and sheet with E4140 ferrules were unnecessary because HIS level of expertise was such that he always withdrew the heat from the metal slowly at the completion of each weld and so "heat treated" the fabrication as he went. This worthy is probably still wondering why he lost our business. I have had customers berate me because parts that I designed (and they built) failed. Imagine my surprise when I found that they had failed simply because the heat-treatment specifications on the drawings had been ignored. "We didn't have time to heat treat the parts. Was it important?" Sometimes this business of being an independent consultant can get to be a bit on the frustrating side. . . .

Anyway, in the metallurgical sense, the term HEAT TREATMENT refers to a series of predetermined operations involving heating, holding (or soaking) and cooling operations applied to a metal WHILE IT IS IN ITS SOLID STATE, in order to change or modify the physical properties of the metal. By heat treatment, metals can be made harder, stronger and tougher—or they can, by a different heat treatment, be made softer and more ductile. As always there are tradeoffs involved; in general the harder and stronger a metal becomes through heat treatment, the more brittle it becomes as well. Metal can be heat treated either before or after it has been machined or fabricated into a component part, or, sometimes, different heat-treat processes are performed at different stages during manufacture. All heat treatments involve heating of the metal, holding it at a given temperature for a specified length of time (soaking) and then cooling to ambient temperature. The individual processes achieve their different results by variations in the temperatures reached, the length of the soaking period and the rate at which the metal is cooled.

MORE ON THE INTIMATE RELATIONSHIP BETWEEN CARBON AND IRON

Almost all of the carbon contained in the carbon steels is present in the form of iron carbide (Fe_3C), known as cementite. Cementite is very hard and very strong. It is also very brittle. In the microstructure of carbon steels the grains are composed of alternating plates of pure iron (ferrite) which is soft, weak and ductile and cementite which is strong, hard and brittle. The result is a laminate structure, illustrated by FIGURE [71], which combines some of the best of both worlds into a strong and tough steel. This particular combination of iron and carbon is known as PEARLITE. The PEARLITIC microstructure makes up at least a part of the microstructure of all carbon steels. If a

Figure (70A): Graphic representation of excess second phase (dark) precipitated from solid solution as a continuous plane of atoms along grain boundaries of solid solution alloys—in space where grains *would* meet if second-phase precipitate were not present.

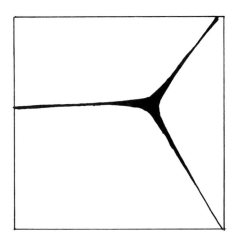

Figure (70B): Microphotograph of actual precipitate along grain boundaries (extreme case).

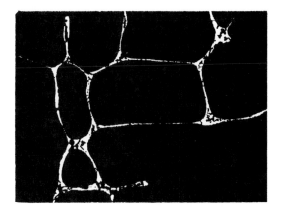

Figure (71): Alternating plates of ferrite and cementite forming a grain of pearlite. Linde Division of Union Carbide Corporation.

steel were to be entirely pearlitic in structure, then the microstructure of a sectioned and polished specimen would appear as FIGURE [72].

However, the maximum amount of carbon that can be held in solid state solution with iron at normal temperatures is 0.83%. This percentage is known as the EUTECTOID composition of carbon and iron. If more carbon is present the composition is termed HYPEREUTECTOID and the excess carbon will separate out of solid solution along the grain boundaries of the pearlite, as in FIGURE [73]. If, on the other hand, there is less than 0.83% carbon present, the composition is termed HYPOEUTECTOID and there will be grains of both pearlite and of ferrite present in the microstructure, as in FIGURE [74]. This is the usual condition for our structural carbon steels. Any other alloying elements will be present as carbides of these elements and may be integrated into the matrix in any of the several ways that we discussed earlier.

Figure (72): Entirely pearlitic microstructure of 0.9% carbon and iron. *Metallurgy*, by Johnson and Weeks, American Technical Society, 1977.

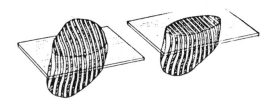

SINGLE GRAIN OF PEARLITE SECTIONED

Figure (73): Hypereutectoid composition of 1.25% carbon and iron. The excess carbon has precipitated along the boundaries between the grains of pearlite.

X500

THE TRANSFORMATION OF IRON AS IT IS HEATED THROUGH ITS CRITICAL TEMPERATURE RANGE

Most metals exhibit a "critical temperature" at which their grain structure undergoes a fundamental change while the metal is in its solid state. Depending on the alloy, the critical temperature range of steels lies in the area from 1300 to 1650 degrees F. As a steel is heated through this range, the crystal structure of the iron changes from the 9-atom body-centered unit cell of alpha iron (ferrite) to the more dense 12-atom face-centered unit cell of gamma iron. Gamma iron is able to hold a lot more carbon in solid solution than alpha iron; so, as the transformation takes place the cementite in the steel separates into carbon and iron and enters into solid solution with the gamma iron. The laminate pearlitic structure disappears. The alloy is still a solid and it is still composed of distinct crystals or grains, whose appearance is now similar to the ferrite grains of FIGURE [68] (without the inclusion). These new grains, however, contain dissolved carbon in solid solution and are known as AUSTENITE.

No further changes of any import take place as the steel is heated until it actually melts at about 2680 degrees F.

COOLING THROUGH THE CRITICAL RANGE

Suppose a piece of carbon steel is uniformly heated to some value above the critical range and held there long enough for the microstructure to become completely austenitic and then allowed to cool. As it passes back through the critical temperature range the microstructure of the iron will change back from the face-centered unit cell of gamma iron to the body-centered configuration of alpha iron. Because the alpha iron cannot hold all of the carbon that was dissolved in the gamma iron in solid solution, most of the

Figure (74): Hypoeutectoid solid solution of 2% carbon and iron; grains of both ferrite and pearlite are present.

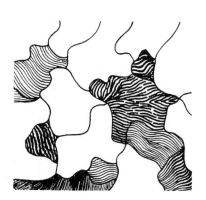

carbon in the austenite is separated out of solution during the transformation. This carbon combines with some of the alpha iron to form cementite, and the laminate pearlitic microstructure reappears. The transformation is gradual and takes place simultaneously at many points throughout the mass of the cooling steel.

What is actually happening here is that, when the beginning of the critical temperature range is reached, a few unit cells of gamma iron at the edges of some of the grains of austenite rearrange their atoms to form cells of alpha iron. Almost all of the carbon that was dissolved in the gamma iron is rejected from this new alpha iron and, separating out of solution, is forced into the surrounding gamma iron which becomes supersaturated with carbon. When the carbon content of the cooling gamma iron reaches a sufficient level of concentration the excess carbon will combine with some of the iron to form iron carbide (cementite).

As we have noted, the transformation of gamma iron to alpha iron is taking place simultaneously at many points throughout the cooling steel. The carbon which is constantly separating out of solution to each side of the continuously forming new alpha iron (ferrite) is trapped between the growing ferrite matrixes so that the ferrite and the cementite are forced to form in alternating PLANES OF ATOMS which grow into the characteristic alternating laminated PLATES of the pearlitic structure. Simple, eh? And so it would be if we could leave TIME out of the equation.

THE EFFECTS OF RAPID COOLING

While the rate at which a steel is HEATED through its critical range has little if any effect upon the structural transformation that takes place, the rate at which it is COOLED through that range is of critical importance. If we take the same piece of heated austenitic carbon steel from the last discussion—still at a temperature above the critical—and plunge it into a cold liquid, the accelerated rate of cooling will result in fundamental changes to the microstructure and to the mechanical characteristics of the finished steel. When the critical temperature is reached, the same things that happened during slow cooling would BEGIN to happen again. But, before the transformation from the austenitic to the pearlitic structure can be completed, the temperature of the steel will have dropped below the point where the atoms can move about freely and the transformation will be arrested before the pearlitic structure can be fully formed. Instead, a hard material called MARTENSITE will appear as a great number of very fine needlelike crystals arranged all helter skelter in interlocking patterns throughout the pearlitic matrix, as shown by FIGURE [75].

The concentration of martensite depends upon both the composition of the alloy and the rate of cooling. Martensite is the hardest, strongest and most brittle of the steel microstructures. The tradeoff between strength and toughness of the alloy steels is basically a tradeoff between martensite and pearlite in the microstructure, and is controlled by the percentage of carbon and alloying elements present in the steel and the rate of cooling from above the critical temperature. This is the basis of all heat treatments of steel. By heat treatment, suitable steel alloys can be made harder or softer, internal stresses can be induced or relieved, mechanical properties increased or decreased, machinability, formability and forgeability enhanced, etc. The basic terms used to describe such thermal treatments and their effects are:

ANNEALING consists of heating the metal to a suitable temperature within the critical range; holding it at that temperature until it is uniformly heated through, its grain structure has been refined (made more uniform) and any internal stresses have been relieved; and then cooling the metal very slowly (usually in an oven or while immersed in a powder). Annealing relieves any internal stresses present in the metal, increases the individual grain size and makes both the grain size and the microstructure more uniform, thus increasing ductility and enhancing formability. Some metals (aluminum, for example) do not possess a "critical temperature" as such. Nonetheless, they are annealed by a similar process. For instance, we anneal aluminum sheet (when it work hardens while being formed) by depositing a very thin layer of carbon onto the surface of the aluminum with a carburizing (acetylene-rich) flame from an oxyacetylene torch and then gently heat the aluminum until the carbon disappears. The carbon acts as a telltale sign and is deposited only to indicate by its disappearance when the annealing is complete.

NORMALIZING is very similar to annealing. The only real difference is that, after heating, the metal is allowed to cool in still air, a faster process which does not yield quite the same results.

Figure (75): Needlelike martensitic microstructure in pearlite matrix.

STRESS RELIEVING is the heating of a ferrous alloy to a suitable temperature within the critical range, holding it at that temperature long enough to reduce internal stresses and to refine the grain structure, and then cooling the steel slowly enough to minimize the development of new internal stresses. Thus both normalizing and annealing are properly termed stress-relieving processes.

As an example, since the heating and cooling involved in the welding process sets up notable residual internal stresses within the metal (and alters the grain structure as well), all critical weldments, especially those involving the medium-alloy steels such as SAE 4130 and 4140, should be stress relieved after welding. If the part is to be heat treated after fabrication we call out a stress relief normalize before heat treat. If not, we stress relieve the welds and the areas adjacent to them by a process called ''torch normalizing.'' Immediately after the weld or the cluster of welds is finished the whole area adjacent to the weld(s) is slowly and evenly heated to a very dull cherry red with a ''rosebud'' tip. This corresponds to the desired stress-relieving temperature of from 1100 to 1250 degrees F. The part is then either immersed in DRY sand or allowed to cool in STILL air. In every case, too little temperature is preferable to too much—the part should never actually reach a red color. In most race car parts (i.e., thin sections welded to other thin sections) 600 to 800 degrees F is actually sufficient, and can be reached in a household gas oven (to the absolute delight of the lady of the house).

A FURTHER PEEK AT THE CONTINUING ROMANCE BETWEEN CARBON AND IRON

In general, the higher the carbon content of a steel the greater its hardness and its ultimate tensile strength, AND the more these properties can be improved by heat treating. As always we cannot get something for nothing. Increasing the carbon content of a steel also reduces its toughness, ductility, impact resistance and weldability. Very often we find a requirement for a steel part that must have a very hard surface for good wear resistance AND a tough, shock-resistant, core for strength and toughness. Common examples are crankshafts, camshafts and live axles or ''hubs.'' We are able to meet this apparent contradiction in requirements by locally increasing the carbon content near the surface of the part.

CASE HARDENING is a generic term for the treatment of a ferrous part in such a way that the case, or outer shell, of the part is made substantially richer in carbon content— and therefore harder—than the inner portion (or core) which remains tough and shock resistant. Case hardening consists of CARBURIZING the steel, followed by a suitable heat treatment. The carburizing results in a hard surface while the heat treatment produces a tough and ductile core. Common processes used include: carburizing, flame hardening, induction hardening, cyaniding and nitriding.

CARBURIZING is the introduction by diffusion of additional carbon into the outer portion of a steel by heating the metal above the critical temperature while it is in contact with a suitable carbon-rich material, which may be a solid, a liquid or a gas. The carburized alloy is usually QUENCH HARDENED after carburizing. Cutting edges were once produced by physically hammering powdered charcoal into the surface of white-hot wrought iron blades.

QUENCHING is the technique of heating a steel to a suitable temperature ABOVE its critical range and then hardening it by immersion in an agitated bath of oil, water, brine or caustic soda. We are all familiar with the legend of how the superb sword blades of Damascus and Toledo (the Toledo of Moorish Spain, not Max Klinger's Toledo, Ohio) were endowed with their extraordinary toughness, flexibility and sharpness by being plunged, red hot, through the belly of a slave. That was quenching in the high-tech world a few centuries back. Quenching techniques (and human rights) have progressed since then but we still quench steel to increase its hardness, tensile strength and yield point. Today we quench in baths of oil, water or various salts that are maintained at specific temperatures which vary with the individual process. Unfortunately, quenching also decreases ductility, toughness and impact resistance, which can be partially restored by subsequent ''tempering'' which will also relieve any internal stresses set up by the sudden cooling.

TEMPERING is the reheating of a quench hardened steel to a specified temperature BELOW the critical range and then allowing it to cool at a specified rate, either in an oven or in a heated bath of oil or salts. Tempering temperatures vary from 300 to 1200 degrees F. Low tempering temperatures give maximum hardness and wear resistance, while maximum toughness results from higher tempering temperatures. Typically, tempering at temperatures up to about 500 degrees F reduces internal stresses with only a very slight decrease in the hardness of the steel, while tempering at temperatures in the range from about 800 to 1000 degrees F results in the optimum toughness for a given level of strength. Increasing the tempering temperature beyond this point normally decreases the hardness and strength of the steel at a faster rate than it increases the toughness. With some high-alloy steels, however, tempering at temperatures in excess of 1000 degrees F is necessary.

SURFACE HARDENING—FLAME AND INDUCTION HARDENING

If a very thin, hard surface layer will do the job, the carburizing process can be omitted. A hard surface can be produced on a part made from a relatively high carbon steel which has already been heat treated to the required strength level by locally reheating and quenching THE OUTER SKIN ONLY. In this case the required heat is produced by exposure to a naked flame (''flame hardening'') or by an induced electrical current (''induction hardening''). The quenching is typically accomplished by a carefully controlled mist. The advantages lie in the ease and speed of the operations (which are very well suited to automation); the fact that the processes produce only minimal physical distortion; and, since no great depth of hardness is required, the option of using less costly lower-carbon steels is sometimes available.

An example is the manufacture of the suspension hub shown in FIGURE [67] on page 95 of PREPARE TO WIN. This very clever arrangement was originally made by shrinking and pinning a standard needle roller bearing inner race over a fully machined and heat-treated hub made from E4340 steel. This is the part shown in PREPARE TO WIN. Later we figured out that the part could be made both lighter and cheaper by deleting the bearing journal and letting the needles roll directly on the surface of the hub, IF we could make that surface very hard indeed, while still retaining core toughness. It turned out that, by induction hardening only that portion of the hub, a perfectly suitable part could be made. It was both lighter and cheaper—an unusual combination in this business.

CYANIDING is the introduction of carbon and nitrogen into the outer layer of a ferrous alloy by holding the metal above its critical temperature while it is immersed in a bath of molten cyanide salts of suitable composition. The cyanided alloy is then usually quench hardened.

NITRIDING is the process of producing an exceptionally hard and wear resistant, but very thin case by exposing steels alloyed with elements which readily form "nitrides" (aluminum, molybdenum, chromium and vanadium) to ammonia for long periods of time at elevated temperatures (850-1100 degrees F). In this case, not only must the steel be a specific "nitriding steel" but it must first be quenched and tempered to the required mechanical properties and finish machined (preferably ground) to a very smooth finish. After nitriding it must be very lightly reground to remove the top of the nitrided layer which is not as hard as the underlying material. The major advantage of the nitriding process is that it is not necessary (nor indeed permissible) to quench the part after nitriding—so that distortion is held to an absolute minimum and excellent core control is obtained. The disadvantage is that the thin, nitrided layer is very brittle making it almost impossible to straighten parts after nitriding. The process is often used to produce the necessary hard and wear-resistant shell on crankshaft journals, the core of which must be very tough indeed.

DO-IT-YOURSELF HEAT TREATING

For millenia the metal smiths quenched and tempered by feel and by observing the color of the hot metal and of the surface oxides formed during tempering. While the results were not perfectly consistent, the alloys were very simple and the results, if not perfect, were a hell of a lot better than could have been obtained by any other method. The color charts are still in print, presumably for the use of downed aviators or mining/farm repairmen. As a point of interest I have reproduced one as FIGURE [76].

Our alloys are no longer simple and people object strongly to aircraft falling out of the sky (and, to a lesser extent, to race cars crashing). The heat treatment of steel is now a complex subject which requires knowledge and equipment beyond that available to the average racer. Un-

fortunately, while most heat-treating shops have both the knowledge and the equipment to do the job properly, it is highly unlikely that the person who actually writes up your job into a shop work order will have any real knowledge of the subject, let alone of your specific needs. There is only one way to avoid giant screw ups: You are going to have to convince the man who DOES have the knowledge to spend some of his valuable time with you.

How you find THE MAN and how you talk him into wasting his time on your insignificant order is up to you. Once you are in a position to speak to him, don't EVEN think about trying to impress him with your knowledge of HIS business. Tell him what the parts are for, what they are made from, what welding rod (if any) was used, what you want to achieve by heat-treatment and what you expect to do with the parts after they are heat-treated (shot-peen, grind or whatever). Make damned sure that you have drilled air holes in any closed fabrication (a #60 hole will do fine—but there MUST be a hole, otherwise the expansion of the trapped air when the part is heated is going to lead to trouble). Make sure that there are no sharp edges or corners—inside or outside—ANYWHERE on the parts to be heat treated (they are guaranteed to come back glass hard and are virtually guaranteed to come back complete with

Figure (76): Color versus temperature chart for steel.

Color	Temp (degrees F.)
"Blood" Red	1050
"Dark Cherry" Red	1075
"Medium Cherry" Red	1250
"Cherry" Red	1375
Bright Red	1550
Salmon	1650
Orange	1725
Lemon	1825
Light Yellow	1975
White	2200
Dazzling White	2350

SURFACE OXIDES FORMED DURING TEMPERING OF STEEL

Oxide Color	Steel Temp (°F)
Pale Yellow	430
Straw	445
Golden Yellow	470
Brown	490
Brown-with-Purple Dapples	510
Purple	530
Dark Blue	550
Bright Blue	570
Pale Blue	610

"quench cracks," which WILL grow). Make equally sure that the complete heat-treatment specification is SPELLED OUT on the work order and that you call out a stress-relief treatment prior to the strength-enhancement heat treatment of any welded part. Tell the man how much, if any, distortion you can live with and, if he says that he requires a holding fixture to eliminate distortion (unlikely), make him one. With long, straight pieces, make sure that they are HUNG in the oven, not just laid on the racks. Make sure that the man understands that you are not going to accept dents in your parts.

Obviously it is best if you can take your parts to a house that does a lot of race car or aircraft work. This is pretty unlikely unless you live in Los Angeles, Kansas City, St. Louis or Seattle. What I do is real simple. I KNOW that I know just about enough about heat treating to get myself in real trouble. I take (or UPS) my parts to Jim Meyer at Jim Meyer and Associates, tell him what I need, let him worry about the heat-treating and shot-peening end of things and happily pay the man for his expertise and connections. It gets done quickly; it gets done right; and, in all probability, going through Jim actually reduces my overall cost. If he were to cost me a ton of money, I would still use him—I don't believe in do-it-yourself brain surgery.

The last time that I suggested in a book that my readers take or send work to a specific person, Pete and Michele Weismann got buried in Hewland dog rings that needed regrinding, which they no longer wanted to do. I'm not sure that they have forgiven me yet! At any rate, I have just talked with Meyer and, as of this moment, he is more than willing to take on outside work. The address is 13720 Florine, Paramount, CA 90723. Phone number is (213) 531-8816. (Don't expect him to spend HIS nickel returning your call!)

A LOOK AT THE MARAGING STEELS FROM A DIFFERENT VIEWPOINT

As we have seen, martensite is the name given to a supersaturated solution of carbon in ferrite. This supersaturation is arrived at by rapid quenching of austenite from about 1650 degrees. Ferrite itself is simply iron with a body-centered cubic crystal structure. The supersaturation with carbon distorts the body-centered cubic crystal to a body-centered tetragonal and results in a very hard, very strong and very brittle microstructure.

The "high strength" alloys of steel have depended upon the formation of martensite—followed first by precipitation heat treatment for hardening and then by tempering for toughening. Martensite requires carbon—lots of carbon—and carbon is, despite all of its strength and hardness, BRITTLE. This simple fact has limited the useful strength level of the high-alloy steels since they were developed.

Even with vacuum-melted steels of the utmost purity, the most exotic alloying elements and multistage highly sophisticated quenching and tempering processes, the steels still get brittle at high strength levels. The sophisticated heat treatments are costly, time consuming and a long way from being fool proof. A great deal of effort has been devoted over the past couple of decades to the development of high-strength steels that do not require all of this sophistication in heat treatment and which are not brittle at high strength levels. Great progress has been made. Some of the manufacturers would have us believe that the problem has been solved. It has not.

MAGIC

The precipitation-hardening MARAGING steels can exhibit strength levels in the 280,000 to 320,000 psi range with a simple precipitation heat treatment. In the process a hardening precipitate is formed in a matrix which, while it strongly resembles martensite in structure, is CARBON FREE. It turns out that while metal-smithing man has always depended upon carbon to impart hardness and strength to soft, useless old iron, THERE IS ANOTHER WAY!

As we have learned more and more about how metallurgy works, we have found that, by alloying virtually carbon-free iron with LOTS of nickel (18-25%) a martensitelike structure can be formed, even when the alloy is cooled slowly. This new structure, instead of being hard and brittle like carbon-based martensite, is tough and only about half as hard as martensite. When alloyed with cobalt, molybdenum, titanium, and/or aluminum this basic nickel-martensitic matrix can be treated to about 280,000-320,000 psi while retaining great ductility. AND the heat treatment is simple and less distortion and crack prone than those required by the carbon-based alloys.

It all sounds like the answer to a RACER'S prayer. But no! As I mentioned before, the martensitic steels so far do not like reversal of stress. They are perfectly satisfactory (in fact brilliant) when subjected to unidirectional stress, as in aircraft landing gear or even in torsion bar, but their fatigue life is severely limited when the direction of stress is reversed, as in driveshaft, hub, antiroll bar, connecting rod, etc. It won't be very long before the maraging steels take over the ultrahigh-strength steel business. I prefer to let the aerospace industry do the experimenting when it comes to materials.

Whenever the subject of the maraging steels comes up I am reminded of two of Murphy's laws of engineering materials:

(1) "Manufacturers' written specifications of performance should always be multiplied by a factor of 0.5."

(2) "Salespeoples' claims for performance should always be multiplied by a factor of 0.25."

CHAPTER FIVE

HISTORIC OVERVIEW OF MAN'S PRODUCTION OF IRON AND STEEL

Believe it or not, I do sometimes ask the opinion of people in the real publishing world before I actually print these books. I sent the first draft of the metallurgy section of this one to a professional whose opinion I truly value. His comment was that he really liked the technical part of it but that I should cut all of the "historical bullshit" out of it because it detracted from the technical content. I have given his advice a lot of thought—and I think that he is wrong. What follows is included partially because I enjoyed writing it and partially because I think that a brief historical summary of man's relationship with the ferrous metals will add to our general understanding of the subject. If you agree with the editor, feel free to skip it.

We have pretty much finished our investigation of ferrous metallurgy. We have probably exhausted the reader. We have certainly exhausted the author. We have by no means exhausted the subject—in fact, we have barely scratched the surface. I have listed some of the books that I think are particularly good in the appendix. Your public library may have one or two of them, or be able to borrow them from another library. Your library probably does have a number of books on the general subject. Most of them will be really dull (librarians, almost by definition, are not technically oriented people and neither are the reviewers of the library journals). Some of them, however, are bound to be both technically correct and well written. You can almost always tell which are which just by flipping pages. If the subject interests you, look in the subject portion of the card catalog under METALS and/or METAL-

LURGY and go from there. I will also point out that just because you think that a book looks good and you check it out from the library, there is no law that says you have to continue to read it after you discover it is not as good (or interesting) as you thought it was going to be.

The history of man's relationship with metals is largely a history of the technology of weapons. I assume the first of our remote ancestors to find a tree limb lying on the ground immediately bashed somebody or something on the head with it—and ate them (or it). So, man progressed from the rock and the club to tipped spears, the throwing stick, the bow and arrow, the sword, the chariot and finally to gun powder and nuclear fission. From the flint chipper to the nuclear physicist the technocrats have always been the weapons producers. And their work has always been tinged with mystery and magic, partially because they have planned it that way and partially because, whether to stave off hunger, to fight off a human invader or to take away something that some other group had possession of, the very survival of the community has always depended upon the success of their efforts.

Man's discovery of iron probably came about after a series of campfires had been built on a piece of ground that just happened to be very rich in iron ores, or when a copper-smelting furnace was cleaned out after iron-bearing ores had been used as fluxes in the production of copper or bronze or when a potter used hematite as a coloring agent in his baking kiln. In any case, porous lumps of metallic iron combined with various impurities (but not much carbon simply because the temperatures that could be achieved were not sufficient to dissolve carbon in iron) could remain, either in the ashes of the fire or in the cooled kiln. They would be neither pretty nor useful but they would be different enough from anything else that man had seen to attract his attention and they WOULD BE HARD. Early man was ALWAYS interested in anything that was hard—hard things penetrate soft things, like skin and muscle tissue. Fortunately, in addition to being hard, these iron sponges were also malleable—at high temperatures.

We will never know how many generations, or millennia, passed before the first metalsmiths learned that by repeatedly heating the sponges to white heat and hammering the bejesus out of them, not only could many of the impurities be squeezed out but the sponges could be welded together into a useful lump of strong, tough and ductile WROUGHT IRON (it is rather like kneading pieces of clay together to make one big lump, except that with the iron sponges, we need heat to do it). We can be certain, however, that it was not long after they got this far that they began to hand forge useful shapes—axe heads, spear points, arrowheads, hammers—from the new, magic metal. In all probability we will never even discover where and when this first happened, because iron, when buried in the earth, oxidizes to nothing and archeologists don't find very many iron artifacts.

We DO know, of course, that early man did not use anything that resembled pure iron, for two reasons. First is the simple fact that pure iron is too soft and weak to be useful, and certainly not pretty enough to be ornamental. The second reason is that early man had no way to create a fire hot enough to melt iron. All that he could do was produce sponges of iron, silicon and slags by the indirect reduction process described in our discussion of the blast furnace. Fortunately for him, the long and repeated exposures to charcoal fires that were a necessary part of the forging process partially carburized the wrought iron and transformed it into an impure and nonhomogenous grade of carbon steel. What the early metalsmiths THOUGHT they were doing was ''purifying'' the iron by exposure to fire. What they WERE doing, without knowing it, was ALLOYING iron with carbon, silicon and so on.

From time immemorial what metallurgists have been doing, or trying to do, in the alloying of metals is to exercise control over the movements of crystal dislocations within the lattice by adjusting the size and the structure of the metallic grains (dislocations CAN move across grain boundaries, but only with difficulty) and by adding other elements, metallic and/or nonmetallic which both alter the crystalline structure and act as ''pins'' or ''keys'' both between crystals in the lattice and as stops for dislocation lines (even a single atom of an alloying element may stop or at least impede the progress of a dislocation line). As you would expect it is only in the past couple of hundred years that anyone has had any idea at all what was happening. Until the 17th or 18th century the body of metallurgical knowledge consisted of what worked.

We have seen that iron, in its pure state, is so soft as to be virtually worthless and that the strength of iron and steel is due primarily to the extraordinary sensitivity of the movement of dislocations within the crystalline lattice of iron to small amounts of carbon. This has been known, if not understood, for literally thousands of years. Simply because I am personally interested, we are going to very briefly explore the progress that man has made in his use of iron.

The cast irons available to our immediate ancestors were, as we have seen, not well suited for structural use. They did make cannon from the stuff—but cast iron cannon had a nasty tendency to blow up, taking the cannoneers with them. (All in all the profession of artilleryman in the early days was a chancy one at best and THEY preferred cannon cast from bronze.) The structural metal of the Industrial Revolution was WROUGHT IRON, which was simply pig iron that had been purified by an incredibly laborious process in which the iron, cast in a blank of suitable size and shape, was repeatedly heated to white heat and HAMMERED or FORGED to literally squeeze the slag and impurities from it. From this wrought iron, carbon steel could be even more slowly produced by carburizing. The whole process was very slow and even after the advent of waterwheel-driven mechanical forges, the output of an individual forge was limited to a few hundred pounds of wrought iron per day.

In the late 18th century the development of the coke-fired puddling furnace raised that figure to about one TON per man per day. This quantum jump in the production of structural iron made the Industrial Revolution possible and paved the way for modern steelmaking.

EARLY STEEL MAKING

Historians and anthropologists tell us that the most significant advance brought about by man's transition from the Bronze Age to the Iron Age was the improvement in edged weapons that allowed the people who first mastered the use of iron to subjugate (or to wipe out, as the case may be) their bronze-using neighbors and, incidentally, to plow the earth more efficiently. As an example, you may recall that when the Biblical Israelites were about to be conquered by the prototype bad guys (the Philistines) David slew the giant, Goliath, with a stone from his shepherd's sling. He had to! The Philistines had learned to smelt and forge iron. They had iron-wheeled chariots, steel spear points, arrow heads and swords. The Israelites had soft copper shields and bronze swords. If David had let Goliath get anywhere near him it would have been all over! (Interestingly enough, the military/political situation in the Middle East doesn't seem to have changed much since then.)

The early ironsmiths could not have done much of this with wrought iron. It is simply too soft and ductile to make good, edged weapons (or plowshares).

When the exhausted smiths had finished the heating, folding and beating process the almost pure wrought iron that they had produced was pretty damned tough. The purity of the iron depended on the thoroughness of the heating, hammering and folding process by which the slag was removed. In the case of exceptional products, such as Damascus, Toledo or Japanese sword blades, this process was (and in Japan, still is) repeated literally thousands of times. The finished blade, examined under magnification, exhibits a characteristic longitudinal wavy layered or laminate pattern, each layer representing a separate hot-folding and beating operation—tiresome, to say the least! The toughness was largely due to the remaining slag which, being mostly silicon, was stringy and, to an extent, limited the plastic flow of the soft iron.

Since it was almost pure iron, it was also far too soft for making blades (or even plowshares) from and so it had to be hardened by replacing SOME of the carbon that had been so laboriously removed. Instead of being interspersed THROUGHOUT the iron, however, this new carbon was placed only near the surface of the raw forging. It was (and is, in classical blade making) done by carburizing the iron to form carbon steel. The blank was packed in charcoal, placed in an airtight box or CASE and heated to a high enough temperature for a long enough time for the carbon to diffuse into the surface of the iron to a depth of 0.020'' to 0.040''. Alternatively, the carbon could be added during the hammering process as powdered charcoal. Either way, although no one knew it at the time, the carbon actually formed an interstitial solid solution with the iron.

Although the carbon diffused into the surface of the iron-hardened outer layers, the steel still had to be quenched by immersing the red hot blank in a cold liquid, usually water, to arrive at the desired levels of both surface hardness and core toughness. I am willing to bet that if man ever develops a time machine, we will discover that quenching began when a smith dropped a hot blank into a bucket or a stream by mistake. Anyway, what happens during quenching is not simple.

THE QUENCHING OF STEEL

The white-hot steel is well above the critical temperature range and so is composed of AUSTENITE which, you remember, is a solid solution of carbon in metallic iron. At room temperature austenite is not a stable compound because there is more carbon in austenite than can be dissolved or held dissolved in iron at normal temperatures. The method in which this "excess carbon" parts from or "precipitates out of" the iron varies with the speed of cooling.

If the steel is cooled slowly, the result will be PEARLITE, the regular laminate of alternate layers of pure iron (ferrite) and iron carbide (cementite) which we first learned about in our investigation of cast iron. The resultant steel is tough and relatively strong, but not particularly hard.

If the hot steel is cooled suddenly, though, the result will be a structure composed mainly of MARTENSITE, a compact carbon/iron crystal that is harder than hell, and brittle to match. It is also very strong. It, too, is composed of ferrite and cementite, but the cementite is very fine grained and evenly distributed throughout the iron, making dislocation movement almost impossible. The faster the steel is quenched, the more martensite will form. The addition of certain salts to the quenching bath modifies the process. Ammonia and other nitrogen-rich compounds, for instance, result in the interstitial diffusion of nitrogen into the surface of the steel in the form of very hard crystals of iron nitride. Interstitial atoms act as pins or keys which prevent or at least discourage dislocation movements so nitriding produces a very hard surface layer.

I'm looking forward to the time machine for this one because the only liquid which occurs in nature which is rich in ammonia is, of course urine. Imagine the reaction of academia when they find that the tradition of the legendary blades of Damascus actually began with the master smith yelling, "piss on it!"

THE TEMPERING OF STEEL

Be that as it may, martensite is TOO hard. It is, in fact, brittle, which is not a very good quality in a sword blade (or a drive shaft, or a gun barrel, or much of anything else). So we come to the final general process in the heat treatment of steels: TEMPERING. In tempering, we simply heat the quenched steel to a temperature somewhere below the transformation range (450 to 850 degrees F covers the normal range of tempering temperatures) and allow it to cool slowly. This transforms some of the martensite to a softer, more ductile crystal structure called sorbite, resulting in a tougher part. The higher the tempering temperature and the longer the steel is held at that temperature the more martensite is transformed into sorbite and the more ductile the resulting steel. The tempering of steel is often referred to as "drawing it back."

It seems interesting to me that the whole process of converting nasty cast iron into useful steel is a series of operations each of which consists of going too far in a given direction and then applying a correction. First we make pig iron, which has too much carbon in it and is brittle and useless. We then remove all of the carbon and find that the result is too soft—so we put some carbon back in and quench the stuff to the point that it is hard and brittle, so we temper it so that it will be tough. Racers are not the only people who do things the hard way!

CRUCIBLE STEEL

Steelmaking as we have described it was a pretty damned laborious process, requiring vast amounts of muscle, skill and judgement. No matter how much of any of the above was employed, the resultant steel was expensive, nonhomogenous, and the chemical composition and resultant mechanical properties were not particularly repeatable. This was sort of ok for tools and weapons (the rich got the really good ones and the infantry got the swords that would break and the muskets that would blow up), but it was not very good for clock springs. In the 18th century the Brits were really into clockmaking (mainly because of an enormous cash prize offered by the Admiralty for the successful development of a really accurate chronometer, so that longitude could be determined rather than guessed at and the empire's trade routes expanded and made more secure).

Several chronometers of sufficient accuracy were developed but the required reliability wasn't there—the damned springs kept breaking.

In the 1740's Benjamin Huntsman, a British clock maker, (in Sheffield, a city about to become famous for cutlery) figured out that the major cause of broken clock springs was the uneven nature of the distribution of carbon in the matrix of iron. (This was particularly clever on his part because metal fatigue had not even been THOUGHT OF yet.) He came up with the concept of CRUCIBLE steelmaking in which wrought iron bars (broken into small pieces so as to present greater surface area) along with a little added carbon, are melted in clay CRUCIBLES (a crucible is nothing more than a pot or a receptacle made from a refractory material, in this case fire clay). Fortuitously, both coke-fired furnaces capable of producing the necessary temperatures (2900 degrees F) and fire clays that could withstand them had recently been developed. When the wrought iron melted, the contained slag also melted and, being lighter, floated to the surface leaving the carbon evenly distributed throughout the iron. The carbon content could be adjusted to the desired level of strength and hardness and the molten steel, free from slag, could be poured off into molds resulting in an ingot of homogenous carbon steel.

Crucible steel was still expensive, partially because the starting product was expensive wrought iron and partially because it could only be produced in very small (less than 100 lb) batches. The solidified ingots, of course, still had to be forged or rolled into shapes. Only the slag was removed (other impurities remained) and the repeatability from batch to batch, while better than forged steel, was not real good. Crucible steel, however, offered the noteworthy advantage of homogeneity—the strength and hardness of the steel was uniform throughout its thickness, although the surface could still be carburized to give a more durable cutting edge. As a point of interest, although modern crucibles are electrically heated, small batches of experimental steel are still made in crucibles. In the days when most of the high-alloy steels came from Sweden, they were known in the trade as "Swedish crucible steels."

SUMMARY

I think that it IS important for us to realize that, for all of our technology, basically what we have done in the past two centuries is to make structural steels cheap and readily available and to improve our methods of joining them. Our predecessors, although they did not understand the physical processes involved, made perfectly good steels, the hard way. Their hand-forged blades were as fine as anything we can accomplish. One other thing that we, pragmatic modern man have accomplished: We have taken out the magic and the mystery from steel and steelmaking. Jim Bowie's blade could no longer be made from a meteor. King Arthur's Excalibur could not now be endowed with mystical powers. Anyone can buy as good a blade as there is, mass produced. It is, however, interesting to note that the custom knifemaker still exists, and the limited production of the good blademakers is sold out years in advance. It is also interesting to note that, to my knowledge, few of them refine their own steels or even forge their own blanks, except in Japan, the current home of mass-production technology and robotics, where the great blademakers are nationally revered. THEY not only hand forge their own blanks, they do their own folding and squeezing—and they do it themselves; the apprentices get to practice on their own blades.

Like all of man's knowledge, the history of steelmaking is a story of men building upon the knowledge, sweat and experience of their predecessors, through a very formalized apprenticeship system. One man found curious little sponges of metal in a cooled potters kiln or in the ashes of a campfire. Generations later another forged a handful of the sponges into a coherent mass of wrought iron. Still more generations passed before a metalsmith reheated and hammered and reheated and hammered until he finally ended up with a useful hammer head, or axe, or whatever. Carburizing, quenching and tempering followed at enormous intervals of time. The progress was never steady, but was frequently halted, and even lost, as tribes, societies and entire civilizations fell. At times the pause would last for centuries, sometimes for millennia, but always, somewhere, the conditions would become right and the learning process would pick up again. Slowly progress was made until, at the time of the Industrial Revolution, technology took over and, from the historical point of view we arrived at our current level in a great rush.

There is a certain inevitability about the development of any technology, and it certainly holds true here. It was inevitable that, if enough camp/cooking fires were built and rebuilt on enough iron-rich earth that some curious individual would find the iron sponges; or that, since hematite is a pretty color, it would eventually be used to color pottery and that, after enough firings, sponges would be found in the cooled kilns. It was also inevitable that some early technocrat would fool around, heating and hammering, until wrought iron came about. And the charcoal involved in heating and reheating would eventually carburize the ductile wrought iron into hard and strong steel. It was certainly inevitable that a hot forging would be dropped into water and that quenching would be developed, and that a hot blank would be set aside to toughen and lead to the development of tempering.

As always, one thing led to another. Benjamin Huntsman couldn't develop crucible steel until the coke furnace was developed to the point where a temperature high enough to melt pure iron was achieved and, even then, unless suitable fire clays had been available the crucible itself could not have been built. It is a historic accident that HUNTSMAN developed the crucible method, that BESSEMER came up with the air-reduction process, that the SIEMENS brothers developed the open-hearth process and so on. But it was inevitable, given the progress that had gone before and the demands of the day, that SOMEONE would do it.

Unfortunately we cannot separate out the beneficial aspects of developing technology. So, in addition to our current stage of metallurgy and physical medicine, we also have atomic fission and biological warfare capabilities.

NON-FERROUS METALS AND THEIR METALLURGY— COMPOSITE MATERIALS

CHAPTER SIX

THE REFINING AND MANUFACTURING OF ALUMINUM

You would never guess it from the price, but aluminum is the earth's most common metal. Some of it is present in practically every handful of dirt found anywhere on the planet, but it never apppears in nature as a free metal. The only practical source is bauxite, a yellow ore which contains from 45% to 60% oxides of aluminum. Ground and kiln-dried bauxite is mixed with a caustic soda (sodium hydroxide) solution and heated. The aluminum oxide dissolves in the caustic soda to form sodium aluminate which, after most of the impurities present have been removed by settling and filtration, is drawn off as a clear liquid. A complex series of processes involving precipitation, washing and high-temperature dehydration produces a fine, white, powdered-aluminum oxide known as ALUMINA.

By weight, alumina is half aluminum and half oxygen. Alumina, sodium aluminum fluoride and aluminum fluoride are then mixed in a carbon-lined cell, or "reduction pot," where direct electric current in vast quantities is applied through a carbon electrode. (The reduction pot is basically an electric smelting furnace in which metallic aluminum is freed as the oxygen from the alumina combines with carbon from the electrode to form carbon dioxide.)

Molten aluminum collects between the carbon lining of the cell and the crust of alumina. It is drawn off and siphoned into crucibles, tested and conveyed to alloying furnaces where other elements are added and dissolved in the aluminum. The resulting alloys of aluminum are then cast into shapes suitable for mill processing into useful shapes and forms. These mill processes, illustrated by FIGURE [77], produce sheet, bar, tube and extruded shapes and are similar to those employed in the steel mills. Like steel, aluminum is also hot forged into structural shapes which, because of the orientation of the grain flow within the forging, are both strong and efficient. Unlike steel, various grades of aluminum are commonly employed in castings.

A unique combination of mechanical characteristics places aluminum at the top of the racer's list of structural materials. It is about ⅓ the weight of steel, yet some of the aluminum alloys exhibit tensile strengths superior to those of the low-carbon steels. It can be cast by any method known to foundrymen, and the castings can be heat treated to moderate strength and stiffness levels. It can be rolled into an almost infinite variety of sheet and bar configurations, drawn into wire forms and extruded into structural shapes. It can be fabricated readily into any form and it can be joined by just about any method—bolting, riveting and welding. Finished fabrications and/or weldments can also be heat treated to high strength and stiffness levels.

Typically, in both the aircraft and race car industries, aluminum fabrications, joined by a combination of mechanical fastening and welding, turn out to be the most cost effective and practical method of producing strong, stiff and lightweight major structures. For our purposes, fabricated aluminum main structures (tubs) have one more major advantage, often overlooked in our love affair with "exotic materials": They crash well. When well-designed and well-thought-out fabricated aluminum chassis DO hit something, they absorb a great deal of impact energy in the process of deforming. SOMETHING has to absorb the energy of impact, and the wall won't move very much. That leaves the car and the driver; any energy absorbed by the car does not have to be absorbed by the driver. Give this a bit of thought when you are next thinking about composite chassis and/or cast wheels!

ALUMINUM ALLOYS

As with most metals, the mechanical properties of aluminum can be enhanced by alloying with other elements. Like the steel industry, the aluminum industry employs a four-digit system to designate and identify the various wrought aluminum alloys. Also in keeping with the tradition begun by the steel industry, there is no single designation system in worldwide use. Needless to say this causes some confusion. In the U.S. system, the first digit identifies the major alloying element:

Figure (77): Processing of cast aluminum billets into mill shapes. Aircraft Spruce and Specialty Company.

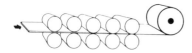

HUGE CAST ROLLING INGOT OF ALUMINUM IS REDUCED THROUGH HOT AND/OR COLD ROLLING MILLS TO THICKNESS DESIRED. ANNEALING AND OTHER HEAT TREATMENTS BEFORE, DURING AND/OR BETWEEN ROLLING OPERATIONS ARE CONTROLLED TO PRODUCE CLOSELY CONTROLLED QUALITY OF FINISHED SHEET OR BAR.

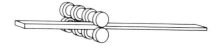

WROUGHT FORMS OF ROD AND BAR ARE ROLLED TO FINISHED DIMENSIONS.

FORGED EXTRUSION INGOT (BILLET) IS HEATED AND FORCED UNDER GREAT PRESSURE THROUGH EXTRUDING DIES TO FORM EXTRUDED TUBE, PIPE, ROD, BAR AND VARIOUS SHAPES.

1xxx series: In this group the minimum aluminum content is 99% and there is no alloying element. The second digit indicates modifications in impurity limits; the last two digits designate the specific absolute minimum aluminum content allowed over the group limit of 99%, in $\frac{1}{100}$'s of 1%. Thus aluminum alloy 1100 is 99% pure aluminum with some specified control of impurities, whereas alloy 1130 is 99.30% pure aluminum with no specified control over the composition of the impurities which comprise the remaining 0.7%.

2xxx through 9xxx series: The major alloying element is identified by the first digit.

2xxx: Copper is the principal alloying element in this group. All of the 2xxx-series alloys require solution heat treatment to realize their optimum mechanical properties, and some require artificial aging as well. In the heat-treated condition their mechanical properties rival, and sometimes exceed, those of low-carbon steel.

3xxx: Manganese is the major alloying element in this group of moderately strong and exceptionally ductile, malleable, weldable and formable alloys. They are not heat-treatable, although their strength levels can be increased by cold working.

4xxx: Silicon alloyed with aluminum causes a substantial reduction in the melting point without producing brittleness in the resulting alloys. The silicon-aluminum alloys are mainly used as welding wire and brazing alloys where a lower melting point than that of the base metal is required. These alloys are not, in themselves, heat-treatable. However, when they are used as filler metal in the welding of heat-treatable aluminum alloys they will pick up some of the alloying elements from the base metal while molten. So, at least to a limited extent, the welds will respond to subsequent heat treatment.

5xxx: Magnesium is one of the most effective and widely used alloying elements for aluminum. Used alone, or with manganese, the result is a non-heat-treatable alloy with tensile values which, while only moderate by comparison with those of the heat-treatable alloys, are the highest of the non-heat-treatable aluminums. These alloys possess very good welding characteristics and are reasonably formable.

6xxx: Magnesium and silicon are the alloying elements in this group of heat-treatable alloys. Although their strength levels are less than those of either the 2xxx or the 7xxx series, these alloys possess good formability and excellent weldability which makes them very popular for semistructural use and for structural use where welding must take place. They all require solution heat treating and artificial aging in order to reach optimum strength.

7xxx: Zinc is the major alloying element in this group. When combined with a smaller percentage of magnesium, it produces heat-treatable aluminum alloys of very high strength, but little ductility. Normally traces of other elements such as copper and chromium are added in order to improve ductility. These alloys require both solution heat treatment and artificial aging. Their formability is very poor indeed and they are weldable only by spot welding.

8xxx:Some other element; this series is not of interest to us.

9xxx:Unused.

The second digit indicates modifications made to the original alloy, if any. The last two digits have no specific significance and are used to identify the different alloys within the group.

THE HEAT TREATMENT OF ALUMINUM

Commercially pure aluminum has a tensile strength of about 13,000 psi. Cold working the metal, by either rolling or stretching (often termed "strain hardening"), can improve this figure to about 24,000 psi. An example is alloy 1100 which, while useful for cheap pots and pans, is hardly suitable for structure. Much greater strengths can be achieved by alloying the aluminum with other elements, but only after the resulting alloy has been heat-treated. In the as alloyed condition, none of the high-strength aluminum alloys has a tensile strength greater than about 35,000 psi.

Enhancement of the strength and hardness of the heat-treatable aluminum alloys is brought about by dissolving portions (or phases) of alloying elements with the aluminum. In many cases further heat-treatment involves controlled precipitation of the hardening phases from solution with the aluminum. The phases differ according to the alloy (and alloying elements) in question but the principles remain the same. The processes are based upon the fact that a greater amount or percentage of the alloying elements can always be retained in solid solution with aluminum at elevated temperatures than can be held in solution at ambient temperature. If an alloy which contains slightly more of an alloying element than can be dissolved in aluminum at room temperature is heated to a point just below the melting point of aluminum, all of the alloying element will be dissolved. If the metal is held at this temperature long enough the dissolved phases will be evenly dispersed throughout the matrix of aluminum by diffusion. If the alloy is then very rapidly cooled (by quenching) the phases will not have time to precipitate out of solution with the aluminum; the result is a sort of supersaturated alloy at room temperature.

This supersaturated state of affairs is the result of a "trick," and it is not a stable condition. The resultant alloy is not only unstable, it is soft. In time the excess amounts of the hardening elements or phases will naturally precipitate out of solution with the aluminum. But they will do so in the form of very fine particles of the phases which will be evenly dispersed throughout the matrix of aluminum as shown by FIGURE [78]. By acting as "keys" between grains and along slip planes, they will cause resistance to slip and thus increase the hardness, yield strength and ultimate tensile strength of the alloy. If this process is allowed to take place at room temperature until the resultant alloy becomes stable, the process is called NATURAL AGING and the alloy is described as being in the T4 TEMPER, as in aluminum alloy 2024-T4. The T3 temper is identical to the T4 except that after solution heat treatment (but before aging) the alloy is cold worked (or strain hardened) by rolling and/or stretching in order to further improve the mechanical properties.

Some alloys, including 2024, harden considerably in a few hours and reach a stable T4 condition in a few days. Others, including 7075, will continue to increase in strength literally for years if left at room temperature. These must be ARTIFICIALLY AGED to the stable condition. The aging process is known as PRECIPITATION HEAT TREATMENT and consists of baking a long time at a relatively low temperature under very carefully controlled conditions. The temperatures and times involved are in the 240 to 375 degrees F and 5 to 48 hour ranges. The resulting stable condition is known as the T6 temper. Most alloys that naturally stabilize in the T4 condition can be artificially aged to the T6 temper. Of course the resulting increase in strength and hardness is accompanied by a decrease in ductility and formability. The 6xxx-series alloys are often formed in the T4 condition and then artificially aged to the T6 temper. Yes, it CAN be done in the average shop but NO, I am neither going to tell you how nor recommend that you do it.

At very low temperatures the precipitation process can be arrested or at least slowed so that the soft, as-quenched properties can be retained for long periods of time. This is why the "superstrength" aircraft rivets made from 2024 or 2017 must be stored in dry ice between quenching and riveting. They naturally age to the T4 temper after being

---

Figure (78): The quenching, precipitation and age hardening of aluminum.

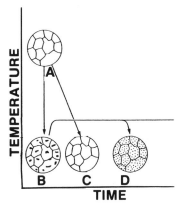

A. SOLID STATE SOLUTION AT ELEVATED TEMPERATURE
B. SLOW COOLING RESULTS IN UNEVEN DISTRIBUTION OF LARGE GRAINS OF HARDENING PHASE
C. QUENCHING RESULTS IN TEMPORARY SOLID STATE SOLUTION AT AMBIENT TEMPERATURE
D. AGING RESULTS IN EVEN DISTRIBUTION OF SUBMICROSCOPIC HARDENING PHASE GRAINS THROUGHOUT ALUMINUM MATRIX

bucked in the dead soft condition—TRICK! For our purposes these ''icebox rivets'' are useless. Because they have a finite storage life (even in dry ice) before they harden, they often appear on the surplus market. They are identifiable by a raised dimple, or dimples, on the rivet head. They cannot be bucked without splitting. Let the buyer beware.

I am aware that all of this may not be terribly clear. Let's consider a copper-based aluminum alloy, such as 2024. At room temperature, less than 1% by weight of copper can remain completely dissolved in aluminum. Just below the melting point of aluminum, however, something more than 5% of copper can be held in solid state solution in the same aluminum. We are aware that if we could evenly disperse 4% by weight of copper, in very fine grains (or crystals) throughout the matrix of aluminum, we would achieve some very desirable physical or mechanical characteristics. The trouble is that, when we try to alloy 4% of copper with molten aluminum, the two metals mix and completely dissolve in each other all right BUT, during the cooling process the copper precipitates out of solution as relatively large lumps that are not particularly evenly distributed throughout the aluminum—somewhat similar to slag inclusions in low-quality carbon steel. The result is a useless lump of expensive metal.

If, however, we heat this useless chunk of metal to a temperature just below the melting point of the aluminum—and hold it there long enough—ALL of the copper will dissolve in the aluminum and it will eventually become evenly dispersed throughout the resultant alloy. If the metal is then quenched the cooling is so rapid that the 75% of the copper that would normally precipitate out of solution just doesn't have time to do so and we have a 4% solution of dissolved copper in aluminum at room temperature; i.e., the aluminum is supersaturated with copper. Of course we cannot fool Mother Nature for very long. Almost immediately the excess copper begins to precipitate out. It will continue to do so at some rate, until the percentage of DISSOLVED copper has been reduced to the maximum that can be held in solution at ambient temperature, a bit less than 1%. The trick is that the copper now precipitates out as almost infinitely small crystals or grains that are very evenly dispersed throughout the aluminum matrix. The result is not actually a solid state solution; it is a combination of a solid state solution and a mechanical mixture. It is, of course, still an alloy.

ALCLAD ALUMINUM

The stronger, heat-treatable aluminum alloys typically display poor resistance to corrosion. To protect sheet which is rolled from these high-strength alloys (including 2024, 6061 and 7075) the metal can be supplied with a very thin coating (or ''cladding'') of pure aluminum which is metallically bonded to both sides of the sheet. The thickness of the pure aluminum (which is highly corrosion resistant) is about 5% of the sheet thickness on each side, or 10% of the total. The mechanical properties of the sheet will be about 6% less than those of an unclad sheet of the same alloy and temper. Although corrosion is not normally one of OUR problems, I normally use alclad sheet, simply because it is easier to polish and to keep looking good.

SUMMARY (SO FAR)

The wrought aluminum alloys are divided into two basic classes: heat-treatable and non-heat-treatable. Non-heat-treatable aluminum alloys have high natural resistance to corrosion and excellent weldability and formability. They are limited to about 40,000 psi ultimate tensile strength and are relatively soft. The heat-treatable aluminum alloys are considerably stronger. In fact, some of them exhibit tensile and yield strengths superior to those of low-carbon steel, making their weight/strength/stiffness ratios very suitable for aircraft and race car structures. Their corrosion resistance is fair. Formability and weldability vary from excellent to impossible depending upon both the alloy and its temper. All of these alloys can, however be purchased in the O or dead-soft condition, formed into the desired shape and THEN heat treated.

ALUMINUM TEMPER DESIGNATIONS

Temper or hardness designators for the wrought aluminum alloys consist of suffixes to the basic four-digit alloy designator. For example, in the designation 6061-T6, 6061 identifies the alloy as an aluminum alloy containing magnesium and silicon. The suffix T6 denotes the degree of hardness, or the ''temper,'' of the alloy. The temper designator also indicates how the temper was obtained. Temper designations differ between the heat-treatable and the non-heat-treatable alloys.

NON-HEAT-TREATABLE ALUMINUM ALLOY TEMPER DESIGNATIONS

F—as fabricated.
O—annealed (dead soft).
H—strain hardened (cold worked) by rolling or stretching. The designation ''H'' is always followed by either two or three digits. The first digit indicates the method used to obtain the temper:

H1 means strain hardened only.

H2 means strain hardened then partially annealed.

H3 means strain hardened, then stabilized by low-temperature heating which slightly lowers the strength and increases the ductility of the alloy. This thermal stabilization is normally done only to those alloys which, unless stabilized, would continue to age-soften at room temperature.

The actual temper is indicated by the second digit, as follows:

2— means ¼ hard
4— means ½ hard
6— means ¾ hard
8— means full hard

Extra digits, if any, merely indicate deviations from standard practice.

Thus Alloy 3003-H14 indicates a manganese-based alloy which has been strain hardened to the ½ hard condition. Alloy 5052-H32 designates a magnesium-based alloy that has been strain hardened to the ¼ hard condition and then thermally stabilized.

HEAT-TREATABLE ALUMINUM ALLOY TEMPER DESIGNATIONS

There are three basic temper designations for the heat-treatable aluminum alloys:
F—as fabricated.
O—annealed (dead soft).
T—heat treated. The letter "T" is always followed by one or more digits which indicate the method or methods used to obtain the temper:

T3—Solution heat treated, cold worked and naturally aged. Alloys in the T3 temper can be bent and moderately stretch formed without significant change to their mechanical properties. Artificial aging (heating) will not cause significant deformation.

T351—Solution heat treated, stress relieved, cold worked and naturally aged.

T4—Solution heat treated, then naturally aged. This temper has essentially the same characteristics as T3 but with slightly inferior mechanical properties due to the lack of cold working.

T6—Solution heat treated, then artificially aged. Sometimes referred to as "fully heat treated" or "precipitation heat treated." Alloys in the T6 condition can be bent (at a suitable bend radius, typically a minimum of 6 times the sheet thickness) without appreciable loss of strength, but very little other forming can be done. They are best not reheated.

T651—Solution heat treated, stress relieved, then artificially aged.

There are more temper designations, but we are not liable to run across them in real life so I see no sense in listing them here.

SPECIFIC NON-HEAT-TREATABLE ALUMINUM ALLOYS

1100 (commercially pure aluminum) is the most corrosion and weather resistant of the alloys. Exceptionally ductile, it is easily worked and is well suited to deep-drawing operations. Widely used for outdoor appliances, it finds little use in racing. Sometimes in the hinterlands when I am unable to locate 3003, I buy 1100 sheet from air-conditioning and roof-gutter installers.

3003 is stronger than 1100 but possesses the same exceptional formability. Almost always used in the H14 condition (½ hard), it is the most widely used of the low-strength, non-heat-treatable alloys. It is easily formed and has excellent welding characteristics, so we can use it for tanks, boxes and tabs, as well as for all of the little angle brackets and whatnots that we are forever making. Its ductility is very high so its fatigue resistance is good, which is a definite advantage when making tanks and brackets. Its mechanical properties are very low indeed—it should never be used for structure.

5052 is somewhat stronger than 3003 and almost as formable. I don't use it much unless I find it cheaply on the surplus market in which case I use it just as I do 3003. About the only specific use for which I normally buy 5052 is for wing skins when the leading edge radius is too tight for me to successfully form from 2024 or 6061. The only temper in which I use 5052 is H32.

SPECIFIC HEAT-TREATABLE ALUMINUM ALLOYS

2024 is the primary aluminum structural alloy of the subsonic aircraft industry. There is a strong possibility that it should also be ours. It is not weldable and it is not very formable, but its tensile strength levels and its stiffness are well above those of any of the other aluminum alloys that can be formed at all. In either the T3 or the T4 condition it demands a bend radius of at least four times the sheet thickness (and six times is better). I, for one, do not find this requirement excessive, or even particularly inconvenient. I use it for most of the structure that I make in the shop—chassis skins, most wing skins, spars (but not ribs). In the field, if the part has to be bent at all, I use 6061. 2024 has exceptional strength and stability at high temperatures. I use it exclusively for my disc brake bells (top hats) and for aluminum flywheels. At the operating temperatures of these components 2024 is considerably better than 7075 which is what most of the better suppliers use. The less-than-better suppliers use 356 cast aluminum and should be shot. Mac Tilton at Tilton Engineering and Robert Kube at RK Precision—who are the BEST suppliers—both use 2024.

6061 is a weldable alloy that has good mechanical properties and is still reasonably formable. For this reason a lot of people who shouldn't do so use it in sheet form for primary race car structure. A quick glance at the values of FIGURES [79] and [80] will illustrate why I don't and you shouldn't. I do use a lot of 6061-T6 extrusions for joining pieces and for corners, and I make most of my fabricated brackets from it. I use it in sheet form for virtually all racetrack repairs simply because it is the strongest of all the aluminum alloys that I can successfully bend over a block and form with a hammer and sandbag.

7075 is the strongest and the stiffest of the commonly available aluminum alloys. It is also the most machinable. In rod and bar form, in the T6 condition, I use it for almost all of the bushings, spacers and the like that we make. I usually use it also for such machined suspension components as steering arms, antiroll bar links and any straight suspension links that I may be making. It machines very well indeed. If I don't use 7075-T6 for these parts I usually use 2024-T351 or T4. 6061-T6 is a viable alternate but it doesn't machine as well. 3003 and 5052 should not be used—they just aren't strong enough. I haven't used much 7075 in sheet form since we stopped using rear spoilers.

FIGURE [79] lists the approximate mechanical properties of the commonly used wrought aluminum alloys. It

Figure (79): Composition, characteristics and applications of common aluminum alloys.

Alloy	Composition (%)	AVAILABLE FORMS*	CORROSION RESISTANCE	MACHINABILITY	WELDABILITY	Minimum Tensile Strength-Annealed (psi)	Maximum Tensile Strength Heat Treated (psi)	Typical Applications
1100	99.00 AL Minimum	B.E.O.S.T.P.W.	A	C	A	13,000	24,000	General Sheet Metal, Spun Parts (Non Structural), Foil
1145	99.45 AL Minimum	S.O	A	C	A	12,000	28,000	Foil, Light Sheet Metal Work
2011	5.5 Cu - 0.5 Bi - 0.5 Pb	B.W	C	A	D	-	60,000	Screw Machine Prods.
2014	4.4 Cu - 0.8 Si - 0.8 Mn - 0.4 Mg	B.E.F.S.T.	C	B	B	27,000	70,000	Forged and Extruded Truck Frames, Aircraft Structure
2017	2.5 Cu - 0.3 Mg	BW	C	B	B	-	62,000	Screw Machine Prods.
2018	4.0 Cu - 2.0 Ni - 0.6 Mg	F	C	B	B	-	61,000	Forged Pistons, Aircraft Cylinders
2024	4.5 Cu - 1.5 Mg - 0.6 Mn	B.E.P.S.T.W.	C	B	B	27,000	75,000	Aircraft & Racecar Structure, Truck Wheels, Screw Machine Prods.
3003	1.2 Mn	All Forms	A	C	A	16,000	30,000	Sheet Metal Work, Cooking Utensils Chemical Eqpt.
3004	1.2 Mn - 1.0 Mg	All Forms	A	C	A	26,000	41,000	Sheet Metal Work Storage Tanks
4043	5.0 Si	W	-	-	-	-	-	Welding Wire
5052	2.5 Mg - 0.2 Cr	B.P.O.S.T.W.	A	C	A	28,000	39,000	Sheet Metal (Non Structural) Appliances, Hydraulics
6151	1.0 Si - 0.7 Mg - 0.25 Cr	F	A	C	A	-	48,000	Moderate Strength Forgings
6061	1.0 Mg - .65 Si - .25 Cu - .25 Cr	B.E.F.P.S.T.W.	A	B	A	18,000	45,000	Truck & Marine Parts, Corrosion Resistant Structures, Pipelines, Racecars
6063	0.7 Mg - 0.4 Si	T.P.E.	A	C	A	13,000	42,000	Furniture, Railings
7075	5.6 Zn - 2.5 Mg - 1.6 Cu - 0.5 Cr	B.E.F.S.T.W.	C	B	P	33,000	83,000	Aircraft Structural Components
7076	7.52 Zn - 1.5 Mg - 0.6 Cu - 0.5 Mn	F	C	B	D	-	70,000	Hi Strength Forgings
7178	6.8 Zn - 2.7 Mg - 2.5 Cu - .30 Cr	E.P.S.T.	C	B	D	33,000	88,000	Aircraft Structural Components
7079	4.32 Zn - 3.3 Mg - 0.6 Cu - 0.2 Mn	E.F.S.	C	B	D	32,000	78,000	Aircraft Structural Components

*Available Forms: B = Bar & Rod, E = Extrusion, F = Forging Stock, O = Foil, P = Pipe,
S = Sheet, T = Tube, W = Wire
Characteristic Ratings: A = Excellent B = Good C = Fair D = Not Suitable

contains a lot of interesting information which we do not commonly require. FIGURE [80], on the other hand, lists the information that we DO require about those alloys that we are realistically interested in. (There are two charts because I tried to combine them and failed.)

ALUMINUM TUBE AND EXTRUDED SHAPES

Aluminum in various alloys is drawn, or extruded, into tubing, pipe and a large variety of structural shapes, angles, tees, channels, hats, zees, I-beams and such. We use the tube for coolant water, wing spars, wing mounts and the like. For water tube I use either 3003-H14 round drawn tube or (if it must be bent a lot) 5052-O round drawn tube. For straight runs I use 0.035'' wall. If it must be bent I increase the wall as necessary to accommodate the stretching that will take place on the outside of the bend. To be perfectly honest, when I need a bend in a water tube, and I am in L.A., I go by my friendly genius tube-bender's shop and dig through his scrap bin until I find what I need. I then weld it onto a straight run. I also carry a selection of his scrapped (not up to his or the aerospace industry's standards but plenty good enough for us) bends around with me. One more reason that I live in L.A. For wing spars and mounting tubes I use 6061-T6.

Extruded aluminum shapes, intelligently chosen and used, make great corner joints for tubs (after Ron Tauranac showed us what idiots we were for using formed and/or welded bulkheads). The trick here is to use only aircraft extrusions which feature a generous radius in the inside corner—as opposed to industrial or hardware store extrusions which generally do not. The best alloy available in extrusion—and the only one to use for structure—is 6061 in the T6 condition. If the extrusion IS 6061-T6, it will be so identified. In the larger sizes the extruded channels make perfectly acceptable rear cross-members (again my thanks to Mr. Tauranac). When I really appreciate the extruded shapes though, is when I have to fix a bent tub in a big hurry. A largish extruded angle blind riveted into the interior corners of a hastily straightened tub or a tee riveted across a bulkhead can do wonders for one's peace of mind. I buy the stuff surplus and I carry a reasonable selection of it around with me. This emergency supply has saved my butt (and those of my friends) many times.

CAST ALUMINUM

It is unlikely that any of my readers are going to need to have castings made. I will therefore not discuss either the techniques or the alloys except to point out that the best general-purpose cast aluminum alloy for our purposes is

Figure (80): Approximate mechanical properties of selected wrought aluminum alloys.

Alloy	Temper	Formability	Weldability	Machinability	Strength (psi) Ultimate	Yield	Shear	% Elongation in 2 Inches	Endurance Limit (psi)
3003	H-14	A	A	D	22,000	21,000	14,000	18%	8,000
5052	H-32	B	A	C	33,000	28,000	20,000	12%	17,000
	H-34	B	A	C	38,000	31,000	21,000	10%	15,000
2024	0	A	F	D	26,000	11,000	18,000	20%	13,000
	T3	C	F	B	65,000	45,000	40,000	18%	20,000
	T4T351	C	F	B	64,000	42,000	40,000	19%	20,000
6061	0	A	A	D	18,000	8,000	12,000	25%	9,000
	T4-T451	C	A	C	35,000	21,000	24,000	22%	14,000
	T6-T651	C	A	C	45,000	40,000	30,000	12%	14,000
7075	0	A	F	D	33,000	15,000	-	17%	?
	T6-T651	D	F	B	83,000	73,000	51,000	11%	23,000
Mg AZ31B	H-24	F	A	A	42,000	39,000	29,000	14%	

Note: Figures are for bars or bare sheets. Alclad sheets are about 6% lower in strength.

356 in the T6 condition. This is sort of the cast equivalent of 6061 and is pretty good stuff. What I WILL point out is that there are a lot of race cars out there with aftermarket aluminum bellhousings and quite a few with cast aluminum hub carriers, as well as a lot of stock cars and road-racing sedans with aluminum hubs. The hubs and hub carriers will fail only due to a crash or just plain old age. The same is pretty much true of differential carriers. The bell housings, on the other hand, are forever cracking, simply due to lousy mechanical design.

All of these parts are made from 356 aluminum, which is eminently weldable—by an expert with a heliarc. Cracks and fractures must be ground out to a deep vee that is actually pretty close to being an equilateral triangle in cross-section. The castings must be both preheated and slow cooled. They should also be re-heat-treated upon completion of the repair. Enough said on the subject, except to state that it helps a lot to weld stiffening webs onto badly designed bellhousings. It's easier to buy a good one to start with. Good ones have stiffening webs in arrangements that make intuitive sense; bad ones do not.

MAGNESIUM

Magnesium is the lightest structural material available to the average racer. It has good mechanical strength and stiffness so, properly used, magnesium can provide strong structures with excellent strength- and stiffness-to-weight ratios. Magnesium alloys are the best machining of all of the structural metals and most of them possess excellent welding, forging and casting characteristics. Unfortunately magnesium sheet is formable only at elevated temperatures so it is a mite impractical for many of our fabrication applications—besides, people are afraid of the fire risk.

That a fire risk DOES exist is undeniable. What many people do not realize is just how slight that risk really is. In dust or powder form or in the form of thin shavings (as in lathe swarf) mag can be truly nasty stuff. It can be set off by a spark or simply by the heat generated by a cutting tool at the wrong speed or feed rate. The resulting fire is about as intense as anything we are liable to experience. In solid form, however, it is such a good conductor of heat that it is very difficult indeed to set alight. This is just as well as it is almost impossible to put out once it HAS caught fire. We all know the horror stories of the magnesium fires at Le Mans and at Clermont-Ferrand, and we have all seen the photos. What we should bear in mind is that in every case that I know of involving a racing car magnesium fire, the magnesium fire has been started by a fuel fire and it was the fuel fire that did the killing. It is my contention that dead is dead. All the mag does is to make the fuel fire harder to extinguish.

The aircraft industry uses mag all over the place and they are every bit as frightened by the specter of fire as racers are—they are just a bit more rational about it. It has always seemed a bit strange to me that the same people who think that I am some kind of callous criminal because I use sheet magnesium in some selected places think nothing of building a car with an aluminum tube roll cage or using a parachute harness instead of a proper safety harness . . .

Anyway, I tend to use AZ 31 magnesium sheet in the H24 condition for cover plates and for flat panels when I am really concerned with weight. I make my engine, wing- and suspension-mounting plates from the same alloy in plate form. Its tensile strengths are roughly comparable with those of aluminum alloy 6061-T6, but it is somewhat stiffer and its formability at room temperature is very poor.

Where mag is really useful, though, is in sand castings. We normally use AZ91C, an alloy of magnesium, aluminum and zinc which combines good castability and weldability with moderately high tensile strength (ultimate tensile strength in the T6 condition is about 40,000 psi with a yield of about 34,000). The English use an alloy that they call "Electron C," which has somewhat higher mechanical strength but is not as weldable. All of the cast magnesium uprights, rack housings, oil pans and so on ARE weldable—but I don't know a lot of people who are both able and willing to do it. The best that I know of are Pete Wilkins, Mark Bohner, Quinn Epperly, Bill Eaton and Nye Frank—all in L.A.; if you need a mag casting welded in the boondocks I wish you luck.

TIP

Magnesium, especially when exposed to salt air, has a nasty tendency to corrode from the inside, where you can't see it, forming a sort of a magnesium sponge. The little white spots that you see on your gearbox casing and on your uprights after you have washed them are indicators. Under normal conditions it takes years for this corrosion to cause any significant damage—but these are expensive and critical pieces, so why take the chance? All I do is spray the castings, inside and out, with WD-40 at weekly intervals or whenever they have been wet. It keeps them looking good and positively prevents corrosion. It also costs nothing and takes no time at all. One does, however, have to be a bit careful in order to avoid spraying the WD-40 onto the brakes. . . .

TITANIUM

For some years now many racers have regarded titanium as some sort of a wonder metal—combining the strength of high-alloy steels with the weight of aluminum (and the price of gold). In some respects, at least, all of the above are true! The trouble is that, for the racer at least, the numbers simply do not add up; titanium is not a practical material for us. Some years from now my grandchildren are going to read this and not believe I said that—just as I have trouble with the fact that aluminum was a wonder material to MY grandfather.

Oxides of titanium comprise about 0.5% of the earth's crust; every ton of matter on earth contains 10 lb of titanium. This "exotic" metal is, then, from 50 to 300 times more plentiful in nature than such "common" metals as copper, lead or zinc. As an oxide it is in common use as a whitening pigment for paint. In fact, every Detroit ring-and-pinion set comes with a tiny tube of titanium dioxide for use as a setup paste. Plentiful though its oxides may be, titanium is the most difficult of all metals to produce. The liquid metal is the closest thing to a universal solvent since the creation of sea water. It dissolves most refractory materials and is contaminated by the rest. What is more, it is almost impossible to remove contaminants that may be picked up during the refining process. Further, the molten metal reacts violently with oxygen so the whole process has to be conducted under vacuum. Hardly any fun at all—and reason enough for the price of the stuff. What's more, the finished product is difficult to machine, difficult to weld and difficult to form (although some of the alloys DO forge well).

The obvious question is, "Why bother with the stuff at all?" The answer is that, as a structural material, titanium has some interesting characteristics that are virtually unique (and which make all the fuss and bother worthwhile) to the aerospace industry, the sea space industry and to very well financed racing teams. First and foremost, titanium, in some of its alloys possesses the highest strength-to-weight and stiffness-to-weight ratios of all structural metals. Further it combines these characteristics with fatigue properties higher than any of the other nonferrous metals. Lastly, although this is not of direct interest to the racer, its mechanical characteristics and strength at extremely high temperatures are outstanding, which is the main reason that it has found such popularity in aerospace.

TITANIUM AND THE AEROSPACE INDUSTRY

It is estimated that the saving of 1 lb of weight in a jet engine will result in the ultimate saving of from 6 to 8 lb in the total aircraft. The use of titanium in gas turbine engines—as forged turbine blades, vanes, compressor discs and housings, fasteners, shrouds and fire shields—saved well over 1000 lb per engine in the days before the fan jets (I cannot come up with any current information). Multiply that by 4 engines and it becomes pretty evident why aerospace loves the stuff—initial cost be damned! Its use is by no means confined to engines; it is used as primary structure and outer skins for hypersonic aircraft simply because it is the only metal that can withstand the heat generated by hypersonic flight. Titanium fasteners are coming into extended use because, in addition to its strength-to-weight ratio, high resistance to corrosion and outstanding strength at elevated temperatures, the metal happens to exhibit a very high ratio of tensile strength to shear strength—and most fasteners are (or should be) installed in shear.

TITANIUM AND THE RACER

If I had unlimited financial backing I would probably be using quite a bit of titanium. I would also be spending A LOT of time talking with the engineers and metallurgists who produce the stuff. Among the "cost no object" uses that I can see are:

Forged hubs (live axles)
Brake disc top hats
Tubular and sheet suspension linkage fabrications
Threaded fasteners
Exhaust systems

EXHAUST SYSTEMS

One of the remarkable features of titanium is that, in "commercially pure" form, titanium tube sand-bends very well indeed, and is remarkably resistant to fatigue from vibration. The very best racing exhaust systems that I have ever seen were sand-bent by Pete Wilkins years ago for Dan Gurney's Eagles and, later, for Pete's early customers (he won't do it any more—at any price). If I were having an exhaust system made today and I could afford the tubing, I would use commercially pure titanium. The finished system is considerably lighter than 321 stainless, infinitely lighter than mild steel, much stronger at elevated temperatures and virtually fatigue proof.

MACHINED PARTS

I can think of no valid reason why I would ever want to machine normal race car parts from titanium. In their stronger forms, all of the titanium alloys are exceptionally notch sensitive. This simply means that fatigue cracks are very liable to start at any sort of surface imperfection, like stone chips, drop marks or tool scratches. This may be ok for military aircraft but I do not want to know about notch-sensitive parts on a race car for which I am responsible. Besides, the stuff is expensive to buy, difficult (and therefore expensive) to machine and has a nasty tendency to gall on steel. Pass! The obvious exception would be hubs if I could afford them. By their very nature, race car hubs are protected from the accidental creation of stress raisers (assuming that the bearings are installed properly—in this case by warming the bearings, cooling the hub and making sure that the titanium is coated with a protective agent so that the bearing cannot gall).

FASTENERS

The aerospace industry uses a lot of titanium-threaded fasteners. They are just as strong as alloy steel parts in tension and stronger in shear, AND they are a lot lighter. Further, they lose very little of their strength at either very high or very low temperatures. The first characteristics would seem to make them ideal for OUR use—and so they would be if that were the end of the story. It is not! The fact that titanium tends to gall on steel can be overcome by the coatings on the bolt and the religious use of antiseize. This tendency also makes the use of titanium nuts mandatory with titanium bolts. The problem lies in the simple fact that, unlike aircraft bolts, OUR bolts come in and out a lot—and in so doing they tend to get scratched (we all know that the proper procedure is to HOLD the bolt and TURN the nut, but sometimes this is simply not possible). The characteristic notch sensitivity of the basic material then makes titanium fasteners, in my opinion, poorly suited to race car use by the average racing team. So does the cost.

WELDING

Titanium, because of its extreme reaction with oxygen when in its molten state, MUST be welded in a chamber which has been purged of air and filled with an inert gas, usually argon. When titanium first appeared on the race car scene (in the late 1960's), those favored few who were given free supplies by the manufacturers as a promotional campaign were all instructed in the proper welding techniques. Because the material was new and everyone was scared to death of it, the instructions were obeyed and failures due to bad welds were virtually unknown. Familiarity, as always, has bred contempt. A great many fabricators will now tell you that the necessity for welding titanium in a chamber is nonsense; that any GOOD welder can weld the stuff with a normal TIG welder with the argon turned up. NO WAY! Don't even think about it! Sound and uncontaminated welds in titanium can ONLY be produced in an inert welding chamber.

The chambers are not difficult to make; temporary ones can be made from plywood and garbage bags. They are, however, expensive to fill and purge so it is best to plan ahead. Anyway, if you are contemplating welding titanium, contact the titanium manufacturer for detailed instructions and make a real chamber. Further, make it large enough to hold anything that you might want to make, plus some, so that you can place an hour or so worth of welding inside and not have to repurge at the end of every bead.

HONEYCOMB

In the 1950's sandwich panels composed of aluminum face skins bonded to a core of hexagonal-shaped "honeycomb" formed from aluminum foil became popular in aircraft component design. The honeycomb core effectively formed continuous shear webs between the face skins, resulting in very light panels of exceptional stiffness which were capable of carrying extreme loads with very little deflection (so long as the loads were spread over large areas). Properly designed, these panels were very effective as floors and bulkheads in both commercial and military aircraft.

In 1966 the Ford J car, later to become the Ford GT Mark IV, burst upon the scene with its innovative aluminum honeycomb chassis structure. The fact that we won Le Mans with it in 1967 was a tribute to development over design and nothing whatsoever to do with the fact that the tub was honeycomb. In fact, the use of honeycomb in this pioneering instance was detrimental to the effort for several reasons:

(1) By the time that we got a satisfactory roll-over cage in the beast, along with satisfactory corner joins, it was not significantly lighter than the steel monocoque that it replaced.

(2) Relocation of inboard suspension pivot points was difficult, making development slower than it needed to be.

(3) Repairs in the field were reasonably close to impossible.

The Mark IV was not only the first significant racing car to use honeycomb for major structure (until the advent of "ground effects" and the development of the "tunnel car"), it was also the LAST. When Colin Chapman set the racing world on its ear for the last time with tunnels, everyone immediately understood the advantages of a very narrow tub (very wide tunnels). In the ensuing scramble for more and more downforce, most of the designers forgot all about torsional rigidity (as well as geometry) and the years of madness were upon us.

Some of the better designers achieved extremely good torsional rigidity with very narrow structures by the INTELLIGENT use of honeycomb. Others preferred to continue with traditional, fabricated aluminum tubs, while John Barnard pioneered the use of integral carbon composite tubs. Properly done, they all work—although the useful life of the sheet aluminum tubs is limited by the fact that they do "loosen up" pretty quickly (see the section on fatigue).

I am not at all convinced that the aluminum honeycomb tub is a viable device for the "kit car" racing car that the American market demands. I will admit that IF the design is clever enough so that ALL of the suspension pickup points are bolt-on substructures and IF the joining of the honeycomb to both itself and the bulkheads is done correctly, AND IF the loads from the engine/transaxle/rear suspension are properly fed into the main chassis structure, then the aluminum honeycomb tub is at least as repairable with regard to minor damage as the fabricated aluminum item. I will also admit that the honeycomb tub SHOULD be cheaper to produce (although this last statement is definitely NOT confirmed by the relative prices of Ralt, Anson and Dart tubs at the moment).

My objection in this regard is that, unlike the fabricated tub, in the event of MAJOR damage, the honeycomb tub is a complete "throw away." I am aware that this is not an item of any real importance to the average Formula car racer in this country who regards ANY chassis as a throwaway item. However, there are a number (admittedly a small number) of shops in this country that both can and will repair fabricated tubs to a state as good or even better than new at a fraction of the replacement cost (this is made possible by the simple fact that the replacement cost of any English tub includes an enormous amount of money for air freight). There is NO ONE who offers the same service for honeycomb tubs, nor is there liable to be.

My further objections center around the difficulty of working with the stuff and the endless opportunities for improper fabrication procedures to cause giant problems down the road. Reinforcing corner joints with pop-riveted

0.049'' aluminum sheet is, in my opinion, just not good enough. When a fabricator decides to rout and fold (or radius bend) aluminum honeycomb to be used for structure by himself—without advice and consent from the manufacturer—I, for one, do not want to know about it. Nor do I want to know about "homemade" honeycomb, a method of producing honeycomb panels with simple curvature by bonding commercial aluminum honeycomb core to pre-shaped aluminum sheets. In this case proper bonding is beyond the scope of the racer/fabricator.

HONEYCOMB AND FIBERGLASS

So, if I do not like the idea of honeycomb tubs, where do I like it? Paper honeycomb stiffens the bejesus out of large expanses of unsupported fiberglass (or Kevlar) at virtually no cost in weight. This gets to be very important indeed when we are talking about ground effects vehicles. Flat panels of honeycomb, either aluminum or glass, make really light and stiff tunnel sides and roofs (again for ground effects cars). Aluminum honeycomb installed with the cells longitudinally oriented makes just about the most efficient energy-absorbing "crushable structure" that I know of (a Tony Cicale original, now adopted by Ralt).

Where I would like to play with honeycomb, though, is in the "hybrid composite" field—very stiff and very light sandwiches made from honeycomb cores of Dupont's Nomex bonded to composite face skins. This type of honeycomb construction has pretty much replaced the original aluminum type in the aerospace industry for these reasons:

(1) The aluminum face skins are, as we have noted, very susceptible to damage. Further, any damage to the skin will almost certainly be transmitted to the core—and such damage is very difficult to repair. Composite face skins, on the other hand, tend to localize impact damage, and both the composite face skins and the Nomex cores are relatively easy to repair.

(2) While shaping and joining of aluminum honeycomb panels are difficult and expensive (and the shaping is extremely limited), both the pre-preg composite face skins and the Nomex honeycomb can be "draped" to predetermined contours during layup. Further, while aluminum honeycomb core must be either frozen into a block of ice or filled with wax before it can be either sawed or milled, the Nomex core can be cut and machined with normal tools and procedures.

(3) The panels are almost corrosion proof, they are nonflammable, nontoxic and they are damned good insulators.

All of this leads me to believe that we could make very good use of Nomex-cored, composite-skinned honeycomb panels for major structure in our racing cars. If I were to be given a commission to design a new car I would look into it pretty thoroughly, particularly as Dupont has a history of being very helpful with design information concerning new uses for their advanced products. As with ALL major structure I would go to some length to design suspension pickup points as bolt-on shear plates; both to discourage crash damage from affecting the integrity of the structure and to allow for relatively simple geometry changes.

COMPOSITE MATERIALS

McLarens (the original trio of Bruce McLaren, Tyler Alexander and Teddy Mayer) started it when they formed their first Formula One tub from a composite sandwich composed of face skins of aluminum sheet bonded to a core of edge-grained balsa wood called MALLITE. The result was a primary structure of unparalleled torsional stiffness and limited practicality. They also seconded the trend when they underlaid a grid of carbon-fiber yarn to the fiberglass body panels of their Can-Am bodywork to stiffen it. Tony Cicale carried it on with the Kevlar body panels of the Cicale 2-liter but ever since John Barnard decided to mold the first of the new generation McLaren Formula One tubs from a carbon-fiber/epoxy resin composite, the enthusiast (lunatic fringe?) press has been filled with (usually) not very well-researched articles on the new wonder material. I've got news: Composite materials are not new and, while they certainly open up some fascinating new roads for the structural engineer to explore, "wonder materials" they are not.

When the word "composite" first came into engineering use, it was used to describe a STRUCTURE, not a material. A composite structure was simply one manufactured from two different materials in such a way that one material made up for some shortcomings of the other so that the final product would perform better than if it had been made from either material by itself. Thus a wooden barrel whose staves are hooped with wrought iron is a composite structure, as is Earl's Supply's stainless-steel-braid-reinforced hose. Let us not, however, play word games. As the term is currently used, a composite material consists of very thin fibers (or filaments) of an element which are arranged in a specific orientation with regard to each other and are combined in a unitary structure by being embedded in and held together by some sort of a matrix. Typically the material consists of fibers or filaments of an element whose fibers exhibit great tensile strength but, by themselves, lack rigidity. Truth to tell, wood is a composite material. Wood consists of thin fibers of cellulose cemented together by and contained within a matrix of lignin. Fiberglass is a more modern example of a truly useful, if not particularly exotic, composite material—thin fibers or filaments of hard and strong but easily scratched and brittle drawn glass in a plastic matrix of polyester or epoxy resins. For that matter the humble sun-dried adobe brick, reinforced with fibers of straw, is a true composite, and some of the ancient Pueblos are still standing.

WHAT IT'S ALL ABOUT: THE BEHAVIOR OF SINGLE CRYSTALS AND THIN FILAMENTS

You will recall from Chapter One that metallurgists have long known that, theoretically at least, single crystals of various elements exhibit tensile strengths far in excess of actual specimens of the materials. This difference in strength between the theoretical (calculated from the strength of the atomic bonds holding the unit crystal cells together) and the actual, measured, performance of the materials are attributed to the influence of grain boundaries and structural imperfections on the behavior of a polycrystalline solid. As an example of the range of strengths under discussion, a single crystal of iron can exhibit an ultimate tensile strength of 1,900,000 psi, whereas pure iron in polycrystalline form has about 4000 psi. The numbers for graphite are 3,000,000 psi and 40,000 psi. In almost all cases the stiffness of the material rises with the tensile strength. Further, single crystals typically exhibit very large ranges of elastic deformation, remaining elastic under as much as 4%-5% strain as compared to the normal range (for metals) which fail at elastic strains of approximately 0.1%. This means that, if we could figure out some practical way to utilize single crystals in structures, we could create some very strong and very stiff structures indeed. This has been realized for a long time. Research into the field has been divided into two areas: single-crystal metallurgy and composite materials. We will deal with single-crystal metallurgy first, and very briefly.

It is now possible to force the growth of metallic single crystals into small structural shapes. This is done by tricking good old Mother Nature at very low temperatures. It is not a cheap process and not all metals lend themselves to this sort of alchemy. Currently the most practical use of single-crystal metallurgy that I know of is the formation of immensely strong jet engine turbine blades as single crystals of titanium or tungsten. At present WE do not need to know any more about the process, which is just as well as we are not going to find out very much more than just that.

FIBER REINFORCEMENT OF METALS

Single-crystal structures are difficult and expensive to come by, but thin fibers or filaments of many elements, including some metals, are not that tricky to produce and they are almost as strong as single crystals. Some decades ago, when the extraordinary strength and stiffness of thin fibers was first being realized, the metallurgists figured out that if some practical way could be found to intersperse the hardening elements of our structural metal alloys into the matrix as fibers rather than as particles, not only would the fibers be strong in themselves but the ductile metal matrix would be able to really grab hold of the relatively long fibers with their greater and more continuous surface area and stronger and stiffer alloys with greater ranges of elastic deformation would result. FIGURE [81] illustrates the idea.

A great deal of research has been done in this area, particularly with alloys of aluminum and copper (the 7xxx series). So far as I can determine, to date there has been no practical success. In fact metallic filaments (or whiskers) have generally proven, so far at least, to be unsatisfactory materials chiefly because they are very susceptible to sur-face oxidation which causes dislocations to appear in their crystal structure. And they are very intolerant of structural imperfections. Some of the nonmetals—chiefly carbon and boron—do not exhibit this unfortunate tendency and can be manufactured in long, continuous filaments which can then be spun into threads and woven into cloth. So it is in this area of nonmetallic fibers that the successful development of composite structural materials has come about.

This section of the book purports to be about metallurgy. Most of the composite materials in which we are directly interested are nonmetallic. This provides me with a very tempting copout. None-the-less we are going to discuss them here and now. First, though, you should read or re-read the articles that Paul Van Valkenburgh did in ON TRACK from August to December 1982, the only well-informed and articulate words on the subject that I have seen published in the motorsport press.

COMPOSITES—WHAT THEY ARE

What we are talking about here is a series of very fine fibers or filaments, in our case either of carbon or of Kevlar (a Dupont aramid), spun into thread and then woven in some definite relationship to each other and saturated with an epoxy resin. Exposed to either a catalyst or to predetermined amounts of pressure and temperature the epoxy resin cures and the result is a strong and stiff sheet or laminate structure of composite material. In their simplest forms the techniques are similar to fiberglass layups and the results are similar, but a lot stronger and stiffer per unit weight.

Figure (81): Reinforcing effect in precipitation-hardened material and in fiber-reinforced material. Greater surface area of fibers gives better matrix adhesion than particulate-hardening phases. *Metals In The Modern World* by Edward Slate, Doubleday and Company, 1968.

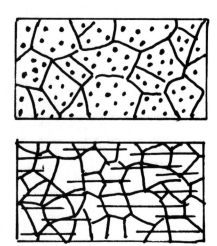

THE RESINS

Without the matrix of resins, the filaments would be just a bunch of threads—strong threads, but far too delicate and flexible for structural use (Kevlar sails are the hot ticket in sailboat racing these days). The resin is necessary to retain the fibers in their proper orientation to each other, to protect them from damage, to bond them together into a strong and stiff structure, and to bond laminates together into predetermined thicknesses. The qualities of the resin are critical to the mechanical characteristics of the finished composite. The resin must perform several functions:

(1) It must be strongly adhesive AND plastic so as to grab and hold the fibers so that the matrix CAN TRANSMIT STRESS TO THE FIBERS.

(2) It must be relatively soft so that it cannot damage (i.e., scratch) the fibers.

(3) It must be so designed that, when the cured composite material is stressed in tension, the STRAINS in the filaments and the STRAINS in the matrix will be very close to equal. Since the matrix will flow in a plastic fashion, the STRESS in the filaments will thus be many thousands of times that in the matrix. In fact, standard practice is to ignore the strength of the matrix in the design of composite structures.

(4) It must be able to perform all of these functions at the temperatures and in the environment to which the composite will be exposed in service.

(5) It would be nice if the resin were nontoxic.

However, the resins are largely a necessary evil in that, while the resin can contribute little to the strength of the completed structure, it will inevitably comprise at least ⅓ of its weight (½ is actually a more typical figure). What this means is that when we are discussing the strengths and the stiffnesses of composite materials, we are actually talking about the combined strength and stiffness of the fibers AND the resins. Since the resins (even the epoxies which are a hell of a lot stronger than the polyesters) have virtually NO strength or stiffness, then a 50% mix of fiber and epoxy will have a maximum strength to weight ratio of 50%

of that of the fibers alone. In actuality it will have less than that because the fiber orientation will not be perfect and neither will the wetting of the fibers by the resin. We are, however, still talking about some pretty impressive numbers and properties.

Little more than a decade ago the available epoxy resins were thermal- and pressure-setting only and there was no hope for us (the racers). The best of them still are, but catalyst-curing epoxies are now available that are pretty damned good. As near as I can tell, Burt Rutan did (or at least caused) most of the development in the course of designing and developing his state-of-the-art foam and fiberglass composite home-built aircraft. There are also pressure/thermal-setting resins available that cure at temperatures as low as 200 degrees F. While ALL of the temperature-curing resins require pressure during the cure, for optimum results so do the catalyst-curing resins. The pressures required by some of the new ones are attainable by the use of simple vacuum bags (the best instructions for vacuum bagging that I have seen are in Pazmany's LIGHT AIRPLANE CONSTRUCTION). The new generation of epoxy resins, unlike the originals, is also unlikely to kill you or even to remove the skin from your hands, a notable step forward.

FIBER ORIENTATION

One of the advantages to fiber composite construction is that the fibers can be directionally oriented within the structure to take maximum advantage of their strength. This is just as well, as the strength of composite materials is highly directional. The filaments themselves, while exhibiting outstanding tensile strength and stiffness, are only so-so in compression and somewhere in between in shear strength. The manufacturers can supply the cloth in any fiber arrangement from unidirectional as shown by FIGURE [82] with upwards of 90% of the fibers parallel to the long axis of the piece and only 5%-10% holding the unidirectional fibers in orientation until the resin sets up. The familiar 50/50 weave is illustrated by FIGURE [83].

Figure (82): Unidirectional woven cloth. Aircraft Spruce and Specialty Company.

Figure (83): Bidirectional woven cloth. Aircraft Spruce and Specialty Company.

This variety allows a laminate structure to be designed so that the orientation of the fibers allows the major loads to be translated into tensile stress in the filaments. As an example, if we were designing a leaf spring to be molded from a composite, we would use a unidirectional weave. Rutan's wing spars consist of spanwise channels cut into the foam cores of his wings, filled with a unidirectional fiberglass in epoxy resin layup and bonded to the outer skins which are also fiberglass in epoxy layups—but with both unidirectional (spanwise) and 50/50 (at 45 degrees to the span) layers. I should point out at this stage that the 50/50 weave "drapes" onto compound curves reasonably well and that the unidirectional cloths do not. Bidirectional cloth is usually oriented at 45 degrees to the axis of the major stress expected in the part being laid up, especially if torsional stress is expected.

THE LAYUP—WET OR PRE-PREG

Like it or not, most of us are familiar with the wet layup process of producing fiberglass parts. Some of us are even pretty good at it. Composites CAN be handled the same way, and for the production of body panels, wings and so on, they usually are. Typically the composites are harder to handle in a wet layup situation—they are harder to saturate than fiberglass, they don't "drape" as well and they are harder to cut. Actually, carbon fiber cuts pretty easily before it cures simply because the individual fibers are brittle and break off cleanly. Kevlar cuts reasonably well with hardened shears before curing, but should be final trimmed while the resin is still tacky because trying to cut it after it has cured will result in a frayed edge. The other difficulty with wet layups of composite fibers is that the inevitable air bubbles are much harder to see than they are with fiberglass, so resin saturation is harder to achieve and voids are harder to avoid.

Aside from the fact that it is a nasty, messy job, the major problem with wet layups of composites is that it is almost impossible to wind up with both the optimum final resin percentage AND complete wetting (and therefore bonding) of the fibers. Either we end up with too much resin and a heavier and more brittle than necessary layup or we end up with air pockets, voids and unbonded areas. Just as with fiberglass the only answer is seemingly endless and very careful squeegeeing out of the excess resin, which is no fun at all. Even with good planning and skillfull application, it is almost impossible to reduce the resin content of a wet layup below 50% by weight. This is a great pity as the optimum makeup is about 25%-30% resin.

Aerospace does not use wet layups. Aerospace uses pre-preg sheets (woven cloths in various orientations which have been preimpregnated with the proper percentage of resin) for complete wetting and optimum final results. They are available in any conceivable combination of cloth, fiber orientation and resin. The resins used are all thermal setting and their shelf life is limited. Some of thermal setting resins cure at 200-250 degrees F (attainable in home ovens for small parts and with heat lamps and care for large ones).

Anyway, the pre-preg sheets are trimmed and laid in place in or on the mold just as in a wet layup.

I have no intention whatsoever of going into either finite element design or into the how-tos of layups and vacuum bagging. Paul Van Valkenburgh covered finite element design very well in his ON TRACK articles and Ladislo Pazmany covered layup and vacuum bagging as well as it can be covered in his LIGHT AIRCRAFT CONSTRUCTION FOR AMATEUR BUILDERS. Aircraft Spruce also carries some instruction books and manuals; Rutan's are particularly worthwhile.

THE UNSUNG JOYS OF COMPOSITES

We all know that the composites are both strong and stiff for their weight. What is not generally realized is that, because individual fibers can rupture without resulting in significant reduction in the overall strength of the composite, they are also remarkably insensitive to localized damage. There are several reasons for this remarkable behavior:

(1) Obviously a broken fiber of whatever material is not capable of supporting any load at all at the point where it is broken. With the composites, however, since the fiber is long and its entire length is embedded in an adhesive and plastic matrix of cured resins, a little way from the point of rupture this same fiber is at its original strength and the matrix can transmit loads to the unbroken portion of the fiber just as if the break had not occurred.

(2) The rupture is highly unlikely to propagate as a crack, both because the fibers react to stress as individuals and because the plastic matrix is not capable of transmitting cracks.

(3) Even if lots of fibers rupture, it is very unlikely that they will do so along a common plane.

FILAMENT WINDING

In addition to mold layups of various sorts, there is another option available to the composite designer. For tubular structures, filaments impregnated with heat- and pressure-curing epoxy resins can be wound around a removable mandrel in such a fashion that both the angular orientation of the fibers and the thickness of the laminate can be controlled so as to best accommodate expected variation in service loads. This is the way in which missile bodies and automotive drive shafts are constructed and the result (of proper design) is a truly elegant and efficient structure. This is not a home-builder or race-shop technique. I can, however, foresee a lot of filament-wound composite race car components down the road.

CARBON FOR BRAKES

Carbon has the highest melting point of all known elements—6300 degrees F. Suitably configured, reinforced carbon makes outstanding brake discs and pads. It is not at all bothered by the heat generated as we convert our cars' kinetic energy of motion into heat energy, and it is much lighter than any other material that will do the job. Strictly speaking the carbon/carbon brakes made famous by the Brabham team are not composites, they are "carbon-fiber-reinforced carbon" (CFRC) structures. Paul Van Valkenburgh beat me to it on this one (in the before-mentioned ON TRACK series) and, since no one outside of the defense/military complex knows more about the stuff than what he had to say, I guess I will have to leave it at that—but get ready; they ARE coming.

COMPOSITES IN OUR WORLD

Structures molded from composite materials are all very well in the giant-bucks worlds of aerospace and Formula One—but what about us? I really don't have a very good answer. It should be pretty obvious that WE are very unlikely to make carbon-fiber tubs—even if we wanted to. At the time of writing I am not tempted to do so simply because I am not willing to trade the energy-absorbing qualities of a well-designed and well-fabricated aluminum tub for the weight saving and stiffness of a composite tub. During a recent conversation with a highly respected specialist in composites I brought this point up. He stated that he was aware of the problem and that what we had to do was to learn to absorb impact by CONTROLLED FRACTURE rather than by plastic deformation—but that we had not yet figured out how to do it. The combination of Kevlar and carbon fiber into a structure also holds out some hope in the energy-absorption department.

God (and anyone who has read either of my previous books) knows that I am in favor of the torsionally rigid chassis. I am not at all against the composite tub. I merely think that it needs a bit of a rethink from the safety aspect.

Personally I believe that what we need for the moment is auxiliary energy-absorbing substructures on the composite tubs. Anyway, I am all in favor of Kevlar bodywork; it is lighter, stronger, stiffer and more impact resistant. It is roughly four times the price of fiberglass but we use less of it to achieve the same strength. It is not that much more difficult than glass to work with and, to my mind, the realistically achievable 30-50% weight saving is well worth the extra cost and trouble.

Any future prototype wings that I make MYSELF will be made by the Rutan moldless foam and fiberglass/epoxy resin sandwich composite system. It is quicker than stressed-aluminum skins over hammer-formed ribs, just as light and a damned sight stronger. Because I really don't like sanding very much, I would vacuum bag the thing. I would form production wings from pre-preg carbon-filament cloth in a female mold made from the prototype.

As for the "advanced" composites; at this point, although I am interested in (even fascinated by) major composite structure for my race cars, I am realistic enough to realize that composites are not practical for me at the moment—later, probably, but not now. I am experimenting with filament-wound carbon fiber in epoxy drive shafts (front engine) and with unidirectional carbon fiber in epoxy single leaf springs. I would be very interested in trying filament-wound trailing arms, wing tubes and torsion bars. I would be delighted to make pre-preg sheet wings and I would really like to be in a position to use carbon/carbon brakes. I foresee carbon-filament wheels and suspension uprights (hub carriers) in the very near future. I also see composites in street cars about 2 years after the Arab nations apply their next petro-stranglehold on the industrial nations.

CHAPTER SEVEN

METAL FATIGUE—OR WHY THINGS BREAK

By the middle of the eighteenth century, after a learning process that extended back for millennia, engineering man had learned to more-or-less accurately determine the static strengths of the materials available to him and to use those materials in the design and construction of structures that would withstand the loads normally imposed upon them. The materials varied from stone and softwoods through hardwoods (bamboo in the orient—an amazing material), bronze and wrought iron to small quantities of precious carbon steel. Failure of well-designed structures was rare—and some of the structures were pretty damned impressive—aqueducts, bridges, cathedrals and sailing ships come to mind. Given the rate at which our freeway overpasses and bridges are collapsing I am not real sure that we are doing any better today.

James Watt (the brilliant 18th century Scots engineer), changed all of that! His development of the practical condensing steam engine in 1769 changed the nature of our world and the structure of our society forever—the world of mechanical engineering most of all. It also began more than a century of spectacular structural failures! By 1781 Watt had devised the mechanisms (including Watt's Link) necessary to convert the reciprocating action of the steam piston to the rotary and linear motions required by industry and the age of mechanization had begun. It was this mechanization (not the Industrial Revolution that spawned it) that gave birth to the mixed benefits of our present industrialized society—and to the twin sciences of engineering and physical metallurgy as we know them today.

Once steam power had allowed industry to move away from the river banks, made ships independent of the capricious wind and mated power to wheels in the form of the railroad, the rest was inevitable.

When various pieces of machinery began to move at reasonable speeds and under reasonable pressures (as opposed to the dead slow, if stately, pace of water and/or wind power), the traditional design parameters for structures and mechanisms—which had been based solely upon the ultimate strengths of the materials involved—quickly proved to be inadequate. The same was true of many of the materials themselves. A period of some confusion, not to mention excitement and physical danger, followed. Eventually the engineers began to realize that, while a structure subjected to a relatively constant load may last virtually forever, any component which is subjected to significant variations in load may well fail unexpectedly in service, even though it has never experienced a load that even approached its static capacity.

Simplistically put, under repeated (cyclic as opposed to continuous) stress the capacity of a metal to withstand stress gradually diminishes and, in most cases, cannot be restored. Metals which are subjected to fluctuating loads can and do break after a finite number of load cycles (or, more accurately, stress cycles) in which the loads applied and the resultant stresses imposed are always below the ultimate strength of the metal. This type of failure is termed "fatigue failure." For the past two centuries the nature, prediction, detection and prevention of metal fatigue has been the subject of a great deal of study, most of it beyond the scope of this book. In the simple interest of survival, however, it behooves the racer to learn the basics of metal fatigue. We shall now attempt to do just that.

Fatigue is estimated to be the primary culprit in more than 90% of all ''in service'' failures of metal parts, which is why we express the expected life of critical aircraft and racing car components in terms of hours of service. Realistically we SHOULD do so in terms of stress levels and load cycles, but service hours, being easy to measure and keep track of, are a lot more practical. The aerospace industry devotes a lot of time, energy and money to the computation (estimation?) of expected average stress and cycles per service hour. They also install recording devices and overload indicators. As a result their record in this respect is very good indeed, although when they DO have a failure it is liable to be a beauty.

For the most part WE guess at all of this and do A LOT of inspecting. Perhaps surprisingly, our record is also pretty good. I should point out that, in our case, there is no practical way to predict (or for that matter, to measure) the stresses involved or the frequency of occurrence of ''operator-induced overloads''—hard landings, curb cloutings and the like. The more competent and experienced estimators involved are only too well aware of this and tend to apply ''safety factors'' of dubious accuracy and generous proportions. Actually, what we engineers call ''the factor of safety'' in our calculations should, in the interest of accuracy, be termed the ''factor of ignorance.'' In the age of the microprocessor, the crystal ball is still a valid and indispensible engineering tool. Knowing this, the more competent and discreet operators do their best to prevent the crystal from becoming cloudy by informing the crew when they have hit things.

Figure (84): Types of load.

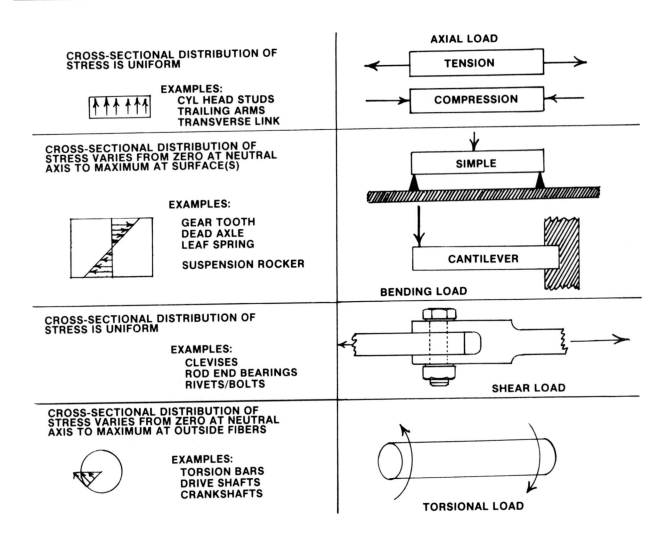

MORE DEFINITIONS

As always, before we can discuss a new subject it is necessary to define the terms which we will use. For once, we have already done so! Please return to Chapter Four and re-read the group of definitions.

A BRIEF REVIEW OF LOAD, STRESS AND STRENGTH

By definition, any load-carrying member must provide resistance to the load. The resistance is supplied by elastic deformation of the material. There is no such thing as an absolutely stiff or an absolutely rigid structure; in order to support a load, any structural member must undergo some measure of elastic deformation, for example, when you step onto a concrete beam, and your mass compresses the concrete a finite, if imperceptible, amount.

There are several ways in which loads can be applied to a member. While the basic TYPES of loads—tension, compression, bending, shear and torsion—illustrated by FIGURE [84] are familiar to each of us, the fact that the distribution of stress across a section of the loaded member differs with the type of load may be less clear.

As a component deforms elastically in order to resist an imposed load, a condition of stress is created within the metal. The sequence of loading can vary from a single application of a simple unidirectional load to a series of fluctuating loads of varying types, intensities and frequencies. Depending upon both the nature and sequences of the load(s) and the geometry of the part, this internal stress condition can vary from a simple single axis tension stress to a complex multiaxis system of shear, tensile and compressive stresses. Further, the stresses set up within a body by the application of an external load are cumulative with any "residual stresses" which have been retained within the member by manufacturing, fabrication or assembly processes. Every stress must produce a strain (i.e., a change in dimension) which may be either elastic or plastic in nature. If the component is to do its job properly, then the stresses which develop inside the part must be balanced by the strength characteristics of the material and the design of the component.

The picture is not simple! This is as far as we are going into the strength of structures, which is a different subject entirely and will, the good Lord willing and the creek don't rise (and you fine people buy enough copies of this book to encourage me), be covered in DESIGN TO WIN.

THE NATURE OF FATIGUE FAILURE

So, what actually happens when a metal part fails from fatigue? NOTHING VERY SUDDEN! This may sound glib but it is, in fact, crucial to our understanding of the nature of fatigue and to the avoidance of failure.

Figure [85] shows a photo of an aircraft crankshaft that has failed from fatigue. The process began with a tiny crack at the surface of the shaft (labeled A). The initial fault (assuming a sound metallurgical structure and lack of stress

raisers to begin with) will, thank God, always be on the outer surface of the part, simply because that is where, by definition, the point of maximum stress must be located. The initial crack is started by repeated application of an applied stress. It is STOPPED (or at least its progress is temporarily halted) by two factors:

(1) Since the load is cyclic in nature, the stress is either removed or reduced when the load cycles.

(2) The crystal space lattice of the metal is disturbed by the presence of the crack. This causes dislocations within the lattice to migrate to the leading edge of the crack and to block its progress through the material—like ants rushing to repair damage to their nest. Dislocations within the structure of a metal can and do cross grain boundaries, but they do so only with reluctance. Alloys exhibit some pretty complex crystal structures, the very diversity of which serves to discourage the propagation of cracks BETWEEN crystals by impeding the progress of the dislocation with physical barriers (dislocations and grain boundaries)—even after a crack has started.

The problem is that, even between cycles, when the stress has been reduced by the cycling of the load and the dislocations have moved in and stopped the progress of the crack, the cross-sectional area of the part has still been reduced by the area of the crack—and there is less material available to resist the next load cycle. Even if the next load to arrive should be of the same magnitude as the one that caused the initial crack, it will produce a higher stress, simply because the cross-section of the part has been reduced by the area of the crack. More importantly, despite the migrated dislocations, the jagged bottom of the initial crack acts as a stress concentrator (the wolves always go after the weakest member of the herd) and, as more load cycles are applied, the stress will cause the crack to enlarge

Figure (85): Fatigue failure of aircraft crankshaft showing characteristic smooth "beach marks" left by progress fatigue transcrystalline fatigue cracks (right side) and crystalline surface resulting in catastrophic failure of weakened part (left side). *Prevention of Fatigue Failure of Metals*, John Wiley and Sons, 1941.

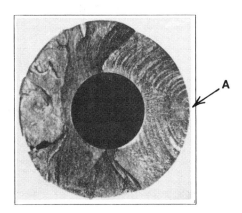

progressively until enough fresh material is engaged to resist the stress—THIS TIME. These fatigue cracks are "transgranular" in nature; that is the fracture actually splits the grains of the metal rather than following grain boundaries, and so the opposing surfaces of the crack tend to be quite smooth in appearance, as shown by the scanning electron microscope photo in FIGURE [86].

As the load (and the stress) continues to cycle, the crack will progress in a "crack/pause/crack/pause" manner. The crack remains stable (perhaps for many hundreds, or thousands, or even millions of cycles) until, inevitably, the stress level reaches the point where the remaining material is no longer able to resist the load. The crack then enlarges and progresses until the load is reduced, the dislocations do their thing and enough fresh metal is again exposed to temporarily resist the load, and the crack cycle starts over.

The sequence of events is repeated, creating the typically smooth opposing surfaces with telltale concentric "beach marks" (clearly visible in FIGURE [85]) which are formed by the progressive enlargement of the crack and which radiate outward from the focus of the original fault. These beach marks are characteristic of fatigue failure. Eventually the crack progresses through the material to the point that the remaining metal is no longer able to withstand the stress imposed and the next load application that is big enough produces sudden and catastrophic failure of the REMAINING PORTION OF THE SHAFT. This last failure is intergranular, in nature.

As illustrated by FIGURE [87] the crack proceeds along the grain boundaries, leaving the individual crystals exposed as a rough and granular surface. This allows the self-appointed "expert" to peer knowingly at the part and proclaim, "Ha! Just as I suspected—a crystallization failure." When you hear this sort of statement, strike the proclaiming person from your list of those to be consulted in the future. He or she is a charlatan. All metal failures are crystalline in nature; since metals are composed of crystals, they have to be.

Remember the crystallographic planes from our discussion of the structure of metals? Well, what is actually happening here, as illustrated by Figure [88], is that when metals fracture they do so only along crystallographic planes. The fracture may be produced either by SHEAR stresses which cause SLIP movement along the crystallographic planes which run diagonally between the corners of the crystal unit cell (the transgranular fracture) or by stresses which cause CLEAVAGE or "splitting" between the planes running across the FACES of adjacent cells (the intergranular fracture).

Figure (87): Intergranular surface after catastrophic failure of 4340 steel part as shown by scanning electron microscope and by etching and enlarging. *Source Book in Failure Analysis*, American Society For Metals, 1974.

Figure (86): Transgranular surface of fatigue failure as shown by scanning electron microscope; and as shown by etching and enlarging. Note that grain boundaries have inhibited propagation of crack. *Source Book in Failure Analysis*, American Society For Metals, 1974.

 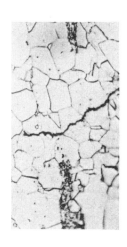

The illustration uses the body-centered cubic crystal unit cell of iron for clarity but the mechanism of fracture planes remains the same for all crystal constructions. As each grain of metal is composed of literally millions of crystal unit cells, all oriented in the same direction, the two types of fractures each leave their characteristic marks which aid the metallurgists in their attempts to determine the nature (and after that, hopefully, the cause) of a given failure.

SUMMARY (TO DATE)

All fatigue failures result from the formation of a tiny fatigue crack at a stress nucleus on the surface of the part. These fatigue cracks propagate THROUGH crystals. Sudden or catastrophic failures result from one-time overloads and move AROUND crystals as a rupture, leaving the outlines of the crystals clearly visible in deep relief. Hopefully we racers will never see a catastrophically failed part—their only possible causes are either a giant underdesign, an enormous manufacturing miss or a really bad crash.

The fatigue crack is ALWAYS gradual and progressive in nature. The initial crack will ALWAYS begin at the point of maximum stress and it will propagate in the direction PERPENDICULAR to the direction of principal stress (which may not always be obvious).

If you look closely enough at any part that has failed from fatigue (assuming that the section has not been peened or beaten beyond legibility by the flailing-around that followed the failure) you will always find either the characteristic beach marks or the smooth area where they were before the polishing action of the opposing surfaces of the crack obliterated them. If the part was designed and built with a large margin of safety, the smoothly radiating beach

marks may comprise a notable percentage of the total-cross-sectional area of the part, as in the shaft of FIGURE [85]. When a part is designed and built with a low margin of safety, as is the case with the valve spring of FIGURE [89], the beach marks may be few and may not take up much of a percentage of the cross-sectional area of the part,

Figure (89): Fatigue failure of highly stressed valve spring (arrow points to origin of failure). *Why Metals Fail* by Barer and Peters, Gordon and Breach Science Publishers, 1971.

Figure (88): Location of fracture planes in body-centered cubic crystal unit cell.

**SHEAR FRACTURE PLANES
SPAN DIAGONALS**

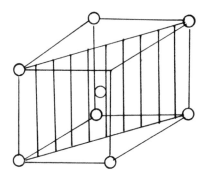

FATIGUE CRACK

**CLEAVAGE FRACTURE PLANES
LIE ACROSS FACES**

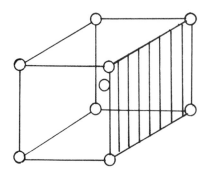

BRITTLE CRACK

but if the failure was initiated by fatigue, THEY WILL BE THERE.

With the valve spring, the initial fatigue crack started at the inside of the coil and, since the spring was very highly stressed, it very quickly let go at 45 degrees to the axis of the wire, characteristic (as we will see) of the catastrophic failure in torsion. The clearly visible granular appearance of the catastrophic portion of the break is evidence of the intergranular nature of the FINAL failure. There are very few parts in any mechanism stressed as highly as the racing valve spring.

By now three factors of importance have become evident:

(1) Since fatigue failures of components start on the surface, if we inspect our parts often enough and well enough the chances of detecting an incipient failure before it causes a catastrophe are very good indeed—if we know where to look and what to look for. This is what dye-penetrant, magnetic particle, sonic and x-ray inspection are all about. It is also what cleanliness, the human eyeball and old-fashioned common sense are all about.

(2) If we can somehow inhibit the formation of cracks on the SURFACES of our parts, we can extend the fatigue life of the parts. This is why we polish parts and go to great lengths to avoid surface scratches. It is also what shot peening is all about.

(3) Just because a part passes inspection today does not mean that it will pass tomorrow. There is a finite point in the stress-cycle life of every metal part when the first fatigue crack starts. Fortunately, with the exception of very highly stressed parts and/or those which undergo cycling at extremely high frequencies (as in valve springs) we will normally have time to detect the fault before failure occurs—if we inspect often enough and well enough. As a point of academic interest, with alloy steels, quenched and tempered to ultimate tensile strengths in the 180,000 to 200,000 psi range, it is usually estimated that fatigue cracks will be detectable by magnetic particle inspection (magna-flux) at about 80-90% of the useful life of the part. This doesn't sound like much of a margin of safety, but a little thought about the service hours involved will show that it actually IS adequate.

Figure (90): The stress ratio and its effect on fatigue life.

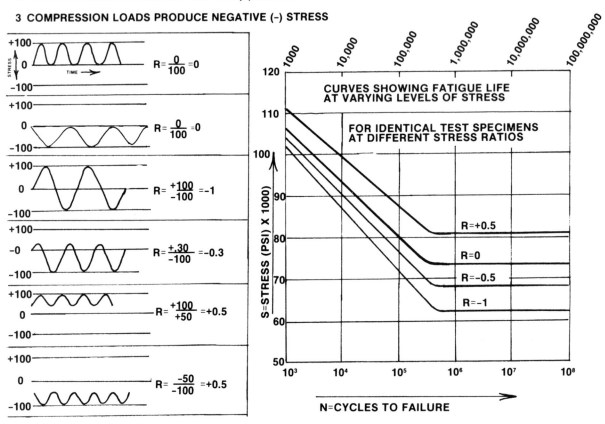

It is important to realize that, in the fatigue history of any part, neither the rate at which stress is built up within the part nor the period of time over which it is maintained are significant. Only the levels of stress experienced, the types of stress and the cumulative number of stress cycles are significant; the higher the stress, the fewer will be the number of cycles required to produce failure, and vice versa. For example, if you intend to bend a wire coat hanger back and forth until it breaks, the farther you bend it each time, the fewer number of times you will have to bend it before it breaks. The speed with which you bend it (so long as it is low enough not to produce significant heat) doesn't matter, nor does the amount of time that you rest between efforts. If you bend it 90 degrees once a week it will fail at exactly the same number of cycles as if you had bent it 90 degrees once a minute. Bending it through 45 degrees instead of 90 will more than double the number of cycles to failure and bending it through 180 degrees instead of 90 will reduce its cyclic life by more than half.

METAL FATIGUE AND THE STRESS RATIO

Just to confuse things a little more, it DOES make a difference to the fatigue life of a part HOW the stress is applied. For example, in a component subjected to compression and tension loads, it matters whether the stress involved is purely tension, purely compression or a combination of the two and, if it IS a combination (stress reversal), whether one is greater than the other. The same is true of torsional stress, except that a metal part cyclically stressed in torsion will fail a lot sooner from fatigue than the same part subjected to the same stresses in tension/compression. If we design a part just right (or just wrong?) we can combine reversed tension/compression stress with reversed torsional stresses and end up with a truly complex, multiaxis series of stresses within one part—MARVELOUS!

To give us some hope of comprehension, a factor termed the STRESS RATIO was developed and should be considered in the design of any part that will be subjected to varying stress, which includes virtually EVERY part of the race car. This STRESS RATIO (usually denoted "R") is defined as the minimum stress experienced by the part divided by the maximum stress to which it will be subjected. To make it all work out, stress produced by a tension load is considered to be positive, while stress produced by a compression load is considered negative. The higher the value of R, the longer the part will last. FIGURE [90] illustrates the idea.

As an example, consider a round test bar of E4130 steel in the normalized condition. The bar has a diameter of 1.1285'' giving a cross-sectional area of 1.000 square inch.

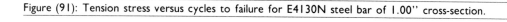

Figure (91): Tension stress versus cycles to failure for E4130N steel bar of 1.00'' cross-section.

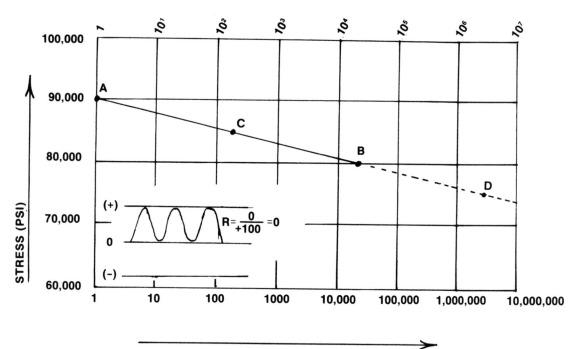

Since 4130 in the normalized condition has an ultimate tensile strength of about 90,000 psi, the specimen will fail when a load of 90,000 lb has been imposed. In this case the failure will be preceded by a marked reduction of area or "necking down" of the specimen but the failure itself will be sudden and the ruptured specimen will exhibit the typical rough crystalline fracture surface of the intergranular crack caused by a one-time overload or catastrophic failure. This point is represented by station "A" on the graph in FIGURE [91].

If, however, we reduce the load to 80,000 lb and we mount the specimen in a cyclic test machine which varies the load from 0 to 80,000 lb in tension only, we will find that failure will occur only after a large number of cycles—in this case 40,000 cycles, as represented by station "B" in FIGURE [91], would not be at all unreasonable. While the number of cycles may not be unreasonable, the horizontal distance required to represent the numbers of cycles that we are talking about on a graph with a linear scale becomes very unreasonable. For this reason, graphs of fatigue cycles normally utilize a logarithmic horizontal scale, as illustrated by FIGURE [92].

Anyway, the bar would then fail from fatigue and the broken pieces would exhibit the typical smooth and progressive beach marks of the transgranular fatigue failure, along with the rough and crystalline intergranular surface at the section where failure finally occurred. If we had stopped the test after, say, 38,000 cycles and examined the part we would almost certainly have detected the fatigue crack(s); had the test specimen been a real part, we would have removed it from service and the failure would not have occurred. If we were half smart we would have noted the time in service to the detection of the crack and made damned sure that all similar parts were removed from service before they accumulated that amount of time, or we would have redesigned the part (or both).

To determine approximately how long the bar would withstand a tension stress cycled from zero to any given level of stress, say 85,000 psi, we merely connect points A and B with a straight line and interpolate, coming up with about 130 cycles to failure at a stress of 85,000 psi (point C), showing that things go to hell in a hurry at the high end of the stress scale. If we reduce the stress by the same amount, however, things get a lot better—about 4,500,000 cycles are required to break the thing at a stress of 75,000 psi (point D). NOW we begin to see the need for the logarithmic horizontal scale.

BUT, if we reverse the 80,000 psi stress as it cycles—alter it from 80,000 psi of tensile stress to 80,000 psi of compressive stress on a regular cyclic basis, as in FIGURE [93], only a small fraction of the previously required 40,000 cycles will break the part, say 10,000. And that is what STRESS REVERSAL can do to us. If the part were loaded in reversed torsion, the slope of the graph would still be similar, but the values would be very much lower.

DETERMINATION OF FATIGUE STRENGTH PROPERTIES

The simple fatigue strength properties of materials are determined experimentally by the use of test machines which are schematically represented by FIGURE [94]. A number of identical test specimens are machined and smoothly necked down from the material being tested. One is mounted in the device; the test load, "W," is suspended from it by frictionless bearings and the specimen is rotated at a preselected and controlled speed by an electric motor. The suspension of the load and the rotation of the specimen ensure that the stress in the specimen is divided into precisely equal portions of tension and compression—the upper fibers of the specimen being in compression and the lower in tension at all times. As the specimen rotates each

Figure (92): The Logarithmic scale.

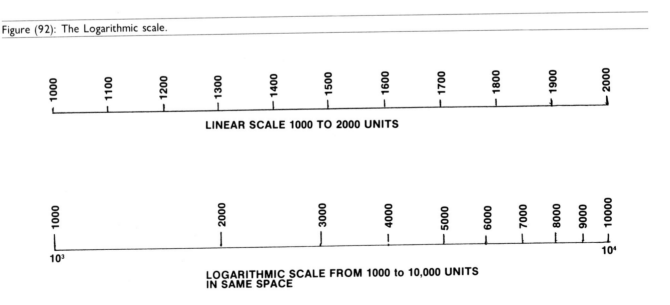

LINEAR SCALE 1000 TO 2000 UNITS

LOGARITHMIC SCALE FROM 1000 to 10,000 UNITS IN SAME SPACE

Figure (93): The S-N curve of E4130N steel (idealized).

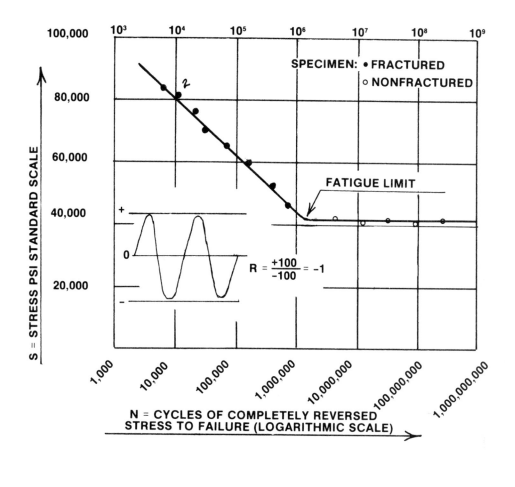

Figure (94): Rotating-beam tension/compression fatigue testing machine.

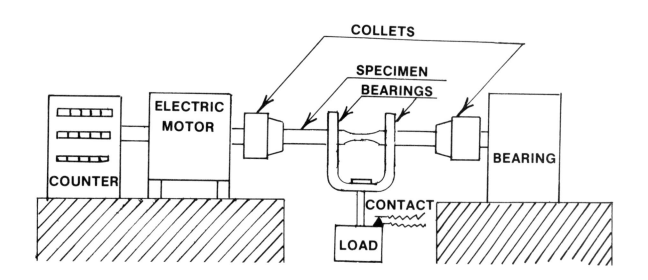

fiber passes through a complete reversal of stress from tension to compression with each revolution. With the machine running at any reasonable speed the specimen will go through a large number of cycles in a comparatively short time (2500 rpm will produce 3,600,000 cycles in 24 hours). Counters are attached to the device and, upon failure of the specimen, a contact is broken and both the motor and the counter are automatically shut off.

In practice many identical test specimens are run simultaneously at differing stress levels until either failure occurs or a predetermined number of cycles have been completed. As you would expect there are many types of fatigue-testing machines. Specimens can be tested under just about any combination of cyclic loads imaginable. The devices vary, but the concepts are the same.

HOW LONG WILL IT LAST?—THE FATIGUE LIMIT

When a graph of stress cycles to failure at various stress levels is plotted, as was done for the bar of E4130N of FIGURE [93], it will show that at some level of stress the test specimens will stop breaking, no matter how many cycles they are subjected to. This is also illustrated in FIGURE [93]. At this point, the curve becomes horizontal—or nearly so. The FATIGUE LIMIT of the material is indicated by the point where the curve approaches the horizontal and is defined as the maximum stress at which the material will withstand an infinite number of completely reversed cycles of stress. It is normally assumed that if a specimen can survive several million stress cycles, it can survive forever.

Although there is no direct relationship between the ultimate strength, the yield strength and the fatigue limit of materials, for most elastic materials the fatigue limit and the yield strength are reasonably close to each other. For

alloy steels, the fatigue limit in reversed tension/compression is usually about 50% of the ultimate tension strength. Unfortunately the fatigue limit for steels in reversed torsion is only about 50% of that for the same steels in reversed tension/compression. It is well to keep this in mind when designing half-shafts, torsion bars and antiroll bars.

While the ferrous alloys normally show a pretty sharp break to the S-N curve and, therefore a definite fatigue limit, the curves for the nonferrous metals normally do not flatten with increasing cycles but continue to fall (although at a lesser rate). This is illustrated by FIGURE [95]. For the nonferrous metals and alloys we specify the number of cycles that the material must withstand (usually 10 to the 7th power or 10,000,000 cycles). The stress that will cause failure at this specified number of cycles is then termed the fatigue strength of the material. In describing the fatigue properties of a metal which does not exhibit a specific fatigue limit, both the stress and the number of cycles must be included. The fatigue limit is also termed the endurance limit and the fatigue strength is sometimes termed the endurance strength, depending on who made up the table that you are using.

Since nothing in God's world is perfect, including both the fatigue testing machinery and the specimens used, the fatigue test data does not repeat itself very well. Truth to tell, we do not end up with the narrow, sharply defined curves that I have been using for illustrations. Instead, identical specimens under the same stress fracture at slightly different numbers of cycles. We end up with a band which encloses an area rather than a curve. The phenomenon of nonrepeating results is known as "scatter" and is illustrated by FIGURE [96], which is merely a rehash of FIGURE [93].

Figure (95): S-N curves for nonferrous metals typically do not flatten but continue to fall (although at a decreasing rate) with increasing cycles. These metals do not, then, exhibit a fatigue limit. In these cases, the stress that will cause failure of the material after an arbitrary number of cycles (usually 10^7—10,000,000) is termed the "fatigue strength" of the material.

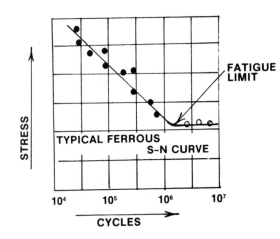

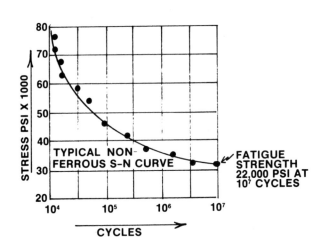

BEWARE OF EXPERIMENTAL DATA—OR NEVER TRUST THE BOFFINS

Test figures—all of them: ultimate tensile strengths, shear strengths, yield strengths, ultimate and yield shear strengths, endurance limits, THE LOT—look really neat in the tables. The tables are in books. Books are made from paper. Paper does a truly poor job of cushioning the impact between aluminum and hard objects such as stone or concrete. The figures are derived in laboratories from smooth and perfect test specimens under precisely controlled conditions of load and environment. The specimens are necessarily small in diameter, and while the exact nature of the effect of physical size on the fatigue life of metals is somewhat confused and unclear it is damned certain that the larger sections that we actually use in our structures have a notably shorter fatigue life than the laboratory specimens from which the tables are constructed.

As an example consider the case of a low-alloy chromium-nickel steel quenched and tempered to an ultimate tensile strength of 120,000 psi. A lab specimen of this alloy used for a torsion test exhibits a fatigue limit (in reversed torsion) of 36,000 psi. However, a 1.188'' diameter bar exhibits an actual fatigue limit of 31,000 psi and a 1.75'' bar only 26,000 psi.

Shucks! We race in the REAL WORLD where our machining, our fabrication, our heat treating and our joining are imperfect at best. Our parts inevitably wind up with scratches which serve as stress raisers and we make mistakes in design, execution and application—sometimes we make mistakes in all three at the same time on the same part. Further, as the tires get better, the engines develop more power, we develop more download or we find a genius driver who is simply able to lean on the car harder and more consistently than the designer thought possible, we will eventually overload every part that we make. Still further, while the prediction of the fatigue behavior of metals as test specimens is really quite simple and reasonably accurate, the same cannot be said of the prediction of the fatigue behavior of structures, especially of complex structures.

By now it is pretty obvious that stress analysis and fatigue prediction are pretty damned complicated and that they are well beyond the scope of this book. VERY TRUE! In fact, before the age of the semiconductor and the microprocessor, the most tedious procedure that I ever read about was Neville Shute Norway's description (in his remarkable autobiography, SLIDE RULE) of the endless stress calculations performed by his design team during the design of the British Dirigible R 101, literally hundreds of thousands of obtuse calculations with pencil, paper and slide rule occupied years of a whole design team's time. Today one man could probably do it in a week.

NEED TO KNOW

Most of us have no real need to know the details of either stress analysis or the calculation of fatigue strength. What we do need to know is what to watch out for. What we have to watch out for (and to avoid like the plague) are CONCENTRATIONS OF STRESS. Basically a stress concentration will occur at any point where the "free flow" of stress along the component is interrupted or piled up by an obstacle such as a hole, a notch, a scratch or a change of section. The obstacles are commonly called "stress raisers" and are to be avoided whenever possible and minimized when avoidance is not possible. Both avoidance and minimization require recognition. Recognition requires little more than common sense. The "flow" of stress around a stress raiser in a metal component under load can be likened to the flow of water around a rock in a stream. The flow will always be smoother and less interrupted if the rock is round. FIGURE [97] illustrates the concept.

Figure (96): Scatter of test results as it affects the S-N curve.

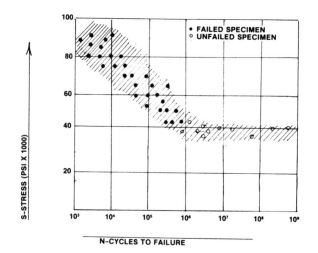

Figure (97): The "flow of stress" concept.

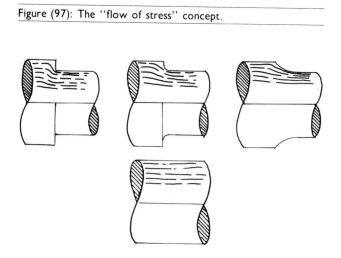

TYPICAL STRESS RAISERS—OBVIOUS

NOTCHES—The term "notch" can be applied to all kinds of discontinuities in structure, bumps, grooves, scratches and such. Notches can be found in machined parts, fabricated parts, weldments, castings and forgings, as well as on drawings. Some cannot be avoided. Some are put there on purpose by people who are ignorant. Others are created accidentally by people who are merely careless. Another common type of notch is the scribe mark (scribing any line on sheet metal except a line to be completely cut away is a cardinal sin and an absolute guarantee of failure—right along the scribed line). Our English friends are particularly adept at this one. So are self-trained metal fabricators. A poor surface finish on a lathe-turned (or, for that matter, milled) part also counts as a notch, as do any tool marks or scratches on the surface of a part. It is important to realize that the presence of a notch does not reduce the fatigue limit of the MATERIAL, only that of the PART. The notch concentrates stress and so raises the level of LOCAL STRESS at a single location on the part.

UNFILLED HOLES—The drilled lightening hole so beloved of racers is little more than a death trap of stress concentration. FIGURES [98A], [98B] and [98C] show what happens to the stress curve of a bar when a hole is drilled in its center, even though the hole is deburred—the result is disastrous. The situation can, however, be worse. FIGURE [99] tabulates actual test numbers obtained from 0.250"-diameter holes bored in a bar of E4130N steel. We should properly deburr ALL of our holes! A much better method would be to smoothly reduce the cross-section of the bar as shown in FIGURE [98C].

In sheet metal, tooling holes should be plugged with rivets and ALL lightening holes MUST be flanged. In the case of riveted structure it is essential that rivet holes be precisely sized and aligned between sheets and that the rivets FILL the holes. As a point of interest the formation of fatigue cracks at the periphery of holes drilled in any material can be significantly delayed by the simple act of peening the

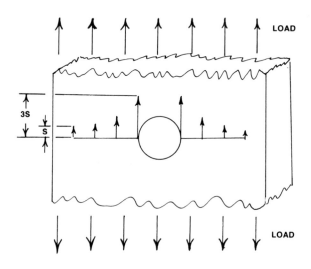

Figure (98B): Stress distribution in bar with central round hole (deburred) when loaded in tension.

Figure (98A): Distribution of stress in entire bar loaded in tension. Note that total stress is only slightly lower than total stress in Figure (99B) because cross-sectional area in bar of Figure (99B) is diminished by the through hole—maximum stress level is greatly reduced.

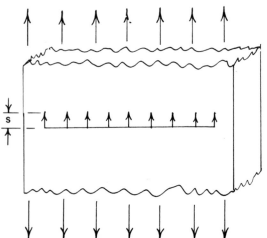

Figure (98C): Reduced cross-section instead of lightening hole.

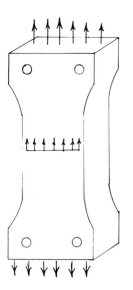

edges of the hole. The edge of the hole is deburred by chamfering and a ball bearing of suitable size is placed on the chamfer and walloped with a hammer. It is that simple. The peening produces a compressed surface layer which inhibits the formation of surface cracks. This works particularly well with brake discs.

STRESS RAISERS—NOT SO OBVIOUS

JOINTS—From both the strength and the fatigue points of view joints in any structure are bad. They are also a necessity. One of the major advantages of the molded composite race car chassis (or of any molded composite structure) is that it has no joints and the thickness of the material as well as the orientation of the fibers can be locally varied so as to ensure a smooth and uninterrupted flow of stress and maximum structural efficiency. If you are reading this book the chances of your having access to enough money to even consider a composite tub are remote (or I am greatly flattered). But, we should all be aware of the advantages of jointless structures and particularly substructures. For instance the now-common practice of milling bulkheads from aluminum or magnesium plate (rather than forming and welding or riveting them from sheet) results in a stronger, stiffer, lighter and more elegant part, as does the milled suspension rocker arm in place of the steel tube weldment. In many cases it also results in a cheaper part that is easier to make—assuming the availability of a tape controlled mill, or even—if the design is clever enough—of a standard mill with digital read outs. As a point of interest, the way to do all of this is with tape or computer control simply because the time taken up in programming is more than made up by the time saved in actual machining, not to mention the time (and money) wasted by mistakes. As tape control and N/C come into more common use, more and more of us will gain access to it and life will become a little bit easier. At any rate, joining is a technique that should not even be considered if it is practical to make the thing in one piece.

PURITY and HOMOGENEITY—Impurities (nonmetallic inclusions) in alloys can strongly influence the fatigue properties of steel. This fact is rather dramatically illustrated by the S-N curves in FIGURE [100] which compares vacuum-melted 4340 with air-melted 4340 from the fatigue point of view. Both steels are heat treated to 230,000 psi ultimate tensile strength. Inclusions (and voids) act as subsurface stress raisers, as shown by FIGURE [101]. Cracks can progress from one inclusion to another, using inclusions and voids as we use stepping stones to cross a stream.

Inclusions and voids are particularly insidious because they are difficult to detect—only x-ray or sonic inspection will find them. When they ARE detected in premachining inspection, they cost the steel producer money. When they are detected during or after manufacture they cost the steel producer AND the component manufacturer money. When they are NOT detected until the part fails, they may well cost someone his ass. This is the major reason that most of us do (and all of us should) insist on vacuum-melted steels for highly stressed parts and on x-ray inspection of all forgings and castings before we begin machining.

Another, and not well enough appreciated, aspect of the inclusion story is the existence of the "free-machining alloys" of both steel and aluminum. Lead is the alloying element in both cases—principally because of its lubricating qualities. The lead is evenly interspersed throughout the

---

Figure (99): The effect of hole-edge finish on the fatigue limit of a bar of E4130N steel with an ultimate tensile strength of 84,000 psi. All holes are drilled with a 0.25 diameter.

Figure (100): The influence of nonmetallic inclusions on the fatigue life of steels—S-N curves of air-melted 4340 and vacuum-melted 4340, both quenched and tempered to 230,000 psi ultimate tensile strength.

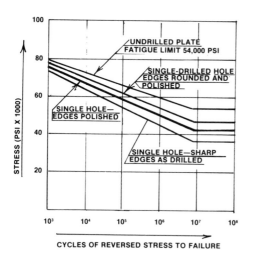

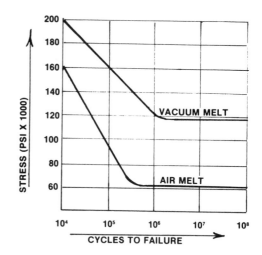

matrix of the parent metal in the form of large, soft inclusions. Its presence typically reduces the ultimate tensile strength of a given alloy by about 15%, which may well be acceptable in some instances (offhand I can't think of any with regard to racing cars). It can also reduce the fatigue limit (or fatigue strength, as the case may be) by as much as 45%. This is definitely not acceptable for racing car components. Avoid the free-machining alloys; be really careful in the surplus metal stores, especially as leaded forms of aluminum alloys 2024 and 6061 in bar form are very popular for production parts.

HARDNESS—In general, the stronger and harder a steel is, the higher its fatigue limit will be BUT the more notch sensitive it will be. Stress raisers that would be trivial in SAE 1018 become critical in 4340M. In fact, not only are the harder steels more prone to the formation of the initial fatigue crack but, once that first tiny crack HAS formed, it will propagate much more quickly in a hard steel than it would in a softer and more ductile steel. So, the use of a "super steel" is no substitute for either good design or good manufacturing practice.

If we are not going to take extreme pains to avoid the creation of even minute stress raisers in design and manufacture, to obtain a good surface finish, and to protect the part from corrosion and surface nicks in service, then there is no sense at all in selecting a high-alloy steel or a high heat treat. In fact, unless we do ALL of the above, the fatigue limit of the part made from the good stuff may actually be lower than if we had made it from a carbon or a low-alloy steel. Unless great care is exercised, over an ultimate tensile strength of about 150,000 psi, the increase in fatigue limit exhibited by laboratory test specimens with increasing hardness is often offset by the increase in notch sensitivity. That it is, however, worth using the higher alloy steels and taking the care required is illustrated by FIGURE [102].

Another point to remember is that the harder the steel, the greater the danger of quench cracks in heat treating. Quench cracks, even in relatively lightly stressed areas, are great stress raisers. The ONLY way to avoid quenching cracks in heat-treated parts is to replace all sharp corners with smooth radii and to COMMUNICATE, effectively, with THE MAN at the heat-treat shop.

While we are on the subject of high-alloy steels and heat treating, it is pretty well known that a very long tempering time will raise the fatigue limit of the finished steel significantly. This is fine for the Bird Works and for government contracts. For the racer, long tempering times mean paying for 24 hours of oven time for a couple of parts—not worth it. Of course, if you live in an aerospace town and are able to both plan ahead and cultivate THE MAN at the heat-treat shop, something might be possible. . . .

SURFACE FINISH—What lies beneath the surface of the metal largely determines the ultimate strength of the material, its toughness, its impact resistance and even the RATE at which cracks will propagate. But it has little to do with the INITIATION of the fatigue failure. Given a sound metallurgical structure, the first crack must ALWAYS be on the surface, and it will occur at the point on the surface with the highest concentration of stress. One obvious way to extend the fatigue life of a highly stressed part, then, is to make sure that the part has a smooth surface finish all over. FIGURE [103] illustrates the effect of various surface finishes on the fatigue life of a test specimen.

Figure (102): S-N curves for some steels.

Figure (101): Subsurface fatigue cracks originating from a void. *How Components Fail*, American Society For Metals.

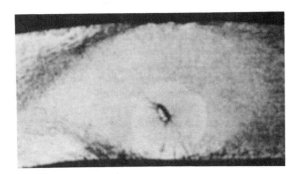

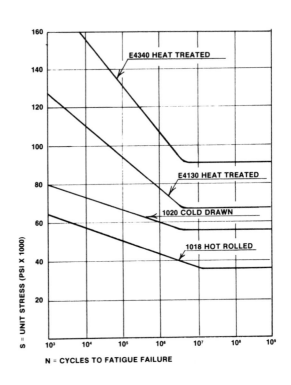

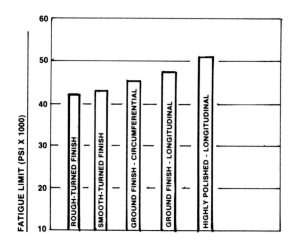

CHANGE OF SECTION—Any time that there is a section change, no matter how small, there must be a fillet radius—and the radius MUST blend smoothly into both adjacent surfaces. There can be no exceptions if we expect the part to live. FIGURE [104] illustrates some of the possibilities.

CORROSION—This is the alteration of the structure of metals by chemical attack, beginning at the surface of the metal. Our structural metals, and their alloys, exist only in a forced or artificial state of stability. In nature they are found only as oxides (which we call "ores") and, given any opportunity at all, they will return to that state. The actual process is complex—beginning with the loss of ions from the crystal lattice, always from positions of maximum stress. This loss of ions, if not halted, will lead to weakening and eventual destruction of the lattice. This is evident to anyone who has ever seen a rusted ferrous part, like an old tin can in the woods or the bodywork of a street car that

Figure (104): Machined radii at section changes.

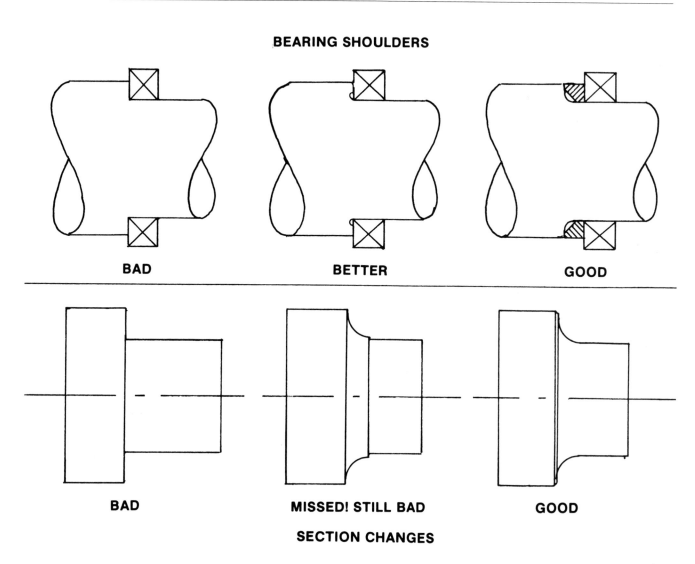

BEARING SHOULDERS

BAD **BETTER** **GOOD**

BAD **MISSED! STILL BAD** **GOOD**

SECTION CHANGES

has been through a couple of eastern winters. What is not so evident, however, is that the initial corrosion pits in the surface of any metal serve as remarkably efficient stress raisers, for two reasons:

(1) They form at the position of maximum stress on the surface of the metal, in other words, where the metal is most vulnerable to the formation of fatigue cracks.

(2) They are jagged as hell.

In case I have failed to convince you with words, FIGURE [105] ought to do so with pictures.

Figure (105): Corrosion-initiated fatigue failure. *How Components Fail*, American Society For Metals.

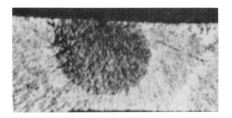

FATIGUE FRACTURE ORIGINATING AT CORROSION PIT

CORROSION-PRODUCED FATIGUE CRACK AT ROOT OF THREAD

SPECIFICS IN THE AVOIDANCE OF STRESS RAISERS
NOTCHES

MACHINING—sometimes I think that machinists (with the exception of Robert Kube) ENJOY making stress raisers. I can think of no other reason for their evident love of sharp corners, even when a radius is specifically called out on the drawing. There are several cardinal rules which should NEVER be broken, and often are:

(1) FILLET RADII—There should be no such thing as a sharp corner on any machined part—internal or external. Every internal corner MUST have a fillet radius, even if it has to be faked by a reentrant radius. And, in the radius department, bigger is ALWAYS better. FIGURE [106] shows the distribution of stress for various radii while FIGURE [107] illustrates some of the penalties that God assigns for ignoring the need for radii.

That the creation of an unintentional "step" by failing to blend a radius into the surface is almost as bad as a sharp corner is graphically demonstrated by FIGURE [108].

(2) SURFACE FINISH—The final surface finish of any part subjected to high levels of stress must be ground and, in some cases, honed or polished. There is no way on God's green earth that anyone is going to turn a surface finish on a lathe that will be satisfactory for a highly stressed machined part. In our case these words refer to hubs, axles, half-shafts, gearbox input shafts and the like. FIGURE [109] shows the effect of surface finish on the fatigue life of test specimens of alloy steels which have been heat treated to varying strength and hardness levels. Once again, the stronger the steel, the more sensitive it is to surface finish.

Many racers believe that a ground surface finish is the living end in fatigue resistance. A properly ground surface finish is indeed a major step in the right direction. But there are some dangers inherent in the grinding process, and they all have to do with heat. Severe grinding produces a lot of heat. If the operator is not both expert and conscientious, the surface can become burned, which will result in the transformation of the surface layer to martensite, which we have already seen is hard, brittle and very notch sensitive. In this case, grinding will have reduced the fatigue resistance of the part rather than enhancing it. FIGURE [110] illustrates. One of the problems is that it is difficult to detect grinding burns (especially if the part has been lightly reground, for instance, by an operator who realizes that he has screwed up). As shown by FIGURE [110], it is also possible to produce small cracks by severe grinding. These are a hell of a lot more detectable than burns. Detection is comforting, but the part is not salvageable. Find the right grinding shop and COMMUNICATE!

(3) TOOL MARK ORIENTATION—The direction in which ANY notch points with respect to the applied stress is critical to fatigue life. Notches at right angles to the direction of stress are deadly, while axial notches may be almost harmless.

Fortunately the most common notch that we create in highly stressed parts is the longitudinal scratch that some-

Figure (106): Flow of stress and stress concentration for different fillet radii.

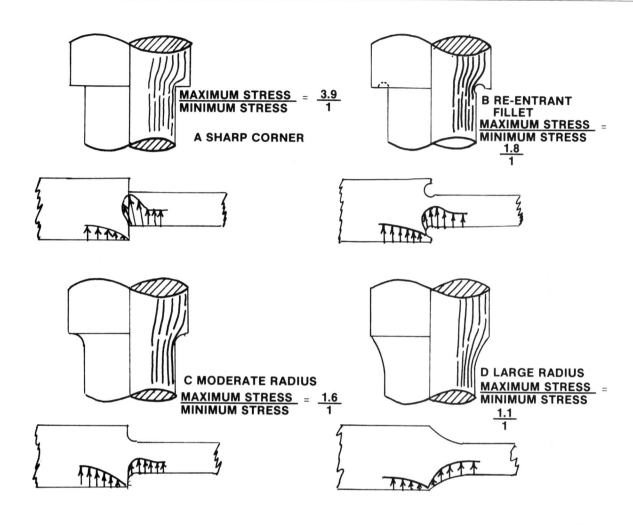

MAXIMUM STRESS / **MINIMUM STRESS** = $\dfrac{3.9}{1}$

A SHARP CORNER

B RE-ENTRANT FILLET
MAXIMUM STRESS / **MINIMUM STRESS** = $\dfrac{1.8}{1}$

C MODERATE RADIUS
MAXIMUM STRESS / **MINIMUM STRESS** = $\dfrac{1.6}{1}$

D LARGE RADIUS
MAXIMUM STRESS / **MINIMUM STRESS** = $\dfrac{1.1}{1}$

Figure (107): Sharp-corner failures. *Tips On Fatigue*, Experimental Aircraft Association.

times appears on our hubs (axles) as a result of the removal (or installation) of bearings. Unfortunately, most of our machined parts have the load applied longitudinally while, at least with turned parts, any tool marks will be circumferential. Drat! Remember this the next time that you are

Figure (108): Machining error causing giant stress raiser. Designer called out radius; machinist missed—or why we *must* inspect each part. *Tips on Fatigue*, Experimental Aircraft Association.

$$\frac{\text{MAXIMUM STRESS}}{\text{MINIMUM STRESS}} = \frac{3.5}{1}$$

Figure (109): Effect of surface finish on fatigue life of test specimens.

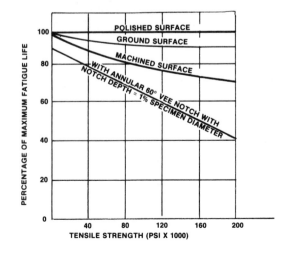

Figure (110): Grinding burns and cracks. *Source Book in Failure Analysis*, American Society For Metals.

EXCESSIVE HEAT DURING GRINDING HAS "BURNED" THE METAL TRANSFORMING THE SUB-SURFACE LAYER (LIGHT AREA) TO HARD AND BRITTLE MARTENSITE

HEAVY GRINDING CAN ALSO PRODUCE CRACKS

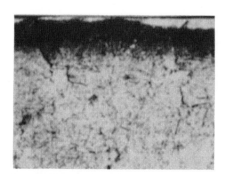

DOING IT ALL WRONG—MARTENSITE <u>AND</u> GRINDING CRACKS

filing or sanding a part—or finish turning one. ALWAYS TRY TO MAKE LIFE EASY FOR THE FLOW OF STRESS.

Before leaving the subject of surface finishes I should point out that, since the OUTSIDE surface of tubular or hollow parts will always be more highly stressed than the interior surface (remember our discussion of tubular anti-roll bars?), the initial fatigue crack will usually form on the OD of such parts. However, fatigue cracks CAN begin on the hard-to-inspect ID—IF a stress raiser is present. FIGURE [111] shows the effect of simply polishing-out the die marks from the inside diameter of a length of 4130 tubing which has been quenched and tempered to a hardness of Rockwell C40 (corresponding to an ultimate tensile strength of 180,000 psi) which, not at all coincidentally, happens to be the upper limit of the heat-treat call out that I use for tubular antiroll bars. The simple facts are that producing a satisfactory surface finish on the ID of any part is more difficult than doing so on the OD and that each of us

is, at least part of the time, lazy. Don't get me wrong—even I do not advocate polishing the ID of every piece of tubing that you use. I am, however, suggesting that if a component made from tube is to be highly stressed, especially in torsion, you clean and inspect the ID before making anything from it and that you select tubing with minimal die marks.

This section should also convince those not already so convinced that welded tubing is not well suited for high torsional stress applications (the weld seam is a stress raiser). I also inspect the bores of hubs and shafts and hone and shot peen as necessary. As a parting shot, the ID of any tubular part is a natural nesting place for moisture and so ID's are prone to corrosion and the attendant corrosion fatigue. Forewarned is forearmed!

THREADS AND SPLINES—These MUST be placed on a diameter that is greater than the operating diameter of the part, or they must be eliminated from the design. Spline roots must never be allowed to blend into the operating dia-

Figure (111): Effect on fatigue life of polishing internal die marks from E4130 tubing heat treated to 180,000 psi.

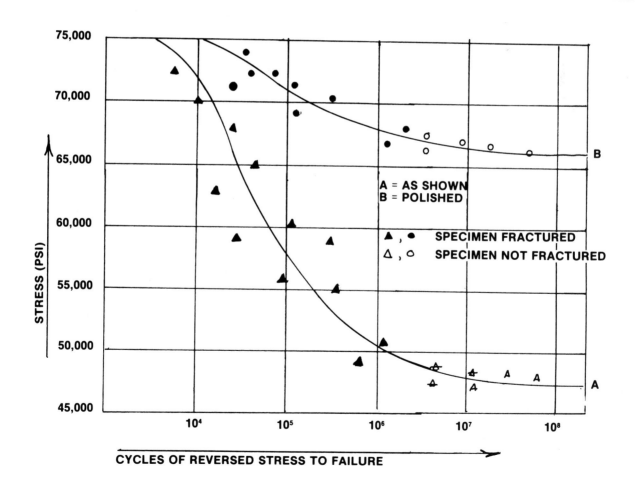

meter. FIGURE [112] shows the right and wrong ways of doing things.

RETAINING RING (CIRCLIP) GROOVES—These must either be placed on a diameter greater than the operating diameter OR placed beyond (outboard of) the operating portion of the part. If they are located in a stressed area the part will fail before its time, as illustrated by FIGURE [113]. Like O-ring grooves, retaining-ring grooves should be designed by the book, in this case the Waldes TruArc Company's book. The book calls out a radius at the bottom of each groove.

WOODRUFF KEY GROOVES

In my opinion it would require an idiot to design a woodruff key into any sort of a modern racing device. Either I am wrong or there are some idiots out there. The key slot is at least arranged parallel to the axis of the shaft which it attempts to destroy, but that is like stating that a broken arm is better than a broken leg. FIGURE [114] is a photo of the crankshaft of my son's Yamaha Sprint Kart crankshaft after it let go. This is a purpose-built racing engine, so it is good to realize that there are idiots in Japan, too.

SECTION CHANGES

Changes of section are inevitable. Sometimes even abrupt changes of section are inevitable. Gradual section changes can be machined from bar stock so long as the change is kept smooth and gradual. Abrupt changes of section should always be machined from forged billets so as to take advantage of the grain flow in order to provide a smooth and uninterrupted path for the flow of stress. As usual there are a few tricks to the change of section bit. Just to illustrate some of the tricks possible, FIGURE [115] shows how the fatigue life of a part can be increased by the REMOVAL of metal.

On the other hand, there are times when nothing will do but to ADD metal, as in FIGURE [116].

JOINTS

Like section changes, joints are inevitable. Like section changes, they are never desirable. All that we can do is minimize the number of joints involved in any assembly and make them as efficient as we can from the flow-of-stress point of view.

RIVETED JOINTS

Rather than devoting a section of this chapter to fatigue and the riveted joint, I am going to cover the subject in the

Figure (112): The do's and don'ts of splined shafts.

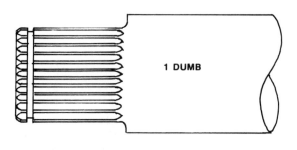

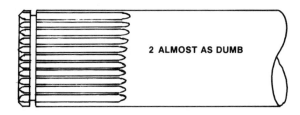

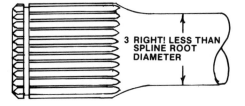

Figure (113): Fatigue failure initiated by snap ring groove in operating (stressed) area of shaft, DUMB! *How Components Fail*, American Society For Metals.

120

Figure (114): Kart crankshaft nose failed in bending; failure initiated at root of keyway marked "A." Andrew Freeman.

section on rivets and riveting. I have two motives in doing this: First of all, this chapter is getting too damned long and, second, I want you all to realize that there ARE real-world practical applications of all this theory—and I feel that separating some of the practical bits from the theoretical text is a good way to achieve this end. For now I will merely say that the riveted joint is particularly susceptible to fatigue, even if (as is usually the case) the joint is perfectly satisfactory from the static strength point of view. The culprits are (usually):

    (1) Oversize and/or misaligned rivet holes
    (2) Failure to deburr the rivet holes
    (3) Poor rivet patterns/joint design
    (4) Inadequate rivets

BOLTED JOINTS

Just about everything that we have just said about the riveted joint holds true also of the bolted joint, but the bolted joint, as used by the racer, is very liable to have a whole bunch of strikes against it going in:

(1) God intended for bolts in tension to clamp surfaces together into RIGID joints. He did not intend for bolts to be used in flexible or even partially flexible joints. In clamping surfaces together, make sure that you have enough flange thickness to achieve rigidity and DO NOT depend on bolts to locate the surfaces. Clamping is the

Figure (115): Increase in fatigue life by REMOVAL of material.

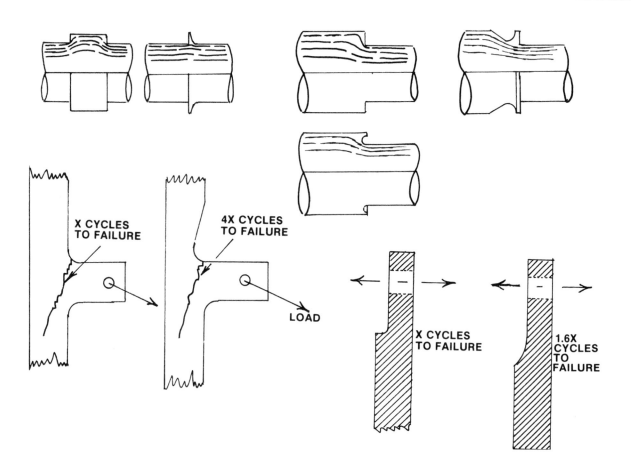

function of bolts in tension. Location is the function of dowels. This is particularly true with respect to flywheels and ring gears—two areas in which our designers are often remiss and, not by coincidence, two areas in which bolt failures are pretty common.

(2) Rivets expand to fill their holes; bolts cannot. If we are able to assemble (let alone disassemble) a bolted joint, the hole(s) must be larger than the bolt diameter. This makes the bolt hole, to some extent, an "unfilled-hole" stress raiser. Bolt holes MUST be deburred, and peening them cannot hurt a thing.

(3) God did not really intend that bolts should be used as axles or trunnions. Aircraft designers found this to be inconvenient and developed a whole series of "airframe bolts" that are perfectly acceptable to use in double shear, so long as the mounting itself is acceptable from the viewpoints of ultimate strength, fatigue life and bearing area. WE tend to use bolts as axles or trunnions for all kinds of suspension bearings and/or bushings. This is ok so long as WE exercise the same care as the aircraft people do: use the right type of bolt (no threads in the bearing area), have ENOUGH bearing area (almost automatically taken care of for the part that pivots by the bore diameter of the bearing/bushing involved, but this means nothing to the mounting lugs). Pay some attention to the section on "sculptured structure" and make damned sure that the bolt is a good fit in a reamed hole. Make equally certain that the bushing or whatever is a precise fit between the legs of the clevis or whatever so as to avoid inducing an unintentional stress in the fitting when the bolt is tightened, as illustrated by FIGURE [117].

(4) If God did not intend us to use bolts for axles/trunnions, then he sure as hell did not EVER intend for us (or anyone else) to use a bolt in single shear. DON'T.

(5) Since threads are, by definition, exceedingly efficient stress raisers, it behooves us to give the bolt manufacturers a bit of a hand in the avoidance of fatigue failure. This includes following the dictums of both this book and PREPARE TO WIN with regard to bolts, and realizing that highly stressed threaded fasteners are not particularly reuseable.

(6) Bolts require holes. Holes weaken whatever they are drilled in. Before drilling a hole in ANYTHING, think about what you are about to do. The man who designed the

---

Figure (116): Tricks to reduce stress concentration.

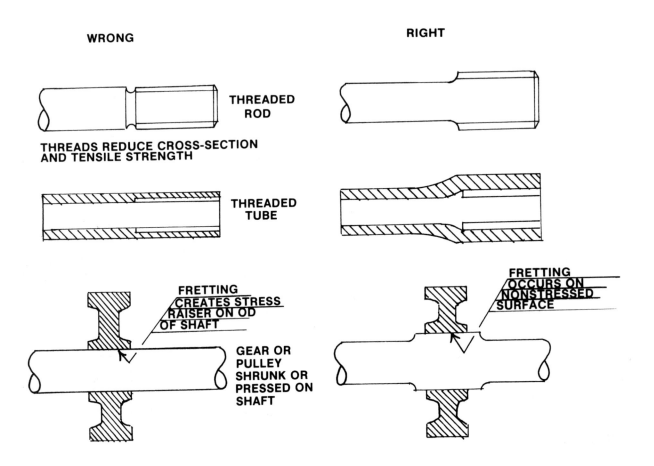

bit that you are about to attack may very well NOT HAVE MEANT FOR A HOLE TO BE DRILLED IN IT. Give the part a chance, as shown in FIGURE [118].

WELDED JOINTS

While a properly designed and executed weld is just damned near as strong as the metals that it joins, a less than very well done weld is very liable to be a veritable nest of stress raisers, which is, of course, why weld failures are not at all uncommon. FIGURES [119], [120], and [121] show some of the common mistakes which give rise to stress concentration and premature failure. Avoiding MOST of these mistakes MOST of the time is NOT GOOD ENOUGH. While there is no such thing as a ''perfect'' weld (just as there is no such thing as a perfectly rigid structure), the dangers here are real enough (and the potential

Figure (117): Fit of bushings/bearings mounted in double shear.

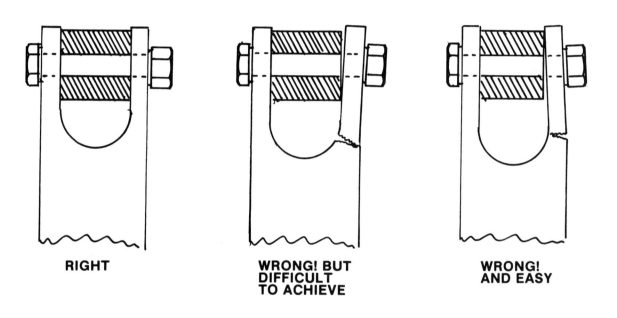

RIGHT   **WRONG! BUT DIFFICULT TO ACHIEVE**   **WRONG! AND EASY**

Figure (118): If you *must* drill a hole . . .

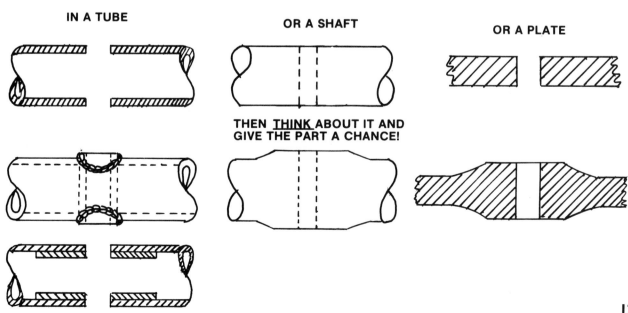

IN A TUBE   **OR A SHAFT**   **OR A PLATE**

THEN THINK ABOUT IT AND GIVE THE PART A CHANCE!

123

Figure (119): Stress raisers created by poor welding technique.

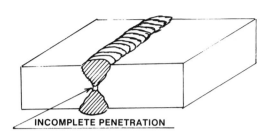

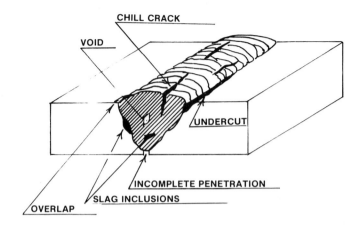

Figure (120A): Weld failures: (left) viewed by naked eye, (right) as seen under magnaflux.

Figure (120B): Why welds fail: 75× enlargement of cross-section of weld shows slag inclusions. Keep the metal clean! *Prevention of Fatigue in Metals*, John Wiley and Sons, 1941.

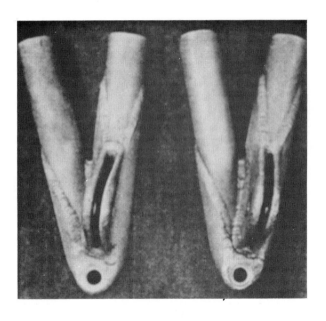

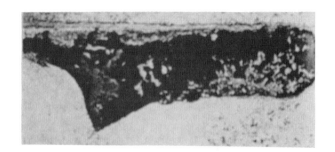

penalties high enough) that we had better be pretty damned sure that the man doing our welding is not only a very good operator (as opposed to one who can make pretty beads) but that he knows about rod selection, pre-heating, post-heating and so on.

FIGURE [121] shows the effect of complete and incomplete welding on both the ultimate strength and the fatigue limit of welded structures. As usual, what may be satisfactory for ultimate strength may well be disastrous when it comes to fatigue life. Note particularly what happens when penetration is incomplete and think about THAT the next time a welder tells you there is no need to vee a section of thick material before welding.

Before we leave the subject of welding: All of us (me included) have been known to weld cracked components. This is usually not a really good idea, especially in the case of the cast aluminum or magnesium components which we usually weld. It is not a good idea because we very seldom have any way to restore the heat treatment that the act of welding destroys. Still, a welded piece is better than a cracked piece, IF THE CRACK HAS BEEN COMPLETELY REMOVED BY GRINDING OR FILING and IF A NEW STRESS RAISER HAS NOT BEEN CREATED. FIGURE [122] illustrates the utter folly of merely welding over a crack.

SCULPTURED STRUCTURE

Sculptured structure is a relatively new term in racing, although it has been around for a long time in aircraft. In many cases it is not only possible, it is desirable, to thin down sections of machined components. There is no sense making the whole damned part thick if it doesn't have to be. On the other hand, a local increase in section thickness is often necessary to provide bearing area for through bolts, etc. FIGURE [123] illustrates the concept. The aerospace people go so far as to chemically mill fuselage and wing

skins so that the rivet lines are thicker than the skins themselves. We only do it on plate and bar stock. The universal milling machine makes this easy. It is also sound engineering and the practice has a certain inherent elegance that I for one appreciate.

Gordon Murray at Brabham is the past master of sculptured structure in racing car construction. The milled from solid I-beam rocker arm is a type of sculptured structure and, of course, the molded composite chassis is merely an extension of machined sculptured structure.

CORROSION

Any material that is elastically strained is much more vulnerable to chemical attack than the same material would be at rest. Therefore, areas and components subjected to high stress levels are liable to weakening and subsequent fatigue failure due to chemical corrosion. There are several

Figure (122): "It's just a little crack, I'll weld it."

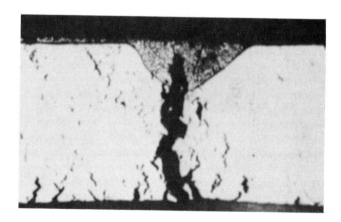

Figure (121): Effect of various welds on ultimate fatigue strength.

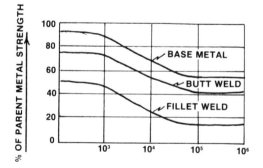

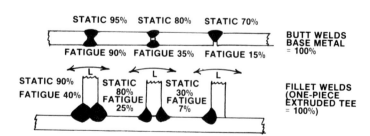

different types of corrosion. Again we have no real need to know much about the process—only how to avoid it. Since galvanic corrosion between unlike metals is not normally a problem in racing cars, all that we have to do is protect our parts from atmospheric corrosion, and THAT is pretty simple to do:

(1) Our engine coolant should always include one of the proprietary corrosion inhibitors. If any part of the engine/radiator system is made from aluminum, then the inhibitor should be formulated for aluminum (GM has a good one, for the old Vega). If the system is all iron and brass, use a little bit of water-soluble oil in the coolant (the oil in Bars Leaks is fine, as is soluble lathe oil). This will stop or at least inhibit internal corrosion in the engine and radiators.

(2) Corrosion on the outside surfaces of parts is visible and easy to avoid. Corrosion on the interior surfaces is not, and it is therefore dangerous. It is easy to say that tubular structures such as suspension links and subframes don't last long enough to worry about corrosion, but it may not be accurate. With the parts that I design and have made, I flood the whole interior with WD-40 (through the relief holes) when the parts come back from heat treat. I then plug the holes with epoxy and paint the parts. If the parts are going to be plated (very unusual for me), I wait until they come back from plating, flood with a mild base (baking soda and water) to get rid of the acid from the plating bath and do the WD-40 bit. I usually either Parkerize or paint hubs, shafts and the like when they come back from shot peening. I strip the paint for periodic inspection and repaint as necessary. Supercritical parts—like half-shafts—I wrap with plastic tape after painting just to stop the paint from stone chipping. I treat aluminum and magnesium castings with one of the proprietary bath compounds and spray them frequently them with with WD-40, inside and out. I tend to anodize most of my aluminum parts—as much for appearance as for protection. When I do plate ferrous parts I use electroless nickel plating for reasons which I have stated previously.

One of the common types of corrosion is termed crevice corrosion for the simple reason that moisture tends to collect in crevices and to remain trapped there after it has evaporated or been dried from surfaces. Trapped moisture will eventually cause corrosion of even protected metal surfaces. A quick wipe with a rag after a run in the wet or a wash is not good enough. It is not necessary to take the car

Figure (123): Cross-sections of typical sculptured structure joints.

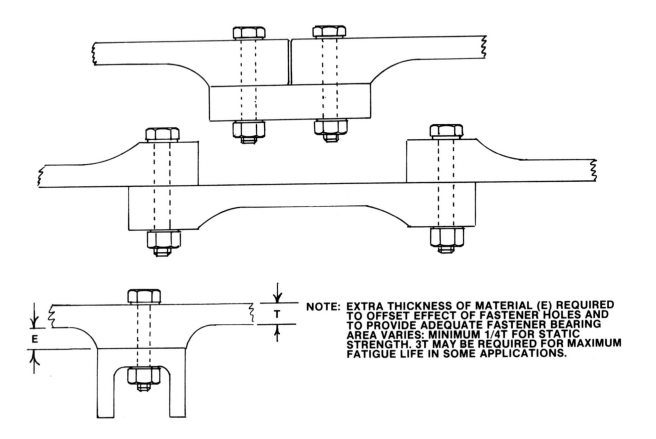

NOTE: EXTRA THICKNESS OF MATERIAL (E) REQUIRED TO OFFSET EFFECT OF FASTENER HOLES AND TO PROVIDE ADEQUATE FASTENER BEARING AREA VARIES: MINIMUM 1/4T FOR STATIC STRENGTH. 3T MAY BE REQUIRED FOR MAXIMUM FATIGUE LIFE IN SOME APPLICATIONS.

apart every time that it gets wet, but it should be thoroughly blown down with compressed air, sprayed with WD-40 in all crevice areas, blown down again, dried with rags and hit with WD-40 again.

FRETTING

Relative motion between clamped surfaces results in a phenomenon known as FRETTING. The relative motion produces GALLING, the physical tearing away of tiny particles of metal from the surfaces involved. These particles very quickly oxidize, becoming rust if the surface was ferrous and a black oxide powder from aluminum and magnesium surfaces. The presence of these oxides is a dead giveaway of fretting.

Any sign of fretting between mating surfaces (including under the heads of fasteners) indicates relative motion between the surfaces due either to insufficient location, insufficient clamping force or overloading. The only logical course of action is to either redesign the thing or to upgrade the fasteners involved. Upgrading the fasteners usually won't get it done and either better location or an auxiliary locating device or devices are in order.

As a specific example, consider the 1981/1982 all-conquering Ralt RT-4 Formula Atlantic car. This car, like its predecessor, the RT-1, came from Ron Tauranac's drawing board with what I can only describe as a woefully inadequate join between the semistressed engine and the monocoque. As shown by FIGURE [124], there was simply no load path at all between the bottom of the bellhousing/transaxle unit and the tub. This was particularly unfortunate in the RT-4, as the major thrust loads from the rear suspension were taken out (or were supposed to be) through this mess—there being no trailing arms involved. The result was excessive understeer, along with serious fretting between the block and the bellhousing. The addition of a pair of simple tension/compression tubes across the bottom of the engine bay, as shown by FIGURE [125], considerably reduced the understeer and did away with the fretting.

Figure (124): Designed-in structural hinge point.

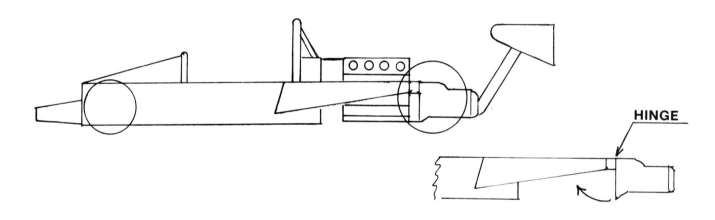

Figure (125): Tension/compression member installed to bridge hinge point.

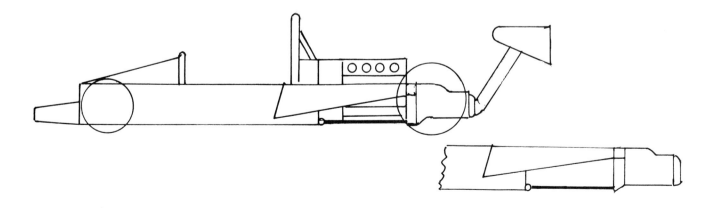

Figure (126): Fatigue failures initiated by fretting. *Prevention of Fatigue in Metals*, John Wiley and Sons, 1941.

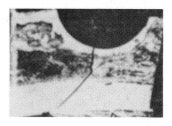

FATIGUE CRACK ORIGINATING IN FRETTED AREA UNDER HEAD OF BOLT

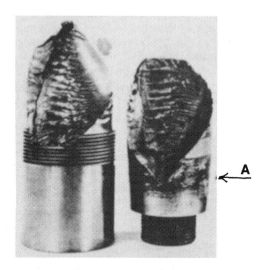

AIRCRAFT CRANKSHAFT WHICH FAILED FROM TORSIONAL FATIGUE. ACTUAL ORIGIN OF FAILURE WAS STRESS-RAISER CREATED BY FRETTING AT "A."

Every year the RT-4 gets better in this respect. The 1984 version is almost adequate as it comes from the works. I suppose that Mr. Tauranac feels that it is best to leave some little thing for the customers to bitch about. (DO NOT read into the above any sort of criticism of Mr. Tauranac's designs. For more than a quarter of a century he has been producing superb racing cars. To my knowledge he has yet to produce a less-than-excellent car, let alone a bad one. As I have said about Foyt, first win your world championships and then criticize those who have.) The Ralt RT-1 revolutionized small Formula car racing, worldwide, to the benefit of the young and aspiring driver, by doing away with the previous necessity of equipping oneself with a new car each season. The RT-3/4/5 family has continued this praiseworthy tradition. We owe Ron Tauranac a debt of gratitude, which I am happy to acknowledge.

Fretting of stressed shafts under pulleys, vibration dampeners and the like is not at all uncommon. Failure due to this fretting IS uncommon—but, as illustrated by FIGURE [126], it does happen. Loctite helps, but the real solution is to locally increase the diameter of the shaft, as shown in FIGURE [118].

The books suggest the use of a soft metal gasket between fretting surfaces. Rick Smisek recently showed me that the use of good old GE high-temperature Silicone Seal does a really good job in marginal cases. As a point of interest, this is almost certainly why Hewland provides a paper gasket between the shift finger housing and the gear case—not to stop the oil from falling out. Again, high-temp silicone does the job just as well.

Figure (127): Effect of grain orientation on ultimate tensile strength and fatigue life of low-alloy steel link with 120,000 psi ultimate tensile strength. *Prevention of Fatigue in Metals.* John Wiley and Sons, 1941.

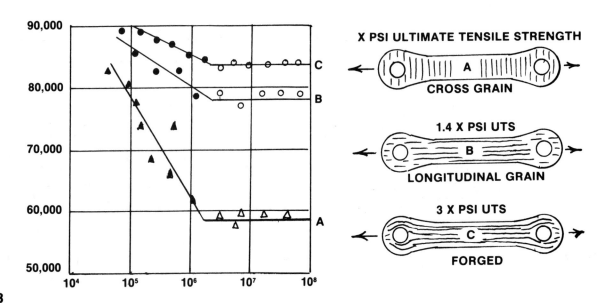

GRAIN DIRECTION

We all know that grain direction is critical when it comes to bending sheet metal. And we have learned that the orientation of tool marks has a notable impact on the fatigue life of stressed metal parts. It should come as no surprise, then, that the direction or orientation of the grain of a stressed metal part has a strong influence on fatigue life. Whenever possible, parts should be constructed so that the natural grain of the metal is parallel to the direction of the principle stress. FIGURE [127] applies.

THE TORSIONAL FATIGUE FAILURE

One of the more common fatigue failures that the racer sees is the fatigue failure of a half-shaft in torsion. If the vehicle in question happens to feature an open differential,

a cam-and-pawl limited slip or a clutch-pack limited slip, not a lot happens—except that the car stops and the race is lost. In the case of the spool or the Weismann locker, however, the car turns with incredible violence toward the shaft that broke. There is no saving this situation. (The same is true of CV joint and/or transaxle output shaft failure.) These failures have ended the careers of some good men. They are preventable. Because of the violence of the ensuing accident and the fact that this type of failure has caused some of my friends to leave the party early, it is worth investigating the phenomenon.

We will begin by going back to our previous discussion of the various types of load that may be imposed on a structure. Referring to FIGURE [128] we will recall that stress is merely "force per unit of cross-sectional area," as in pounds per square inch. When the direction of the stress is perpendicular to the cross-section of the component, it is

Figure (128): Normal stress and shear stress.

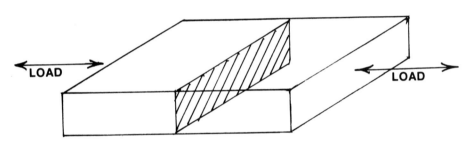

A LOAD APPLIED AT A RIGHT ANGLE TO THE CROSS-SECTION OF A PART RESULTS IN A NORMAL STRESS IN THE MATERIAL

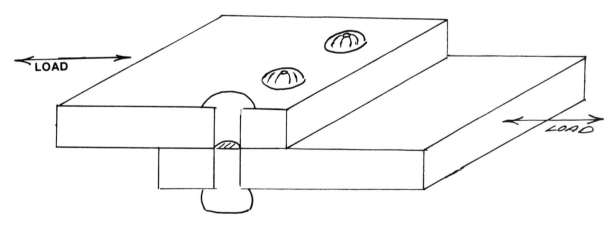

STRESS IN THE PLANE OF THE CROSS-SECTION OF THE PART (THE RIVETS IN THIS CASE) IS TERMED SHEER STRESS

termed a "normal" stress (in the geometric sense of the word) and can be either a compressive or a tensile stress. We racers don't much concern ourselves with compressive stresses.

On the other hand, when the direction of the stress lies IN the plane of the cross-section the stress is termed a "shear" stress. Returning to our friends the crystallographic planes, it becomes clear that, in order for a part to fail from a tensile stress, the material must literally be pulled apart. For a part to fail in shear, however, all that has to happen is for adjacent crystallographic planes to slip over each other sufficiently for them to part company. This requires less force than pulling the stuff apart and explains why the listed shear strength of a given metal is less than its ultimate tensile strength.

Both the direction and the distribution of the stresses in a shaft subjected to a pure torsional load are, to say the least, complex. To begin with, there are both shear and tensile stresses at work—at the same time. Shear stresses can form on two separate groups of crystallographic planes: on the planes parallel to the axis of the shaft (the longitudinal shear planes) or on the planes perpendicular to it (the transverse shear planes). These planes are illustrated in FIGURE [129].

Tensile and compressive stresses, on the other hand, occur on the two diagonal planes located at a 45 degree angle to the shaft axis (and at 90 degrees to each other). These are shown in FIGURE [130].

Tensile forces will act on one set of these diagonal planes while compressive forces act on the other (as a point of in-terest, this situation reverses when the direction of stress is reversed). Tensile forces do not act on the shear planes and shear stresses do not act on the diagonal planes.

The actual failure mode of a material stressed in torsion depends upon the nature of the loading (i.e. the relationship between the shear stresses and the normal stresses), the properties of the material and the shape of the structure. Torsional cracks caused by a single overload may follow the longitudinal or the transverse shear planes, or they may follow the diagonal planes of tensile stress. The fracture will take place along the shear planes if the stress in shear reaches the ultimate shear strength of the material before the stress in tension reaches the ultimate tensile strength, and vice-versa. In ductile materials the fracture will usually occur along the transverse shear plane but may in some cases follow the longitudinal shear plane. About the only ductile torsional failure that WE are liable to see happens when someone forgets to heat treat an axle, an input shaft, an antiroll bar or a half-shaft (or when someone makes one of the above from a non-heat-treatable material). FIGURE [131] shows one such part. They usually appear to have been twisted into two parts.

Brittle materials which fail catastrophically from a torsional overload will almost always crack on the 45 degree spiral angle perpendicular to the direction of the principal tensile stress. This is illustrated by FIGURE [132] and is a dead giveaway that the failure being investigated was caused by torsional stress.

The lack of beach marks and the granular appearance of the entire fracture area indicates that the failure was caused

Figure (129): Torsional cracks along shear planes in torsionally loaded shaft.

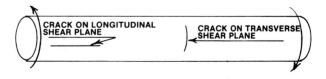

Figure (130): The diagonal planes of tensile stress in a torsionally loaded shaft.

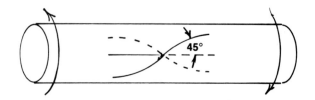

Figure (131): One-time overload failure of ductile part stressed in torsion. *Prevention of Fatigue in Metals*, John Wiley and Sons, 1941.

by a giant one-time overload; in this case applying second-gear Can-Am-type torque to a flat tire! To see what it actually looks like, twist a length of blackboard chalk in two.

The torsional fatigue crack, as opposed to the catastrophic overload rupture, will always be initiated by a shear stress and will invariably begin along one of the shear planes. Our everyday torsional fatigue crack, then, will begin as a tiny crack originating at a surface stress raiser and running either parallel to the axis of the part or at right angles to it. Once formed, however, the torsional fatigue crack can grow along either the shear or the diagonal plane or both. Usually it will grow along the same crystallographic shear plane until the shaft is sufficiently weakened that the next load in the cycle will cause sudden failure of the remainder of the shaft. This final catastrophic failure will almost always take place along a spiral path at 45 degrees to the axis of the shaft. Careful investigation with the naked eye will usually reveal that the true cause was fatigue. FIGURE [133] shows what happens.

Figure (133): The torsional fatigue failure.

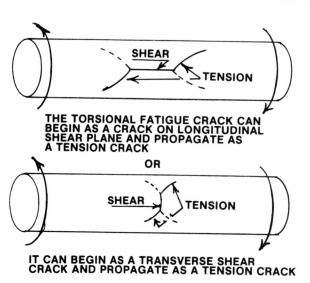

THE TORSIONAL FATIGUE CRACK CAN BEGIN AS A CRACK ON LONGITUDINAL SHEAR PLANE AND PROPAGATE AS A TENSION CRACK

OR

IT CAN BEGIN AS A TRANSVERSE SHEAR CRACK AND PROPAGATE AS A TENSION CRACK

Figure (132): Half-shaft failed from one-time torsional overload. Note 45 degree angle of fracture and granular appearance. Andrew Freeman.

FIGURE [134] shows a half-shaft from a Can-Am car. The shaft failed as a result of torsional fatigue. The origin of the fatigue crack was at the natural stress raiser at the end of a spline. The crack propagated along the longitudinal shear plane until the weakened shaft failed along the 45 degree diagonal tension plane. The longitudinal shear plane is beautifully defined—a textbook example of both bad design and bad maintenance. With respect to the design, regardless of the nonfunctional "bump" (remember that bumps are one form of the dreaded notch) between the end of the spline and the shaft itself, the root diameter of the spline is smaller than the diameter of the shaft and the thing was an explosion waiting for Mr. Murphy to select a time and a place for the happening.

The designer would actually have been better off if he had reduced the shaft diameter to a value less than the root diameter of the spline. Better still, he could have gone to a larger CV joint and done it right, AS HE DID ON THE OTHER END OF THE SHAFT. Be that as it may, the simple fact remains that, if the shaft had been inspected on the night before the race, the fatigue crack would have been detected, both shafts would have been replaced (if one is gone, its identical twin is going) and we might have won the race. It wasn't, Murphy prevailed and we didn't. Let this be a lesson to us all!

TRIVIA

In the avoidance of metal fatigue there is no such thing as a trivial detail. One of the best illustrations of this fact that I know of is the fatal crash of an earlier era aircraft caused by the fatigue failure of a propeller blade, which was initiated by the ill-chosen location of a stamped serial

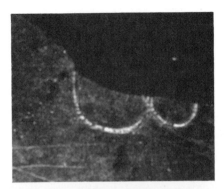
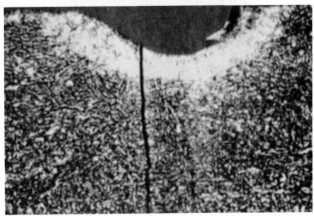

Figure (135): Fatigue cracks originating at electric etching pencil marks. *Source Book in Failure Analysis, American Society For Metals.*

Figure (134): Half-shaft failed from torsional fatigue. Note exceptionally well defined shear plane of failure. Andrew Freeman.

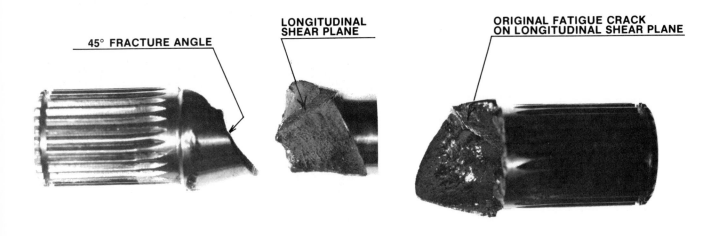

45° FRACTURE ANGLE

LONGITUDINAL SHEAR PLANE

ORIGINAL FATIGUE CRACK ON LONGITUDINAL SHEAR PLANE

number. For a graphic illustration of the principle, see FIGURE [135]—and forever regard the electric etching pencil as well as number and letter stamps with suspicion. Or take a look at FIGURE [136] and then take a look at your connecting rods. Lest you think for a moment that sharp corners are important only if they happen to be internal, consider the example of FIGURE [137] and forever pay attention to the notation of the drawing that says, "break all sharp edges."

EASING OUT OF THE SUBJECT

The subject of stress raisers is something like the subject of giving advice to one's son. Not only is it really easy to become tedious but it is simply not possible to describe EVERY possible pitfall. The instructor must depend on a combination of the student's native intelligence and his remembrance of specific examples to keep the student out of trouble until he has developed his own eye for stress concentrations. For this reason, along with laziness, we are going to drop the subject right here.

APPROACHING THE PROBLEM

In many branches of engineering, fatigue failure can be irritating, embarrassing and even costly, in terms of downtime for replacement of failed parts. With racing cars and with aircraft, we are not talking about embarrassing or expensive—we are talking about DEAD. For this reason, if for no other, the engineering standards and practices which we exercise in our relationship with the racing car and its component parts must be equal to those developed (and, hopefully, practiced) by the aerospace industry. Since aerospace has spent a great deal of time and money amassing a vast amount of experience in the field, it makes sense to borrow as much of its knowledge and expertise as we can. It is very good at avoiding failure due to metal fatigue.

The history of fatigue failure in the aircraft industry is a history of nicks, notches, gouges, sharp corners, section changes, keyways, oiling holes, inclusions (including welding slags), corrosion pits and other such crimes against nature. It is, in short, a history of human ignorance, laziness and carelessness. It is most emphatically NOT a history of inadequate metals, metallurgy or even of inadequate application. Ninety-nine and 44/100ths percent of the times that metal has failed in service from fatigue it has done so because human error made failure inevitable.

It makes a certain amount of sense to look at the racing car as an enormous collection of potential fatigue failures just waiting to happen. Given this approach, the problem seems insurmountable. The only logical approach is to sit back and hope that it doesn't happen. This is not an unpopular concept. But it does not work.

If, however, we look at metal fatigue as a large number of simple potential problems, it all becomes quite manageable—not EASY, but manageable. A few simple questions should be asked about every component on the car:

(1) What loads can be expected, and what stresses will the loads produce in the part? We need to consider magnitude, direction and cyclic frequency.

(2) Is the material suitable?

(3) Is a more suitable material available and, if so, is it feasible to use it?

(4) Is there ENOUGH of the material to withstand the stress?

Figure (136): Effect of reduction of stress concentrations in little end of internal-combustion engine by relatively minor redesign of transition radii. *Three Keys to Success*, Climax Molybdenum Company.

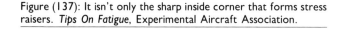

Figure (137): It isn't only the sharp inside corner that forms stress raisers. *Tips On Fatigue*, Experimental Aircraft Association.

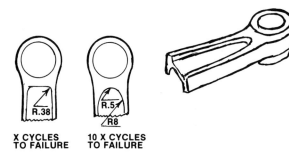

X CYCLES TO FAILURE　　**10 X CYCLES TO FAILURE**

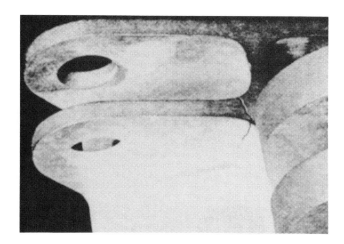

(5) Is the shape chosen optimum for

(a) the loads and stress involved

(b) the DIRECTION of the loads and

(c) the fatigue life of the part?

(6) Is the part properly made and, if not, can it be saved?

(7) Has the optimum post-manufacturing treatment been carried out?

(a) Should the part be stress-relieved, or heat-treated, or shot-peened, or all three?

(b) Should the part be painted or plated to protect it from corrosion?

If this procedure were carried out in detail during the design phase, and if designers were infallible, then everything would be peachy and we could get on with the racing. This is NOT the way the world works—particularly the world of English and German kit race cars, regardless of price. (One of the worst offenders in this respect that I have ever seen is the Porsche 956.) Unfortunately racing cars are designed by fools like me—and only God can design a tree (nature allows damned few stress raisers in living organisms). It therefore behooves each of us to examine each and every part of our racers with a very suspicious eye—from the header tank to the brake pedal—and to keep doing so forever.

SUMMARY

Any metal component subjected to cyclic stress can fail from fatigue even though it has never been subjected to a load sufficient to cause a stress approaching the ultimate strength of the material. The fatigue crack will always begin at one tiny spot where, for whatever reason, the metal is repeatedly stressed beyond its LOCAL endurance level. This spot will almost always be on the surface of the part (only in the case of an inclusion or a void can it be inside) AND it will always be a stress raiser of one sort or another (even if it is only the least perfect spot on a part with a good surface finish). Further, the crack can almost always be detected prior to failure of the part by a trained and curious eye with a bit of help from nondestructive testing equipment. Further yet, the formation of the fatigue crack could almost certainly have been prevented by one or more of the following persons: the designer, the machinist, the fabricator, the welder and/or the mechanic. The bottom line is real simple: when the surface stress rises above the local fatigue limit (and the local fatigue limit is notably decreased by the presence of stress raisers) then failure WILL OCCUR if that stress is repeated sufficiently.

It follows then, that the most effective way to avoid fatigue failure of metal components subjected to cyclic stress is to avoid the creation of stress raisers. In order of ease, the places to avoid their creation are:

(1) On the drawing board. It is always easier (and cheaper) to design a part correctly than it is to redesign and remanufacture it.

(2) In the shop. Again, it is easier to make it right the first time.

(3) During inspection, either before the part is assembled/installed or during routine maintenance.

I will leave you with my final words on the subject of metal fatigue, repeated from the introduction to this section of the book: **"THERE IS NO SUCH THING AS METAL FAILURE—ALL COMPONENT FAILURES ARE HUMAN IN ORIGIN."**

SHOT PEENING

This started out to be a full chapter on shot peening. It turns out that, no matter how much I like and am fascinated by the process—and no matter how misunderstood and underappreciated it may be—there is just not enough to the subject to make up a full chapter in a book of this nature. Logically, since shot peening is a process designed and developed to enhance the fatigue characteristics of metals, it belongs in this chapter—so here it is . . .

GRAIN BOUNDARIES, COMPRESSION AND CRACK PROPAGATION

We have seen that grain boundaries and dislocations within the metallic crystal lattice serve as barriers which prevent (or at least discourage) the propagation of cracks. Over the centuries experience has taught fabricators that thin surface layers of highly compressed metal also serve as highly effective crack propagation barriers. Almost all fatigue and stress corrosion cracks originate at the surface of the part; therefore, if we can introduce a highly compressed layer of material at the very surface of the part, the fatigue life of the part should be notably improved—and that is what shot peening is all about.

SHOT PEENING—WHAT IT IS

Shot peening is a cold-working process designed to both increase the fatigue life and discourage stress-corrosion cracking of highly stressed metal parts. The surface of the finished part is heavily and continuously bombarded with ROUND STEEL SHOT UNDER PRECISELY CONTROLLED CONDITIONS. Each midget cannonball acts as a tiny peening hammer, compressing a small area of the surface layer of the metal. When the complete surface has been evenly peened by a great multitude of impacts, the result is a residual compression stress of predetermined depth and stress level in the surface layer of the part. This layer is permanent and will effectively discourage the formation of both fatigue and stress corrosion cracks. Shot peening is used to both increase the fatigue life of existing components and to allow the use of higher stress levels (thus permitting weight reduction) in new designs. The treatment is universally applied to highly stressed parts in the aerospace industry and SHOULD BE in motor racing. There are several reasons that it is not; chief among them, ignorance.

CONTROL IN SHOT PEENING

The whole object of shot peening is to produce a compressively stressed layer in which the amount of stress, its uniformity and its depth are predetermined and can be repeated from part to part. It is not practical to inspect either the level or the distribution of stress in the finished part, so full control of the peening process is an absolute necessity. Control is achieved by selection of shot size, hardness and speed of the shot, the size of the nozzle and its distance from the part, exposure time and both the rate and nature of the relative motion between the part and the shot nozzle. This is not a task for the amateur.

SHOT PEENING—WHAT IT IS NOT

Shot peening is NOT:

(a) Sand blasting. Sand blasting is a cleaning process, so is grit blasting.

(b) Glass bead blasting. It is true that a compressive layer can sometimes be produced in SOME materials by controlled glass beading with ROUND glass beads. The process, however, takes place under carefully controlled conditions and cannot be carried out in your own shop glass beading cabinet.

(c) Peening with steel shot in your "in-shop" blasting cabinet. Again, the required control just is not possible. Neither, in fact, is the velocity of shot, not to mention the expertise of the operator.

Just to illustrate the point, Figure [138] puts some numbers to my claim that none of the above are any sort of a substitute for shot peening.

MAKING BELIEVERS OF MY READERS

No one ever believes what I have to say about shot peening. I have more-or-less gotten used to this. I have made so damned many graphs so far that making a few more is not going to upset me. Maybe they will convince someone. See FIGURES [139] through [141].

WHAT TO PEEN

There are a number of racing parts which should be shot peened as a matter of course. They include:

(a) Springs: coil, leaf and/or torsion bar. Any reputable spring maker will have already shot peened his springs. Even Detroit does. Some of the advertised el-cheapo suspension springs are not shot peened. The lack of shot peening gives you one more reason not to buy them. The antiroll bar is nothing but a torsion bar. Virtually no one shot peens them. This is dumb; we have enough trouble with antiroll bars yielding. I must admit that I am not at all sure what the actual effect of shot peening a low-carbon-steel English antiroll bar would be, but it couldn't hurt. I don't shot peen them for the simple reason that I don't run the stock bars.

(b) Drive axles. The axles (or half-shafts) are just about the most highly stressed parts of the drive line. They should be shot peened (they should also have a much better surface finish than most of them come with). The good ones are. I usually repeen the spline roots and the radii at the section changes.

(c) Hubs (or stub axles). I am not a trusting soul. I repeen all of the radii on the hubs of every race car that I become responsible for. I have seen the things break, and I have not been favorably impressed by the results.

(d) Connecting rods. There are some surprises here! It has been proven, time after time, that a rough surface IN COMPRESSION will be more crack resistant than a smooth surface in tension. This means that there is no need to polish a connecting rod that is going to be shot peened.

Figure (139): Effect of shot peening on fatigue life of E4340 steel test specimen.

Figure (138): The effects of various blasting and peening processes on E4130 tube heat treated, quenched and tempered to 208,000 psi (which is a lot harder than *we* would ever take 4130).

CONDITION	FATIGUE LIMIT
As received	45,000 psi
Sand blasted with round sand	42,000 psi
Sand blasted with sand dust	44,000 psi
Blasted with steel grit	45,000 psi
Shot peened	55,000 psi

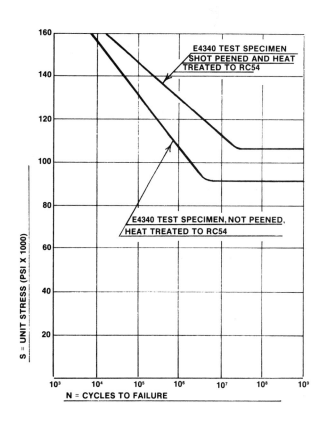

Anyway, ALL connecting rods should be peened. What is more, they should be peened with the bolts removed, simply because the radius where the register for the bolt head and/or nut joins the rod is one of the most highly stressed areas of the rod and peening with the bolts in place means that the most critical area is going to be missed—DUMB!

(e) Gears. The fillets at the tooth roots of gears are areas of extremely high stress and should be shot peened. This is especially true of Hewland crown wheel-and-pinion gears—in particular the pinion. In this case special shot, hardened to Rockwell C55-C65, should be used. The tiny indentations produced by the shot don't hurt anything; in fact there is evidence to suggest that they help by forming tiny oil reservoirs. Theoretically I suppose that we should shot peen all of our Hewland stuff. I do the pinions, the input and output shafts and let the rest go. If I were running a series in which the change gears were very highly stressed (Can-Am, champ cars, long distance, or Formula One), I would peen all of the gears.

WHO SHOULD DO YOUR SHOT PEENING

Obviously you are not going to send your parts to Joe Backyard for shot peening. The big names are The Abra-sive Finishing Company, PeenRite and The Metal Improvement Company. Each has offices throughout the country, although widely spaced. The yellow pages are probably your best bet. Anyone who advertises shot peening to ''aerospace/military specifications'' should be capable of doing the job properly. This does not mean that you can just mail or drop off your parts with instructions to ''shot peen the parts.'' That is about like telling the heat-treat shop that you want the parts heat treated. One more time you are going to have to talk to THE MAN. As with the heat-treat shop, The Man is most unlikely to be the one who writes up your order. It is up to you to find him and to establish communications. He will need to know what the material is, what hardness it is heat treated to, what surfaces must be masked, what sort of service the part is going to see along with some notion of the way it will be loaded (tension, bending, compression or torsion). After that it is sort of like dealing with your doctor—either you trust him or you change doctors.

Figure (140): Effect of shot peening before chromium plating of hardened E4340 steel part.

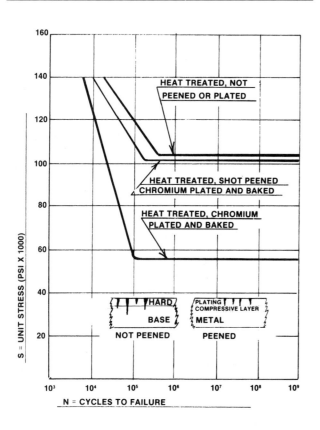

Figure (141): Effect of shot peening on fatigue life of heat-treated and ground 4340 test specimen.

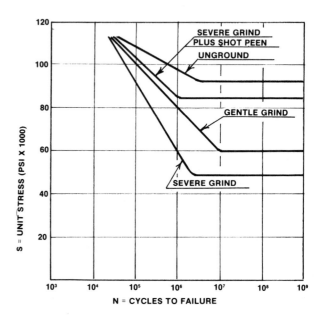

CHAPTER EIGHT

THREADED FASTENERS—AN EDUCATED RE-LOOK

As you might expect, there is very little new in the world of threaded fasteners that applies to the racer. New and intriguing trick fasteners may be a daily occurrence in aerospace but, due to the highly specialized nature and the cost of the new stuff—not to mention its availability—these parts are only of academic interest to us. However. . . .

THREAD TALK

In PREPARE TO WIN I had quite a bit to say about the do's and the don'ts of threaded fasteners, but little to say about the whys. I refrained from writing a dissertation on the actual mechanics of the threaded fastener simply because I could not write it without getting into terminology that I felt my readers were not fully prepared for. Hopefully the metallurgy section of this book has introduced and explained the basic terminology of strength of materials and it is now time to write the dissertation. I do so partly to point out the practical value of a little metallurgical knowledge and partly in the hope that an understanding of the whys of the matter will encourage more racers to take the time (there is no additional dollar outlay involved) to find and to use proper fasteners and thus reduce the incidence of fastener failure. Those of my readers who think that I am fanatic on the subject (I am) will realize why, and perhaps become just a bit that way themselves.

First let's examine the actual function of the BOLT. The bolt is designed simply (and solely) to clamp parts together. Bolts are not meant to LOCATE members; location is the function of dowels, piloting diameters and the like. For ex-

ample, bellhousings are typically located on engine blocks by dowels and then clamped in position by bolts. The same is true of flywheels, at least of well-designed flywheels. Hewland gear cases are doweled onto the differential case and clamped by studs, while Hewland differential side covers are located by concentric piloting diameters and clamped by studs, as are the transaxles to the bellhousings.

On the other hand, bolts can be, and frequently are, used as trunnions for bearings—but only when the bolt itself is well supported in DOUBLE SHEAR. In no case should any rotating member be allowed to turn directly on a bolt. The proper way, indeed the only safe way, is to use the bolt to clamp a bearing between supporting members, as in FIGURE [142]. Note that nothing in this assembly rotates on or has any relative motion with respect to the bolt.

If the bolt is to clamp parts together, sometimes against the opposition of considerable and cyclic force, then the installed bolt itself must obviously be under a load in tension, otherwise the clamping force will not exist. This is why we take considerable care in the tightening of our bolts. We may not realize it, but in tightening a bolt to a specified torque value we are actually stretching the bolt and loading it in tension to a predetermined level of stress (the English and the Australians term our torque wrench a tension wrench). The fact is that the level of installed tension (commonly termed ''pre-load'') in a bolt is more important to the strength and the fatigue resistance of the bolted assembly than is the ultimate strength of the bolt.

A bolt that is pre-loaded or stretched to its designed stress level will resist a given external load for the maximum number of fatigue cycles and will also provide the maximum resistance to loosening from vibration. A bolt that is installed in an understressed condition will loosen under load and will then fail, either by rupture or by loss of clamping force. A bolt that is overtightened, on the other hand, will fail either during installation or prematurely from fatigue under cyclic stress.

THE MECHANICS OF TIGHTENING THREADED FASTENERS—OR HOW TIGHT IS RIGHT

During tightening, any threaded fastener is subjected to two very different stresses:

Figure (142): Bolt loaded in double shear.

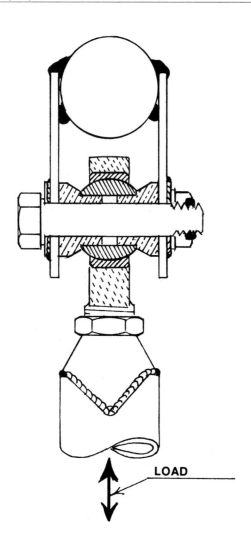

LOAD

(1) The tension stress set up by the actual stretching of the bolt as it is tightened.

(2) The torsional stress due to friction between the male and female threads and between the undersurface of the bolt head and the washer. This stress varies from virtually zero at the time thread engagement begins to a very high value indeed at the end of the tightening operation.

The tensile stress in the bolt is what we are looking for. It is the force that will clamp the parts and lock the male and female threads together so that the assembly will not loosen in service. The male threads elongate as the bolt stretches while the female threads compress, resulting in an increasing interference condition which resists loosening due to vibration and so on. Unfortunately a large percentage of the actual torque required to tighten any threaded fastener is used up in applying the torsional stress necessary to overcome friction. This means that, while the calculation of the proper amount of pre-load is not all that difficult, its accurate measurement IS.

The torque required to produce a given tensile stress varies with plating, lubrication (or lack of it) length of engaged thread and class of thread fit. As an example of the magnitude of what we are talking about, FIGURE [143] shows the effect of different levels of lubrication on the tightening torque required to achieve various levels of installed stress and corresponding pre-load.

Figure (143): Effect of lubricating cadmium-plated 3/8-24 MS 20006 (160,000 psi, uts) on torque required to achieve a given installed stress of pre-load.

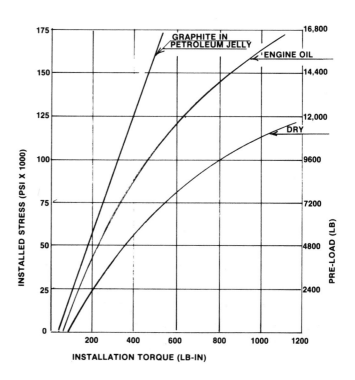

What we are really looking for is a level of installed tensile stress that is somewhere below the yield strength of the bolt material. Standard torque tables are usually compiled for plated fasteners, without lubrication. I printed the standard torque tables for AN bolts in PREPARE TO WIN, and these values are absolutely safe for properly designed, double-shear assemblies using elastic stop nuts. Tension assemblies are different.

Critical tension assemblies subjected to high levels of cyclic stress such as cylinder heads, connecting rods, flywheels and the like require specialized fasteners. Each such fastener usually has its very own recommended torque value. These values are arrived at experimentally either by torquing a series of joints to bolt failure and setting the recommended torque value at about 60% of the level at failure or, preferably, by actually measuring the elongation of the bolts and specifying the torque required to elongate the bolt sufficiently to develop the optimum amount of pre-load required for the assembly. The optimum pre-load is normally just below the yield strength of the bolt, or about 60% of the ultimate tensile strength.

In critical aerospace applications, stress-sensitive washers and various types of stress-indicating bolts are used to ensure proper bolt pre-load. Most clued-in engine builders measure the actual stretch of the connecting rod bolts rather than using an indicated torque value. Only in this way is it possible to avoid fastener failures by taking full advantage of the high stress levels available in the current generation of high-strength bolts.

As a point of interest, we can now readily obtain bolts with an ultimate tensile strength of 220,000 psi, a yield strength of 185,000, a shear strength of 132,000 and a tension endurance limit of 80,000 psi for 8 million cycles. Bolts are available (and nuts to match) up to 300,000 psi, but they are difficult for us mortals to obtain. FIGURES [144A], [144B] and [144C] show the ultimate tensile strengths, shear strengths and fatigue limits of various aerospace-quality bolts. There IS a difference.

The only good point about the torsional stress produced by the friction of tightening is that it goes away shortly after tightening is completed (without relative movement there is no friction). Everything relaxes just a little bit and the bolt is left under tension only. This means that, assuming a rigid joint and no cyclic stress, the maximum stress level that the bolt will ever see occurs during tightening.

Strange as it may seem at first, it is actually better to overtighten a bolt than to undertighten it! As an example,

Figure (144B): Shear strength comparison.

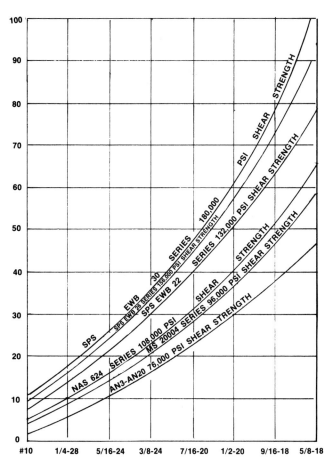

Figure (144A): Ultimate tensile strengths of various series of aerospace bolts arranged by bolt diameter.

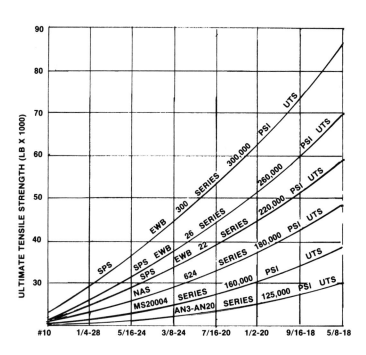

in a laboratory test a 180,000 psi NAS bolt with a shank diameter of 0.374'', when tightened to a residual stress level of 72,000 psi and subjected to a cyclic tension load of 12,000 lb failed after 4900 cycles. An identical bolt, pre-stressed to a level of 108,000 psi and subjected to the same cyclic load, went more than 6 MILLION cycles before failure.

Interestingly enough, a residual stress (pre-load) of 108,000 psi works out to 60% of the Ultimate Tensile Strength (UTS) of the bolt and a cyclic load of 12,000 lb works out to about 60% of the ultimate strength of the bolt. The cross-sectional area of a ⅜'' bolt is $(0.375 \div 2)^2 \times 3.1416 = 0.11045$ in² so the ultimate strength of a 180,000 psi bolt will be $180,000 \times 0.11045 = 19,880$ lb. 60% of 19,880 lb is 11,928 lb. In our earlier discussion of strength of materials we discovered that a rule of thumb states that the yield strength of most steels is about 60% of the UTS. None of this is coincidental. It DOES pay to properly tighten bolts!

Theory be damned! It is easy to overdue this tightening bit. We have seen that, due to the torsional resistance to tightening caused by thread friction, the highest total stress that a bolt will ever be subjected to occurs during the act of tightening, so that, if the bolt doesn't fail while being tightened, then, within the parameters of its assembled endurance limit, it never should. BUT, if Super Mechanic with his eighteen-inch wrench exceeds the elastic limit of a bolt while tightening it, then the bolt MUST undergo plastic deformation. It will do so locally, beginning at the root of the starting thread and progressing through the bolt section with the highest unit stress, the unengaged threads, and the bolt will never return to its original length. Even so, the theorists proclaim, the installed stress is maintained. And it is this installed stress or pre-load that both maintains thread tightness and determines joint strength.

You read a lot of this sort of thing in fastener manuals. It is perfectly true—FOR RIGID ASSEMBLIES. There are no such assemblies in the racing car and WE should never pre-load a bolt (or a stud) quite to its yield strength. When you feel a bolt yield while being tightened, take it out and throw it away—don't even look at it. Every time that you remove ANY bolt, look at the threads for signs of elongation. If there is any sign at all (as in FIGURE [145]) or if the threads are damaged in any way, give the bolt a floatation test (a popular test from my U.S. Navy days: Throw the metallic item under question into the nearest large body of water; if it floats, save it).

Figure (144C): S-N curves showing the effect of upgrading bolts upon fatigue life.

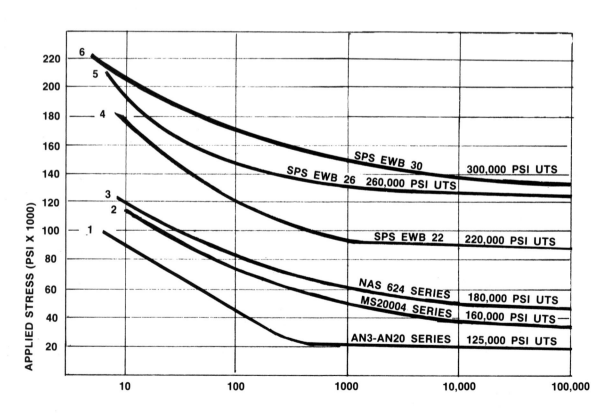

THE DOUBLE-SHEAR JOINT

As I have stated, most of our critical chassis bolt applications are designed so that the bolt is loaded in double shear. This is good. It is not, however, a panacea. The usual idea of our double-shear joint (see FIGURE [142]) is to transfer a load from an articulated member to the main structure. The load will inevitably be either a tension or a compression load and it will be transferred by converting it into a bending load in the trunnion which transfers to the lugs or ears that form the double shear supports. From the ears the load flows into the structure to which the lugs are fixed.

While double shear is a stable system of load carrying, the design and fabrication of a proper system requires some thought. The first rule is that the bolt MUST be a close fit in the holes through the lugs (both of them) and the two holes must be aligned. A loose bolt is subject to both rela-

tive movement and high bending stress and therefore to premature failure from bending fatigue. It will also introduce high bending stresses at the corners of the lugs—not good. Of course a loose bolt in ANY application will allow the clamped member to move under load, thus introducing unplanned relative motion between members into both the vehicle dynamics and the fatigue life picture. None of the above is desirable, and ALL will inevitably result from loose-fitting bolts in double shear.

The design of the lugs in the double-shear joint is at least as important as the strength of the bolt, perhaps more so. We (the racers) typically do a miserable job in this area. A thin lug (like a piece of 16-gauge mild steel with a hole drilled in it) is dead easy to make and will introduce no bending stresses into the bolt. It will also have insufficient bearing area for the bolt so that the stress at the edge of the hole (even if it happens to be a properly sized hole) will be infinitely greater than the stress in the rest of the lug (return to FIGURE [98] for stress concentrations around holes) and the hole will have a nasty tendency to elongate under load. On the other hand, an overly thick lug, in addition to being unnecessarily heavy and difficult to make, will transfer the bending stress caused by the load from the lugs into the bolt, which will then bend and again overstress the edges of the lug. SHUCKS!

The fastener industry recommends that each lug have a minimum thickness of about ⅓ the bolt diameter, when the strength of the lug is about equal to the strength of the bolt in double shear. (Maximum recommended thickness is about equal to the bolt diameter.) Aerospace engineers spend a lot of time worrying about this sort of thing. I do not, except in off-road applications. I tend to use bolts that are a lot stronger than they need to be, calculate the tear-out load for the lug, multiply it by four, use the next greater thickness of standard sheet metal for the lug, weld the next undersized washer to the outside of each lug, drill an undersized hole and ream the assembly to size. This results in a lug that will never fail under load, doesn't transfer much bending load to the bolt, has sufficient bolt bearing area so that the holes will not elongate in service, is not excessively heavy and is easy to make. It works out that I make most of my lugs from 0.095" sheet steel.

This has probably been a lot more detail than I can justify—I include it, not to make the reader paranoid (regardless of what Steve Nickless thinks), but to point out that EVERY detail of the racing car deserves to be thought about before it is put into metal. The popular attitude that finding weak points is what vehicle testing is for is just plain irresponsible (and stupid). Always remember that when one part of the car fails, the ensuing gyrations and/or the final sudden stop are liable to damage a lot more parts which will require both time and money to repair or replace. Besides, it is embarrassing for the designer, and someone is liable to get hurt. It is a hell of a lot cheaper to make it right the first time and to devote expensive testing time to making the car go fast.

Figure (145): Stretched tension bolt. Stress has exceeded elastic limit (yield strength) of bolt, resulting in deformation of unengaged thread. This bolt is junk.

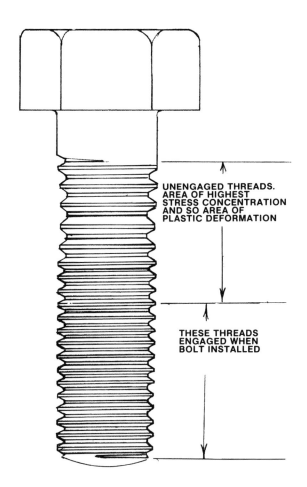

UNENGAGED THREADS. AREA OF HIGHEST STRESS CONCENTRATION AND SO AREA OF PLASTIC DEFORMATION

THESE THREADS ENGAGED WHEN BOLT INSTALLED

WHY THE THREADS ARE SO LONG

While shortening the threads and dressing the ends of nonaircraft bolts so that you can use them on your race car, you may well wonder why the damned fools who designed the things made the threads too long to start with. Well gentle reader, as is usual in the very real world of commercial engineering, there are perfectly good reasons behind this seeming idiocy. Most obviously, the use of a very long thread allows a reasonable stock of bolts to cover a wide range of applications. Not so obvious, but a lot more important, is the fact that neither the manufacturer nor the seller has any idea what the bolt is going to be used for. While neither of these may have any sort of conscience, the SAE does—and since it gets to lay out the fastener specs, we get long threads. We get them so that ANY bolt you buy in a hardware store or industrial supply house will, within the envelope of its material strength and detail design/fabrication, be safe when it is used in tension.

A little while ago, while discussing shear applications, I stated that, "tension is different." We chassis and suspension people are so used to double-shear bolt applications that we lose sight of the simple fact that, in the real world, most bolts are installed in tension. Let's look at the tension bolt for a moment.

THE BOLT IN TENSION

We have been taught that the ideal length of engaged thread in a tension bolt (or stud) application is 1.5 times the bolt diameter. Being weight conscious, we tend to regard any more thread than that as being a waste. What we are ignoring is the word "engaged"—and we can get ourselves into a lot of trouble by doing so. Referring to FIGURE [146] we first see a tension bolt with 1.5 times the diameter of engaged thread—the ideal setup, right? WRONG! What we have achieved here is the placement of the weakest part of the bolt (the root of the starting thread) at the interface between the clamped parts. If the bolt is properly tightened, the bolt itself will be subjected to a pre-load that will stress the bolt to a level close to its yield point. This is fine; indeed it is the stress level at which the bolt was designed to operate. BUT if there should occur any relative movement between the clamped parts, the bolt will be subjected to an additional stress, either in tension or in shear—and the bolt will eventually fail, at the thread root as the illustration shows.

The proper way to install a bolt which will be loaded in tension is shown in FIGURE [147]. The thread is extended into the hole in the top member so that the weak-starting thread root is removed from the danger zone of shear stress. It is all very well to say that the assembly should be

Figure (146): Tension bolt—wrong.

Figure (147): Tension bolt—right.

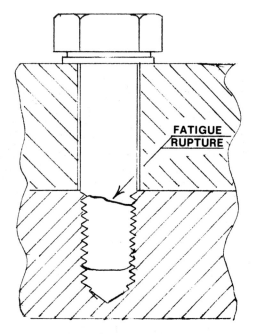

WRONG—STARTING THREAD AT CLAMPED SURFACE INTERSECTION

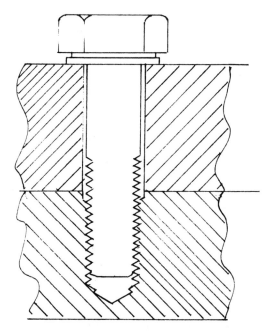

RIGHT—UNENGAGED THREAD EXTENDS ABOVE CLAMPED SURFACE

designed so that there will be no relative motion between the clamped parts, or that bolts should be used as clamping members only, not as locators—but we do not live, or race, in a perfect world.

THE ROLLED THREAD VERSUS THE CUT THREAD

Male threads can be manufactured either by cutting (on a lathe or with a thread die) or by rolling. In the rolling process the cylindrical bolt (or stud) stock is passed between rotating threaded rollers under extreme pressure and the thread is cold formed by mechanical displacement of metal into the grooves in the rollers. Except for the temperatures involved, the process is similar to forging; the grain of the metal follows the contour of the threads and the thread surface is not only smooth, it is actually burnished by the rollers. As you would expect the resulting threads are both strong and resistant to fatigue.

One of most unpopular proclamations that I made in PREPARE TO WIN was that either die cutting or lathe cutting threads onto a bolt is a crime against nature. I have been attacked by just about every machinist that I know, stating that any competent machinist can turn good threads onto any piece of bolt stock that I can come up with. NO ARGUMENT. I never stated that GOOD threads could not be turned on a lathe. They can be—assuming that the operator knows what he is doing, and uses a properly sharpened tool and the right speeds for the thread and the metal. The trouble is that no matter how competent and careful the man may be, he is interrupting the flow of stress through the bolt by CUTTING threads ACROSS the grain of the metal. There is no way that even the very best lathe-turned threads are going to be:

(1) As strong as rolled threads

(2) As resistant to fatigue as rolled threads. Turning involves tearing metal and leaves rough spots which form perfect stress raisers.

To the best of my knowledge, ALL commercial bolts and studs that we are liable to come across are manufactured with rolled threads (only very large threads are commercially cut anymore). As you might expect, however, there are various ways of rolling threads and the results tend to vary directly as the cost of the equipment. The right way is to cold roll the threads in a single pass through polished rollers which have radiused thread roots. Threads should be rolled AFTER the bolt/stud has been heat treated. (Threads rolled before heat treatment are not much better than cut threads.) A quick, naked-eye comparison between the threads on a "super whatever" bolt and an AN/MS/NAS bolt will illustrate my point.

So we not only have to guard against the well-meaning fool who decides to modify an existing bolt or to make one, but also against the cost-cutting beancounters who run the industrial fastener corporations, upon whom the SAE has no practical way to enforce its standards.

There is no way on God's green earth that anyone is going to cut even a decent thread with a thread die, and this includes "just cutting a couple of more threads onto this here bolt."

One picture is said to be worth a thousand words. FIGURE [148] shows a comparison of the grain structure between lathe-cut and rolled threads under 80X magnifica-

Figure (148): Comparison of cut and rolled male threads. *How Components Fail,* American Society For Metals.

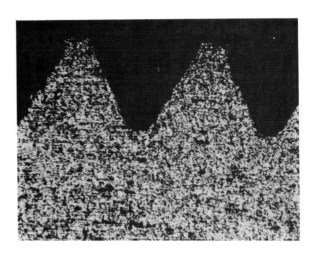

LATHE-TURNED THREADS ON STEEL BOLT (X80)

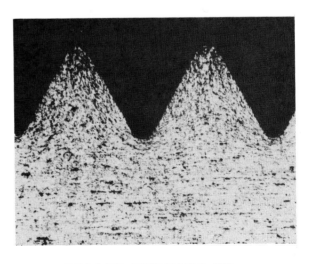

ROLLED THREADS OF AIRCRAFT BOLT (X80)

tion. FIGURE [149] is a 200X magnification of what appears to the naked eye to be a perfectly formed lathe-cut thread. Enough said.

THE HEX-HEADED BOLT VERSUS THE SOCKET HEAD CAP SCREW

The socket head cap screw (i.e., Allen bolt) has two advantages over the standard hexagon-headed bolt:

(1) The head takes up less space.

(2) High quality socket-head cap screws are more readily available than are high-quality hex bolts.

For the racer, they also have three DISadvantages:

(1) If they are to be loaded in tension, the limited bearing area under the head will prevent tightening the bolt sufficiently to take full advantage of the strength of the alloy; unless, of course, a hardened washer is inserted under the bolt head.

(2) If they are to be used in shear (loaded in bending), the excess thread must be removed before they can be properly installed.

(3) The heads are case hardened and are therefore difficult to drill for safety wire.

For shear applications where WE are almost certainly not going to tighten the bolt enough to take full advantage of the strength of the bolt alloy, there is no practical difference between using a socket or a hex head. I use hex-headed AN bolts for reasons which I have stated many times. If I don't have access to AN bolts I usually use a modified socket-head cap screw simply because, as we will see later, it is

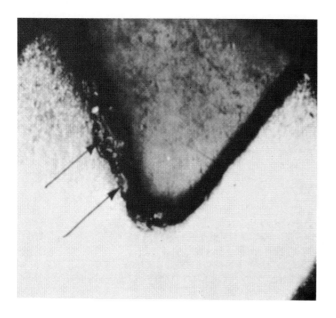

Figure (149): Enlargement (200×) of root of lathe-turned thread. Note torn metal indicated by arrows. *Why Metals Fail* by Barer and Peters, Gordon and Breach Science Publishers, 1971.

liable to be a superior fastener. BUT, the lack of bearing area under the socket head itself can lead to big trouble when the bolt is stressed in tension by the ignorant or the unwary.

The reason that we are readily able to obtain high-quality socket-head cap screws is simply that the machine tool industry uses them to hold machine tools together (because the heads fit into counterbored holes and thus allow parts to slide past each other without snagging on bolt heads). The machine tool industry also uses hardened and ground "machine washers" under the heads of socket-head cap screws because, if they don't, they cannot tighten the things sufficiently to develop the required clamping force, let alone lock the threads. What this means is that, when you decide to use an SPS Unbrako for a head bolt you had damned well better use a hardened and ground washer under the head or the head will sink into whatever washers you do use; you will lose torque and the head will lift.

As a matter of course, I use hardened and ground washers under the head of EVERY head bolt (including those of my son's Yamaha kart engines). They are available from industrial hardware stores, machinery supply houses and from your local farm equipment dealer (yes, I mean like John Deere, Caterpillar, International Harvester). These people REALLY know about fasteners, fatigue and metallurgy and, from the metal fatigue point of view, put out some of the best-designed equipment in the world.

TRIVIA

Some years ago during a discussion having to do with connecting rod bolts, Keith Duckworth made a statement to the effect that we had once had the perfect screw thread form and had then thrown it away. He was referring to the much-despised (in the U.S.) Whitworth thread. Actually, it is not the thread form that a generation of American mechanics learned to despise, but the nut and bolt hex sizes which differ from ours and simply do not make sense to us (like other British habits such as cold toast and almost-raw bacon). When Mr. Whitworth designed his thread form he was thinking very hard about fatigue in bolts under tension so he designed radiused thread roots and peaks into the system. FIGURE [150] shows that he knew what he was talking about.

In the praiseworthy interest of international unification (ignoring, of course, the metric system) we (the U.S., Great Britain and Canada) shelved Whitworth for UNF and UNC in 1948. Interestingly enough, SPS introduced its Hi-R thread form some years ago in order to reduce stress concentrations and improve fatigue life in highly stressed aerospace fasteners. A comparison of FIGURE [151] with the Whitworth thread form of FIGURE [150] looks like one more example of the reinvention of the wheel.

THE STUD

We use a lot of studs, particularly in the engine and in the transaxle/differential housing/bellhousing family. Our rationale for this practice is that we don't want to hurt the female threads in castings by repeated removal and installation of bolts. Technically speaking, this line of thinking is incorrect; repeated insertion will not damage proper threads. From the practical point of view, however, I maintain that we are, in this respect, correct in our thinking. Further, we have an unfortunate tendency to use studs as locating devices and this we should not do; studs, like bolts, are meant to be clamping devices only. Location should be by means of dowels or, in Mr. Hewland's case (he understands these things very well; he has even finally figured out that people are bolting wings to his shift-finger housings and rear covers and has now doweled them as well) by locating or piloting diameters on the clamped parts. A locating dowel can be a HOLLOW cylinder surrounding a stud just as easily as it can be a SOLID one in a separate hole.

Me, I LIKE studs. Some of my best friends are studs, or think they are. As fasteners, studs make assembly easy because, even if the part to be installed cannot be located by the studs, it can be guided into place on them. This is of particular interest when the part is hot and heavy (as in a Ford 9'' differential) or when it is awkward (as in a Hewland Transaxle complete with rear suspension assembly into clutch spline and onto bellhousing). In many cases, though, we do the stud thing wrong (applause from the ladies?).

First of all, a stud properly requires an interference fit between the male and female threads, otherwise it will eventually back off while the nut is being loosened. This means that we should theoretically use a class 3B tap to form the female threads in a hole that is going to receive a stud (in the Unified Thread System, class A denotes female threads, class B denotes male threads, class 1 is a loose fit, class 2 is a normal fit used for most threaded fasteners, and class 3 is an interference fit). NOBODY does this—including me. I use Loctite stud lock to achieve my

Figure (151): Standard UNF thread form versus SPS "Hi-R."

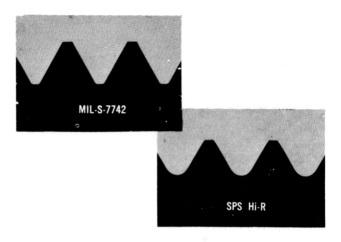

Figure (150): Comparison of Whitworth and UNF threads. Any thread is a stress raiser, smoothly radiused threads are better than sharp threads. But, might makes right and the Whitworth thread form is extinct. *Prevention of Failure in Metals*, John Wiley and Sons, 1941.

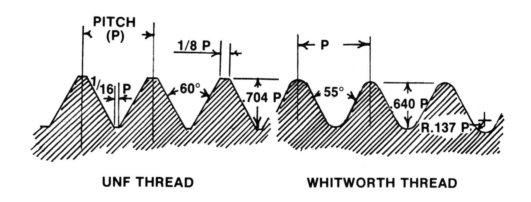

UNF THREAD   WHITWORTH THREAD

TENSION FATIGUE LIMIT ZERO TO MAXIMUM STRESS

THREAD FORM	MEDIUM CARBON STEEL—58,000 PSI UTS	ALLOY STEEL 109,000 PSI UTS
NO THREAD	37,000 PSI	73,000 PSI
UNF	13,000 PSI	19,000 PSI
WHITWORTH	21,000 PSI	22,000 PSI

interference fits. I have never been accused of being a trusting soul, so I also use some form of threaded insert for any female thread that I think is going to see much disassembly. More on both inserts and Loctite later.

When there is going to be very little stress involved AND we are certain that the stud will do no locating, then our standard practice of tightening the stud into a tapped hole so that the thread root of the stud ends up at or slightly above the surface of the hole borders on being acceptable. The problem is that tightening the stud is bound to pull up the material at the edge of the hole forming a ridge around the stud which will prevent proper clamping of the mating surface. (Take a good look at the area surrounding the side cover studs on your Hewland.)

If, on the other hand, the stud is going to do any locating at all and we locate the starting thread at the joint surface, the bending load which does the locating, when added to the tension stress already in the tightened stud ensures us that we will eventually achieve a fatigue failure—right at the starting thread. See FIGURE [152]. The solution is to counterbore the hole so that tensioning the stud cannot raise a ring of parent metal around the hole, and relieve the starting thread so that it is not a stress raiser. The stress-relieving groove at the last thread must also extend below the first female thread when the stud is bottomed.

VERY HIGHLY STRESSED BOLTS AND STUDS

You have doubtless noticed that on some very highly stressed bolts and/or studs the diameter of the shank has been reduced over a part of its length. The thinking here is that for maximum clamping force AND resistance to fatigue, we want an even distribution of stress throughout the bolt. Since the weakest portion of the bolt is obviously the minor diameter of the threaded portion, when the bolt is

tensioned the stress will be concentrated in this area while the shank will be more lightly stressed. If the diameter of the shank is reduced to slightly less than the minor diameter of the thread (leaving selected areas at the standard size for locating the fastener in its hole) and the diameter change is properly radiused, then the tension stress will be evenly distributed throughout the length of the bolt and maximum advantage can be taken of the strength of the alloy used while maximum resistance to fatigue is also achieved. FIGURE [153] illustrates and also gives the proper dimension for the stress-relief groove at the starting thread.

WE normally only see this sort of thing on connecting rod and cylinder head bolts. Farmers and truckers see it all the time on farm equipment and diesels.

A PRACTICAL VIEW OF THE BOLT PICTURE

Everything that I said so many years ago about bolts and their relationship to the racing car stands. Judging from your letters, I seriously underestimated the difficulty of obtaining aircraft hardware in the hinterlands (alternatively I may have OVERestimated the ingenuity and determination of the racer—but we won't go into that). Living and working in southern California DOES have its compensations. I still STRONGLY prefer the AN, MS and/or NAS items— and in many instances I insist on them. But I, too, spend a lot of time in East Jesus and I DO recognize reality if my nose is rubbed in it often enough. If you cannot find the right stuff locally, I will now offer a few acceptable alternatives that I probably should have mentioned originally:

(1) Both Earl's Supply Company and Aircraft Spruce and Specialty maintain stocks of AN/MS/NAS hardware and offer UPS service.

(2) Since most racing cars are designed around junk bolts, any premium-grade, internal-wrenching (i.e., Allen) bolt will do the job in just about any application (with the exception of highly stressed engine bolts) as in cylinder head, connecting rod and flywheel. "Premium Grade," in my book includes:

(a) Standard Pressed Steel's Unbrako line, THE BEST industrial bolts that I know of. There are several members of this family. One thing to be a little careful of is that the K16 type, while it is rated at only 150,000 psi UTS has twice the FATIGUE LIFE of the standard Hi-Life Unbrako, which is rated at 190,000 psi UTS. Remember what I said about hard sometimes equals brittle?

(b) Hollo-chrome.

(c) Allen.

(d) Camcar.

And no others. As a generalized tip, the manufacturers of GOOD Allen Bolts always describe their products as "socket head" or "Internal Wrenching" CAP SCREWS. If you cannot find one of these brands where you live then I can only suggest that you move. The best sources are industrial and machinery supply houses and industrial hardware stores.

Figure (152): Studs and stud-hole design.

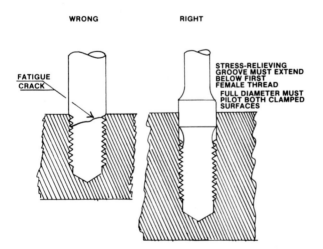

WRONG   RIGHT

FATIGUE CRACK

STRESS-RELIEVING GROOVE MUST EXTEND BELOW FIRST FEMALE THREAD

FULL DIAMETER MUST PILOT BOTH CLAMPED SURFACES

The basic problem here is the inordinate amount of work that is required to convert even a good industrial tension bolt into an acceptable race car double-shear bolt:

(1) Find a bolt with the required diameter, thread pitch and an acceptable grip (unthreaded or shank) length.

(2) Cut off the surplus thread. Leave sufficient thread to fully engage the threads of the nut plus a minimum of three full threads. Standard AN thread lengths are:

Bolt diameter and thread pitch	Thread length (for full-height nut)
#10-32	13/32"
1/4-28	13/32"
5/16-24	17/32"
3/8-24	41/64"
7/16-20	21/32"
1/2-20	25/32"

(3) Chamfer (put a lead on) the cut-off end so that you can screw a nut onto it, preferably without cutting the nylon locking ring. I use, in descending order of preference, a belt sander, a disc grinder, a grindstone or a file. I am too lazy to chuck each bolt into a lathe.

(4) You may also get to drill the thing for safety wire. Since all internal wrenching bolts are case hardened, they are every bit as destructive toward drill bits as they are toward hacksaw blades. The tip here is to grind a small flat on each side of the bolt head in the area of the hole-to-be AND to SERIOUSLY center punch a starting pocket. It helps both operator and drill bit temper to grind the flats approximately parallel to the corresponding flats of the internal hex and to use a sharp drill bit, the right drill speed and a lubricant.

A great many of the bolts and machine screws on the typical racing car fall into the "noncritical" class. You are not going to break the #10-32's that hold the mirrors on, the 1/4-28's in the fuel cell hatch nor the 5/16-24's that serve as throttle and clutch stops. The 7/16"-bore rod end bearings so loved by small Formula car constructors don't require NAS bolts for the simple reason that the loads involved are too low to cause a problem if you were to use a 7/16" nail. This means that there are many applications where, when nothing better is available, an SAE Grade Five (three line) bolt will do the job, but not on one of my cars.

For a realistic indication of what is actually required, assuming top-quality hardware, properly scheduled and performed maintenance and scheduled replacement of parts, take a good look at the bolts on the current Brabham Formula One car. For an equally valid indication of what is required to do the job on a very good amateur car take a look at David Bruns' and Paul White's latest brainchild, the

Figure (153): Tension bolts with reduced shank diameter for more even distribution of installed stress and enhanced fatigue life.

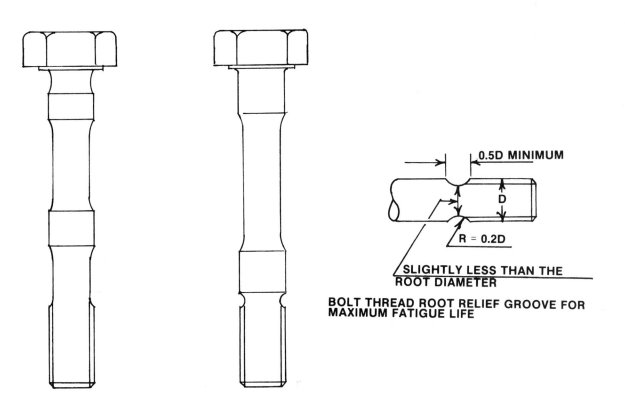

0.5D MINIMUM

D

R = 0.2D

SLIGHTLY LESS THAN THE ROOT DIAMETER

BOLT THREAD ROOT RELIEF GROOVE FOR MAXIMUM FATIGUE LIFE

Swift Formula Ford. For reasons involving quality control (or lack of it) and price, I don't much like using SAE Grade Eight bolts but I will use them in a pinch. I still REFUSE to use or to keep in stock "super whatever" and "superior to SAE Grade Eight" bolts. More on this subject later.

We should be sensible about this business of bolts and the racing car. If your racer arrived from the manufacturer with an aircraft bolt (or a good socket-head cap screw) holding a particular widget on, you can bet that it is there for a reason (the builder does not enjoy spending money) and you will replace it with an inferior bolt at your peril. On the other hand, replacing a British Allen bolt with an SPS Unbrako socket head cap screw or replacing an original grade-nothing bolt with a modified SAE Grade Eight or an AN bolt is not only perfectly safe, it is a positive step in the right direction. One has to use one's head.

My standard practice is to keep only Mil Spec bolts in open stock (i.e., the stock that anyone other than myself can get at). That way I KNOW that no one is going to substitute an inferior bolt without my knowledge. Since there is no realistic way that I can foresee every fastener need that is going to come up in the course of a season—even if I had room to carry them—I also carry, in my own private stock, a pretty comprehensive selection of SPS socket-head cap screws and SAE Grade Eight bolts in various diameters and grip lengths. I then modify to suit when it becomes necessary.

I also keep in stock a few ridiculously long bolts in each diameter so that, when the need arises, I can break my oft-quoted cardinal rule about NEVER die cutting threads onto a bolt. I only do it when I absolutely have to and then only with bolts in double shear. I DO replace the thing at the next opportunity. One last word on the subject—I would much rather use a modified Grade Eight bolt than to die additional threads onto an NAS bolt!

CAUTION! PELIGRO! DANGER!

There are some applications where it is just NOT SAFE to use anything other than the best bolts available. These applications—regardless of what came on the car—include, but are not limited to:

(1) Brake disc to top hat bolts. Having once been witness to the results of the shearing of these items (and not having liked what I saw even a little bit) I use 180,000 psi NAS 624-series 12-point bolts with proper NAS beveled washers under the bolt head and high-temperature "jet" or "K" nuts. DO NOT USE STAINLESS BOLTS IN THIS APPLICATION.

(2) Crown wheel (ring gear) to differential housing or spool bolts. A fair percentage of the failed Hewland crown-wheel-and-pinion sets that I am called in to autopsy have failed simply because the crown wheel loosened on the carrier with subsequent predictable and catastrophic results. Hewland assembles the things with bolts that are marginally satisfactory for one-time use, and then uses soft-iron lock tabs to hold the bolts in place. This is insanity! Even though the Hewland manuals specifically warn against reuse of the bolts, lots of people do use them over.

Some people even get away with it—for a while. Eventually either the bolts stretch or the lock tabs squeeze out (the shock loads involved are fearsome); the ring gear gets just a little loose on the carrier and AWAY WE GO. Another possible scenario which I have seen a few times is that one of the stretched bolts fatigues and breaks off. Stress raisers being what and where they are, the bolt breaks at the thread root. This leaves just enough grip length so that the bolt head and shank, due to the proximity of the Hewland side cover, cannot escape. Instead the head of the bolt becomes a dull but effective fly cutter until it either destroys the side cover OR removes enough of same so that it CAN escape and wedge itself between the pinion and the ring gear. . . . in either case, END OF DEAL! The solution is to use a Ford Motor Company bolt, part #B8AZ-6379A, bolt, fly/whl. This is Ford's standard V-8 manual flywheel-to-crankshaft bolt. It has to be shortened about $\frac{1}{8}$'', drilled and chamfered for lock wire. It will then fit Hewland FT and larger applications (I am not sure about MK9/8/5) and it WILL NOT FAIL. I use them with no washer at all, Loctite Threadlocker 271 or, when I can find it, 262 and safety wire. These bolts are reuseable until thread damage is visible in the form of flattened thread crowns (I have never seen one elongate).

(3) Flywheel to crankshaft bolts. Nothing good has ever been reported about the flywheel parting company with the crankshaft! On V-8's, I use the same Ford Motor Company bolt described above. For the Cosworths I use a suitably modified SPS Unbrako socket-head cap screw, WITH THE CORRECT GRIP LENGTH. This is a pain in the butt. Not only must a bunch of thread be removed and the end of the thread dressed, but the head must also be shortened. These bolts cannot be reused (not even once!) and the shortened inhex will occasionally strip when you are trying to remove them. (Heat the bolt to red hot to kill the Loctite, hit it HARD at the root of the inhex with a punch, wait for it to cool and remove with an Allen key or chisel—effective technique courtesy Steve Jennings.) On the other hand, the flywheel WILL NOT COME OFF. This last statement cannot be made if other bolts are used. Take your choice. Make sure that there is enough of a chamfer in the flywheel to clear the radius under the bolt head.

(4) Any suspension pivot bolt with a diameter of less than $\frac{5}{16}$'' on a car weighing 900 lb or less, $\frac{3}{8}$'' on 1500 lb cars or $\frac{7}{16}$'' on cars up to 2500 lb. When cars get heavier than that we are out of the league that I prefer to play in. My feeling is that the behemoths are liable at some time in their lives to run on the high banks; therefore, they deserve the best suspension pivot bolts that can be found.

(5) Shift linkage universal joint to tube/rail bolts. This may sound like a very strange place to require good bolts. It is not—for the simple reason that no one, to my knowledge (except David Bruns) designs cars with BOTH a decent shift linkage layout AND proper universal joints. Why this should be I do not know. It just IS! From Formula Ford to Formula One, most shifting problems can be traced directly to less-than-optimum shift linkage. Most racers never do anything about it. When everything loosens up

and becomes sloppy and horrible the normal answer to the driver's piteous complaints is to slot the cheap and nasty universal joints that came on the car and to really graunch down on the ¼'' throughbolt that secures the universal joint to the rail. With any kind of luck at all the operator will even drill and deburr a hole in the universal joint at the end of the hacksaw slot so that the whole thing won't split in two starting at the jagged end of the cut. Eventually, however, the bolt gives up (by now it is almost certain to be in an oversize hole). If we are lucky it happens while the nut is being tightened after a gear change and the result is a couple of skinned knuckles and a new bolt. If we are not lucky the mechanic ignores it when the bolt ''feels funny''; it happens later and the result is a DNF. The use of a 12-point NAS 624-series bolt and a shear stop nut will prevent the latter occurrence simply because the nut will strip before any harm can be done to the bolt. The right way to do the whole thing will be described later.

NUTS

In most racing applications the actual tensile strength of the nut used in an assembly is of secondary importance. Notable exceptions to this statement are found in the engine. In just about all of our applications the assembly will be loaded mainly in shear (hopefully in double shear) and the nut is only required to:

    (1) Retain assembled torque/clamping force and
    (2) Not fall off.

So long as the temperature stays below the boiling point of water, just about ANY properly tightened elastic stop nut will do the job.

The Formula One brigade, accustomed by now to virtually unlimited budgets, tends to use ''jet nuts'' or ''K nuts'' for just about everything. I admit that these are fine pieces indeed—light, temperature resistant, positively locking, handsome and almost infinitely reuseable (see FIGURE [154]). They are also diabolically expensive and their haphazard use smacks, to me, of conspicuous consumption. I use plain old nylon insert elastic stop nuts almost everywhere. I have never had one back off. I DO use the AN/MS stuff rather than the industrial variety.

Since I am at least as weight conscious as the next man I do use shear (½ high) nuts on double-shear applications and yes, I do use shear bolts when I can find them surplus and I do trim the excess thread length from standard airframe bolts when I use them in double shear. Single shear, a mortal sin to begin with, I consider to be a tension application so far as fasteners are concerned.

For high temperature and/or high stress and/or severe vibration applications I use all-metal 6-point ''jet nuts'' which I purchase from Earl's Supply. If I were really in the bucks I would use the NAS 679 series high-temperature lock nuts which are formed from sheet metal and are REALLY light (see FIGURE [155]). If we are talking about turbocharger-type heat we should talk to either the manufacturer of the turbo or to SPS.

Nylon insert elastic stop nuts should not be used on modular wheels, at least not with outboard brakes. Bill Jongbloed uses an all-metal lock nut manufactured by Fastron that is light, has a lot of bearing area, holds its torque indefinitely while in very close proximity to the brake disc and is relatively inexpensive. It also tends to chew up the male threads when reused. Bill does not recommend reusing the nuts. Being no fool, he uses SPS Unbrako cap screws to hold his wheels together. I do not reuse the cap screws either.

HOW THE STOP NUTS WORK

There are three basic forms of elastic stop nut: those that use a nylon locking collar; the ''slotted beam,'' ''segmented'' or ''flex lock'' all-metal nut; and the ''elliptically offset'' or ''triangular displacement'' all-metal nut. The all-metal types are termed ''elastic stop nuts'' simply because they form their lock by controlled elastic deformation of a portion of the thread cylinder. The operating principles of all three are similar, and I am going to take the time to explain them for the simple reason that no one else does.

The most common (and least expensive) of the self locking nuts utilizes a nylon locking collar (FIGURE [156]) and

Figure (154): The ''Jet'' or ''K'' nut.

Figure (155): NAS 679 high-temperature nut.

Figure (156): Elastic stop nut with nylon locking collar.

is available either as an AN/MS or as an industrial part. We can be certain of the material, design and quality control on the AN/MS parts. The ID of the nylon insert is slightly smaller than the major diameter of the bolt thread. The nut will spin freely on the bolt until the bolt threads engage the locking collar where they impress (but do not cut) mating threads in the nylon. This compression forces the upper flanks of the nut threads into metal-to-metal contact with the lower flanks of the mating bolt threads forming a "friction hold." This hold plus the compression of the nylon are sufficient to ensure that a properly tightened nut will not loosen on the bolt at temperatures up to 250 degrees F. These nuts cannot harm the bolt thread and they can be reused many times.

In the all-metal elliptically offset or displaced thread elastic stop nut, as illustrated by FIGURE [157], the nut threads are divided into two separate sections. The lower section consists of retaining threads which are manufactured in the form of the normal cylindrical helix, while the top portion of the thread is distorted or offset into either a triangular or an elliptical shape.

As the bolt thread enters the distorted locking section of the nut thread, the out-of-roundness is displaced to a cylindrical section. This displacement is actually elastic deformation of the nut metal. When the male thread protrudes two or three threads beyond the top of the nut, this elastic deformation has created a friction hold sufficient to lock the nut against minor vibration, even though it may not yet be seated against the work surface. When it is seated and fully tightened the base of the nut presses down on the clamped surface while the locking threads press in against the bolt, lifting the nut and forcing the upper flanks of the retaining

threads hard against the lower flanks of the bolt threads, as shown in FIGURE [158]. The fastener is now fully locked.

These nuts are available in tensile strengths to 300,000 psi with temperature ranges up to 1400 degrees F. When manufactured to Mil Specs they are almost infinitely reuseable and will not harm male threads. On the other hand, some of the industrial copies are not meant to be disassembled and can wreck male threads in a single removal.

The thread of the all-metal "slotted beam" or "segmented" elastic stop nut, as shown in FIGURE [159] is also divided into two separate areas: the retaining threads and the locking threads. In this case the top locking threads

Figure (158): Cross-section of installed elastic stop nut.

Figure (157): The all-metal "distorted thread" or elliptically offset elastic stop nut.

Figure (159): The all-metal "segmented" or "slotted-beam" elastic stop nut.

A RELAXED

A RELAXED

B ENGAGED

B ENGAGED

are radially slotted and deflected inward to produce a controlled friction lock at the top of the nut. Again they are available in various configurations, alloys and tempers to about 180,000 psi and 1400 degrees F and, manufactured to Mil Specs, are reuseable and harmless.

WASHERS

Washers basically serve as bearing surfaces to prevent bolt heads and nuts from digging into the surfaces to be clamped and to provide more accurate torque readings. We also use them as shims. The only functional requirement is that they have a hole the right size, that they be flat (which is just about guaranteed by the manufacturing process) and that they be hard enough to prevent the nut or bolt from squeezing them under load. For shear applications I still prefer to use the AN/MS items. AN/MS washers are the only ones that come in both 0.031 and 0.063 thicknesses and in oversize diameters for use with fiberglass. Besides, they are lighter and a damned sight more handsome than SAE washers. Again Earl's can supply via UPS if you cannot find a local source and the bill may be a pleasant surprise—at least when compared with what the "super whatever" distributors charge for inferior stuff. In tension applications I use hardened and ground machine washers.

LOCK WASHERS

So called "lock washers" are popular in certain circles. There is only one basic problem with lock washers: they don't work. Think about it: the lock washer is supposed to function as a spring BUT, at a very low level of bolt preload the spring washer is squashed flat. Once a fastener has loosened to the point where a split lock washer becomes a spring, the assembly is far too loose for any sort of safety.

SPEAKING OF WHICH

Some of you people out there STILL don't believe what I said in PREPARE TO WIN about "super whatever" and "superior to SAE Grade Eight" bolts. I will therefore repeat my words: "THEY ARE JUNK!" They have always been junk and, presumably, they will always BE junk. In these cases "superior to Grade Eight" actually means "HARDER than SAE Grade Eight"—and usually means HARD as in GLASS and HARD as in BRITTLE. If the SAE members felt any need for a series of bolt specifications superior to their Grade Eight, they would come out with Grade Nine specs (this was actually being considered a few years ago but, so far as I know, nothing came of it). If the SAE had some way of enforcing their CURRENT specifications, I would be happier and so would they.

The "super whatever" claims are pure moonglow, a sales gimmick designed to seduce the unwary and the ignorant. If you use this stuff on race cars, sooner or later you are going to have a fastener failure, usually due to poor quality control. Seldom does a month go by without someone who should know better coming up to me with a snapped (not bent) "super whatever" bolt to ask me what I think. I usually tell the individual I think he should have his brains tested. In addition to being junk, these bolts, compared to aircraft stuff, are expensive. Do yourself a couple of favors and don't use them.

It seems I failed to convince a great many people on this subject the first time around. This time I have hunted up some graphic examples of what can go wrong in the manufacture of bolts. FIGURE [160] is a collection of microphotos of manufacturing defects that are not visible to the naked eye. With aerospace fasteners we can be pretty damned sure that the manufacturer's inspection and quality control programs are going to catch these foul-ups. With commercial fasteners we have no such guarantee. With "super whatever" type fasteners we can be pretty damned sure that they will be ignored. With regard to the worthies who sell the "super whatever" stuff, remember that one of Murphy's laws states, "All claims made by a manufacturer's sales representative should be multiplied by a factor of 0.25." These people are SALESMEN, not engineers. Their ignorance is awesome.

METRICS

As the world moves inexorably toward total metricization (in its refusal to change, the United States now finds itself in the lonely but somewhat select company of such industrial giants as Liberia, Burma and Papua New Guinea) we, the racers, will have to find more and more high quality metric fasteners. Even though U.S. industry now uses (very quietly) quite a few, it isn't easy to find metric hardware, let alone GOOD metric hardware. The best source that I have found is: Metrics Inc., 410 S. Varney St., Burbank, CA 90502. This worthy stocks hex-headed and internal-wrenching bolts in all common metric diameters and thread pitches (of which there are too many) as well as plain nuts, elastic stop nuts, all-metal lock nuts, flat and lock washers. It also stocks the copper-coated all-metal lock nuts that are magic for exhaust systems.

This is good information to have when you need a season's supply of something, but not a lot of help when you need a couple of items in a hurry. You would do well to make the acquaintance of a GOOD parts man in a Fiat, VW, Honda, Datsun or Toyota shop. They all have good hardware of all descriptions, but it is somewhat of a bear to identify. The Japanese quality is every bit as good as that of the Germans and Italians and a damn sight cheaper. In my opinion that statement applies to the cars as well as to the hardware.

If you need aerospace quality in metric fasteners you are in big trouble unless you happen to know someone who works for Matra or Aerospaziale. The same is true of rod end and spherical bearings. I can only suggest converting to inches by the selective use of drills, reamers, sleeves, bushings and threaded inserts as necessary.

THREADED INSERTS

Again there is little new to describe. I still use Helicoils, Keen-Serts or Rosans in nonferrous castings. I have just about stopped using Riv-Nuts and such in sheet metal and

Figure (160): Defects in the manufacture of bolts, which are not visible to the unaided eye.

GOOD FORGING PRACTICE

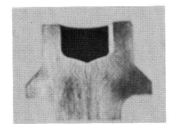

PROPER FORGING PRACTICE PRODUCES UNIFORM AND SMOOTH GRAIN FLOW

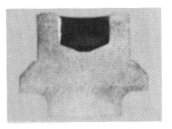

BOLT MANUFACTURED FROM STOCK WITH SEAM

LAP IN THREAD ROOT

SEVERE GRINDING BURNS REVEALED BY ACID ETCH

BRITTLE CARBURIZATION LAYER ON TOOTH CREST DUE TO IMPROPER HEAT TREAT

fiberglass because I finally got tired of having them twist out at the wrong time. I am presently using nut plates (anchor nuts) of one type or another (FIGURE [161] shows some of the available configurations) wherever I need female threads in a blind or partially blind panel. The only new tip that I have with respect to the nut plate is that I have finally figured out that it is a damned sight more practical to carry around a bunch of $\frac{3}{32}$'' blind rivets than it is to drill out the $\frac{3}{32}$'' holes that come in #10-32 nut plates to $\frac{1}{8}$'' so that you can use standard pop rivets. It is also more than worthwhile to either make or buy a simple drill jig if you are going to install very many of them. I obtain my nut plates from Earl's Supply or from Cal State Aero.

QUARTER TURN TO LOCK PANEL FASTENERS

I still use a lot of Dzus buttons to hold various body, auxiliary and access panels in place. I don't like Cam-Locs much and I refuse to use whatever the deformed nails are that hold Ralt side pods more-or-less in place. I use the old reliable EFF series of plate mounted Dzuses held to the panel with two rivets (see FIGURE [162]). This is made a lot easier for me by the fact that Earl's Supply now stocks them in most diameters and grip lengths.

The EFF series of Dzus fasteners require no tooling and are so easy to use that it seems silly to use anything else. It seems equally silly to install either a Dzus button or a Dzus wire onto a fiberglass panel without an aluminum back-up plate. Fiberglass may have many virtues (off hand I cannot think of any other than cost) but a bearing material it is not! The back-up plates should have enough area to do some good, require very little thickness (0.031'' is enough) and should be dimpled in the center to match the dimple in the Dzus plate. They should be flush riveted to the inside of the fiberglass panel. This is just one more of the seemingly endless preseason tasks that convert the standard kit car to a practical race car. All of the details pay off during the season when time is critical.

If I ever have a program with money again I will probably convert to Dzus's relatively new ''supersonic'' line (see FIGURE [163]) which is stronger and more vibration

Figure (162): Dzus EHF panel fastener.

Figure (163): Dzus ''supersonic'' line of aircraft panel fasteners.

Figure (161): Some of the available anchor nut configurations.

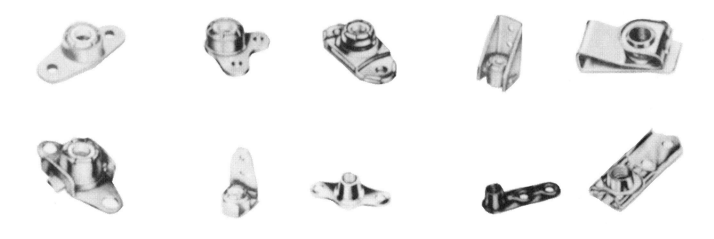

resistant than the standard line OR to its "quick-acting threaded fasteners," (see FIGURE [164]) which feature a bayonet-type thread and are still stronger and even more vibration resistant.

Previous comments regarding back-up plates also apply to these advanced fasteners—even more than they do to the standard line.

As a point of interest, Dzus also manufactures a very complete line of really good toggle clamps, which we don't use very often but which we can never find when we do need them (see FIGURE [165]).

PIP PINS

It seems that each year I use more and more quick-release pins of one sort or another. I use pip pins in all sorts of applications—from holding things in place in the trailer to holding the antiroll bar links in place when I think it is going to rain. I strongly favor the retention of front substructures with pip pins through double-shear brackets so that I can replace them in a hurry. I am giving serious thought to using pip pins to hold the spring/shock absorber units in place while testing in order to reduce the downtime while changing springs. I use either roll pins or taper pins to lock various things that I don't want to move AT ALL, like shift linkage adjustors and universal joints.

Much as I admire all types of quick-acting pins, I really dislike cotter pins. It therefore gives me great pleasure to announce that I no longer use them at all, although I do carry a reasonable assortment around with me just in case. They have been replaced with a combination of AN 415 lock pins and AN 416 cowling pins as shown in FIGURE [166]. These clever little devils do the same job of last-ditch safetying in a fraction of the time and with a fraction of the bother. The AN 415-2 (2.00" × 0.080") lock pin does an admirable job as a wheel safety pin for Ralts and Marches at a fraction of the importer's price. It blew the kart racers away when my son Christopher showed up with nary a cotter pin on his Sprint Kart. Now the aircraft pins are pretty common in karting and are sold by all the kart shops at exorbitant prices—which may indicate a couple of things about karters and racers (it certainly indicates something about my business acumen).

BETTER RACING THROUGH CHEMISTRY—THE LOCTITE STORY

A lot has happened at the Loctite Corporation since I first sung its praises in PREPARE TO WIN. Loctite acquired the Permatex Corporation and integrated, streamlined and expanded both product lines. The quality remains superb. The products are now divided into five major categories: threadlocking, sealing, gasketing, retaining of cylindrical components and bonding. Its catalog is complete, detailed, informative and free. Obtain it from your local distributor and read it.

In the beginning we racers used only a couple of Loctite products: Nutloc (blue) and Studlock (red). No more! At the moment I carry with me four separate threadlockers, two sealants, one gasketing compound, two retaining compounds, a primer, two adhesives and an antiseize compound. I also carry Loctite's do-it-yourself O-ring kit, but seldom use it.

Basically the Loctite compounds are anaerobic liquids. This means that they fill the voids between mating parts, and IN THE ABSENCE OF AIR and IN THE PRESENCE OF METAL they will "cure" or self harden from the liquid state to a plastic film which adheres to the surface imperfections on both parts and which must be sheared before the mating metal parts can move relative to each other. The mating parts are not only locked together, they are sealed against leakage and/or corrosion. Of the various compounds that are available I use:

Figure (165): Dzus toggle latches.

Figure (164): Dzus quick-acting threaded fasteners.

THREADLOCKER 242 (blue). A general-purpose, medium-strength compound which, as the name suggests, does most jobs—so long as the thread in question is engaged for a minimum of 1.5 diameters.

THREADLOCKER 271 (red). A high-strength compound for small fasteners. (Loctite's definition of small is somewhat different from ours: To it any fastener under 1'' in diameter is small.) This compound is especially effective in aluminum and magnesium castings and is very resistant to fuels, oils and solvents (after it has set). Where once I helicoiled all of my Hewland transaxle and bellhousing studs, I now use 271. Contrary to popular opinion it has the same temperature range as 242 (to 300 degrees F). Its shearing or breakaway torque is, however, some 2½ times greater.

THREADLOCKER 262 (red). A hard-to-find, high-strength compound with controlled torque tension—whatever that may be. It is specifically compounded for high-strength fasteners which will be subjected to heavy shock/vibration loads and high levels of stress. I use it on ring gear bolts, universal and CV joint bolts, axle-retaining nuts, flywheel bolts and the like. It has about 15% greater breakaway torque than 271 and the same 300 degree F temperature limitation.

THREADLOCKER 290 (green). Believe it or not, this is a penetrating compound which locks ALREADY ASSEMBLED threaded fasteners. I first ran into it under the name Loctite Super Wick-In in Australia. The fluid is drawn into assembled and torqued threads by capillary action and cures to a medium strength similar to that of 242. Like all of the Loctite compounds, 290 does not like oil or grease, so I spray the assembly-to-be-treated with Loctite Primer N, Brake Clean or some similar aerosol cleaner before I apply the magic. Since I end up running a lot of cars that have been assembled by folk I do not know, I find Loctite 290 to be great comfort.

Figure (166): Two types of pins.

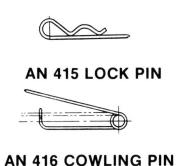

AN 415 LOCK PIN

AN 416 COWLING PIN

POROSITY SEALANT 290 (green). Same stuff—we just didn't know it. In addition to locking threads, 290 will wick itself into any porous metal (including both ferrous and nonferrous castings and welds) and cures to form a tough, elastic and pressure-resistant seal that is resistant to fuels, lubes and solvents. It brushes on and the excess cleans off with a rag. I use it as a matter of course on the weld seams of all tanks, reservoirs and hard lines.

PST PIPE SEALANT WITH TEFLON. I no longer use Teflon tape. PST is a hell of a lot more convenient, easier to use, cannot shred and get into filters, jets and so on, seals better, and I don't have to worry about which direction to wrap the tape. PST is not just another pipe dope, it is anaerobic and completely fills the voids between the mating threads.

RETAINING COMPOUND 601 (green). This is serious stuff. It is designed to retain bearings, sleeves, pins, bushings or other cylindrical objects in bores which have become distorted, oversized or otherwise buggered. It works. Shear strength is 3000 psi and the temperature range is up to 300 degrees F. I use it where and when I need it. If things get really desperate, Retaining Compound 680 has a shear strength of 4000 psi and Retaining Compound 620 has the same strength as 601 but is good to 450 degrees F. My experience tells me (although the Loctite Corporation does not) that all of these compounds will also work on threads. It should be noted that disassembly will not be easy and that the shear figures that I have given are for steel. Used with either aluminum or magnesium the figure drops to 600 psi in all cases. When the designer has been cheap and used a right-hand thread where he should have used a left-hand thread, I find that 680 works wonders until I can figure out a mechanical lock.

GASKET ELIMINATOR 515. I used to carry around a whole bunch of gasketing glops, ranging from the various silicone sealants to Hylomar. No more! Now I carry Gasket Eliminator 515 with a tube of GE's high-temperature silicone sealer as a back-up. 515 has two major advantages over anything else that I know of: It peels off the disassembled surface as a ribbon rather than having to be scraped or scrubbed off AND it fills voids between mating surfaces better than any other gasket goop. Used with Loctite Primer N it will fill and seal voids up to 0.050'' which makes it a really good buggered-surface repairer as well as a gasket eliminator.

NICKEL ANTISEIZE 771. When I cannot find my very favorite antiseize compound (Copaslip, which is hard to find, expensive and worth it) I use Loctite 771, which is probably every bit as good.

LOCTITE PRIMERS. Primers decrease cure time, clean parts and improve the void-filling capability of the various anaerobic compounds. They are a minor pain to use. I carry Primer N with me and use it when I think that I need it, like when I want the Loctite to cure in a hurry.

SPEEDBONDER 319. This is a general-purpose bonding agent with good impact resistance and a very fast cure. I use it to rig quick and dirty holding fixtures. Used with Primer N, bonded metal parts can be handled in less than a minute and reach fixture strength in 15. It also fixes broken china and stuff around the house, thus earning valuable points for us housemates.

QUICKSET ADHESIVE 404. I use it to splice my own O-rings from the Loctite O-ring kit. I used to carry a Parker O-ring kit around. I always had every O-ring except the one that I needed. Now I carry the specific O-rings that I think I might need (in sealed containers) and the Loctite do-it-yourself kit. It will not make dynamic seals but it works just fine for static O-rings.

QUICKMETAL PRESS FIT REPAIR. This is a new product that I have been carrying for about a year. It is supposed to be a PERMANENT repair for worn shafts, housings, keyways and the like. I hope that I never need it but I have a hunch that one of these days it is going to save my butt.

INSTANT GAS TANK REPAIR. I have a couple of these kits in the glovebox of the truck. They also work on metal fuel churns (NOBODY enjoys welding on a fuel container, even when it is filled with water).

KILLING THE LOCTITE BOND

Every so often we run into a situation where cured Loctite prevents us from removing something, usually a cheap and nasty internal-wrenching bolt that has stripped its in-hex. The solution, since Loctites are temperature limited, is heat—lots of heat. Steve Jennings taught me that if the head of the offending cap screw is heated to bright red with a small tipped welding torch (to localize the heat), allowed to cool and struck a sharp blow with a hammer, the damned thing will usually come out.

LOCTITE AND SLIPPERY COATINGS

The Loctite compounds are designed to work on clean metal; they will not function on either oily or dirty metal. This means that BOTH surfaces must be cleaned prior to application. Since most of our solvents (and the racer's normal cleaning agent, gasoline) leave an oily film on everything that they touch, it is easy to achieve a false sense of security with Loctite. I tend to use one of the brake cleaning compounds to clean the parts for the simple reason that they work and are easy both to find and to carry around. Loctite Corporation would prefer us to use its cleaners, but they are VERY expensive and the Brake Clean seems to work just fine. Use whatever you prefer, but get all of the oil, grease and dirt off before you apply Loctite.

THE JOINING OF MATERIALS—RIVETING, BONDING & WELDING

CHAPTER NINE

The evolution of joining by riveting and welding has been just about complete for a very long time, and we racers don't do much bonding. This will therefore be a short chapter.

RIVETING—NEW STUFF

Since PREPARE TO WIN, the Cherry Rivet Division of the Townsend Corporation has introduced a new industrial structural blind rivet, the Cherry Q, at a fraction of the cost of its aerospace structural rivets and with virtually the same strengths. Unlike Cherry's other rivets, the Q requires no special tooling and can be pulled with any standard hand or pneumatic puller. FIGURE [167] shows the rivet and its characteristics. Material for material the Cherry Q has about 75% more shear strength and 80% more tensile strength than the best of the "pop" rivets. I use both the BS and the MS series. My discovery of the Cherry Q has encouraged me to stop wasting my time sourcing USM's Flush Break line, which is even harder to find. Rivet salespeople are about as knowledgeable as threaded-fastener salespeople. Do not allow their hype to confuse the Cherry Q with Cherry's other commercial blind rivet, the Cherry N which is just another pop rivet.

Premier Fastener Corporation offers a hand-operated blind-rivet squeezer that is superior to all of the others that I have tried. It is made in England, has a long snout so that it can reach into tight places, long handles so that normal human beings can pull even $^3/_{16}$'' steel mandrel rivets and can be purchased, with a certain amount of coaxing, from your local Premier distributor. Premier, whose threaded fasteners are junk, also handles the outstanding Avex line of nonstructural blind rivets (although at exorbitant cost compared to what your Avdel distributor charges for the same item). Speaking of Avex rivets, they now offer an oversized (in head diameter only) dome-head rivet which is excellent for use in fiberglass. I still use no other brand of nonstructural rivets.

TOOLS

If you are shooting a lot of blind rivets you may want to consider the purchase of either a pneumatic or a hydraulic blind-rivet puller. Aircraft Spruce offers the very good Trojan model HR-77 hand-operated hydraulic unit for about $60. When it comes to pneumatic units, the one to avoid is Rodac (I have seen the pot metal castings explode under normal air-line pressure). Mine is made by USM, is the bottom of the line and has given me 15 years of excellent service.

FLUSH RIVETING

Due to the relatively light gauges of sheet metal that we use we can seldom CUT a countersink for flush rivets. This means that we have to dimple in order to use flush rivets. You can purchase $\frac{1}{8}$'', 100 degree combination punch and dimpling die sets for your Whitney punch from Roper Whitney. This set works fine with Avex flush rivets but for structural rivets of any sort you will need a 120 degree taper. Aircraft Spruce offers a neat 120 degree flush-dimpling tool that fits in your hand pop-rivet pliers. You will need a bunch of extra pulling nails. Alternatively, you can have the Whitney punch dies ground to 120 degrees. FIGURE [168] shows both.

It has just dawned on me that it is not common knowledge that the cutting of countersinks in thin sheet metal is a bad

Figure (167): The Cherry Q rivet.

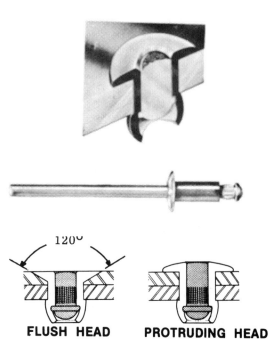

CHERRY Q RIVET IDENTIFICATION CODE

First letter is rivet material:
A = 5052 Aluminum   B = 5056 Aluminum   C = Stainless
M = Monel   S = Steel
Second letter is mandrel material:
A = 7178 Aluminum   S = Steel   C = Stainless
Third letter is head style:
P = Protruding   L = Large   C = Flush
Fourth letter is type of rivet:
Q = Cherry Q Rivet, structural, self-plugging
First number is rivet diameter in 32nds of an inch:
For example, −6 is 6/32nds or 3/16'' diameter
Second number is rivet maximum grip length in 16th of an inch:

For example, −8 is 8/16ths or 1/2'' grip length

MINIMUM RIVET SHEAR AND TENSILE STRENGTH (lbs.) CHERRY Q RIVETS

RIVET DIAM.	BS SERIES ALUM RIVET STEEL MAND. GRADE 19		MS SERIES MONEL RIVET STEEL MAND. GRADE 40		CC SERIES STAINLESS RIVET STAINLESS MAND. GRADE 51	
	Shear	Tens.	Shear	Tens.	Shear	Tens.
1/8	350	325	650	525	700	600
5/32	525	450	950	900	1050	1000
3/16	750	650	1450	1100	1650	1300
1/4	1250	1050	2350	2150	2450	2250

practice and that I had best explain. FIGURE [169] shows the various ways of preparing sheet metal surfaces for flush rivets. You will note that in example A (the machining of a countersink in thin sheet metal which is to be joined to a similar sheet), there is precious little rivet bearing area left and the sheets are actually being held together by blind faith. The same is true of example C (a thin sheet joined to a sheet of thicker cross section). Examples B and D show the right way to arrange countersinks in these cases. Section E illustrates the reason that the aircraft industry rejected the 100 degree industrial countersink in favor of the 120 degree AN countersink. Section F merely shows that it is possible to dimple a thick sheet, but not with our hand equipment. Dimpling is easy—although with 2024 T3, you may have to locally anneal the dimpled area. Anyway, you cut countersinks in thin sheet metal at your peril.

Every so often I come up with the need to squeeze rather than to buck a solid rivet, such as on the trailing edges of wings. I used to borrow an expensive air/hydraulic rivet squeezer from Jan Rury. Jan got smart and moved to Tahoe. I then discovered that a standard compound lever welding toggle clamp does a super job on $3/32$'' and $1/8$'' solid rivets—flush, dome or flat head in either A (soft, formed from 1100 aluminum with a tensile strength of 16,000 psi) or AD (formed from 2117 aluminum alloy and heat treated to the T-4 condition with a tensile strength of 38,000 psi) specification. My clamp is about 8'' long, says Knu-Vise #P-1800 on it and is shown in FIGURE [170]. I bought it at Douglas Surplus a long time ago. Any compound lever parallel arm clamp will do; merely polish the pedestals, adjust the width to the desired finished rivet thickness and have at it one handed.

Figure (168): Flush riveting dimplers.

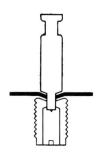

100° DIMPLING DIES FOR #5 JUNIOR WHITNEY PUNCH

120° DIMPLING DIES FOR POP-RIVET PLIERS FROM AIRCRAFT SPRUCE

TIP-RIVET INSERTION

I have recently been dipping each blind rivet in epoxy before I insert it into its hole. This makes damned sure that the hole is completely filled and seals the rivet against moisture.

Figure (170): Toggle clamp.

Figure (169): Preparation of holes for flush riveting.

A. COUNTERSINK CUT IN THIN SHEET METAL REDUCING RIVET BEARING AREA

B. COUNTERSINK DIMPLED

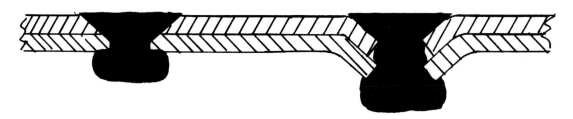

C. COUNTERSINK CUT IN THIN/THICK SHEETS— REDUCED BEARING AREA IN THIN SHEET

D. COUNTERSINK DIMPLED IN THIN SHEET, CUT IN THICK—ACCEPTABLE

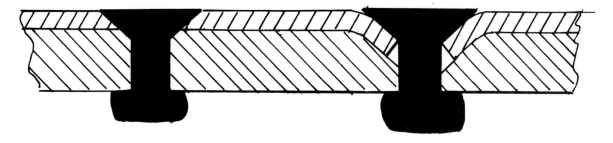

E. 120° AIRCRAFT INDUSTRY COUNTERSINK. COMPARE BEARING AREA WITH 100° INDUSTRIAL COUNTERSINK ABOVE

F. COUNTERSINK DIMPLED IN BOTH THICK AND THIN SHEETS

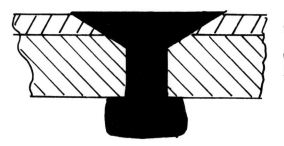

TIP-RIVET REMOVAL

Instead of using a dolly (or nothing) to back up the panel when I am either punching the mandrel out of a blind rivet or knocking the stem of an already beheaded rivet out of its hole, I now use a couple of pieces of heavy bar stock with generously radiused corners and a few ¼'' holes drilled in strategic locations. I hold the appropriate chunk behind the panel, wiggle it around until the shop-formed head of the rivet to be removed falls into one of the holes, hold a punch on the other end of the rivet and hammer the thing out. Assuming that the back-up bar is properly positioned and firmly held, the mandrel or rivet pops right out and it is almost impossible to distort the sheet metal.

THE DESIGN OF RIVETED JOINTS

You may recall that during our discussion of metal fatigue I stated that I would cover fatigue and the riveted joint at a later time. That time has come. I have already stated that, although structural joins are never good, from the practical point of view they are inevitable. Let's see what is wrong with the riveted joint—and how we can use our new-found knowledge of metallurgy and strength of materials to minimize the unfortunate aspects.

The first problem with the riveted joint in sheet metal is that the loads involved are virtually always tension/compression loads which place the sheets in tension/compression, but the rivets in shear. The tension load in the sheet metal tends to elongate the round rivet holes into little ellipses whose major axes lie in the direction of load. We know (from PREPARE TO WIN) that single-row rivet joints are to be avoided. What I did not mention in PREPARE TO WIN is that, in the normal multiple-row riveted joint, regardless of the spacing and/or pattern of the rivets or the number of rivet rows involved, the load is not evenly distributed among the rivets. The row of rivets nearest to the load is going to get a disproportionate share of the load and will therefore be more highly stressed.

This phenomenon can be graphically illustrated by my all-time favorite physical demonstration. As shown in FIGURE [171], if a heavy rubber band in the relaxed condition is pinned to a piece of wood by three equally spaced pins and then stretched, the three pin holes will be distorted to different degrees with the hole nearest the load receiving the greatest amount of distortion. With the rivet pattern, while the first row will always receive an unfair portion of the LOAD by varying either the diameter or the spacing of the rivets, the level of STRESS can be evened out among them. For our purposes, this solution is usually a lot more work than it is worth. Our usual problem with riveted primary structures does not have to do with varying stress levels in the rivets, or even with the strength of the rivets or the joints. Rather it is the problem of what happens to the rivets themselves in service and it is caused by inadequate JOINT design due to a combination of cost cutting and ignorance.

In the construction of the racing car, the usual riveted joint is the simple LAP JOINT illustrated by FIGURE [172], with either a single row of rivets or an offset double row. It is quick, it is easy, it is cheap and it is inexcusable. The problem is NOT one of ultimate joint strength. Instead it is a "down the road" problem of what happens after the monocoque has a few thousand miles (and a few thumps) on it. The whole damned thing "loosens up" and gets "wanky" or flexible. This happens simply because, while the ultimate strength of the riveted joints may be perfectly adequate to withstand the loads involved, from the fatigue point of view the design is just plain not good enough.

The inadequacy of the joint design is often compounded by the use of unsuitable rivets (like Avex rivets, which have no place in structure) and/or by unsuitable alloys of sheet metal. What happens is that when a tension load is applied to the riveted lap joint, the two sheets attempt to align themselves with each other as in FIGURE [173] and, in so doing, undergo elastic distortion. This gives rise to a bending stress at the first line of rivets. This distortion is impercepti-

---

Figure (171): Model illustrating uneven distribution of stress in multirow rivet pattern.

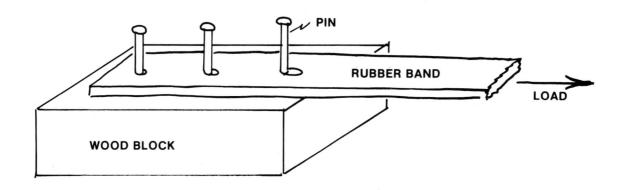

ble to the human eye and, of itself, is relatively harmless. The problem lies in the fact that the bending stress causes the load on the rivets to change from pure single shear to a combination of tension and single shear. Both the rivets and the rivet holes also undergo elastic distortion, which causes them to rub imperceptibly against each other and to wear. The more they wear the greater the cyclic stress becomes until eventually, after many tens of thousands of cycles, each individual rivet is just a little bit loose—either axially, so that clamping force is lost, or radially so that it is no longer a tight fit in its hole (or both).

Little by little the whole structure "loosens up" and, if we happen to be talking about the monocoque, the whole car's responsiveness and general handling goes to hell in a handbasket. The usual syndrome is gradually increasing understeer over a long period of time accompanied by a growing feeling of general sloppiness and an unwillingness to respond to changes in roll stiffness distribution. At the same time, any electrical ground that the designer was foolhardy enough to route through the main structure of the chassis is liable to deteriorate and become intermittent in operation—as will whatever circuit is dependent upon it—driving all concerned up the nearest wall. The process is slow but steady and the use of adhesives to bond the panels together only slightly retards the action.

Once a tub has loosened, the only cure is to rerivet the chassis, a tedious, if not particularly difficult, process. A trick which works well on a brand new chassis is the insertion of a row of what is known in the aircraft trades as "stress confuser" rivets. If we could somehow clamp the edge of each sheet to the sheet beneath it, as illustrated by FIGURE [174], then, while the sheets would still distort under tension loads, the distortion would take place in an area AWAY from the rivets. This would separate the load-carrying shear stress in the sheet metal from the distortion-caused bending stress, and subject the rivets to shear stress only—a better state of affairs altogether. While the use of a multitude of C clamps is impractical from the viewpoints of weight, cost and aerodynamics, the driving or squeezing of extra rows of rivets through the edges of the panels as illustrated in FIGURES [175] and [176] will accomplish the

---

Figure (172): Riveted lap joint at rest.

Figure (173): Lap joint under tension load—rivets taking shear load and sheet-bending load.

Figure (175): Simple lap joint with added rivets at sheet edges as stress confusers—at rest.

Figure (176): Lap joint with added edge rivets under tension load—edge rivets cannot take shear load but do take sheet-bending load and pass shear load onto main rivets. Stress is confused and fatigue life of joint is appreciably extended.

Figure (174): Sheets clamped at edges to prevent bending loads from reaching rivets—rivets in shear only.

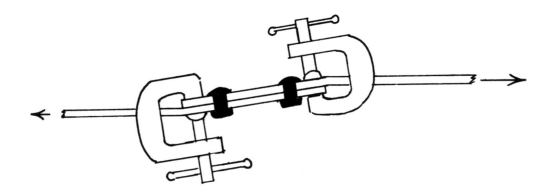

same end. The sheets will still bend imperceptibly under load but, now, because the extra rivets can accept no loads other than those caused by distortion of the sheets (there can be no such thing as shear stress through half a hole), they will distort at the edges of the overlapping sheets only. The shear stresses will be passed along to the original row of rivets, which are thus relieved of any tension load caused by bending stress, and will function infinitely longer without loosening.

With a clean sheet of paper, one would not use the lap joint at all. A better way is the BUTT JOINT with doubler, illustrated by FIGURE [177]. For outside skins this joint is also aerodynamically superior, so long as the doubler is on the inside. This joint is properly termed a "single shear" butt joint. While the sheet metal can still stretch under a tension load (and the rivet holes elongate differentially) and the shear stress is unevenly divided among the rivet rows, the sheets are aligned with each other and no bending stress will be developed under load so the rivets will remain in shear. The "double shear" butt joint of FIGURE [178] is a stronger and more fatigue resistant joint with more stable rivet support but has both aerodynamic and appearance disadvantages, and is heavy.

Virtually the same results can be obtained by increasing the thickness of the doubler plate in the "single shear" lap joint. This method, however, still concentrates most of the load on the row of rivets set nearest the edge of the doubler —not good! The BEST way to attack this problem is to use a tapered doubler plate and yet another row of rivets (of reduced diameter) near the edge of the tapered plate, as shown in FIGURE [179]. Virtually the same result is achieved by the use of two doublers as shown in FIGURE [180], with the first doubler being very thin in section. In actual practice a single-shear butt joint with the doubler plate twice the thickness of the sheets being joined, works just fine with a standard double-row staggered pattern of equal-diameter rivets. This system is shown in FIGURE [181]. It IS more work and it IS heavier. Since most of our current rules are such that we end up with a certain amount of ballast anyway, I consider the couple of extra pounds attendant with fatigue-resistant rivet joints to be a more-than-worthwhile tradeoff. I would feel the same way if the car ended up overweight by the amount of the doubler plates involved. NOTHING can take the place of a rigid chassis.

I am not advocating the complete redesign of existing tubs. I am, however, advocating the addition of stress-confusing panel-edge rivets when reriveting a tub and the application of a lot of thought to joint design when reskinning.

BONDING

I still do not use or recommend adhesive bonding of metals as a primary method of joining race car structures. I have three reasons:

(1) We have neither the equipment nor the patience to achieve a reliable bond.

(2) Adhesive bonding, properly designed and carried out, is very effective in tension and in shear. Bonding is not at all effective in peel. We have a lot of difficulty arranging things so that there is no tendency for our adhesives to peel.

(3) The potential penalty for a bonding failure just is not worth the weight saving that could be achieved.

I still do, however, bond all of my riveted joints, as a secondary joining method, as an antichafe strip and as a moisture seal. I still use 3M's 8101 Structural Adhesive but I have recently been using Aircraft Spruce's APCO 9912 A and B two-part epoxy adhesive with very good results; it makes less of a mess. I keep tabs on what is happening in the adhesive-bonding line, as well as on the practical side of composite construction through Aircraft Spruce which is closely tied in with the Rutan Aircraft Company—where Burt Rutan, the Colin Chapman of the world of general aviation and the man who introduced practical composite construction to the skilled homebuilder, holds forth.

WELDING

The last method of joining metals that we will consider is FUSION WELDING. I am, once more, not about to write anything that resembles a welding handbook—there are too many good ones available. This time I just want to talk a little bit about welding from the metallurgical point of view, and maybe scare some of my readers into thinking a bit more about the techniques and materials that they have been using.

Fusion welding is nothing more than a casting process. The pieces of metal to be joined are locally heated at the desired interface to their melting point so that both pieces and any filler metal involved are in the liquid state. These liquid metals flow together and their individual atoms form an intimate mixture which, upon cooling, solidifies into a single crystalline structure. During solidification the crystal dendrites originate from the interface between the solid (and therefore cooler) base metal and the molten metal of the zone of fusion and grow toward the center of the cooling weld. The crystal growth continues until all of the liquid has been consumed. The result can be a strong and homogenous welded joint which is virtually as strong and fatigue-resistant as the original metal. The result can also be a good deal less than this; say, a hard and brittle interface with "cast in" stress raisers of various sorts—an invitation to disaster.

As you would expect, there are, geographically speaking, two critical areas in any weld. Both are located near the interface between that portion of the metal which did not melt and the weld zone. The first is termed the "heat effected zone" and the second "the zone of fusion."

In order for a strong, fully bonded and fatigue-resistant weld to form, the solidified zone of fusion must be free of inclusions of foreign material and of the scales and oxides that form when metal is heated in the presence of oxygen. Cleanliness of the parent metal and of the filler rod is obviously part of the answer here—he who welds dirty, oily, scaled, painted or plated steel with a coat hanger for a welding rod deserves whatever he gets.

Metallurgically speaking, what we are trying to achieve in the welded joint is a homogenous solid solution alloy

Figure (177): Single-shear butt joint with doubler.

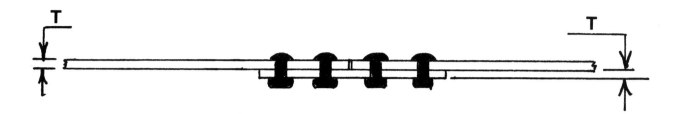

Figure (178): Double-shear butt joint.

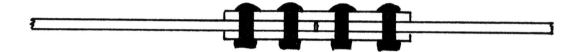

Figure (179): Single-shear butt joint with tapered doubler.

Figure (180): Single-shear butt joint with auxiliary doubler.

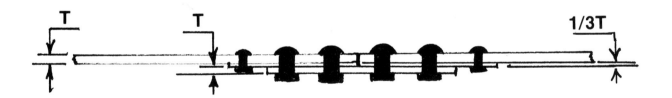

Figure (181): Single-shear butt joint with thick doubler.

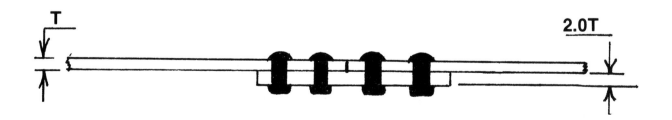

with a refined grain structure that is closely akin to that of the base metal and which contains no inclusions, voids, unwelded seams or cracks. It is not easy to do. The structures of both the heat-effected zone and the zone of fusion depend upon the composition of the parent metals and upon the rate of heating and cooling.

We are first going to take a look at what actually happens during welding from the metallurgical point of view.

THE METALLURGY OF THE FUSION WELD IN STEEL

I pointed out at the beginning of this section that fusion welding is in reality a casting process. The base metal and the filler metal experience exactly the same RANGE of temperatures as were used in the original production of the metal. And they undergo exactly the same structural changes. The trouble is that the best that we can hope for is for the completed weld to be in the as-cast condition. This is ok if we are dealing with low-carbon steels or with 1100 or 3003 aluminum. If we are dealing with 6061-T6 aluminum (or any heat-treated aluminum or magnesium alloy), however, the weld and the heat-effected zone are going to be considerably more ductile and weaker than the rest of the part, unless we heat treat the completed part. With the medium carbon and medium alloy steels, on the other hand, the quickly cooled weld and heat-effected zone will be harder, stronger and more brittle than the surrounding area —unless the weld area is stress relieved. Actually, with 4130, 4140 and/or 4340 (which are the only alloy steels that we should ever consider welding), we should heat treat every component except for the chassis itself, simply because in doing so we gain a lot of strength and fatigue life at no cost in toughness. Even when we are going to heat treat an alloy steel fabrication, it must be stress relieved first.

Let's take a minute and see just what happens when we weld steel. We'll start with standard old low-carbon, mild steel of the 1010/1015/1018/1020 family. You will recall that in low-carbon steels, almost all of the carbon is in the form of iron carbide, Fe3C, known as cementite. Cementite is very hard and very strong, but has virtually no ductil-

ity at all. In the microstructure of carbon steel, the grains are composed of alternate plates of pure iron (which is soft, weak and ductile) and of cementite (which is strong, hard and brittle). Figure [182A] illustrates. The result is a laminate microstructure that is both strong and tough. This "pearlitic" structure is a part of the normal structure of steels. The limit of carbon that can be held in solid state solution in iron is, however, 0.83%. This percentage is known as the eutectoid composition of carbon and iron. If more carbon than that is present, the composition is termed hypereutectoid and the extra carbon will separate out of solid solution along the grain boundaries of the pearlite, as in FIGURE [182B]. If there is less than 0.83% carbon present in the alloy, the composition is termed hypoeutectoid and there will be grains of both pearlite and pure iron (known as ferrite) present in the matrix (the usual condition for steels) as in FIGURE [183].

Any other alloying elements in the alloy will be present as carbides of those elements and may be integrated into the matrix in several ways as we discussed earlier. So much for our review.

Figure (182B): Microphoto showing hypereutectoid composition.

X1000

Figure (182A): Alternating plates of iron and cementite.

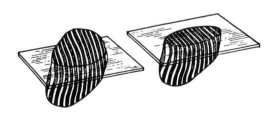

SINGLE GRAIN OF PEARLITE SECTION

THE TRANSFORMATION OF IRON IN THE CRITICAL TEMPERATURE RANGE

You will also recall from our earlier discussion that, as iron is heated, it goes through some remarkable structural changes. In the critical temperature range between 1,300 and 1,350 degrees F, the basic crystal matrix structure of iron changes from body-centered cubic to face-centered cubic—from alpha iron to more dense gamma iron. At the same time the grain structure of the carbon/iron alloy also changes; as the atoms rearrange themselves into a face-centered matrix, the iron carbide separates into carbon and iron and the carbon goes into solid solution with the iron—the laminated pearlitic structure disappears. The alloy is still a solid and is still composed of distinct grains, whose appearance is now similar to grains of ferrite. These new grains, however, contain dissolved carbon in solid solution and are called austenite.

No further changes of any import take place as the steel is heated until it actually melts at about 2,680 degrees F. When the steel melts, the crystal structure is destroyed and the atoms of both iron and carbon (plus any other alloying elements) move randomly around in the liquid with no fixed relationship to each other.

Figure (183): Microphoto showing hypoeutectoid composition.

MICROPHOTOGRAPH X500

COOLING

As the zone of weld fusion is moved along the join, the molten metal cools and the effects are reversed—with some critical variations. We know that the crystallization of a molten metal is a gradual process, beginning at crystal nuclei located at random throughout the liquid and continuing in a random but progressive fashion until solidification is complete. With pure metals, the temperature does not change during crystallization. With the iron-carbon alloys, however, crystallization takes place over a RANGE of temperatures. First some crystals of pure iron soldify while the carbon (and other alloying elements, if any) is concentrated in the remaining liquid. At a slightly lower temperature, crystals of austenite begin to solidify; this austenitic crystallization continues as the temperature continues to drop until the whole mass becomes a solid. While this austenitic crystallization is taking place, the metal is semisolid or mushy and has virtually no strength. It can even be poured.

When the solid state is reached, the white-hot alloy is still too hot to have much strength and it can be readily hammered or forged into various shapes. As cooling continues, the solid solution of iron and carbon progresses from white heat through the various stages of red. At the critical temperature of from 1,350 to 1,300 degrees F, the structure changes from the face-centered cubic structure of gamma iron back to the body-centered cubic matrix of alpha iron. The alpha iron cannot hold all of the carbon in solid solution. Thus, most of the carbon in the austenite is separated out of solution with the iron and becomes cementite. The laminated pearlitic structure appears and we are back where we started from. This is a more-or-less accurate picture of what happens when low-carbon steels are welded and allowed to cool slowly.

THE EFFECTS OF RAPID COOLING

While the rate at which a steel is HEATED has little if any effect upon the structural changes that take place, you will recall from our discussion of heat treating that the rate at which it is COOLED is of critical importance. If we take a piece of carbon steel at the temperature at which solidification is just complete and the steel consists of an austenitic solid state solution of carbon in iron, and plunge it into a cold liquid, the accelerated cooling rate will result in fundamental changes to the structure of the cooled steel. When the critical temperature is reached, the same things that happened during normal cooling would start to happen again. But, before the transformation from the austenitic to the pearlitic structure can be completed the temperature will have dropped below the point that the atoms can move around freely and the transformation will be arrested before the pearlitic structure is formed. Instead, a hard material called MARTENSITE will appear as a great number of very fine, interlocking needlelike crystals interspersed throughout the microstructure. The faster the metal is cooled, the more martensite will be formed. The resulting martensitic structure is the hardest, strongest and most brittle of the steel microstructures. This is what happens when we quench a weld in steel—glass.

The final structure of the steel in the zone of fusion of a weld, then, can be profoundly influenced by the rate of cooling. Extremely rapid cooling will produce a brittle martensitic structure which is in no way desirable. A less radical quench will produce a composite structure of mixed pearlite and martensite. Slow cooling (as in still air) will produce a fine-grained pearlitic structure while very slow cooling (as in an oven) will produce a coarse-grained pearlitic structure. Further, we learned in our discussion of heat treating that a hardened steel can be tempered by reheating to a temperature below the critical range and held at the temperature long enough for the structural changes that were arrested by quenching or cooling to progress to a predetermined desirable level and for the grain structure to become refined. The same is true of welds. Since the tempering temperature is held below the critical range, the reheating does not allow the changes that were arrested during rapid cooling from above the critical range to be completed, so that the strength and hardness obtained by quenching are not lost. Instead, tempering results in a variation of the structure produced during rapid cooling. For example, martensite, upon being reheated to 800 or 900 degrees F, is not transformed to pearlite. Instead the sharp martensite crystals are rounded and form a structure known as SORBITE. The hardness and the strength of an alloy will not be as great after tempering as they were after quenching, but the toughness and impact resistance will be greatly improved while the strength and hardness will be much greater than an unquenched alloy. What, you may well ask, has all this got to do with welding? Read on!

WELDING 4130

There are a lot of myths surrounding the techniques of welding 4130 steel. Most of them are just that—myths. To be sure, care must be exercised. We have a narrow choice of suitable filler rods. Pre- and post-heat are important and become critical in thicker sections and all welds should be stress relieved after welding. But there are no great secrets involved.

Most racing welders do not believe that it is necessary to stress relieve welds made in 4130, especially TIG welds. They are wrong. Maybe explaining why will make some converts to the cause of righteousness. Contrary to popular opinion, the necessity for stress relieving 4130 weldments has little if anything to do with carbon content or weld contamination, and the superior shielding afforded by TIG welding does not help at all. In fact, as we will see, the need for stress relief is GREATER with TIG-welded 4130 than it is with oxyacetylene welds.

4130 is an "air hardening" steel. During welding, by whatever process, both edges of the joint are heated to the molten condition and then allowed to cool in air. This results in the creation of a series of "layers" in the heat-effected zone adjacent to the weld itself. In a short distance measured at right angles to the line of the weld we will find

metal that has been heated considerably above the critical zone, just above it, not quite up to it, nowhere near it and only slightly heated. As the weld puddle progresses, the heated metal behind it will be cooled both by exposure to the air and by the quenching effect of the adjacent cooler metal. The heat-effected zone will thus cool more rapidly than if the whole part had been evenly heated and cooled as a unit. The weld is, in effect, quenched and is therefore considerably more brittle than the surrounding material. It doesn't take a cold liquid to achieve a quench—all it takes is a source of RELATIVE cool. The weld is liable to be largely martensitic in structure and to fail under impact. In addition, the grain structure will vary throughout the entire heat-effected zone, with the larger grain size being found in the portion that has been hottest.

With TIG welding, the heat-effected zone is geographically narrower than it is with torch welding. Far from being an advantage, this produces a steeper temperature gradient in the heat-effected zone and, with air-hardening steels, a more brittle weld than a good torch weld—regardless of how skilled and careful the operator is about slow withdrawal and post purging. The solution is simple, inexpensive and not even time consuming. At the completion of welding, the entire area surrounding the welds should be evenly heated to about 1,200 degrees F (somewhere between "dark cherry" and "medium cherry") and allowed either to cool in STILL AIR or covered in LIME or DRY SAND. Still air is best arranged by placing shields around large parts (like tube frames) or by placing a sheet metal box over the part until it has cooled. This, as you will have deduced by now is also the reason that 4130 should always be preheated (gently warmed to 300–400 degrees F) BEFORE starting a weld. It is all a case of keeping the temperature gradient in the heat-effected zone as gradual as practical. With higher-alloy steels such as 4340, pre-heat and post-heat are an absolute necessity. Strictly speaking, it probably isn't NECESSARY to either pre-heat or to normalize welds in 4130 if the sections are .065" or less in thickness, but it is damned good insurance.

FILLER METAL FOR 4130

A great many different formulations of filler rods CAN be used with 4130. Very few SHOULD be. Again it is perfectly true that in thin sections (0.095" and less) enough of the alloying elements in the 4130 will be picked up in even a low-carbon filler rod to bring the strength of the weld almost up to that of the base metal, but the pick-up will not be particularly uniform at best, so why depend on it?

If you are certain that the weldment will not be heat treated, then Linde's Oxweld #1 steel rod or its equivalent (0.13% to 0.18% carbon, 1.10% manganese and 0.25% silicon) is the rod to use. Its carbon content is high enough so that the finished weld, properly stress relieved, will be as strong as the base metal and it is easy to use. If the section is greater than 0.095" and/or the part is to be heat treated you NEED Linde's Oxweld 32 or its equivalent (a filler rod with about 0.10% to 0.15% carbon, 1.10% manganese, 0.25% silicon AND 0.30% chromium). Otherwise the weld is not going to respond to heat treatment properly and you are going to end up with either a weak or brittle weld. The common practice of using #502 stainless rod to weld 4130, because it is easy and makes pretty beads, should be discouraged: The inclusion of nickel in chromemoly welds leads to brittleness. The use of Everdur is just plain dumb.

I am fully aware that current practice in the aerospace industry is to use a vacuum-melted 4130 filler rod. They take a great many precautions in their welding that we do not—and their welders are better at it than we are. Me? I learned a long time ago that I cannot always depend upon fabricators or welders to read drawings or to pay any attention to filler material specs; so, if 4130 is to be welded, I make damned sure that Oxweld 32 is the ONLY rod used. As usual, don't pay too much attention to the opinion of your welding supply salesman.

GAS WELDING

TIG welders cost a lot of money. In all probability, most of the welding done by my readers will be oxyacetylene or gas welding. There is absolutely nothing wrong with gas welding—properly done—on most materials. True, the higher the alloy, the less satisfactory the results are liable to be, but it is highly unlikely that anyone is going to attack anything more exotic than 4130 with a torch, and 4130 was originally developed for gas welding. Anyway, I think that we should look into both the composition and the purpose of the oxyacetylene flame.

When acetylene (C_2H_2) is burned completely in air, combines with the oxygen in the air to form carbon dioxide and water vapor. 2.5 volumes of oxygen are required to burn 1.0 volume of acetylene completely. In oxyacetylene welding, about 1.0 of these 2.5 volumes of oxygen is supplied as commercially pure oxygen under pressure through the blowpipe, and the remaining 1.5 volumes come from the surrounding air.

The combustion at the tip of the welding blowpipe utilizes only the oxygen from the blowpipe and is actually a two-stage process. In the first stage, as combustion of the carbon takes place in the presence of oxygen, the temperature of combustion breaks the acetylene down into gaseous carbon and hydrogen, which then combine with some of the oxygen present to form carbon monoxide and hydrogen ($C_2H_2 + O_2 = 2CO + H_2$). Since both hydrogen and carbon monoxide are combustible gases, in the presence of additional oxygen, they will burn and react in a double barreled reaction:
$$2CO + O_2 = 2CO_2$$
and
$$2H_2 + O_2 = 2H_2O$$
forming water vapor and carbon dioxide.

THE THREE TYPES OF OXYACETYLENE FLAMES

By regulating the relative amounts of acetylene and oxygen that flow through the blowpipe and through the welding regulators into the mixing chamber we can achieve three very different types of oxyacetylene flame: the NEUTRAL FLAME, a one-to-one mixture of oxygen and acetylene which produces a flame with a very clearly defined inner cone surrounded by an outer "envelope" of bluish flame; the EXCESS ACETYLENE FLAME, which still has the clearly defined inner cone within the bluish outer envelope of the neutral flame but also features a whitish intermediate cone between the two; and, finally, the EXCESS OXYGEN FLAME which has a "violent" two-zone appearance in which the inner cone is short and jagged with a purple tinge.

We will examine the neutral flame first. What is actually happening here is that when the 1-to-1 mixture of oxygen and acetylene (C_2H_2) burns at the tip of the blowpipe, it goes through the reactions previously described. In the inner cone the acetylene is broken down into gaseous carbon and hydrogen and the carbon combines with an equal volume of oxygen to form carbon monoxide. In the outer envelope the carbon monoxide and hydrogen combine with oxygen from the air to form water vapor and carbon dioxide. The neutral flame is the flame most often recommended for fusion welding of the low-carbon steels.

With the excess acetylene flame, carbon is present in a proportion in excess of that required for complete combustion. We have seen that the inner cone represents the primary combustion of the carbon from the acetylene and the outer envelope represents the combustion of the carbon monoxide and hydrogen with oxygen from the atmosphere. The excess carbon of the acetylene-rich flame combines with oxygen from the atmosphere to form a third zone: the whitish "acetylene feather" located between the inner cone and the outer envelope. The length of the feather depends on the amount of excess acetylene. Because of the presence of excess carbon in the feather, this acetylene-rich flame is termed a "carburizing flame." This is the flame that SHOULD be used for most of our welding.

On the other hand, when an excess of oxygen is present at the blowpipe tip, we have a dual-zone flame like the neutral flame, but the inner cone is shorter, sharper and has a purple tint. The cone is harsher and more violent than that of the neutral or carburizing flame. In this case, the acetylene breaks down as usual into gaseous carbon and hydrogen and the combustion of the carbon in the presence of some of the oxygen from the tank forms the inner cone. But this time there is more oxygen present than is required to burn with the carbon, and the hydrogen combines with this excess oxygen to form water vapor—at the surface of the inner cone instead of in the outer envelope as is normal. At the same time some of the carbon monoxide from the initial breakdown of the acetylene may also combine with excess oxygen to form carbon dioxide. These two gases are normally stable, even at the temperature of the outer flame envelope. However, the temperature at the edge of the inner cone is high enough to make them unstable, and they become very strong oxidizing agents. For this reason, the excess oxygen flame is termed the "oxidizing flame." It is the flame that I very often see ignorant welders TRYING to use.

THE PURPOSE OF THE FLAME

The obvious purpose of the welding flame is to heat the metal. This function is accomplished by the inner cone. However the outer envelope of the welding flame also has a function which, if not so dramatic, is of equal importance. During welding, the outer envelope of the oxyacetylene flame excludes air from the molten weld puddle. "Big deal," you say? Think back to our discussion of the steel making process. One of the critical aspects during the refinement of steel is to prevent oxidation. This is why deoxidizers are added to melts and why high-alloy steels are refined under vacuum. At ordinary temperatures, any oxygen combined with the iron in any steel will be in the form of iron oxide which is weak, brittle and totally undesirable in steel. At elevated temperatures iron combines readily with oxygen to form iron oxides which then remain as inclusions in the cooled steel. It is therefore necessary to protect steel being welded from the oxygen in the atmosphere. In TIG and MIG welding, this protection is provided by the inert gas (argon or helium) which shields the weld area. In arc welding and in the various brazing processes, the protection is provided by the flux. In oxyacetylene fusion welding the protection is provided by the shielding action of the outer envelope of the gas flame.

HOWEVER, it is not quite that simple. In order to provide the required protection the envelope must be of the right composition. Pretty obviously, for instance, an atmosphere rich in oxidizers is going to be of no help at all in shielding the molten metal from oxidation—and that is exactly what we have with an oxidizing flame. When you see someone attempting to weld steel with even a slight excess of oxygen you are watching ignorance at work—and the creation of a burned and brittle weld.

This oxidation bit is also one of the major reasons that I do not want to know about hot rolled steel. When we receive it, it is covered with "mill scale" which is nothing more than iron oxide. Among the things that we don't need while trying to protect hot steel from oxidation is a layer of iron oxide on the part that we are welding. So all of the mill scale must be removed from hot rolled steels before they can be welded (a pain). Along these lines, I should point out that ANY metal should be cleaned of ALL scale, oxide surfaces and protective coatings before welding. This means emery cloth and a wipe with MEK. Failure to clean the metal properly MUST lead to inclusions in the weld. I have never succeeded in convincing anyone of this.

On the other hand, with 4130, for instance, we must use a SLIGHTLY carburizing flame. The slight amount of gaseous carbon in the flame has a fluxing effect which is a definite help in reducing surface oxidation of the heated steel but is not enough to cause carbon pick-up by the base metal. Although the welding handbooks usually suggest a neutral flame for all fusion welding of the low-carbon steels, I favor a slightly carburizing flame for ALL ferrous welding. It is a "softer" flame, not quite as hot as a neutral flame. As such, it reduces the overheating of the parent metal and widens the temperature gradient in the base metal so that there is less danger of creating hard spots. Admittedly, the welding process is slower than with a neutral or oxidizing flame, but welders should never be in a hurry anyway. And the weld will be infinitely better, especially if the regulators should allow the flame to adjust itself toward oxidizing in the course of welding. I don't much like flames that I can hear (for thin gauge racing car work). I would much rather use a bigger tip with a softer flame and take a little more time.

The whole idea is to heat a small area at the edges of the two parts to be joined until a small pool of molten metal is formed. The torch is then moved to push this pool along the junction of the two parts being joined and filler rod is added as required. As the puddle moves along the join, the rear edge of the puddle should be continuously solidifying while new metal is becoming molten at the leading edge. The edges of the base metal should be melted first and the puddle moved forward by advancing the melting EDGES. It is important that the puddle not be allowed to flow forward onto solid edges; a cold lap is the inevitable result. The torch should be held so that the inner cone just barely touches the surface of the molten puddle. If the inner cone is dipped into the puddle, oxidation of the weld metal is inevitable ("pop pop pop"). The outer envelope of the flame MUST protect the white-hot and molten metal at all times. Allowing the atmosphere to come into contact with metal above red heat again guarantees oxidation of the weld. One of the more common procedural errors is to move the flame to one side when the puddle begins to grow too large. You can pull it back a bit, but you cannot move it away from the puddle without causing oxidation.

For a man who stated not too long ago that I had no intention of writing a welding handbook, I have rambled on far too long. If you are going to do any welding at all, the smartest thing that you can do is to read several books and then have someone who knows what he is doing teach you how to weld. If you are going to do MUCH welding, take a course at one of the tech schools that offer aircraft welding. You will be doing yourself (and anyone who drives, owns or works on the racing cars on which you intend to weld) a big favor. As with everything else that is worth doing in life, practice makes perfect.

WELDING THE NONFERROUS ALLOYS

All that I am going to say here is that welding a heat-treated alloy effectively anneals the heat-effected zone and that the strength of the finished weldment must therefore be calculated for the material in the annealed condition—or the whole thing must be re-heat-treated. This is just one of the reasons that I believe that "roll cages" of aluminum tubing are misnamed and that ANY manufacturer and/or sanctioning body that allows their use is either criminally ignorant or just plain criminal. It is also the reason that those manufacturers who fabricate such things as rocker arms from weldable aluminum alloys but do not heat treat the weldments because "there is no need, it is made from a heat-treated alloy," need to read a book or two. Their customers need to have their brains tested. It is also why welding a cracked casting seldom works for very long. Some of the aluminum alloys CAN be successfully heat treated in the field. I do not do it and I am not about to tell you how to do it. If you are really interested ask your heat-treat shop.

CHAPTER TEN

PLUMBING REVISITED

Plumbing and plumbing associated failures are less frequent than they were a few years ago—almost certainly because more of the right stuff is being used. Even the English "kit car" manufacturers have mainly caught on. My ego would like to think that PREPARE TO WIN has contributed in some measure to this apparent improvement of the breed. In recent years most of the failures that I have seen have been due either to misuse of the right stuff or misinformation about what comprises the right stuff. The problems, while reduced, are still a long way from being solved. This will not be a short chapter, nor will it increase my popularity in some circles.

THE WATER SYSTEM

The only additional comments that I have here are:

(1) Due to an entirely understandable desire to reduce the cost of manufacture, the kit car producers have just about stopped bending aluminum water tubes. I really don't blame them—from sheer laziness so have I.

Actually, there is more to it than that. With the advent of the lamentable "full smog" engine, the underhood temperatures of street cars, domestic and imports alike, have risen to unprecedented and fearsome levels. The junk molded water hoses that Detroit loved just couldn't take this new environment, so the reputable manufacturers have developed a whole new generation of vastly improved molded water hoses (and bushings, and elastomeric gaskets, fuel lines and so on). If something good can come of our idiotic EPA emissions requirements, then it must be a

REALLY ill wind that blows no good at all. While I am still enamoured of Gates Green Stripe water hose and use it exclusively for my straight-line applications, I now make extensive use of the formerly despised molded rubber hoses in various convenient shapes—but ONLY of those hoses manufactured by either Gates or Dayco and ONLY those with woven fabric cores. You are pretty safe using Detroit, Japanese or German original-equipment water hoses but you have to be a little careful here because, dealers being what they are, are liable to save a few bucks in the water hose department and stock a cheaper substitute rather than the OEM item. Do not use Italian, Taiwanese or South American water hoses. The safe way is to buy from a good parts house (they will have a larger selection than anyone else anyway) and use nothing but Gates and/or Dayco. Pay no attention to what the "I've been selling this stuff for twenty-five years and I know what I'm talking about," counter man has to say about either quality or availability.

I use the exact (or at least a very close approximation thereof) degree of bend that was molded into the hose. If the bend in a molded hose is either opened or closed very far there is a very real chance that the hose will collapse, with entirely predictable results. This simple fact seems to have largely escaped the attention of our friends across the pond. It also means that we will spend an inordinate amount of time searching for the RIGHT water hose. The incredible lack of standardization throughout the automotive industry with regard to water hoses (also fan belts, oil filters, fuel filters, etc.) ensures us that you WILL find it—

eventually. The right hose is indeed worth the search. I know of one highly regarded operation that managed to burn down three engines in a row before the much-maligned (and innocent) engine builder found the severely underbent and collapsed water hose at the bottom of one of the radiators (it WAS hidden by a side pod, but that is a feeble excuse). Pity that no one was present with a tape recorder. . . . If I have any doubts at all I insert a light coil spring in the hose, especially if it happens to be on the suction side.

I religiously replace even the best molded hose at the midpoint of each season, or when they start to feel the least bit ''mushy.'' If I were building my own cars I would still bend the tubes and use Gates Green Stripe.

(2) Because I sincerely dislike burns on my body I use Stant brand lever-releasing pressure caps in the 14-15 psi range. I don't use more system pressure because:

(a) The caps are hard to find.

(b) We don't need higher pressures anymore; the POM's have reversed their historic trends and the typical English kit car now overcools.

Instead of safety wiring the pressure cap I now use a small lock pin through the lip to make sure that it doesn't loosen.

(3) I still consider the water system de-aerating swirl pot (as described in PREPARE TO WIN) to be an absolute necessity on any racing car. Thanks to a tip from Alan McCall (clever man!) I now make them considerably larger than I used to (½ gallon minimum). The big one can save you when a head gasket begins to weep.

(4) I run a lot of block pressure, usually by means of a venturi-shaped restricter where the water exits the engine. This goes a long way toward the prevention of hot spots and attendant steam pockets in the cylinder head. I have also taken to running a SMALL line from the bottom of the header tank to the inlet side of the water pump, just to make very sure that there is always a positive head of water at the inlet of the pump to prevent cavitation. I strongly prefer to make the header tank noncirculating as shown in FIGURE [184].

In this case I run a good sized hose (say, dash 10 or dash 12) to the inlet of the pump simply to facilitate the filling

Figure (184): Water system schematic.

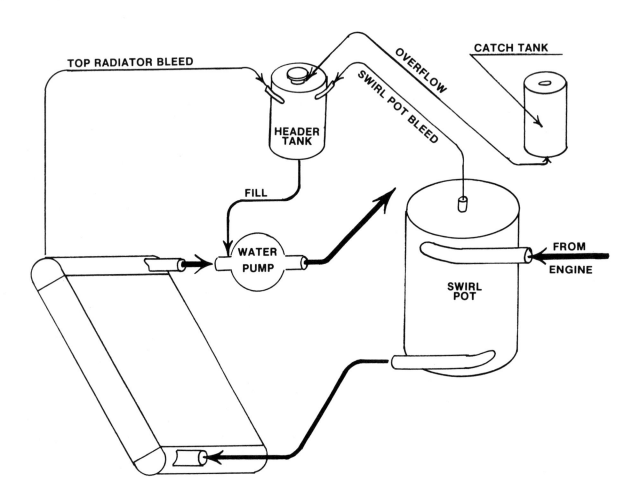

of the system. If, for whatever reason, the header tank is a part of the coolant circulating system then the size of this line must be severely restricted (say ¼" ID) in order to prevent any sizeable portion of the coolant from following the path of least resistance from the header tank to the water pump, bypassing the radiator(s) entirely. Don't laugh—I have seen cars delivered from "the works" with just such a system (and, no, it didn't work).

(5) Most engines (and particularly Cosworths) like to run at about 90-95 degrees C water temperature. They were designed to run there; they will make more power there and they will last longer there—it is all a question of running clearances and cooling efficiency. This means that either we should run thermostats (which I am seldom brave enough to do) or that we should sometimes restrict the flow of air to our water radiator(s). The normal method of doing so with duct tape is ok for warming up but dumb to practice and qualify with. (No one tapes radiators for the race—we would all prefer to give up a little power in return for some excess cooling capacity in case of trouble.) We spend our lives and our money trying desperately to reduce aerodynamic drag and then we go out with an aerodynamic brick wall installed in the cooler duct—real smart!

Instead, form a piece of sheet aluminum into a radiused duct area and cooler restricter as shown by FIGURE [185]. Do not alter the flow of air into the ground effect tunnel(s) if any. Remember that, in order to do its job , the restricter must block off part of the cooler as well as part of the duct. Make very sure that your artistic addition cannot chafe the cooler. If nothing else, it will look as if you are trying. I attach mine with either nut plates or Riv-Nuts.

As for those people who try to reduce drag by directing the air ABOVE the cooling ducts in their side pods when they don't need one radiator (or the oil cooler)—one more time we are watching ignorance at work. They are actually INCREASING the total aerodynamic drag of the vehicle. In this situation, if you are worried about cooler drag, the

Figure (185): Low drag cooler/cooler duct restrictor.

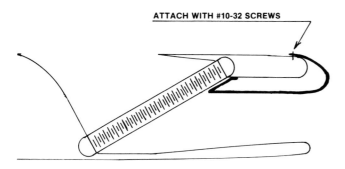

ATTACH WITH #10-32 SCREWS

right thing to do is to remove the cooler and close in the gaps in the duct floor and ceiling where it was, WHILE LEAVING THE DUCT ITSELF ALONE.

(6) Lately I have run across a few people who no longer believe that it is necessary to bleed the top(s) of the radiator(s) back to the header tank. These worthies claim that if the cooling system is properly designed and bled there can be no bubbles, and that a running bleed is therefore unnecessary. I wonder how they feel about the requirement for dual-ignition systems in piston aircraft engines. Since I am all too aware that head gaskets DO develop seeps from time to time—AND that when an engine is changed in a flaming hurry it is possible that the water system will not be properly bled—I will continue to take the time, spend the money and cheerfully accept the minimal weight penalty entailed in making the water system self bleeding. I use dash 4 hose because dash 3 is too liable to clog with trash or make the bars leak and I blow through the lines on a daily basis to make sure that they are clear.

(7) Modine and Tyndall both market all-aluminum racing radiators. Harrison makes aluminum radiators in various configurations for Corvettes. All three are good units. Size for size there is no measurable difference in thermal efficiency between them. The Modine unit is the strongest, the Tyndall is both lightest and cheapest (by a lot). All are reasonably easy to modify. Those who tell you that the traditional copper/brass radiator is thermally more efficient than an aluminum radiator are correct—on an absolute basis. On a BTU per pound of cooling system basis, however, aluminum wins. Given a choice, I run aluminum every time.

(8) Vee belts do a very good job of driving the water pumps on street cars. They (and their pulleys) are cheap, adjustable, easy to obtain or replace and they work—at street-car-engine rpm. Any attempt to drive the water pump of a racing engine with the stock setup is an invitation to disaster. Except for Show Room Stock classes, the racing engine is going to use a lot more rpm than the street engine. The stock belt and pulley setup was carefully designed to drive the water pump at its optimum speed at an engine rpm corresponding to a road speed of about 65 mph in high gear, and for the belt not to come off the pulleys at whatever maximum rpm the engineers at the factory thought that the engine might see—usually far short of racing rpm. What usually happens is that the overspeeded belt literally turns itself inside out; it jumps off the pulley and the water pump stops. Alternatively, the water pump, if it is not slowed down by the installation of an appropriately larger driven pulley, may well cavitate at racing rpm and then the engine will overheat even if the belt does stay on. Most racing engines drive the water pump with a toothed Gilmer belt and cog wheel pulleys. These offer a virtually unlimited choice of drive ratios, and are light, efficient and expensive. Fortunately Dayco had a lot of experience in stock car racing in the days when NASCAR regulations insisted on vee belts. They developed a series of belts that WILL NOT turn themselves inside out. They are no longer specifically designated as racing belts but they have a black-and-white checkered flag type emblem both on the wrapper and on the

belt. Most good hot-rod and high-performance houses carry them. A careful search through your dealer's and your high-performance parts house's catalogs will usually unearth a whole series of drive and driven pulley setups which will allow you to accomplish a couple of very desirable ends:

(a) Slow the water pump down by using a smaller drive and/or larger driven pulley.

(b) Use a short belt to drive the water pump—and to do nothing else. This will give you the maximum possible belt wrap on both pulleys and is one of the best methods known to man or mechanic to make sure that the belt stays on. There are also trick anticavitation water pump impellers as well as pulley setups available for most U.S. V-8's. Ask your local race engine builder.

OIL AND FUEL HOSES AND HOSE ENDS

The passage of a few years has seen some changes here! In PREPARE TO WIN I made brief mention of the fact that Earl's Supply Company had recently introduced its own line of hoses and hose ends and that these items were in every way comparable and interchangeable with Aeroquip's. All of that is still true. The difference is that Earl's, the new kid on the block a few years ago, has become the industry leader (the motor racing industry, that is). The reason is simple: Earl's hose ends are, in my opinion, superior to Aeroquip's for racing use.

Before I hear words like "conflict of interest," this is probably the time to state that I work very closely with Earl's Supply Company. I have used its products ever since we returned to this country in 1965—and I have never had a failure. I do not endorse Earl's products because I work with the company. I work with the company because the products are so good that I CAN endorse them. Having disposed of that question, it is time for a very brief history lesson and a brief explanation of the innermost workings of the replaceable hose end.

A LITTLE BIT OF HISTORY

Like most, if not all, of our really good hardware, our plumbing bits originated in the aircraft industry. In the beginning there was the hose clamp and a natural rubber hose wrapped with bicycle tape (in the very beginning there was a twisted piece of fence wire, once known as the "Dusenberg hose clamp"). So long as all that was involved in fluid transmission was gravity feed to a low-pressure carburetor, water hoses to and from a radiator and (maybe) some very low pressure oil lines, the right hose clamp was satisfactory (after those involved had learned to bead the ends of the hard lines). In fact, the hose clamp was in all probability better than the hose that was available. In most passenger car applications the right hose clamp is STILL perfectly satisfactory.

As military and commercial aircraft became more sophisticated, lubricants had to be conveyed over longer distances and at higher pressures; the high pressure fuel injection sys-

tem came into being; retractable landing gear, variable-pitch propellers, flaps, bomb bay doors, gun turrets and the like were developed and actuated by hydraulic systems. In short, the conveyance of various fluids became both more complex and more critical. At the same time the increased weight and landing speeds of the aircraft (as well as the effect on the paying passenger) made putting down in a convenient cow pasture to effect a quick repair a bit on the impractical side. The pressures, temperatures and number of cycles involved rendered the old faithful hose clamp obsolete. Neither were the old hoses up to the new tasks. Extensive use was (and is) made of "hard lines" or rigid metal tubing but, due to the articulation of the actuated parts and to the danger of vibration there was a need for flexible hydraulic hoses. Among the needs that had to be met was the crucial requirement that mechanics in the field (and I mean in the back-of-beyond, not the airfield as in LAX) be able to repair or replace damaged components from a minimal stock of parts and with common hand tools—while being shot at. In those days we still knew how to make equipment with which to fight a war. A whole generation of lightweight and flexible medium pressure hoses and hose ends were developed to meet the need. Through innovative design and engineering excellence the Aeroquip Corporation became the world's leader in the design and manufacture of flexible hoses and replaceable hose ends.

The original hoses were flexible only in comparison to the hard lines that they replaced. They featured thick walls of synthetic rubber reinforced with both external and internal braided, protective sheaths of fabric and/or metal which both protected the hose from abrasion and increased its pressure capacity. The hose ends were of the "single nipple" configuration illustrated by FIGURE [186].

Figure (186): Single-nipple hose end.

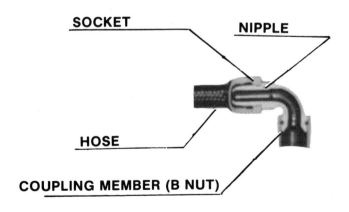

THE SINGLE-NIPPLE REPLACEABLE HOSE END

In use, the female threaded socket is slipped over the cut end of the hose and the male threaded nipple is threaded into the socket, and into the hose liner. As the tapered nipple advances into the threads of the socket the hose is wedged firmly into the annular space between the ID of the socket and the OD of the nipple. The interior shape of the socket is designed to receive and wedge the hose, and is provided with annular barbs to help prevent the hose from backing out during assembly and to help retain the hose under pressure. This wedging of the hose between the socket and the nipple both retains the hose and provides the primary (in this case the only) seal for the assembly.

The single-nipple hose end is a relatively inexpensive part to manufacture and it is perfectly suitable for use with relatively thick-walled hose that it was designed for, especially if the hose ID is greater than ⅝″. In the smaller sizes the necessarily heavy wall of the nipple reduces the cross-sectional area of the assembly sufficiently to cause significant reductions in flow capacity. While the reduction is not particularly important in many of our applications, the fact that the single-nipple hose end, when assembled on modern, thin-walled flexible hose, is liable to leak under pressure (or even to blow off the hose) IS of considerable significance—not to say, concern. Read on!

As the complexity of the modern aircraft increased at a greater rate than did the power available to make them fly, the importance of component weight changed from critical to super critical. Advances in both synthetic rubber technology and in manufacturing techniques led to the development and almost universal use of ultra-light and extremely flexible low- and medium-pressure hose. Such hose is made of very thin walled synthetic rubber which is protected against both abrasion and aneurysm by a partial stainless-steel braided sheath molded into the hose liner and a full-coverage stainless wire braided outer cover bonded to the hose.

Again the Aeroquip Corporation led the way. During the development phase of this type of hose, now almost universal on racing cars, it was discovered that the traditional single-nipple hose end could not be successfully adapted for reliable use. The basic problem was that if the hose end were to be designed so that it would compress the hose sufficiently to positively prevent blow-off, the soft inner liner would be very likely to cold flow under compression. Sometime after assembly this cold flowing would reduce the thickness of that portion of the hose that was wedged between the nipple and the socket and, if fortune smiled, the assembly would only begin to leak. If fortune did not smile, the hose end could blow off the hose. Conversely, if the initial compression were reduced to the point where the hose liner would not cold flow, neither a positive seal nor secure hose retention could be ensured. I quote from Aeroquip's AIRCRAFT CATALOG NO. 105: "The inner tube of this hose [Aeroquip's lightweight engine hose #601] is soft and would tend to 'set' or 'flow' under the high compression of the usual type of fitting. A new type of fitting has been provided through Aeroquip research and development. Known as the Aeroquip Little Gem this fitting attaches without harmful compression. . . ."

THE DOUBLE-NIPPLE HOSE END

The "fitting" referred to is the "nipple and cutter" or "double nipple" hose end, which I reckon to be one of the more clever devices of recent years. In this design (see FIGURE [187]) the female threaded socket is slipped over the cut end of the hose and the male threaded nipple is screwed into it just as in the single nipple. The difference lies in the detail design of the nipple itself—a deceptively complex part. This nipple is, in effect (and sometimes in fact), two separate parts—hence the name. Just as with the single nipple, the nipple tube slips inside the hose liner, but it is not threaded. Concentric with the nipple tube and attached to it is the sharp-edged "cutter." An annular chamber of very closely controlled dimensions is formed between the inside surface of the cutter and the outside surface of the nipple tube. The outside of the cutter has male threads which match the female threads of the socket. As the nipple/cutter assembly advances into the socket threads the sharp, leading edge of the cutter separates the soft, inner hose liner into an inner tube and an outer tube. The resulting inner tube, which is all synthetic rubber, is captured (but not compressed) inside the annular chamber between the nipple tube and the cutter to form the primary seal of the assembly. The outer tube and both layers of protective braid are wedged into the space between the outside of the

Figure (187): Double-nipple hose end.

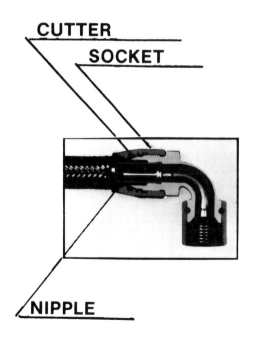

CUTTER

SOCKET

NIPPLE

nipple/cutter assembly and the inside of the socket, both of which are designed and shaped to ensure positive hose retention. Thus the sealing function and the hose-retention function are accomplished separately and, since the contained fluid is not in contact with the threads of either part, there can be no seepage past the threads. Since the portion of the nipple that slips inside the hose is not threaded, it can be designed with a very thin wall, and flow restriction through the assembly is minimized. Very clever—and it cannot have been easy to develop.

In the last years of World War II and again during the Korean Conflict the stuff was turned out by the shipload, and soon found its way onto the surplus market. About that time Earl Fouts decided to set up Earl's Supply Company as an aircraft surplus house in Gardena, California. One of his neighbors was Quinn Epperly. George Bignotti was in and out of Quinn's frequently. One thing led to another: George's Indy cars sprouted surplus Aeroquip; the rest of the Indy contingent weren't far behind; Lance Reventlow's Scarabs followed suit—and soon everybody who was anybody in racing was plumbing their cars with surplus hose, hose ends and adapters from Earl's Supply. In some ways it turned out that Earl had grabbed a tiger by the tail. . . .

In the fullness of time Robert McNamara became Secretary of Defense and tried to run the DOD as he had Ford Motor Company (for the better, in my opinion—at least he REALIZED that they were wasting billions of dollars and TRIED to do something about it). "Cost plus" military contracts became a thing of the past (only to be replaced by cost override clauses) and the surplus market dried up. The Aeroquip Corporation did not consider the automotive high-performance/racing market to be worthwhile (talk about misreading a market!) and refused to sell to lowly "surplus dealers." Earl's Supply Company was faced with the choice of either abandoning the market that it had established and built up or of designing and manufacturing its own line of hose and hose ends. Fortunately for the racers, the company decided to bite the bullet and became manufacturers. Neither Earl nor his son Bob saw any sense at all in going to the expense and effort necessary to design and produce a hose end to arrive at a product that would only be "as good as" Aeroquip's so they set out to improve upon the recognized standard of a very sophisticated industry.

Against all odds they succeeded. Earl's Swivel Seal ™ hose end is, for racing purposes, superior to Aeroquip's Little Gem ™ —not because it is more reliable (they are each as reliable as a mechanical device can be, i.e., foolproof but not idiot proof), or because it is cheaper (it is, but only slightly) or even because Earl's offers more configurations and better service than Aeroquip (both true). The advantage lies in the fact that Earl's got very clever indeed and improved upon the original design of the double-nipple hose end by making the Swivel Seal radially adjustable with respect to the hose AFTER it has been finally assembled onto the hose. This does away with the previously necessary (and frustrating) process of "clocking" angled hose ends so that they would end up pointing in the required

Figure (188): The types of configurations are almost endless.

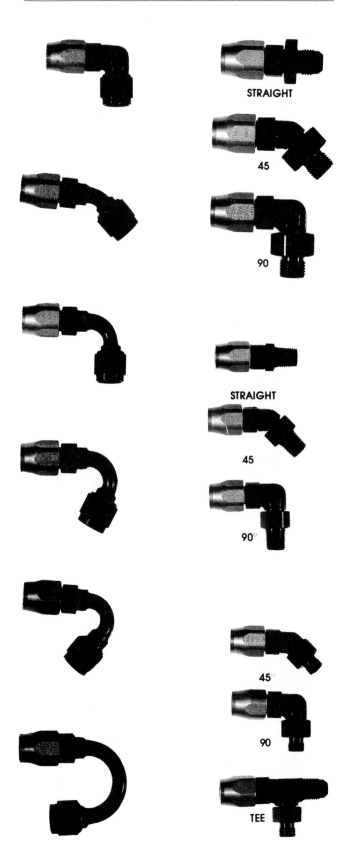

STRAIGHT

45

90

STRAIGHT

45

90°

45°

90

TEE

direction and could be installed onto their respective adapters without putting a torsional preload or even a kink in the hose—or, in the case of short hose runs, so that they could be installed at all. There are two possible dangers here: a torsionally preloaded or twisted hose is considerably weakened and prone to aneurysm AND, under just the wrong combination of conditions, a torsional preload can force the hose to attempt to unwind like a twisted rubber band, and the hose end becomes self loosening on the adapter.

Anyway Earl's, by the simple but brilliant expedient of designing the cutter so that it is positively sealed to and retained on the nipple (but is free to rotate on it), has done away with all that. With the company's kind permission I will reprint the explanation of the workings of the Swivel Seal that I wrote for its catalog some years ago (referring to FIGURE [189]): "The Swivel Seal is supplied preassembled from the four major components illustrated—a socket, a cutter, a nipple and a coupling member. In this illustration the coupler is a female B nut which threads onto and seals against standard Earl's Supply, AN and MS 37 degree male cone adapter fittings. The B nut is free to rotate on the nipple but is retained to it by a pin which is inserted through a hole in the nut and bent into a matching 360 degree groove machined into the nipple. When the B nut is tightened onto the adapter fitting the female seat of the nipple seals against the male cone of the adapter. The threads have no sealing function.

A Viton O ring is placed in the appropriate groove on the hose end side of the nipple. The cutter, which is machined with a matching O ring recess, is then pushed over the nipple and retained on it by a pin in the same way that the coupler is retained on the other end of the nipple. The cutter is now sealed to and retained on the nipple—but can be rotated with respect to it. This feature is unique. The assembly of the cutter on the nipple leaves an annular chamber between the cutter and the outer surface of the nipple tube.

The nipple tube protrudes well beyond the sharp edge of the cutter.

To assemble the hose end onto a hose, the socket is first slipped over the end of the hose and the nipple tube is inserted into the nitrile inner hose liner until the cutter edge butts against the liner. Threading the cutter into the socket then forces the inner tube onto the edge of the cutter which separates the liner into an inner tube of synthetic rubber and an outer tube which includes the intermediate partial coverage reinforcing braid. The inner tube is forced into the annular chamber between the I.D. of the cutter and the O.D. of the nipple tube and there forms the primary seal of the assembly. The outer tube, along with the full coverage outer protective braid, is captured between the O.D. of the cutter and the I.D. of the socket—both of which are shaped for the purpose. This controlled wedging action retains the hose end onto the hose. The O ring between the cutter and the nipple provides a secondary or "anti-seepage" seal. The design thus provides positive hose retention and a positive seal—with the sealing and retention functions separated. This "double nipple" configuration hose end offers both more positive seal and stronger retention than either the "single nipple" or the "push on" type. IN ADDITION, SINCE THE CUTTER CAN BE ROTATED ON THE NIPPLE, THE NIPPLE AND COUPLER CAN BE ROTATED WITH RESPECT TO THE HOSE AFTER ASSEMBLY. This feature is unique to the Swivel Seal hose end and allows angled hose ends to be aligned or "clocked" to suit the requirements of the individual assembly without either disassembly or overtightening. . . . "

When the racing/high-performance market proved to be considerably larger than anyone had predicted, Aeroquip, caught in a recession, decided that our money was green after all and, mainly through industrial distributors, started a campaign aimed at the racers. This program really hasn't worked out too well simply because the industrial people (with one notable and lovely exception—and SHE was a racer before she was a distributor) are not tuned in to any of the racer's frequencies. It HAS made it slightly easier for the racer to obtain emergency parts in the hinterlands.

Predictably, the market has attracted some new manufacturers—and some pretty heavy hype. Mainly the newcomers are mass merchandising inferior products that LOOK like the right stuff, but are not. To my knowledge only Earl's and Aeroquip currently manufacture double-nipple hose ends for use with lightweight, thin-wall stainless steel braid protected hose. One of the hypesters has been spending a lot of money trying to convince the unwary and the uninformed that both Earl's and Aeroquip (to say nothing of the U.S. Navy Bureau of Aeronautics, the U.S. Air Force and the CAA) are WRONG—that not only is the single-nipple hose end eminently suitable for use with lightweight hose but that the assembly of the double-nipple hose end often leads to the inadvertent creation of a "flapper" or one-way valve and that, therefore, the single nipple is the only way to go. God knows that it IS possible to make a "flapper"—but you really have to work at it. In all the years that I have been using double-nipple hose ends I have

Figure (189): Details of Earl's Swivel Seal design.

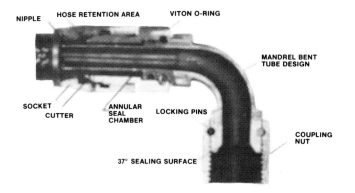

seen exactly one—and that one was made by a very competent man who just got careless once. Of course, being competent he DID find it before it got onto a car (by the simple expedient of trying to pass clean solvent through the assembly in BOTH directions as a final test before installation). The double-nipple configuration of hose end is the ONLY type currently approved for use with lightweight hose by the people who refuse to take ANY chances with equipment—the USN BuAer, the USAF and the CAA. There has to be a message there someplace!

THE FUTURE

This does not mean that it is impossible to design an alternative hose end configuration that will be suitable for use with lightweight hose. Western Coupling came very close a few years ago with a modified push-on, barb-style—but it seeped and was reuseable only with difficulty. It wasn't particularly well marketed and I haven't seen one in years. Earl's, after several years of development, has very recently introduced the Auto-Fit hose end. This fitting represents a new concept in the design of single-nipple hose ends. It combines the threaded socket and wedge-shaped, hose-retention area of the conventional single-nipple hose end with the barbed nipple of the push-on hose end. In this configuration the seal is effected by compression of the hose against the annular barbs (labeled A and B in FIGURE [190]) by the wedging action of the threaded socket—whose interior shape is similar to that of the Swivel Seal socket.

The hose retention function is carried out both by the barbs and by controlled and relatively mild wedging of the hose and braid between the nipple barbs and the socket. Unlike the conventional single-nipple hose end, the threads are not part of the seal and the amount of crush necessary to ensure hose retention is reduced below the point where there is any danger of cold flow. The people at Earl's are

Figure (190): Earl's Auto-Fit hose end.

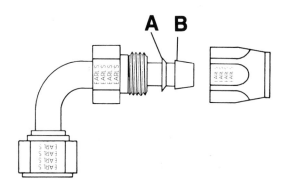

A B

very cautious—this particular hose end was in development for two years that I know of, and it has been through a lot of testing. It works just fine. In its final configuration there have been no failures and no seepage. The Auto-Fit hose end is as safe and as secure as the Swivel Seal. It is not radially adjustable after assembly (they are working on that!). Also, being of single-nipple design, its inside diameter is slightly less than that of the Swivel Seal so there is some flow reduction. It is presently available in straight, 45 degree and 90 degree configurations for hose sizes from dash 4 through dash 12. The Auto-Fit is obviously less expensive to manufacture than the Swivel Seal and, unlike some manufacturers, Earl's is passing the savings along to us: The Auto-Fit is considerably less expensive than the corresponding Swivel Seal.

So much for the history lesson. None of the foregoing should be taken to mean that I advocate the indiscriminate use of expensive plumbing bits. I do not. I also do not believe in settling for second best if it means a decrease in reliability—let alone vehicle safety. It DOES mean that I do not approve of the use of street car plumbing, such as Earl's Econ-O-Braid hose or Econ-O-Mate and Econ-O-Set hose ends (or any of the imitations thereof) on racing cars. Neither do the folks at Earl's. I do use their Econ-O-Flex yellow hose for vents, engine down-tubes and the like. I also use their whole street car line throughout my tow vehicles and personal cars. I have had one engine fire when an OEM fuel hose turned out to be something less than adequate for underhood temperatures and I am damned well not going to have another.

HOSE

There are at least three reputable manufacturers of stainless steel, braid-protected hose in this country. If there is any functional or visual difference between them, I have not found it. This is just as well, since I cannot tell who made any particular length of good hose and I am not convinced that anyone else can either. However, quality control being what it is, some substandard stuff does slip through inspection and some people have been burned. To the best of my knowledge the only actual failures of quality hoses have been caused by the outer sheath of protective braid not getting bonded to the hose liner in manufacture, resulting in a hose that, in a suction application (as in the scavenge side of a dry sump oil system), can collapse—causing instant disaster. In this case the braid not only wasn't bonded to the liner, it wasn't even attached—you could pull the liner out of the sheath like pulling a candy bar from its wrapper. It should have been impossible for ANYONE to assemble a hose end onto this defective hose without realizing that something was wrong—but, as usual, it wasn't.

I suppose that this is as good a time as any to insert Smith's treatise (or diatribe?) on modern manufacturing, quality control and the responsibility of the end user in the age of mass production:

Just about everything that we use (including our racing cars) is, to some extent, mass produced. This is a necessary evil attendant upon our way of life. It is the ONLY way that the cost of goods can be brought down to the level where the masses (us) can afford the proliferation of technical goodies that we enjoy.

It is not economically feasible to inspect each mass-produced item for faults before it is sold. Instead a small percentage of each production run is normally "sampled." If and when a sample is found to be faulty the line is stopped and the defect in the manufacturing process that caused the fault is rectified. Hopefully all of the parts finished since the last satisfactory sampling will be inspected and the bad parts (if any) will be rejected, reworked or whatever. The system works pretty damned well and, although we bitch about quality all the time, we actually purchase very few defective items. But, no matter how stringent the quality control inspections may be, SOME defects will always sneak through. I firmly believe that the end user must share the liability for the use of such parts with the manufacturer.

For example, I x-ray inspect my brand-new wheels—and I expect my engine builder(s) to x-ray inspect brand-new cranks, rods, valves etc., BEFORE they are assembled into my engine. If I spend ten minutes trying to screw a nut onto a bolt only to finally discover that the nut slipped through inspection with no threads, then I must share the blame—I should have seen it (or at least felt it)! If I assemble a hose end onto a hose when the sheath is not bonded to the liner, or if I install a hose end in which the seating taper did not get machined, a portion—even a major portion—of the fault is mine. The liberal judges who have taken over our court system do not agree with this notion of mine—or, for that matter, with any aspect of personal responsibility other than taxpaying. But that is not my department. The judge is not going to be of any use to you, the racer, if you install a defective part. So, form the habit of visually inspecting every part before you assemble it or install it. If it doesn't "feel right" going together or going on, there is always a reason. Take it apart (or off, as the case may be) and find out what is wrong before it strikes you dead. Once a failure has happened, assigning blame is not going to help anything or anybody.

Back to hoses . . . Someone can always do it cheaper—and just because a hose is sheathed in shiny wire braid does not mean that it is quality hose. In this case most of the "someones" seem to be located in Taiwan. There are a number of braid-protected (and even STAINLESS braid-protected) hoses being sold, sometimes as first-class stuff, that are as much decorative as they are functional. I have no objection to this sort of thing so long as the end user is informed that what he is buying is not of race car quality. Unfortunately this is not always the case, some of the merchandisers are ignorant and some are just plain dishonest.

Fortunately there are a couple of relatively easy ways to judge the quality of lightweight fuel and oil hoses. FIGURE [191] shows the three possible configurations of stainless steel braid-protected synthetic rubber flexible hoses. Part A shows the right stuff—in this case Earl's ES 400 Perform-O-Flex competition hose. Note that there are actually two protective sheaths of stainless wire braid: the full-coverage

outer sheath that everyone knows about because it is highly visible AND the partial-coverage inner braid located between the inner liner and the outer rubber jacket. If the hose you are looking at does not have BOTH sheaths AND, if the outer sheath is not bonded to the rubber jacket, then, regardless of what the salesman is telling you, you are NOT looking at race car quality hose.

Part B shows Earl's Econ-O-Braid hose. Notice that the inner protective braid is fabric, not stainless steel wire. The outer braid is not bonded to the liner so that you would notice. This particular hose is a lot cheaper than the right stuff. It is perfectly suitable for street and custom cars, ski boats and so on. In my opinion (and in Earl's) it is just not good enough for race cars.

An alternative on this same theme is the use of tin-plated copper braid with the same hose construction—cheaper yet, and serviceable, but not for racing.

Part C shows the moonglow hose from across the Western Ocean. The purpose of the braid is decorative. The quality and pressure and temperature capabilities of the hose are unknown.

If, for whatever reason, I am not going to use the very best, then I pass the whole braided hose bit and use Earl's Econ-O-Flex heavy-wall, fabric-braid-protected hose. It is

---

Figure (191): Three configurations of metal-braid-protected hose.

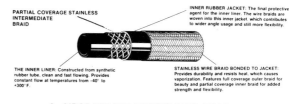

A. AIRCRAFT AND RACING SPEC HOSE
(EARL'S PERFORM-O-FLEX™)

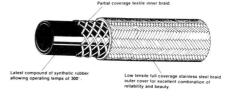

B. HIGH-PERFORMANCE STREET HOSE
(EARL'S ECON-O-BRAID™)

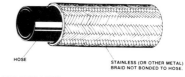

C. MOONGLOW

heavier than the others, but it is hell for stout and has the same temperature rating as the right stuff. Unlike some of the cheaper thin-wall hoses, it will not kink and it will not collapse under any suction that we are going to pull. It also comes in four colors. I use it on all of my street cars and tow vehicles. I guess that I just don't like imitations.

HOW TO DO IT

At the beginning of this chapter, I stated that most current plumbing failures are the result of misuse of the right components. Again with Earl's kind permission I am going to repeat my words in the assembly and installation of hose and hose ends from its catalog. Both the words and the illustrations also apply to Aeroquip—but not to other brands:

MISTAKES—OR HOW TO SCREW UP THE FOOLPROOF STUFF

The most common errors committed during hose end assembly are:

(1) Not cutting the hose straight. This makes it impossible to engage the sharp edge of the cutter squarely with the hose inner liner and can, in extreme cases, result in the creation of the dreaded ''flapper'' or a leaking assembly (or both). In addition to the normal radiac wheel or fine-toothed hacksaw method of cutting hose, it is also possible (and easy) to cut the stuff with a really sharp, wide-bladed chisel—and a really BIG brass or copper hammer. This is, in fact, my usual method. The tricks are :

(a) The hose must be backed by something really solid. (I use an old chunk of 4'' round steel bar that I clean up on a lathe when the chisel scars get too bad.)

(b) You have to hit the thing REALLY HARD—one shot is all you get.

(c) The area of the hose that is about to be attacked must be very tightly taped. I prefer masking tape to duct tape.

(d) This method is definitely NOT SUITABLE for Teflon hose—it crushes the Teflon.

(2) Fraying and/or partial unraveling of the outer protective metal braid when cutting the hose—either through not taping tight enough or from the use of either a coarse-toothed or dull hacksaw blade. This unraveling makes it difficult (in extreme cases, impossible) to fit the socket over the hose at the beginning of the assembly procedure. It usually results in a multitude of tiny puncture wounds on the hands of the operator as well as the addition of small quantities of blood (a poor lubricant) to the assembly.

(3) Failure to use a lubricant on the cutter, making it more difficult than it should be to start the annular separation of the inner hose liner.

(4) Failure to use an antiseize compound on the cutter threads. This can lead to the formation of a permanently assembled hose end by galling the male and female threads together forever. With a lot of bad luck it can also result in a complete inability to finish assembling the part.

(5) Failure to tighten the socket sufficiently onto the nipple. This results in a lesser amount of hose retention

Figure (191A): Assembly tips for Earl's Perform-O-Flex hose.

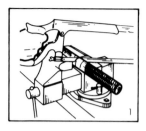

1. Cut hose to required length.

a Measure distance between ports or adapter fittings along the path that the hose run will follow -allowing for bend radius, hose end length and offset to obtain length and hose required.

b Cut the hose square with a radiac wheel or a sharp 32 teeth per inch hacksaw blade. It is necessary to wrap it tightly with masking tape before cutting and to cut through the tape. This helps to prevent the stainless wire braid from fraying.

c Trim any frayed end of the braid with a sharp pair of metal snips or diagonal cutters and remove the tape.

2. Place the socket in a vise and insert the end of the hose into the socket until the hose butts against the bottom of the threads provided for the cutter. Gently pull the hose back until there is a 1/16" to 1/8" gap between the end of the hose and the bottom of the socket - mark hose at bottom of socket with a felt pen so that you can detect any tendency of the hose to be pushed out as you complete the assembly.

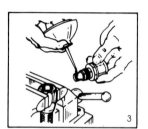

3. Lubricate the inside of the hose, the cutter threads and the socket threads. Just about any kind of clean oil will do but I prefer to use an anti-seize compound on the threads. Place the nipple in a vise. Flex muscles.

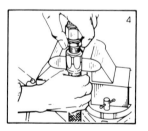

4. Push the hose and the socket onto the nipple until the socket threads can be started on the cutter. Start the threads and go as far as you can by hand. Depending on the size of the hose, some force may be necessary in this part of the operation.

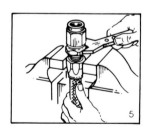

5. To complete the assembly it doesn't matter whether the nipple or the socket is held in the vise. Holding one or the other in the vise and using a suitable wrench on the other, tighten the socket onto the cutter threads until the socket is within .060" of bottoming on the nipple. Do not use an adjustable or over-size wrench or you will damage either the nipple or the socket.

6. Check the mark that you made on the hose in step 2. If the hose has backed more than about 1/16" out of the socket as you assembled it, curse and return to step 3.

7. Clean the hose and the hose ends with CLEAN solvent.

8. It is most unlikely that you will have available any method of pressure checking the assembly before it is installed. Before letting the assembly out of your sight, check the assembly by running the system at full pressure while you observe the hose, hose ends and adapters for leaks.

than was designed in and can obviously lead to either leakage or, in really extreme cases, blow-off. The maximum allowable gap between the faces of the assembled nipple and cutter is 0.046''. Everyone, including me, eyeballs this dimension.

(6) Failure of the operator to notice when the hose tries to work its way back through the socket as the cutter advances onto the socket during assembly. This is a particularly nasty happening because the completed assembly may look perfectly normal when, in fact, the hose is neither properly retained nor properly sealed—a disaster looking for a place to happen. Murphy's laws assure us that the disaster will happen at the worst possible time—such as leading Indianapolis by miles with 25 laps to go (yes, it DID happen and no, I'm not going to tell who it was). The ONLY way to positively prevent this embarrassment is to mark the hose as described in assembly step 2 and to check the mark after assembly—EVERY TIME.

(7) Attempting to replace a hose end without recutting the end of the hose. It is miracle enough that the cutter does its thing the first time. Asking it to do it again in the old wound is a bit much; the odds of success are not in your favor. These odds, in fact, strongly favor the creation of a flapper, a blown-off hose end or a giant leak. Cut the hose back to virgin rubber and start over.

(8) Attempting to assemble a previously used hose end with a ring of inner liner rubber trapped in the annular sealing chamber. As you would expect, this just doesn't work at all.

REUSE

All double-nipple hose ends are completely reuseable, as is the hose. As usual, Earl's has come up with an advantage. When disassembling a double-nipple hose end it is not at all uncommon for the inner tube of the hose liner, which is captured between the nipple and the cutter, to be torn off by the friction between the rubber and the walls of the chamber (which rotate in opposite directions during disassembly) and to remain trapped in place. When this happens the rubber MUST be removed before the nipple can be used again —and it is a bear to get out. With the Swivel Seal the chances of this happening are diminished, simply because the cutter can rotate with respect to the nipple (if we allow it to) so that the rubber in torsion is required to deal with only one moving surface. The procedure is as follows:

Place the socket in a soft-jawed vise and, with one wrench on the nipple and another on the cutter, hold the nipple and turn the cutter until the socket is disengaged completely—then pull the hose off the nipple. This method will only work with the angled Swivel Seals. With the straight parts you hold the socket in the vise and turn the nipple.

If you should be so unfortunate as to end up with a ring of rubber trapped between the nipple tube and the cutter ID, do not despair. Merely grind one end of an old hacksaw blade into a flat hook (see FIGURE [192]), insert the hose into the chamber containing the recalcitrant rubber and pull it out.

LEAKS

If a double-nipple hose end fitting leaks it has either been assembled incorrectly or the sealing surfaces on the adapter and/or the nipple have been damaged (or, just possibly, someone has tried to assemble a 37 degree AN seat onto a 45 degree SAE cone). Damage to the cone or the seat can be caused by a multitude of sins—dirt and overtightening being the most common. We are not about to do away with either one. The good news is that we now have an instant fix for the damaged sealing surface: the CONICAL SEAL.

"And what the hell," you may say, "is a conical seal?" "Just about the neatest thing to come out of California since the founding of the wine industry," say I. Have a look at FIGURE [193].

Figure (192): Homemade hose removal hook.

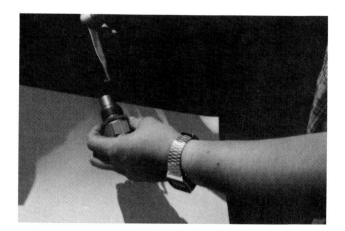

Figure (193): The conical seal.

The conical seal is formed from a very malleable alloy (either aluminum or copper) that "flows" into any imperfections in the sealing surfaces. The yield point of the alloy is low enough to form a leakproof joint at standard assembly pressures. It is installed by simply pushing it over the end of the male cone and assembling the hose end in the normal way. Equally spaced "friction flats" on the conical seal retain the device on the male cone and prevent misalignment. I have used them about eight times in the past six years. One of those times a dash 3 size won a race for us. I carry a full range of the things in my toolbox and consider anyone who knows about them and does not do so to be foolish.

There is one other common cause of hose end leaks: People don't tighten them. The only way that I know of to be certain that every hose end is properly tightened is for everyone concerned to form the habit of NEVER leaving an adapter, a hose end (or, for that matter, anything else) loose, finger tight, or "partially tightened." Even when you know that you are going to take the thing off again in two minutes, properly tighten it—EVERY TIME. Otherwise, Murphy will eventually get you.

To finish our discussion of leaks, I will state one more time that there is no need whatsoever to put Teflon tape, gasket goop or anything else on either the sealing surfaces or the threads of the coupler or the adapter—it only makes a mess.

Figure (194): Some of the available hose end configurations for use with Teflon/stainless hose.

HYDRAULIC SYSTEMS

Just about the whole world has now figured out that the familiar stainless braid-protected Teflon hose that we introduced on the GT-40's some 18 years ago is the only flexible hose to use on the race car braking system. Combined with the right hose ends, it is lighter, stronger and better looking than anything else, AND its use results in a much firmer brake pedal and an increase in effective available pedal travel. As always, however, all that glitters is not gold and there are pitfalls in store for the unwary and/or uninformed. Since I am talking here about possible sudden failure of the braking system, these pits tend to be particularly deep and nasty.

As you would expect, there are exactly two manufacturers whose hose and hose ends I will allow on the braking systems of my racing cars. To no one's surprise, they are Earl's Supply and Aeroquip. Again Earl's offers a greater variety of hose end configurations—including a hose end tee which I now use instead of the usual AN tee adapter and three separate hose ends at the rear brake line junction (at the front I use a double banjo directly at the master cylinder). I have found that a great many racers do not understand the inner workings of these hose ends either, so stand by for one more explanation. Refer to FIGURE [195], an Earl's Supply Fluor-O-Seal which is functionally identical to the Aeroquip Super Gem.

The sleeve is inserted between the Teflon tube and the stainless steel protective braid before assembly. When the nipple is screwed into the socket, hose retention is assured by the wedging of the the braid between the ID of the socket (which is shaped and sized to obtain a predetermined amount of crush) and the OD of the sleeve. At the same time the action of the tapered ID of the socket against the OD of the somewhat flexible sleeve forces the annular barbs on the ID of the sleeve into the Teflon tube AND butts the taper at the face of the sleeve against the seat on

Figure (195): Earl's Fluor-O-Seal hose end.

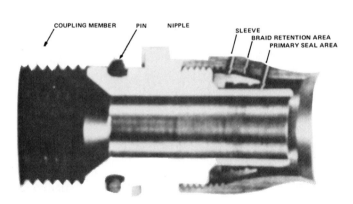

the nipple, forming a two-stage seal. In this way the sealing function is separated from the hose retention function and the strongest possible assembly is obtained. The sleeves are available in either stainless steel or brass. I prefer the brass because it is softer and should seal better, but I have never had any trouble with the stainless.

ASSEMBLY

Once more this comes straight from Earl's catalog:

DOING IT RIGHT

There are not a whole lot of no-no's in the actual installation of flexible plumbing runs. About the only things that can be done REALLY wrong are to install a hose under tension (either axial or radial, and THAT will be pretty obvious when you go to hook up the hose) or to install a hose in such a way that it will interfere with something (or be interfered with) under some combination of dynamic conditions. It is not unusual for a really neat and convenient hose location to suddenly become all wrong when the suspension travels; or the front wheels turn; or the fluids involved get hot and burn the driver (or heat the fuel/brake fluid); or the exhaust gets hot and boils the brake fluid; or the car gets off the road and tears off whatever hoses were dangling (even a little bit), leaving the driver with no brakes, clutch, fuel delivery, oil, and/or water—but with a fearsome temper. The no-no's that I want to warn you about include:

(1) Leaving insufficient clearance between each hose end and anything that it might contact or vibrate against. While the hose is flexible, the hose ends are not.

(2) Allowing a hose to come in contact with a sharp corner, a nut, a bolt, a rivet stem or anything else that is not perfectly smooth. This one includes failure to install a grommet at each point at which a hose passes through a panel.

(3) Allowing a hose to rub against ANYTHING, even when the surface against which it will rub is flat and smooth. The stainless braid makes a very efficient file and will abrade through anything that it moves against. This is particularly true in those instances where brake and clutch lines pass through the fuel cell compartment. In this case I encase the hoses in a thin-walled aluminum tube. Spiral wrapping is a neat and convenient way to prevent chafe damage under normal conditions.

(4) Kinking the hose, either by bending it too tightly (Earl's includes minimum bend radii tables in its catalog) or by placing the hose in a torsional bind.

(5) Overtightening the hose ends onto their adapter fittings or into their ports. Both the seal and the self-locking feature are provided by the design, not by sheer muscle. It helps a lot to use the wrenches made for the job. FIGURE [196] shows them.

(6) Allowing things to hang by their hoses. This is particularly true of brake calipers. It is the single most common cause of failure in brake system hose ends and is the main reason that I do not allow the use of 90 degree hose ends at the caliper. What happens is that the hose end gets bent at its weakest point and, sometime later, it fails at the

Figure (195A): Assembly tips for Earl's Fluor-O-Flex hose.

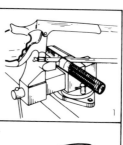

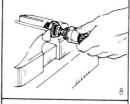
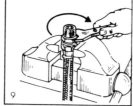

Brake lines are critical items. The potential penalties for improper assembly are severe. Although there is nothing complicated about the procedure and no special tools are required, extreme care must be used in assembly. We strongly recommend that the following procedures be used.

1. Cut the hose to the required length. We recommend the use of a radiac wheel but it can be done satisfactorily with a 32 teeth per inch hacksaw blade. In either case, the hose must be tightly wrapped with masking tape and the cut made through the tape. Do not cut FLUOR-O-FLEX hose with a chisel, snips, pliers, or a shear as these may crush the Teflon sleeve.

2. Deburr the Teflon and trim any loose ends of braid with sharp snips or diagonal cutting pliers.

3. Install the socket on the hose with the threaded end of the socket toward the cut end of the hose. This will be a lot easier and you will end up with fewer holes in your hand if you clamp the socket in a vise. Push socket on well beyond end.

4. Place the hex portion of the nipple in the vise. Insert the end of the hose onto the nipple and bottom the hose against the chamfer seat of the nipple with a rotary motion of the hose. This will size the I.D. of the Teflon tube and start the necessary separation of the tube from the braid.

5. Separate the braid from the O.D. of the Teflon Tube with a small screwdriver or a scribe. Be careful not to scratch or nick the Teflon.

6. Install the sleeve between the braid and the Teflon tube. Make sure that none of the braid is trapped between the Teflon and the sleeve. Bottom the tube against the shoulder of the sleeve and make sure that the sleeve is inserted square.

7. With the nipple held in the vise, push the hose and the sleeve onto the nipple until the sleeve bottoms. Remove the hose and make sure that the Teflon tube is still bottomed against the shoulder of the sleeve and that the sleeve is still square.

8. Push the hose and sleeve back onto the nipple and bottom against the chamfer. Start the socket onto the nipple threads and hand tighten.

9. Place the socket in the vise and complete the assembly by tightening the nipple onto the socket with a wrench until the gap between the face of the socket and the hex of the nipple is .023" to .046" – use a feeler gauge.

10. Blow the assembly clean and pressure test before running the car.

stress raiser from fatigue. Not pleasant at all! Since I don't even trust myself much, let alone anyone else, I use Earl's banjo hose ends on all of my calipers.

MAINTENANCE

Plumbing systems require virtually no maintenance at all. What maintenance there is is largely a question of preventing abuse:

(1) Inspect the whole system frequently for signs of chafing, abrasion, crushing or seepage.

(2) Keep both the hose and the fittings CLEAN:

(a) Before removing any hose end from its adapter or port, wash the assembly down with solvent—or even with gasoline—and blow it both clean and dry so that no grit or dirt can find its way into the threads or sealing surfaces.

(b) As soon as the hose has been removed install a clean protective plug into the hose end and a clean cap over the adapter.

(c) Always inspect both the hose end and the adapter for damage or dirt before reassembly.

(d) Race cars, particularly open-wheeled race cars, are forever getting corners either knocked off or folded back against the chassis. In either case the flexible brake lines and their hose ends are going to be stretched and distorted. Scrap them—it just isn't worth the chance.

The only way to end up with a truly neat, serviceable and workmanlike plumbing installation is to think it all out ahead of time. He who grabs a couple of coils of hose and a shoebox full of hose ends and adapters and gets stuck into it will inevitably end up with an unmanageable, unpresentable and expensive bunch of silver worms. Planning is merely a question of working out what has to run where and

what line size is required and then deciding on the routing and grouping of the hoses and the configurations of hose ends and adapters that will result in the neatest, most maintainable/workable and economical installation. It helps a lot to work out a schematic listing of the length of hoses, the styles of hose ends and the configuration and sizes of adapters that will be needed. When laying out the plumbing try to keep normal maintenance functions and operations in mind. Too many good-looking installations end up causing needless work—like deplumbing the transaxle oil cooler to change gears; or having to disconnect a bunch of oil hoses to change the filter; or having to bleed the clutch and brakes every time that the engine is changed. You should be vitally concerned with arranging the minimum number of connections to be undone for an engine change and, even more important, the absolute minimum possibility of damaging things during engine changes. Improbable as it may seem, this happens all the time because hoses that had to be disconnected are left dangling where they can be run over by the cherry picker or crushed between either the incoming or the outgoing engine and the chassis or whatever. Of course, if it doesn't have to be disconnected, it is not going to get dirt in it—and it will not have to be either reconnected or bled.

It always looks better if the plumbing lines are arranged to run together in logical groups (of about the same temperature, among other things). It also makes it a lot easier to support the hoses. Hoses, flexible or not, are meant to carry fluid—not to hang something from. They are not even SELF supporting. In fact they need a lot of outside support—at about 18 inch intervals. I use a lot of ti-wrap saddles and ti-wraps—they are both cheap and fast.

Figure (196): Aluminum hose end wrenches.

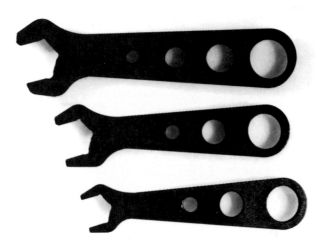

Figure (197): Use tie wraps to support plumbing hoses.

PLUMBING SIZE DESIGNATIONS

A fair bit of confusion has been expressed regarding the AN and NPT size designations used in both race car and aircraft plumbing. We will attack the AN system first.

THE AN SYSTEM OF TUBING SIZES

The AN (Air Corps/Navy) standards were established prior to World War II in order to organize and standardize the sizes, configurations and specifications of military aircraft hardware into a servicewide system of interchangeable, standard parts. The system soon became industrywide, has been greatly expanded in the ensuing decades and has gone through a couple of name changes.

With respect to plumbing, the number that we usually refer to as the ''AN number'' is actually a size designation and comprises only a part of the full AN identifying number. It is properly referred to as the ''AN dash number'' and does not define the ID of a flexible hose but refers to the OD (in $\frac{1}{16}$ths of an inch) of the metal hard line, which is considered to be the equivalent (in flow rate) of the flexible hose. The OD was used as the standard simply so that the metal flared-tube compression sleeves and coupling nuts used with hard lines (see FIGURE [198]) could be standardized.

Accordingly, each AN tube diameter was assigned a corresponding thread diameter and pitch for its coupling members. This thread designation refers to the threads of the hard line coupling nut, the flexible hose end coupling nut and the AN adapters that go with them. Any AN dash 10 coupler will fit and seal on any AN dash 10 male adapter. It does not, however, mean that any dash 10 hose end can be used with any dash 10 line. Hopefully the table and the thread silhouettes in FIGURE [198] will clarify the situation.

PIPE THREADS

Those of you who have read PREPARE TO WIN are aware that I consider the tapered pipe thread to be an abomination. This opinion, no matter how well founded, has done nothing toward the abolishment of the tapered pipe thread in racing. We are, it seems, stuck with the damned things so we may as well learn to identify them. NPT (national pipe-tapered) numbers refer to the INSIDE diameter of the piece of pipe that receives the male thread. The threads themselves are so designed that the male thread is an interference fit in its female counterpart—that is what keeps the drain lines and some of the water supply lines in your house from leaking. Unfortunately a great number of our castings come equipped with female pipe threads; so, some of the AN adapters are manufactured with tapered pipe threads on one end and AN threads and sealing cones on the other. Although I flatly refuse to use pipe threads on the braking system I must admit that I am usually too lazy to change them on existing fuel and oil systems—so long as

---

Figure (198): AN thread sizes and silhouettes (exact size).

MALE AN THREAD SILHOUETTES (ACTUAL SIZE)

     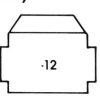 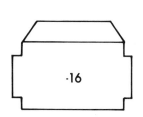

AN Size	Metal Tube O.D.	Thread Size UNF
3	3/16	3/8-24
4	1/4	7/16-20
5	5/16	1/2-20
6	3/8	9/16-18
8	1/2	3/4-16
10	5/8	7/8-14
12	3/4	1-1/16-12
16	1"	1-5/16-12
20	1-1/4	1-5/8-12

I do not intend to remove the adapter from its female housing very often. The use of Teflon (either in tape or paste form) is an absolute necessity with pipe threads. FIGURE [199] shows how the system works.

British castings come with British straight pipe threads. BSP thread pitches are close enough to NPT so that running the appropriate NPT tap through the BSP hole works pretty well.

HARD LINES

My thanks to John Gianelli for bringing to my attention a point that I had forgotten. In PREPARE TO WIN I stated that I convert all of my brake and clutch hard-line fittings to AN configuration. I still do—and I always will. A little bit later I stated that "American double flares are easily formed on hard lines by any of the proprietary flaring tools." This is also perfectly true. What I neglected to point out, though, is that the "American" double flare is an SAE 45 degree flare and is not suitable for use with the AN fittings, which are 37 degree cones. In fact, I use an AN single flare with the AN 818 compression sleeve/AN 819 coupling nut combination which is the only way that I

connect hard lines to flex hoses, as shown by FIGURE [200]. To do so I use a Rol-Aire 37 degree flaring tool from Aircraft Spruce. Do not attempt to use a 45 degree SAE flaring tool with the AN fittings.

CONCLUSION

It seems as if this has been a long chapter, for a rehash. I hope that I have not rambled on at too great length on the subject. I feel that a detailed treatment is in order due to the number of ignorance-type failures that I have seen in the past few years. I think that the seeming increase in this particular cause of failure is due to a combination of factors: first, the proliferation of imitation "right stuff" that is currently being hyped and, second, we experienced racers don't spend enough time teaching.

My generation was the first to use all of this semiexotic stuff and at first we were scared to death of it—so we took the time to learn how it all worked, how to assemble it and how to use it. The trouble is that WE have known about it for so long that it is now second nature to us and we assume, without thinking about it, that the young people know as much about it as we do. They don't—simply because we haven't taught them. The really good young ones ask (by definition there can be no such thing as a stupid question). The rest just plow ahead and all of a sudden the plumbing that we have taken for granted for a decade starts to give us trouble. Being human, we blame either the younger generation or the manufacturer. Maybe this will help the young ones.

Figure (199): Male NPT thread silhouette (exact size).

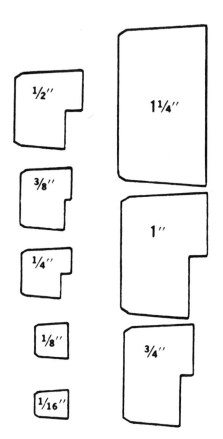

Figure (200): AN compression sleeve and coupling nut for single-flared, hard lines.

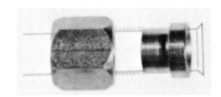

CHAPTER ELEVEN

BRAKING SYSTEM

THE BRAKES

The typical racing brake system has been developed to a state of effectiveness and reliability well in advance of the rest of the racing car. Almost all "braking problems" are caused by maladjustment (more often in the chassis than in the brakes themselves), by driver abuse (king of the late brakers), by lack of maintenance or by badly adjusted front-to-rear brake balance. With few exceptions—all of which can be avoided by intelligent and informed component selection—there are virtually no design defects within the currently available RACING brake systems. Even the once despised AP/Lockheed master cylinder is now a perfectly good unit (they DO listen to our piteous complaints from the field—at least the good ones do). Because of this refinement of design and because of the simple fact that we spend less than 5% of our typical lap time under the brakes anymore, do not expect to find any sizeable increments of lap time by improving your braking system. You can, however, achieve "tactical" advantages, such as being able to pass under the brakes because you can develop more braking force early in the slowing down process than your opponents can. Read on. . . .

Keeping it all working is a question of routine replacement of seals and fluid and of keeping things in adjustment. Preventative maintenance is not just the best kind; it is the ONLY kind. It is folly to expect brake seals to last more than half a season on a racing car. You can talk all day about the seals on your street car lasting a half million miles, but it is simply not the same thing. Not only are the conditions of use totally different but, as they say about airplanes, "you can take a perfectly good part up in the air, and it will stop working." WE can take a perfectly good, brand-new and certified AIRCRAFT part (like a toggle switch or a magneto), install it on a racing car, and IT will stop working. Like everyone else, Murphy works overtime in this business.

It would be possible to write a whole book on the design and maintenance of the braking system. I have no interest in doing so. Fortunately Fred Puhn, with assistance from Mac Tilton, has done just that. HP books, upon whom blessings be, is about to publish Fred's BRAKE HANDBOOK. I have read the manuscript. It is clearly written, well organized and it contains everything that any of us are ever going to want to know about braking systems. I will buy it when it comes out and I suggest that you do also.

THE DISC BRAKE ROTOR

Drum brakes are dead. Solid discs remain on cars which don't require ventilated rotors simply because they don't have enough tire to stop hard—like Formula Fords and Super Vees. Just about every other serious racing car uses proper-ventilated disc-brake rotors. There are three basic types: the straight vane, the curved vane and the sphericone. Straight vanes came first and, because they are considerably cheaper to produce, are still the most common. When Phil Remington was chief engineer at Shelby's he came up with the curved-vane rotor in order to arrest the propagation of heat cracks before they became full radial cracks. The sphericone is a relatively new configuration from Automotive Products/Lockheed. It greatly increases the surface area without much increasing the mass. Basically, as shown in FIGURE [201], it consists of alternate stalagmites and stalactites growing inward from the opposing disc friction surfaces. It is in almost universal use in Formula One and long-distance racing. I have no idea how it is cast and would really like to know.

At the moment there are, to my knowledge, six manufacturers of RACING brake discs: Automotive Products and Girling in England, ATE in Germany, Brembo in Italy, Gregg Industries of El Monte, California, and Hurst Airheart. If Bob Gregg happens to have what I need in stock I usually run his discs because they are as good as anyone's and, believe it or not, I don't want to injure our national balance of payments any more than I have to. If Bob doesn't have what I want I run curved-vane rotors from AP simply because they last longer. If I were running Trans-Am or NASCAR I would run the sphericones. If I had unlimited money I would try carbon filament discs and pads—the idea being that the vehicle's rotational moments of inertia (as well as overall mass) are considerably reduced with attendant beneficial results to both linear acceleration and deceleration. Although it is most unlikely that I will ever have unlimited money, I expect that I will be using carbon brakes in the not very distant future; the advantages are tremendous and the price is coming down.

In the meantime I slot my discs. For years I cut radial slots on a mill with a rotary table. When I first saw the rectangular cross slot pattern of FIGURE [202A], I felt really dumb. I now do it the easy way, as in FIGURE [202B]. It is still important to get a radius in the slot so I use a ball

Figure (201): The sphericone disc. Tilton Engineering, Inc.

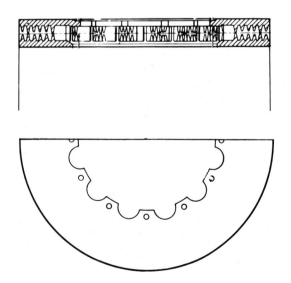

Figure (202A): Machining cleaning slots on a brake disc—the hard way.

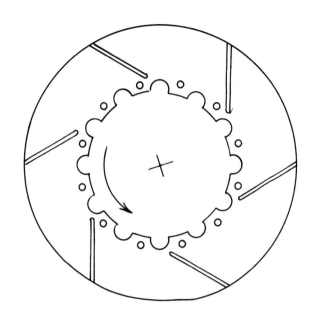

Figure (202B): Machining cleaning slots on a brake disc—the easy way.

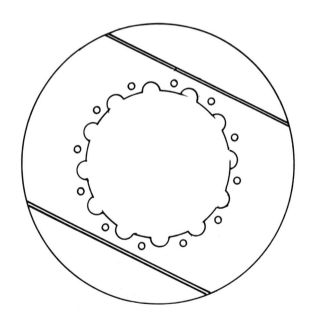

end mill. It is still equally important not to carry the slot all the way to the ID of the disc face. If I had the time I would drill my discs in the overlapping pattern shown by FIGURE [203].

The uninformed who drill the holes in a circumferential pattern on equal radii as shown by FIGURE [204] end up with grooved pads and cars that will not stop. Those who try to race anything (including karts) with ¼'' discs end up with warped discs, even if they are made of cast iron. Those who try to make discs from steel plate are in real trouble.

THE TOP HAT OR BRAKE BELL

In most racing applications the brake disc is attached to the hub or axles by means of a separate mounting bell or ''top hat.'' These days I will grudgingly admit that the now popular method of bolting the cast iron disc directly to an aluminum top hat can, like certain other unnatural acts, be made to work—IF the correct bell material (2024-T3 or T351) is used and IF the bolting flange has both sufficient thickness and sufficient edge distance to stabilize the bolt in single shear and IF proper bolts are used. BUT, it can never be made to function as well as the castellated dog-drive disc. The manufacturers are simply too cheap to spend the money necessary to mill the drive dogs and they can get away with the bolt-on part, even though there have been a number of failures (only, I must admit, of the badly designed ones) and even though it leads to premature cracking of the discs and probably increases taper wear of the pads. After all, what do you expect for $40,000?

Mac Tilton now markets a really clever bolt-on drive dog which converts bolt-on top hats to dog drive. I couldn't figure out how in hell he was making them at the price. It turns out that they are sintered. So my earlier statement about sintered metals having no place on the racing car is retracted.

Anyway, given any choice at all, I run dog-drive discs. I no longer make my own top hats because I can buy proper 2024-T351 items from Mac cheaper than I can make them. As yet, I have not converted an Atlantic car but I would very much like to do a back-to-back comparison some day. And I am willing to bet that the driver's feel would be better with dog drive. I know that the discs would last longer. I would not even consider running a Can-Am or champ car with bolt-on discs—let alone a sedan. On the Atlantic cars I at least throw away the junk bolts that they come with and use NAS 1104 bolts with NAS washers and jet nuts.

THE BRAKE CALIPER

Racing-brake calipers are manufactured by AP, Girling, ATE, Brembo and no others. All of the other so-called racing calipers are junk and should be replaced if the regulations allow and if it is your intent to race seriously. There is also no such thing as a racing caliper on the ''slider'' design so beloved of the passenger car manufacturers (they are cheap to produce and more than adequate for street use). The only exception that I can think of to this statement occurs when a street car that was born with drums at the rear is converted to four-wheel disc brakes. In this case, unless a GOOD fully floating axle is installed, the rear discs

Figure (203): Overlapping (Porsche pattern) holes drilled in brake disc.

Figure (204): How not to drill discs—holes in circumferential pattern reduce effective pad area by 50%.

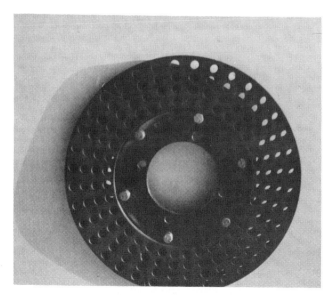

are very liable to wander about so much (in the axial sense) that pad knockback can become a very serious problem. Under these circumstances a good slider will be more effective than a racing caliper. The best sliders that I know of are manufactured by Girlock in Australia, are OEM on the 1984 Corvette and are imported by Tilton Engineering.

One of the dead giveaways of bad caliper design is the common practice of expecting the steel pad backing plate to slide across an aluminum caliper body without digging in. It will not. Another dead giveaway is the use of caliper piston seals of round cross-section. They cause too much piston retraction and are simply not suitable. My last word on calipers is that I would much rather run a good cast iron caliper than a bad aluminum one.

THE STAGGER PISTON CALIPER

After God knows how many years of requests from the long-distance racers, AP has finally begun to produce a racing four-pot caliper with unequal piston bores. As I pointed out in TUNE TO WIN, taper wear of the brake pads is basically caused by the simple fact that the trailing edge of the pad runs hotter than the leading edge and so wears faster. If the leading pistons of a four-pot caliper are made larger than the trailing pistons (since the line pressure is the same for all of the pistons), relatively more force will be applied at the leading edge of the pad and, if the ratios were correctly worked out, taper wear will be virtually eliminated. This is a more efficient method of reducing taper wear than shaping the pads as I described in TUNE TO WIN. It's about time!

BRAKE PADS

Nothing new here except that the price has escalated all out of proportion to anything sensible. I now mill the pads flat again when they get a little tapered (with a carbide cutter and a STRONG vacuum cleaner to grab the dust before I can inhale it). I still want a pad material with a high coefficient of friction at relatively low temperatures so that the driver does not have to wait for the pad to get hot before the brakes really hard. I use Mintex 171FF or Ferodo 2459 for Atlantic and Super Vee, Ferodo DS 11 or 2459 or Mintex 171FF for Can-Am, and Hardie Ferodo 1103 for distance racing. I have not been able to make Hardie Ferodo DP 11, Hardie Ferodo Premium, or Ferodo 2430 work. If in doubt, DS 11, while a bit slow, is always safe—except for sedans and distance cars. For Formula Ford, I use Mintex 121FF.

THE BIAS BAR

As late as yesterday I thought that I had said all that there was to say about the brake bias bar. Wrong again! I have just come back from a combined pro/national race. While I was there one of the national competitors came up with an interesting problem, one that had not occurred to me: "How in hell do I, a vastly inexperienced driver, tell which way to adjust the brake bias?" It turned out that he already knew which end of the car he wanted to put more braking effort on—he couldn't figure out which way to turn the adjusting screw. What's more, his level of driving experience was such that the message from the car as to which way he was adjusting things wasn't getting through to him. The only way he could tell what was going on was by brake pad wear. We had a discussion about how to tell from the driver's point of view, but it dawned on me that I probably needed to come up with a foolproof way to tell which way does what. Here it is, as shown by FIGURE [205].

The object of the exercise is to move the spherical bearing TOWARD the master cylinder that you want to put more braking effort on. Take any old bolt and a plain hex nut. Start the hex nut onto the bolt. Reach through whatever you have to reach through and hold the bolt and nut just behind the brake bias bar with the head of the bolt on the same side of the bias bar as the adjuster. Hold the nut stationary against the edge of the bias bar tube and turn the bolt. The way that the end of the bolt moves is the way that the spherical bearing will move if you turn the adjuster the same way as you have just turned the bolt. Now mark your adjuster in some clever fashion so that you will, forever and ever, know which way biases the brakes to the front. I usually just put a curved arrow in the direction that biases the front with the letter "F" at the end of the arrow. DO NOT:

(1) Trust your friends for advice on this matter.

(2) Trust any marks put on the car by either the manufacturer or a previous owner.

(3) Believe the importer of your car.

Figure (205): The brake bias bar. Tilton Engineering, Inc.

1. CLEVIS   **5.** PIVOT SLEEVE
2. BARRELL NUT   **6.** SPHERICAL BEARING
3. JAM NUT   **7.** PUSH RODS
4. RETAINING RING **8.** ADJUSTING SHAFT

BRAKE FLUID

Since I wrote PREPARE TO WIN the Department of Transportation has gone mad and played around with the DOT specs for brake fluids so that DOT3 and DOT5 don't mean much any more. Just to make matters worse, neither Delco 550 Supreme nor Wagner Lockhheed FC 59250 are currently available. There is, however, one bright spot in this sea of bureaucratic gloom. Ford Motor Company C6AZ 19542A brake fluid is, at the time of writing, still available and it is just what it has always been—a damned good racing brake fluid (even if it WAS developed to solve the problem created by idiots resting their left feet on the brake pedals of their Lincoln Continentals). The only viable alternative that I know of is the Automotive Products/Lockheed 550 Racing Brake Fluid that Mac Tilton imports at vast cost. It is really good stuff, but I sincerely believe that the Ford product is just as good—at a small fraction of the price. This is the only area that I know of where Mac and I disagree. Stop And Go Products (1835 Whittier Ave., St. A5, Costa Mesa, CA 92627, 714-646-0525) has developed a racing brake fluid as good as the best and sells it at a reasonable price under its own name.

Castrol LMA, available at any NAPA store and most discount houses, is the next best brake fluid available and is suitable for many car/driver/circuit combinations, up to and including Super Vee (on average circuits—not for Elkhart Lake, Long Beach or Trois Rivieres). I use it in our street cars.

No brake fluid will work in a racing car if it has been allowed to absorb moisture from the atmosphere. Small cans are still the rule and using fluid that has been bled through the system, even if it looks clean, is asking for trouble. Use it in the clutch system.

The silicon-based brake fluids have made progress since PREPARE TO WIN. Some of them are now almost useable in racing cars—but not quite. They still have high-frequency-vibration frothing problems and they are still compressible at high temperatures, which is why it takes a few laps for the pedal to get spongy when gullible people try to use silicones to race with. The only advantage that even the most eager salesman claims for the silicones is that they are nonhygroscopic. We replace all of our brake fluid long before it has a chance to collect moisture so I have never understood why anyone would spend the money for the silicones anyway. Tilton sells a neat litle bellows diaphragm that fits in the top of your master cylinder reservoir and keeps the atmosphere away from the fluid.

BRAKE BALANCE

I still consider driver-adjustable front-to-rear braking force balance (or "brake bias") to be a must in anything that purports to be a serious racing car. Ron Tauranac has shown us the easy way to achieve it, without the angle drive which I described in TUNE TO WIN. Look at any Ralt RT 4 or RT 5.

One of the factors that I define in preseason testing, with each car, is just how much additional rear brake bias it takes to get things right in the wet (it is always more than you think).

In addition to his excellent pedal/bias bar assemblies, Mac Tilton now sells a very serviceable driver-controlled bias adjuster. He also has a very interesting five-position proportioning valve which installs in the rear brake line and is adjustable by the driver. It was developed by Automotive Products for European rally cars—which are liable to encounter snow, ice, dirt, gravel, mud, dry concrete and wet bricks in one ten-mile stretch of road. It has a lot less hysteresis than the familiar Kelsey Hayes and/or Chrysler units. If I did much snow driving or if it rained in southern California (or if I weren't so lazy) I would install one in my Honda. I mention the device because the short-track roundy round racers are starting to install them across the FRONT WHEELS, the idea being that they can either still brake straight with a lot of cross weight in the car or they can use left front brake bias to turn the car into the corners. There are A LOT of ways to skin a cat! Clever man, Mr. Tilton. I talk with him a lot—and I learn something every time I do.

I do not believe in the time-honored theory of setting cars up with excessive rear brake bias in order to reduce corner entry understeer ("make the car point"). This is a classic example of balancing the handling of a car by killing the end that IS working—DUMB. Of course, like everyone else, when I run out of time and the car still won't point, I crank on the rear brake—but I know that I have failed in my efforts to properly set the car up.

BRAKE FADE

It is time to clear the air of the popular misconceptions concerning the dreaded brake fade. The racing car is subject to three distinct forms of brake fade:

(1) Green fade. This is a natural by-product of the brake bedding process (except with Mintex 17 FF pads) and was both defined and described in PREPARE TO WIN.

(2) Pad fade or compound fade. This is similar in feel and result to green fade. It occurs when the temperature generated by the brakes exceeds the upper temperature limit of the friction material. The symptom is a normal pedal (high and firm), but virtually no stopping power. Pumping does not help. While it is now quite uncommon in racing, compound fade is easy to achieve in a street car—any street car—and the aspiring racing driver would be well advised to deliberately fade the pads in a street car from time to time simply so that he will remember what it feels like and not confuse his crew when he experiences the third type of brake fade, which is NOT all that uncommon.

(3) Fluid fade. This happens when the temperature of the caliper cylinder (or the piston) reaches the boiling point of the brake fluid and tiny bubbles of compressible gas form in and are diffused through the previously incompressible brake fluid. The pedal then goes to the floor, giving rise to frantic pumping of both the brake pedal and the driver's heart and, upon the driver's eventual return to the pits, a wild-eyed statement to the effect that, "the brakes faded

and scared the hell out of me." After I get done explaining to the driver that if he really did experience a partial loss of braking effectiveness AND stayed on the road, then he hadn't been using the brakes as hard as he should have been (think about that one!), I gently point out that he had better be able to differentiate between pad fade and fluid boil. Not only are the symptoms diametrically opposite, but so are the cures and a lot of time can be wasted in chasing the wrong culprit. Brake fluid that has been overheated once has lost its effectiveness and must be replaced.

Basically, if the pedal goes all soft and horrible, you have not faded the brakes, you have boiled the brake fluid. The only cure is to either upgrade the fluid or to keep it cooler. This can be achieved either by increasing the cooling to the CALIPER or by insulating the caliper pistons. Additional disc cooling or going to a harder pad compound is NOT going to fix it.

On the other hand, if the pedal stays high and firm but the car won't stop, you are experiencing pad fade and, as-suming that the pads have been properly bedded, the only way that you are going to cure the problem is by going to a harder (more temperature resistant) pad or by increasing the effective heat sink of the disc—by increasing its mass, its surface area and/or the effectiveness of its cooling. The quickest and least expensive way out of trouble in this area is the harder pad material—but we can only go so far in this department. Water cooling (by a mist inserted as far up-stream in the cooling duct as possible) works just fine. As usual, Tilton knows how to do it and sells all the right gear. It is important to realize that the system works by reducing the temperature of the brake-cooling air, not by spraying water on the brake disc. The idea here is to inject a very fine spray of water as far upstream as possible in the cool-ing air duct so the evaporation of the water will be able to reduce the temperature of the cooling air by the maximum possible amount before the air gets to the brakes. We want all of the water to have evaporated BEFORE it gets to the disc. The system works best on hot, dry days. The trouble is, of course, that you have to carry around (and to both ac-celerate and decelerate) a fearsomely heavy amount of water. I prefer to use more disc and more air. I would rather pay the money for sphericones than start a race with 10 gallons of water on board.

SOFT PEDALING

But, the pedal can also bounce off the floor for other rea-sons. Chief among them is either badly designed or worn-out seals. Poorly designed caliper seals (featured by many U.S.-made, so called ''racing calipers'') retract the pistons so far that most of the available pedal travel can be used up in just moving the pads far enough so that they contact the discs. A dead giveaway in this department is the use of a round O-ring for a caliper seal (with or without a Teflon back-up ring). Since AP realizes that continuous light pad contact doesn't hurt anything at all, and that disc run out prevents continuous contact anyway, they usually insert a very light barrel spring inside the caliper piston to make sure that their properly designed seal in its properly de-signed trapezoidal groove doesn't retract the piston too far. A too-thin backing plate (sometimes featured by the U.S. manufacturers) also uses up pedal travel, as does taper wear of the pads.

Add all of these features together and it doesn't take much imagination to realize that, when the manufacturer does everything wrong, there is not liable to be a lot of pedal travel left with which to stop the car. I defy ANY-ONE to be truly quick around a circuit which requires the use of brakes when he (or she) has to pump the damned things every time that they are applied. Like I said, ''RAC-ING calipers are manufactured by AP/Lockheed, Girling, ATE and Brembo.''

While deteriorated caliper and master cylinder seals will normally evidence their presence by visible weeping of brake fluid, this is not always the case. If you cannot get all of the air bubbles out of the brake system and are faced with a deteriorating brake pedal, replace the caliper seals and/or the master cylinder seals—including the little round one at the end of the master cylinder return spring (which is often the unsuspected culprit).

If all of your efforts to stop fluid boil come to naught, a ceramic insulating spacer inserted into the caliper piston and bearing on the pad backing plate will insulate the piston and cylinder (and therefore the fluid therein) to a surprising degree. Be very careful in your selection of material—it must be suitable for the temperature, the compressive stress

Figure (206): Brake caliper piston insulator.

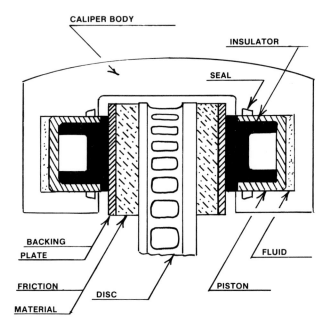

and the shear stress involved. Carbon fiber is perfect, but there are several ceramics available. Bakelite will work. Tempered masonite will not. Of course this scheme sacrifices some pad thickness but, except for distance racing, this shouldn't present a problem. FIGURE [206] illustrates.

BLEEDING THE BRAKES

The other cause of the soft brake pedal is improper bleeding procedure. I have changed the system that I rec-ommended in PREPARE TO WIN in one respect: I no longer do any pressure bleeding at all. Not only is it not necessary; it is very liable to create bubbles by forcing the brake fluid to move with extreme and unaccustomed velocity through tiny orifices, and to cavitate. Since no one wants to believe me in this matter I will reprint as FIGURE [207] Mac Tilton's treatise on the subject (with his permission):

Figure (207): Mac Tilton's treatise on brake bleeding.

Brake bleeding procedure. The most misunderstood area in brake system maintenance is brake bleeding. There has been more misinformation and old wives' tales passed on regarding brake bleeding than we care to relate. Proper brake bleeding requires the minimal amount of equipment and the minimal number of people. It is an exceptionally simple procedure and there is really only one way to do it correctly. The equipment required is two clear bottles, two clear plastic hoses that will fit the bleeder screws, proper bleeder screw wrenches and an adequate supply of fresh brake fluid. If the car has dual master cylinders or has a compound or dual system master cylinder, **both systems must be bled simultaneously.** Quite often a brake system can be bled without even pumping the pedal if the master cylinders and reservoirs are mounted high enough. When this condition is present, quite often gravity is all that is required.

Start by placing a small quantity of brake fluid in each clear bottle and by attaching the plastic bleeder hose to the bleeder fitting and submerging the end of the hose below the brake fluid level in the clear bottles. Next, crack the inside bleed fitting and hold open. Have someone depress the brake pedal with their **hand,** pumping in slow, steady movements. Have someone observe the fluid reservoir and add fluid before it reaches within one-half inch of the bottom of the reservoir. Continue pumping with the brake fittings open until a steady flow of clear, air-free fluid is observed coming from the caliper. Make sure that the hose is always held underneath the brake fluid level in the bottle. This prevents the caliper from sucking air on the return stroke of the master cylinder. After a steady stream of air-free fluid is observed, close the bleeder screw on the downward stroke of the pedal, release the pedal and observe its travel. Now go to the other calipers and repeat the same procedure.

At the completion of the second set of calipers, the brake system should be bled thoroughly and only minimal pedal travel should be observed. It is not required that you have your resident gorilla depress the pedal on the car as hard as possible and then crack the bleed fittings. In fact, this procedure causes air in the system. This air is generated by the surge of fluid through the small orifices of the brake plumbing system. This surge causes cavitation, which is a form of boiling caused by low pressure areas in the system. Pressure bleeders should not be used, even those with the rubber diaphragm, because of the fluid surge problem and because of the uncertainty of the condition of the fluid stored in the pressure bleeder.

COOL OFF

If you beat your driver about the head and shoulders often enough he will eventually form the habit of doing a cool-off lap before he comes in to talk with you during or after practice/qualifying—or even during a scheduled pit stop (cool-off in this case is a relative term). He will then arrive without smoking brakes which will be deprived of the undoubted benefits of cooling air while the car is stationary in the pits. He will also avoid heat soaking the calipers and boiling the fluid. The cool-off procedure also helps the tires (a lot), and there is no way that it can hurt either the engine or the gearbox. Besides, it shows the car owner that the driver cares about his (the car owner's) investment.

BRAKES AND THE OVAL TRACK

Since I have been involved with Super Vees on oval tracks, I have often heard words to the effect, "Since we don't use the brakes at Phoenix or MIS or Pocono, it doesn't matter what pads we put in." *Nonsense!* Every so often an accident in the making forces the driver to use his brakes—hard. If he has to wait for DS-11 to warm up he stands a much greater chance of becoming a part of the accident than he would if he were using instantly effective Mintex 171.

CHAPTER TWELVE

PRE- AND POSTNATAL CARE FOR THE RACING WHEEL AND TIRE

THE MODULAR WHEEL

When I wrote PREPARE TO WIN the three-piece "modular" racing wheel was in its infancy. One-piece, sand cast magnesium alloy wheels were the norm and the Melmag wheel with its honeycomb center section bonded to stamped magnesium rims was supposed to be the wave of the future. That particular wave broke early because the engineers involved did not take all of the factors into account; the tension loads involved, aided by brake and tire heat, destroyed the adhesive bond (adhesive bonding, you will recall, is very effective in shear and not as effective in tension). Today the cast magnesium wheel has become ridiculously expensive. After a somewhat shaky (not to say terrifying) start, the three-piece modular wheel, with a sand cast magnesium alloy center section (or spyder) and detachable rim halves of either spun or pressed aluminum alloy clamped to the center section by a series of machine screws, is in almost universal use.

Properly designed and executed, this type of construction offers significant advantages over cast rims—particularly with regard to flexibility of design, to cost (both original and replacement) and to safety. There is very little difference in weight between a well-designed modular wheel and an equally well designed cast wheel, but the modular wheel is very liable to have a lower moment of rotational inertia. The modular construction means that the teams (and the manufacturers/dealers) have to stock fewer and less expensive parts.

The wheel width and/or offset can be varied almost at will. Most of us realize all that. What I have never seen mentioned in print, though, is the ability of rims spun or pressed from sheet aluminum to absorb gross amounts of energy in crash situations—energy that would otherwise have to be absorbed either by the chassis or by the occupant. We are talking about SIGNIFICANT amounts of energy here! The cast wheel does not act as an energy sponge.

Another aspect that no one ever seems to mention is that because the formed rims WILL distort (plastically) when they DO hit something unyielding (the cast ones tend to crack or even to shatter), the penalty for clipping curbs and such is a lot less severe than it used to be. I have, in fact, seen races WON by cars after hitting things that would for sure have broken cast rims. Since the future of road racing is pretty obviously in the streets I find this feature to be of considerable interest.

Anyway, while there are a few good modular wheels on the market, there are also a lot of mediocre ones and a few just plain bad ones. Since hype is the order of the age, the following discussion of the design features of the modular racing wheel should help you to differentiate between them.

THE CENTER SECTION

The center section, or spyder, of the racing wheel (of whatever type) must meet some pretty obvious requirements. It shouldn't break; it should be resistant to metal fatigue by design (no stress raisers and a sound casting); it should at least allow (if not promote) free passage of brake cooling air; it should be as light as is consistent with strength; and, it should be easy to both clean and inspect. It should also meet one design criterion that is not so obvious: In its plane of rotation it should be just as stiff as the designer can make it! The importance of wheel stiffness is not widely appreciated. It should be. Testing has conclusively demonstrated that a stiffer wheel, at either end of the car, results in more positive steering response/corner entry characteristics and faster and more positive transient response. This is almost certainly due to more linear slip angle generation. In motor racing any type of lag or sloppiness is bad.

I believe that a "spoked" design meets these criteria better and more efficiently than the popular "grid" or "web" design originated by Jim Hall and currently featured (although both the designs and the castings tend to be inferior to Jim's) by BBS and its imitators. The grid usually does not have the section depth to achieve adequate stiffness AND it is too complex to achieve consistently good sand castings (take a good look at one—typically they are a textbook example of bad castings and stress raisers). What is very liable to happen here is that, since the mass of metal at the intersection of the webs is necessarily much greater than that of the spokes themselves, it is very difficult to achieve a constant cooling rate as the molten metal solidifies and we are very liable to end up with "micro-shrink" cracks in the castings. These micro shrinks are some of God's favorite stress raisers. Further, the very design of most of the things prevents a smooth flow of stress.

I believe that the minimum acceptable number of spokes is four and that six is a considerably better number. The spokes should be tapered with the larger cross-section toward the center of the wheel and should have generous radii where they blend into both the center boss and the rim bolt ring. This is equally true of one-piece cast wheels. Spokes can be efficiently designed with either an I-beam, a T-beam or a semicylindrical cross-section. While some porosity is almost inevitable, the casting must be free of large voids and gross porosity. It doesn't do a lot of good to design a stiff and efficient spyder, pay the money for an aircraft-quality casting and then machine stress raisers into the finished part through the use of insufficient radii; yet a lot of wheel manufacturers do just that.

THE RIMS

There are positive points to be made in favor of both spun and pressed rims. I really don't care which method is used nor do I particularly care whether the spinning is accomplished by man or by machine. I care only about the quality of the finished product. Basically this means that I want to see BIG radii where the metal changes direction and that I do NOT want to see the thickness of the metal decreased in these radii. It also means that I want to see a rim of the diameter, profile and width that I am going to use sectioned so that I can SEE the thickness variation. And I do not mean that I want to look at the demo part. I want a production part sawed apart in my presence. I want the ma-

terial used to be aluminum alloy 6061 and I want it heat treated to the T-6 condition after forming. I do not want to know about 2000, 3000 or 5000 series alloy rims or about non-heat-treated rims. I want the center casting to be clamped between the two rim halves, rather than placing both of the rim halves on one side of the casting. I could care less about who is using the same make of rims in some other class of racing or in some other configuration.

FASTENERS

Multipiece wheels should be assembled with machine screws and self-locking nuts. Rivets are simply not suitable. The rivet is primarily a shear fastener and the function of the fasteners in the modular wheel is to clamp the members together by tension. I use SPS Unbrako machine screws with all-metal elastic stop nuts, preferably of the slotted beam variety. I use $\frac{1}{4}$" for Super Vee and Atlantic and $\frac{5}{16}$" for Can-Am and sedans, regardless of what the wheel came with. I torque the fasteners to the manufacturer's spec, check the torque frequently and do not reuse either the nuts or the machine screws. I use full-thickness AN washers under both the bolt heads and the nuts. The thick aluminum tapered washers featured by Gotti are both elegant and effective, but not necessary.

THE CARE AND INSPECTION OF THE RACING WHEEL

Bill Jongbloed makes some of the best racing wheels in the world. He takes a lot of flak because his customers don't take care of their wheels and because he tends to get a bit outspoken at times. He does not suffer fools gladly. Sometimes he does not suffer them at all. Some years ago he wrote a short but effective treatise on preventative maintenance of the racing wheel—his or anyone else's. With the permission of all concerned I am reprinting it as FIGURE [208]. Maybe the doubters will believe BOTH of us.

I order my modular racing wheels unassembled and unpainted—not because I like ugly wheels or because I like to assemble wheels. It's because the chip-resistant epoxy paints now in common use (Jongbloed now uses a brittle lacquer for reasons that will become obvious in a moment) make it impossible to properly inspect a casting, and because I do not trust the minimum-wage help employed by the wheel manufacturers to properly assemble a wheel.

The paint is flexible enough to both fill (and hide) small casting voids and to allow the development of small fatigue cracks in the metal underneath the intact paint. If, as is usual, the manufacturer delivers them painted anyway, I curse the man, bead blast the paint away, deburr the castings to get rid of the obvious stress raisers and x-ray inspect them. Due to the cost involved I only take one view (axial) to make sure that there are no big voids or occlusions. I then Zyglo the casting and paint it with a spray can of cheap lacquer (Krylon is my favorite for the purpose—it comes off easily for inspection and is brittle as hell so it is very liable to crack due to wheel strain BEFORE the wheel does). At the same time I deburr and dye-penetrant inspect the formed rims.

Figure (208): Bill Jongbloed's article on wheels.

A Wheel Concern/Bill Jongbloed

How many racers do you know who actually take the time, at some point during the year, to really inspect their wheels? Let's face it: During the season there isn't enough time and during the off season there are simply too many other neat things to do.

Now let's look from another perspective: What single component is the first one to accept the stresses of cornering? Wheels would be the obvious answer. However, while many teams strip down their chassis to inspect the suspension, the wheels generally sit in the corner. Therein lies my concern as a manufacturer. With tire and chassis development progressing as fast as it is, the loadings on wheels are spiraling up. Remember, wheel failures usually happen during cornering. You proceed directly off the road in most cases ...

By now you're thinking, "Who is this guy, some prophet of doom?" In fact I'm not at all but, having designed and manufactured wheels for going on seven years now, I've had more exposure than most. My concern is that I don't see enough basic preventative maintenance. Not just on my wheels but wheels in general, one-piece and modular.

I'd like to suggest some basic guidelines for maintenance, starting with one-piece cast wheels. First, though, let's look at how much energy is being stored up in a wheel-tire combination. On a modern Can-Am rear wheel-tire combination, the force with which the tire pressure (20 psi) is trying to burst or separate the outer half from the inner half is nearing 4000 pounds. And that's lying on the ground before you bolt it to the car! Sounds pretty impressive. By realizing how much energy you have

bottled up, what you read next might have more effect on you.

One-piece cast wheels are quite popular and, in many cases, have been in service for the longest time. In my opinion once a year (at minimum) tires should be dismounted and steam cleaning should be undertaken. This lets you give the wheels a good visual inspection. If they pass a visual inspection, then beadblasting is heartily recommended so that a zyglo dye penetrant inspection can be done. First, though, any abrasions should be ground and sanded as *all* sharp corners can develop into cracks. A die grinder is best but a drill motor with a rotary file will do OK. If the wheels don't pass then you have a candidate for an end table (with a history). Just get the glass cut.

In some cases, if you have a localized deformation on the rim lip it may be repairable. Say "may" because cast material doesn't like to be bent, let alone bent back. It doesn't take much to surpass a casting's elongation limits. Some people weld them up; I don't usually recommmend that as it will leave cracks or gas holes in mag unless the welder is very good.

Also remember that both aluminum and magnesium anneal when welded. Therefore, your wheel will be soft in that area and in the immediately surrounding area. You could have it heat treated but, since warpage would probably occur during the quench, you would simply have produced a heat treated end table. After *any* welding zyglo is, in my opinion, mandatory. Tossing a wheel is not cheap but crashing and possibly getting hurt costs much more.

Modular wheels are increasingly popular, but they also cannot be mounted and forgotten about. Modulars offer certain advantages but, like freedom, they come with responsibility. Whereas

on a one-piece wheel you have only one component, these wheels generally have two rim halves, a centercasting, numerous bolts, nuts, washers and a sealing apparatus. Again, thorough once-a-year inspection should be at minimum using the zyglo process preceded by cleaning as mentioned earlier. At all factories they are assembled neatly and cleanly; be sure that when you disassemble and reassemble, you do the same.

Be sure to follow the procedures that the manufacturer recommends. Remember that any time you have a wheel apart, closely inspect the rim halves— especially the inner rim. Inner rims take the heaviest load and are the least visible. One thing I recommend is that since locknuts work the best the first time, you replace them each time you disassemble a wheel. It's cheap to do and good insurance. When you install bolts and they are a tight fit, wind them down—*don't* beat on them! That will invariably leave chips between the wheel components. Use the proper torque setting as recommended and remember never to torque with an inflated tire as your reading won't be accurate. If your wheels are of the riveted variety, then you won't be able to change pieces but periodical inspection would catch a rivet that was working loose. Remember that rivets are normally a shear-type fastener and are being used in a predominantly tension application. Check them.

I hope that in the future we all will cast a more observant eye toward the wheels that are gathering dust in the corner. Keep in mind that if we take it upon ourselves to do a good job, then the sanctioning bodies won't have to make more rules. After all, wouldn't you rather inspect wheels on your own than be told to do it by a technical inspector?

Only then will I run the wheel—no matter WHO made the thing. AND I visually inspect them every time that they are dismounted and before each race event. Don't be bashful about returning a wheel that is either badly machined or doesn't pass x-ray or Zyglo—the manufacturer should have found the defect(s) before you did and the unit should have been destroyed, not sold. I serial number the wheels, keep a time-elapsed log on them, try to keep the in-service hours roughly even and dye-penetrant inspect at eight- to ten-hour (running time) intervals.

I prefer black anodized rims to polished ones. The reason is just what you would think—I don't have time to keep wheels both polished AND inspected. Rims are easy to inspect because you KNOW where the initial cracks are going to appear: They will be at one of the radii and they will be circumferential. There is no way to heal these cracks once they appear. For obvious reasons the outermost rim is the one that gets checked and inspected most frequently. Unfortunately it is the innermost rim that takes the heaviest load. I do not carry rims around that have even small cracks or nonreparable dents. I will not give them away, or even sell them. Our home features a lot of lawn chairs, coffee tables, trash cans, foot stools and garden hose reels made from old rims (and some not-so-old ones). On the road I comply with Bill Jongbloed's request and throw the damaged parts into a convenient lake to become fish habitats. I saw a spoke out of my cracked spyders and use the remains to make bump steer and/or alignment wheels.

RUN OUT

Any wheel that is formed from sheet metal, as opposed to being machined from a casting, will inevitably show some measurable run out at the rim. The run out may be either radial or axial (or both). Even if it has virtually none when received from the manufacturer (and I would refuse to accept a new rim with more than about 0.010'' of run out), the tender ministrations of tire machines, levers and racing drivers will soon provide some. Contrary to some of the alarmist articles that I have read, small amounts of either radial or axial run out at the rim will not have a discernable effect upon either the tire or the driver. I don't know at what point run out begins to present a problem but certainly 0.030'' is acceptable to the tire.

All of this is assuming that we are talking about radial or axial run out measured at the rim—not about nonflat or skew-machined mounting surfaces, a feature of some of the highly touted riveted wheels. I should also mention that just because a wheel is machined from a casting is no guarantee that it has no run out. It is also possible to achieve radial run out while drilling the drive peg or lug stud holes—which is why racing wheels should be piloted on the hub.

The actual problem with wheel run out is that we have all become accustomed to using the rim itself as the reference plane for suspension alignment. We simply cannot do it with formed rims—at least without some preparation. When you are trying to set your toe in (or out) to ± 0.010'' and the rim that you are using for reference has 0.060'' of run out, a certain lack of compatability becomes obvious.

There are as many solutions to this minor problem as there are racers who are aware of it. We can always measure camber directly on the tire (so long as the camber gauge is not resting on a raised letter or whatever), but toe presents another problem. It is possible (and practical) to use the time-honored method of chalking a band around the circumference of the tire, scribing a reference line in the chalk dust and measuring the toe to this reference line (and this is a method that merits more consideration than we give it because it is accurate and the equipment is both easy to make and portable). We can also use any of the "string around the tires" or "straight edge held against the tire and measure to the chassis" methods. I watch a lot of people aligning a lot of cars. In my opinion the methods that do not reference the centerline of the car do not work very well and are not particularly repeatable. For the sake of convenience this means that toe is going to have to be measured at the wheel rim.

I get to play with a lot of race cars over the course of a season. Before I can achieve anything meaningful I have to at least verify the alignment. To do so on a car that I have never seen before I tape a felt-tipped pen to something solid (like a concrete building block), jack up each wheel in turn and slowly rotate the wheel while using the marker as a dial indicator to mark points on the rim that lie in the same plane of rotation. Eventually I end up with two spots on each rim that are 180 degrees apart and in the same plane of rotation. So long as I always measure from those two points, run out is eliminated and I can proceed with confidence.

It is also possible to come up with an almost infinite variety of adapters which bolt or clamp onto the machined portion of the wheel. Which method you decide to use doesn't really matter so long as it provides you with a convenient, repeatable and true reference plane. I still do it my way—referencing the centerline of the vehicle (see PREPARE TO WIN)—and I now use alignment wheels which I make from unserviceable spyders and aluminum plate.

TIRE DIAMETER VERSUS RIM DIAMETER

Every manufactured part must be made to SOME tolerance. This is true of both tires and rims—they are manufactured to a given design diameter plus or minus a dimensional tolerance. Even if both are within tolerance, if the tire diameter happens to be all the way toward the high side of its tolerance AND the rim is all the way toward its lower limit, there is a possibility that the tire may slip circumferentially on the rim under either braking or accelerative torque. When this happens the tire very quickly goes out of balance—and some air may be lost.

The time-honored way to detect tire rotation on the rim is to put a chalk mark on the tire opposite the valve stem and check to see that it stays there. That is what I used to do with cast rims—until Lola came up with a batch of undersized wheels, which REALLY spun. Then I borrowed a trick from the motorcycle and sprint car racers: I secured each tire to its rim with six short sheet metal screws through the outer bead-retaining flange and into (but not through) the tire bead. This is a pain in the butt, but it does fix the problem.

Each manufacturer assures me that there cannot be a diameter problem with HIS rims—only with his competitors'. What I do now is to borrow Pat Shelby's Motor Rim and Wheel Association rim diameter bead gauge and check all of my new rims. I also carry the sheet metal screws around with me and, if I have any doubts at all, I use them. A hole must be predrilled in the rim flange and a drill stop had better be used when drilling into the tire bead or you are eventually going to ruin a perfectly good, brand-new tire. A lot of people laugh at me when my metal screws make their appearance—but I notice who they come to for parts when THEIR tires start to slip.

CAST WHEELS

Although I prefer to use modular wheels from the viewpoints of safety and cost, I am willing to admit that they are labor intensive. If I were running a low-bucks racing team AND I could buy GOOD cast wheels at almost the same price as good modulars of the same weight I would probably opt for the cast wheels simply to reduce the work load and increase the operating efficiency of the team. This is not about to happen. When I have a choice I run Jongbloed Modular Wheels simply because they are at least as light, as strong and as stiff as anything that is available and Bill Jongbloed's quality control tends to be better than most— HE CARES. The price is also usually less than the competition but this is not a factor in my book. A great many of the advertised cast "mag racing wheels" are actually made from aluminum and are either so heavy or so lacking in stiffness as to be useless. Be careful. Among the good ones are Panasport and Momo. I do not consider cast wheels to be reparable—at all.

I have witnessed altogether too many wheel failures. None of them have had pleasant results. The number of wheel manufacturers whose products I will purchase when I have a clean sheet of paper keeps getting smaller. At the moment, the only readily available wheels which I am willing to run in the dry on a car for which I am responsible are Momos and Jongbloeds.

Momo has just brought out a low-pressure, diecast small car wheel that is considerably less expensive than its previous outstanding sand-cast wheels. Like the sand-cast wheel it is very light, strong and stiff. The US distributor is McNeil Motorsports. Jongbloeds are still my favorite wheels, simply because of their lightness, stiffness and inherent energy-absorbing characteristics.

SAFETY BEADS AND SAFETY STUDS

I no longer use safety studs to ensure that a deflating tire will stay on the rim—only because I am now convinced that an ADEQUATE formed or machined safety bead will do the same job. If I were running a series with really wide tires, like Can-Am or IMSA, I would run the studs. I check the beads on my wheels both to make sure that they leave an adequate tire bead seat outboard of the bead (I have seen a number of wheels manufactured so that the tire bead sat on top of the safety bead when installed rather than outboard of it) and to make sure that the safety bead is both large enough to do some good and has a gentle enough slope so that a tire can be mounted. Never trust the manufacturer!

REPAIR

I mentioned earlier that proper racing formed-aluminum rims are heat treated to the T-6 condition. This means that the common practice of annealing the dented section before attempting to hammer it straight is not real smart. In fact, the practice should be discouraged. I anneal only as a last resort. My system of minor dent removal is, I believe, more sane—if more trouble. I carry with me a couple of segments sawn and formed from 2''×6'' oak which match the curvature of the rims I am using—one is an inside form and the other an outside. I use them as hammer forms to straighten mildly dinged rims. Badly bent ones are not, in my opinion, reparable. The amount of force required to hammer even mildly distorted rims is more than we are used to. I use a #3 rawhide mallet rather than the #1 that I use for everything else and I wail on the things pretty hard. As long as we realize that the rim is only going to move a tiny bit with each blow and so long as we exercise a certain amount of restraint and control, the minor dings WILL come out and the wheel will be as good as new.

When I do have to anneal a rim to make it straight again, that rim gets relegated to the rain tires. I have been known to more or less straighten some pretty far out wheels—and to indelibly mark them "TOW ONLY" simply because I dislike transporting (or even going to the pits) on good rubber. Just to be on the safe side, I usually paint these tow wheels some really distinctive color.

ASSEMBLY

I refuse to have anything to do with rims that must be disassembled to mount/dismount tires and it is simply not necessary to take a wheel apart to visually inspect it. My modular wheels come down only when I have to replace a damaged part or when it is Zyglo time.

I order my wheels unassembled for ease of initial inspection AND because I do not trust the manufacturer's hired help to assemble them properly. The first step in assembly is to make sure that there are no burrs, scratches or rough spots that will tend to keep the rim/center surfaces from actually mating. Because I would rather be safe than sorry, I assemble my modular wheels with a very thin coating of GE high-temperature (orange) silicon seal on the mating surfaces, in addition to the usual O-ring seal supplied by the manufacturer. To be triple safe I form a "wet finger" fillet of silicone seal in the drop center between the spyder and the rim halves when the assembly is completed.

LIFE EXPECTANCY

There is no valid answer to the often asked question, "How long should we continue to use a racing wheel?" What we are talking about here is metal fatigue. In all probability the highest non-crash-induced stress that a wheel ever sees is the tensile stress induced by "popping the bead" when the tire is mounted. I do not believe that it is possible to predict the life of a racing wheel by stress analysis because we cannot even approximate either the stress levels that will be encountered or their frequency. Frequent inspection is the only answer that I know of. We are, of course, helped by the gradual nature of failure from metal fatigue. If we are conscientious about it we will find the early fatigue cracks well before a failure occurs. The problem lies in the all-to-human temptation to say, "It's just a little crack; I'll grind it out and it'll be OK this time." Wrong! Once metal fatigue has progressed to the point that WE can detect fatigue cracks in a wheel it is coffee table time.

Another factor to consider is the expected use—a gentlemanly stroll around Laguna in a vintage exhibition is simply not the same thing as Turn Nine at Riverside in a Trans-Am car. Speaking of Turn Nine, never forget the effects of banked turns (on all of the suspension/chassis components, not just the wheels). The three-spoke DiMag SuperVee wheels gave no trouble whatsoever until the SuperVee circus got to Phoenix, where they broke like popcorn. This is something for those of my readers who go forth to Daytona once or twice a year to consider.

THE RACING TIRE

I said virtually everything that I have to say about the racing tire in TUNE TO WIN. To my regret I haven't learned a lot about them since. So what you get here is a mini tirade about some of the less desirable design features of the current generation of racing tires—and a few tips on making them last longer.

In contrast to the rest of our racing equipment, the unit cost of the racing tire has risen very little since TUNE TO WIN. BUT, because the tires do not last anywhere near as long as they did, tire cost as a percentage of the annual budget has gone up considerably. If you are going to be fully competitive you will find that your season's tire bill will rival your engine rebuild bill. I have never understood this. Sometimes it looks to me like Akron has taken a page out of the chassis designers book of a few years ago when download was supposed to be everything and torsional rigidity no longer mattered—except that with the tire, soft seems to be everything, or at least the easy way out. I would think that compound technology should by now have reached a point where a tire could be made with a considerably longer consistent life than our current gumballs evidence—with little if any sacrifice in performance.

When there is an all-out war between rival tire companies, each company is obviously going to produce the stickiest tire that it can come up with—and qualifiers and a dozen different compounds and constructions are going to be the order of the day. This is completely understandable (although qualifiers should be outlawed). It is also good for the sport and for the industry, and it won't cost the competitors anything. The front runners will get sponsorship money, testing fees and free tires, plus a performance edge. The mid-field runners and the back markers won't benefit

in terms of relative performance, but it won't hurt them either because, let's face it, more tires simply are not going to move them up. They will benefit financially from both the inevitable crumbs that will fall their way and from being able to buy slightly used tires very cheaply. All of this is fine when there is a tire war in a professional series.

However, to my way of thinking, every amateur series and those professional series in which one tire company has (for whatever reason) a monopoly should require a spec tire—and that spec tire should be like the old Goodyear Tasman Formula Atlantic Tire: cast iron. At the moment it takes a minimum of two and probably three sets of tires to run up front all weekend at, for God's sake, a Super Vee road race—with spec tires. The SCCA seems unable to come up with spec tire rules for Fords, Sports 2000 and so on (but then, they are not able to do much of anything else either). The fact that Jacques Coutre and his Russell school people (in concert with Mazda and Firestone) realize this and have started their spec car, spec engine, spec tire, no mods pro series without Denver leads me to think that Jacques and Joe Aguirre just may be the hope of the future for the aspiring young racing driver. THEIR tire idea is simplicity itself. The entry fee includes one set of spec tires. They are marked. AND, except for accident and puncture damage, they are all that you get for the meeting. If you want to burn them up in practice, go ahead, but you are going to start the race on them. Flat, spotted and/or punctured tires will be replaced by good USED tires from a common pile in the pits. To me this is an excellent rule. Would that Denver would follow suit! Since Denver is not capable of doing so, I do wish that Akron would do us a favor in the tire department.

The late, late word from the first 1984 SCCA national at Sebring is that Goodyear may well have done just that. A new Formula Ford compound—harder, faster, longer lived and more consistent—was introduced and dominated. Presumably this breakthrough will be extended to other classes and Goodyear will reap the deserved benefits of working harder and better than the opposition—and will make up in number of customers and good will what they lose in tires sold per customer.

As I am about to deliver this book to the publisher, the late word is that Goodyear has somehow convinced the SCCA to allow them to change the Super Vee spec tire to this new hard and fast compound and we will get to use it (without prior testing) at Long Beach—next week. If it actually happens I will add my comments after Long Beach.

It is now the day after Long Beach 1984. The new tire worked JUST FINE. So far as I could tell, it is at least as quick as the old tire when new and it stays fast A LOT longer. Thank you, Goodyear.

No matter what improvements are made in our tires, it will still behoove us to look for ways to cut the tire bill without reducing performance. There are a few; they are not inconsiderable, and they are unlikely to change.

THE DREADED HEAT CYCLE

We used to be able to run our racing tires until we could literally see the cords, and still be competitive. No more!

Today the tire will inevitably have "gone off" or lost its grip long before the tread is worn out. The competitive life of the modern racing tire is measured in number of heat cycles, not miles of service or depth of tread.

But there are heat cycles and there are HEAT CYCLES. The first rule of saving tires is very simple: Don't abuse them. Put the heat into your racing tires gradually—every time—and do a cool-off lap before you come in. The effect on tire life will astonish you. It will also give you time to get yourself into tune with the world upon leaving the pits and to collect your thoughts before your return.

To back up these words of advice I am reprinting (with permission) Goodyear's official words on tire break in:
RACE TIRE BREAK IN PROCEDURE *The proper procedure of "breaking-in" a race tire consists of running a few miles of warm-up, a few miles as hard as possible, and then letting the tire cool. Below are several basic reasons for this method.*

Running a few miles of warm up allows the new tire's internal construction to adjust to the forces acting on it. Tire irregularities from storage and shipping are re-shaped into the desired size and contour for racing. The tread surface is skuffed and cleaned of dust, oil and other foreign materials. Improper tire balance can also be discovered at this time. Speed should gradually be increased during these few miles of warm up until the driver feels comfortable with the tires and is ready to go as hard as possible.

Running the next few miles (usually 3 to 5 miles for Sports Car Racing—it varies with vehicles, course conditions and driver ability) as hard as possible completes the tire's adjustment to its new lifestyle. This adjusting process results in the generation of extra heat (when compared to a previously broken in tire) and may actually overheat the tire if hard running is continued. A common complaint heard from drivers starting a race on new tires is that they worked great for the first couple of laps and then "went away" or "gave up". What ACTUALLY happened was that the tires overheated due to the extra heat created in a new tire. As the tread temperature went through its optimum range the tire felt as good as it ever will, and when the temperature continued to climb above this optimum range the tread compound started to permanently change and it will never again be as good as was intended. Running a new tire through its optimum temperature range is great for a short qualifying effort—but not during a race.

Letting the tire cool can be accomplished in several ways. It is best to allow enough time to cool to ambient temperature with the tire at rest—but if stopping to change or to cool tires is not practical, a couple of slower laps will be of some benefit.

The best approach to a race weekend where new tires are going to be used is to first set up the car on a good used set and then break in the new tires with a short qualifying attempt. Save this set for the race and you should have a predictable set of tires with a minimum of problems.

S. Reed Kryder
Race Tire Engineering
1-21-81

If, after reading the above a few times you come to the twin conclusions that:

(1) You should break in the tires that you intend to race on as soon as possible after your arrival at the race track, and that

(2) If you are good enough, precise enough and lucky enough in traffic you will be faster if you qualify on a brand-new set of tires—BUT remember that these tires will then not be either as fast or as blister resistant as a properly broken in set then you can go straight to the head of the class.

Normally the front tires "go off" before the rear tires do. This results in understeer increasing with mileage. Putting a new set of fronts on with a worn set of rears, however, unbalances the car. Popular opinion not withstanding, this phenomenon has nothing to do with greed, incompetence or lack of concern in Akron. In most cases, the front tires go off first simply because the car is set up with too much understeer. Some understeer is an absolute necessity. A little too much understeer is safe and comfortable. It is also slow and it hurts the front tires—a lot. Do yourself a favor, reread TUNE TO WIN, and dial the understeer out; you'll go faster, have more fun and use up far fewer tires.

Quite a few circuits are harder on the tires on one side of the car than they are on those on the opposite side. When testing (or even during official practice) on these circuits, I swap my tires from side to side about every 10 to 20 laps. Naturally this does not work if you are running tire stagger, but if you are not it can just about double the effective life of a set of tires.

THE COST OF QUALIFYING

For qualifying, especially if you have a valid shot at the pole, it pays to remember that the first fast lap that a set of road-racing tires ever does is going to be their fastest lap. It is all downhill after that (gradual, but still downhill). Since the easiest time and place to win a motor race is during qualifying (if you are on the pole and you get beat, WE KNOW whose fault it is), it is worth a set of new tires to get there. Not breaking them in won't ruin them (so long as they don't blister) but it will make them slower and reduce their effective life by a few heat cycles. I normally break in the race set when we first get to the track (beforehand if it is Long Beach, Detroit, Montreal or a CART show where we are going to receive very limited practice and qualifying time) and then see how things are going for qualifying. If we need an extra little bit I will qualify on a new set and then use them for testing or for practice at the next race. We are, however, talking about a maximum of two qualifying laps—any more will almost certainly overheat them and then we are very liable to blister them.

It behooves the racing driver to learn how to get it on at the required time. Sprint karts are excellent training for this—as is any sort of racing where the cars qualify one at a time. As a point of interest, the average set of current road-racing tires has definitely gone off after 8 heat cycles on the average race track. Again as a point of interest, my son has the same problem in sprint karts.

TIRE PRESSURE

I determine the optimum hot-tire pressure by testing. Invariably this turns out to be somewhat less pressure than the tire engineers want me to run. So long as the tread temperature is not approaching the compound limit, I let the stopwatch decide.

On a road-racing circuit I want the hot tire pressure to be the same on the left side as the right side (this may not be true of the front and the rear). That way the car's characteristics will be the same in each direction and the braking will be stable. I go to some trouble to determine exactly what cold tire pressure will result in the hot pressure that I want to run—at each corner of the car. If I have money available I use nitrogen instead of air and, when I do not, I use MY compressor instead of the tire company's, simply because I KNOW that mine has been blown down and contains as litle moisture vapor as I can arrange. Theirs may or may not.

I often mount and balance my own tires. It saves a lot of time and trouble while testing. I even sometimes do so at the race track if I don't think that the individual tire crew is competent or if the line is unduly long. I use Roger Krause's outstanding tire machine and balancer because I can't build one for the price he sells them at.

I keep my rain tires and any other tires that I am not going to use immediately in dark garbage bags (actually I use Japanese Dunlop draw string tire covers that I brought back from Australia, but they are not available here and while garbage bags lack elegance, they do just as good a job of retarding ultraviolet damage). I do not transport on good tires.

THE RADIAL RACING TIRE

There can be no serious doubt that the racing tire of the immediate future will be of radial ply construction. The good old U.S. of A. is the only nation in the world still racing on bias ply tires and even WE are catching on. Champ cars will almost definitely go radial in 1984 and the rest cannot be far behind. What wonders await us? I'll be damned if I know—I have never raced on radials. The one thing that I do know is that radials, in order to develop their maximum lateral adhesion, require more camber thrust than bias ply tires do. I do not pretend to know why. They are also a hell of a lot more tolerant of negative camber under the brakes. It would seem logical to steepen the camber change curve of the suspension to accommodate the radials, but, so far at least, the Formula One teams seem to have gotten their best results simply by running obscene amounts of static negative camber. It is going to be interesting.

CHAPTER THIRTEEN

SPRINGS AND SHOCK ABSORBERS

I thought that I had adequately covered the design and selection of suspension springs and their relationship to wheel rate, roll resistance, ride height and corner weight in TUNE TO WIN. At least in some respects, I failed. Time after time I find myself either testing or racing with operations who have opted to purchase low-dollar (on a comparative basis) springs from a spring manufacturer, a sales operation, or from a racing car importer. One of two things (occasionally both) inevitably happens:

(1) The springs take a set which changes the loaded heights so that the corner weights change and, at least until the springs have taken their final set (if ever), the car's behavior keeps changing due to changes in ride height and corner weights so that we waste a lot of time adjusting things instead of getting on with the job.

(2) The springs were designed to a free length rather than to a loaded height and every time that we want to change springs we have to readjust ride height, chassis rake and corner weights—again wasting a lot of time and, to some extent, masking the actual effects of the spring change both because the driver's memory of the way things were deteriorates with time spent sitting around and because the chances of getting everything exactly the way that it was are not real good.

There is a third possibility: The springs were designed to either a loaded height or a free length AND they have settled, in which case each spring will have a slightly different height at installed load, making the adjustment of corner weights a pain and the accurate setting of ride heights problematical.

Once and for all we are about to put this one to bed. We are about to cover the basic factors of spring design AND a simple, cheap and effective method of dealing with good springs that happen to be designed to free length rather than loaded height. We will also cover the only effective method of dealing with BAD springs.

BASIC SPRING DESIGN

Most racing cars use helical compression springs—simply because, from the point of view of strain energy storage capacity, the helical spring is the most efficient practical configuration for metal springs. Every compression spring is designed to have a specific resistance to compression. This is termed the spring rate and is expressed (in this country) in pounds of load required to cause one inch of compression. For reasons of cost and simplicity most of our helical springs are constant pitch, constant diameter linear springs; i.e., if a load of x pounds will cause a compression of y inches then a load of 1.5x pounds will compress the spring 1.5y inches and a load of 2x pounds will compress it 2y inches and so on, as shown in FIGURE [209].

So that they will seat squarely against their seats and adjustment collars, racing springs almost always have ground and closed ends as shown in FIGURE [210]. This feature subtracts slightly from their linearity in that compression force required to collapse the ground ends is less than the actual "rate" of the spring. To correctly measure spring rate it is necessary to compress the spring a given amount (1.00" is usually used for racing springs), take a reading of the load in pounds at that point, compress the spring one inch farther, take another reading and then subtract the two readings to obtain the actual spring rate in pounds per inch. This figure is the rate of the SPRING. It is NOT the wheel rate of the car with the spring installed. (You can go back and read TUNE TO WIN pages 64 through 66, until you fully understand the distinction between spring rate and wheel rate and the relationship between them.)

LOADED HEIGHT AND FREE LENGTH

In addition to being designed to a specific rate, each spring is also designed to support a certain load at a specified height and finally is constructed to both a specified free length dimension and a height at which the coils touch each other (solid stack height). In racing, the loaded height is the installed height of the spring and is critical, while the free length is only important. We want our springs to have a free length sufficient so that the spring will not become unloaded with the suspension at full droop. The reason for this usually overlooked design parameter is that, when the suspension is fully extended, the car is usually flying through the air. When it lands, we want the springs to begin their

Figure (210): Helical compression spring with closed and ground ends.

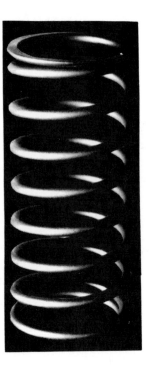

Figure (209): Linearity of helically wound compression spring. Spring rate is 600 lb/in.

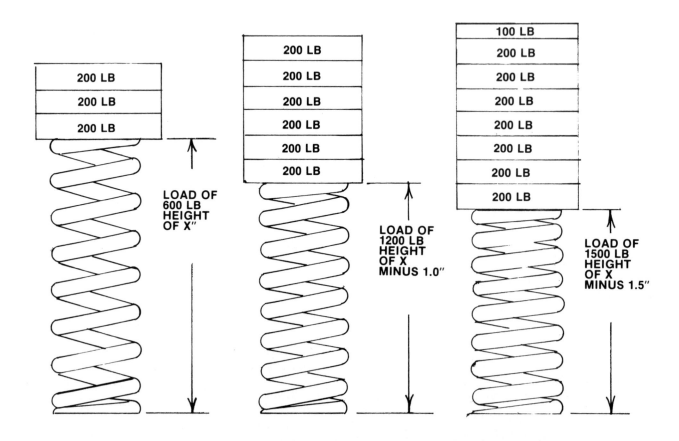

resistance to compression immediately. If the suspension has to move a finite distance before the springs begin to compress, then a greater amount of suspension travel will be required to absorb the force of landing and we will have to run our ride height higher than we would have to if the springs had been properly designed. Not good!

Another side of the same coin is the fact that we wish to be pushing each of our tires into the track with as much force as we can arrange at all times. If a spring is so short as to uncouple in some combination of droop and roll, then that tire is unloaded at a time when the spring could have been loading it. This can lead to such things as partial loss of traction at one end of the car and inside wheelspin.

On the other hand, we don't want our free length to be so long that changing springs becomes a pain. Compromise is the name of the free length game. The solid stack height, on the other hand, only has to be less than the space available for the spring at full shock absorber compression.

It used to be that we could, if we were willing to do a few calculations, always design our springs so that they would not uncouple at all. That was when we had long springs and sane wheel rates. Now we have short springs to suit our rocker-operated suspensions and the rates tend to be very high, both because of the mechanical advantage of the rockers and because of the recent developments in tire technology due to the advent of the ground effect racing car.

It is not at all unusual to end up with a spring envelope that DEMANDS that the spring uncouple. One common solution is to restrict the droop travel of the suspension. This has always seemed rather silly to me. I do not like "darty" racing cars and I do not like racing cars which have to be "thrown" at corners. To my way of thinking, it is a hell of a lot more sensible to use a longer spring than the one supplied with the car (assuming that it can be fitted), so that we can keep the wheel loaded by design, or to use either a progressively wound spring (expensive) or a helper spring with a rate such that it will be a spacer in normal operation but will keep the tire loaded when the suspension is in droop.

The helper spring can be a helical coil spring, a flat die spring or even a stack of Belleville washers. The flat "anti-rattle" spring once popular on March Formula Atlantic cars is NOT what I am talking about. It didn't have enough rate to do anything but prevent the adjustment threads on the shock body from being destroyed. Anyway, the performance improvement from such simple steps can be staggering—sometimes we simply do not see the forest for the trees.

The "load at height" of the racing car spring is critical. First, and obviously, since the height at which each spring will support any given load is a fixed dimension and the static load that the car places on each of its springs is virtually fixed, if the loaded height is too high, we will not be able to let the car down to desired ride height. If, on the other hand, it is too low, we will not be able to get the car off the ground. The range of adjustment of the spring platforms gives us some tolerance in this regard. I try to arrange things so that, with the spring platforms in the center of their adjustment, I am at designed ride height. This gives me adjustment and latitude for error in both directions.

LOADED HEIGHT, RIDE HEIGHT AND CORNER WEIGHT

The actual ride height of the car will be a function of the load at height of the springs and the adjustment of the spring platforms, not of the spring rate. If you installed solid steel bars of the same length in place of the suspension springs, you would not affect the corner weights. As illustrated by FIGURE [211], when the springs are installed on the car, the weight of the car applies, for all practical purposes, a fixed load on the springs. This load will compress each of the springs a fixed amount. The actual amount is a function of the free length of the spring, its rate and the geometry of its installation on the vehicle. If we design our springs so that each of the alternate front or rear springs, regardless of its rate, will support the fixed load placed upon it by the car AT THE SAME HEIGHT as all of its mates for the same position on the car, then we can return our spring platforms to the same adjustment every time we change springs. Assuming that we are using very good springs, our ride height, our chassis rake and our corner weights will, by definition, remain as they were before we changed the spring. This may not sound like a big deal. It is! Especially with single tube gas shocks, adjusting ride height and corner weights every time we change springs is a time-consuming bitch. Not only does it interfere with testing/practice/qualifying time, it costs a fortune in wasted man hours and lost track time. It is also completely unnecessary.

THE FIX—ONE

The first solution to the problem is the one that I advocated in each of the previous books. Order your springs from the Chassis Components Division of Rockwell International Corporation, Springs and Stampings Business, 500 East Ottowa Street, Logansport, Indiana, 46947, (219) 753-5181. The man to talk to is Jim Fiedler (pronounced "Fiddler"). Jim and his merry men have been making virtually all of the springs for the knowledgeable pros for years and they make PERFECT springs—every time. Their prices are typically about 50% higher than what you have to pay for ordinary springs from your importer and bad ones from some suppliers—a genuine bargain. Before you rush to your phone, read what follows, make sure that you understand it and do your homework. I don't want Jim mad at me—it would complicate my life a lot!

The first thing that you have to figure out is what spring rate(s) you want. That's up to you. There is no way that I can give detailed advice in a book. Typically your standard English Kit Formula Ford/ Sports 2000 comes too soft. Atlantics and Super Vees need an assortment on either side of what they come with. Fifty pounds of spring rate is about the right sort of step to work in. I almost always go in even increments of 50 pounds. When money is tight I try to borrow good test springs so that I can figure out exactly what

I want before spending the money. Speaking of money, I NEVER sell Rockwell Springs with the car at the end of the season. They are worth more to me than what I can get for them—unless, of course, the purchaser is willing to part with the replacement price.

Next you must measure the loaded height and measure/ calculate the load at this height. With the car aligned and on the ground, driver and half a fuel load in place, measure the distance from the top of the spring to the adjustable spring perch, assuming that the perch is close to being in the center of its range of adjustment. If it is not, change your loaded height (but not the load at that height) to compensate so that the loaded height that you call out will put the perch near the center of its adjustment. There are three ways to figure out the design load at this height:

(1) Measure the load on the stock spring when it is compressed to its installed height (the ACTUAL installed height, not the figure that you have adjusted to get the platform in the right place) on an ACCURATE spring checker.

(2) Calculate the load from the free length of the stock spring, its installed length and the known ACCURATE spring rate. Subtract the installed length from the free length and multiply the result in decimal inches by the spring rate to arrive at the load at installed height. For example, a spring with a free length of 7.00'', a rate of 600 lb./in. and an installed height of 5.75'' would have a load of (1.25 × 600 lb) 750 lb at its design height of 5.75''. This method will not be strictly accurate due to the before mentioned necessity of closing the ground ends of the spring before measuring the rate, but it is normally plenty close enough.

(3) Calculate the load at installed height from an end elevation drawing of the suspension, as illustrated by FIGURE [209], and a known corner weight.

The third step in the design of your spring is to figure out the maximum free length that you can live with. With the suspension at full droop, measure the distance between the top spring retainer and the adjustable perch. That is your maximum free height. With the spring removed, move the suspension into full bump. Measure the distance between the top spring retainer and the adjustable perch. This is the maximum height that you can allow for the ''solid stack'' of the spring—the height at which it will coil bind.

The last thing that you have to supply to Rockwell is the desired spring inside diameter. I design for Konis because springs so designed will fit virtually any shock.

What you are not going to do is to give a steel specification, a heat treatment specification, a shot-peening call out, a wire diameter, the number of coils or the working stress level. As the cliche goes, Jim Fiedler has forgotten more

Figure (211): Loaded height of coil spring.

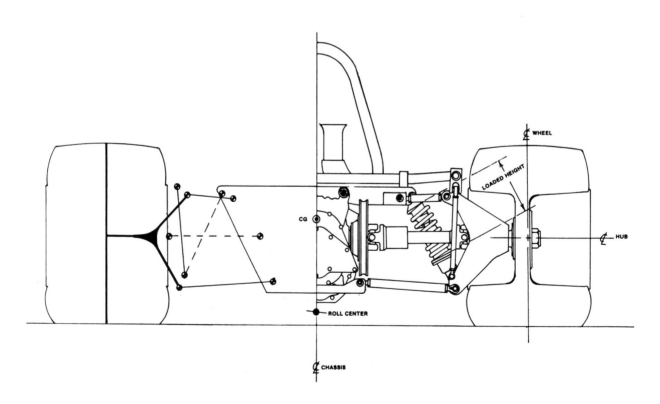

about designing springs than you are ever going to know. If he wants more information than you are supplying him, he will ask. Just to make sure that there are no communication gaps, I follow up my phone orders with a written specification—this protects all involved.

THE FIX—TWO

I can hear it now, ''Great, Smith, if all of your readers were millionaires! But what about Joe Average Racer, who just happens to own a reasonable selection of perfectly good springs that fit his car and whose only fault is that they all have different heights at the same load because they were designed to a common free length?''

What you do, dear reader, is measure the heights of your INDIVIDUAL springs at the required installed load and then make a series of cylindrical aluminum spring spacers—one for each spring—so that the loaded heights of all of your front springs can be made identical and the same for all of your rear springs. And, yes, you can substitute springs at the other end of the car by making up different spacers. You then mark each spring and its spacer(s) and carry on just as if you had Rockwell springs.

THE FIX—THREE

The last plaintive cry that I can hear is, ''But I bought a whole bunch of mail order springs and they all took different sets and some of them are leaning over to one side. What do I do now?'' What you do in this situation is take your springs to the nearest deep body of water and give them the old floatation test. You throw them in the water and if they float you save them. Sorry about that!

MEASURING THE RIDE HEIGHT

Being a lazy devil, I stopped groveling around on the ground to measure ride height a long time ago. What I do now is put all of my shock pivot bolts (or inboard upper suspension link bolts if they are more convenient) in a lathe and drill a center mark on the head with a center drill. I then set the car up to desired ride height in the shop where I can lie on the clean floor. With a pair of calipers I then measure and record the distance between the center of the top (or bottom, as the case may be) bolt and the adjustable spring perch. When I change springs I merely duplicate the distance, and everything—ride height, corner weights and all—is back to square one. I also, in the shop, figure out how many turns of rear ride height adjustment it takes to match each turn of front ride height adjustment so that the chassis rake stays the same.

I really don't like trying to measure ride height at the track—it is inaccurate, undignified and dirty. If you MUST do so, then you will need some sort of level surface to measure to; the track surface simply won't do. As good a method as any is to obtain a 4' × 8' sheet of ONE INCH pressboard; rip it into two 2' × 8' lengths, coat the lengths with polyurethane paint and lug them around with you—including into the pits for practice. They can be leveled with shims if you feel it necessary. I don't, because I change my wheel alignment and/or ride heights by numbers of turns without measuring.

SHOCK ABSORBERS

For twenty years or so I have felt that racing shock absorbers are manufactured by Koni and by no one else. Nothing has recently happened to make me change my mind. I will admit that with a relatively inexperienced driver I often prefer to use Bilsteins (if they have actually been designed and developed specifically for the individual race car either by Bilstein IN GERMANY or by the manufacturer working with Bilstein in Germany) simply because the inexperienced driver has quite enough going on to keep his mind and senses fully occupied without worrying about shock adjustment. HOWEVER, I am convinced that before any driver can realize his full potential he is going to have to learn to use Koni's double adjustable shocks to their best advantage so that he can set his car up for its optimum performance on different circuits. There is simply no other way to get those last few tenths of a second. The problem lies, as always, in learning how to do it. I suggest that a good place to start is by rereading what I had to say about shocks in TUNE TO WIN. With Koni's permission I will now quote from its current racing catalog/instruction manual:

BUMP DAMPING *Bump damping controls the unsprung weight of the vehicle. It controls the upward movement of the suspension as when hitting a bump on the track. It should not be used to control the downward movement of the vehicle when it encounters dips. Also it should not be used to control either roll or bottoming.*

Depending on the vehicle, the ideal bump setting can occur at any point within the adjustment range. This setting will be reached when ''side hop'' or ''walking'' in bumpy turns is minimal and the ride is not unduly harsh. At any point other than this ideal setting, EITHER the ''side hopping'' will be more pronounced OR the ride will be unduly harsh. [In the racing car the penalty of a too harsh ride is a reduction in the ability of the tire to put its tractive effort to the road—and is evidenced in the tire spinning, sliding or locking at an earlier value of acceleration than necessary, C.S.]

ADJUSTING THE BUMP CONTROL

STEP 1—Set all four dampers on minimum bump and minimum rebound settings.

STEP 2—Drive one or more laps to get the feel of the car. NOTE: When driving the car during the bump adjustment phase, disregard body lean or roll and concentrate SOLELY on how the car feels over bumps. Also, try to notice if the car ''walks'' or ''side hops'' on a rough turn.

STEP 3—Increase bump adjustment 3 clicks on all four dampers. Drive the car one or two laps. Repeat step three until a point is reached where the car starts to feel hard over bumpy surfaces.

STEP 4—Back off bump adjustment two clicks. The bump control is now set. NOTE: The back off point will probably be reached sooner at one end of the vehicle than the other. If this occurs, keep increasing the bump control at the soft end until it, too feels hard. Then back it off 2 clicks. The bump control is now set [for this racetrack, C.S.]

REBOUND DAMPING *Once you have found what you feel to be the best bump setting on all four wheels, you are ready to proceed with adjusting the rebound.*

The rebound damping controls the transitional roll (lean) as when entering a turn. It does NOT limit the total amount of roll; it does limit how fast this total roll angle is achieved. How much the vehicle leans is determined by other things such as spring rate, sway bars, roll center heights, etc.

It should be noted that too much rebound on either end of the vehicle will cause an INITIAL loss of lateral adhesion (cornering power) at that end which will cause the vehicle to oversteer or understeer excessively when entering a turn. Too much rebound in relation to bump will cause a condition known as "jacking down". This is a condition where, after hitting a bump and compressing the spring, the damper does not allow the spring to return to a neutral position (ride height) before the next bump is encountered. This repeats with each subsequent bump until the car is actually lowered on to the bump stops. . . .

ADJUSTING REBOUND CONTROL

STEP 1—With rebound set on full soft and the bump set from your testing, drive the car one or two laps, paying attention to how the car rolls WHEN ENTERING A TURN.

STEP 2—Increase rebound damping three sweeps (¼ turns) on all four corners and drive the car one or two laps.

STEP 3—Repeat step 2 until the car enters the turns smoothly (no drastic attitude changes) and without leaning excessively. Any increase in rebound stiffness beyond this point is un-necessary and may in fact be detrimental. EXCEPTION—It may be desirable to have a car that assumes an oversteering or understeering attitude when entering a turn. This preference, of course, will vary from one driver to another depending on individual driving style. . . .

Needless to say, the foregoing, while perfectly true, is somewhat simplified. It is, however, the best information for adjusting shock absorbers that I have seen in writing and as such is a damned good starting point. To learn how to use the shocks in detail, start from there and experiment, realizing that rebound is more important than bump, that too little rebound control leads to slow and sloppy transitions and response, while too much jacks the car down on its suspension AND makes things harsh in general. Too little bump control again makes the car soft and sloppy while too much bump will lead to a decreased ability to put the power down, premature sliding and brake lock up.

In general, increasing rear rebound control will reduce wheelspin, and decreasing front bump control will reduce corner entry understeer. Always remember that the PRIMARY purpose of the shock absorber is to dampen the release of energy stored in springs by suspension movement. Therefore, any effort to use really heavy springs with shocks valved for soft ones is foredoomed to failure (and confusion). The whole exercise is not easy!

When the Koni trailer arrives at the racetrack where you are, spend as much time with the technicians as you can, without becoming a pain in their butts. These people KNOW about shocks and what they can do for you and they are more than willing to share the information. Take advantage of it; too few do. Don't waste your time talking to the reps from the other manufacturers.

SPRINGS AND FATIGUE

To illustrate that nothing really changes, in 1937 A. L. Boegehold wrote in METAL PROGRESS, "The coil spring for the individually suspended front wheels of the automobile is an interesting metallurgical study because of the high stresses induced from the loads imposed. When the wheel moves upward to the bump position the stress in a typical spring is 117,000 psi in torsion—almost to the elastic limit." THERE ARE NO OTHER PARTS OF THE CAR STRESSED SO HIGHLY AS THE SPRINGS.

The helical steel coil spring is still a very highly stressed item. You will recall that it was the search for homogenous and dependable spring steel that sent Mr. Huntsman off on the road that led to the development of the first crucible steels. Nothing much has changed—human nature ensures that just as soon as the metallurgists come up with either a spring steel capable of withstanding either higher stress or more cycles, we engineers will redesign the springs to take advantage of the expanded horizon and the nature of springs will be what it has always been—a failure looking for a place to happen.

Anyway, helical compression springs are regularly stressed to levels in excess of 200,000 psi (in corrected unidirectional torsional stress). The steels used must have very good strain-energy storage capacity and fatigue characteristics, which means that they will be made from a high-alloy steel and heat treated to high levels of strength and hardness. They are therefore notch sensitive, which does not exactly enhance their fatigue properties. In any type of spring, the region of highest stress will be at the surface of the spring. In the helical spring it will be at the surface on the inside of the coil. It stands to reason then, that the strength of the surface layer and its freedom from the dreaded notches will determine the fatigue life of the spring—and so it does. As you would expect, good springs are ALWAYS shot peened to stringent specifications.

Most of the springs advertised in the classified section of our beloved lunatic fringe publications are absolute JUNK. They are made from cheap wire, badly designed, badly coiled (often hot coiled, an outmoded process for springs in our range), badly heat treated, badly finished and brilliantly plated and marketed. One dead giveaway of spring quality is plating. If someone offers you a plated spring it is JUNK. Even if it wasn't junk before it was plated, it is afterward.

I do not understand why, in the whole damned world, only Rockwell seems to make acceptable suspension springs. According to Jim Fiedler there is no magic involved, or even a whole lot of high tech. You use the

RIGHT spring wire (heat treated and pretempered 9245 chrome silicon for cold winding and annealed 9260 for hot winding in the unlikely event that the individual spring design does not lend itself to cold winding), design and coil the spring properly, stress relieve the cold-wound springs at 800 degrees F, quench, temper and stress relieve the hot-wound units, shot peen and preset the springs; and that's all there is to it—HE SAYS. Somehow I think that Jim is oversimplifying the process just a bit. If it were that easy anyone could do it, and a lot of people would.

In the days when highly stressed springs were wound from 6150 chrome vanadium wire there were several possible problems with the manufacture of well-designed springs. These problems were twofold: decarburization during heat treatment and quality control. The current use of quenched and tempered chrome silicon alloy steel wire for highly stressed cold wound springs has removed the heat-treating problems. Spring design and quality control are matters of engineering procedure. Of course the el-cheapo manufacturers still use chrome vanadium, or, worse, silicon-manganese wire, still hot coil, don't shot peen, etc. In case you had any doubts, the foregoing should go a long way toward explaining why I buy my springs from Rockwell International. And, yes, they make valve springs to the same state of the art that they make suspension springs.

SPRING CONFIGURATIONS

There are several types of springs that are suitable for automotive use: The leaf spring, the coil spring, the torsion bar, the elastomeric spring and the gas spring come to mind at once. At one time or another I have used them all (the CELLASTO polyurethane "bump rubber" is, in reality, an elastomeric spring which we use as a progressive helper spring). In all probability I will use each of them again—and again. From the practical point of view I prefer the coil spring for the racing car. It is the most efficient, practical configuration from the point of view of strain-energy storage capacity per unit of weight, so it is reasonably light. Used coaxially with the shock absorber it requires the least space. Since the shock absorber requires a major structure at each end (due to piston velocities, the shock load can exceed the spring load), the coil spring requires virtually no ancillary structure. Ride height and corner weight adjustments are simple, rate changes are easy and, equally important, excellent coil springs are quickly and economically available. None of the above statements are true of leaf springs. Tubular torsion bars are more efficient energy storage devices and so are lighter—but they require major structure at weird locations, are very expensive and are hard to change. I don't like torsion bars much.

If I were involved in the design of a new passenger vehicle, however, I would give serious consideration to the use of a transverse composite single leaf spring of unidirectional glass or carbon filament in an epoxy matrix. This would be the lightest practical spring configuration and, although space constraints would seem to limit its use in racing, it should be perfectly feasible on road-going vehicles, from large trucks to small commuter cars. (Since I wrote this paragraph the new-generation Corvette has come out with just such a spring to control its independent suspension systems—at both ends of the car.)

We were informed in the early 1970's that the age of the elastomeric spring was upon us. After a brief appearance on the Hesketh Formula One car it disappeared. I am informed that the age of the gas spring in racing is now upon us. This may be true, but I have seen little evidence of it so far. Things are seldom as simple as they first appear. I think that it is important to keep our priorities straight here. Unless we can realistically expect a clear-cut performance gain from experimenting with different spring configurations, we should concentrate our resources in areas where performance CAN be gained. The function of the automotive suspension spring is pretty damned straightforward. The spring exists to isolate the sprung mass from excessive vertical accelerations caused by movement of the wheels and tires relative to the chassis under the influence of various accelerations. PERIOD. It seems unlikely to me that there is much performance to be gained here and I see vast possibilities for confusion. Until I am convinced otherwise I will keep my springing and my damping separate. For reasons of cost, simplicity and adjustability I will arrange whatever raising rate I may desire mechanically rather than by progressive springs.

THE BUMP STOP

In TUNE TO WIN I sang the praises of the cellasto polyurethane progressive bump stop, and explained how it works. I don't think that ANYONE believed me. Some racers still believe that bump rubbers should not be used AT ALL. This is an obvious hangover from prehistoric hard black rubber bump stops. Still others INSIST on cutting the cone off their cellastos and then bitch about how sudden they are. Please reread what I said in TUNE TO WIN. Then and only then read what Koni has to say:

BUMP STOPS *Since racing dampers are usually required to limit the travel of the suspension, all KONI racing dampers come supplied with a specially-designed cellular polyurethane bump stop. This provides safe and controlled [i.e., progressive] bottoming of the suspension as well as preventing internal damage within the damper from metal to metal contact. All too often we have seen racers using the bump rubbers solely as a suspension travel indicator. This is unfortunate since the information derived from this practice is virtually useless when compared with the realistic benefits, in the form of increased cornering power, which are obtained from the correct use of the bump rubber combined with the proper spring rate. . . .*

What they are saying here is that if you are not USING the bump stops, you are running stiffer springs than you need and are therefore giving away some cornering power.

SPRINGS AND CORROSION

Next to a file mark, the last thing that we need on the surface of the most highly stressed component of the racing car is a corrosion pit. Some of the English springs come prepitted at no extra charge. Regardless of what the books and the platers say about the elimination of hydrogen embrittlement by baking after plating, I refuse to plate my springs. I paint them—using my favorite Zynolite Epoxy Rust Mate—and I make sure that they stay painted. As a point of interest, the chrome silicon spring wire that Rockwell winds most of their racing suspension springs from is particularly susceptible to both hydrogen embrittlement and damage from acidic cleaning baths.

CHAPTER FOURTEEN

LOAD TRANSFER AND SUSPENSION GEOMETRY

LOAD TRANSFER: BARS AND SPRINGS AND THINGS

In 1983 I did a lot of Super Vee racing, not because I like the cars (I don't, but that's another story), but because I have at last realized that the combined efforts of the CASC and the SCCA have finally managed to kill Formula Atlantic and by running Super Vee I got to race with Price Cobb, who just happens to be one of my all-time-favorite race drivers. To my astonishment I have learned more in a low budget, limited test time program with dumb cars than I have in years. I never cease to be amazed at how a really good racing driver can focus the mind and clarify the thinking of the development engineer.

When Price informed me that we were going Super Vee racing the first thing that I did was to read the rule book. My first thought upon doing so was that IT HAD BEEN 19 YEARS since I had raced a car without a limited slip differential! At once I started thinking about cars with narrow tires, wings, adequate horsepower, no torque and no limited slip. The combination at first seemed dumb. After almost a full season it still does. But what the hell—the series works. It's wonderful what even a TINY bit of organizational effort can achieve. If you want to see what A LOT of organizational effort can accomplish in our world, take a look at CART, NASCAR, The World of Outlaws, Stadium Motocross or Formula One.

Not being one of the world's great original thinkers, I also talked about Super Vee with everyone who would talk with me (for some reason a lot of people are not particularly willing to enter into technical dialogues with me). I was less than astonished to find that EVERYONE agreed that the major problem encountered would be trying to tune out the "inherent" entry understeer and the equally "inherent" exit oversteer resulting from "unavoidable" inside rear wheelspin and that the operation that achieved the best compromise between the two was sure to win the race.

I try to come up with a plan of action long before I start testing. In this case I felt that the big thing would be to get the car to turn in and to "take a set" without the driver having to "pitch" the car. The big pitch ALWAYS leads to power oversteer, lifting of the inside rear wheel, tire smoke and a vast lack of acceleration. As Shakespeare said about something entirely different, "full of sound and fury, signifying nothing!" My ideas of things to try included:

(1) A wide front track to both give a good "stance" (try turning in quickly on a tricycle sometime) AND to reduce the amount of lateral load transfer at the front in order to get more work from the inside front tire. To my surprise and dismay, Ralt had already done that.

(2) A lot of Ackerman steering effect in order to get some more work out of the inside front tire. This was a pretty good advantage for about half the season (as it had been for three years). To my surprise and dismay Ralt came out with it at mid-season—thus depriving us of an advantage we had enjoyed for years.

(3) A lot of front negative camber in order to keep the outside wheel from going to positive camber (relative to the road surface) in roll. I felt that the narrow Super Vee

spec tire would probably be relatively insensitive to camber under the brakes. This turned out to be correct.

(4) Sufficient droop travel in the suspension to make very sure that we never jerked a wheel off the ground while it was still loaded.

I also felt that the stock antiroll bars—at least at the rear—were probably too stiff for a car without a limited slip. It seemed to me that, since an antiroll bar basically transfers load from the inside wheel in a corner to the outside wheel at the same end of the car, what was needed in this class was the lightest rear bar that we could get away with. So I made some lighter-than-stock bars. To my great good fortune, Rick Smisek, Price's crew chief, is about as willing to accept racing dogma as I am and really enjoys thinking things through from basic principles.

What we proceeded to do was the exact opposite of what everyone else was doing. On the road courses, at least on the ones with predominately slow and medium speed corners, we substituted rear spring for rear bar (the spring, if it still has tension in droop, will plant the inside rear wheel rather than lifting it). We ran relatively light front springs to kill the initial understeer (and thus allow Price to drive the car into corners rather than pitching it), unbelievable amounts of front negative camber, tons of Ackerman effect and virtually no rear bar. We did it one step at a time, usually at race meetings, because the budget didn't allow for much testing. The results were startling. Until the team ran out of money, Price completely dominated Super Vee. This pointed out a couple of things that I already knew but tend to lose sight of:

(1) There is absolutely no substitute for a real racing driver.

(2) There is absolutely no substitute for a logical testing program.

(3) There is absolutely no substitute for either teamwork or clear thinking.

(4) It does me a power of good to have someone or something kick my crutches away every so often and force me to really think. I do not believe that I am at all unique in this respect.

(5) Our use of the limited slip differential for the past many years just may have changed to an unhealthy dependence upon the thing—and I would like to explore this avenue for a few minutes.

LOAD TRANSFER AND THE LIMITED SLIP

The limited slip differential, as we have seen, does just what its name implies: It LIMITS the onset of wheelspin caused by lateral load transfer. No limited slip can ELIMINATE inside wheelspin under conditions that combine high values of lateral load transfer between the driven wheels with large amounts of available torque—in other words, when vehicles with high power-to-weight ratios are exiting slow and medium speed corners. Only a locking differential or a locked rear end can do that. We will, however, see (later) that the locked rear end has serious disadvantages on road courses and that effective locking differentials are

scarce as hen's teeth. Just to make matters more interesting, as professional road racing moves into the city streets it is going to feature more and more slow corners, fewer and fewer fast corners AND the regulations are going to see to it that the cars have less and less available download. We had better take a good hard look at the basic situation at the driven wheels.

LOAD TRANSFER AND THE ANTIROLL BAR AS HISTORY

The antiroll bar was developed a very long time ago in order to limit the amount of body roll produced by lateral acceleration during cornering without the necessity of using suspension springs so stiff as to produce a harsh ride. Basically, in the days when we carried 30 psi and up in our narrow racing tires, we could not put enough spring on the car to keep chassis roll within acceptable limits without causing tire hop over bumps and under lateral accelerations, so we used antiroll bars to restrict the amount of roll generated by lateral acceleration. Detroit, in fact, still calls the thing an anti-SWAY bar while the rest of the passenger car world calls it a "stabilizer bar." It is neither—it is an antiroll bar. It made its initial appearance at the front of the car (where the engine and most of the weight WAS). Logically enough the rear bar made its appearance at about the same time that the engine moved to the middle of the chassis. EVERY self-respecting racing car has featured an antiroll bar at each end for decades now and, in the interest of tightened response and reduced understeer, most self-respecting passenger cars have now added a rear bar to the front one that they have had forever. The passenger car people use them to limit body roll. WE also use them to limit body roll—BUT we also use them as a quick adjustment to the basic understeer/oversteer balance of the racing car, AND as a crutch. It is this last bit that I want to investigate here.

LOAD TRANSFER AND THE ANTIROLL BAR TODAY

In the days of narrow tires we used antiroll bars of pencil slimness and we basically used them as trim tabs. When the tires very suddenly became wide, the suspension designers did not keep up and, for a while at least, we all tended to use something resembling a "solid axle conversion kit," usually at both ends of the car, to make up for certain geometric deficiencies in the suspension linkage of REAL racing cars and to make up for the height of the center of gravity in sedans. We didn't do it with the springs because the idea was that we needed a relatively soft ride rate to keep the tires in contact with the track but needed to limit in order to both keep the dynamic camber within something that resembled reason and to tighten up the transient response of the vehicle. All of this was pretty much true in the days before wings became effective.

Once the chassis-mounted wing became truly effective, we HAD to up the ride rates in order to keep the ride height somewhere near constant, both to keep the cars from grinding themselves to bits against the racetrack at high speeds and to keep the download-generated bump travel from producing bags of negative wheel camber at those same high speeds. There followed a period of some confusion, during which we started to dimly realize that MUCH longer suspension links would produce bump camber curves which would be A LOT less sensitive to ride height changes, without having any detrimental effect on roll camber compensation. It is interesting to see that Honda has realized this while the rest of the Japanese passenger car manufacturers have not.

The early ground effects cars with their sliding skirts and need for a constant ride height AND pitch attitude taught us that we could stand a lot more ride rate than we had thought. When they wisely took the sliding skirts away from the ground effects cars, constancy of ride height became sacred and ride rates became truly insane: We expressed spring rates in the same number of thousands of pounds that we had been used to expressing in hundreds of pounds (without, however, anywhere as dramatic an increase in actual ride rates, because all of the designers now realized that the suspension links HAD to get a lot longer and, in an effort to clean up the sacred tunnels, everyone installed high-ratio rocker arms of one sort or another at both ends of the car so that motion ratios became more extreme).

Anyway, when the spring rates climbed toward infinity everyone more or less forgot about the bars (download was everything) and they were pretty much ignored for a while. The acceleration of tire technology was increased at the same time because, suddenly, the tire became the ONLY spring on the car. The end result of all this madness is that while ground effects are now outlawed in Formula One, are about to be in Formula Three, and are severely and sensibly limited in champ cars, Atlantic and Super Vee, we now have tires that will stand a lot more wheel rate than was the case a few years ago—without losing their ability to stay on and comply with the racetrack. How the wizards of Akron have managed this, I have no idea.

The basic division of duty between springs and antiroll bars has always been that the suspension springs determine the vehicle's ride rate and basic roll resistance while the antiroll bars add their torsional resistance to the roll resistance of the springs to determine the total roll resistance of the vehicle. What many people do not appreciate is that, within reason, the suspension spring and the antiroll bar are interchangeable so far as roll resistance is concerned. In other words, we can reduce the roll resistance of an antiroll bar by x pounds per degree of roll without affecting the balance of the chassis due to roll couple distribution—SO LONG as we add that same x pounds of resistance per degree by increasing the spring rate at that end of the car an appropriate amount.

Obviously there is a tradeoff here—and it will be different for each car (as will the amount of spring that will replace a given torsional bar resistance). Up to the point where wheelspin becomes a problem, how things are proportioned in this department is probably not a real problem. I still tend to run relatively stiff bars on ovals and on circuits with predominantly fast corners. BUT, when wheelspin rears its ugly head I feel that we should think about putting off its onset by reducing the amount of load transfer between the driven wheels.

THE LIMITED SLIP—AGAIN

The limited slip, once wheelspin has begun, behaves much like the open diff, only less so. The limited slip acts about like a whiffle tree which connects two horses to a wagon (to you city people, the mechanism is exactly the same as a brake bias bar—originally called the whiffletree—in reverse). So long as both horses are pulling, everything is fine. But let one horse fall down or ease off and we are in big trouble accelerationwise. Going back to the curve of coefficient of friction versus percent slip of the tire (TUNE TO WIN, FIGURE [3], page 17), we can see that once a tire starts to spin, the coefficient drops like a rock and the effect on acceleration out of the corner will be fearsome. Anyway, I would really like to do some testing along these lines.

Also, any artificial reduction in driven wheel droop travel will obviously unload the inside wheel if enough chassis roll is generated—or when a hill is crested under a combination of turning and acceleration. No one ever said that it was going to be easy to go truly fast. Every time that we learn something, the bottom line is that we have added one more variable to the performance equation. Perhaps the first time in the career of the aspiring racing driver that I feel that there is any real hope for him is the day that he finally realizes in his heart of hearts that the simple fact that he is the most talented DRIVER ever born is just not going to be enough to get the job done and that he is going to have to learn about testing and car setup.

THE BLADE ADJUSTABLE ANTIROLL BAR

As I stated in TUNE TO WIN, I am a firm believer in the cockpit adjustable antiroll bar, which I consider to be one of the best ideas to come out of the 1960's (bad ideas from the same period, in my opinion, include wings and turbochargers). Credit for the idea could go to either Bob Riley (the Australian Bob Riley, not the equally talented designer of the same name at Ford Motor Company), who made one for Frank Matich, or to someone at All American Racers, who came up with a somewhat complicated and expensive hydraulic version at about the same time. Be that as it may, sometime in the early 1970's, Mark Donohue—a clever man if ever there was one—came up with the now ubiquitous blade adjustable bar illustrated by FIGURE [212]. Moving a lever in the cockpit rotates the blade which makes the ARM or LEVER (which actuates the antiroll bar) either stiffer or more limber and thus applies more or less force to the bar itself. When the blade is vertical, the total resistance of the system is at its maximum and when the blade is horizontal, resistance is at its minimum.

Clever! But does it work? The answer is yes and no. The device DOES vary the effective roll stiffness supplied by the bar. Unfortunately it also introduces into the system an undamped leaf spring—the blade or blades themselves. It turns out that the force that is NOT applied to the bar when the blades are away from their stiffest position is used up in deflecting the blades. This energy does not resist the rolling moment generated by the lateral acceleration of the center of mass but is stored in the blade. The result is that the roll resistance generated by the antiroll bar/adjusting blade system becomes a compound and incomprehensible function of the torsional resistance of the bar and the spring rate of the blade(s) in its (their) instantaneous position of adjustment IN TWO PLANES. The undamped leaf spring(s) introduces a phenomenon known as "roll rock" into the behavior of the vehicle. After cornering force has generated roll and the roll has been resisted by the bar, instead of everything settling down into a nice, stable and predictable state of affairs and load distribution, the blade oscillates back and forth. This, of course, causes the car to roll gently back and forth, to the consternation of the driver who is sensitive enough to notice it. This phenomenon is usually reported to the hapless crew as, "it feels like it is hitting the bump stops in corners." I am not sure how much this sort of thing actually detracts from lap time (although there is no way that it can help) but it DOES distract and annoy the driver, which sure as hell detracts from performance.

The blade adjustable system has a couple of other bad things going for it as well:

(1) If the cross-sectional area of the blade is less than sufficient in relation to the torsional resistance of the bar, when the power is applied coming out of corners (particularly slow corners) what happens is that the blade bends, little force is applied to the bar and the car "falls over" on the outside wheel simply because the blade itself does not offer enough resistance to allow the bar to resist the forces involved.

(2) If the blade is made of less-than-optimum material or has been given a less-than-optimum heat treat (either or both of which are liable to happen in that small island across the Atlantic), the thing will be overstressed and will eventually fail from fatigue.

Lately the designers seem to have realized that this system of driver adjustable roll couple distribution leaves a little something to be desired in the linear and predictable generation of roll-resistance department. Some of them have attempted to alleviate this undesirable situation by doing away with the short link connecting the end of the adjusting blade to the inboard end of the suspension rocker and inserting the end of the blade (ball shaped for the purpose) into a tube on the end of the rocker, as shown in FIGURE [213], apparently figuring that by forcing the end of the blade to follow the arc of the rocker, some of the monkey motion would be done away with and linearity would be restored.

Figure (212): The blade adjustable antiroll bar.

While this splint on a broken leg DOES reduce the monkey motion, it also makes it impossible to "zero the antiroll bar" in order to adjust corner weight. If the antiroll bar (or the chassis, or a rocker) is even slightly out of true when the blades are inserted into their sockets, the bar will be twisted to an extent which will depend on how much out of line things may be, and an amount of corner weight will be jacked into the chassis. The only way that this corner weight can be taken out is by elongating the holes that mount the antiroll bar pivot blocks to the chassis and tilting the bar. In addition, the linkless blade adjustable antiroll bar makes it a bit difficult to set tilt into the chassis for an oval track without jacking weight (the elongated mounting hole trick does work in this instance, but it IS a bit on the Mickey Mouse side). Further still, in order for the system to function with anything that resembles linearity, one blade must be much less stiff than the other AND the bar itself should be allowed to shift a bit in its mounting brackets.

As usual the good Mr. Tauranac has figured all of this out and come up with a workable and practical system while his erstwhile rivals are still floundering around. He even supplies (on demand) "oval track bars" in which the blade receptacles are offset to allow for chassis tilt. His latest configuration, of which I thoroughly approve, is shown by FIGURE [214]. I reckon that the guide bearings at the end of the blades are a typical Tauranac development—practical, clever, light, cheap and effective.

You will have determined that I think that the blade adjustment system was and is a bad idea. You are correct. So, in fact, did Mark Donohue. The last conversation that I had with Mark was about, among other things, blades. He allowed as how, while it had seemed like a good idea at the time, it had, in his opinion, turned out not to be.

As I stated in TUNE TO WIN I firmly believe in cockpit adjustable bars—but I believe in sliders as described in TUNE TO WIN.

When, as often happens, I am faced with the necessity of running a car equipped with blade adjustable bars, I have several ways to go. If the bar is equipped with a single blade I throw it away and either make a new tubular bar or substitute a solid or tubular arm. Period. While I lose the definite advantage of driver adjustability, back-to-back tests have consistently shown a reduction in lap times of at least one-half second. If I feel that driver adjustability is going to be an absolute necessity during the course of the race (as it always is on oval tracks) then I am liable to qualify with nonadjustable arms and race with the blades installed at the front. A blade installed at each end of the bar seems to be preferable from the stability point of view to a blade at one end and a nonadjustable arm at the other. To be effective, the blades have to be pretty damned stout—minimum thickness of the OPERATING blade seems to be about 0.375''—which means that it really isn't a blade at all and has two effective positions: full hard and full soft.

Figure (214): Linked-blade adjustable antiroll bar with blades ending in guided rollers (detail below).

Figure (213): Linkless-blade, adjustable antiroll bar. Blade ends are balls riding in sockets welded to inboard end of rocker arms. Thin blade on left side of car is fixed in "hard" position. Thick blade on right side of car is adjustable.

As those of you who have read much of my output (or spent much time talking with me) realize, I am a big believer in linear roll resistance. In the unlikely event that I ever got to work with a clean sheet of paper on a racing car (as opposed to the offroad racers that I presently design) I would start out with a REAL antiroll bar—i.e. a full-width tubular bar with long links leading to an outboard location on a suspension arm. In the interest of aerodynamics I would put the thing in line with one of the control arms. If back-to-back tests were to show that I was wrong I would happily eat my words and install a conventional short bar, either with long links and a driver operated slider or with Ron Tauranac's end guided blades.

Many racers see no practical advantage in having BOTH the front and the rear antiroll bars driver adjustable. I disagree. I always try to start the race with the bars in such a configuration that the driver has adjustment in the direction of both understeer and oversteer. Since I consider the blades to be two-position devices, this means that I need to start with one bar full hard and the other full soft. I prefer to start with the front full hard and the rear full soft—both because what the driver almost always needs during the race is less understeer and because with the rear bars that I use, the blades don't have much effect. (If the blades are strong enough so that the car doesn't fall over during acceleration out of slow corners, then they are stiffer than MY road racing bars.) Of course, the possibility does exist that Mr. Tauranac's new development will result in a multi-position effective adjustment range.

SUSPENSION AND SUSPENSION GEOMETRY

Most of you who are reading this have read TUNE TO WIN. Hopefully those who have not will instantly buy a copy. Many of you will have played my ''paper doll game'' from TUNE TO WIN and driven yourself to the edge of madness with it. I still think that, short of a CADCAM, the simple paper doll game is the very best method that I know of to get a realistic feel for what a suspension system is really going to do under various conditions of load—and to very quickly evaluate the effects of changes in the geometry. I am using the computer for more and more calculations these days, but I still do a lot of playing with ½ scale, x/y axis models. Maybe I am a touch-and-vision oriented person (God knows that I do have my troubles with number crunching).

HOWEVER, if it is accuracy that you are after, there are now low-cost ways of achieving it. If you are into computers and programming, it is simple enough to come up with a workable x and y axis program that will compute the behavior of any proposed suspension linkage. Remember that the roll center moves laterally as well as vertically. How sophisticated the program gets is up to you. Theoretically it should compute lateral load transfer, integrate that with roll center movement, camber change and a host of other variables and then come up with a force capability for each tire under the various conditions. There is no end to how far you could go in writing such a program. I have a feeling

that the law of diminishing returns probably takes over pretty soon after lateral movement of the roll center. Since we are still a lot less than certain about the details of what happens where the rubber meets the road I see no sense at all in complicating our lives with what are very liable to be meaningless numbers. This is all going to change in the very near future for the simple reason that the clued-in tire manufacturers who are truly into the top ranks of motor racing are fast finding out what IS happening at that crucial interface. If you think that racing doesn't contribute to the improvement of passenger car tires, drive your street car on Goodyears, Pirellis or Michelins and then on ANY other brand—it cannot be coincidence.

If you are not into computers, a clever man named George Anderson, who calls himself Walter Mitty Racing (3221 East Calhoun Parkway, Minneapolis, MN 55408), has developed a good computer program for suspension analysis. When you have finished with the paper dolls, you send him your design parameters (x and y axes, on his form) and for a relative pittance he runs the program and you get a printout of static conditions; camber for all conditions of bump, droop and roll (and some combinations thereof); roll center height; lateral displacement; plus virtual swing arm length for the same conditions. For a few bucks more he will rerun the program with whatever modifications you decide are in order.

MR. ACKERMAN AND HIS PRINCIPLE

Last time around, in TUNE TO WIN, I explained the concept and the mechanics of Ackerman steering geometry (wherein inside tire scrub in a turn is avoided by arranging the steering linkage so that the inside front wheel is steered through a greater arc than the outside one). I further pointed out that the Ackerman principle, while it works just fine for street cars, ignores the existence of slip angles and assumes that the geometric turn center is located on a line extended from the rear axle, which it never is in the real world. I still further pointed out that ''some designers'' had even employed ''anti-Ackerman'' (in which the outside wheel turns farther), that few employed full-Ackerman, and that I usually used something pretty close to parallel steering.

Well, you may also recall that, in the forward to the same book, I explained that vehicle dynamics is a field in which our knowledge is always expanding—and that I reserved the right to change my thinking with regard to any aspect of the art. In the case of the geometry of the steering system I have done just that. A few years ago I got to thinking seriously about steering geometry as it relates to our long-standing, universal problem: UNDERSTEER. My thinking went along these lines:

(1) Once a turn has been initiated and the various transients have settled down, lateral load transfer ensures that the inside front tire (with respect to the center of the turn) will be relatively lightly loaded. Ignoring the existence of downforce, the current generation of racing cars seems to transfer about 80% to 90% of the vertical load on the inside front tire to the outside front.

(2) If the car is well balanced and well driven, the actual tire steer angles will be small, and the steering input will be smooth. The lateral load transfer between the front wheels will be gradual, BUT since the yaw response time of the racing car is very quick indeed (it had better be), it will take place over a very short period of time.

(3) The outside front tire, therefore, is supplying almost all of the tractive effort at the front end of the car. The inside tire is along, however, not just for the ride. The slip angles involved make nonsense of Mr. Ackerman. What we want is for the inside and outside front tire slip angles to be equal—or so we have thought for years. BUT:

(A) For about a decade now, static front toe out has been a very common fix for initial understeer (or "lack of point"). We road racers stole it from the stock car people who have been using it from the beginning of time. It works. It takes more of it to work at low speed than it does at high speed.

(B) The preponderance of vertical load on the outside tire ensures that, as soon as lateral load transfer begins, all of the toe out will be on the inside front tire. What static front toe out does, then, is to increase the steer angle (and therefore the slip angle) of the inside front tire. It is easy enough to visualize how this will encourage the car to turn in. If our original theory regarding Ackerman geometry and the racing car were correct, once the car has turned in and taken its set, front toe out should be detrimental to the generation of front adhesion. BUT such is not the case: Front toe out helps in all of the phases of cornering, not just in the initial point department. So we just may have been missing something here.

(C) None of us LIKE to use static front toe out because we are afraid that it will make the car unstable under the brakes and we are afraid that it will increase the rolling resistance of the front tires to the point that it might slow the car down in a straight line. Some of us have been using toe out in bump at the front to achieve pretty much the same effect. I have never been able to successfully substitute toe out in bump for static toe out, but I have been able to reduce the amount of static toe out required. When we arrive at the street courses we use both.

(D) Several major factors in our operating conditions have changed since the late and great Colin Chapman postulated his anti-Ackerman theory a couple of decades ago:

(a) Our tires have become a lot stickier. The coefficient of friction of a good racing tire 20 years ago was in the neighborhood of 0.8. Today 1.4 is not uncommon.

(b) The contact patch has rotated 90 degrees. Twenty years ago the contact patch of the racing tire was a long and thin oval. It is still oval, but now it is short and wide.

(c) Slip angles have decreased notably.

(d) The addition of DOWNLOAD to the traction scene has drastically altered the load picture of the inside front tire. Under lateral acceleration we transfer only the physical end of the vertical load picture. The download remains where it was. So the inside front tire is no longer UNloaded, its load is merely decreased.

(e) What we really want in the front tire slip angle department is for both the inside and the outside tires to be at their individual OPTIMUM slip angles. Due to the factors mentioned above (and the phase of the moon) these optimum angles are the same for the heavily loaded outside tire and the lightly loaded inside tire.

(f) If we were to increase the Ackerman effect the geometric result would be the same as static front toe out—as soon as the front wheels were turned. There would, however, be no toe out when the wheels were in the straight-ahead position (regardless of download) so our fears of braking instability, increased rolling resistance and darting could be forgotten. Further, unlike static toe out, the greater the steering input, the greater would be the difference in steering angle between the two front wheels—with the inside wheel ALWAYS assuming the greater steering angle.

(E) The actual result of all of this playing loose with Ackerman and Euclid would be twofold: the elimination of any possibility of dragging the inside front tire and an effective increase in the inside front tire slip angle.

At the time that all of this ran through my head, I was running a Ralt RT-1 Formula Atlantic car. It featured easily changed Ackerman geometry—so what the hell, I tried it. I increased the Ackerman and lo and behold, IT WORKED. The understeer was reduced—considerably—at both high and low speed. I have played with it ever since and have come to some interesting conclusions:

(1) Every car that I have increased the Ackerman effect on has responded with decreased understeer. Every driver has noticed it (and loved it). It works at both high and low speed but any given amount is more noticeable at high speed. The driver usually reports that the car feels "freer in the corners" and that understeer is reduced in all phases of cornering.

(2) We are talking about some pretty damned small differences in steering angle here. But, when we are fooling with the front toe we are also talking about some pretty small angles. I have a strong feeling that as the optimum slip angle of the racing tire decreased over the years, the tires have become more sensitive to small changes in slip angle.

(3) When the Ackerman center is moved TOO far forward, things go "overcenter" and the understeer actually begins to increase (although the initial point or "turn in" will continue to be more positive). The first indication that we have gone too far is when the car becomes darty over bumps and under the brakes—just as if it had too much front toe out or too much toe out in bump. This point of an excess of goodness varies with each car (it probably has to do with the ratio of wheelbase length to track widths) but is typically reached when the Ackerman center is placed somewhere between 25% and 50% of the wheelbase dimension forward of the rear axle center. BUT, the optimum amount of Ackerman effect varies with the speed of the corners involved. The car will not only tolerate more Ackerman on slow courses, it almost demands more.

(4) Up to the point of diminishing returns, more is better.

(5) Ackerman effect and static toe out are cumulative in effect. What I do now is put in enough Ackerman that the car begins to become unstable, back off from that point a bit and call that my optimum Ackerman for the course. When we get to the street courses, like Trois Rivieres and Long Beach, I add static toe out until the car and driver are happy. I carry about three alternative Ackerman setups around with me.

The million-dollar question is, of course, WHY? I'm not sure. The improved initial point is easy to figure out. The inside tire simply steers more and points the car. One theory is: that is all there is; after the car has pointed and taken its set, lateral load transfer has reduced the vertical load on the inside front tire to the point that its steer angle no longer matters. This MIGHT be true on cars which do not feature front downforce, but if so it does not explain why increased Ackerman works better at high speed. And

it sure as hell doesn't explain why it reduces understeer on corner exit when the inside front is virtually unloaded.

We learned in TUNE TO WIN that a tire's ability to generate cornering force decreases as the vertical load on it is reduced and that, up to a limiting angle, its cornering force will increase with increased slip angle. I feel that the improvement in initial point is just as simple as it seems but the rest of the answer has to do with a complex tradeoff between decreasing vertical load and increased slip angle due to increased steer angle. Somewhere in the equation, reduced inside tire drag at today's lower slip angles may come in as well.

I am certain that you are now as unsure of WHY increased Ackerman steering geometry works as I am. I can only apologize; that's the best that I can do at the moment. As with so many things, I wish that I could do some meaningful testing here. There just HAS to be a lot to be gained, especially on the ovals. Maybe someday. . . .

Figure (215A): "Classic" Ackerman steering geometry in left turn.

Figure (215B): "Modified" or increased Ackerman steering geometry in left turn.

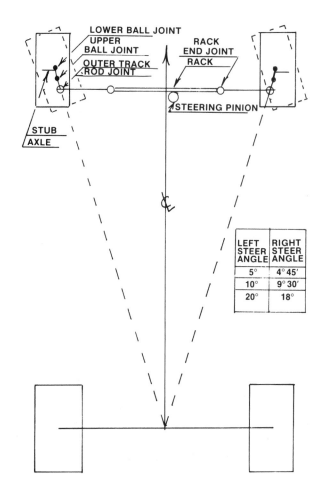

LEFT STEER ANGLE	RIGHT STEER ANGLE
5°	4° 45'
10°	9° 30'
20°	18°

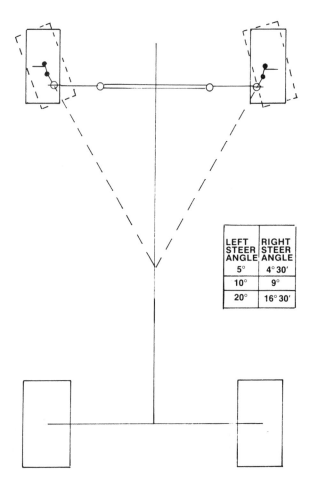

LEFT STEER ANGLE	RIGHT STEER ANGLE
5°	4° 30'
10°	9°
20°	16° 30'

Anyway, it dawns upon me that what I am talking about may not be entirely clear. FIGURES [215A], [215B], [215C] and [215D] illustrate how we play with the Ackerman geometry and the effect of changing it around. Note that you can change the effective toe out in turns (the marvelously descriptive British term for the Ackerman effect) by moving the rack (or idler, or cross link) toward the axle center as well as by changing the inclination of the steering arms. This method also quickens the effective steering ratio at high steering angles, which is no bad thing, especially off road. Moving the actuator away from the axle center slows the ratio at high angles and we don't want to know about that.

When trying to figure out Ackerman, it is well to be aware that two-dimensional models (as advocated in TUNE TO WIN), while beneficial, are not entirely accurate. The effects of caster, king pin inclination and antidive (if any) make steering geometry a three-dimensional problem. I work out what I think I want in two dimensions (plan view), with a fudge factor for caster, KPI and antidive, and then finalize things on the car.

PRIORITIES

To add to what I had to say about wasting time at the racetrack in the first two books, I have recently prioritized the way I go about things at the racetrack. Assuming that I am operating from a background of SOME knowledge of car, driver and racetrack and that we are talking about practice for an event rather than a test day with a specific series of items to evaluate, I will obviously show up with my best estimate (guess) already on the car. From there on, my priorities are:

(1) Establish the basic chassis balance with regard to springs, bars, static alignment, shock adjustment, et al.

Figure (215C): Another way to skin a cat—modified Ackerman steering geometry of Figure (215B) increased (and progression changed by moving rack toward axle center).

Figure (215D): Parallel steering geometry.

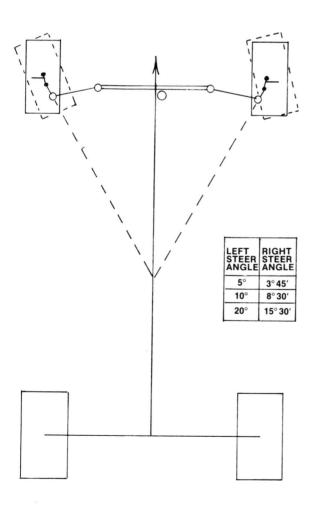

LEFT STEER ANGLE	RIGHT STEER ANGLE
5°	3° 45'
10°	8° 30'
20°	15° 30'

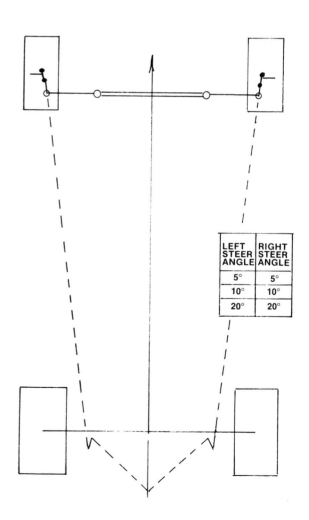

LEFT STEER ANGLE	RIGHT STEER ANGLE
5°	5°
10°	10°
20°	20°

(2) Establish the basic aerodynamic balance.

(3) Either increase or decrease the wheel rate by equal percentage points, front and rear, until the ride rate is optimized.

(4) Either increase or decrease the roll resistance by antiroll bars by equal percentage points front and rear until an optimum has been established.

(5) (oval track only) Tilt the chassis until it no longer helps.

(6) (oval track only) Load the left front tire until that no longer helps.

(7) Add download in proportional increments front and rear until it slows the lap time.

(8) I am willing to change gear ratios at any point in the proceedings.

ROD END AND SPHERICAL BEARINGS

I still prefer to use NMB rod end and spherical bearings at all critical suspension points (i.e., everywhere except the antiroll bars). I now buy them from Paul Baker at Baker Precision Bearings. He is knowledgeable, fair, will not substitute manufacturers without asking and can somehow find the bearings I need when no one else can.

ALIGNMENT

Nothing is new here. I now measure my toes by means of trammel bars. I make them for each car from 1'' square steel tube. They pip-pin into a fixed position at the front and rear of the car and establish instant reference parallels by means of fishing line stretched tightly between carefully placed holes or pins on the bars. It literally takes less than a minute to set the system up and costs about $2.00 to make. A level surface is not required.

It is important for you to know the ''adjustment sensitivity'' of your car, i.e., the physical effect of ½ turn of adjustment at every adjustment point. With this information written down, you can add or subtract a given amount of toe, camber or caster in the pits without worrying about a level surface or even taking the time to measure—or you can jack 10 lb of weight into the locking front wheel, etc. Without the information, YOU ARE GUESSING. It is dumb to guess when you can KNOW. We do enough guessing when we HAVE to. I mark the day's starting point for both toe and camber with a felt pen on masking tape wrapped around the control arm next to the adjustment point, and I keep track of how many quarter turns of adjustment have been made so that I can return to square one when confusion threatens to take control.

CURRENT KIT CAR FOIBLES

There are certain factors in vehicle dynamics that some of our English cousins do not seem to grasp. Chief among them are the benefits of wide track widths (especially at the front), torsional rigidity of the chassis WITH THE ENGINE INSTALLED, suspension travel in droop, Ackerman steering effect and front toe out. I make no effort to explain any of this, it just IS. The typical result is a car that, when set up to ''factory specs,'' understeers to the point that it has to be pitched at corners. As I have been pointing out for years, while pitching the car into the corner and exiting in a lurid slide is more fun than almost anything else that you can do with your clothes on, and while it may impress the ignorant—IT IS SLOW. The traction circle ensures us that the fast way around ANY corner will always involve DRIVING THE CAR INTO THE CORNER.

RIDE HEIGHT

Efforts to control the ride height of ''ground effects'' cars by restricting droop travel seem to me to be the wrong way to go—except on ovals and billiard tables. Every time that I have increased the droop travel, especially at the front, the result has been magical at the bumpy tracks, especially those that combine corners with crests of hills. When we get to the billiard tables it is always easy enough to restrict the travel if we want to. Pretty much the same thing holds true of ride rate in my experience. Every time that I install the railroad car springs that everyone tells me we need with ground effects, we go slow and every time that I go back to ''rational'' ride rates, we go faster. It seems to have to do with keeping the tires on the road. Efforts to determine optimum ride height by installing tie wraps on the shock absorber piston rods and then seeing how far up the tell tale gets pushed are just plain silly. What this tells you is how big the worst bump on the course is. Efforts to keep the car off the bump rubbers by this method are even more silly. As I explained in TUNE TO WIN and in the shock absorber section of this book, so long as you are using truly progressive cellular polyurethane bump rubbers, they are there to be used. Not using them means that you are either going to run the car higher than its optimum ride height or you are going to run it stiffer than its optimum ride rate.

CORNER WEIGHT

After years of using expensive and bulky "grain" scales in the shop and expensive and not-very-satisfactory "Lo-Boy" scales at the track (and trying every "weight jacker" and "portable" scale that came along and finding none of them to be satisfactory) I have discovered the RuggleS-'cales, designed and manufactured by Joe Ruggless of JPR Development.

As illustrated (FIGURE [215E]), Joe simply added a precise lever system to the old reliable bathroom scale and came up with a portable system that is reliable, repeatable and *cheap*. All parts are fixture built and the price is so reasonable that it just isn't worth making your own. Genius! We owe Joe Ruggless a debt of gratitude.

ANTISQUAT AND ANTIDIVE

I thought that I had covered the subject rather well in TUNE TO WIN, and one more time it seems that I did not do it as well as I had thought. The problem seems to be that I didn't do a good job of explaining what squat, antisquat, dive and antidive are. I think that we can clarify the point by looking at the racing car as a brick-shaped unsprung

mass suspended on four wheels with drive torque transmitted by trailing arms from the driven rear wheels to a vertical arm extended downward from the center of gravity of the sprung mass.

Such a vehicle is shown in side elevation by FIGURE [216]. The trailing arms are pivoted at the vertical arm, but the arm is rigidly attached to the sprung mass (which is exactly the same configuration found in the automobile—I have merely simplified it for clarity). Part A shows the vehicle at rest. The trailing arms are parallel to the ground and well below the center of gravity. When drive is applied—as in Part B—the trailing arm pushes against the vertical bar. This sets up a couple about the cg, load is transferred from the front wheels to the back and the rear of the vehicle "squats." Note that the squat is caused by the load transfer, not vice versa. If we raise the front of the trailing arm on the vertical bar as in Part C, the length of the moment arm between the pivot and the cg is reduced and, for the same amount of drive thrust, less load transfer and less squat will result. It really is that simple.

Antisquat was pretty popular in the days of narrow tires, soft springs, short suspension links and steep camber curves. I tend not to run very much of it. With today's cg heights, we don't get much squat and with today's ride rates and rear suspension curves the effect of squat on camber is minimal. Further, as I mentioned in TUNE TO WIN, antigeometry has the unfortunate side effect of tending to lock the suspension solid. Rearward load transfer under acceleration is no bad thing. Rear-wheel-drive cars, like primates, need to squat in order to go. Antidive is the exact opposite of antisquat; just turn the thrust arrow in the illustration around. Everything that I had to say about the effects of the "antis" and the methods of measuring and changing them in TUNE TO WIN still goes.

Figure (216): Antisquat.

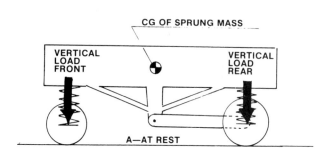

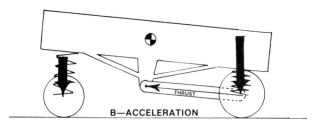

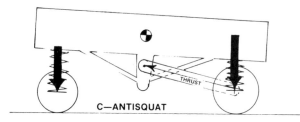

RAISING RATE SUSPENSION SYSTEMS

After some years of vacillation and confusion it looks as though the mechanical linkage raising rate suspension system is here to stay—at least at the front of the car. I covered the whys and wherefores of raising rates in TUNE TO WIN and I have no intention of recovering that ground; none of my opinions have changed. What I do want to cover is the now universal method of achieving the raising rate by the use of either a push rod and a bellcrank (FIGURES [216A] and [216B]) or by a pull rod and a rocker (FIGURE [216C]). In either case, altering the length of the pull or push rod will alter the geometry of the system, changing both the rate of increase in wheel rate and the zero point of the rate change curve. Therefore the length of the operating

Figure (216A): Mechanical linkage raising rate suspension by push rod and bell crank.

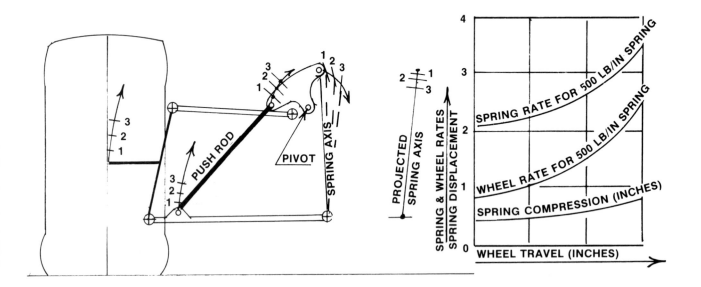

rod is a critical part of the design parameters of the suspension system and it should not be fooled around with by the uninitiated, imprecise or unwary. Changing the length of the operating rod is NOT a valid method of altering ride height.

It is also critical to ensure that the pull/push rod (and/or the bellcrank) does not contact any part of the chassis during wheel travel. As you would expect, this leads to a sudden increase in wheel rate (to infinity) and a car that is given to sudden and unpredictable slides—and which doesn't respond very well to changes.

Figure (216B): Push rod lengthened, progression changed.

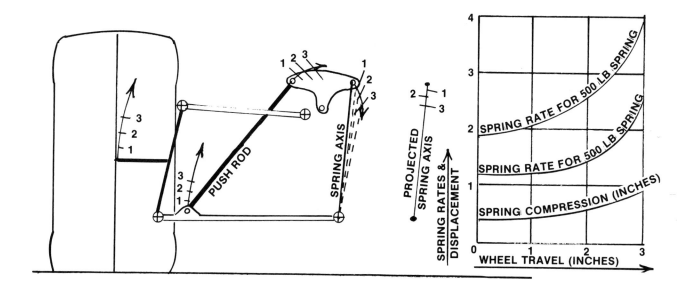

Figure (216C): Pull rod raising rate linkage.

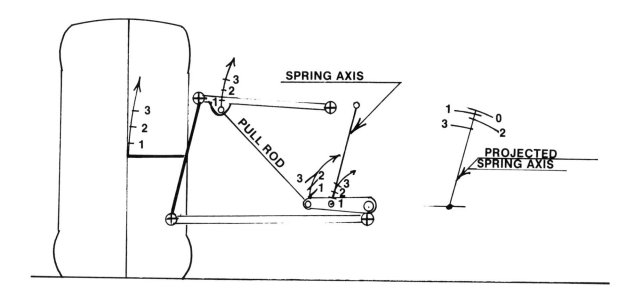

CHAPTER FIFTEEN

GEARBOX AND FINAL DRIVE

ABOUT THE DOGS

First, I have to retract one of the statements made in PREPARE TO WIN: Peter Weismann no longer regrinds the dogs on Hewland gears. MRW Precision Machining (415 South 6th St., St. Charles, IL 60174) does. I should mention that the economics of regrinding are more than a little uncertain. When a dog has been hurt to the point that it needs regrinding, the case hardening is worn through and the reground dog face will be soft. Unless the gear is re-case-hardened, the dog won't last very long. I think that it is better for the driver to learn how to shift properly. There are drivers whose dogs last all season and there are drivers, equally fast (or slow) who regularly go through five gears and three dog rings per day (per session in extreme cases). I don't know what the answer is. For sure it isn't experience. Maybe if the driver were required to pay for the things out of his personal pocket, or were beaten about the head and shoulders . . . I wish I could say that the driver who abuses his gearbox will never get anywhere in racing, but I can name at least two former world champions who regularly tore the things to pieces (selectively—they did not DNF because of it). Neither does the answer lie in the speed with which the gears are shifted. The two easiest on the dogs that I have worked with—Peter Revson and Danny Ongais—are among the fastest shifters ever known. Maybe the destroyers own stock in Hewland (or in Haas).

SHIFT-FORK ADJUSTMENT

I forgot to mention what a delight it is to measure the axial shift-fork position for fourth and fifth gears in the Hewland transaxle. If there is an easy way, I would appreciate hearing about it. I use a 45 degree dentist's mirror-on-a-stick, bent feeler gauges and choice adjectives in three languages. Fortunately it doesn't have to be done very often.

As our engines get less torquey and more peaky we find ourselves using first gear in our five-speed boxes more and more often. This would be ok if Mike Hewland had intended first to be used for any purpose other than starting. That he did not is evidenced by the extreme unsupported cantilever of the first/reverse rail and by the original configuration of the first/reverse shift forks fitted to all Hewland five-speed transaxles—they did not fully straddle the gear. The fix (or at least the crutch) is to install a (7075-T6) cylindrical aluminum spacer over the rail. This spacer must be machined to a precise length so that, when first gear is fully engaged, the spacer just bottoms between the fork shoulder and the gearbox casting, as happens by design with the rest of the forks.

This modification must be accompanied by the use of a "new-pattern" straddle-type first/reverse fork (which was actually first made by Huey Absalom for McLaren's six-speed a very long time ago and introduced by Hewland in

1982) and by a very careful radial alignment of the fork and the rails as described in PREPARE TO WIN. In addition to modifying the box as described in the first two books, you should also install a positive stop in the first/reverse lock-out plunger in order to both limit the transverse travel of the shift selector finger and to give the driver something solid to slam up against when reaching for first. A length of $\frac{3}{16}$'' bundy tube inside the spring does just fine. I size it so that the shift finger stops about 0.06'' after it is completely into the first/reverse gate. The shift forks should be replaced when the wear grooves get to be about 0.010'' to 0.015'' deep.

DETENTS

With the advent of the ground effects racing car, the achievable rate of deceleration has taken a quantum leap forward (or backward, as the case may be). This is especially true when ground effects are paired with Mintex 17FF pads and a driver who wastes no time building up his rate of deceleration. The initial reversal of acceleration is now so great that those of us who were addicted to light shift detents have had to either tighten up our detent springs or not radius the detent grooves so much. This keeps the inertia of the shift finger, linkage and lever from pulling the box out of gear when the driver really climbs on the binders while in a gear located on the back side of the shift gate. Lightweight shift levers and knobs are definitely a plus in this respect.

Every so often we don't catch an incipient pinion bearing failure in time and the thrust washer at the back of the Hewland gear case eats into the rear wall of the case. The damage is usually reparable. If the thing has only eaten its way in 15 or 20 thousandths, we just mill the bore for the thrust washer flat and make a thicker washer. When real damage has been done it will be necessary to machine an insert to replace the rear pinion bearing bore as well as to provide a thrust surface. This is not a job for an apprentice milling machine operator. Robert Kube, one of the very best that I have ever known, is set up to do the job—it will be perfect and the price will be a pleasant surprise. RK Precision, 3734 S. Lowell, Santa Ana, CA 92707 (714) 545-7712.

SHIFT LINKAGE

Most shifting problems are still the result of poorly designed and/or maintained shift linkages and have nothing to do with either the driver or the box. This is just as true in champ cars and in Formula One as it is in Formula Ford. I ranted and raved at the constructors about this earlier—and promised to describe the right way to do it later. Now is the time.

First of all, the physical layout of the linkages must make engineering sense and cannot contain any acute angles (15 degrees is about as far as you can safely go). There should be no bent linkage tubes. If there is simply no way out of the situation without the use of a bent tube, then make sure that it is truly rigid in compression, in tension and in torsion. This is true of ALL of the shift linkage tubes, which

will be loaded in compression on 50% of your shifts. Some of the abortions that people come up with are truly awful in this respect; for the shock of your week, have someone actually shift your kit car racer while you watch the linkage tubes bend and bow. In addition to pointing in the right directions the shift linkage tubes should be of the maximum practical diameter (stiffness comes from diameter, not wall thickness).

There is little sense in going to the trouble to lay out a really good shift linkage and then using sloppy universal joints. There is only one joint suitable for shift linkage: the Apex heavy-duty MS20271 series handled by Earl's Supply, Baker Precision Bearings and Aircraft Spruce in sizes from $\frac{3}{8}$'' to 1'' bore. They are expensive. Enough of them to completely outfit the average race car cost about as much as one badly missed shift. I have been using them for years. They will last forever—without developing ANY slop—so long as they are not asked to handle a direction change in excess of about 12 degrees. The only possible problem in their use comes from their characteristically thin wall. With enough abuse it IS possible to elongate the through holes and thus develop radial play in the assembly. I cannot see this happening if the holes are properly made (start small with the joint installed on its shift tube and the hole carefully centered, and ream the last 0.015'') and a solid-aluminum slug is press fitted into the shift tube to prevent crushing the assembly with the through bolt. I use washers machined with a radius to match the OD of the joint both under the bolt head and under the nut.

The next requirement is for the shift tubes to move freely through the various steady bearings which are required for support. I hard-chrome and grind the tubes where they pass through support bearings and do not lubricate them (the lubricant merely acts as a dirt magnet and leads to friction). I use either the sloppy-iron rose joints that most of the cars come with or bronze-raced Heims. The whole assembly must be fairly frequently disassembled and really cleaned.

All of this probably sounds like a typical case of Smith's overkill (often called over-Carroll). It is not. The money that a really good shift linkage saves in wear and tear on the shifting dogs will more than repay the efforts required to lay out and build one. The look on your driver's face the first time that he gets to use a good one is a bonus.

If you cannot afford the Apex joints (and they are cheaper than replacement stockers) then drilling and slotting what you have will help, so long as you are clamping on a solid slug, not a tube.

THE RING AND PINION

The only things that I forgot the first (and second) time around are:

(1) The sharp edges of both the pinion-and-ring gear teeth should be deburred and slightly radiused with a rotary stone. The possible problems here are twofold:

(a) Crack propagation can start from a quench crack originated on a thin, sharp edge during heat treatment.

(b) If the ring and pinion is set up slightly too deep into mesh it is possible for the sharp edge of the ring gear tooth to dig into the pinion tooth root as it rotates past. This will create a narrow zone of abnormally high stress, which will lead to premature failure.

(c) It will pay big dividends to shot peen the pinion gear teeth to Pratt and Whitney gear specs. I consider this to be preferable to the fairly common practice of slightly softening the ring gear.

(2) I didn't skip this one, but I will restate it because it is evident from the number of failed pinions I see that people don't believe it. When setting up the ring-and-pinion on a racing car, the static pattern MUST be heavy toward the nose of the pinion gear. Under racing loads, the pattern will inevitably move toward the rear of the pinion tooth. If we have set the mesh in the center of the tooth (as in a street car) this means that under acceleration, only about 60%-70% of the pinion tooth area is available to carry the load. This is the major reason that pinion teeth "pull out" for "no apparent reason." A close look at the failure interface will invariably show the characteristic beach front marks of fatigue failure. FIGURE [217] illustrates.

I had my say about ring gear bolts and bolting procedures in the threaded-fastener section of this book. The part number is still FoMoCo B8AZ-6379-A. I replace my ring-and-pinion sets at a predetermined mileage or when they start to look like they might want to go away, whichever comes first. If the unit is still looking good when I pull it out, I put it carefully aside—along with all of its shims and a note

Figure (217): Fatigue failure of pinion due to pattern being too far to rear—note polished and fatigue cracks and granular appearance of successive fatigue failure. Andrew Freeman.

telling me which shims go where—and I have a ready-to-install emergency spare with no setup or break-in required. I also sell this spare with the car. I buy my spare ring-and-pinion sets all with the same pinion depth and I take the time before the season starts to set up however many spare sets I think I am going to use and I carry them around complete with their shims and new pinion bearings. I don't have to take the time to set them up, but they MUST be properly broken in.

BREAK-IN

In PREPARE TO WIN I described the proper way to break-in a ring-and-pinion, but neglected to say why. Many people apparently did not believe me. This time I will explain the whys. When a ring-and-pinion set is manufactured, even if the gears are lapped together on a fixture (and Hewland's are), there inevitably remain some high spots on each gear. The purpose of the break-in procedure is to wear these high spots down WITHOUT partially annealing (or burning) the adjacent areas of the gear teeth by the heat of friction generated by the wearing-down process. The only safe way to achieve this end is to load the gears for a short time (by applying drive torque) and then to remove the load and coast while the high spots cool down before repeating the process. We start with a light load and gradually increase both the amount of load and the time of application. It is a simple process, does not require a racetrack (a drag strip, local oval or even a parking lot will do fine) and doesn't take very long—ten minutes is usually plenty. The ever-popular, if futile, exercise of doing ten or twenty laps with a constant, moderate load on the drive gears is exactly what we DON'T want to do. This procedure puts heat into the gears and keeps it there and is one of the main causes of the pits that later appear in the surface of the pinion gear.

LUBES

Shell no longer makes SL7923 gear oil. This presented a distinct problem for me until I discovered Southwest Petroleum Company's Gear Oil #101—which they apparently blended for the turbo Porsches. I am very happy with it and, from the smell of it, it will probably work with the Weismann differential.

Of the readily available racing-gear lubes I favor Pennzoil and will run Kendall and Quaker State. I still do not believe in multigrades for racing and I am convinced that the future for all types of lubrication is in synthetic oils. I am equally convinced that, by and large, this particular future is not yet here. Unless you can talk a real oil company into blending a specific synthetic to meet your individual operating conditions (including a specific type of limited slip diff), my advice is to stay away from the current synthetics—particularly if you have to pay for them. Strangely enough, our demands on either gear or engine lubes are usually not that severe and old-fashioned dinosaur oils, properly blended, will do the job very well. The synthetics that will offer REAL advantages to us will come from the oil companies, not from a backyard alchemist allied with a snake oil salesman.

Understandably, the oil companies are more interested in industrial applications than they are in racing and, to date, none of the U.S. majors have come out with synthetic racing lubes. This is in stark contrast to the Europeans and the antipodes who, realizing what is going to happen the next time that the Arabs apply a stranglehold on us, are well and truly stuck into synthetics.

Having said that, I must admit that both Amsoil's and Red Line's synthetic racing gear lubes are as good as anything that I have ever used, with a Salisbury-type diff (they will probably work just fine with a cam-and-pawl but not at all with a Weismann), and that I am very happy with Red Line racing engine oil.

When I wrote the first edition of this book I had some pretty positive things to say about the future of synthetic oils. I was not wrong in the gist of what I had to say. Where I *was* wrong was in thinking that the big oil companies would lead the way and that the racer's answer would not come from "backyard alchemists."

My standard offer to the snake oil salesmen who hound me is that if they will sign a contract to supply free products for a couple of years, match the contingency awards posted by the oil companies, pay for the track rent necessary to establish that their product is indeed useable AND pay for any damage caused by their product, I will do a comparison test against whatever I am using. If theirs proves to be better—or even equal—I will use and endorse it. To date no one has accepted the offer.

CONSTANT-VELOCITY JOINTS

The almost universal adoption of the CV joint on racing half-shafts has made life a lot easier for us. It has also made it somewhat more messy. CV joints, by their very nature, require an extreme pressure grease. Until synthetics are developed for our use this means a molybdenum disulfide grease, black and nasty. As I understand the situation, moly is pretty much moly; the effectiveness of the grease depends on the base grease and the amount of moly. Most of the commercial moly greases are not very good, turning either to clay or to water under severe operating conditions, so that the joints require frequent service (like every couple of hundred miles). No fun at all.

For years we all used Duckham's racing CV joint grease which we imported from the U.K. Good news: Swepco's Moly Grease #101 is BETTER. In a Formula Atlantic car, CV joint service intervals with Swepco are at least 1200 miles (this is as far as I have ever gone between services; at that, everything was perfect).

You will hear all sorts of racers swear by all kinds of lubes. In my experience, most of them are running low-pressure cars with small tires, and virtually any sort of gear lube or joint grease will do just fine. The racing car with the least pressure that can strain things is the Formula Atlantic car—it requires both horsepower AND tires.

Properly lubricated, the CV joint should be trouble free; it is not—because of some manufacturing peculiarities. One of the problems is that, as manufactured, the cages tend to be too tight on the balls. It doesn't seem to matter who made the things or whether they are helically grooved

Rzeppa joints (the right kind—as in Porsche/VW/BMW) or straight-grooved Birfields (the wrong kind as in Hewland and Japanese); EVERYONE makes the cages too tight. At best this causes some unnecessary drag on wheel travel (one of the major reasons for using CV's to start with) and at worst, leads to fractured cages. The answer is simple enough: Take the things apart while new and relieve the cages with a rotary stone sufficiently so that the balls will just fall through. With some of the Lobro joints (made for Porsche and used on all Can-Am and most Indy cars and available from your Lobro distributor for about 25% of what your Porsche dealer gets for them), the balls themselves are slightly oversized and tend to bind slightly. The fix is a slightly smaller ball from your bearing house.

On some designs, particularly those with inboard rear brakes, the CV joint boots, even though they seem to clear everything by miles, are continually getting rubbed and/or burned. What is happening is that the centrifugal force of axle rotation expands the diameter of the boots by a factor of two and they hit things that appear to be impossible for them to reach. The solution is to insert a ti-wrap around the minor diameter of each boot bellows.

It IS necessary to vent the CV joint boots so that they can breathe as the shafts change angle and plunge. Many racers insert a split pin or a length of bundy tubing under the ti-wrap with which they clamp the minor diameter of the boot to the shaft. I don't clamp the minor diameters of my CV joint boots at all. There is no functional need to do so (the centrifugal force of shaft rotation prevents the grease from coming out). If the minor diameter is not sealed, any over-supply of grease will come out harmlessly AND, if the grease goes watery, the telltale drip from the stationary car will warn you before anything gets hurt.

THE HALF-SHAFT

The half-shaft is probably the single most highly stressed nonengine component of the racing car. The poor thing operates in fully reversed torsion which is the absolute worst condition for fatigue life. It is tortured every time we shift gears, accelerate out of a slow corner or lock up the rear brakes. I replace the half-shafts on a strict mileage basis and throw the old ones away. With anything bigger than an Atlantic car I have my shafts made, rather than buying them from the importer (mainly because I want to know what they are made from and how they have been heat treated).

The ONLY two materials from which to make racing car half-shafts are vacuum-melted 4340 and 4340M (300M). The shafts should be designed so that the minor diameter of the spline is at least 5% larger than the major diameter of the shaft and all the rules of stress raisers and section changes should be followed religiously. It is critical that you get the length right so that they neither bottom out nor run out of travel due to plunge on wheel travel. This must be checked at full bump and at full droop, as well as at ride height. They should be heat treated to Rockwell C42/44 for 4340 and C50/54 for 300M. Both 4340 and 300M tend to surface decarburize during heat treat so they must either be copper plated prior to heat treatment or have the decarburized layer ground off afterward. The shafts should be shot peened to Pratt and Whitney axle specification after heat treatment. Anyone who uses a CV joint on one end of a half-shaft and a Hooke's type universal joint on the other is displaying ignorance. It is neither necessary nor desirable to provide bumps and/or grooves for the CV joint boots.

Because the acceleration loads are considerably greater than the braking loads, every half-shaft will take a slight set in the direction of the most load. For this reason it is forbidden to change the position or orientation of the shafts. The inboard end of the right side shaft must remain in that position for life. If you keep your shafts free of nicks and scars (a double wrap of electrical tape does just fine) the initial fatigue cracks will inevitably appear at the spline roots (or the shaft may begin to twist at the spline roots JUST before the cracks appear). While the nature of the beast and its conditions of service assure us that the elapsed time between the appearance of the first fatigue cracks and the catastrophic failure of the shaft will be pretty damned short, in any kind of racing other than endurance and the champ car 500 milers, a dye-penetrant inspection on Saturday night will pretty much ensure that the shaft will not fail on Sunday. Anyone who starts an endurance race or a 500 miler with half-shafts that are the least bit suspect is out of his mind and deserves whatever happens to him. So do those fools who make half-shafts from 4130.

THE LIMITED SLIP DIFFERENTIAL

Before the wing made its lamented appearance on the racing car, every successful design/development engineer and every successful racing driver was fully aware that the limited slip differential was a very important part of the performance equation. Experimentation and back-to-back tests of diffs and modifications thereof were an accepted and challenging part of our life. After a period of Darwinian selection, the Weismann "locker" (actually a very clever true torque sensing AND locking differential) became king of that particular hill. EVERYONE who went really quick in the real Can-Am, the original Trans-Am and in Formula 5000 used a Weismann, as did the faster champ cars in the prewing days. Most of the Formula One teams used them, although what was actually being used was usually a well-kept secret. Even Pete Weismann, while he obviously knew who owned them, seldom knew who in either Formula One or Indy was using them on any given day. Those of us who asked Pete what oil to use and how to maintain them and then did as we were instructed had no trouble with them at all.

The limited slip differential exists for one reason only: to prevent (or at least to discourage) the inside wheel (with respect to the turn center) from spinning when the vertical load applied to it is decreased by lateral load transfer in cornering. Engine torque, like water and electricity, will follow the path of least resistance, and once we get one wheel spinning, without a limited slip or a locker, ALL of our torque is going to go up in smoke. Fine, you say, but the locked differential or spool will achieve the same end in a more positive fashion, is lighter, less complicated, more reliable and cheaper. Right you are, BUT by dragging the in-

side rear tire under deceleration like a sea anchor so that the car tends to rotate about it, the spool causes corner entry understeer which must be overcome either by pitching the car, by biasing the rear brakes or, if all of the corners are in the same direction and about the same speed, by running a larger outside rear tire (tire stagger). On the average oval track, all of the corners ARE very close to the same speed and tire stagger works just fine, so long as you get it right and it doesn't change. It has its limitations when it comes to road courses.

The need for a limited slip is basically a function of the accelerative force-generating capacity (lateral and longitudinal) of the driven tires and of the excess torque available for acceleration. We learned in TUNE TO WIN that the force-generating capacity of a pair of tires on the same axle line is a function of the area of the contact patch between the tires and the road, the coefficient of friction between the rubber and the road, the camber angle of the tires with respect to the road surface, the vertical load on the tires and the amount of lateral load transfer between them. The slower the road speed, the less engine torque is required to maintain speed and therefore the more excess torque is available for acceleration. The slower the speed of the corner the easier it is for the driver to approach the theoretical maximum cornering speed of his car. The slower the corner, the less downforce will be generated by whatever devices we have to generate it. Therefore, the slower the average corner of a given racetrack, the more we need an effective limited slip differential.

When the wing appeared on the racing scene—and particularly when it became very effective—it appeared to many racers that the download applied to the driven wheels would do away with the need for a sophisticated limited slip simply because the download would be so great that lateral load transfer would no longer matter and any old limited slip would do. These are the same people who later thought that ground effects did away with the need for a torsionally rigid chassis.

Anyway, aided and abetted by the advent of the ground effects car, this attitude more or less prevailed for several years. Just about everyone in big-time road racing was using Salisbury clutch-pack limited slips because they were easy to maintain and supposedly worked just as well as the Weismann, at least when download was plentiful. The fallacy of this argument could be seen by anyone who cared to watch even the ground effects Formula One cars smoking the inside tire off really slow corners. Porsche used spools in the turbos for several reasons: There was no limited slip available that would handle the torque, the 935's only ran against each other so they could afford to give away some performance, and the insane rear engine layout meant that they could use some spool-induced entry understeer.

This situation went on until March realized that, download or no, the cam-and-pawl didn't work worth a damn. Needing an edge over the Ralt Honda in Formula Two he prevailed upon Hewland to adapt the BMW Salisbury to the FT-200 transaxle. March had a notable advantage for some years, until the rest of the Brits caught on and the small car march to Salisburys and modified Salisburys was on (pun intended).

At the moment, the situation is confused. Champ cars run spools on the ovals and Hewland-type Salisburys on the road courses. Some of them try to run spools on the road courses. Color them slow. Lots of large sedans run spools on road courses. I consider these people to be foolish. Some sedans run Detroit lockers; suitably modified (with Banjo Matthews springs), they are better than spools, but not much. Can-Am cars, fast Formula Two and Three cars and many of the GT cars run Salisburys. Formula Atlantic runs the cam-and-pawl, except for one smart Italian/Australian who runs a Salisbury, and beats EVERYONE, including the visiting foreigners. Formula One runs Salisburys, except for Ferrari who, at least sometimes, runs a Weismann-like device of its own manufacture.

If all of our corners were quick ones, and if all of our cars had effective downforce generators, it wouldn't much matter what sort of diffs we used. BUT the current trend is toward street courses with their natural preponderance of slow- and medium-speed corners; the powers that be are wisely reducing the download by quantum jumps and the limited slip is coming back into its own. There is going to be a lot of development in this area in the next couple of years. We should take a look at it.

To be truly effective the racing differential should be able to continuously sense the amount of torque that each wheel can accept and then so proportion the input torque that no SINGLE wheel ever gets more torque (in either direction) than it can accept. In other words, if we are going to get wheelspin, we want BOTH wheels to spin so that our rate of acceleration is limited by the amount of traction that the weak tire can generate. In practical terms this means that the diff should be open or nearly so on deceleration in order not to cause corner entry understeer and that it should be locked or nearly so on acceleration. It must be consistent and predictable in operation. The transition from power-off-open to power-on-locked, while it must obviously be rapid, should not be violent.

To date, none of the limited slips fulfill all of the above requirements. In fact, the "limited slips" (as opposed to the locking differentials) cannot work very well with high-torque outputs simply because they are all planetary gear systems of one sort or another. When one tire unloads to the point that it begins to spin, the limited slip takes the easy way out and converts engine torque into wheel rpm, which we term inside wheelspin. Only the locking differential has any real hope in the coming age of turbo power. To my mind this means that those of us who wish to win had better encourage Pete Weismann. Let's take a look at what is available.

The Detroit locker is violent and unpredictable in operation and because of this it is simply not possible to place the car precisely where you want it on the racetrack or to apply the throttle as early as the tires will allow on corner exit. Given any kind of choice at all, no one in their right mind uses a Detroit locker.

The cam-and-pawl (or ZF) is smooth and progressive in operation with a soft transition—but it only locks about 80%, and that only when brand-new. Given any reasonable amount of torque and slow corners it will self destruct at a rapid pace and is generally an unsatisfactory device. At the moment, only Formula Atlantic cars and slow Formula Two and Three cars are using the cam-and-pawl.

The Salisbury type of multidisc limited slip, after some years in limbo, is enjoying a rebirth. In its unmodified form, direct from Hewland, it works very well. It does cause some entry understeer—but not a lot—and it is very smooth, progressive and easy to drive. It does a much better job of limiting inside wheelspin than does the cam-and-pawl and is much less expensive to maintain. Just about all of the current generation of Formula One and Can-Am cars use them as do the vast majority of the champ cars that go quickly on road courses. They work exceptionally well in street cars—BMW, Porsche and Mazda that I know of offer them as very worthwhile options—especially if you drive in snow country.

The "break-loose" torque is adjustable by shims. One hundred twenty lb/ft is a very good starting point—more results in more entry understeer and less results in more inside wheelspin. Those who attempt to reduce understeer by removing the Belleville washers that provide the pre-load are displaying their ignorance of how the thing works and wind up with ill-behaving and unpredictable cars. It is, however, possible to modify the behavior of the Salisbury by playing with the angles of the ramps that locate the cross. The idea is to reduce the amount of slip limitation while decelerating without affecting the power-on characteristics. It is not easy to accomplish. What usually happens is that the experimenters end up with a violent and unpredictable car which displays an annoying tendency to split the differential case wide open. However, the more sophisticated Salisburys are reported to be very effective units indeed.

The True Track is not proven reliable enough for racing use and, in my opinion, is unlikely to be—too many parts, too many built-in stress raisers and too much generation of heat.

The Gleason "Torsen" diff is based upon the simple fact that a worm-and-wheel gear setup can transmit torque in one direction only. It has A LOT of parts. The worm gears are very small for the amount of torque that they will have to transmit under racing conditions and the shock loads that they will receive. The whole thing is filled with stress raisers. The worm-and-wheel is a very inefficient gear configuration at high speeds and it generates a lot of heat—which is destructive and wastes power. As the GLEASOM, this diff has been around for a long time and has never been very successful, possibly because of a lack of development and possibly because the concept is just too complex and too inefficient to succeed.

The Gleason Gear Works of Rochester, New York, one of the world's premier gear houses, has now come to some sort of arrangement with the Gleasom family and is producing the Gleason Torsen (for "torque sensing") diff. (The similarity of the two names is bound to cause some confusion.) As always with nonracing engineers, Gleason has grievously underestimated the loads involved in racing, and the units that I know of that have been tested, while they have performed well, have failed early. Gleason engineers certainly have the expertise and the facilities to solve the metallurgy problems. Whether they have the will, remains to be seen. Our recent off-road tests with the prototype racing units both ended in early fragmentation. I don't hold out a lot of hope for the unit, but for sure I will keep a close eye on its development.

To my mind the Weismann locker is far and away the best of the diffs. It is fully locked under power; it creates very little heat and so wastes virtually no power; it is a true locking differential and so it doesn't mind at all when you get one wheel out in the dirt and it LOVES the rain. It does cause some corner-entry understeer, but nothing extreme. If the driver does it all wrong it will also cause terminal corner exit understeer—as in HELLO WALL. The spool does the same thing when one climbs on the power while holding understeer steering lock on the car. But we do not pay our drivers to do it wrong. It is not as forgiving a unit as the Salisbury and it requires a lot more maintenance.

So far as I know virtually no one presently runs a Weismann diff. There are a couple of reasons. One of them is that the Weismann has acquired an entirely undeserved reputation for unreliability. Another is that they are supposed to be "hard to drive." If "hard" means that they require a certain appreciation of their characteristics and a lot of awareness and discipline on the part of the driver, then this one is true—but surely, that is what drivers are paid for. (Another of Smith's laws is that if you are not paying the driver, you do not have a RACING TEAM—you have either a hobby or a school.) The third reason is that Pete and Michelle are tired of the grief piled upon them by incompetent operators and really don't want to build them anymore.

Me, if I were running champ cars or Can-Am, I would be running a Weismann and experimenting with modified Salisburys—and watching the Torsen. If I were running Trans-Am I would be running a Weismann, building a Salisbury (so far as I know there is no RACING clutch-pack that can be adapted to the big sedans) simply because I would want a backup to the Weismann in case I ran out of diffs. If I were running an Atlantic car I would run the only surviving Hewland FT-sized Weismann and I would obtain a couple of Salisburys from the U.K. and start playing games. If I were running off-road I would run a Weismann and experiment with both the Detroit locker and the Torsen. In each case I would be playing with the Torsen not because I think that it is going to be better than the Weismann (in fact I doubt that it will ever be as good), but because Pete Weismann is no longer interested in making diffs and I would want some alternative to the Salisbury.

COOLING

Even the best designed and manufactured gears generate a lot of heat. The final-drive lubricating oil of any racing car that puts out much over 250 bhp is going to require a cooler. Mr. Hewland realizes this and provides an integral gear pump on the FGA and larger transaxles. On front-engined cars, we have to provide some sort of pump.

Mechanical pumps are a pain to package; for years I used Jabsco Water Puppy 12-volt pumps with nitrile impellers. They work fine, don't draw a lot of current and are pretty insensitive to trash passing through. They are also hard to find with the nitrile impeller. I now use a 12-volt Nippondenso pump, part number 41910-0607, that I buy from Mac Tilton. This is a positive-displacement pump so it must be protected by a pretty good sized screen filter. I put a switch on the pump circuit and a temperature gauge in the cockpit. The driver is instructed not to switch the pump on until the unit's temperature is over 200 degrees F. Naturally I use one pump on the gearbox and one on the diff. I use Earl's Temp-A-Cure coolers on everything.

With the beam axle, it helps the cooling A LOT if you seal the axle tubes so that the gear oil has to stay in the banjo and not flow down the axle tubes under cornering loads. It also helps the ring and pinion. If you are not up for installing seals around the axles, a pair of simple baffles at the point where the axle housing joins the diff housing will help considerably. If the axle shafts don't enter the diff splines freely, straighten the housing; you are turning a lot of useful horsepower into heat.

THE CLUTCH

In the days of my youth the racing clutch was a source of constant worry. If the damned thing got me off the line I usually said a quick prayer of thanks and then refused to touch the clutch pedal again until it was time to stop. A little-appreciated side benefit of the weakness was that all of us learned to shift properly. All this has changed; the racing clutch is now reliable to the point of boredom and the driver who can shift is an endangered species.

As always, the clutch for racing use is manufactured by the Borg and Beck arm of Automotive Products. They even have a multiplate unit designed for dirt-track and off-road use. If these clutches are maintained according to the simple and comprehensive instructions provided by Tilton Engineering they will give no trouble—for a very long time. When they do start to get cranky in the release department, send them back to Mac. If you get really smart you will form the habit of inspecting the pressure plate every time that you are able to see it and, when you are no longer able to insert your fingernail between the diaphragm fingers and the pressure plate cover at the point where the fingers disappear behind the cover (with the assembly bolted up) you send it back to Mac BEFORE it starts to give trouble. As a matter of course I have Mac rework my units from new because I don't think much of English threaded fasteners in general.

Repeated abuse—like slipping the clutch or practicing standing starts without allowing the unit to cool down between attempts—will inevitably result in a warped pressure plate and/or intermediate disc(s). Maximum recommended out-of-flat is 0.005'' measured with a straight edge and a feeler gauge. You can actually get away with 0.008'' before you start to run out of release. The problem with all of this has to do with standing starts. If you have much warpage in the pressure plate department, or if the pivot ring is worn, the car will creep when first gear is engaged and you are waiting for the flag to fall (or the light to turn green). At best this is embarrassing and/or costly; at worst it is damned dangerous.

On four-cylinder engines, the magnesium clutch rings DO break from time to time, especially if some well-meaning soul has inscribed top dead center marks on their outside surface (remember where the point of maximum stress is always found). Flexible, warped or out-of-flat flywheels will also fracture the mag rings. With the Cosworth BDA's, switching at vast cost to the 12-bolt Formula Two unit cures the problem. Tilton now has a B & B clutch that stands on six steel pedestals—problem fixed!

With the Borg and Beck clutch it is essential to use a throw-out bearing that has both the correct diameter and the correct radius to match the diaphragm fingers. It is equally important that there be no plastic parts in the bearing (like ball cages). I routinely throw away what comes on the car and buy a bearing from Tilton.

SUBSTITUTES

Both Quartermaster and RAM are now producing low moment of rotational inertia multidisc clutch units in the U.S. RAM has had the decency and ingenuity to design their own unit. The Quartermaster is a direct and blatant copy of the Borg and Beck. I have used the RAM off-road with great success. I have not tried the Quartermaster and probably never will. As an engineer I do not approve of unlicensed copying of designs for profit (as opposed to copying someone's clever idea for personal use) and I refuse to support corporations that do so.

GROUND EFFECTS AND THE CLUTCH SLAVE CYLINDER

The advent of the tunnel-type ground effects racing car (which I heartily disapprove of) has caused the designers to switch to the McLaren/BMW style of clutch-release mechanism in which the slave cylinder is in unit with the release bearing and concentric with the input shaft—i.e., inside the bellhousing. This has accomplished several ends. First of all, it has cleaned up the side of the transaxle allowing the use of a smooth and uninterrupted fairing on the inside of the tunnel and it has narrowed the transaxle itself, allowing wider tunnels. Second, it has vastly increased the life expectancy of the throw-out bearing itself. Instead of being rudely accelerated from zero to 10,000 rpm in about a nanosecond every time the driver pushed the clutch pedal, it now rotates at engine speed all the time—a state of affairs that the bearing finds more healthy. I still use one of Tilton's GOOD bearings—no plastic bearing cages for this boy! Third, we no longer have to worry about adjusting the clutch free play; it is self adjusting. Of course, EVERYTHING has to be spot on its designed dimension or we are

going to wreck either the clutch or the main bearing thrusts. Under no circumstances can we trust the manufacturer to get this one right. Check it yourself—and recheck it with each engine that you own.

This all sounds too good to be true; there has to be a catch somewhere. The catch is simple: the fine folks across the pond don't seem to understand all that they know about dynamic seals and some of them attempt to use O-rings to seal the concentric slave cylinder. They neither use a seal compound compatible with brake fluid nor shield the poor thing from that most abrasive of matters, sintered metallic clutch lining dust. Talk about no hope! The predictable result is a somewhat shaky seal life of about 400 miles, after you have changed to a Viton O-ring. The only real answer is to redesign and remachine the whole mess and use a proper square section seal. Saab has just such a unit on the 900 Turbo. It is well designed, well manufactured, relatively inexpensive and works just fine. Of course you have to machine your own adapter for it. Tilton also sells one that is equally good and which comes with a throw-out bearing with the correct diameter and radius for the Borg and Beck clutch.

This is as good a time as any to point out the single shortcoming of the whole concept. If anything goes wrong with any of the seals, you are going to have to tear off the whole transaxle/rear suspension assembly to fix it—and this could be disastrous in terms of missing a session (or a race). Of course you can always get along without the clutch, so long as there is no standing start involved—AND you don't spin. . . . So it pays to be very sure of the seals and the plumbing joints. We went so far as to make up a simple little test fixture so that we could make damned sure that the thing did not leak before we buttoned it up. I use very heavy copper seal washers for the banjo bolts and anneal them every time that they are reused. I also preplan the emergency transaxle/bellhousing removal and replacement; and I make the crew practice it.

Gary Anderson has shown us the intelligent way to go on the Anson Super Vee: a simple mechanical linkage that accomplishes exactly the same purpose at zero cost and zero risk. This is, in fact, not the only clever tweak on this underrated and underdeveloped car. I have a feeling that we will hear more from the good Mr. Anderson.

LAST WORDS

After years of making every conceivable sort of gear-carrying box/bin, I finally got smart. I now carry them, two to four gear sets to a drawer, in a standard everyday steel 24-drawer cabinet from Grainger. It is the cheapest, most convenient and most secure method that I have yet come up with.

CHAPTER SIXTEEN

CHANGES IN THE WORLD OF VEHICLE AERODYNAMICS

GROUND EFFECT

When I wrote TUNE TO WIN, ground effect had not yet had a significant effect on motor racing. Six years later, as I write the final chapters of ENGINEER TO WIN ground effect seems to have shot its bolt and is on the way out. To which I can only say "about time!" Although (with the exception of champ cars and IMSA) ground effects racing cars will soon be nothing more than an unpleasant memory, their effect on our lives has been so pronounced and there is so much misinformation floating about that I feel that I must devote some considerable amount of time, space and effort to explaining this aberration—or at least trying to. Besides, I expect that the champ car rules will allow tunnels for the foreseeable future and since champ cars will inevitably take over big time American road racing, it behooves us all to attempt to understand the phenomenon.

I am trying to write this series of books as a progression of knowledge, each building on the previous. If I succeed this will accomplish two ends: I will not have to spend time rewriting what I wrote some years ago and you will not have to spend money for what you have already paid for. Before proceeding, please go back and reread the aerodynamics sections of TUNE TO WIN.

ANY vehicle, wheeled or otherwise, when moving in close proximity to the surface of the earth, is of necessity operating in what the aerodynamicists term "ground effect" and so is technically a "ground effect vehicle." In the case of the aircraft, ground effect is usually defined as whenever the altitude is less than half of the wingspan; some interesting changes in flight characteristics take place at these altitudes both because of the "packing effect" of the air between the lifting surfaces and the earth (or sea) and because of the shearing forces between the accelerated air attached to the aircraft and the stationary ground. The behavior of aircraft in ground effect is actually the behavior of a THREE-DIMENSIONAL wing in ground effect.

This behavior is mathematically highly complex and is well beyond the scope of this book. Except for military pilots flying close ground support, it really doesn't matter much (even crop dusters don't normally operate THAT close to the ground), except when leaving or returning to the roost—which is a totally different set of circumstances. On the other hand, the aircraft, when close enough to the ground, DOES compress a layer of air directly beneath itself and it IS possible (if not advisable) to "ride the cushion" with slight forward stick pressure right down on the deck, and the aircraft will follow gentle undulations in the terrain all by itself. This sort of thing is not conducive to continued good health (imagine the effect of a small canyon, for instance) and so is discouraged by all of the powers that be. We are not going to talk about airplanes.

Obviously the racing car is by definition a ground effect vehicle. The airstream flowing beneath the moving car is both attached to the vehicle and in constant contact (and combat) with the surface of the track. Both the drag and the stability of the vehicle are profoundly influenced by the reaction of the moving, attached and semiattached airstream with the stationary ground. We are not going to talk very much about that, either.

What we ARE going to talk about is the current manifestation of the species "ground effect racing car." It was jointly sired by General Motors R&D and by the redoubtable (and remarkable) Jim Hall with the Chaparral "Vacuum Cleaner" Can-Am car of 1970, raised to full-fledged international outlawry by the equally remarkable Gordon Murray with the Brabham "Sucker" Formula One car of 1978, revived in legal configuration by Colin Chapman with the Lotus 79 and—although detested by drivers, designers, sanctioning bodies, track owners, race promoters, tire companies journalists and paying spectators alike—virtually ubiquitous (except for stock cars) by 1980. Personally I feel that the advent of the ground effects racing cars was even worse for the sport than the admission of the turbocharged engine without a logical equivalence formula. It is my firm opinion that ANYTHING which detracts from the level of driver skill required to negotiate any given corner is bad for the sport.

At the peak of their efficiency, the ground effects cars transformed corners which had been taken by only the very best at 120 mph on tiptoes to corners that were taken by everyone and his dog at whatever maximum speed the cars were capable of reaching on that part of the racetrack. Once upon a time, watching the very best drivers go through the delicate sequence of braking at the last point that would allow the car to be rebalanced before turning it in, balancing it and then tiptoeing through a truly high-speed corner on the very edge of a swaying tightrope was, for those of us who understood what we were seeing, an awe-inspiring sight—and served as a graphic example of the difference between men and boys. It was also a source of truly great satisfaction for the drivers—one of the all-time-great feelings! In all too many cases ground effect took that away from us—and from the drivers.

Overtaking under the brakes almost became a thing of the past both because so many corners became flat out and because the literally tons of available downforce shortened the time and the distance spent braking to the point where passing under the brakes became impossible rather than difficult. (It is MEANT to be difficult; that is one of the things that people consistently refuse to understand about this business of driving racing cars as fast as they CAN be driven: IT IS MEANT TO BE A VERY DIFFICULT THING TO DO.) Along these lines I reject the theory that the harnessing of ground effect to the racing car is bad because the increased corner speeds reduce the amount of time available for the driver to do his thing. That, to my mind is what racing is all about—the driver's thing SHOULD be damned difficult to do, or at least to do supremely well!

Not only did the ground effect racing car remove a great deal of the spectacle and required skill from the sport, it escalated the physical dangers, again for several reasons. Once upon a time, if you roared off the racetrack at corner A, you were going, say, 120 mph and would likely get the thing slowed down quite a bit before you hit anything solid.

With the full ground effects car you would have been going over 160 when you went off and, unless the layout of the barriers were drastically changed, your chances would be considerably reduced. Further, the never-ending search for more download inevitably led to wider tunnels and narrower, less crashworthy tubs. The driver lives inside the tub and, while the tunnels certainly reduce the chances of cars tangling wheels and also absorb SOME energy in crash situations, they won't absorb much and are a poor substitute for a crashworthy chassis.

One of the least-understood factors with regard to the safety of the ground effect vehicle is what happens when the car gets a little too far sideways. What happens is that the tunnels stall. The effect is about the same as if the wings had fallen off a non-ground-effect car—the hapless driver becomes a passenger with little if any control over his immediate destiny. This is the major reason that the drivers hate the things (and why some of the very best retired early), not the discomfort and not the physical strain imposed by the insane wheel rates and g forces; simply that NOBODY likes being a helpless passenger.

It is interesting to note that after some years of ineffective efforts to limit the downforce generation of ground effect tunnels, the powers that be in Formula One have come to their senses and outlawed ground effects altogether. Formula Three gets it next year and, presumably, the rest of the FIA-controlled formulas soon thereafter. On this side of the pond, CART and USAC, in order not to bankrupt their car owners, have announced their intent to stay with their present limited ground effect rules for the foreseeable future, and I would not expect IMSA to change their rules for the same reason. GOD KNOWS what SCCA will do with Super Vee and the presently moribund Formula Atlantic. Hopefully they will also go to the flat-bottom rules and I will make a fortune marketing conversion kits for Ralts. Whatever happens it seems that we on this side of the pond are going to have to live with limited ground effects. It would therefore be best if we understood something about them. . . .

THE BASIC IDEA

As always, the basic idea is very simple. Mother Nature sees to it that the racing car, along with you, me, everything and everybody else on earth, is surrounded by and constantly pushed upon from all directions by the pressure of the atmosphere above us—14.7 psi at sea level under standard conditions. If we can somehow devise a way to reduce that pressure on the underside of the racing car while maintaining it on the upper side we will achieve a negative pressure differential between the topside and the underside and the car will be pushed down onto the racetrack by a force equal to the mean pressure differential multiplied by the planform area of the car.

That even a seemingly negligible pressure differential can yield results that are significant indeed in terms of download is demonstrated by the fact that the 1982 VDS Tony Cicale-designed Can-Am car had a planform area of some 10,000 square inches. If the mean pressure under the car could be reduced by a mere 0.1 psi (an easily attainable figure) the result would therefore be 1000 lb of download. The underbody area of a typical Super Vee or Atlantic car is about 4500 square inches—and, yes, mean differentials on the order of several times 0.1 psi are attainable at high road speeds.

STILL MORE HISTORY

The history of the development of the ground effects racing car is a classic example of tunnel vision (pun intentional). So many of us were so close to seeing the light for so long, and none of us DID. At least as early as M.G.'s mid-1950's assault on Bonneville, the designers (at least some of them) realized that underbody turbulence and ground effects shear were responsible for a significant portion of total aerodynamic drag. Under the premise that if it's not there it cannot cause drag, a transverse flexible skirt was placed under the nose of the M.G. streamliner in order to discourage as much air as possible from flowing beneath the car. Legend has it that it worked; although the steeply in-curving sides of the body were completely unsealed and so lots of air had to migrate under the car from the sides, the decrease in drag more than offset the increase in frontal area. Although we experimented with similar devices during the 1960's (usually chevron shaped with the point of the vee facing forward so as to dump the air out the sides and thus kill, or at least wound, both lift and drag), it was a decade and a half before we came up with the now familiar "spook" front spoiler for racing sedans.

In the mid-1960's, while tuft testing in the interest of reducing drag, we noted that the tufts along the underside of the body sides inevitably tried to flow to the underside of the car, indicating that the underside was a region of relatively low pressure. We also realized both from the point of view of drag and from that of download that this was a good thing. This was the real reason that racing cars stopped having curved and sexy, compound lower bodies about 1967 and became slab sided with sharp bottom corners (we were also trying to carry more fuel in a shorter length so the rounded corners had to go anyway). Some of the cars started sprouting various chines and fences in an attempt to further discourage this unwanted transverse migration of air to the sacred under-regions. About this time Jim Hall reintroduced the wing to the racing car and we all started to think (and some of us to learn) about the dynamics of lift.

Dimly we perceived that actual evacuation of the underside of the racing car could be a very good thing indeed. Our perception was temporarily brightened when GM and Jim Hall sprung the Vacuum Cleaner on an unsuspecting world. In case you are too young to remember this remarkable device (or have forgotten it, unlikely) this was a Chaparral Can-Am car which featured a series of peripheral skirts which effectively sealed the underbody of the car. It also featured an auxiliary snowmobile engine which drove a dirty great pair of rear-mounted fans which evacuated the entire underside of the car. Adhesion was instantly redefined. Driven by Jackie Stewart this device struck terror into the opposition like nothing before or since. The unreliability of the auxillary engine kept it from winning races and the whole device was outlawed before it became reliable. Jim called a halt to his remarkable career of innovation, went back to basic principles and started his second career of winning races. No one has ever done it better.

For a couple of years after that little episode, since the FIA and the SCCA had made it illegal to use any sort of auxillary motor to power the evacuating fans, when most of us thought about the sucker principle at all we blithely assumed that we simply could not afford to use any of our precious engine power to drive evacuation devices and so we smugly ignored the whole thing—until Gordon Murray did his homework regarding the benefits of increased download versus the amount of power required to generate it. He also READ the regulations and discovered that, although an evacuation fan was most definitely a movable aerodynamic device and therefore clearly outside the law (as are throttle butterflies, throttle slides and the ventilated brake disc), if he were to arrange things so that the fans, in addition to evacuating the underside of the car, pulled cooling air through the radiators, he could state that cooling was the primary function of the system and he just MIGHT get away with it. And get away with it he did—for one race. Niki Lauda won the Swedish Grand Prix of 1978 in the one and only appearance of the Brabham Sucker before it too was outlawed, and relative sanity briefly prevailed.

Prevailed, that is, until Colin Chapman, in an effort to reduce drag and, for once, end up with a Lotus that was fast in a straight line, cleaned up the underside of the Lotus 78. The effort succeeded; one thing led to another in the fertile brain of the good Mr. Chapman and the tunnel car was born with the Lotus 79. Sliding skirts followed very quickly indeed and the era of Formula One go-karts was on. When the sanctioning bodies outlawed sliding skirts, the designers replied with two-stage driver adjustable ride height systems. When these were outlawed in turn we saw insane ride rates in order to keep the fixed skirts on the track surface. It never dawned upon the rule makers to raise the level of the fixed skirts to a rational dimension above the bottom of the chassis and so return to sanity. Finally (and rightly) they outlawed the whole ground effects concept. Coincidental with the beginning of this period of international madness Bernard Ecclestone started the ongoing process of converting Formula One racing from a spectator sport to a spectacle or a happening, really BIG sponsorship money appeared, the egomaniac struggle between Ecclestone, Balestre, FOCA, FISA et. al., began—and we were off!

WHAT IT IS AND WHERE IT'S AT

When the ground effects car made its first appearance some of the less-informed members of the motoring press immediately attempted to convince us that the ground effects tunnel functions as an upside-down wing, and that the sides of the tunnels increase the efficiency of these "wings" of remarkably unfavorable aspect ratio by acting as end plates. If nothing else, this was amusing. Things just aren't that simple—they never are. The best words that I have seen in print on the subject are (as usual) Paul Van Valkenburgh's—in ON TRACK, December 2, 1982.

Virtually everyone reading this chapter will already know that the current "ground effects" racing car generates download by the use of one or more three-sided tunnel (or tunnels) whose bottom surface is open to the track surface, whose front opening is of relatively small area and whose rear portion is an expanding diffusor. Stating that these tunnels function by using the track surface as the other side of a rectangular venturi may be a vast over-simplification—but the idea is in the right direction.

The way it actually happens is depicted by the drawings of FIGURE [218]. FIGURE [218A] shows the whole catastrophe with the side view of the ground effect pod shaded. In the interest of clarity, FIGURE [218B] shows only the pod in side elevation—the wheels (and everything else) having been removed. The vertical sides and skirts (if any) are not shown, nor are the coolers and their ducts. At some point out in front of our pod we have undisturbed air at standard atmospheric pressure. From this point, labeled "a," we will trace the progress of a single molecule of air as a streamline and trace its progress to and through the pod back to the free air behind the car. As we will see when we get to Bernoulli, The Creator has so arranged things that the sum of the pressure head and the velocity head at any point within a fluid must be constant. Therefore, at some point ("a' ") behind our car, the air MUST return to the condi-

tion of point "a." I will point out right now that I am fully aware that this utopian state of affairs assumes no turbulence and no flow separation and so does not actually exist in the real world. It will do just fine for our present examination. In the real world, depending on road speed, point "a" is somewhere between one and two car lengths ahead of the racing car and point "a' " is a somewhat greater distance behind it.

If we graph the velocity of our molecule of air as it approaches and passes through the tunnel we see the curve of FIGURE [218C]. The air decelerates as it approaches the stagnation point; accelerates wildly as it passes around the nose and into the nozzle and then decelerates smoothly as it exits the tunnel. Interesting—but not surprising. When, however, we plot the air PRESSURE distribution along the path of our molecule of air we will find something similar to FIGURE [218D]. The area of negative pressure greatly exceeds the area of positive pressure and we have, to an extent, suceeded in lifting ourselves by our bootstraps. Actually, of course, we have done nothing of the kind—we have merely increased and accelerated the mass flow of air BENEATH our vehicle. The same AMOUNT of air has to flow at all points between the ground and the streamline and, like the water in a river, when the area through which it must flow is reduced (at the flat region of the tunnel) then the velocity of the flow MUST increase—and Bernoulli

Figure (218A): The ground effect tunnel.

Figure (218B): Streamlines around ground effect tunnel.

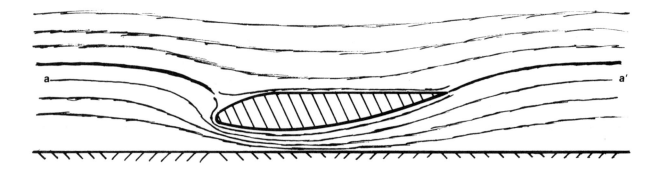

assures us that when the velocity increases the pressure will drop. Actually, from the instant that the streamline begins its downward path, the area through which the mass of air must flow is reduced and so is the pressure. We have therefore generated download at a nominal cost in induced drag. We don't notice the induced drag simply because, by cleaning up the normal turbulent underbody airflow we have lost at least as much drag as we have generated—so the download is effectively free.

AN INTERRUPTION TO EXPLAIN SOME NUMBERS

Fluid mechanics tend to talk about both lift and drag in terms of dimensionless coefficients—which I explained in TUNE TO WIN. While this makes the study of fluid mechanics possible, I, for one, find it difficult to visualize or otherwise make reality of this sort of thing. I like to think in terms of pounds of force at some given road speed. One hundred miles per hour is a convenient speed value, easily obtainable as a constant in testing and fast enough to give consistent results. Besides, it is easy to multiply or divide by—and so racers tend to talk about both lift and drag as so many pounds of force at 100 mph. To convert the figure to another road speed, one simply multiplies the figure in pounds of force by the square of the difference in velocity: To convert 100 pounds of drag (or download) at 100 mph to the equivalent figure at 160 mph, $100 (160/100)^2 = 100 \times (1.6)^2 = 100 \times 2.56 = 256$ lb @ 160 mph. To go the

Figure (218C): Air velocity along streamline passing through ground effect tunnel.

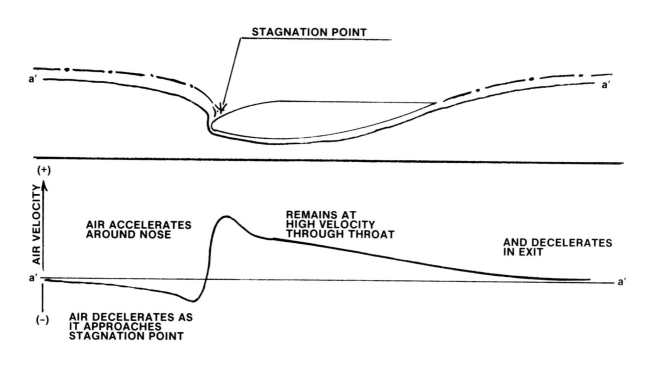

Figure (218D): Idealized air pressure distribution around ground effect tunnel.

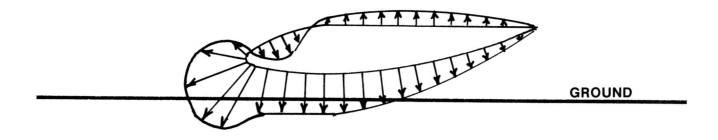

235

other way—say to 60 mph—the equation becomes 100 $(60/100)^2$ = 3.6 × 100 = 36 lb @ 60 mph.

Among other things, this may make the fact that both lift and drag vary as the SQUARE of velocity become very real in your mind. As often happens in racing, the ACTUAL numbers aren't terribly important to most of us, only to the people who are designing and/or developing the cars. What is important to US is the improvements that WE may be able to make in those numbers.

Returning to the Bonneville M.G. streamliner idea, IF the skirt across the nose were to be exceptionally effective and IF the sides of the body had been sealed with equal effectiveness so that little if any air could flow under the car, then the theorists tell us that the most we can hope for is a mean negative underbody pressure of about 80% of the base drag at the tail of the vehicle. This base drag would typically be about ⅓ of the frontal pressure. This in itself would make a notable contribution to the reduction of aerodynamic drag, but wouldn't do a whole hell of a lot for the generation of downforce—an inactive measure, as it were.

To inject a bit of reality into this discussion, let's talk about what might be attainable at 160 mph by this method. The rise in pressure ahead of the car at 160 mph is equal to ½ of the mass density of air denoted in this instance by the symbol ''r'' (my word processor does not know about the conventional symbol, the Greek rho) multiplied by road speed in feet/sec squared—or delta $P = r/2 \ (V^2)$. At 160 mph this works out to 0.002378/2 × $(235 \ fps)^2$ = 66.6 lb/ft² or 0.4625 psi—a 3.15% rise above atmospheric pressure.

Assuming an excellent design, the base drag at the tail of the vehicle will be about 33% of the frontal pressure—in this case 22.2 pounds per square foot or 0.154 psi. If we achieve a mean pressure difference of 80% of this figure we are talking about 17.75 pounds per square foot or 0.121 psi. The total download on the car, then, would be 17.75 pounds per square foot times the planform area of the car. In the case of a typical Formula Atlantic/Super Vee we are talking about 35 square feet of planform area or 35 × 17.75 = 621 lb of download at 160 mph. Not at all inconsiderable but not very impressive, either. The cost in drag would be relatively high.

On the other hand, if we allow (or even encourage) the air to flow freely beneath the car, control its velocity while it is doing so and convince it not to separate from the bodywork, we can generate quite large negative pressures at no or at least very little cost in drag. In fact, if we do it just right we can get download while reducing drag—something for nothing (but only because the airflow underneath the pre-ground-effects racing car was truly bad). Doing it just right has not yet been achieved—but we are getting closer. There are several semiconflicting aims:

(1) To achieve maximum acceleration of the airflow in the tunnel.

(2) To avoid the generation of positive pressure at the tunnel entry, both to avoid generation of lift and to prevent the possibility of a region of positive pressure migrating rearward to the infinite detriment of downforce generation.

(3) To keep the flow attached all the way to the tunnel exit in order to avoid turbulence which will both create drag and degrade download.

(4) To optimize the longitudinal location of the tunnel's center of pressure and to maintain said center of pressure at the same longitudinal location with increasing road speed (an often overlooked point that is critical to the understeer/oversteer balance of the car at varying speeds). In the interest of survival, if the center of pressure cannot remain constant, what we need is for it to move rearward. We DO NOT NEED dynamic oversteer increasing with road speed.

(5) To make the whole thing relatively insensitive to changes in pitch angle and ride height.

To no one's surprise, all of this has turned out to be easier said than done. In the first place, although Bernoulli's theorem still holds true, in order to apply it we must first define the complete flow field around the pod. To solve for the flow field about a general shape such as the ground effect tunnel is highly complex and requires both very sophisticated measuring devices and sophisticated computer analyses which are well beyond the scope of this book, the knowledge of the author and the resources of most racing teams. They may even be beyond the present capability of the aerospace industry. What the fluid mechanics are wont to say about all this is, ''Sure we understand it—we just can't solve for it.'' As a result, even with all of the super equipment and computer programs and resultant high-dollar number crunching, the effects of real-life flow separation within the tunnel are typically not completely accounted for, which makes the results of computer-aided wind tunnel simulation of ground effect vehicles questionable at the very least.

Lift and drag theory developed for wings in free air doesn't work either. The aspect ratio is so low as to be ridiculous and we are deeply and completely in ground effect—a situation foreign to the aircraft industry—so that the shear forces make a nonsense of accepted theory. Cut, measure and try has been the name of this game from the very beginning. However, in order to achieve even reasonable results, the measuring, cutting and trying MUST be combined with a basic knowledge of aerodynamics and a lot of good old common sense. The measuring is typically done by means of multiple manometers strategically mounted in the tunnels and on the underbody so that an accurate picture of the overall pressure pattern can be obtained. Basic aerodynamics and common sense are needed to interpret the pressure data in terms of what the flow is actually doing, and how and where to change the design in order to obtain more of what we want (download) and less of what we don't (drag).

What follows is far too generalized for me to be very happy with it, but I have no logical choice—ground effects testing and development require reasonable sums of money and I stopped working with the big teams before ground effects came into being. I claim no direct expertise. The people who DO development work guard their results very closely indeed (as well they should). I do however listen well and I am capable of deductive reasoning, at least to some extent.

Back in the 18th century, Daniel Bernoulli figured out that the sum of the pressure head within a fluid and the velocity head of that fluid must remain constant. Essentially his theorem is a statement of the conservation of energy. What Bernoulli's theorem means to us is that when a fluid stream is accelerated, its internal pressure will be reduced. This is what makes the fuel flow from the float bowl of a carburetor into the venturi. The float bowl is exposed to atmospheric pressure (or ram head pressure as the case may be) while the airstream entering the carb is accelerated through a converging venturi. The pressure at the throat of the venturi is therefore less than that in the float bowl and the fuel is pulled from the bowl into the moving airstream. The delivery pressure of the fuel pump has nothing to do with this; the fuel pump exists only to keep the fuel in the float bowl at its desired level. Referring back to FIGURE [218], what we are doing in the ground effect tunnel is accelerating the air through a smoothly converging nozzle, maintaining the increased velocity along the flat section and then smoothly exhausting the air through a diverging diffusor out the rear of the car where it rejoins the free airstream.

MORE NUMBERS

Just to put some numbers on things, if we assume a maximum negative pressure reading of 7 inches of water (not unrealistic at all) obtained at the flat part of the tunnel at 100 mph, this would translate to 36.4 psf (one inch of water is equal to 5.2 pounds per square foot). At 160 mph this would (on paper) increase to 93.2 psf [$36.4 \times (160/100)^2$]. This converts to 0.647 psi or a DECREASE of 4.40% from standard atmospheric pressure. If we assume that the base pressure at the exits of the tunnels is 22.2 psf as in our earlier example and take a wild stab at an average figure under the vehicle of, say, 45 psf, then our earlier planform area of 35 square feet would result in the theoretical generation of 1575 lb of download at 160 mph—a notable increase indeed! Further, if all went well, this could be achieved at little or no cost in drag.

SOME LIGHTS AT THE END OF THE TUNNEL

There are not a lot of hard and fast rules in the design of ground effects tunnels. Instead there is a host of general guidelines :

(1) The forward edge of the air inlet must be radiused.

(2) There must be no separation of flow in the converging section or in the flat section. Most of the people involved seem to realize this. What some of them apparently do not fully realize is that separation of flow in the diffusor should also be avoided. Looking at FIGURE [219], if we have separation within the diffusor, then the trailing streamline, instead of rising as it flows rearward, flows in a more horizontal fashion. Since God (as interpreted by Bernoulli) tells us that the sum of the pressure head and the velocity head must remain constant, this means that the leading airstream must start at the same level that the trailing airstream ends up at and not only will the separation cause drag, but the mass flow of air through the tunnel will be reduced and WE AIN'T GONNA GET THE DOWNFORCE! The fluid mechanics refer to the diverging exit of the tunnel as "the DRIVER"—with good reason. If the exit is wrong, the tunnel won't work! On the other hand, some slight turbulence in the airstream may help keep the airflow attached to the walls of the tunnel. This is just as well, as there is no way that the air entering the tunnel is going to be in a laminar condition anyway. If testing reveals local separation, the placement of vortex generators upstream of the separation point may well prevent the separation without a major rework.

(3) The transitions from the inlet to the flat section of the tunnel and from the flat section to the diffusor should be gradual (i.e., radiused).

(4) The longer the flat section or throat, the more download will be generated—and the more drag will be induced. The shorter the flat section, the less download will be generated—and the less drag will be induced.

(5) The farther forward the flat section or throat is located, the farther forward will be the center of pressure.

Figure (219): Separation of flow in the ground effect tunnel.

(6) The intersection between the vertical walls of the tunnel and the roof must be generously radiused. Otherwise the boundary layers on the adjacent surfaces will interfere with each other and corner separation will inevitably result.

(7) The inboard side of the tunnels must be tightly sealed to the chassis—leakage of air here will be disastrous.

(8) The entire pod/tunnel complex MUST be rigid. If the tunnel does not hold its shape, the download generation will be inconsistent with regard to both the location of the center of pressure and to roadspeed.

(9) A major portion of the total download is generated by the flat area of the tunnel. The throat exists ONLY to generate download. The entrance exists merely to smoothly accelerate the airstream into the flat area and, while the accelerated air in the diffusor is at a pressure less than atmospheric, the diffusor's major purpose in life is to exit the accelerated air from the flat area in a smooth flow so as to avoid separation and drag-causing turbulence. Therefore, the longer we make the flat area, assuming that we can keep the flow attached, the more download will be generated—and the more drag will result.

(10) The diffusor must gradually and constantly increase in area with no abrupt direction changes of any wall. The angles of divergence, both in side elevation and in plan view, must be such that separation does not occur. This is one reason why the narrow transverse transaxle is such an advantage.

(11) The airstream in the tunnel must not be allowed to impinge upon the rotating rear wheels. This is difficult to arrange in conjunction with #7 above and is an often-broken rule. The price in drag is notable. It is another reason why the narrow transaxle is an advantage.

(12) The greater the running clearance between the outer side of the tunnel (or skirt) and the ground, the greater should be the distance between the track surface and the roof of the tunnel. In other words, as the regulation makers raise the minimum skirt height, the designers SHOULD raise the roofs of their tunnels in order to achieve a greater mass flow of air, which will then be less affected by the increased leakage or migration of air from the sides of the pods into the tunnels. How much is, of course, the secret to success.

(13) The greater the distance from the track surface to the roof of the tunnel, the steeper the diffusor angle can be before separation results.

(14) The greater the distance from the track surface to the roof of the tunnel, the less critical variations in ride height and pitch angle or rake become.

(15) Attempts to reduce understeer by increasing chassis rake will inevitably choke off the front of the tunnels and make a diffusor out of the flat area of the tunnel—both of which will reduce download and, assuming that the tunnel center of pressure is as far forward as it should be, increase understeer. This is known as chasing your tail, and is a popular pasttime in some circles. The longer the throat area of the tunnel, the more critical the car will be with respect to rake, pitch angle and ride height.

(16) If you are really clever, by shaping the outer sides of the pods you can generate a rolling, flowing vortex that will serve as a surprisingly effective air magnet to pull air which has migrated under the chassis back out—sort of like a Gurney lip turned 90 degrees. Take a look at the sculpted side of a March Indy car (or a Swift Formula Ford) and visualize the air flowing along the body side and rolling off the lower lip like a curling wave and pulling air from under the car with it. Clever men—Robin Herd and David Bruns.

(17) You are going to do A LOT of cutting and trying. If I were designing a ground effect car, or modifying the pods of an existing one, at least on the test pods the roof of the tunnels would be easily replaceable and the interior corner radii would be some sort of flexible silicone or urethane so that I could change things around very easily indeed.

(18) It seems to me that the optimum configuration of a ground effect tunnel for Indianapolis is unlikely to be the optimum configuration for Long Beach. Of course I have been saying the same thing about wings for so long that I have grown tired of saying it and still no one will fund a simple R & D program to determine the actual optimum wing configuration for the three different types of courses high-speed straight(s) combined with high-speed corners as in OVAL TRACK, high speed straight(s) with low-speed corners as in LONG BEACH and DETROIT, and high-speed straights combined with medium-speed corners as in MID-OHIO and ELKHART LAKE. The other types of courses are variations of these three and a compromise setup is required.

(19) No matter how well you do the ground effect bit, the tunnels by themselves are not going to supply enough download to make a car competitive. Even if they could, you would still need wings in order to change the aerodynamic balance of the car quickly and practically in order to meet the varying demands and needs of different circuits, drivers and tires.

(20) The center of pressure of the tunnels should always be placed far enough forward so that the angle of attack of the front wings, or canards, to achieve vehicle balance does not even APPROACH the stall. When wings approach the stall point, separation of flow takes place on the underside of the wing and the air behind the wing is turbulent "low-energy" air. This would not be critical if that very same air were not about to enter either the ground effect tunnel or the radiator air entry duct (or both). In the case of the ground effect racing car, however, that is exactly where the air behind the front wings is going and separation in this area is going to rob the tunnels of mass airflow which is going to decrease downforce, and, by increasing the effects of transverse migration of air into the tunnels, increase drag. Carried to extremes this upward deflection of the airstream can also rob the heat exchanger inlet ducts with predictable results. FIGURES [220A] and [220B] apply. When more front download is required it is always better to run a front wing with a larger chord—even though the increased wetted area will necessarily cause more profile drag—than it is to increase the angle of attack. For the same reason it is preferable to run a Gurney at the rear of the airfoil than to increase the angle of attack above

about 3 degrees. In my opinion, double-element front wings (as opposed to Fowler flaps—see the forthcoming section on wings) with small angles of attack on the secondary wings are a very good idea on ground effect cars.

For the same reason, the nose itself must be as narrow as practical so as to achieve the maximum possible front wing effective span and the most favorable attainable aspect ratio—both so that high angles of attack are not necessary and the download required from the front wing can be generated with minimum induced drag. FIGURE [221] shows what can be achieved here.

HOW MUCH OF IT THERE WAS (OR IS)

In the early days of ground effects we saw some pretty impressive claims about the amounts of download generated—2 tons and up, at 175 mph. At the risk of having my historic RACECAR pit pass holder ripped off my belt and broken across someone's knee, my Aussie slouch hat hung from a flagpole and my presence drummed out of the paddocks of the world, I will state heresy one more time: It is my belief that the ground effects vehicle, even when skirts were legal, never delivered anywhere near as much download as people thought it did, and that a significant part of the performance increase actually came from a dramatic reduction in aerodynamic drag.

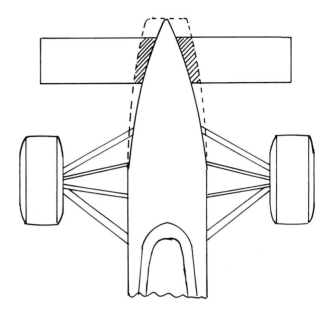

Figure (221): Gain in wing area by narrowing nose.

Figure (220A): Front wing at efficient angle of attack. No flow separation. Clean, high-energy air entering ground effect tunnel and radiator duct.

Figure (220B): Front wing stalled. Turbulent, "low-energy" air entering ground effect tunnel and radiator air duct to detriment of download, drag and cooling.

I have no way of proving my claim (although I seriously doubt that anyone is going to claim that the ground effects tunnels of the all-conquering Ralt Atlantic, Super Vee and/or Formula Three cars are particularly well designed). I can quote a couple of instances. I have never conducted a back-to-back test with and without tunnels, but a back-to-back at Mid-Ohio with and without fixed Atlantic legal skirts resulted in a lap time difference of just under one second. I know of one very good driver who accidentally removed a skirt while testing at Sears Point and neither the driver nor the stopwatch noticed it. Further, if the tunnels generate so much download, why did the Formula One cars run such enormous amounts of wing during the entire ground effects era? Still further, if they were cornering at the higher quoted "g" figures, why did the lap times not reflect the cornering (and resulting straight entry) speeds?

I think that a lot of people got carried away with the romance and glory of test figures—and a lot of other people lied. Real life very seldom reflects any very accurate relationship with experimental figures. In this instance, forgetting about wind tunnel figures which, until a couple of years ago, long after the departure of the skirts, were REALLY suspect, most of the actual test data was recorded at road speeds around 100 mph and then interpolated to the higher speeds. This doesn't work because, although download (and drag) both increase as the square function of road speed, it appears that leakage increases and efficiency DECREASES, if not at the same rate, at least at a rate that is considerably above linear.

Further, even if a road-racing car should develop literally TONS of download at its top speed, it spends a precious small percentage of its total lap time at anything that approaches that speed. The very fastest lap speed AVERAGES in Formula One are around the 140 mph mark. This means that the average speed of the corners is far below that level. The square function of road speed versus download tells us that, at the cornering speeds where it really counts, the download is a hell of a lot less than the quoted figures.

Champ cars are a different case in point, at least on the ovals. Their average ground speed is such that the tunnels DO contribute enormous amounts of download. And that, of course, is why their setup is so critical and why so few teams succeed in getting their cars to work properly. I note that on the road courses the best teams run all the wing that they can find. IMSA GT/GTP cars are so slow compared to what they should be doing that I can't figure out ANYTHING that is happening there. I have no current experience at all with World Manufacturers Championship cars.

It would be fun as well as instructive to optimize a car in both configurations (with and without tunnels) and then to do a real comparison. It would also be both expensive and academic. There is no doubt in my mind that any given car will be faster with effective ground effects tunnels so, as long as the regulations permit, we are all going to run tunnels. Period. The idea is to concentrate our already severely limited development money on improving what we have.

In closing this section I will publicly state what I have been trying to tell the sanctioning bodies for years: It is fruitless to attempt to measure skirt height referenced to the ground. To be either meaningful or practical the height of the skirts or "coachwork" must be referenced to the bottom of the primary structure of the car. And the tunnels themselves should have about 250 lb of sandbags evenly distributed along each of their lengths whenever the measurement is taken. With gas shocks we can't even get our ride height to repeat to within ⅛'' of any specified dimension—the diameters of individual tires vary by ¼'' or so; the tires grow when they are hot (or overinflated); the scrutineers never seem to be able to find a level surface; and the whole procedure is a great waste of time that serves no purpose other than to fray the patience of the competent. If the rule were to read that no portion of the vehicle's coachwork could extend below a plane some dimension ABOVE the plane of the bottom of the major chassis structure—defined as to location and area—then any idiot in the world could instantly define the legality of the car. More and more of the sanctioning bodies are seeing the sense of this. I would also point out that if the dimension above the bottom of the chassis were to be made something in the neighborhood of 2.0'' or more, the question of skirts would become largely academic with no adverse effects on the quality of the racing. Further, since the seal between the tunnels and the ground would then be very ineffective, no matter what the ride rate, the horrifying effects of getting too far sideways would largely be negated, even at champ car speeds. The tunnels would still generate enough download that no one would be tempted to remove them and go back to the old wheel tangling configuration, but they would not generate great gobs of it—and a return to rational ride rates and better low speed corner behavior would be the inevitable result. Further, since the penalty for getting a little too far sideways would be a lot less severe, racing would become not only safer for the participants but more spectacular (or less boring) for the viewer.

It is pretty obvious that NONE of the sanctioning bodies have the technical expertise necessary to write rational racing regulations (and/or driver qualification requirements) in this day and age—although CART certainly comes close. I think that the rules for ANY series of races should be arrived at by locking ALL of the designers and engine builders involved, along with a representative selection of the more technically inclined drivers, car owners and chief mechanics into a room with bathroom facilities, sending food in at intervals and refusing to allow ANYONE to come out until a set of regulations had been agreed upon. This is pretty close to what CART does, but the designers are not included. They should be. There is NO ONE ELSE technically qualified to do the job.

A RETURN TO THE RELATIVE SANITY OF BODY SHAPE AND WINGS

I said most of what I had to say about drag and wings in TUNE TO WIN. I have, however, learned a couple of things in the ensuing years.

THE SHAPE OF THE NOSE

The most efficient nose cross-sectional shape for the open-wheeled racing car is flat on the bottom with sharp corners to vertical sides and a completely rounded top. If this sounds a lot like a current Ralt or Brabham or McLaren or Ferrari or March, then it just goes to show you that all good development roads lead inevitably to the same point.

THE FRONT WINGS

Our front wings operate in ground effects at all times. The basic problem with the front wing is that ground effects shearing forces are very liable to cause separation of flow on the undersurface of the wing at relatively low angles of attack. This separation may not cause a decrease in the amount of download generated. Let's face it, even after a wing is fully stalled it will continue to generate download (somewhat less, but still lots of it). The basic problem with the stalled airplane wing is not just loss of lift but so great an increase in drag after the stall that the lift still being generated by the wing can no longer support the aircraft. With the racing car, a partial stall of the front wing may not even be noticed unless someone marks streamlines on the undersurface; but the additional drag and turbulent wake will for sure slow the car. There are several ways to alleviate the problem. They all have to do with working the bottom surface of the wing less hard.

(1) The best way is to have Bernard Pershing design a wing configuration that will function well in ground effect and to design the nose of the car so that the wing has the maximum possible effective span—as shown by FIGURE [221].

(2) The next best thing is to install a small (³⁄₁₆'') Gurney on the upper surface at the rear of your current wings. As shown by FIGURE [222], this will create a low pressure area and encourage the flow on the lower surface to remain attached. The cost in drag will be negligible and you will be able to generate the same download at a lesser angle of attack.

Figure (222): "Gurney" added to upper surface of wing trailing edge to delay separation.

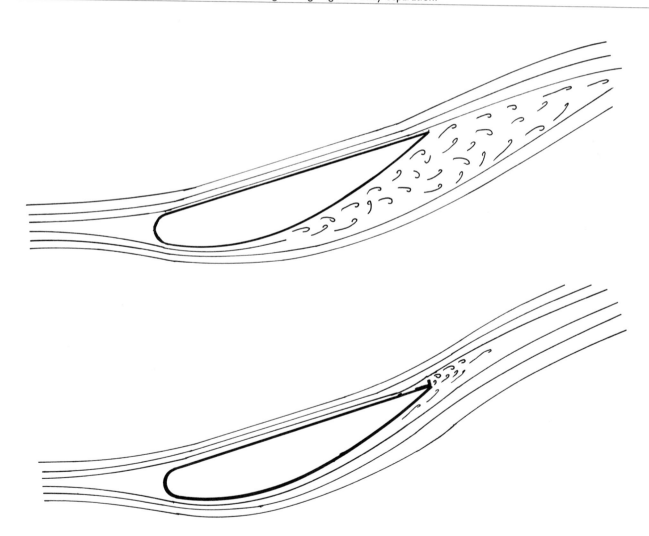

241

Figure (223): Front wing extension.

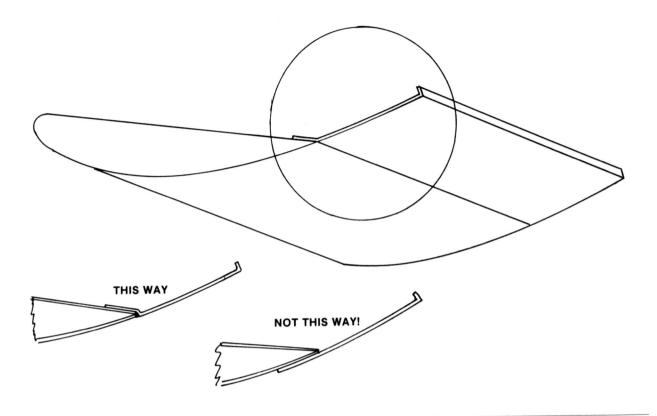

THIS WAY

NOT THIS WAY!

Figure (224): Vortex generators mounted on underside of front wing to delay separation.

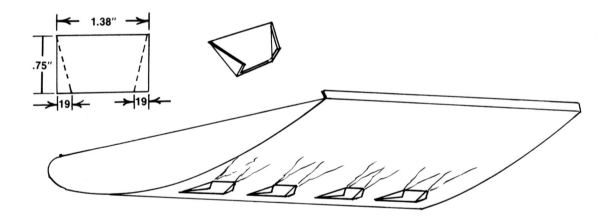

(3) If you still need more front download, make an extension for your current wing as shown by FIGURE [223]. Note that the extension must continue the curve of the UNDERSIDE of the wing and that the underside must remain a smooth and unbroken curve. This will both increase the chord of your wings and allow you to run them slightly nose up so as to reduce the relative work required of the lower surface.

(4) If you are still experiencing separation at the level of download that you need, try installing vortex generators (see FIGURE [224]) on the underside of your wing. They will generate controlled local turbulence and delay the onset of separation. You may feel that these devices are crude and unprofessional. I suggest that you take a good look at the upper surfaces of the wings of the next commercial airliner you board. The little vanes jutting vertically from the upper wing surface at about 25% of chord width are vortex generators. Even the big boys can't design three-dimensional airfoils to perfection.

(5) My personal preference for front wings (on road courses) is a dual-element wing. The configuration depends on whether we are talking about a ground effect car or a conventional car. With the conventional car I prefer a Fowler flap and with the ground effect car I prefer a dual-element wing with the main plane at zero angle and the secondary wing placed at a low angle of attack but with relatively large vertical separation from the main plane—all in the interest of avoiding separation.

THE REAR WING— THE DUAL-ELEMENT WING VERSUS THE SINGLE-ELEMENT WING

I am frequently asked whether I prefer dual-element or single-element wings. What we call the dual-element or the multi-element wing is nothing more than what the aircraft people term a slotted flap wing. THEY use slotted flaps to generate large amounts of lift at relatively low speeds and very high angles of attack (as in during take off and landing)—at some considerable cost in drag. So do WE—although WE have to be a bit more careful about drag than THEY do. THEIR big worry about drag comes after take-off and THEY retract the flaps before drag becomes a problem. We would if we were allowed to—we are not allowed to—so we reduce our drag by never running the main planes of our wings at high angles of attack.

Anyway, my answer to the original question is YES. It is another case of different horses for different courses. If all of the corners are going to be about the same speed—and very fast when compared with the straights (as in oval track), then we are in a situation very similar to that of the modern aircraft at cruising speed and altitude. Since the high coefficient of lift offered by the dual-element wing is not needed, it seems obvious to me (and to the fluid mechanics) that the most efficient setup will be a properly designed single-element wing. On the average road-racing circuit, on the other hand, we are in the landing/take off situation where we need all of the low- and medium-speed

download that we can get and a good dual-element wing is the answer despite the induced drag penalty. On the slower street courses it seems very probable that triple-element wings or even quadruple would be faster yet. In this case it seems probable that, the more engine power that is available, the more elements could be efficiently used.

In any case, the trick is always to balance the car and then add download until the download slows the lap times, then back off a bit. As I explained in TUNE TO WIN, corner exit speed is always more important than ultimate straight-away speed. I have never won a race by going faster than the others in a straight line. Cars for which I was responsible have won both Le Mans and Daytona, the two longest straights in the world.

SLOT-GAP GEOMETRY OF THE DUAL-ELEMENT WING

In TUNE TO WIN I explained the importance of slot-gap geometry in the dual-element wing. There are, of course, two distinct types of multi-element wings: the Fowler flap and the venetian blind flap are illustrated by FIGURE [225]. There doesn't seem to be any general consensus as to which is more efficient—either for aircraft or for racing. I must say, though, when we are talking about

Figure (225): Various flap configurations.

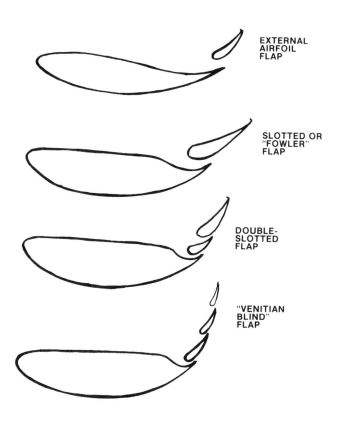

EXTERNAL AIRFOIL FLAP

SLOTTED OR "FOWLER" FLAP

DOUBLE-SLOTTED FLAP

"VENITIAN BLIND" FLAP

243

DUAL-element wings, it would be very unusual to see anything other than a Fowler type on a modern aircraft, and both Pershing and Liebeck use Fowler flaps exclusively.

The multiple venetian blind may be a different case in point. In any case it pays to play with the gap. What happens here, as illustrated by FIGURE [226], is that by moving the flap in the fore and aft sense with respect to the main plane and/or by changing the gap dimension (and in the case of the Fowler flap, by changing the geometry of the slot) between the flap and the main plane, we can regulate both the mass of air that passes through the gap and the amount that this air is accelerated. I do it by asking Bernard Pershing and then playing with poster paint, kerosene streamlines and segment times. On the average track the optimum gap for the Ralt wing works out to about $\frac{7}{16}$''.

WING CONSTRUCTION

Several of the fabricators who specialize in the manufacture of racing car wings, rightly feeling that the riveted-together trailing edge both looks bad and tends to vibrate the rivets loose, have begun to fold the trailing edge over and to join the fold with epoxy adhesives, as in example B in FIGURE [227].

This would be just fine if the surface were joggled first, as shown in example D, and the inevitable join line were filled with Bondo or epoxy.

Unfortunately this is seldom the case. What we usually see is a blunt step on the critical undersurface of the wing, as in example A. While the fabricators may tell you that this makes no difference, they will be WRONG! What happens is that the boundary layer separates at the step, generating drag and costing download. FIGURE [228] is a photo of the streamlines on the underside of just such a wing. Note that the boundary layer actually REVERSES at the step in the skin. SHUCKS! Note also that a full 10% of the undersurface of the wing is doing no work at all, simply because of the wake generated by the un-faired-in mounting post. SHUCKS AND SHUCKS. It is my firm conviction that none of us (the racers, that is) are capable of designing wing profiles for racing use and that we had best leave the field to those few souls who are so qualified.

Figure (227): Alternate techniques for joining trailing edges of sheet metal wings.

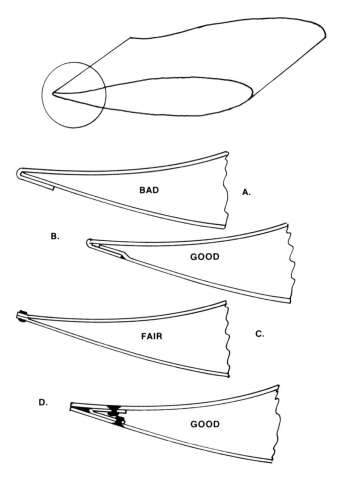

Figure (226): Slot geometry of well-designed Fowler flap. Note that shape of throat remains constant as flap angle is changed.

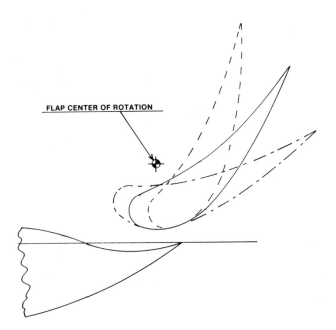

FLAP CENTER OF ROTATION

DEVELOPMENT

I am often informed that there is nothing further to be gained from the detail design of wings. I can't believe that people really think that! What they are actually saying is that our current wings generate as much download as we are able to utilize. I agree—but I only agree at very high road speeds. I have NEVER had a car with what I considered to be sufficient download at relatively low road speeds—first, second and third gear corners (five-speed box). Top end DOWNLOAD is not the problem. The twin problems are too much top end drag and not enough low end and mid-speed download. Intelligent and innovative wing and wing end plate design can achieve notable improvements in both. The basic idea, according to Bernard Pershing, is this:

The race car wing is a three-dimensional aerodynamic device. The airfoil is a two-dimensional aerodynamic device. Therefore the search for a "trick" airfoil will not be as fruitful as the design of an integrated wing/end plate system with design features to reduce drag at a given download.

What follows (FIGURE [229]) are the actual test results and segment times from a back-to-back test of the standard Ralt RT-1 wing and end plate mounting system with a Pershing dual-element wing and three-dimensional end plate mounting system. The test was conducted at Willow Springs; the driver was completely familiar with both the track and the car. The aerodynamics were first optimized (on other tires) with the standard Ralt wing. Each run consisted of 5 laps. No changes were made other than substitution and adjustment of the rear wing. The recorded lap and segment times are averages with any abnormally high or low times discarded. The day stayed constant and the tires, if anything, deteriorated.

Figure (228): Flow reversal on underside of unstalled wing due to blunt lap of trailing-edge fold. Note wake of unfaired mounting tube.

You will note that, since the results were both more clear cut and better than had been anticipated, we went back to baseline just to be sure. It is really easy in this business to fall victim to a couple of Murphy's laws of research: "Enough research will tend to support your theory" and, "If enough data is collected, any conclusion may be proven by statistical analysis."

An appraisal of the results reveals several things:

(1) Something improved markedly because the lap times improved significantly.

(2) That the Pershing wing resulted in a reduction of drag for the same amount of high speed download (as indicated by the driver feel of car balance and by turn 9 exit rpm) is indicated by the improvement in trap times 1 and 6.

(3) That low-speed download may have been improved is indicated by the improvement of trap times 4 and 5.

(4) In the evaluation of drag, driver readings of engine rpm are right next door to useless simply because our tachs cannot be read accurately enough to detect the small changes in top end speed that result from relatively small changes in drag coefficient. Straight-line trap times tell the story. I have always felt that a tachometer could be built that would operate like an aircraft altimeter with the inside pointer indicating 1000's of rpm and the outside indicating 100's (see FIGURE [230]). This would be useless for racing, but great for testing.

(5) Our wing systems are not as good as we think they are. Ralt is still using the identical wing, although it is now center post mounted. It is a damned good wing, but it can be improved upon.

Ok, but you can't afford Pershing and/or can't afford to build a new wing. This I can relate to. But anyone can afford to experiment with the slot gap between the main plane and the flap. And anyone can afford to radius the leading edge of his end plates. And anyone can afford to mount his Gurneys on top of the wing rather than underneath where they do almost as much harm as good. The list goes on.

The same year that we did the wing comparison we did some nose work on the RT-1 and picked a solid and repeatable 0.25 seconds down the Riverside long course straight, at virtually NO COST. Anyone can do this sort of thing. Very few do. It has to do with the importance of seemingly insignificant increments of lap time as discussed in TUNE TO WIN.

I am reminded, constantly, of the probably apocryphal story of why British aircraft of the pre-Mitchell (the designer of the Supermarine racers and the Spitfire) era were, from the drag point of view, aerodynamic disasters. It seems that the standards of engineering practice at the time were set by British Railroads. According to the younger engineers the opinion prevalent in the upper echelons of the aircraft industry was something like, "Streamlining cannot be very important. If it were, British Railroads would pay more attention to it."

Figure (229): Test results: Willow Springs 3-6-81, Berg, Ralt RT-1 wing/side plate comparison Ralt versus Pershing. Temperature—75 degrees F. Wind—none.

CONFIGURATION	LAP TIME	TRAP #1	TRAP #2	TRAP #3	TRAP #4	TRAP #5	TRAP #6	RPM BRAKE POINT FOR TURN 1	RPM TURN 8 ENTRANCE / EXIT	RPM TURN 9 ENTRANCE / EXIT	AERODYNAMIC BALANCE
RUN #1. RALT R WING AT OPTIMIZED FLAP ANGLE + SLOT GEOMETRY	1:20^58	12.28	12.78	15.62	10.31	12.88	16.61	9000+	8700/9000	9050/8500	PERFECT
PERSHING R WING-MAIN PLANE @ DESIGN, FLAP @ 30°	1:20^71	12.27	12.86	15.71	10.32	12.91	16.64	9000+	8700/9000	9000/8500	PRONOUNCED UNDERSTEER
PERSHING R WING-FLAP @ 25°	1:20^30	12.19	12.75	15.62	10.33	12.87	16.58	9000+	8700/9000	9000/8500	MILD UNDERSTEER
PERSHING R WING-FLAP @ 20°	1:19^85	12.08	12.68	15.60	10.26	12.84	16.51	9100	8800/9100	9700/8500	PERFECT
BASELINE RALT-AS RUN #1	1:20^94	12.27	12.74	15.68	10.29	12.91	16.58	9000+	8700/9000	9050/8500	PERFECT
RALT WING WITH FLAP	1:21^09	12.51	12.91	15.73	10.34	12.87	16.61	8800	8700/9000	9050/8300	PRONOUNCED OVERSTEER

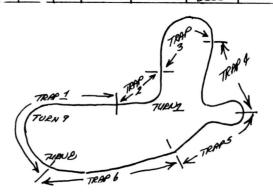

A DEPARTURE FROM OUR NORMAL ARENA

To my way of thinking the best racing in the world takes place on dirt—sprint cars. Because technical innovation is (and damned well should be) actively discouraged, there is no place for me in that world, but I dearly love to watch the sprinters—on dirt only. For some years now most of the sprint car associations have allowed the use of wings. FIGURE [231] shows the state of the art. A glance through the pages of OPEN WHEEL, my third favorite racing magazine (if you are curious, ON TRACK and INDY CAR are numbers one and two and Pete Lyons ties with Denis Jenkinson as my all-time-favorite racing writer), will show you several things:

(1) All of the sprint car people appreciate download and know how to get it.

(2) All of them use enormous and probably very effective flat end plates.

(3) Some of them use some reasonably sophisticated airfoils.

(4) None of them seem to care anything at all about drag.

(5) The first sprint car operation that hires Bernie Pershing—and listens to him—is going to clean house.

Purely as a point of interest, I also enjoy watching top-level motocross and the very top class of road-racing motorcycles. I am afraid that I very much prefer to watch men than machines. I definitely do not agree with Herr Neubauer's statement that restrictive regulations should not be allowed because their adoption would result in Grand Prix racing degenerating into a contest between drivers.

Figure (230): Testing tachometer allows accurate assessment of corner exit speeds. Reads 8380 rpm.

Figure (231): Sprint car wing.

CHAPTER SEVENTEEN

TOOLS & TIPS

POWER TOOLS

You will be buying power tools of one sort or another for the rest of your life. As an example, although I don't do a hell of a lot of work with my hands, I now own one each:

Black and Decker ¼'' angle-drive drill motor
Makita ⅜'' vari-speed drill motor
Makita rechargeable ¼'' drill motor
Black and Decker 12-volt drill motor
Ingersol Rand high-speed pneumatic drill motor
Dayton pneumatic die grinder
Makita 110-volt die grinder
Makita vari-speed 110-volt saber saw
Craftsman 6'' ''Skil'' saw
Makita 4'' 110-volt hand-held grinder
Makita 1'' hand-held 110-volt belt sander
Makita reciprocating/orbital finishing sander
Makita 110-volt sheet metal shear (useless)
Black and Decker 110-volt sheet metal nibbler
Chicago Pneumatic rivet bucking set
USM pneumatic blind rivet gun
Snap-On ⅜'' drive air ratchet

I don't do much work with my hands; I have all of the above, they are all in perfect working order—and I want more. I want a good pair of electric sheet metal shears to replace the nibbler and the Makita shear; I want a small bench belt/disc sander; I want one of Aircraft Spruce's hand-operated hydraulic blind-rivet pullers—and the list goes on. I assume that it will stop when I do.

I once felt that one should buy the best tools available for use at home or in the shop but take only real cheapies on the road. I have changed my mind, first, because I truly dislike working with inferior tools and, second, because not much seems to take wing and fly away anymore. I came up with a very convincing third reason a couple of years ago when the back of the pressure chamber of a cheapy (Rodac) pneumatic blind-rivet puller that Bob Earl was using fractured and put a large dent in a corrugated steel wall about an inch from Bob's ear.

Anyway, I now recommend buying only the very best tools that you can afford. You will never regret it. I used to believe that Bosch made the best electric power tools in the world and that they were worth every cent of their admittedly exorbitant price. I felt the same way about Ingersol Rand and Chicago Pneumatic in air tools. Although I am willing to admit that both Sioux and Dayton make excellent products.

Nothing has changed my mind when it comes to wind power, but there is good news in the world of electric hand tools. The Japanese have arrived. Just as with rational sized automobiles and with machine tools, the design, quality and quality control of their BEST tools are outstanding. To no one's surprise the value per dollar makes everything else on the market look a bit silly. The name to remember is Makita. With some exceptions, which I am about to list, I believe that, for our use, their tools are every bit as good as Bosch—at a fraction of the price. They are marketing through a strange combination of industrial supply houses, discount shops and Snap-On dealers. Availability is reasonable and the warranty and service are apparently pretty good. They have the only cordless tools that I have ever seen that are worth owning. Although they are virtually unknown in the racing/aircraft or automotive service industries, they are very big in the building trades and among the very fussy craftsmen who specialize in the construction and repair of wooden boats (now THERE is a true lunatic fringe group!). It is interesting to note that after a century of key-operated Jacobs-type chucks, it took the Japanese to figure out that you snap the chuck key into a recess cast into the drill motor when you are done with it, sort of like the change purse built into Hondas.

There are a couple of clouds in this paradise: The chucks on Makita drill motors, although they are marked ''Jacobs,'' are so soft as to be useless and must be replaced with real units very soon after purchase. Their electric ''beverly shear'' hardly works at all—but then, neither does anyone else's. The only sort of hand-operated power shear that I have ever seen that WORKS is configured like a pair of shears with a moving blade between two stationary blades—it is magic and I am going to get me one.

Anyway, SOME power tools are indispensable. These include, but are not limited to:

A GOOD 110 volt ⅜'' vari-speed drill motor. It must be capable of 2000 rpm or it won't do a good job of what we use it for the most—drilling holes in thin sheet metal.

A GOOD electric die grinder, capable of 20,000 rpm with sufficient torque to remove some metal. This pretty much limits the selection to Makita and Bosch. Electric is a hell of a lot more convenient than air simply because we can ALWAYS find 110 volts somewhere. A die grinder with a reasonable selection of CARBIDE burrs, sanding drums, abrasive cutting wheels (no more than 0.060'' thick) and SAFETY GLASSES will get you out of more trouble than you ever thought that you could get into. The miniradiac wheel is also perfect for cutting braided hose.

A ⅜'' drive pneumatic ratchet wrench. I am the only road racer I know of who even owns one. On the other hand, every street car and/or industrial mechanic uses nothing else (they are a great way to beat the flat rate book) and off-road and stock car mechanics follow suit. Some years ago I took the time to get used to using the thing and I use it a lot, but very selectively. The ratchet feature allows me to break nuts loose and to finally tighten them by hand while taking advantage of the speed and ease of the power drive to spin them on and off. I have my clutch set at 15 lb/ft of torque so that nothing can be accidentally overtightened. The road racers may laugh, but they have never seen the men of NASCAR at work. I have—and I was impressed.

THE BAND SAW

Legend has it that a band saw is an absolute necessity for the manufacture of race car parts. I disagree—strongly. I have never owned a band saw, nor do I wish to. For most of what I do, 0.063'' is as heavy as sheet metal ever gets and good snips will handle that very nicely. Admittedly I do own an electric shear and a nibbler with which I rough cut my sheet metal. More to the point, I also own a GOOD saber saw which allows me to make hammer forms, cut up to ¼'' plate and in general wreak whatever minor havoc that may be required. My whole philosophy is that I do not want to own anything that will not fit into the back of my Honda, nor will I allow my racing possessions to become so numerous that they will not ALL fit into the small trailer that I share with my son's Sprint kart. Overheads are not my thing. Like all gypsies, mobility is. I buy the best saber saw blades that I can find and I use the correct blade for what I am cutting. I cut my tubing with a hacksaw—and the proper blade.

THE WORK BENCH

For some years after Black and Decker introduced their Workmate portable folding workbench I refused to buy one on the premise that nothing that cheap could be any good. I was wrong. I cannot believe that I got through 45 years without one. At the moment I almost refuse to leave the house without the thing. To go with it I mounted a good 4'' Wilton vise on a length of 2''×6'' which clamps on the Workmate. With my collection of electric tools and a generator I have a portable shop that fits into my space requirements. Thank you, Black and Decker.

POWER FOR THE POWER TOOLS

Most road racing takes place under relatively primitive conditions. Compressed air is usually not available and even 110-volt, 60-cycle power is liable to be a long way from where we are working, AND in short supply. This means that some sort of portable generator is a virtual necessity.

The portable generator should start easily, every time, and keep running without fuss. It should put out the rated current without fluctuation and it should have an automatic load/speed control loop. It should have a fuel capacity large enough to allow it to run for several hours. It should be as light and compact as is consistent with reliability; it should run in the rain; and IT SHOULD NEVER SHOCK ME. It should give no trouble whatsoever, but if it should (you take things to a racetrack and they stop working—it is a form of magic), then parts and service should be available nationwide. I have used every brand of portable generator known to man. It is my conviction that Honda makes portable generators and everyone else makes toys. God (and my family) knows that I have nothing against toys—but I prefer to make my living with TOOLS.

THE AIR COMPRESSOR

Portable air compressors must meet the same criteria as generators. I buy mine from Grainger. They are cheap and they work just fine. So that I don't have to pay for and lug around a monster generator AND so that I can hook the compressor into the track's 110 line when it is available, I favor relatively small compressors with capacitor-start motors hooked up to large tanks—we don't use a hell of a lot of air at the track anyway.

TO BUILD IN
OR NOT TO BUILD IN

I do not believe in either buying my trailers with generators and compressors or in building them into the transporter, for a couple of reasons. The first reason is that, at those tracks where garage space IS available, I want my compressed air in the garage, not in the trailer. My second reason is that it is almost impossible to perform even the most routine service on built-in units (like changing the oil or blowing down the compressor to get rid of moisture). So the oil never gets changed, the belts get loose and the units generally get filled up with grundge until such time as one or the other stops working (at a time and in a place selected by Mr. Murphy). We are then faced with the need to perform major surgery on a filthy unit which is totally inaccessible. I don't want to know about any part of that scene. I simply stick both units under the workbench with their own little chocks and tie-downs and take them out when we get there. Both units are on wheels; they require no more space than the built-ins and, while they do not look as elegant, they work where I need them—and all the time.

I do provide the trailer with an external plug for either the generator or someone else's 110, and I carry two 50-foot, 12-gauge extension cords for the same reason: I want power where I am working.

SOURCES

The top of Sears' line of power tools is very good indeed, and the guarantee is iron clad and nationwide. They have frequent sales, at about 25% off. Most of the stuff that they put on sale, however, is the bottom of their line and not worth having. What Sears does not advertise, however, is their repossessed and reconditioned tools. If you cultivate a salesman in your nearest big Sears tool department you will find out in advance about their sales AND where and when they are going to unload the repos and the reconditioned stuff—50% is not uncommon and the tools are almost always guaranteed.

Swap meets are an excellent source of tools at the right price, if your conscience is such that you don't worry too much about the origin of the goods. Me, I don't like the idea of receiving stolen goods—at all—AND I don't enjoy the ambience of swap meets. The same pretty much holds true of the strangers who wander around selling tools from car trunks. There are, of course, any number of legitimate small businessmen who go from shop to shop selling legitimate merchandise from their cars at very attractive prices—them, I patronize.

The discount tool stores stock an amazing amount of Taiwanese trash. I have never figured out who is gullible enough to buy the junk. In my experience, the discount stores, unlike surplus and salvage stores, are a waste of time.

The REAL tool and supply houses (i.e., those who supply the trades) will usually discount even the best tools up to about 20% if they are convinced that you are a pro. It usually doesn't take a lot to convince them.

TIPS
METAL WORKING NO-NO'S

A dismayingly large percentage of the foul-ups that I see in metal work are repeats—a whole bunch of separate people making the same mistakes over and over. The mistakes fall into two basic classifications:

(1) Use of the wrong material(s). I sincerely hope that the first section of this book has gone a long way toward preventing this one.

(2) Use of the wrong or improper technique(s) in design, fabrication, welding and/or machining, which we we will now address.

The mistakes that I see ALL THE TIME include:

FABRICATION

SCRIBING A BEND LINE ON SHEET METAL: Scribed lines are meant to be cut, not bent or folded. If you scribe a bend line on any material known to man, you have just created a monstrous stress raiser and the material will fail from fatigue along the scribed line long before its time is due. You will notice that I did not say that the metal MAY fail early; I stated that it WILL fail early. We used to mark bend lines with soapstone, or with a pencil line on a strip of masking tape (never with a pencil line directly onto metal). I now use a felt pen for the simple reason that I always have one in my pocket—and the mark comes off with thinner.

CUTTING TO AN INSIDE CORNER IN SHEET METAL: This is a continuation of the story begun above. All inside corners MUST begin with a round hole punched or drilled (and deburred) in the appropriate location. The metal is then cut TO the hole—not through it. Snip tracks continued beyond corners are one of the all-time-great stress raisers. See FIGURE [232].

BENDING SHEET METAL TOO SHARPLY: The usual culprit here is the standard, everyday sheet metal leaf brake which all of us use to bend sheet metal. As nearly as I can figure out the device was designed to be used in heating/air conditioning work where the standard material is very thin, annealed and galvanized low-carbon steel sheet—which requires no bend radius at all. Consequently the leaf brake, as purchased, features a knife-edged hold down finger. In OUR world, every piece of metal that we bend requires a minimum bend radius of its own thickness. What actually happens here is that, any time that we bend metal we are purposely producing plastic deformation; the material on the inside of the bend is compressed while that on the outside is stretched. The smaller the radius for a given thickness of material and degree of bend, the less compression takes place on the inside surface of the metal and the MORE stretching occurs on the outside. Refer to FIGURE [233A]; with a zero radius, NO compression takes place and the only strain involved is stretching of the outside fibers. It doesn't take a PhD in strength of materials to figure out that this is an unhealthy state of affairs.

FIGURE [233B] lists the minimum recommended radii for most of the metals that we work with; we depart from these recommendations at our peril. The easy way to get

Figure (232): Cutting sheet metal to an inside corner.

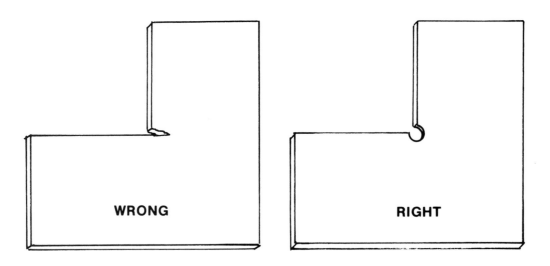

WRONG

RIGHT

Figure (233A): Bend radius = material thickness. Plastic deformation combines elongation and compression and is spread over much larger area.

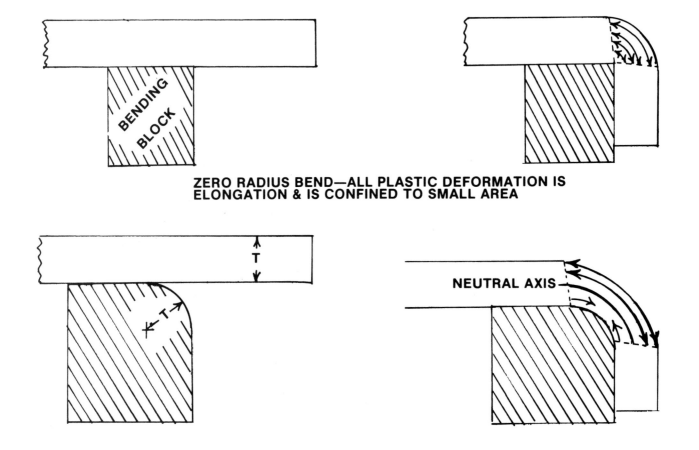

BENDING BLOCK

ZERO RADIUS BEND—ALL PLASTIC DEFORMATION IS
ELONGATION & IS CONFINED TO SMALL AREA

T

T

NEUTRAL AXIS

around this little problem is to grind (or have ground) a 0.06'' radius on the hold down finger of your brake AND to make up a series of radius dies of various thicknesses— and to kill the first man that you find not using them. You can make suitable radius dies either by bending sheet metal shims of various thicknesses or by welding a suitable diameter round bar or rod to a "hold down bar." Both methods are shown in FIGURE [234]. In either case the setback of the hold down bar of the brake must be adjusted before the radius device is used.

SHEET METAL, VOLUME ONE from the Experimental Aircraft Association will tell you all that you ever need to know about bending sheet metal. Pazmany adds several GOOD tips in his books. I am not about to duplicate their efforts. The March 1984 issue of SPORT AVIATION covers about all that any of us need to know about bending sheet metal, and has a good article about wingtip modifications for the reduction of drag.

BENDING SHEET METAL PARALLEL TO THE GRAIN: Whenever possible, sheet metal parts should be bent across the natural grain of the material. This is not always possible. When bends must be formed in the same sheet at right angles to each other, try to orient the part so that all of the bends are at 45 degrees to the grain. When you MUST bend parallel to the grain, double the bend radius.

DRILLING OVERSIZED AND NONROUND RIVET HOLES: Rivets, either blind or solid, should be a loose fit in their holes, but only by a few thousandths of an inch. This is why we use a #30 drill bit (0.1285'') to form the hole for a ⅛'' (0.125'') rivet and a #10 bit (0.193'') for a ³⁄₁₆'' rivet, etc. The holes should also be perfectly aligned, and they MUST be deburred. Depending on your rivets to swell sufficiently to fill oversized holes is asking too much.

Figure (234): Radius shims and bars for sheet metal brakes.

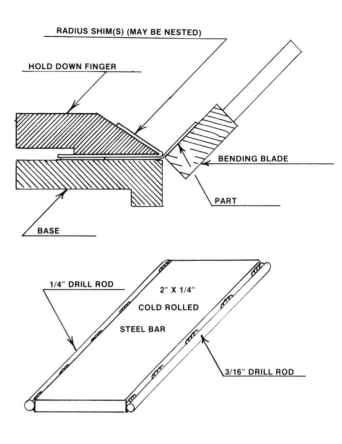

Figure (233B): Approximate minimum bend radii for 90 degree cold bend in aluminum and steel sheet.

	Alloy	Temper	.032	.063	.125	.188	.250
	3003	H14	1t	1t	1t	1t	1t
	5052	H32	1t	1t	1t	1t	1½t
	5052	H34	1t	1t	1½t	2t	3t
ALUMINUM ALLOYS	2024	T3	4t	5t	6t	Forget it	
		T4	4t	5t	6t	Forget it	
	6061	T4	1t	1½t	2t	3t	4t
		T6	1½t	2t	3t	4t	4t
	7075	T6	5t	6t	7t	Forget it	
STEEL	1010/1020	Cold Rolled	1t	1t	1t	1t	1t
	E4130	Normalized	3t	3t	3t	4t	4t

minimum radius in terms of thickness (t) for indicated sheet thickness

DRILLING OVERSIZED AND/OR NONROUND BOLT HOLES: Oversized bolt holes mean loose bolts. It is that simple. Bolt holes, as I have said many times before (and will continue to say until I die) should be drilled $\frac{1}{64}$'' undersize and reamed to the finished dimension.

MACHINING

LEAVING SHARP CORNERS AND/OR NOTCHES ON MACHINED PARTS: This can be a matter of ignorance: "What difference can a sharp OUTSIDE corner make?" (refer back to FIGURE [138] and to the section dealing with heat treating quench cracks). Or it can be a matter of laziness or cost cutting. Every machine drawing must, as a matter of course, include a specific radius callout for EVERY inside corner and/or section change and should include those familiar words, "break all sharp edges." Everyone involved should form the habit of breaking those edges. This is an excellent job for relatively unskilled labor.

WELDING

FAILING TO PROPERLY PREPARE PARTS FOR WELDING: If all rust and scale are not removed from metal before it is welded, the zone of fusion is going to be contaminated, whether or not the actual welding process is protected by a shield of inert gas.

FAILING TO "VEE OUT" HEAVY SECTIONS PRIOR TO WELDING: If parts whose thickness is $\frac{1}{8}$'' or more are not veed out prior to welding, penetration is not going to be complete and the weldment will fail from fatigue before its time.

CREATING TINY LITTLE WELD BEADS: These may be pretty but often have little or no penetration.

UNDERCUTTING THE WELD: This is particularly liable to happen with very thin sections.

USING THE WRONG FILLER MATERIAL: This is particularly popular with 4130.

FAILING TO STRESS RELIEVE 4130 WELDMENTS.

RAPIDLY COOLING HOT FERROUS METAL: The number of broken parts directly traceable to water quenching of recently welded ferrous parts must make Christ weep. The same is true of hot BENT ferrous parts. We can get away with almost anything when we use low-carbon steel, but we cannot get away with water cooling hot parts. Develop some patience: Drink a cup of coffee, go drool over the secretary, go abuse the boss (even if he is me—in fact ESPECIALLY if he is me), but WAIT for the parts to air cool. This is especially true of you good sedan and off-road folks who are in the habit of hot bending steering arms, drag links and the like. Do-it-yourself heat treating ranks right up there with do-it-yourself vasectomies.

PAINTING ON PARTS SUBJECTED TO NON-DESTRUCTIVE TESTING: He who attempts to magnaflux, Zyglo or dye penetrant inspect a painted part is only kidding himself—especially with the flexible urethane and epoxy paints now in common use. Painted parts MUST be stripped before they are inspected. This is particularly true of castings.

DESIGN ERRORS

It is not only the people on the floor who screw up—so do the designers. OUR common errors include (but are not limited to):

Failing to analyze or to appreciate load paths and so designing in offset loads and unintentional couples and/or arranging welds or rivets in tension instead of shear.

Using convenient and cheap joint designs with inadequate fatigue characteristics.

Designing-in stress raisers through inadequate fillet radii and/or extreme section changes.

Machining across grain structures rather than using forgings.

Choosing materials poorly, due to ignorance, laziness or cost cutting.

Failing to call out proper welding filler rods, stress-relief procedures and heat treats.

Failing to shot peen critical components subjected to high levels of cyclic stress.

NOT CHECKING DRAWINGS AND DIMENSIONS THOROUGHLY BEFORE RELEASING THEM TO THE SHOP.

METAL SELECTION

The major culprit here is the indiscriminate use of 4130 chrome moly steel. I have said it before and I will be saying it for as long as I am in racing: 4130 IS NOT A GENERAL-PURPOSE STEEL. It does not forge well and it does not take a good thorough heat treatment in sections thicker than about ¼''. It is meant to be used in tube and sheet form. It should NOT be used for knuckles, axles, drive shafts, spindles or gears. It is also expensive and using it for lowly stressed parts is silly.

METAL WORKING TIPS

DIMPLES: Dimpling dies are expensive to buy and time consuming (although not difficult) to make—so few of us own them. There are a couple of ways to form dimples in light gauge sheet metal without dies. Aircraft Spruce sells a pretty simple dimple roller which works reasonably well on very thin sheet aluminum if you are patient enough. A ball bearing of appropriate size inserted into a punched hole in sheet metal backed up with a shot bag and then walloped with a brass hammer forms an instant dimple for small holes. Larger holes can be gradually dimpled using a rounded rawhide mallet with a shot bag for back up.

SHRINKING/STRETCHING/FLANGING: Most amateur racers form curved flanges in sheet metal by hammering over forms as described in PREPARE TO WIN, simply because most do not own shrinking or stretching equipment. If you are going to do much sheet metal forming, maybe you should. Hand-operated shrinkers/stretchers as illustrated in FIGURE [235] are available at about $80 each or $120 for a combination tool from a number of houses, including U.S. Industrial Tool & Supply. Aircraft Spruce and most houses offering aircraft sheet metal tools offer "fluting pliers" which are really excellent ways to get stretched metal out of the way on flanges.

THE PAINTING OF METAL OBJECTS

There are those who maintain that I have never had a "job" in my life—and, I suppose, that, looked at from a warped point of view, there could be some justification for that statement. Most people seem to feel that one should make one's living doing something that one would rather not do at all—apparently so that one can cultivate expensive hobbies to alleviate the misery of one's work and so that one can look forward to an annual vacation and eventual retirement. This is not quite the way that I see it. The first man that I ever worked for on a full-time basis (I was 14) told and taught me many of the precepts that have shaped my life. One of his statements that I have never forgotten is that the real secret to success in life is to figure out exactly what you WANT to do—and then to devote every minute of your waking life to learning how to do it really well. No matter what you do, if you do it well enough, you will make money. So I will cheerfully admit that, except for one very brief and predictably unsuccessful stint at trying to sell sports cars, I have always managed to be well paid for doing something that I would cheerfully have paid someone to let me do. Of course, since I started with no money at all, I couldn't possibly have afforded to do any of the nutty things that I have done as hobbies—so I had to get good enough at them to get paid for it—or wait until I had earned enough money to afford hobbies. THAT road never much appealed to me.

Anyway, believe it or not, I occasionally do some consulting work for REAL companies. It is always something that I enjoy and learn from and it is always in conjunction with people who are both competent and pleasant. During one of these stints I ran across the world's best paint for metal objects. It seems that the corporation in question had carried out its own aerosol spray paint evaluation, testing every brand and specification of spray can paint that it could find. It turned out that Zynolyte Epoxy Rust Mate by Zynolyte Products, Compton, CA, makes every other aerosol paint on the market—including Rustoleum—look sick. It adheres better than anything else, it resists corrosion better than anything else and it resists chipping better than anything else—and we are talking about a factor of about two. The stuff is available nationwide in a wide variety of colors. It is expensive to buy but worth every penny. From time to time it even appears on "special" at the big paint discount houses like Standard Brands and Homeowner's Emporium. I have stopped using my beloved slime-green zinc chromate on all of the trailer parts, nose frames, antiroll bars, springs and so on because I have at last found a paint in spray cans that sticks on, stays on and doesn't chip. This should go some way toward increasing my personal popularity with both those who pay me and those who work with me—which would definitely be a good thing. I still use chromate on the hidden, unanodized aluminum areas and as a primer for any painted aluminum.

PAINTING THE EXHAUST SYSTEM

The super wealthy may run titanium exhaust systems and those afflicted with turbochargers had better run 321 stainless. Neither stainless nor titanium headers need to be painted, nor should they be. The rest of us run low-carbon-steel exhausts which, unless they are either painted and painted properly or oiled every time the engine is stopped, soon become an unsightly mass of rust. Once upon a time the only exhaust header paint available was VHT by the Sperex Corporation—and it was magic. When it was applied according to the directions on the can it would last a full season with no trouble at all. At present there are at least eight brands of "high-temperature exhaust system paint" on the market in spray cans. Alas, for once they really don't make things like they used to. The fact that the silicone resins used in the manufacture of the stuff now sell for about $35/lb may have something to do with it. Most of the brands of so-called "header paint" that I have tried have been right next door to useless. The best two are VHT and Zynolyte, with VHT ahead. But even VHT doesn't seem to be what it was . . . HOWEVER, there are a few procedures that will help.

First is the simple and inescapable fact that, if success is contemplated, the headers must be sandblasted or bead-blasted before painting. Period. Second is that preheating the headers—to about 400-500 degrees F helps a whole bunch. They can also be baked in a hot oven immediately after painting, but the lady is very liable to object and your food may taste funny for a while. Third is the most ignored rule of painting: MORE IS WORSE. You need only enough to completely cover the surface and impart the color. Fourth, most people paint with the spray nozzle far too close to the work. Follow the directions. Myself, I use a Red Devil spray can handle, spray from 15'' to 18'' away

Figure (235): Sheet metal shrinker and stretcher.

SHRINKER   **STRETCHER**

from the work and use only flat-black on my headers. I chose that color because it is the natural color of the hand-prints that are bound to get on the pipes.

PROTECTING ALUMINUM

The average racing car seems to contain about an acre of sheet aluminum, most of it exposed to view. It can be painted or polished, or, if you are a slob, it can be left to look after itself. I tend to polish the visible bits rather than paint them simply because paint is heavy and, since it has to be touched up frequently in order to look decent, the car tends, like me, to get heavier as it gets older. AND it is difficult to keep a touch-up job looking like anything other than a touch-up job. Polishing is not a lot of fun—but it is easy, costs only time and weighs nothing. The parts that cannot be seen I tend to cover with a very light coat of zinc chromate. I admit that it is a horrible color, but it is the ONLY stuff in a spray can that will really stick and it was designed to do the job. It must meet Mil Spec P-8585A or it is the wrong stuff, regardless of what the counter man says. I buy it in 12 packs from the local general aviation store.

The trick here is to realize that all sheet aluminum has been surface oiled for protection. Unless you get off every bit of the oil, nothing will stick to it except dirt and finger-prints—not even zinc chromate. Wiping the sheet with thinner or solvent simply will not get the job done; it merely dilutes the protective oil and moves it around. There are two choices: buy some ALUMAPREP #33 at about $15/gallon (or METAL PREP #79, which actually etches the surface) or use hot water and a strong solution of good old TIDE, followed by a thorough, cold water rinse. It works just fine. Do not breathe the zinc chromate fumes—and fog-on the lightest coat possible—more just looks worse, weighs more and costs money. The aircraft industry uses a chromate coat so light that it is transparent.

To keep polished aluminum bright, Alodine 1001 from Aircraft Spruce works better than anything else that I have tried. Do not confuse Alodine 1001 with Alodine 1201, which is an excellent prepainting treatment for aluminum.

The relatively small parts—brackets, tanks, links, control arms and the like—that I don't want to keep polished I have anodized in whatever color strikes my fancy at the time.

THE TRIOK

Some truly clever people have come up with the ultimate small sheet metal tool—a combination shear, brake, press brake and roller that is simply the most versatile and useful device I have yet seen. It is even reasonably priced; I am saving my pennies.

I do not see how any serious racing team can afford not to have one of these in the truck/trailer. It's available from Michael Brayton Racing.

PAINTING THE RACE CAR

I strongly prefer to run my fiberglass in its original gel coat. Further I prefer the darker colors, simply because they require a lighter coat of gel coat and therefore the parts don't weigh as much as the lighter colors. I prefer gel coat to paint because it is both a lot lighter (since it is there anyway) and because it is damned near indestructible. Race car fiberglass seldom lasts long enough for the gel coat to fade. If it does, marine stores and swimming pool supply houses sell fiberglass brighteners that work well.

However, there ARE those parts of the car that MUST be painted—and there is also the pitiful prospect of having to touch up the paint after damage, abrasion or stone nicks. This is as it should be, if for no other reason than to discourage people from complex, multicolor paint jobs. I like one color with, if anything, a very little tasteful striping. Be that as it may, the reality of the matter is that a lot of parts have to be painted and a lot of parts have to be touched up—frequently. Since no one in his right mind uses anything but a two-part epoxy paint on race cars (and no, I'm not going to get into THAT because I don't know anything about it), it would seem a bit difficult to obtain and carry touch-up paint around. Not so! Every model airplane store in the country carries PACTRA Formula U Polyurethane Fuel Proof (nitro methane is what we are talking about here) High Gloss Paint in spray cans. The color range is pretty complete. The trick is to have your painter mix the Imron or whatever he is going to use on your jewel to match the PACTRA and—presto—you have spray cans of touch-up paint. It is damned good stuff: chip resistant and, to a degree, even brake-fluid resistant.

I cover the leading edges of the wings, air ducts, noses and so on with one of 3Ms clear vinyl tapes (helicopter tape). While expensive, the tape works wonders for the longevity of the parts, gel coat and paint. Ron Minor's Auto Racing Specialties (651 N 27th Ave., Phoenix, AZ 85009, 602-242-3398) stocks an almost equal clear vinyl tape for $15 per three-inch-wide roll.

CHAPTER EIGHTEEN

BEANCOUNTING FOR THE NON-BEANCOUNTER

"Moneymen are like house cats—they may appear domesticated—but they are NEVER tame" Neville Shute Norway.

"I am the decision maker. YOU are the beancounter. Your job is to keep track of my beans, not to tell me what to do with them!" Mickey Thompson [to his comptroller], circa 1980.

One of the unpleasant realities of life as a racer is the ongoing necessity to keep track of the money, no matter whose it is or how much or little of it there may be.

If you are running your racing operation on your own bucks you are almost certain to be woefully underfinanced. In this case a reasonable prediction of your actual needs, plus a means of keeping track of where it is all going may well prevent (or at least put off) the dreaded "mid-season broke blues."

If, on the other hand you are so fortunate as to be operating on someone else's (including dad's) money, one of the primary requirements in the essential art of keeping the sponsor happy is a regular, organized, concise, accurate and verifiable report of how much money has been spent, where it has both come from and gone to, how much more is required, when and why. It is almost certain that whoever is supplying the funds which allow you to race is very well aware of the true value of a dollar. It is equally probable that he (or she) expects you to take care of the racing monies as if they were your own—which, in a way, they are. Besides, a regular and reasonable accounting will help keep the sponsor's REAL accountants off your back and

will eventually help you (or him, or them—or all of you) to ward off the unwelcome attention of the IRS.

Always remember that in ANY race team/sponsor relationship, somewhere in the corporate offices there lurks a Brutus in a green eyeshade just waiting for the perfect moment to stab you in the back. Corporate accountants (unlike independent accountants) HATE racers—for several reasons. One is that, as a class, they are totally unable to come to terms with what they imagine our sense of values and lifestyle to be. Another is that, for some obscure reason, they all seem to be convinced that we are a group of irresponsible and profligate wastrels whose greatest ambition is to spend vast amounts of precious corporate monies holding unspeakable orgies in exotic locales. Perhaps we should invite the beancounters to a weekend in the rain at Summit Point! A third reason is that these people tend to be very possessive when it comes to corporate funds. When we, the racers, have somehow been granted control over some amount of corporate money but are not subjected to either the corporate accounting procedures or the corporate bureaucracy, the beancounters get paranoid. These people are in daily and (in the business sense of the word) intimate contact with the man who is responsible for your racing destiny. He values their advice. They are constantly doing their level best to shoot you down. You have only three defenses: racing successes, a happy sponsor and good accounting. It will take all three to keep your sponsorship coming.

If, like Mickey Thompson, you have your priorities straight and your beancounters under control you are the master of your own destiny and you may be excused from reading the rest of this chapter. If, like most of us, you are trying to operate on nonexistent, personal funds and/or scarce and skinny chunks of other peoples money and sponsorship, read on.

In the case of the IRS, however, NO ONE has THEM under control—including, it sometimes appears, the executive, legislative or judicial branches of the federal government. If anything, these people view the racers with an even more jaundiced eye than corporate accountants do—and they are apparently fast becoming a law unto themselves. It often seems that they consider the individual or corporation under investigation to be guilty until proven innocent. Should the IRS (or one of its computers) decide to pick either yourself or your sponsor as one of their targets for today, there is going to be trouble. The only person who is going to get you out of the mess is YOU.

There is a popular and charming folktale to the effect that all that one has to do in order to avoid trouble with the IRS is to save all of one's receipts and canceled checks in old shoe boxes. When notified of an investigation, the story goes, one merely walks into the district office of the IRS, dumps the shoeboxes on the desk of the investigating agent and tells HIM to sort them out. After all, we are taxpayers and he is a government employee! While comforting, the folktale is WRONG! It is, in fact, about as wrong as can be. The way that the system works (in fact, if you think about it, the only way that it CAN work) is that the person or corporation responsible for paying the taxes is also responsible for keeping the records AND, no record = no deduction. It is difficult enough to convince these people that you are entitled to deduct all or even a part of your racing expenses when you DO have good and verifiable records. Without them there is NO WAY.

After rereading the above paragraph it dawns upon me that I should make one of my personal positions clear: We have lived, "on the economy," in enough other countries (Australia, England, Italy and Switzerland) to fully realize that, while our government may not be the most efficient imaginable and while our system of personal and corporate taxation may not be the most equitable and efficient that can be conceived (I am a long time advocate of the "flat tax rate"), they are both one hell of a lot better than those of any other nation on earth. The same goes for our civil servants. I vote, and I pay taxes—therefore, I am entitled to bitch. I am human, therefore I DO bitch about the government, the welfare state, taxes and creeping socialism. But I also appreciate that we in the U.S.A. have it better than any nation of people have ever had it—in the history of mankind! I will now climb down off my plastic milk carton (the high-tech racer's replacement for the traditional street-corner orator's soap box) and get on with what you have paid me to write about. The lecture was for free.

The bottom line of this introduction to beancounting is very simple. The first time that the money man, his beancounters, or the IRS want to know where the money went, and you cannot satisfy their curiosity in very short order,

you are going to become very unhappy. Hopefully I can convince you of both the importance and the truth of the foregoing statements before your first auditor does.

SO! You are going to have to do some book keeping, or, if you are very lucky, your lady is going to have to do some. Every REAL RACER views accounting—any form of accounting—with a combination of terror and disdain. Both are born of ignorance. As a matter of fact, so do I—STILL! But I learned a long time ago that keeping the books is an inescapable part of what I really want to do with my life. With a lot of help I have, over the years, developed a bookkeeping system (not an accounting system) that takes very little of my time, is accurate, complete and verifiable. What is more important, it works.

Most accountants do not really like my system very much. It is too simple—and it is not one of the formal ac-

---

Figure (236): Typical chart of racing accounts.

ACCOUNT NUMBER	DESCRIPTION
82-100	Capital expenditures
82-200	Overhead and shop expenses
82-300	Travel
301	Fares
302	Lodging
303	Meals
304	Rent cars and taxis
305	Licenses, permits and tolls
306	Fuel and oil
307	Maintenance of company vehicles
308	Modifications to company vehicles
309	Insurance
82-400	Cost of contract labor and services
82-450	Cost of outside services
82-500	Freight and duties
82-550	Cost of raw materials
82-600	Public relations and entertainment
82-650	Administration and communication expenses
82-700	Miscellaneous and consumable items
82-750	Unclassified expenses
82-800	Direct racing expenses
801	Engine program
802	Final drive
803	Chassis, suspension and tires
804	Body and aerodynamics
805	Brakes
806	Racing fuel oil and additives
807	Paint
808	Track rental
809	Research and development
810	Entry fees
82-900	Income
901	Prize monies
902	Contingency monies
903	Tow/starting monies
904	Sale of goods
905	Miscellaneous income
906	Sponsorship monies

counting methods with which they are familiar. My only answer is that, if I am going to do a proper job of what I am paid to do, I can afford a maximum of about fifteen minutes per day for bookkeeping. I cannot afford an accountant or usually even a secretary. None of the conventional systems meet that basic requirement. Mine does. The Smith system was never meant to be a super trick, double-entry, double-throw-down formal accounting system. It is designed merely to provide a competent (and flexible) accountant/tax person with the raw material, categorized and in rough chronological order, that they need to construct whatever type of more formal documentation may be required. The system also provides a concise and understandable running summary of just where the money is coming from and going to. It does this with about fifteen minutes of extra work per day (extra, that is, over and above the time normally spent writing checks, doing the banking and so on).

THE CHART OF ACCOUNTS

It all begins with a very basic "chart of accounts." The one that I am currently using (for Formula Atlantic) is shown in FIGURE [236]. You may well find that this chart does not completely suit your individual operation. It was never meant to be graven in stone! I change mine around frequently, depending on the size and nature of the operation and upon my latest ideas to simplify things. The chart of accounts is not at all sacred. It merely provides a series of convenient and readily identifiable boxes in which we can segregate our beans for easy translation into tax accounting categories—by a tax person. The chart of accounts also serves as a basis for budget preparation (more about that later).

THE BOOKS

The next step is to obtain a pad of 13-column analysis paper from the local office supply store and to set up however many "daily disbursement" sheets as your chart of accounts requires. A typical sheet is shown in FIGURE [237]. Placed in a three-ring binder (far and away the best are made by Cardinal, the clever people who discovered that if you make the rings D-shaped rather than round the pages lie flat when you open the binder) these sheets form the basis of a very easy and very accurate accounting system.

Figure (237): Daily disbursements sheet.

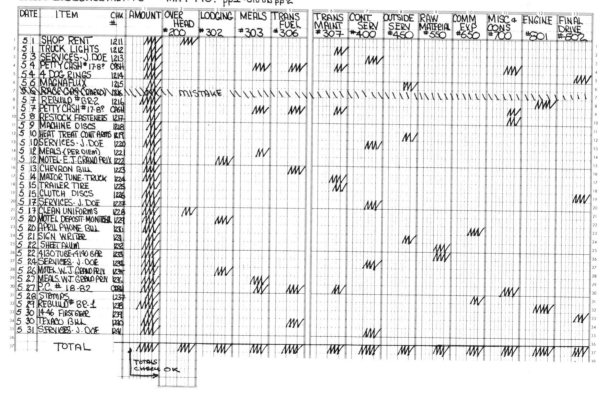

259

Each financial transaction having to do with racing is entered in the left column by date, item, check number and amount. The amount is ALSO entered in the appropriate vertical column (on the same horizontal line). When totaled the expenditures on the page are automatically subtotaled by account number.

The grand total of all of the account number totals should match the total of the "amount" column on the left, give or take a few bucks. I don't much worry about an exact match—the accountants are much better with calculators than I am and they are not going to take my word for it anyway. If things match within about 1% I don't chase the arithmetic. Once you get the system working, virtually every penny that you spend will automatically fall into one of the chart of accounts classifications and will (almost automatically) be entered in the appropriate column of the daily sheets, thus leaving a trail that any accountant in the world can follow. The trick is to discipline yourself to enter each day's transactions into the system EVERY DAY FOR THE REST OF YOUR RACING CAREER.

I total the columns when the page is full or at the end of the month, whichever comes sooner. At the end of the month (or the quarter, depending on the size of the opera-tion and the requirements of the accountants) I transfer the figures to the summary sheet, illustrated by FIGURE [238]. One glance at the summary sheet brings you (or your sponsor) up to date without requiring either of you to know anything about accounting. I submit good photostats of both the daily sheets and the summary to the sponsor and (separately) to his accountants on a monthly basis.

THE COMPUTER AS A RACING BEANCOUNTER

The question of whether a personal computer should be used for all of this stuff is bound to come up. The answer is HELL YES! Anyone who has access to a computer and doesn't use it is wasting the most valuable commodity of all: time. I have all of my accounting information, from budgets to petty cash records, on electronic spread sheets. I usually transfer information to the computer once a week when things aren't particularly busy—more often when they are. So far as what hardware and software to use, I am simply not expert enough to make valid comments. I am most emphatically NOT a computer person. To me, the computer is a tool—nothing more. I neither know nor care how it works.

Figure (238): Financial summary.

I use a KAYPRO II (only because the KAYPRO IV had not been introduced when I bought mine). It is semiportable, reliable, does everything that I presently need to do, has an aluminum case (you will recall that I hate plastic) and is made by friendly people who really seem to care about their customers (and are only 80 miles away). I use WORDSTAR as a word processor, BASIC as a language and am presently using PERFECT CALC as a spread sheet. PERFECT CALC really doesn't suit my needs very well so I will probably change to LOTUS 1-2-3 for accounting. That ends Smith on computers.

RECEIPTS

There is no such thing as too much back-up. Insist on a receipt for everything that you buy. Even if you have to write one yourself on a 3''× 5'' card it will serve as a more-or-less legitimate reminder of the transaction (no one is going to expect you to be perfect—not even the IRS). I keep the receipts in a sturdy envelope until the transactions that they represent have been entered in the daily sheets. I then file them inside manila envelopes which live in a hanging file in the office (or, sometimes, in the trailer). On a less permanent basis I keep the receipts in 5''× 8'' manila envelopes inside an accordion file which travels with me on the road. In any case, the envelopes are identified with the account number, the name of the account and the letter or number of the slot where they are supposed to live. The outside of the accordion file has an index, and there is an index card at the front of the hanging file in the office. Unless I need one as proof of purchase for a warranty claim or as back-up to a question by an accountant, I will probably never see any given receipt again once it enters its envelope. If the accountants insist, I photocopy all of the receipts on a monthly basis and send them on.

THE CHECKING ACCOUNT

It is a good idea to pay as many bills as possible by check rather than with cash. You are automatically provided with a record of the transaction and, even if you should lose both your check ledger and your canceled checks, everything can be reconstructed from the bank's files. We are all aware that keeping track of a checking account can be a major pain. It doesn't have to be that way! There are methods that can render it practically painless.

Step one is to establish a "racing only" checking account. All racing bills will be paid from this account and it will not be used for anything else. Step two is to select the right check and check ledger formats. I use a full-sized, three to a page, business check ledger with integral stubs, large "what for" windows on both the checks and the stubs and self-carboned duplicate deposit slips. I keep the whole thing in a minibriefcase, zip-closed, three-ring binder provided by the bank (if you look through their check ledger catalog thoroughly enough). This thing comes complete with pockets and an attached transparent, heavy plastic envelope which I use to hold the day's receipts until I am ready to enter them. Some of them even have handles. For years I have been going to have a leather one made in Mex-

ico (I am a certified leather freak) but now that devaluation has ended professional motor racing in Mexico for the foreseeable future, I guess that I missed the boat and will have to make do with plastic (I hate plastic—especially vinyl). Anyway, I keep a minicalculator (TI 50, in case anyone is curious) in one of the pockets; resale cards, business cards, 3''× 5'' and 5''× 8'' cards in the other pockets; deposit slips in the back of the book and the checks in the front. The thing is large enough so that I am unlikely to leave it behind as I regularly do my eyeglasses, etc. I am really religious about filling out the "what for" windows on both the checks and the stubs and about keeping an accurate running balance as I write each check.

When the monthly statement arrives I balance the account—i.e., I make sure that my running total agrees with the bank's ending balance—again within a reasonable figure. It almost always does and when it does not I check that the bank statement agrees with the amount for which I wrote each check, that their record of deposits agrees with mine and that their total of the debits and deposits is correct before I go looking for the inevitable mistake in my arithmetic. When I am satisfied that all is well I take a wide-tip highlighting pen and color-in the stub of the last check included in the monthly statement. This gives me a quick indication of where to start next month's arithmetic rework. I do the rechecking simply by starting at the last known good point with a printing calculator and going through the book until I find the mistake. It never takes very long and I always feel really dumb.

I tape each canceled check to its original stub and file them in a separate, standard three-ring check binder. I photocopy the canceled checks and their stubs along with both sides of the monthly statement. The copies go to the accountants and the originals remain with me. Everyone concerned now has readily available (the check number is listed by account number in the daily sheets) proof of payment for virtually every bill.

On the deposit side I fill in the deposit slip in some detail: where the money came from, the check number, the date and anything else that I consider to be pertinent. I tape the actual deposit receipt to the original of the deposit stub and submit the carbons to the accountants. I enter the deposit by date, number and amount on the check stubs.

At the end of the day I enter the day's transactions by check number and account number in the daily sheets. As each transaction is entered I draw a wide, highlight-pen line through the appropriate check number on the stub so that I have a visible indication that the transaction has been properly recorded and I can forget about it. The secret is to do the work on a daily basis (I do it before I go home) and not to succumb to the human temptation to let it slide and catch up later.

THE SAVINGS ACCOUNT

I don't believe in letting any sizeable amounts of money lay about in a checking account where it draws no interest. I also do not believe in allowing whoever is paying me to run his operation to get behind in his payments. Under normal circumstances I insist on having a minimum of one month's operating costs under my control at all times. To this effect I am more than willing to work out an approximate monthly cash flow requirement as a part of the budget. Someday the full-service banks may offer interest-bearing business checking accounts (as most of them now do personal accounts). Until they do I will have a racing savings account to go with the checking account. Most banks will set things up so that funds are automatically transferred from the savings account to the checking account as they are needed. I usually just call the bank manager or the bookkeeper and ask them to transfer a specific amount on a weekly basis. I write the origin and destination of all deposits and withdrawals directly in the passbook and send monthly copies to the accountants. The interest that the money earns before it is needed to cover checks pays for a surprising number of tires. . . .

THE CREDIT CARD

Like everyone else, I prefer to put as many of my purchases as I can conveniently arrange on plastic, for several reasons:

(1) I am automatically provided with at least two records of the transaction.

(2) I don't have to write and/or keep track of so many checks.

(3) The use of a card significantly reduces the amount of cash that I have to carry around. Few merchants will take an out-of-town check, let alone an out-of-state one (especially if one happens to be from California, the supposed home of the rubber check). Everybody accepts MasterCard and VISA. Most merchants will take American Express.

(4) Refunds in the case of defective merchandise, unused airline tickets and the like are a lot easier and more convenient if the purchase was made by a card. The actual procedure varies from card to card but basically one writes a couple of letters and doesn't pay the bill. This beats fighting over a warranty claim or waiting forever for a refund.

(5) The use of a card gives me at least two weeks free use of the money that I have just spent. In the case of merchants who are really lax about sending in their receipts (especially airlines—but not travel agents) the interest-free loan can be as much as ninety days. I pay off the total card balance monthly, but I do appreciate the free float.

I give the towing crew as many oil company credit cards as I can obtain. I used to virtually forbid them to pay cash for fuel and I did not expect them to price shop while towing. The rash of significant discounts for cash has somewhat changed my thinking in this respect. ARCO really started something. If we are talking a few percentage points for the use of the card, it is worth it to me. When we are talking a difference of 20 cents and up per gallon, it is not.

If I were running my own operation I would give the senior member of the towing crew a VISA or MasterCard for motels and the like. It has been a long time since anyone for whom I have been running a racing operation has been willing or able to supply any credit cards other than gas. What I normally do is to give the person in charge one of my own cards to be used in tight spots only, and a generous

supply of company cash. He also gets a list of my friends throughout the hemisphere who can be called upon in time of need.

BANK CARDS

I have had a lot of experience with various credit cards and with the people who administer the accounts (believe it or not, there really are human beings in there somewhere, although it takes some perserverence to actually speak or correspond with one). The companies are not really run by obtuse computers, it just seems that way. Presently I am carrying American Express, a Hertz Card, a telephone company card, a raft of oil company cards and a Master-Card issued by Finance One in Hicksville, N.Y. If and when I feel the need for another card I will obtain a VISA issued by either Chase Manhattan or by CitiBankCorp.

You will doubtless wonder why, although I live in and operate from California, I do not carry California Bank Cards. When the Bank Cards first came out I applied for and was granted a BANKAMERICARD. For several years this was the only card that I carried and I was delighted with it. If I needed to temporarily exceed my credit limit I called someone in Pasadena, explained the situation and it was taken care of. When I needed to increase my limit on a permanent basis I called the same person, explained, and it was taken care of. The same was true of glitches in the billing. No problems. As the use of the cards proliferated, BANK-AMERICARD somehow became VISA and the administration of most of the accounts, at least in southern California, was transferred to a truly idiotic operation entitled The Pacific Bank Card Association, with whom I have found it very inconvenient to do business. The accounts were regularly screwed up, there was no one with any authority at all who could be talked to on the phone, they didn't answer correspondence and I sent my card back in tiny little pieces. This decision on my part has imposed no hardship, as the East Coast and Midwestern operations are hungry for business, have higher credit limits and are a lot easier to deal with. They also, at least at the time of this writing, have real people that I can talk with on the telephone. The same is true of American Express and the card is good anywhere in the world, with no credit limit. It also carries some cheap and useful optional travel insurance and doesn't even rip you off (much) on the exchange rate for foreign currencies.

THE TELEPHONE CREDIT CARD

I reckon that the telephone credit card is one of Ma Bell's bigger rip-offs. I get to dial the number direct, give my credit card number to a computer and I pay the operator-assisted rate! Like the airlines, the phone company rips off its most frequent and heavy users. Like the airlines they can get away with it simply because most business people are traveling or calling on the corporate nickel and could care less. I usually travel (and call) on the racing budget's nickel and I do care, every hundred bucks that I spend on an air ticket is one tire that I don't get to buy! There is nothing that I can do about the airlines. I almost never know my schedule far enough in advance to qualify for one of the special fares, and I can virtually never schedule my return very far in advance. It really doesn't matter much, as I usually can't meet the rest of the requirements anyway. So much for the airlines; I'll just keep piling up the frequent-flyer points and paying through the nose.

As you would expect, I have to use the phone a lot when I am away from home. Until recently there was no viable alternative to the credit card. Putting calls on the motel bill is even more expensive and collect calls are the same price as the card and a pain for all concerned. I used the hell out of the card and I bitched a lot. For once, technology and capitalism have answered my prayers. The SPRINT long-distance system and its fast proliferating imitators have ripped off the phone company (sort of the way that UPS has ripped off the Post Office—better service at a lower price). The situation is too fluid for me to make any specific recommendations, but shop around. What you need is a system that allows you to call numbers in the most extensive area AND allows you to call from anywhere in the country. Interestingly enough, since I wrote what I thought was going to be the final draft of this chapter some months ago Ma Bell, doubtless in response to economic pressure, has reduced the charges for the non-operator-assisted use of its credit cards—they are still a hell of a lot more expensive than SPRINT. I still carry the phone company card. I also check the bill when it comes in. It never fails to astound me how many times I am billed for calls to places that I never heard of. I assume that this is just normal computer glitches at work. The phone company business office never disputes my calls; they just remove the call from the bill.

CONFUSION AND THE CARD

The surest way for me to become hopelessly confused with my credit card bills (and my racing accounts) is to use the same card for both business and personal transactions. The solution is simple. I use the business cards ONLY for business, just like the bank accounts. We have family VISAs through CitiBank and they are used for personal stuff. My phone card or SPRINT is simply not used for personal calls. The gas cards are not a problem; I just keep the receipts separate.

RACING ON PLASTIC

I have never been able to make my peace with the economic realities of life in the latter half of the twentieth century—let alone in the last quarter of it. I simply cannot bring myself to either live or do business on credit. I take out loans on real estate and nothing else. I pay my bills when they come in, and I expect other people to do the same. I am not even a little bit proud of this attitude; it is just plain dumb—but that is the way I am and I cannot change it and be comfortable. None of this, however, has prevented me from watching my friends and acquaintances explore the elastic limits of various types of plastic by racing on creative management of credit cards—sometimes LOTS of credit cards. Carefully and cleverly done this practice surely can extend the time when the racer runs out of wherewithal. If any reasonable amount of restraint has been exercised, the cards may even get paid off before the

racer, his wife, his children and his race car are hauled off to debtor's prison. The finance charges are, to put it mildly, excessive, but using up your cards is a lot easier than trying to convince your banker to extend a line of credit for your racing activities. Even bankruptcy, a lifelong disgrace under the old system, is no longer considered to be any big thing. So each of us will continue to do what racers have always done in order to go racing: whatever it takes.

THERE AIN'T NO (PLASTIC) FREE LUNCH

The credit card is a convenient and useful device. It can lead the unwary into a world of hurt. The money manipulators who dreamed up the credit card system, who make it SO easy for us to obtain them and who spend literally billions promoting their use, are not entirely altruistic. The cards make money for the issuing corporations in three ways:

(1) The member merchants pay a service charge on each credit card transaction. The amount varies with the amount of business that the merchant does with the card company and with how much clout he has. It is typically in the 2% to 6% range. This doesn't sound like much and it wouldn't be, if it were an annual rate. The fact is that it is more like a weekly or even daily rate.

(2) The card carrier pays a nominal annual fee for the use of the card AND, if he does not pay off his balance, on time, each month, he also gets to pay a whopping great finance charge. This is no surprise, nor is there anything wrong with it. The rub comes in when you read the fine print. If you are not current, the finance charge is usually computed, not only on your previous unpaid balance, but also on all subsequent purchases—from the date of purchase. Needless to say this can add up in a big hurry and it is the reason why they make it so tempting to make only the minimum monthly payment.

(3) Many human brains have trouble making the connection between handing an innocent piece of plastic to a merchant and paying for it at the end of the month—or sometime. The same, to a lesser extent, is true of checks. If we had to lay out cold cash for everything, as our grandparents did, we would probably buy a lot less and we wouldn't be so far in hock to the modern equivalents of the old company store. The so-called "consumer economy" is a product of easy credit. To some extent each of us is a victim.

So long as we regard the cards as cash they are not only a real convenience, they CAN be a money saver. Because of the time that it takes the billing to go through the various electronic devices and mailings involved the credit card can provide interest-free use of money (read loan) for a short time. The danger lies in the finance charges; avoid them when you can and at least be aware of what you are doing to yourself when you can't.

Another factor which we should be aware of is that the merchant, since his credit card receipts are discounted, may be willing to give you a discount for cash or the equivalent (i.e. traveler's checks—one of the advantages of the credit card system is that if the merchant obeys the rules of the game he cannot get stuck with a bad debt. He is therefore not going to be very anxious to discount your bill AND take your check.). This discounting can be a good deal for all concerned (except, of course, the credit card company)—especially if the merchant is paying on the high end of the scale. They are often more willing to discount American Express and Diners Club than MasterCard and VISA simply because it takes the merchant a lot longer to collect from the former (bank card receipts are treated as cash by the banks). It doesn't hurt to ask. If you do pay in cash GET A RECEIPT!

YOU AND YOUR BANK

Most people seem to give little thought to the selection of a bank. This is a mistake—especially if you are self employed. The bank exists to make a profit through the use of the money that you place on deposit with them. In return they offer interest on your money, security for your funds, and services. Many people do not seem to realize that banking is a two-way street and never ask about or make use of the services and expertise offered by the banks. Individual needs vary a lot, but the services cover a wide range—from free traveler's checks through free checking accounts to foreign exchange, currency transfers and loans. Perhaps most important, however, is the knowledge and expert advice available from the officers of any good, commercial (i.e., full-service) bank.

I tend to pick my banks on the advice of businessmen in the community or my tax accountant. I then tend to keep all of my accounts in the same bank—business and personal. What I have actually done is to find a bank manager or assistant manager that I get along with and who is both willing and able to provide the services that I require. I then follow him around from branch to branch or even from bank to bank until one of us leaves the area. I find that I get along better with the smaller banks; they tend to employ real people and to be better geared to my rather modest requirements than the multibranched monsters. They also don't make many enormous loans to South American, Balkan or African states. I have had no particularly good experiences with the foreign-based banks, either English or Japanese, in California (although my experiences with English and Australian banks during the years that we lived there were uniformly delightful).

Anyway, it is important to establish some sort of business relationship with an officer of your bank so that when you need advice (or a service) you can get it and so that when you need something done by telephone from 3000 miles away you are not just another account number. Things are pretty tough right now in the banking business and they are being pretty damned competitive, and cooperative. THEY DO NOT WANT TO LOSE ANY ACCOUNTS—even small ones.

PETTY CASH

It is not possible to pay for EVERYTHING with a check or a credit card, nor would it be practical to do so if it were possible. (Carroll Shelby, upon whom praises be, used to say that the perfect racing parts department was a kid with a motorcycle and a roll of ten-dollar bills.) Few merchants will accept a credit card for a purchase of less than $5 and I usually don't find it worth my time to write a check for less than that; $10 is a more realistic lower limit. So we all handle a fair bit of cash. The trick in keeping track of it is simplicity itself; GET A RECEIPT FOR EVERYTHING, LABEL THE RECEIPT BEFORE YOU LEAVE THE STORE AND FILL IN A PETTY CASH SHEET EVERY NIGHT. It is a source of continuing amazement to me how quickly I can forget that I bought something—and, equally, how quickly I can forget what it was that I bought when all that I have for a reminder is a cash register tape or a receipt with a part number on it. Step two is to categorize the petty cash sheet (shown in FIGURE [239]) and to enter the purchases into the daily sheets (I usually do it weekly).

Figure (239): Typical petty cash sheet.

12 PESOS = $100 $0.86 CDN

PETTY CASH SHEET # 81-19   NAME ANYFACE   DATE 8-11-81

COUNT NO.	DATE	LOCATION	ITEM	LOCAL	U.S.
302	7-25	Laredo Tx	Motel		31⁸⁵
650	7-26	N Laredo	Customs Fee	P800	66⁶⁷
305	7-26	N Laredo	Truck Gas	P1100	91⁶⁷
306	7-30	N Laredo	Truck Gas Plus	P2100	175⁰⁰
302	7-30	Oklahoma City	Motel		34⁶³
302	7-31	Des Moines	Motel		26⁸⁵
302	8-1	Brainerd	Motel		29⁰⁰
806	8-1	Brainerd	Race Gas		156⁰⁰
302	8-2	Billings	Motel		34⁰⁰
307	8-3	Great Falls	Repair Trailer Tire		12⁰⁰
302	8-4	Calgary	Motel	C41⁰⁰	35²⁶
307	8-5	Edmonton	Wash Truck + Trailer	C8⁵⁰	7³¹
700	8-5	Edmonton	Fantastic, Paper Towels	C7⁶¹	6⁵¹
307	8-7	Golden BC	Trailer Brake Controller	C41⁰⁰	35²⁶
302	8-7	Golden BC	Motel	C38⁰⁰	32⁶⁸
306	8-7	Golden BC	Truck Gas	C43⁰⁰	36⁹⁸
307	8-8	Westwood	Wash Truck + Trailer	C6⁵⁰	5⁵⁹
307	8-9	Westwood	Truck Muffler	C43⁰⁰	36⁹⁸
700	8-9	Westwood	Paper Towels	C6⁵⁰	5⁵⁹
307	8-10	Westwood	Starter Solenoid	C9⁶⁵	8³⁰

TRUCK FUEL	(306)	303⁶⁵	
T. CK MAINTENANCE	(307)	105⁴⁵	
MOTEL	(302)	224²⁷	
MISC + CONSUMABLE	(700)	12¹³	
ADMIN	(650)	66⁶⁷	
RACE FUEL	(806)	156⁰⁰	

TOTAL BRAZZ

TOTAL	P4000 C244.76 324³³
TOTAL U.S. $	568¹⁶
ADVANCE	1500
REMAINING ADVANCE	631⁸⁴
NEW ADVANCE	400
NET ADVANCE	1031⁸⁴

None of this presents a problem when you are handling the money yourself. Trouble begins when other members of the operation are called upon to handle cash—and handle it they must. I have tried, I think, every imaginable system for keeping track of the petty cash. None of them have worked 100%. The one that seems to work best—and which I have used for several years now—is for me to run a "cash float" for each member of the team who needs to handle company cash. The amount of the float varies with the circumstances. The person to whom the money is issued signs a receipt for it when he gets it, keeps his own petty cash sheet and the receipts are subtracted from the float at more-or-less regular intervals. No receipt = no deduction. It is THAT simple, although there have to be some exceptions to the "no tickee, no laundry" rule. An obvious example is the "mordidas" so necessary to operate south of the border. Another is the lost receipt when the purchase is obvious (or even sometimes when it isn't, one has to be flexible, and morale and trust are a hell of a lot more important than a few bucks). In these cases I write the receipt myself and explain the situation to the accountants.

I issue each member of the crew a three-ring binder, a sheaf of petty cash sheets, a small accordion file labeled with the basic categories for the receipts, a calculator and hope for the best. It almost always works out—if we get together and balance things out at least every couple of weeks. One very quickly figures out who is good at keeping track of money and who is not. The floats are then adjusted accordingly. It sometimes turns out that the gofer is better at it than the crew chief. If so, let the gofer handle the bread—the chief will probably be grateful to each of you. . . .

When the time comes to enter the petty cash sheets into the bookkeeping system I fill in the left-hand column ("category") with the appropriate account number, total the entries for each account number and insert the totals into the daily sheets with the chronological number of the petty cash sheet entered in the "check number" column. As you would expect, I photocopy the petty cash sheets: one copy to the team member, one to the accountants and the original for my files.

ROAD EXPENSES

For the small racing team, keeping track of living expenses on the road is easy. Everyone stays together and everyone eats together so there is normally one motel bill per night and one meal bill per meal. The poor devil in charge of money keeps the receipts and makes sure that they are properly entered and filed and that is that. End of story.

As the operation gets larger, however—either in size or in scope—problems arise. Either by plan or by mischance people end up in different places at the same time, there aren't enough credit cards to go around, not everyone eats together all of the time, the crew is towing while the driver and the team manager are flying, a sponsor or a prospective sponsor has to be entertained. . . . Rather than attempting to keep track of and entering three meals per day for a group of people (an almost impossible task) I use a per diem system. The team picks up the motel bills and pays for the cleaning of team uniforms. Each team member is issued (and signs for) a fixed amount of cash per day on which he is expected to feed himself while he is away from home base. I allow no room service charges of any type on the motel bills and so inform the motels (with the obvious exception of the boss's and/or the sponsor's rooms). The working crew has been heard to piss and moan to considerable extents over this rule of mine, but it saves me HOURS of poring over badly detailed motel bills trying to figure out what the charges were and whom they should be charged to, as well as trying to collect. It also prevents the motels from ripping us off—unintentionally or otherwise.

First-term racing team managers are often shocked (and occasionally embarrassed) to find that the home-base checks with which they cheerfully intend to pay the crew's compensation and per diem on the road are absolutely worthless to the crew. No one is going to cash an out-of-town check, let alone an out-of-state one, and don't even think about a California check! I normally carry enough cash and/or traveler's checks to take care of things and I refresh the kitty with a wire transfer from the home bank to a cooperative local bank when and where it becomes necessary. I pay per diem in cash and offer the individual crew members personalized payment options. They usually elect to take part in cash and part by check which they then mail home. Obviously I have to get receipts for the cash (also for per diem payments).

THE BUDGET

Even when you are racing on your own money and there is damned little of it, you should take the time and trouble to prepare a written annual budget. It is good practice for the time (you hope) that you will be operating on someone else's money. More important, with a written budget you can sit down and actually figure out where you can cut financial corners while doing the least possible amount of damage to the program. It also helps to know pretty closely what your actual cash flow requirements are going to be on a monthly basis. Attempting to run a racing program without a written budget is like trying to figure out gear ratios for a new racetrack without a gear chart or a course map—possible, but time consuming. How much detail you go into is up to you. I go into quite a bit. But I am playing the game with someone else's money and the people who supply it, rightly, want to know where it is that I intend that it should go.

FIGURE [240] is a not terribly detailed hypothetical budget for a first-year Formula Atlantic effort, with the assumption that the operation already owns some sort of trailer, tow vehicle, driver's gear and normal tools. I have also assumed that the driver will travel with the car and work on same so that he can get along with one qualified mechanic. It is a rock-bottom budget to be competitive. There are enough spares included to take care of, at the race track, damage that is quickly reparable. There are no frills.

THE RACER AND THE LAWMAN

This section probably does not belong in here with the beancounting, but it doesn't logically belong anywhere else. SO! There are some areas where the racing operation,

regardless of size, is liable to run afoul of various enforcement agencies. They are: payroll taxes and deductions, the use of "undocumented workers" (i.e., wetbacks—in our case Kiwis and Aussies) as mechanics and the misuse of a sales tax exemption number.

The common practice of having each team member sign a contract stating that he is acting as an "independent contractor" providing specialized services in return for a monthly contract fee may or may not be legal in any given

---

Figure (240): Budget chart.

```
                                                          Sign Writing                    XXX
                                                          Fibreglass Work                 XXX
        PROVISIONAL BUDGET, 198? FORMULA ATLANTIC SERIES              SUB TOTAL      XXXX          XXXXXX

ASSUMPTIONS:                                       V  CAPITAL - SUPPORT EQUIPMENT
                                                       Honda Generator               XXX
(1) 12 month program                                   Air Comp. & Tank              XXX
(2) 10/12 race series                                  Nitrogen Set Up & Rattle Guns XXX
(3) Entry fees and travel schedule similar to 198??    Quick Jacks                   XXX
(4) All U.K. components to be purchased at one time in January  Tire Mount/ Balance eqpt.     XXX
(5) Driver's expenses except for room and per diem are not     Alignment Wheels              XXX
included                                               Scales                        XXX
(6) Shop space to be rented from an existing operation in the Los   Small Drill Press (trailer)   XXX
Angeles area and to include use of shop equipment.     Vises (trailer)               XXX
(7) Promotional, PR and Entertainment expenses are not included    Awning & indr/outdr carpet(trailer) XXX
(8) Existing equipment assumed to include truck, trailer and   Floodlights (trailer)         XXX
normal tools                                           Race Gas Tank (truck)         XXX
                                                       Knock Down Engine Hoist       XXX
I  OVERHEAD                                             Bins & Spare Parts Boxes      XXX
      Incorporation Fees              XXX              IN-Pit Radio                  XXX
      Shop Rent @ XXX/month           XXXX            Walkie Talkies                XXX
      Insurance (transport & off track)  XXXX         Radar Gun                     XXX
      Major Medical Insurance         XXXX
      Communications  (phone/postage) XXXX                       SUB TOTAL      XXXXX      XXXXXX
      Race Entries                    XXXXX
      Entrant's License               XXX       VI CAPITAL EQUIPMENT- RACING
      Track Rentals for Testing       XXXX          (A) CHASSIS
      Year End Accounting             XXXX                 Rolling Chassis            XXXXX
                                                           Chassis Spares (see att. # 1) XXXXX
                  SUB TOTAL      XXXXX      XXXXX    (B) ENGINE
                                                           2 Jennings/Cosworth BDAs   XXXXX
II COST OF CONTRACT SERVICES                        (C) FINAL DRIVE (see att. # 2 )   XXXXX

      Team Manager/Development Engineer  XXXXX                    SUB TOTAL      XXXXX      XXXXXX
      Chief Mechanic                  XXXXX
      Helper                          XXXX      VII OPERATING COSTS
                                                    (A) ENGINE PROGRAM
                  SUB TOTAL      XXXXX      XXXXXX          8. Rebuilds @XXXX          XXXXX
                                                           2 Starter Motors (Toyota)  XXX
III TRAVEL                                                 Auxiliary  Start Set Up    XXX
      Transporter (50,000 miles @X/mille  XXXXX            Leak Rater                 XXX
      Crew Per Diem(XX for YYY days)  XXXX                 2 ATDC Rev Limiters        XXX
      Lodging ( XX/rm x Y x Z days)   XXXX                 4 Howard Ignition boxes    XXX
      Team Manager to U.K. if necessary  XXXX             Batteries (Yuhasa)         XXX
      Team Manager & Driver Air Fares XXXX                2 Blow ups @XXXX           XXXX
                                                          Lightweight flywheels (Tilton) XXX
                  SUB TOTAL      XXXXX      XXXXXX         Spare Parts, unlisted      XXX
                                                                   SUB TOTAL      XXXXX
IV OUTSIDE SERVICES                                 (B) TIRES
      Inspection                      XXX                 Pre Season Test (y sets @XXX) XXXX
      Specialist Machining/Fabrication  XXXX             12 Races x 2 sets @ XXX      XXXXX
      Paint                           XXX                 1 set wets + spare F & R    XXX

                                                                   SUB TOTAL      XXXXX      XXXXXX
                  1                                                  2
```

state. BUT it sure beats doing all of the accounting necessary for a payroll system, figuring the deductions, withholding, reporting and so on. The independent contractor is self employed and is responsible for his (or her) own income tax reporting and paying. Of course, under the independent contractor system no one is covered by any sort of medical insurance, or even by worker compensation, but we are a pretty healthy group and the sanctioning body covers us while we are at the track and our auto insurance covers us while on the highway, so most of us just take our chances. I pay the medical bills for those who get hurt at work, even when (almost always) it is his (or her) own damned fault. It is a good idea to carry major medical on each employee, it's not that brutally expensive. Of course if you are a real company none of the above applies. The company will have its own payroll system and insurance plans and the race team will merely fit into the existing framework.

```
    (C) BRAKES
            3 sets drilled rotors          XXXX
            18 Sets Mintex pads            XXXX
            Caliper seals & Pistons          XX
            Master Cylinders & Kits         XXX
            Brake Fluid                     XXX

                    SUB TOTAL             XXXX      XXXXXX

VII CONSUMABLE ITEMS
            Threaded fasteners              XXX
            Rivets                          XXX
            Ti-warps, clamps, saddles etc   XXX
            Electrical kit                  XXX
            Epoxies & sealants              XXX
            Plumbing Supplies               XXX
            Aluminum sheet, tube, bar & extr. XXX
            Steel sheet, tube, bar          XXX
            Fibreglass repair kit           XXX
            Cleaning Supplies               XXX
            Uniforms                        XXX
            Cleaning of uniforms            XXX
            Unlisted misc. items           XXXX

                    SUB TOTAL             XXXX      XXXXXX

IX DEVELOPMENT COSTS
            Mfr of suspension components   XXXX
            Design & Mfr of aero components XXXX

                    SUB TOTAL             XXXX      XXXXXX

X JESUS FACTOR @ 10%                     XXXXX      XXXXXX


            GROSS OPERATING BUDGET       XXXXXX
            LESS PROBABLE CAPITAL REMAINS XXXXX

                    NETT BUDGET          XXXXXX


ATTACHMENT # 1 - CHASSIS SPARES
            Wheels - 3 sets (Jongbloed)    XXXX
            Rod end & spherical bearings    XXX
            Hub Bearings                    XXX
            Anti-roll bars (6) - fabricate  XXX
            Springs -12 (Rockwell)          XXX
            Shocks -6- (KONI)              XXXX
            Noses -3- (U.S. Made)           XXX
            Front substructures -2- (U.S. Made) XXX
            Front wing assy -2- (U.S. Made) XXX
            Rear Wing assy -1- (U.S. Made)  XXX

                            3
```

```
            Radiator (1)                   XXX
            Oil Cooler (1)                 XXX
            Instruments                    XXX
            Corners & shear plates        XXXX
            Wild Guess at annual damage   XXXX

                    SUB TOTAL             XXXXX     XXXXXX

ATTACHMENT #2 FINAL DRIVE SPARES
            Clutches, compete (2)          XXX
            Cost to modify clutches to
                    Tilton Spec            XXX
            Clutch driven & int. plates    XXX
            SAAB throw out systems and spares XX
            Weismann Diff                 XXXX
            Salisbury Diff                XXXX
            Crown wheel & pinion sets (3)  XXX
            Crown wheel bolts (FoMoCo)      XX
            Pinion depth setting fixture   XXX
            Fork setting fixture           XXX
            1sr/rev fork (3) [Formula One]  XXX
            2cnd/3rd & 4th/5th Forks (1 ea) XXX
            Fork shims (asst)               XX
            Dog Rings (24)                XXXX
            1st/rev sliders (6)            XXX
            Side carrier & pionio shims     XX
            Hewland Bearings, Seals, Circlips,
                    springs, detents ertc  XXX
            Selector fingers, bushes, seals XXX
            Linkage U-Joints (APEX)         XX
            Magnetic drain plugs            XX
            Gear Oil & CV Grease           XXX
            CV Joint Spares                XXX

                    SUB TOTAL             XXXXX     XXXXX

FIRST GEAR SETS  @  XX
            13/47 (1)
            14/46 (2)
            12/35 (2)
            13/35 (2)
            14/34 (2)
            14/32 (1)
                    SUB TOTAL               XXX     XXXXX

SECOND GEAR SETS  @  XX
            14/34 (1)
            14/32 (2)
            14/33 (1)
            15/33 (2)
            15/32 (1)
            15/31 (1)
            16/32 (2)
            16/31 (1)
            16/30 (2)

                    SUB TOTAL             XXXX      XXXXX

TOP GEAR SETS  @  XX
            15/33 (1)
            15/32 (1)
            15/31 (1)
            16/32 (1)
            16/31 (2)
            16/30 (1)
            17/31 (2)
            17/30 (2)
            17/29 (2)
            18/30 (1)
            18/29 (1)
            19/29 (1)
            19/28 (2)
            19/27 (1)
            20/28 (1)
            20/27 (2)
            25/33 (1)
            21/26 (1)
                    SUB TOTAL             XXXX      TOTALXXXXX

NOTE:  Depending upon the driver's penchant for destroying drive
dogs, this list may have to be revised upwards.



ATTACHMENT # 3  ESTIMATED CAPITAL REMAINS AT END OF SEASON

            Rolling Chassis               XXXXX
            Chassis Spares                 XXXX
            Final Drive Spares             XXXX
            2 Engines                     XXXXX
            Support Equipment              XXXX
            Truck & Trailer               XXXXX

                    TOTAL                 XXXXX
```

It is virtually impossible to legally employ a foreign national in the U.S. at this time. Any noncitizen, in order to work in this country, must have a work permit issued by the U.S. Department of Immigration and approved by the labor department. To get the permit he or she must prove that he will not be displacing a citizen from the job. All of this would be simple if that were all there was to it. The problem is that Jimmy Carter let in so many people under special provisos that there are no permits left and the process takes years. In the meantime, the average racing mechanic, who came in on a tourist visa, is not legally allowed to work. Since Englishmen, Australians, New Zealanders and Canadians are provided with natural protective coloration in this country, almost everyone pays them under the table, in cash, and depends on the size of the country and the magnitude of the illegal immigration problem to keep from getting caught. I don't know of anyone who ever has been. The trick is to apply for a multiple-entry tourist visa so that the person in question can cross into Canada and Mexico (or wherever) for races there (do not, however, allow them to cross in or with the tow vehicle; fly them or have them drive a private car). The next trick is to apply for a green card (i.e., residence permit) through a GOOD immigration lawyer, who does NOT specialize in agricultural workers, immediately upon arrival in this country. The rub here is that the applicant must apply for permission each time that he wants to leave the country—and it may not be granted. Anyone contemplating the addition of noncitizens to their staff should have a long talk with a good immigration lawyer before committing himself. It is a complicated mess and it is never going to get better. The reputation of immigration lawyers for ethical behavior is about on a par with that of used car salesmen, so some caution in the selection process is indicated.

In every state that I know of where it is possible to obtain a "sales tax exemption permit" or a "resale certificate," the permit is issued with the proviso that it will be used only for the purchase of goods to be resold and that the permittee is responsible both for the collection of sales tax when the goods are resold and the payment of those taxes to the state on a regular basis. I don't know much about the procedures in other states, but in California it is REAL EASY to get oneself into deep trouble through the misuse of a resale certificate. The State Board of Equalization can pull a surprise audit at any time—and does so with surprising frequency. IF they find that someone has been defrauding the state of their rightful 6.5%, big trouble is on the way. It simply is not worth it. I pay the tax, unless, of course, I really am going to resell the item or ship it out of state. In those cases I collect either the tax or a resale card from the purchaser, or I keep proof of some sort that I shipped the merchandise out of California.

The same is true of the U.S. duty on racing cars and parts. At the time of this writing it is ONLY 2.9% (the category number is 1055.46) and I just flat pay it. I also use a customs broker rather than trying to do it myself—that is the way that the system is set up and, while it is possible to circumvent the system, it isn't worth it in terms of time and trouble. It is worth cultivating a good broker, preferably a small one. I file the consumption entry form for whatever I brought in and carry copies of all of them in the trailer to display to the U.S. Customs people at the border when we come back from either Canada or Mexico. These people can be just downright unreasonable.

That wraps up Smith on beancounting. I am certain that I enjoyed writing it even less than you enjoyed reading it (those of you who have perservered). It is hardly any fun at all. My way will not make it fun. It will, however, make it less painful and less time consuming. It may also save your tail one day.

CHAPTER NINETEEN

BITS & PIECES

No matter how hard I try, it seems that I always end up with a bunch of bits and pieces that I feel should be included in each book but which I cannot logically fit into the framework of the book. The first time, in PREPARE TO WIN, I went back and found a place for everything. The second time around, in TUNE TO WIN, the last chapter was entitled "EVERYTHING ELSE" and was a catch-all. This time I am going to openly admit it: This chapter consists of all of the unrelated bits and pieces that I want to include but which are not long enough to form separate chapters and do not fit into the existing chapters.

THEFT

When I was working for Carroll Shelby I developed a theory that NO ONE considered it wrong to steal from Shelby; after all, we had all that Ford money. I think that the attitude is akin to cheating on taxes or ripping off the insurance companies. Anyway, we lost a lot of stuff—from the pits, from the racetrack garages and even from the trucks. Since Shel retired from our game (and a black day that was!), I have lost very little. I have, however, noticed a pattern. Nothing ever goes away at an amateur race—regardless of level. Nothing ever goes away at professional races where the spectators are enthusiasts. The "happenings" are another case. I have had tools and equipment walk away from the garages (but not the pits) at Watkins Glen and at Mosport (both notorious for a small but highly visible percentage of animals among the spectators). I have had valuable equipment disappear from the pits (during a practice session) at Montreal, where there are lots of spectators who don't have passes and don't belong there and NO marshalls for the Atlantic sessions. It doesn't happen at Trois Rivieres where we leave everything in the barn for three or four days with no security at all. The people are genuine enthusiasts (for this reason Trois Rivieres is my favorite event of the year). It doesn't happen at Long Beach where Cal Club, for all of its many shortcomings, does provide experienced marshalls and the LBGP supplies garage security. The same is true of Detroit. It doesn't even happen at Daytona or Sebring where the stuff is in the unguarded pits forever. I firmly believe that RACERS, be they participants or spectators, are honest. As an example, in my years of racing I have never had a bad check, or a bad debt, from a racer. A little late in paying, maybe, but the debt gets paid. It's those OTHER people that you have to worry about—the nonracers who are hunting souvenirs and figure that we are all filthy rich anyway. As a final example, we have sold some 20,000 mail-order books from the house. We have had exactly ONE bad check.

THE ELECTRICS

As I have pointed out before, I am an electrical idiot. I do not understand electrics (or electronics) and I therefore view anything having to do with either as a potential casualty. This tends to make me very careful. I will not use anything electric on the racing car that I am not absolutely sure of (or at least as sure as I can be). Since TUNE TO WIN I have come up with a few new items:

(1) THE STARTER: I now use a Toyota winterized starter motor that I obtain from the man who remains my favorite engine builder, Steve Jennings. This is the famous Formula Two starter motor. It is expensive. For engines other than Cosworth BD's, its use requires the manufacture of an adaptor. It is worth it.

(2) THE JUMPER BATTERY: I do not approve of the English screw-in jumper battery plug. I also do not approve of any location other than on major structure at the rear of the car and facing directly to the rear. I use Donna Wilson's quick-connect battery booster cable plugins and I use welding cable for battery wire. These plugins are lightweight, idiot-proof AND, if the driver SHOULD take off with the booster connected, they will uncouple themselves thus eliminating the possibility of the race car dragging a flailing booster battery behind it in pit row.

(3) THE BATTERY: English racing cars come with Varley Gel Cell batteries. There was a quality control problem with Varleys a couple of years ago but it seems to have been solved. That leaves two problems:

(a) They are brutally expensive.

(b) People REFUSE to read the charging directions which are clearly printed on each battery and insist on either adding acid to them or charging them on a real battery charger. The Varley then dies and everyone says that they are junk.

Until recently I used a Yuhasa gel-cell battery. The part number is NP-15-12. The thing retails for about $50, fits in Varley space and it works just fine. Yuhasa is, however, the only satisfactory manufacturer of these batteries. I note in AUTOSPORT's Formula One write-ups, most of the Formula One teams now use Yuhasa batteries.

I now use an absolutely magic unit. Dunlop of Australia makes a gel battery called Pulsar. The model 5 is a little different in shape than what we are used to so it requires a new box/holder. It has the most actual capacity and cranking power of any small battery that I have ever seen. It is lighter than a Varley, a lot cheaper and it is bulletproof. They are available from Momo Course Ltd., 2040 South Grand Ave., Santa Ana CA 92705 (714) 641-7397 or from Steve Jennings Racing, 1401 S. Borchard, Santa Ana CA 92705 (714) 547-3717.

(4) THE FUEL PUMP: I still prefer the old standby Bendix (now Facet) ELECTRIC pump. Solid state pumps scare hell out of me and I do not use them. I use Holley pressure regulators where required.

FUEL

The days when we could race on Chevron Supreme pump gasoline are gone—presumably forever. I now use Daeco on the West Coast and CAM 2 on the East Coast. I have tried other brands of "racing gasoline" with mixed results. When I cannot obtain proper racing fuel I use 110/130 aviation gas with 0.5% by volume engine oil added.

If all else fails I run the highest octane leaded street gas I can find with either VORTEX or MOROSO octane booster. I really don't like doing this because the octane booster leaves deposits on carbs and jets and things AND it removes all of the skin from my hands.

I carry my fuel in plastic "super jugs" from Daeco or in a race gas tank built into the tow vehicle. I filter the fuel out of the race gas tank and I pour it into the race car through a filter and a chamois built into the funnel.

SAFETY

One way or another, most of what I write has to do with safety. Right now I want to take a couple of minutes to talk about the specifics of driver safety, starting with the driver's equipment.

THE HELMET: It is my firm conviction that racing helmets are made by SIMPSON, BELL and no one else. It is my further conviction that racing helmets are of full-face design, have the smallest eye holes that the driver can see through, and are modified ONLY by the manufacturer. Any time that a helmet is USED (as in a crash) it MUST go back to the manufacturer. The energy-absorbing foam that keeps the driver's brain from becoming scrambled eggs is NOT REUSEABLE AT ALL. I also believe that the driver should use, at all times, a medical air bottle and that the inlet port for same should be installed by the helmet manufacturer. It SHOULD go without saying that the helmet should fit properly. The number of drivers I know who wear helmets that are too big is astounding. Color them dumb. The maximum life of a racing helmet, even if it is not used, is about two seasons. He who wears a helmet that snaps together rather than buckling on deserves whatever happens to him.

THE DRIVING SUIT: It is my firm conviction that driving suits are made by Bill Simpson. Period. It is my further conviction that driving suits are composed of FOUR layers of Nomex and that they are to be worn at all times with full underwear. Period. You will no doubt note that Bill Simpson's name keeps appearing whenever I mention driver safety. There is a reason for this. HE CARES!

THE SAFETY HARNESS: REAL safety harnesses have six straps, not five, and certainly not four. The shoulder straps are three inches wide, not two, and are of the same material as the lap straps. I prefer Simpson's harness over all others but am not insistent so long as the others meet the above criteria. Real safety harnesses are so tight that getting into them is a pain, and getting into them by oneself is impossible—at least in a single seater. Real safety harnesses include a "horse collar," both to provide neck support and to help prevent the shoulder harness from breaking collar bones in accidents. The best safety harness in the world will do no good if its mounting to the chassis is inadequate. Do not trust your car's manufacturer in this respect. Go back and read PREPARE TO WIN, page 90; watch again the video of Gilles Villeneuve's fatal accident and then have a good look at your harness attachments.

I worry a lot. I also think about racing safety a lot. Since the first edition of this book, I have come to a couple of strong conclusions: I am never again going to run a car without a removable steering wheel or one without a driver's medical air supply (which, it finally dawned on me will also work both under water and under mud, so long as the driver remembers to activate it).

Using the removable steering wheel is simply a case of trying to facilitate the driver's exit in an emergency, or his removal after an accident. And, yes, you do need one in a sedan, even with a good full cage.

Waiting until the car is on fire to set off the halon extinguisher is all very well, so long as you have a guarantee that the driver is going to be conscious after the impact that led to the fire. I have never seen such a guarantee and I want my drivers to hit the thing before impact—you almost always know when you are going to hit hard. And if you think about hitting the fire switch often enough, the chances are pretty good that you will do so when the need arises.

A friend of mine, now departed, once remarked that if you drive these things long enough, sooner or later one of them will bite you. Nikki Lauda, the most precise and intelligent of drivers admits to making a couple of mistakes big enough to cause either a spin or a thump, every season. So let's not hear "It can't (won't) happen to me."

THE SEAT AND DRIVER PERFORMANCE

In the days when we all drove M.G.'s (on street tires) and liked each other, we sat on top of the seat with no lateral support at all—and didn't miss it. This is no longer the case. As lateral g loadings increase, the fit of the driver in the seat becomes more critical. These days the driver must be wedged very firmly indeed into his proper position and the combination of seat and safety harness must be capable of keeping him there with virtually no effort, conscious or otherwise, on his part—under g forces that would have seemed ridiculous a decade ago. This means that unless you have been ungodly lucky and your driver happens to be a perfect fit in the seat that your car came with, you get to make a seat, or at least to modify an existing one.

There are lots of ways of doing this, ranging from ignoring the whole thing to shaping an aluminum seat. The easy way is with two-part foam. BUT, before we start to actually make a seat we have to position the driver properly in the car both with respect to his fore and aft positions and the inclination of his torso. Up and down is easy—since the driver is heavy, we want his butt on the floor, although I usually compromise by inserting a ⅜'' Ensolite pad under him. I start out with the stock seat. The important thing here is to get him arranged so that his legs are bent slightly at the knee (straight legged may look fast and elegant, but the human knee/leg/ankle assembly was not designed to operate pedals while fully extended) and so that his arms are bent more than slightly at the elbow, for the same reason. When EVERYTHING that can be adjusted has been fiddled with—all three pedal heights; steering wheel height and, if necessary, inclination (the new generation of kit cars come through with silly steering wheel inclinations, something like a bus, which require remaking the steering column with a universal joint so that the driver can operate the

steering wheel properly); gear lever position; and placement of the left foot rest; and when Fred declares that everything is perfect, including the under-thigh support (usually ignored, but very important)—THEN make him drive the thing for 50 miles or so at speed and readjust as necessary.

Now you know where HE has to be and it is a relatively simple matter to make him a proper seat. Remove the safety harness, measure the ultimate position and inclination of the stock seat and install some sort of a temporary driver's backrest, such as a flat sheet of aluminum, an inch or so behind where Fred is going to end up, or the stock seat moved an inch or so back (you may not need anything at all in a current single-seat monocoque). Dress Fred in his driving suit, with underwear and driving shoes, and obtain a couple of super-heavy-duty garbage bags. Tape one of the garbage bags to the floor with the closed edge well ahead of the desired midpoint of the seat bottom. Extend the bag, open end up, up the back of the temporary seat. Mix a half pint of each part of a 2 lb/cubic foot density foam and pour the result into the bag. Quickly insert Fred on top of it. One has to play with the garbage bag a bit while the foam is happening to ensure that the hardened foam ends up in all the right places. In a few minutes you will have a form-fitting, hardened-foam seatback. If you didn't mix enough foam, merely mix and add more—it will stick to what is already there.

The foam tends to run away with itself so some trimming will be necessary. Make sure that the seat extends far enough around the torso to hold the driver in place but not so far as to restrict his arm movements or to make it impossible for him to get into the car. I form the under-thigh support as two separate channels with a divider a couple of inches high (it just happens if you have placed the bag correctly). I do this separately, since I find one bag of rapidly growing foam quite enough to deal with at a time.

You now have a couple of choices. You can use the foam seat as a plug, make a mold and lay up a fiberglass seat. This is pretty elegant, but A LOT of work, and, as we shall see, not so safe in a crash. I prefer to artfully lay duct tape over the foam, place the result into a simple fabricated sheet aluminum channel (if required) for rigidity and that is my seat. If I feel particularly elegant, after I am certain that everything is just right, I take the thing to a good trim man and have it covered in top-quality vinyl. Whatever you decide, don't do ANYTHING until your man has driven the car with the foam in place and it has been carved away where necessary to achieve the perfect fit.

I must point out that all of the self foaming compounds are polyurethanes and that they give off a very toxic gas when they burn. This means that the danger of toxic gas ingestion is added to the other, obvious, dangers during a race car fire. I don't worry about this too much. First of all, I believe that every driver should use a medical air bottle attached (properly) to his helmet. This will give him one minute of protection from toxic gas ingestion. If he is not out of the fire in 60 seconds, toxic gas ingestion may be the best thing that he can hope for. Secondly, I feel that the added control and efficiency that a proper seat gives to the driver goes far enough towards the prevention of an accident that it is worth the slight risk involved.

There are a number of racing seats available for sedans. Recaro is excellent and very expensive. You get what you pay for in this world and it has been my experience that after Recaro it is all downhill in the upholstered racing seat department. I, for reasons of both ergonometrics and safety, like the fiberglass shell that Paul Van Valkenburgh designed a decade ago, which is still being marketed by (I think) Racemark. Beware of imitations. With a little bit of luck all that a good fiberglass shell needs to be converted to a proper racing seat is some strategically placed temper foam. If you don't know about temper foam, you should. It is some form of high-tech magic that was originally developed for burn patients and the like to do away with painful pressure points on the injured, immovable and sensitive human body. It is also used to make the astronauts' couches. It is a very firm foam which reacts to body heat and, in a few minutes, shapes itself to the individual body that happens to be sitting in it. It is available in three densities from: TEMPERFOAM-EXPLOSAFE, 1310 Idylwild Drive, Lincoln, NE 68503.

It is not cheap but it is worth every penny. To be effective it must be covered with an absorbent and breathable cover —NOT PLASTIC. Failing that, Ensolite works just fine— the REAL Ensolite, not the blue polyfoam. Ensolite is available from good back-packing stores as a sleeping bag mattress. Better (i.e., firmer) Ensolite is available at clued-in aircraft trim and seat shops. If your luck runs out in the size and shape of your driver, it is a simple enough matter to foam a custom seat over a fiberglass shell.

THE SEAT AND DRIVER SAFETY

From the crash safety point of view I am not real happy with most of our current racing seat technology for a couple of reasons. The first reason has to do with proper body support so that the driver can do his job. Most of what comes in our racing cars, regardless of the price, is simply inadequate. The second, and equally important, reason has to do with safety in the crash situation. The experienced racing driver, when he finally realizes that a crash is inevitable, will amost invariably try to spin the car so that it hits whatever it is going to hit backward. When successful, this action accomplishes several worthwhile ends: It keeps the driver's feet from being crushed in a frontal impact; it imposes a lot of additional energy-absorbing structure between the driver and the point of impact; through the medium of the seat, it provides support area for the driver's body, thus spreading the impact over a wider area and reducing the unit stress on the body; and, of course, it removes the impending disaster from the driver's sight.

While "backing it in" is almost certainly preferable to going in front first, there are a couple of problems inherent with the philosophy. The first problem (with the mid-engined car) is that if the engine/transaxle package has not been designed so that its mountings will withstand a severe rear end impact, this heavy lump is liable to tear out of its mounts and cause spinal damage to the driver. To this end,

transverse cast aluminum engine mounts should be outlawed and the engine/trans mounting system of EVERY racing car should be very carefully reviewed by prospective purchasers. The second problem is not quite so simple and has to do with the prevalent use of foam-rubber seat padding and the "rebound" type of secondary impact. What can happen here is a sequence like this:

(1) The car hits a solid object—while traveling backward. The structure of the automobile begins to collapse while the driver moves rearward relative to the seat, compressing the foam cushion that his seat has been provided with.

(2) A couple of microseconds after the initial impact the car's structure rebounds, but the driver is still moving rearward at virtually undiminished relative velocity because the foam rubber does not slow him down.

(3) When the cushion is finally compressed the driver hits the actual support structure of the seat. The driver's body will still be traveling at pretty close to its maximum velocity—backward. Unfortunately the seat structure, due to the "rebound," may well be moving forward by this time and the result can be a "head on" between the driver's spine and the seat support structure—and a greatly enhanced possibility of spinal injury.

This goes a long way toward explaining why unpadded seats are preferable to the ever popular and brutally expensive Recaro/Scheel units—at least in a crash situation. My own opinion is that the seat that offers the best driver support while driving is also the safest in an impact: the seat that we foam in place to fit the individual. Not only will the "rebound impact" between the driver and the seat support be eliminated but the foam itself will absorb one hell of a lot of energy in the process of being crushed by the driver's rearward momentum. For sedan use it is a simple enough exercise to foam a seat inside a framework that can be securely enough fastened to major chassis structure. Don't ever forget that a seat that comes loose in an impact is almost certain to result in severe injury. Along these lines, the safety harness should always be secured to the chassis —not to the seat.

THE ROLLOVER STRUCTURE

At the time of this writing it looks very much as though the SCCA is going to require forward-facing rollover hoop braces in 1984. In my opinion, this is dumb, for three reasons:

(1) With the diameters and wall thicknesses that will be required, in a really severe rollover at speed while going backward or in an endo situation, the braces are liable to buckle in compression. If this happens the driver has a 50/50 chance of being speared in the head or in the torso by the brace that was supposed to protect him.

(2) In any crash situation involving lateral forces, the driver's head is going to contact the braces. There is no way that this can help the driver's head. It is all very well to say that the braces must be padded, but we all know that the padding that will be used in 95% of the cases is right next door to useless.

(3) Since the designers will feel that this is all just

another load of SCCA BS it seems improbable to me that they will do a very good job of designing the braces. This means that, in many cases, the bars will not be anywhere near as good as they could be. The thought of the SCCA policing the system is so ridiculous as to be unworthy of discussion.

Don't get me wrong—I am all in favor of proper longitudinal bracing of the rollover structure. Further, such bracing not only can be accomplished with forward-leading diagonals—they should be REQUIRED as an integral part of the car's structure. Properly designed and executed, not only do such braces prevent collapse of the rollover hoop, but they go a long way toward the prevention of head and neck injuries caused by the ingress of foreign objects, such as catch fence poles, race car wheels and the like. I merely want to point out that a 1" rollover hoop brace subjected to a compression load is ridiculous. If we are to have such braces (and I strongly believe that we should) then they should be required to be REAL braces—say 1⅜" × 0.095" wall low-carbon steel tube.

On the other hand, since virtually none of the cars raced in the SCCA competition uses the engine as a fully stressed member, there is no valid objection to a rearward brace or braces of worthwhile proportions, and that is PERHAPS what should be required—at least on retrofits—along with a REAL rollover hoop and enforcement of the design, material and height regulations presently supposedly in force. If I had my way I would go further still and require a full cage and driver capsule on every racing car. Period. Surely if the sprinters and the midgets can run cages, we road racers shouldn't be afraid of losing our macho image!

THE WINDSCREEEN

Pat Shelby, whose progress as a racing driver (after a somewhat late start) lends still more credence to the value of genes, has recently pointed out to me that NOWHERE in either of the previous books have I stressed the absolute necessity of keeping the driver's head from being buffeted by the airstream. This is probably because approaching senility has made me forget my own head being knocked about and how very unpleasant it is—and the simple fact that most of my recent drivers have been somewhat less than real tall (Danny Ongais, Tim Coconis, Allen Berg and Price Cobb come instantly to mind). ANYWAY, if the driver's head is being knocked about by the airstream he simply CANNOT do a proper job of driving. That is what windshields and windshield extensions are for. They cost like nothing, they are easy to make, they do not HAVE to be ugly (they don't even have to be transparent) and they are crucial to the total performance picture. Look at current Formula One and Indy car photos for inspiration.

THE NECK

Along these same lines, the sports doctors tell us (and practical experience backs them up) that it is important that the driver keep his head and neck straight, as an extension of the spinal column, rather than adopting the once stylish procedure of leaning his silly neck into the corner like a goose. It has to do with sensory perception, feedback, the inner ear and such. In today's cars this requires a very strong neck—and the lightest crash helmet produced by either Simpson or Bell. This in turn means a faithful course of neck exercises best prescribed by a doctor specializing in sports medicine. It is my contention that any driver who has not taken himself to such a physician and had a specific course of physical conditioning prescribed to meet his (or her) individual needs is a fool.

THE ENGINE

Just a couple of recent paranoid notes on engine details:
(1) I now safety all of my block-freeze plugs with #10-32 screws and washers (see FIGURE [241]) AND I

Figure (241): Saftied freeze plug.

Figure (242): Properly designed air intake bell.

safety my main oil gallery plugs. Yes, I had a freeze plug come out in a test session and, yes, I saw another team's main gallery threaded end plug come out.

(2) We have known for years that intake bells should have a full return radius (see FIGURE [242]) for maximum airflow. This is one of the little things that keep being rediscovered. There are now some neat and good flowing intake adaptors available for Holley and Rochester carbs as well as for Webers. Use them.

THE OIL COOLER

The oil cooler SHOULD be mounted in such a fashion that the inlet port is located on the bottom of the cooler and the outlet on the top. This simple step will do away with the possibility of the oil following the path of least resistance and partially bypassing the cooler. If this is not feasible, the cooler MUST be mounted with both ports at the top. If you are using either Earl's or Serck coolers (they are completely interchangeable) DO NOT mount them by the handy little tabs at the four corners. Cut the tabs off and mount them in sheet metal channels with big rubber bands.

THROTTLE CABLES, LINKAGES AND THINGS

Everything that I have previously said on this subject still stands. I am now using Cable Craft throttle cables just about exclusively. They are every bit as good as American Chain and Cable (a lot better than Morse) and are locally made to order with one-day service. I still use right- and left-hand threaded spacers at both the pedal and throttle ends to give myself easy and quick adjustment.

You will remember from both previous books that I really disapprove of most throttle spring setups and strongly prefer to use compression springs even if it is a lot of work. When I must use extension springs I use the tricky little barrel springs with separate swiveling end hooks that are the only decent part that BLMC ever made. Since they don't have a lot of tension I use at least two, and often three, on a little swivel plate (as shown by FIGURE [243]) so that the springs are always pulling straight and don't get tangled in each other. This type of spring is also available in a variety of sizes and tensions from any good spring specialty house, such as Associated Spring.

STREAMLINE TUBING

Every racer is in love with streamline tubing—it just looks so great. Given a big budget there is no doubt in my mind that 4130 streamline tubing is the ONLY stuff to make suspension arms from. Trouble is, it is hard to find, costs a fortune, AND nobody in his right mind is going to go to the trouble and expense of replacing the perfectly good suspension arms that came on his racer with streamline tube just for the probably theoretical benefit of a miniscule reduction in drag. Well take a look at FIGURE [244] and let a whole new world open before your very eyes! My bet is that Patterson Engineering is about to be buried in orders—and they have never heard of me. . . .

DRILL JIG

Every so often someone comes up with a gadget so simple and so brilliant that it takes my breath away. Usually it also makes me feel real dumb for not having thought of it myself. I have been drilling safety wire holes in bolt heads for more years than most of my readers have been alive. During those years, I have broken countless drills (about twenty percent of them inside the damned hole), drilled

Figure (243): Properly done throttle return spring arrangement.

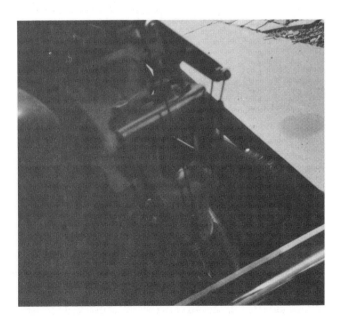

Figure (244): An inexpensive alternative to streamline tubing.

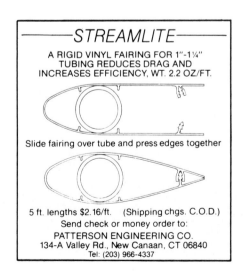

countless off-center holes and wasted enough hours to write another book. Over the years I have tried several commercial drilling jigs. Not one of them has worked worth a damn. In fact they have been so useless that I have always given up in disgust and gone back to the time-honored center punch, vise and drill press (or center punch, vise and hand-held drill motor) method of breaking drills.

Those days are over. A clever man named Tuck Jones now markets a drill jig that just plain works. As FIGURE [245] shows, you merely insert the bolt to be drilled into the appropriate hole, tighten the drill bushing to hold the thing still and start drilling. Of course, it is necessary to withdraw the drill bit every so often to clear the chips and it does help to use a lubricant and you do have to chamfer the holes when you get done but the bottom line is good news indeed: The damned thing works!

At the time of this writing Tuck gets $50 for it and, in my case, it will save that in drill bits within three months. He is thinking of modifying it so that it will also do Allen bolts.

BUMP STEER

You may recall that I had many words to say about bump steer in PREPARE TO WIN. I even went so far as to make three drawings of my faithful old dial indicator setup. After twenty years of faithful service, I have retired the thing. I have done so not because senility has set in and I no longer believe in bump steer or because I am too lazy to do it but because someone has finally built a better mousetrap. In this case the clever devil is Rodger Shapiro of The Driving Force, Inc. He figured out that since bump steer is a relative measurement (i.e., change of toe), not an absolute or linear measurement, we are not really interested in know-ing how much of it there is, but in making it go away. "So what?" you say. "Who doesn't know that?"

We may all realize it but Mr. Shapiro is the first to make the connection that we don't need dial indicators or measurements to make it go away—all we need is a flat surface to attach to the wheel and some way to eyeball change of toe. It really is as simple as it appears in FIGURE [246]: Remove the spring/shock units from the car, fasten the marine plywood plate to the wheel and tire with a bungee cord, lay the two rollers against the plate, pull the wheel through its travel range, eyeball the toe change by looking for a gap between one roller and the plate and make adjustments until there is no more to change. Eureka!

My previous record for checking the bump steer on all four wheels was about thirty minutes. The time has now been reduced to about half that—and I don't have to carry delicate dial indicators. Thank you, Mr. Shapiro. It's one more example of the fact that if you have been doing something in a given way because "That's the way we've always done it," chances are, there is a better way!

THE VALUE OF EXPERIENCE

In closing, I wish to take a few minutes of your time to discuss the actual value of experience in motor racing. I am heartily sick and tired of hearing statements such as, "Of course so and so (or such and such an operation) wins all the time—look at the experience they have" or, "You can't beat Joe Quick here—it's his home track and he knows it backward." As Colonel Potter of the late and sincerely lamented 4077th MASH would say, "HORSE PUCKEY!"

Another of Smith's laws states that experience is only valuable if you have both the capability and the inclination

---

Figure (245): Jones safety wire drilling jig. Andrew Freeman.

Figure (246): Bump steer measuring device. Andrew Freeman.

to learn from it. The corollary is that it is a lot less expensive—in terms of money, time and embarrassment—to learn from OTHER PEOPLE'S experience. This, of course, is what learning (and teaching) is all about.

There is a story about Napoleon and HIS opinion of the value of experience. It seems that in the latter stages of Nap's years of greatness—when it seemed that he couldn't lose even a skirmish let alone a campaign or a war—during the weekly press conference one of the UP stringers voiced his opinion that Napoleon's successes were due more to the experience of his generals than to his own strategic genius. Napoleon thought about it for a while and then replied, "Yes, our generals are now very experienced and capable generals, and we certainly realize the value of experience. But, of itself, experience has little value. For example, there is, within my armies, an artillery mule who has been with me ever since I left Corsica as a corporal. He has not missed a campaign or a battle. He now has more combat experience than anyone in all my armies—including even myself. But, despite all of that experience, HE IS STILL AN ARTILLERY MULE!"

You will hear that Penske, or Bignotti, or Andretti, or Foyt, or Yarborough, or Swindell, or Wolfgang, or Petty, or Prudhomme, or Williams, or Ferrari win because of their experience. Bullshit! Look back into history and you will invariably find that they have been winning for a very long time—and they are beating and have always beaten people with even more experience than they have. They win because they are smarter and work harder than the opposition does, and because they USE their experience. I once heard Jim Hall, who may have been the best racer of this generation, say, "I learned to win by losing." Presumably Jim didn't like losing very much.

There is another side to the experience picture. There is an old saying that experience breeds contempt. I don't know about contempt, but for sure experience can breed carelessness. Some months ago I had the good fortune to spend a few weeks in Australia working with Pat Purcell and John Skola, as fine a pair of racers and human beings as I have known. Pat and I had, with some difficulty, prevailed upon our engine builder to put in some late hours to finish an engine so that we could go testing. He promised that it would be sitting in our shop by 6 AM if we left him the key. At 6 AM we arrived and, to our astonishment, there, sitting on the floor was the engine—complete with a profane note. Since we were there, Pat and I decided to show the rest of the crew, who were due to arrive at 7, what a pair of experienced racers could do.

When the crew arrived, engine and gearbox were in the car and we were about to fire it. Skola idly asked if we had installed a crankshaft pilot bearing. Pat and I looked at each other somewhat blankly and said, "NO!" We then asked each other if we had SEEN a pilot bearing in the crank when we installed (together—40 years of experience) the clutch. The answer was another resounding "NO!" We then tried to rationalize; after all, we HAD lined up a multi-disc clutch and the transmission had slipped right on. After all, we asked, "What are the odds against THAT happening without a pilot bearing to center the aligning tool?" Common sense and cowardice won over pride and ego—we took the transmission off and looked. To this day I don't know what the odds are of getting a triple-plate Borg and Beck clutch so perfectly aligned that the transmission slips right on when there is no pilot bearing in place to center the alignment tool. Whatever the odds, Pat and I had proved the value of experience by achieving this difficult feat with ease. It is always the old hand that falls out of the rigging—the new one is too scared. On that note I will take my leave, until either DRIVE TO WIN or DESIGN TO WIN is finished.

CORPORATIONS THAT THE RACER SHOULD KNOW ABOUT

EARL'S SUPPLY COMPANY
825 East Sepulveda
Carson, CA 90745
(213) 830-1620

Manufacturer and supplier of Swivel Seal and Fluor-O-Seal hose ends. Perform-O-Flex and Fluor-O-Flex hose and Temp-A-Cure oil coolers. They stock a complete line of aircraft and racing hardware and support equipment.

TILTON ENGINEERING, INC.
P.O. Box 1787
Buellton, CA 93427
(805) 688-2353

Brakes, braking systems, clutches, flywheels and related gear; parts for everything from Formula Ford to Grand National cars.

WILLIAMS LOW BUCK TOOLS, INC.
4175A California Avenue
Norco, CA 91760
(714) 735-7848

An excellent line of first-class but economical major sheet metal tools—a tubing notcher, a 4' shear, a beader, etc.

ROGER KRAUSE RACING
2896 Grove Way
Castro Valley, CA 94546
(415) 886-4636

A portable and economical tire-mounting machine and balancer.

W. W. GRAINGER INC.
5959 W. Howard St.
Chicago, IL 60648
(312) 647-8900

A nationwide chain of industrial supply houses for power tools, compressors, etc. at the best prices I know of. Wholesale only, but easy to get along with.

TUCK JONES ENGINEERING
P.O. Box 331
Gualala, CA 95445

Inventor and manufacturer of the only safety wire drilling fixture that works.

McNEIL MOTORSPORTS
2040 S. Grand Ave.
Santa Ana, CA 92705

Alister McNeil operates it and handles a limited line of products, each the best in its field.

THE DRIVING FORCE, INC.
P.O. Box 1431
Pleasanton, CA 94556

Developer and manufacturer of the best and simplest bump steer measuring device that I know of.

CHAMPLIN MOTORSPORT
Box 114
Middlesex, NJ 08846
(201) 356-1132

Chip Robinson, one of the best of the current crop of young drivers, stocks Hewlands and NMB rod ends at attractive prices and is the only stockist of Rockwell suspension springs that I know of.

U.S. INDUSTRIAL TOOL & SUPPLY CO.
13541 Auburn
Detroit, MI 48223

Aircraft hand and power tools—write for catalog.

AIRCRAFT SPRUCE AND SPECIALTY COMPANY
201 W. Truslow Ave
Fullerton, CA 92632
(714) 870-7551

Composite materials and parts, supplies and tools for the homebuilder of aircraft. Their catalog is one of the GREAT ones.

JIM MEYER AND ASSOCIATES
13720 Florine
Paramount, CA 90723

Metallurgical consultant and supplier of forgings to the racing industry.

BAKER PRECISION BEARINGS
2865 Grundry Avenue
Long Beach, CA 90806
(213) 424-8118

The best racing bearing store in the country.

MICHAEL BRAYTON RACING
503 E. Broadway
Anaheim, CA 92805
(714) 533-6604

The supplier for the incredible TRIOK sheet metal shear/brake/roll.

TORINO MOTOR RACING, LTD.
1350-M W. Collins
Orange, CA 92668
(714) 771-1348

The only known (to me) supplier of Copaslip antiseize, AN to BSP adaptor fittings and/or Hylomar gasket sealant at reasonable prices.

JPR DEVELOPMENT
P.O. Box 2066
Canyon Country, CA 91351
(805) 251-9357

The provider of the best (and cheapest) corner weight scales I have seen.

NOTE:

PREPARE TO WIN contained a list of Los Angeles bargain houses. Some things have changed. Douglas Surplus is no longer in business. Washington Hardware no longer stocks much that is of interest to us. The same is true of Vogel Tool. Race Car Parts has become Russell Performance Products. I do not consider their line of plumbing hardware to be of race car quality.

The one that I did not list in PREPARE TO WIN was Cal Aero Supply, 13840 Paramount Blvd., Paramount, CA. I did not list them because they were in the process of moving and I thought that they had gone out of business. What they are is your basic, old-fashioned surplus fastener house. You have to do some hunting but the base price for steel surplus is under $1.00/lb. They usually have a pretty good selection of AN bolts and washers plus plate nuts and the like.

RECOMMENDED READING

I see very litle sense in my covering ground that others have covered well. Any of my readers who are interested in going further into any of the subjects I have discussed (all of you, I hope) are hereby urged to obtain the following works. I am not listing prices simply because they change too often.

LIGHT AIRPLANE CONSTRUCTION FOR THE AMATEUR BUILDER by L. Pazmany, available from L. Pazmany, P.O. Box 80051, San Diego, CA 92138. This is THE BEST book of its type ever written. No one who intends to do any sheet metal fabrication or fiberglass work can afford to be without it—end of statement. The good Mr. Pazmany has also published the construction manual for his Pazmany PL-4 homebuilt airplane, an exceptionally clever design. Not all of the information in the construction manual is contained in the guide. The construction manual is worth buying just to see how simple, clever and complete the man's work is.

I have previously mentioned the manuals published by the Experimental Aircraft Association, upon whom blessings be. This time I am going to be specific. You should own:

SHEET METAL, volume one and volume two
TIPS ON FATIGUE
WELDING TIPS
BUILDING THE METAL AIRPLANE

They are available at nominal cost from The Experimental Aircraft Association, Wittman Airfield, Oshkosh, WI 54903-2591. It is well worth joining the association just to receive their monthly magazine, SPORT AVIATION. Anyone who is in the Elkhart Lake area and does not visit their museum at Oshkosh is missing something really worthwhile.

The U.S. government has published a number of excellent manuals. Aircraft Spruce stocks them. You should have:

CAM 18—MAINTENANCE, REPAIR AND ALTERATION OF AIRFRAMES, POWER PLANTS AND APPLIANCES This is a reprint by the EAA and is also available from them.
ACCEPTABLE METHODS, TECHNIQUES AND PRACTICES This is a reprint of FAA manuals, AIRCRAFT INSPECTION AND REPAIR and AIRCRAFT ALTERATIONS.

You also need **THE STANDARD AIRCRAFT HANDBOOK** by Leavell and Bungay (Aero Publishers) and **THE STANDARD AIRCRAFT WORKER'S MANUAL** by Fletcher Aircraft. Both are available from any general aviation store or from Aircraft Spruce.

Strangely enough, it turns out that in the world of engineering, the people who make the tools usually know best how to use them—and they generally publish the information very cheaply.

If you are going to do any machining at all, you need a couple of cheapies:

HOW TO RUN A LATHE from South Bend Lathe, 400 West Sample Street, South Bend, IN 46625
THE STARRETT BOOK FOR STUDENT MACHINISTS from the L.S. Starrett Company, Athol, MA 01330

If you are going to weld, you need:

THE OXY-ACETYLENE HANDBOOK from The Union Carbide Company, Linde Reference Library, 47-36 36th Street, Long Island City, NY 11101
THE PROCEDURE BOOK OF ARC WELDING from The Lincoln Electric Company, 22801 St. Clair Ave., Cleveland, OH 44117
WELDING GUIDELINES, WITH AIRCRAFT SUPPLEMENT by William H. Kielhorn from Aviation Maintenance Publishers Inc., P.O. Box 890, Basin, WY 82410

If you are seriously going to make parts for racing cars you should own:

MACHINERY'S HANDBOOK from Industrial Press Inc., TDS Building 424, Raritin Center, Edison, NJ 08817
KENT'S MECHANICAL ENGINEER'S HANDBOOK, VOLUME TWO, DESIGN AND PRODUCTION edited by Colin Carmichael, from John Wiley and Sons
JIGS AND FIXTURES FOR LIMITED PRODUCTION by Harold Sedlik, from Society of Manufacturing Engineers, P.O. Box 930, One SME Drive, Detroit, MI 48128 (or the Whole Earth Household Store)
SHOP TACTICS by William Adler from Running Press, Philadelphia, PA (or the Whole Earth Household Store)

You should read (your local library may well have these, or can get them):

INTRODUCTION TO ENGINEERING DESIGN by Thomas Woodso, from McGraw Hill
THE DESIGN OF DESIGN and **THE SCIENCE OF DESIGN** by Gordon L. Glegg, Cambridge University Press
THE ELEMENTS OF STRUCTURE by W. Morgan (1973)

Before playing with composites you should read **THE NEW SCIENCE OF STRONG MATERIALS** by J.E. Gordon from Walker & Co, NY (620.11 at your library) and you should buy:

MOULDLESS COMPOSITE SANDWICH HOMEBUILT AIRCRAFT CONSTRUCTION by Burt Rutan from Aircraft Spruce
THE RUTAN AIRCRAFT FACTORY OWNER'S MANUAL from Aircraft Spruce

There are also a few catalogs that you cannot afford to be without:

Earl's Supply
Aircraft Spruce and Specialty
Baker Precision Bearings

If our discussion of metallurgy whetted your appetite I heartily recommend:

100 YEARS OF METALLURGY by W.H. Dennis, The Aldine Publishing Co., Chicago, IL (1964). Library of Congress Catalog Card #64-12248.